A list of the principal works of Thomas Mann

will be found at the end of this volume

LETTERS OF THOMAS MANN

1889-1955

(homo)eroticism : 103-105
morality/immorality : 104-108

LETTERS OF THOMAS MANN

1889–1955

———————— • ————————

Selected and translated from the German by
Richard and Clara Winston
Introduction by Richard Winston

Alfred A. Knopf   New York   1971

CONTENTS

ILLUSTRATIONS

Following page 142

*Unless otherwise credited, photographs are from the
Thomas Mann Archive in Zurich, Switzerland.*

PREFACE

This collection of the letters of Thomas Mann is based on the three volumes of German *Briefe* edited by the late Erika Mann and published by S. Fischer Verlag between 1962 and 1965. Although Erika Mann in no way attempted to influence the translators' selections, it should be clearly understood that her work alone made the present edition possible. The problems she faced, and the judgment with which she mastered them, can be fully appreciated only by those who have looked into the vast correspondence deposited in the Thomas Mann Archives in Zurich, and in various other public and private collections.

Out of the 1,331 letters in the German volumes, we have selected 483. To these we have added four German letters, and fifty-three that were originally written in English, or are extant only in English translations made by Mann's various secretaries.

In the German edition, the long span of years between 1889 and 1936 is covered by the first volume, which contains approximately one third of the total number of letters. The remaining two thirds derive from the last years of Mann's life. This disproportion is reflected in the translation. Partly it is due to the natural circumstance that more recent letters have greater chances of survival, partly to the immense increase in Mann's correspondence during his later years. But certain unnatural circumstances rooted in the history of the times account for the disappearance of a large number of the letters that Mann wrote before 1933. The saddest lack is the almost total loss of his letters to his wife from the years 1904 to 1933. These vanished, along with many of his early manuscripts, in the following way.

On January 30, 1933, Adolf Hitler became Chancellor of Germany. On February 11, 1933, Mann set out on a lecture tour, and because this was to be something of a gala visit to foreign countries, Katia Mann accompanied him. He lectured in Holland, Belgium, and France, then went to Switzerland for a vacation. In the meantime the Nazis instituted a reign of terror, and Mann received warnings that his life would be in danger if he returned to Germany. Thus began the exile which was to last the rest of his life, for even after the war he could not bring himself to live in Germany again.

Mann had left behind in Munich all his manuscripts and all the letters he had exchanged with his wife and members of his family. His house, along with the rest of his property, was confiscated by the Nazis. Erika Mann risked her life to return briefly to Munich in May 1933 and succeeded in rescuing the manuscript of her father's work in progress, *Joseph and His Brothers*. The rest of the manuscripts and papers were entrusted to a Munich lawyer, Dr. Valentin Heins, who offered to keep them safe and meanwhile to wage a legal battle to obtain the release of the entire Mann property, which according to the laws of the Weimar Republic had been illegally seized. In those early days of the Hitler dictatorship legal resistance to the Nazis still seemed possible—and occasionally proved successful. It was some time before Hitler completely "coordinated" the German judiciary.

Among the papers that Dr. Heins placed in his safe were bundles of letters from Thomas to Katia Mann written over a period of twenty-nine years: all the letters of his courtship days, and a great many from the first decade of their marriage, when the couple were sometimes separated for considerable periods. As Erika Mann explains:

"In their totality these letters constituted a kind of autobiography which, if they did not encompass that period of his life, at least richly illustrated it, and in many respects provided far more detail more exactly than any autobiographer would ever be able to recall. The collection was irreplaceable."

Soon realizing that the legal battle was hopeless, the Manns seized an opportunity to send a messenger—armed with a diplomatic passport and a formal letter of authorization signed by Thomas Mann—to take the manuscripts from Dr. Heins and bring them out of Germany in the diplomatic baggage. But the lawyer flatly refused to surrender the manuscripts (see p. 492). They formed a valuable part of the Mann property, he declared, and since that property had been confiscated, he would be legally liable. To this day the matter has remained somewhat mysterious, since obviously the Nazi authorities did not know that Dr. Heins had the manuscripts or they would have arrested him immediately.

Preface

The mystery deepened after the war. Dr. Heins had survived the bombings of Munich, but his office in the heart of the city had been hit. Fortunately, he had removed all his papers to a place of safety—all except the manuscripts and letters of Thomas Mann. These, he claimed, had been consumed in the flames that destroyed his office.

A small selection of Mann's letters to Katia Pringsheim during his courtship were preserved by a lucky chance. During his work on *Royal Highness* Mann wished to use his "wooing" letters and borrowed them from his wife to make excerpts. These excerpts, copied without salutations or complimentary closes, remained with the manuscript of the novel and fortunately escaped destruction. They are translated here in their entirety, and must stand for a far larger body of connubial communication. There is only one letter from Thomas to Katia Mann after 1933, because from then on the couple were never separated.

Many of Mann's friends and correspondents likewise spent the twelve years of Nazi rule in exile, and during their wanderings found it impossible to preserve cherished letters. Other letters sent to friends who remained in Germany were lost during the upheavals, fires, and bombings of wartime. Extensive correspondences with Bruno Frank, Hans Reisiger, and Emil Preetorius have been lost. The bulk of Mann's lifelong correspondence with S. Fischer, his German publisher, had to be abandoned in Germany and has disappeared.

The loss of so many letters must be bitterly regretted, for each of his intimate correspondents evoked a different aspect of Mann's complex personality. But more than enough letters have remained to make the problem of choice a troublesome one for the German editor, and still more troublesome for those who have had to make a selection from a selection. The editor's impulse in dealing with these letters is to include every single one. But the exigencies of space and structure compelled many painful decisions. Sometimes excellent letters were omitted because they repeated things Mann had already said in a previous letter, or because they would have obscured the pursuit of a certain leitmotif.

One solution to the problem of space would have been to publish extracts. But extracts do not show the living correspondent, and an editorial decision was therefore made at the start to print letters in their entirety or else to eliminate them. There are, however, occasional deletions in some letters. These were made in the German edition by Erika Mann, a very few of them for reasons of privacy, and a somewhat larger number to avoid repetition. All such omissions are indicated by ellipses within brackets. Ellipses without brackets are Mann's own punctuation.

A word of explanation is needed concerning the letters marked "original in English." During his years in America Mann learned to speak English effortlessly, and he traveled about the country lecturing in English. As a consequence, he attracted thousands of correspondents, to whom he invariably replied with self-sacrificing courtesy. But to write English with ease, style, and discrimination was beyond him, especially during his earlier years in America, and he resorted to various expedients to deal with this correspondence.

The majority of his replies were dictated (in spite of his intense dislike for dictation) in German to a secretary who took them down stenographically and then translated them. The secretaries did not preserve their notes, so that the originals have been lost. Moreover, the translations, hastily done, are very uneven in quality. For this reason we have in some cases—and in accordance with the wishes of Erika and Katia Mann—made slight stylistic alterations in the texts of these letters. Lacking originals, we have had to depend on our familiarity with Mann's style. On the whole, however, we have risked very little such editing, and have left the letters of Mann's later years in America unaltered, partly because more of them were dictated directly in an English which bears only slight touches of awkwardness, partly because he was better able to correct the translations of his secretaries. It has been assumed that from about 1943 on Mann had become sufficiently acclimated to be considered "responsible" for the English form of his letters. But it must be remembered that he never felt able to express himself adequately in written English, and that a letter in English always cost him a disproportionate amount of time.

Like all exiles, however, Mann formed the habit of interlarding English words and phrases in his German sentences, especially in letters to members of his family or letters to fellow exiles in America, and letters intended for translation anyhow, where the exact English word would be a convenience for the secretary-translator. These English intrusions were usually deliberate with Mann. The Magician, as his family affectionately called him, loved the conjurer's effect of blending languages.[1] It seemed to us necessary, therefore, to indicate the presence

---

[1] He used this effect as a literary device throughout *The Holy Sinner*, but this was not due to the influence of life in exile, as has been mistakenly assumed. He had begun such experimentation as far back as his first novel, *Buddenbrooks*, which opens with a passage in dialect, and he continued it in *The Magic Mountain*, writing an entire chapter in a mixture of French and German.

Preface

of such English words and phrases. This has been done by printing them in italics. Mann's occasional use of italics for emphasis has been indicated by footnotes wherever it would not be obvious from the context.

The footnotes, based largely on the notes to the three German volumes of letters, are intended for the general reader rather than the specialist—since it is a fair assumption that specialists read Thomas Mann in the original. To some readers the information given in footnotes will seem gratuitous, to others insufficient. We have tried to strike a mean between saying too much and too little. Identification is provided at the first mention of a name. *In the index, the black-letter numeral opposite a name indicates the page on which the person is identified.*

In order to save space, complimentary closes and signatures have usually been omitted. They have been retained wherever they seemed to throw some special light on Mann's relationship with his correspondent.

In conclusion, it is a pleasure to acknowledge the kindness of all those recipients of letters who so generously placed copies at our disposal. We wish also to thank Katia and Erika Mann for their unstinting aid; Dr. Hans Wysling, curator of the Thomas Mann Archives in Zurich, and his assistant, Marianne Fischer, for their endless patience and knowledgeability; William A. Koshland of Alfred A. Knopf, Inc., for constant encouragement and good advice throughout the years this project has engaged us; and Sophie Wilkins for many perspicacious editorial suggestions.

RICHARD AND CLARA WINSTON

INTRODUCTION

In his literary works Thomas Mann skillfully concealed the autobiographical elements on which he drew so heavily. Like Goethe, on whom he only half seriously modeled himself, all his works were "fragments of a great confession"; but in his literary demeanor he strove always for complete control of the artist's confessional impulse. It is impossible not to see aspects of the author in Hanno Buddenbrook, Tonio Kröger, His Royal Highness Klaus Heinrich, Felix Krull, Hans Castorp, Joseph, even Adrian Leverkühn; but it would be absurd to identify the author with any one of these extraordinarily lifelike fictional creations. Each lives within his own time and sphere.

Mann himself had the gravest doubts about the possibility of direct autobiography. ("On the whole I feel great timidity about directly autobiographical writing, which seems to me the most difficult kind of all, an impossible task from the point of view of literary tact.") He himself essayed it only twice: in *A Sketch of My Life*, which he wrote in 1930 to satisfy the demands of a public curious about the recipient of the Nobel Prize, and in *The Story of a Novel* (British title *The Genesis of the Novel*), his account of the genesis of *Doctor Faustus*. Both these exercises in the autobiographical vein reflect his scruples about the form, for they are ingenious blends of confession and deception.

For a narrative of Mann's life in his own words, therefore, we must turn to the letters. There is a vast body of them. In his lifetime, his daughter Erika Mann estimates, he probably wrote more than twenty thousand letters by hand—this in addition to the thousands he dictated during his later years, especially from 1938 to 1952, the years in America. Very few were written with any thought of publication; and while Mann was not one to wear his heart on his sleeve, he revealed himself in

Introduction

these letters with the integrity that he brought to all his dealings with the written word. Until his diaries are unsealed in 1975 (his will provided that they were to remain unopened until twenty years after his death), the letters will continue to provide our most intimate glimpses into his life, mind, and workshop.

There is scarcely a letter, even the most trivial business jotting, which does not contribute some piece of information or some psychological nuance that adds to our understanding of Thomas Mann as man and artist. From the gay note of the fourteen-year-old boy to the last undaunted letter from what was to be his deathbed, they cover in time two thirds of a century, in space the distance from Lübeck in northern Germany to Santa Monica on the West Coast of the United States, in subject much of the thought and emotion that entered into Mann's magnificent works of fiction and imposing body of essays. They provide a running account of his personal affairs, and a commentary on his times. They record the development of Mann's political opinions from his early nationalistic defense of Germany and antipathy toward democracy, to his commitment to the Weimar Republic, his opposition to Nazism in the late twenties and early thirties, and his uncompromising call for Hitler Germany's defeat in the Second World War. As we read them, we may see the evolution of his active role in the social and political life of his new country, America. These letters reveal his relationships with other great men of his time, and with unknown readers who turned to him for advice on grave personal decisions—much to his embarrassment. Here are glimpses of him in the intimacy of his family and in the public arena; here is light on his preoccupations during the work on each of his major novels. Many of the letters ring the changes on the themes of his fiction.

The following sketch of Mann's life is intended solely for the modest purpose of setting the scene for the reader of these letters. No attempt is made here at a critical evaluation of any of Mann's works. The reader curious to sip the *mer à boire* (to use one of Mann's favorite phrases) need only refer to the more than seven thousand items recorded by Klaus W. Jonas and Ilsedore B. Jonas in *Fifty Years of Thomas Mann Studies*[1] and *Thomas Mann Studies*,[2] vol. 2. The occasional comments on the works included in this Introduction are drawn from Mann's own observations— since these also constitute an element of autobiography.

·   ·   ·

[1] University of Minnesota Press, 1955.
[2] University of Pennsylvania Press, 1967.

Introduction

From the outset, Mann knew he was destined to be a writer. The very first preserved letter mentions a play he has written entitled *Aischa*, and is intrepidly signed: "Th. Mann Lyric-dramatic author." The following year, when he was fifteen, the city of Lübeck celebrated the hundredth anniversary of the grain firm his great-grandfather had established there. Mann saw the flags flying over the city and port, saw the deputations filing by to congratulate his father, the man of the hour, and his heart was heavy. "I knew even then that I was not the successor of my father and my forefathers, at least not in the way that was tacitly expected of me. I knew that I would not lead the old firm on into the future."

But although he was not to carry on the merchant tradition of his ancestors, he did not repudiate the solid virtues he had inherited. "How often in my life," he wrote in "Lübeck as a Way of Life and Thought," "have I not observed with a smile that the personality of my deceased father was governing my acts and omissions, was serving as the secret model for them? Often I literally caught myself in the act. . . . He was by no means a simple man, not robust, rather nervous and susceptible to suffering; but he was a man dedicated to self-control and to success, who had early achieved prestige and honors in the world—this world which was his, in which he had built his handsome house. We two brothers, my older brother and myself, are well aware of what our natures owe to our mother and her blithe southern disposition, what Goethe calls *Frohnatur*; but our father endowed us with 'the serious conduct of life,' *des Lebens ernstes Führen*, the ethical note that so strikingly coincides with the bourgeois temper."

Thomas Mann's older brother, Heinrich, led the way into literature. The decision was made easier for both brothers by their father's premature death and the liquidation of the firm in 1891, when Thomas was sixteen and Heinrich twenty. Their mother, Frau Julia Mann, moved to Munich, Germany's city of artists, and Thomas followed two years later, after he had completed his studies at the Lübeck Gymnasium. He had been an indifferent scholar—"school I loathed, and to the end failed to satisfy its demands"—but had already tasted the joys of publication. He and some school friends had succeeded in bringing out two issues of a magazine called *Der Frühlingssturm* ("Spring Storm") in which a certain Paul Thomas (these were Mann's given names) "shone as a writer of philosophic and revolutionary articles." Thereafter he dropped "Paul" and used only his middle and last name.

In Munich the nineteen-year-old Thomas lived with his mother, and for a short time worked in the South German Fire Insurance

Introduction

Company. "A singular interlude. I sat surrounded by snuff-taking clerks copying out accounts and secretly wrote at my sloping desk my first tale, a love story called 'Gefallen' ['Fallen']." It was a singular story for a young "revolutionary": at a time in which writers like Frank Wedekind were calling for sexual freedom, Thomas Mann brilliantly pointed up some of the ambiguities of emancipation for women, and came to the defense of the traditional double standard of morality. "Gefallen" was published in a magazine and brought a congratulatory letter from the established poet Richard Dehmel. With this success in hand, Mann claimed and won his own emancipation. He left the insurance firm and registered at the University of Munich, where for some years he "attended lectures which seemed likely to prepare me in general for my rather indefinite calling, courses in history, political economy, literature, and art."

A succession of short stories followed. Thomas also collaborated with his brother on the publication of a magazine, and spent somewhat more than a year in Italy with him. By the spring of 1898 enough stories had accumulated for the publication of a first book. Samuel Fischer, who was to be his lifelong publisher, suggested that he try a longer work in prose, and Mann began work on *Buddenbrooks*. Simultaneously, he accepted an editorial job on the German literary magazine *Simplicissimus* and took a moderately active part in the life of Munich literary circles.

The bulky manuscript of *Buddenbrooks* was finished at the turn of the century, and the single existing copy, handwritten on both sides of the page, was dispatched to S. Fischer Verlag. Meanwhile Mann had entered military service as a "one-year volunteer"—as a certain class of conscripts was whimsically called in Wilhelmine Germany. His brief experience with army life, and his negative attitude toward it, are amusingly reflected in his letters. While he lay in the garrison hospital with an inflamed tendon of the foot, he heard from S. Fischer. The publisher wished him to shorten the novel by half. Mann answered promptly from his hospital bed: the length of the book was an essential quality of it, he told Fischer, and should not be lightly tampered with. A long period of anxious waiting for a reply followed. He wrote gloomily to his brother at this time: "If I only knew what is to become of *Buddenbrooks*. . . . I must fear that it will be left on my hands." But at last, in February 1901, Fischer wrote that he would publish the novel uncut, probably in three volumes. "I shall have my picture taken, right hand tucked into the waist of my dinner jacket, left resting on the three volumes."

Buddenbrooks had a mixed critical reception and sold slowly at first.

Introduction

But it caught on after publication of a cheap edition. By 1904 it had sold more than thirty thousand copies, had been translated into Danish and Swedish, and Thomas Mann had at one leap become a noted literary figure. As he wrote a quarter of a century later: "It was fame. I was snatched up in a whirl of success. . . . My mail was swollen, money flowed in streams, my picture appeared in the papers, a hundred pens made copy of the product of my secluded hours, the world embraced me amid congratulations and shouts of praise."

The successful author had begun to frequent the home of Professor Alfred Pringsheim, one of the chief centers of artistic life in Munich. He fell in love with Katia, the gifted daughter of the house, and began a courtship which he would subsequently describe, with delightful self-mockery, in his novel *Royal Highness*. The anguish and exuberance of wooing are recorded in the charming letters to Katia Pringsheim. All the letters still in existence have been included here. The reader of the translation necessarily misses the abrupt, triumphant intimacy of the shift from the formal *Sie* to the familiar *du* in the last of this group of letters. The wedding was held on February 11, 1905; and from this unusually harmonious marriage sprang six children in what Thomas Mann liked to call "rhymed pairs": girl, boy; boy, girl; girl, boy.

Mann had successfully accomplished the transition from art to life which he withheld from one of his most famous characters, Tonio Kröger—the hero of the novella of that name, written shortly after the completion of *Buddenbrooks*. Happy in his new role of husband and father, he even then began his struggle against the mistaken identifications of the artist with his creations which were to trouble him throughout his life. Writing to his friend Kurt Martens, who had done a critical essay on him and his brother Heinrich, he protested: "It won't do to attribute to me 'icy misanthropy' and 'lovelessness toward everything of flesh and blood.'" The novel *Royal Highness* was also in a sense an answer to such charges. Completed early in 1909, it was "an attempt to come to terms, as a writer, with my own happiness." But with the theme of personal felicity it combined the problem of "representation," of the exceptional man's role in society, which was likewise to preoccupy Mann all his life.

A growing family, the building of a country home in Bad Tölz, new friendships with other writers such as Arthur Schnitzler and Hugo von Hofmannsthal, even his sister's death by suicide, did not interrupt Mann's slow but steady productivity. In January 1910 he began work on *The Confessions of Felix Krull, Confidence Man*, which he planned as a kind of parody of the classical German *Bildungsroman*. He approached this ingenious study of *persona* with great zest, but found the tone difficult to sustain and broke off, not to resume work on the novel for forty years. A stay in Venice with his wife in the spring of 1911 provided the germinal idea for *Death in Venice*. "The tale as at first conceived was as modest as all the rest of my undertakings: I thought of it as a quick improvisation which should serve as interlude to my work on the Krull novel. . . . But things . . . have a will of their own . . . and Aschenbach's story proved perverse in more than the sense I had planned for it."

The novella was not yet complete when Katia Mann fell ill and was compelled to stay several months in a sanatorium at Davos, in the Swiss Alps. Thomas Mann spent three weeks with her there in May and June of 1912, and returned home to Munich with the plan for a novella humorous in treatment, concerned with "the fascination of death, the triumph of extreme disorder over a life founded upon order . . . a droll conflict between macabre adventure and bourgeois sense of duty." He even began writing the first chapter of what was to be *The Magic Mountain*, but at bottom he realized that the simple story he had contemplated was growing into a major enterprise. He could scarcely have envisioned the novel's taking him more than ten years to complete; nor could he have anticipated—consciously at least—the outbreak of the First World War, which was to turn his creative energies into other channels and force him to neglect fiction for years.

In those last years before the war he entered public life in a small way by becoming a member of the advisory board to the Munich censorship authorities. The position accorded with his deep feeling for the obligations of "representation," and also reflected the conservatism of his sentiments at the time—a conservatism which led to a widening split between himself and his radically republican elder brother, Heinrich. He considered that he had accepted the post in order to protect writers against undue interference. But the equivocal nature of his role—reflected in the series of letters to and concerning Frank Wedekind—soon forced him to submit his resignation. Simultaneously, he resigned from the writer's league. "I entered the former as well as the latter for honorable reasons, out of a desire to be active in social and professional affairs. But one is ill thanked for that sort of thing. . . ."

The outbreak of the First World War, the "thunderclap," as he would call it at the end of *The Magic Mountain*, involved Mann for the first time in the major political and social questions from which he had hitherto held publicly aloof. His temperament quickly led him to identify with the cause of Germany. He felt that the world for centuries had imposed political humiliation and impotence on Germany, had refused to grant her "a little space on earth." He declared himself "profoundly convinced . . . that all historic justice, all real modernity, future, certainty of victory, lie with Germany."

This position set him at odds with many European intellectuals, men like Romain Rolland, Henri Barbusse, and Heinrich Mann, who took the road of internationalism and opposition to the war. "A certain radical intellectual, humanitarian-pacifist group represents the war pretty much as a swindle," Thomas Mann commented. Political disagreements led to a growing estrangement between himself and his brother, and to intense personal bitterness after Heinrich, in November 1915, published an essay on Zola which he used as a vehicle to attack his younger brother's views. Partly to answer Heinrich, partly to make what he regarded as a contribution to the war effort on the intellectual front, partly to keep occupied (since he found that he could not go on with the works of fiction he had begun), but above all to clarify his own thinking, he set to work on a voluminous essay, *Betrachtungen eines Unpolitischen* ("Reflections of a Nonpolitical Man"). This "effusion or memorandum," as he called it, in which he tormentedly wrestled with the problem of Germany, preoccupied him until the end of the war. By the time it was published in 1918 it was already outdated, both for the times and for the author—although Mann was later to argue that in reality it had come out at the right moment. In struggling to define for himself the nature of nationalism and the relation of Germany to Europe, he had moved closer to the internationalism he decried. In later life he rejected many of the arguments he had advanced in the *Betrachtungen*, but continued to regard the book itself as an important and necessary stage in his development, "a last great rearguard action of the romantic middle-class mentality in the face of advancing 'modernity,' an action conducted not without gallantry."

Heinrich Mann sensed a coming change of views in his brother before Thomas himself did, and toward the end of the war—when the collapse of Germany was already imminent—he offered a reconciliation. Thomas read his letter as "dictated by nothing but moral smugness and self-righteousness"; he saw their political conflict as colored by what he called *das brüderliche Welterlebnis*, "the fraternal constellation," and rebuffed his brother with heartbroken pride. A gingerly rapprochement was finally achieved four years later, when Heinrich fell seriously ill. But relations remained tense, and a source of grief, until Thomas's growing affirmation of democracy and support for the Weimar Republic restored cordiality and, in time, affection. Throughout the long and painful estrangement Thomas had continued to regard his differences with Heinrich as "a symbolic antithesis—on the basis of a strongly felt brotherliness." He saw himself as representative of individualism and Protestantism, his brother of collectivism and Catholicism. This was an antithesis he presented artistically in *The Magic Mountain*, for in April 1919 he resumed work on the novel he had abandoned during the war.

It was characteristic of Thomas Mann that a time of social and personal upheaval found him going to his desk each morning from nine to twelve-thirty or one o'clock, patiently spinning his tale of a society above the clouds which limned the world of the flatland below. Battles were raging in Munich as German federal troops suppressed the Bavarian Soviet Republic. "It was wild, but we are well and have personally passed through all the storms unaffected. In fact, when I count heads in my family, I find them actually increased by one. On Easter Monday (with the heavy artillery blasting away) my wife brought into the world an infant boy who is to be named Michael."

He had had enough of politics for the time being, and in the aftermath of the war preferred to tend quietly to his own affairs. But politics let no one in Germany tend to his own affairs, and shortly after his precarious reconciliation with his brother at the end of January 1922, Mann began to elaborate his newly forming attitudes in a major address, "On a German Republic." It was a call to the youth of Germany to consecrate their idealism to the beleaguered Weimar Republic. Publication of the address brought him the hatred of the ultranationalists, who had hitherto regarded him as one of their own. Mann continued to maintain that his views had not changed: "This essay is the direct continuation of the essential line of the *Betrachtungen*." But in fact the rise of Fascism in Italy and the first stirrings of Nazism in Germany had made him aware of the antihuman and antihumanistic tendencies of the rightist position.

The fantastic German inflation, which destroyed the substance of the German middle class and left a great scar upon the German psyche, forced Mann to scramble for a living once more, after years of relative prosperity. He interrupted his work on the novel to give lectures and readings even though, as he wrote to his brother, "German lecture tours scarcely pay nowadays. I have just been in Dresden for 50,000 marks . . . and would have come out in the red had I not stayed in a private house and not had to go to Berlin anyhow, so that it covered at least the cost of the trip." Without some source of foreign money it was virtually impossible to live, and the most desirable of foreign currencies was the

Introduction

dollar, which was soon to be worth billions of marks. In order to earn dollars, Mann began contributing articles to *The Dial*, the remarkable American literary magazine of the twenties. These *German Letters* helped him to tide his family over the period of the inflation. They also marked the beginning of an increasingly close relationship with America. A demand arose for the works of the writer whom the editors of *The Dial* had introduced as "generally and rightly looked upon by his countrymen as their most distinguished man of letters." Soon Alfred Knopf, who had presented Mann to the American public by bringing out *Royal Highness* in the middle of the war (when German books were scarcely a popular item), published *Buddenbrooks* in H. T. Lowe-Porter's translation and reissued *Death in Venice* in the Kenneth Burke rendering. Thereafter, for the next three decades some work by Thomas Mann appeared in America almost every year.

Around this same time Mann's reputation was spreading rapidly throughout the world. In the mid-twenties, translations of his works appeared in almost all the languages of Europe, and by 1928 the Japanese reader could purchase *Tonio Kregeru* in what is reputed to be an excellent translation. Rumors began to circulate that Thomas Mann was being considered for the Nobel Prize. Writing to his daughter Erika—now launching on a stage and literary career of her own—Mann mentions them wryly. The rumors swelled after German publication of *The Magic Mountain* in November 1924. Planned originally as a slight, humorous story about the same length as *Death in Venice*, it had wound up as a two-volume novel of some twelve hundred pages, leisurely, discursive, crammed with the ideas that had preoccupied Mann during and after the writing of *Betrachtungen eines Unpolitischen*. In a period of much experimentation with form in the arts, Mann had written what appeared on the surface to be an ordinary realistic novel which might be taken for a conventional satire on sanatorium life in the Swiss Alps. In fact, *The Magic Mountain* went beyond the more conspicuous experimentalism of Expressionists and Symbolists to incorporate symbolism into the very structure of the novel. "The book itself is the substance of that which it relates: it depicts the hermetic enchantment of its young hero within the timeless, and thus seeks to abrogate time itself by means of the technical device that attempts to make completely present at any given moment the entire world of ideas that it comprises."

Mann had not worked on *The Magic Mountain* during the war itself—partly because he never lost sight of his original intention of writing a humorous story. In the end, it was the humor that enabled the novel to sustain its heavy freight of ideas and symbolic purport. Even so, it remained the most "difficult" work he had written, and he had few hopes for it. "Would anyone expect that a harassed public, economically oppressed, would take it on itself to pursue through twelve hundred pages the dreamlike ramifications of this figment of thought? Would . . . more than a few hundred people be found willing to spend money and time on such odd entertainment, which had really little or nothing in common with a novel in the usual sense of the word?" But his forebodings proved unfounded. In addition to its novelties—such as its consistently musical, symphonic structure, or its hidden numerological references—*The Magic Mountain* contained enough old-fashioned, solid, vigorous characterization, enough traditional pathos and story, to make it popular in the same way that *Buddenbrooks* had become popular. Moreover, the time was ripe for a summing up of all that prewar Europe, now forever gone, had meant. Surprisingly large numbers of Americans as well as Europeans sensed that *The Magic Mountain* offered such a summing up. They read the story and absorbed the allegory, even if they did not consciously and critically understand it.

Mann's pleasure in the literary success of *The Magic Mountain* was somewhat alloyed by the personal complications that arose out of it. For his portrait of Mynheer Peeperkorn in the novel, Mann had borrowed some of the features of Gerhart Hauptmann, Germany's foremost dramatist. Literary busybodies attempted to whip up a public scandal, and Mann, who above all hated to be accused of disloyalty and disrespect, was forced to appeal directly to Hauptmann himself. "I have sinned against you. I was in need, was led into temptation, and yielded to it. The need was artistic." The older writer forgave; he himself was only too familiar with the artist's proclivity to borrow from reality. Moreover, he was probably flattered by the portrait.

Around the same time Mann was drawn into another literary dispute with Josef Ponten, a nationalistic novelist whose acquaintance Mann himself had sought several years earlier. Ponten developed an almost obsessional jealousy of Mann. The personal rivalry was complicated by what Ponten regarded as Mann's desertion of the conservative cause. In personal as well as public letters of denunciation Ponten made *The Magic Mountain* his special target. Nevertheless, he continued to insist on his devoted friendship, so that Mann was constrained to answer him in long letters of self-defense and remonstrance. "Good God, it seems as if nothing in the world exists but you and me and the problem of our relationship to each other." The relationship survived

Introduction

precariously for a while, until Ponten's commitment to Nazism put an end to it.

With uncommon prescience, Mann had been one of the first to take note of the phenomenon of Adolf Hitler. In the early twenties, when scarcely anyone was aware of the existence of a National Socialist movement, Mann had mentioned Hitler with distaste in one of his *German Letters* to *The Dial*. By the late twenties his support of the Weimar Republic, his warnings to German youth against a revival of nationalism, and his efforts at rapprochement with the French—marked by a notable visit to Paris in January 1926 and his publication of an account of it, *Pariser Rechenschaft*—had made him and his brother Heinrich favorite targets of the Nazis. By 1928 Mann was writing: "The thunder and lightning hurled down on me by a young dynamiter and fascist 'revolutionary' in an article entitled 'The Disenchanted Mountain' is well worth reading as expressive of the state of mind of a certain type of political or pseudopolitical youth." As the clash of ideologies intensified and the Storm Troops began their battles in the streets and meeting halls of Germany, Mann leaned more and more toward the camp of humanitarian internationalism and social democracy. If before and during the war he had claimed for himself the epithet "nonpolitical," he now found more and more of his time and thought taken up with politics and polemics. The letters—we present here only a scanty selection from now-forgotten battles—reflect the bitterness of that period and the passion with which Mann threw himself into an uncongenial task. He had no natural gift for journalism; his inclination was to turn every reply to an attack into a principled statement of his views; and this could be done only at the cost of neglecting fiction, which he always considered "the main thing."

He particularly regretted the cost at this time because he had embarked on another of his "novellas," a longish short story to be part of a religious and historical triptych, a "psychology of the myth" of Joseph and his brothers. As he wrote to his close friend Ernst Bertram: "What attracts me and what I should like to express is the transformation of Tradition into Present as a timeless mystery, the experiencing of the self as myth." But the reconstruction of ancient civilization could not be confined; what Mann deprecatingly called his "epic-writing pedantry" and "mania for treatment *ab ovo*" soon led him back from Joseph to Jacob and his ancestors. He found himself at work on a novel destined to grow into a vast narrative of the origins of individual consciousness and the rise of the humane tradition. Before he was finished, the novella had turned into a tetralogy. That he chose the Semitic world of ancient Palestine for his setting was an unobtrusive but firm response to the increasingly racist tone of German society and political life in the period between the wars. Perhaps a similar motive, conscious or unconscious, underlay his preoccupation with Sigmund Freud, which resulted in the essay, "Freud's Position in the History of Modern Thought."

"The Continent lay under threatening weather"—to quote a prophetic sentence from *Death in Venice*—but the clouds briefly lifted, at least for Mann personally, in November 1929. The Swedish Academy at last made the announcement that he had received the Nobel Prize for Literature. "The famous award . . . found me not unprepared," Mann wrote shortly afterwards. "It lay, I suppose, upon my path in life—I say this without presumption." With his delight in playing a public role, he thoroughly enjoyed the interviews, the ceremonies at Stockholm, the meetings with the King of Sweden and with dignitaries of church and state, as well as with painters, publishers, and writers. But he was taken aback by the public's voracity for a new star, by the requests for money that poured in from all quarters, and by the demands of his correspondence, "swollen disastrously by the world's herd instinct."

The year 1929, which brought Mann the Nobel Prize, an increased demand for his books all over the world, and hence the temporary cessation of the financial problems which had beset him since the catastrophic inflation of the early twenties, was also the beginning of the worldwide Great Depression. By 1932 there were more than six million unemployed in Germany. Economic crisis accentuated the polarization of political life in the Weimar Republic. While Mann was participating in the celebrations of the hundredth anniversary of Goethe's death, the Nazi Party was tripling its representation in the Reichstag. Storm Troopers began ranging through the streets of Germany, savagely attacking Jews, Communists, and Social Democrats.

Mann tried to continue his work on *Joseph and His Brothers*, but his concern with the debasement of German social and political conditions constantly obtruded. In August 1932, after a particularly bloody Nazi fracas in Königsberg, he published an article entitled "What We Must Demand" in the *Berliner Tageblatt*. In it he denounced Nazism as a "national disease," a "hodgepodge of hysteria and mouldy romanticism, megaphone Germanism that is a caricature and vulgarization of everything German." Two months later, in deliberate defiance of the advancing wave of nationalism and reaction, he delivered a speech that made headlines throughout Germany: addressing a meeting of socialist workers in

Introduction

Vienna, he declared his solidarity with them. As he would afterwards write to Karl Kerényi: "I am a man of balance. I instinctively lean to the left when the boat threatens to capsize on the right, and vice versa." At the beginning of the new year he leaned even farther to the left by agreeing to appear before the Socialist League of Culture in Berlin on February 19th. For this occasion he prepared a speech in which he proclaimed his sympathy with the ideals of socialism. The speech was published, but the meeting was never held. On January 30, 1933, Adolf Hitler became Chancellor of Germany.

Ten days before that, Mann had written sanguinely to an old friend: "Yes, things look bad in Germany, but . . . they are surely not so bad as they look." And for a few weeks after the Nazi seizure of power, he held to this conviction. He went ahead with his own plans, and on February 10 in Munich delivered a lecture on the "Sufferings and Greatness of Richard Wagner," challenging the spirit of triumphant Nazism by declaring that Hitler's favorite composer "today would probably be called a cultural Bolshevist."

Heinrich Mann had fled Germany precipitately after January 30th, but Thomas Mann departed calmly for Holland, accompanied by his wife, without any suspicion that he would not see Germany again for sixteen years. He was merely setting out on a rather demanding lecture tour which involved his speaking in Amsterdam, Brussels, and Paris. After two weeks of exhausting travel and lecturing, he and Katia went to Switzerland for a rest. They arrived in Arosa on February 26, 1933. On February 27th the Reichstag went up in flames, providing the Nazis with a pretext for initiating a reign of terror. The Manns decided not to return home for the time being. "Our bags were already packed. Then from all sides came friendly admonitions and warnings that at present my personal safety could not be guaranteed. . . . Moreover, the question arises whether henceforth there will be any room at all in Germany for the likes of me, whether the atmosphere there will be breathable for me."

Within a few weeks there could no longer be a question. Hitler had assumed dictatorial powers, political opponents were being systematically beaten, arrested, and murdered, and it became apparent that terror was the guiding principle of the new regime, not a temporary expedient. The frightful process of *Gleichschaltung* began; the first concentration camps were set up for those who would not fall into line. Clearly Thomas Mann, in general guilty of "pacifistic excesses" and "intellectual high treason," more specifically guilty of so recently defaming Richard Wagner, would have no place in the New Germany. Reluctantly—"I am much too good a German for the thought of permanent exile not to weigh heavily indeed upon me"—Mann resigned himself to the prospect of finding a new basis for his life at the age of fifty-seven. He had left without even his manuscripts, and within a few months the Hitler government confiscated his house in Munich. In May, Erika daringly slipped into Munich and brought out the precious manuscript of *Joseph and His Brothers*.

There was at any rate no lack of friends and colleagues in exile. The foremost writers of Germany had left immediately after the seizure of power. Many of them gathered for a time in or near Sanary-sur-Mer in France, where the Manns spent the summer months of 1933 at the invitation of René Schickele. Here Mann formed close friendships with such men as Lion Feuchtwanger, Julius Meier-Graefe, Franz Werfel, Schickele, and others. Here too, after a separation of many years, he saw a good deal of his brother Heinrich. The "Emigration," as these exiles came to be known collectively, soon scattered as its members sought new homes all over Europe and even in the Americas. But although Mann would later point out that the German Emigration did not really exist "as an intellectual and political entity," it did remain a spiritual concept with a measure of coherence within enormous diversity. All the exiles were united at least in implacable opposition to Nazism.

After some hesitation, the Manns decided to settle in Zurich, the most cosmopolitan German-speaking city outside the Nazi orbit. In Küsnacht, a Zurich suburb, they rented a large house overlooking the lake—"much too dear in the long run." These words suggest the difficulties that Thomas Mann encountered, though to a lesser degree than some of the other exiled writers, when he cut his ties with Germany. The German government not only confiscated his real property inside Germany, but also sequestered his bank accounts—including the proceeds of the Nobel Prize. With characteristic dignity Mann scarcely ever mentions financial problems in his letters; but they were real and pressing.

He was even more concerned about the upheaval in the lives of his children, particularly the two eldest, whose promising literary and theatrical careers had apparently been deprived of their foundation. But with a courage, energy, and adaptability that many of their elders might envy, Klaus and Erika found a footing in the unstable conditions of exile. Klaus Mann began editing an exiles' magazine, *Die Sammlung*, in Amsterdam. In Zurich Erika Mann reopened her satiric literary cabaret, *The Peppermill*, which had been a great hit in Munich at the beginning

Introduction

of the year, and the Swiss public took to it. (With fatherly pride, Thomas Mann noted: "The little restaurant *Zum Hirschen* . . . is jammed night after night; the cars of Zurich high society park in front of it; the audiences rejoice and the press is unanimously delighted. . . . I take more pleasure in this success than in the applause that *Joseph and His Brothers* has met with. This is the imperceptible and painless creeping abdication of advancing age in favor of the young folks.") Golo Mann abandoned his efforts to finish his studies in Munich, although he was on the verge of his *Staatsexamen*, and took a teaching position in St. Cloud, near Paris. But before leaving Munich he managed to pack up and send to an address in Switzerland some of the research materials that his father needed for continuing his work on the Joseph story. The younger children, Michael and Elizabeth, resumed their schooling in Zurich. Monika moved to Florence, where she had friends.

Writing had become difficult, for there were a thousand distractions, but Mann doggedly continued to work on *Joseph*. In one respect he was more fortunate than most of the exiles. Although the Nazis had confiscated his property, they inconsistently permitted his books to be published. Perhaps they wished to hoodwink the world into thinking that the Nobel Prize winner was not among their opponents, and that he chose to live abroad for nonpolitical reasons.[3] Or perhaps they could find no bureaucratic pretext for acting against him, since they had not yet taken the step of depriving him of citizenship, as they had promptly done with his brother Heinrich. In any case, this loophole was welcome to Thomas Mann, for he wished above all else to remain in touch with his public in Germany. His writing, he believed, might have a humanizing influence upon the German people, might remind them of those civilized values which National Socialism was bent on destroying.

Die Geschichten Jaakobs, the first volume of *Joseph and His Brothers*, accordingly appeared in October 1933 in a Germany whose government was committed to an official policy of anti-Semitism. The press response inside Germany to this excursion into the world of the ancient Hebrews was such that Mann felt "wounded and repelled to the depths of my soul." And the mere fact of his still being able to publish inside Germany sometimes aroused bitter comment among the emigrés whose books were being banned and burned. Some exiles felt that he was allowing his name to be exploited by the Nazis; that if he had truly made a clean and public

---

[3] After the war Goering, in prison, exclaimed: "The Mann case was handled all wrong. I would have done differently." See *The Story of a Novel*, page 143, for Mann's ironic comment on this remark.

break with the totalitarian regime, his books would not continue to come
out as if nothing had happened. Mann himself remained convinced that
he might have some influence upon the course of events in Germany if
he kept the channel of communication open; but the arguments of men
he respected weighed on his conscience during the years before he
deliberately provoked the Hitler government to expatriate him.

American publication of the first volume of *Joseph and His Brothers*
had been set for the middle of 1934—there was no longer a lag of decades
between the appearance of Mann's works in German and in translation.
Alfred Knopf had the happy notion of inviting the author to the United
States for the occasion, and the month of June was selected so that
Mann's birthday could also be celebrated. On May 19 Katia and Thomas
Mann embarked on the *R.M.S. Volendam* for their first transatlantic
crossing. Mann was naïvely delighted by the sea voyage in itself; he
recorded his impressions in many letters and in a chatty and subtle essay,
Voyage with Don Quixote.[4]

The enthusiasm with which he was received in America rather
stunned him. Everywhere he was followed by hordes of journalists,
everywhere greeted by the foremost figures in American life and letters;
and everywhere, with patience, courtesy, and modesty, he played the
part that was required of him, representing to America the best qualities
of Germany at the very time that Germany was beginning to be seen as a
land of terror and brutality. It was a hectic ten days: a dinner at the home
of Alfred Knopf, a reception given by the New York PEN Club, a lunch
with the editors of *The Nation*, a lecture on Goethe at Yale University,
a radio address, countless interviews and talks. For the climax of the
visit, Alfred Knopf had arranged a grand testimonial dinner in the
Hotel Plaza on Mann's birthday, June 6; it was attended by some three
hundred eminent guests. Although his English at this time was strictly
bookish, Mann performed the feat of responding in English to the
welcoming speeches.

"The adventure has been lived through and now seems only a
dream," he wrote to his German publisher on his return from those ten
crammed days. "A rather confused but pleasant dream." Neither he nor
Alfred Knopf suspected that this brief excursion would lead Mann to
forge ever closer ties with America, that within a few years his entire

---

[4] In *Essays of Three Decades* (New York: Alfred A. Knopf; 1947).

Introduction

family would be making their homes in the United States. For the present, Mann was thinking more of the time he had lost. "Our trip to America . . . cost me a month of time. . . . Yet it was really nothing but a grand spree—a term which covers both the impressive and the unnecessary aspects of the whole thing. I do not want to regret such gamboling, for there is something right and good about harvesting sympathies that have been sowed and have grown over the years, especially when the harvest has been blasted by hail in one's native land."

The "hail" was meant in a double sense, for Mann was also referring to the bloody purge of June 30, 1934, in which Hitler destroyed the opposition within his own party. A month later came the death of President Hindenburg, followed by Hitler's consolidating his dictatorship by combining the offices of president and chancellor in his own person. Mann was plunged once more into the kind of intellectual and moral crisis he had suffered during the First World War, when he abandoned fiction to work on the *Betrachtungen eines Unpolitischen*. For a while he thought of writing another such "profession of beliefs," but after several months of inner turmoil and virtual creative paralysis he rejected the idea, and toward the end of the year resumed work on the third volume of the Joseph novel. But he remained dissatisfied with the way the book was moving, and sometimes wondered whether he still had the energy "to carry this work to an end worthy of its beginnings." In these circumstances he half welcomed, half resented the prospect of another long interruption, and after some hesitation he accepted Harvard University's invitation to come to the United States to receive an honorary doctorate, along with Albert Einstein.

Further honors came in America. On this second visit he and Katia were asked to a private dinner at the White House, as if he were the envoy of a government in exile. "As a dinner very bad," he noted dryly. But he conceived a lasting admiration for President Roosevelt. Later, the President's aims and personality would influence his conception of Joseph the Provider, overseer of the ever-normal granary.

Without his knowing quite how it had happened, Mann found himself standing, for most Americans, as the symbol of the "better Germany," to use the phrase current at the time. He himself saw ambiguities in that concept, and in his fiction and his essays subsequently explored the light and shades of Germany's divided soul. But he accepted his representatives role, and for this reason it saddened him that some persons, both in America and Europe, regarded his position as equivocal. He did not like being accused of indecisiveness, and by the end of the year he had become

Introduction

convinced that a forthright "here I stand" was needed. An article by the Swiss critic Eduard Korrodi, alleging that exile literature was predominantly Jewish and hence not German, provided the pretext he sought. In his reply to Korrodi, published as an Open Letter, he corrected the misapprehension but declared his own allegiance to the Emigration and bluntly challenged the Nazis to deprive him of his citizenship.

The Open Letter stirred much excitement: rage on the part of the Nazis, gratification on the part of the exiles, distress and alarm on the part of such friends as Hermann Hesse, who at this time (he later changed his mind) objected not to Mann's condemnation of Nazism, but to the underlying assumption that the artist must be *engagé*. For Mann, however, the writing and publication of the letter cleared the air and his conscience. He was able to write his lecture "Freud and the Future," which he read in Vienna at a celebration of Freud's eightieth birthday. Then he returned to the third volume of the Joseph story and in August 1936 finished the final chapters of *Joseph in Egypt*.

By now he felt that he had written himself out on the Joseph subject for the time being. He decided, as was his habit after completing a major book, to seek relief and relaxation by doing a novella on Goethe. But it was the old story: the short narrative he planned had a will of its own, and Mann found himself embarked on a novel about the visit that Goethe's erstwhile sweetheart paid to Weimar in old age. *The Beloved Returns*, that unique fictional disquisition on the realities and shams of greatness, provided Mann with many opportunities to embed sharp commentary on Germany and the Germans within a new treatment of his old theme of art and life. So adroitly did he indict German weaknesses, while keeping strictly to the Goethean tone, that passages from his novel were afterwards quoted at the Nuremberg trials under the misapprehension that they were authentic remarks of Goethe.

The National Socialist regime waited for a full year after the Open Letter before taking the action that Mann had expected at once: the formal declaration that he, his wife, and his four younger children (Erika and Klaus had long since been expatriated) were no longer German citizens. He had even been forced to provoke this final step by accepting the Czech citizenship offered him by the Beneš government of Czechoslovakia. Two weeks later, he received a curt letter from the philosophical faculty of Bonn University withdrawing his honorary doctorate. His lengthy reply was virtually a pamphlet and was published as such almost at once in most of the major languages of the world. Mann bluntly called the rulers of Germany robbers and murderers, and asserted that the sole

Introduction

purpose of the National Socialist state was to prepare the German people for the coming war.

Publication of the Bonn letter transformed Mann overnight from a celebrated novelist into a political personality, a leader in the fight against totalitarianism, a spokesman for the Emigration. The logical consequence was his founding, with the Swiss publisher Emil Oprecht, of "the longed-for free German journal," *Mass und Wert*. Funds for the new magazine were supplied by a wealthy patroness; Ferdinand Lion was entrusted with the day-to-day editorial work (he was later replaced by Golo Mann); but Thomas Mann himself participated actively in the solicitation and selection of manuscripts. For a time *Mass und Wert* served as a major forum for the emigré writers, a substitute for the German periodicals that were now closed to them.

Mann took on further public duties in the cause of anti-Nazism. In April 1937 he made a third visit to the United States, where his daughter Erika had preceded him, to speak in behalf of the University in Exile then being founded at the New School for Social Research in New York. He made many speeches and formed a number of friendships with Americans who afterwards figured largely in his correspondence—in particular Agnes Meyer, the journalist and wife of the publisher of the *Washington Post*, and the psychoanalyst Caroline Newton. The Manns began to entertain the notion of spending part of every year in the United States, and they at least considered the idea of moving permanently to America. But the only practical step taken was Mann's consent to arrangements for an extensive lecture tour of the United States in 1938. Thus, as had been the case with his initial exile in 1933, the period of exile in America began unexpectedly. Events on the world scene transformed a lecture tour into exile at a further remove.

In February 1938 the Manns arrived in New York aboard the *Queen Mary*. Three weeks later, Hitler sent his rearmed Wehrmacht into Austria and proclaimed the annexation of that country to the German Reich. The very name of the ancient seat of an empire disappeared; Austria became the Ostmark. The SS ranged through the streets of Vienna; native Austrian Nazis threw off their disguises and denounced Jews, pacifists, socialists, and communists; and thousands of refugees from the Reich who had found temporary haven in Vienna now fled desperately once more. Many were trapped at the border; many succeeded in escaping into Czechoslovakia only to be trapped there the following year.

Almost on the spur of the moment, Katia and Thomas Mann decided to make their home in America. Agnes Meyer, already a close friend, helped to arrange the technicalities, and on May 5 the Manns went to Canada in order to reenter the United States as official immigrants. A material basis for living in America was provided almost immediately after this act of faith. Princeton University offered Mann the post of lecturer in the humanities. His duties would allow him ample time for writing—although the preparation of three public lectures was no small requirement.

Mann did not take this step without feelings of guilt, as if he were deserting Europe in her hour of need—although it would have made no sense for him personally to go down to destruction with the Old Continent. "You do understand our decision, don't you?" he wrote rather anxiously to Erich von Kahler, soon to be his neighbor in Princeton. "The shock of the crime against Austria was severe; the parallel with 1933 forced itself upon us; we felt it as a 'seizure of power' on the continental scale. . . . That by leaving Europe at this point we shall very possibly escape the war is actually a thought of secondary importance. My reason cannot believe in the war. . . . But on the other hand, reason also tells me that nothing but war can be the result of what is brewing in Europe now."

It took no special prescience to see that; but the contrast between Mann in 1914 and 1938 is interesting. The First World War had come as a total surprise to him, the "nonpolitical man." But in the years before the outbreak of the Second World War he had acquired a political sophistication which enabled him to form subtle, highly differentiated judgments on complex world situations. Sometimes, in fact, he judged so subtly, mediated so adroitly between extremist views, that journalists and the public, always seeking certainties, crassly misunderstood him.

During the summer of 1938 the Manns returned to Küsnacht to prepare their permanent departure from Europe. After a farewell public reading from *The Beloved Returns* at the Schauspielhaus in Zurich, they traveled to Boulogne and embarked on the *Nieuw Amsterdam* September 17th. The day before, Prime Minister Neville Chamberlain had flown to Berchtesgaden to persuade Hitler not to invade Czechoslovakia. The ship was crowded with Americans and refugees fleeing a Europe that seemed on the brink of war. The day after the *Nieuw Amsterdam* arrived in New York, Thomas Mann stood on the platform at Madison Square Garden addressing a gigantic "Save Czechoslovakia" mass meeting. But Czechoslovakia was not destined to be saved. Even as the Manns were moving into their new home in Princeton, Hitler, Mussolini, Chamberlain, and Daladier met in the historic Munich conference. "The shame,

Introduction

the disgust, the shattering of all hopes," Mann wrote. "For days I was literally sick at heart. . . . The way that history has taken has been so filthy, such a carrion-strewn path of lies and baseness. . . . Who knows what further atrocities this way may still pass through."

Yet Mann still had his own desk, "with every item arranged on it exactly as in Küsnacht and even in Munich." He enjoyed Princeton: "The landscape is parklike, well suited to walks, with amazingly beautiful trees which now, in Indian summer, glow in the most magnificent colors." Physically, his exile was not painful; but the situation of most of the emigrants was far from idyllic. America was now beginning to fill with professors without chairs, actors without theaters, writers without publishers, with refugees who above all had lost their language and with it their means of livelihood. In Czechoslovakia there were further tens of thousands who had fled Germany, fled Austria, and were now endangered once more. America's restrictive immigration laws, and the failure, willful or otherwise, of American consuls in Europe to understand the predicament of the refugees, made it extremely difficult for them to obtain visas. Mann fully understood what they were facing, and he used all the influence he had among Americans in positions of power in an effort to help. He and his wife wrote countless letters, secured affidavits, lent money, sponsored committees, addressed meetings, procured jobs for those who were fortunate enough to reach America. And, of course, he wrote: political, polemical essays such as "This Peace"; imaginative, ironic studies such as "Bruder Hitler" (first published in English under the title "This Man Is My Brother"). He contributed a moving preface to Erika and Klaus Mann's book, *Escape to Life,* a survey of the whole phenomenon of the German Emigration. And in the midst of these activities he managed to push on in the memorable Seventh Chapter of *The Beloved Returns,* the great interior monologue in which he performed what he called his *unio mystica* with Goethe.

In 1939 all three of the Mann's younger children were married: Michael to Gret Moser, a Swiss schoolmate; Monika to the Hungarian art historian Jenö Lányi; Elisabeth, the child "heroine" of *Disorder and Early Sorrow,* to G. A. Borgese, the noted Italian professor of literature, who was more than twice her age. Writing to Heinrich Mann, whose wedding also took place that year, Thomas Mann commented somewhat wryly: "Medi has married her anti-Fascist professor, who at the age of fifty-seven probably no longer expected to win so much youth. But the child wanted it so and brought it off. He is a brilliant, charming, and excellently preserved man, that must be granted, and the bitterest hater of his Duce, whom out of pure nationalism he regards as the worst of the worst."

In the summer of 1939 Mann returned to Europe, for the first time as a visitor, accompanied by his wife and daughter Erika. They came close to being trapped on the Continent, for they were in Sweden attending a PEN Club congress when Hitler's troops marched into Poland. But they were able to obtain a flight to London by way of Amsterdam, and sailed for home on board the American liner *Washington*.

At the outbreak of war Mann was in a state of painful perplexity (see the letter to his son Golo, page 313). He could not want the brutalization he knew to be the inevitable concomitant of war, and at the same time he longed for the war to proceed to the complete destruction of Nazism. Germany herself, he could not help realizing, might be destroyed in the process. He had come very far from the nationalism of *Betrachtungen eines Unpolitischen*, so far indeed that he was prepared to face the possibility of a liquidation of the Reich, if that would serve the cause of a future international community. Such thoughts were in his mind when he wrote the foreword to the first wartime issue of *Mass und Wert*, and a pro-British essay to which he gave the title "This War."

After the lightning German conquest of Poland, there was little military action throughout the winter of 1939–40. But in April 1940 the German armies overran Denmark and Norway, and in May they began their invasion of Holland, Belgium, and France. By the end of June France had capitulated. Hitler was triumphant on all fronts.

Even before the fall of France, Mann had realized the terrible danger to the German anti-Nazi intellectuals who had taken refuge there, his brother Heinrich among them. His son Golo, who had been in Switzerland as editor of *Mass und Wert*, had made his way into France at the beginning of the invasion and there volunteered as a Red Cross driver. Since then, nothing had been heard from him. Assisted by his daughter Erika, Thomas Mann was instrumental in setting up the Emergency Rescue Committee to work with President Roosevelt's Advisory Committee on Political Refugees. Procedures were devised for issuing emergency American visas to refugees in France. An underground railroad was organized to help the refugees escape over the border into Spain. In connection with this work Mann wrote a vast number of letters, of which only a few samples are given here. As he commented sadly in one letter: "Our house has become a rescue bureau for people in danger, people crying for help, people going under. Our effectuality does not match our efforts, and we seem fated not to be able to bring over my own brother and son."

Heinrich and Golo Mann, Franz Werfel, Leonhard Frank, and many other noted German writers were at last smuggled safely across the Pyrenees into Spain. In the middle of October they arrived in New York aboard a Greek ship. In welcoming them, Thomas Mann compared their rescue to the British feat of evacuating a whole army from defeated France. "We are celebrating a retreat so difficult and so successful that it deserves to be called a victory, a civilian Dunkerque." But in the meantime tragedy had struck his family. Monika Mann and her husband had sailed for Canada aboard an evacuation ship full of children. The ship was torpedoed, many of the children were lost, and Monika's husband was drowned before her eyes. She herself was saved by her prodigious feat of clinging to the edge of a boat for twenty hours.

Many of the German writers, including Heinrich Mann, had gone to the West Coast soon after their arrival, partly because jobs in Hollywood had been arranged for some of them, partly because a sizable colony of German exiles already existed in and around Los Angeles. Mann felt strongly drawn to this group, which included some of his closest friends, and he was also attracted by the beauty of the landscape and by the climate—not yet ruined by smog. His duties in Princeton had proved more onerous than he had expected; and the nearness to Washington and New York imposed social and other obligations that robbed him of time for writing. He was past his sixty-fifth year, and could not adjust to what he referred to as America's good-hearted but naïve demands upon his time and energy. He had now resumed his work on the Joseph novel, and the long-interrupted task demanded a steadier and quieter life than he had been able to lead in the East.

With many misgivings, therefore, the Manns gave up their home in Princeton. After an exhausting month of cross-country lecturing, they moved into a rented cottage in Pacific Palisades, a suburb of Los Angeles. Here they had earlier bought a plot of land, and during the first months of their stay in Pacific Palisades Mann announced to Erich Kahler: "Our plans for building have been subject to many vacillations. . . . But now it seems after all as if we will begin and from the autumn on live under our own, that is, under the Federal Loan's, roof."

By autumn Mann was somewhat wiser in the ways of American building contractors; the family was not able to move into 1550 San Remo Drive, Pacific Palisades, until the following February. Before that time, the expenses of building had caused considerable financial stress,

Introduction

which Agnes Meyer contrived to relieve by arranging Mann's appointment as consultant in Germanic literature to the Library of Congress.

"As in the East, there is no lack of interruptions and episodes here," Mann wrote to Erich Kahler shortly after arriving on the West Coast. His efforts in behalf of other exiled writers continued in California; he gave speeches, attended committee meetings, prepared lectures—all in addition to the vigorous social life among the exiled writers. But he was also making real progress at last on *Joseph the Provider*, the fourth and final volume of the Joseph story. In the late autumn of 1941 he undertook another taxing lecture tour, speaking on "The War and the Future" throughout the South, East, and Middle West. He had barely returned home when Japanese bombs fell on Pearl Harbor, and within four days his adopted country was at war with the country of his birth.

Mann had no problem of divided loyalties. He fervently wished for the total defeat of Adolf Hitler's Germany. His own contribution to the war effort consisted both of radio broadcasts which were beamed to Germany and of lectures given throughout this country—lectures in which he tended to speak more of the shape of the coming peace than of the war itself. This was the more necessary because the war was going very badly for the Allies. Throughout 1942, while the Japanese advanced steadily in the Pacific and the Germans occupied the remainder of France, invaded North Africa, and pushed on to Stalingrad in Russia, Mann continued his major task: finishing *Joseph the Provider*. Completion was delayed by a trip to the East crowded with encounters and speeches, but on January 5, 1943, he was able to announce to Agnes Meyer: "*Joseph* is finished. Yesterday noon I wrote the last lines. . . . And so it is done and may well stand as a monument of persistence and endurance, for I am more inclined to see it as that than as, say, a monument of art and intellect." He did not seriously mean this deprecating comment. Only a few weeks before, speaking on "The Theme of the Joseph Novels" in the Library of Congress, he had remarked: "Faust is a symbol of humanity, and under my hands the Joseph story insisted on turning into something of the same sort."

The allusion to Faust was significant. Already stirring in his mind was the idea of a story about an artist's pact with the devil. For a while he could dwell a little longer in the biblical world; he had recklessly agreed to write an introduction to a projected book, *The Ten Commandments*. Within a short time the project had turned into a novella about Moses, ultimately published as *The Tables of the Law*. It was completed in less than two months—a fantastic pace for him. As he wrote, with some pride,

Introduction

to his son Klaus, then in the American army: "I have knocked off a hundred pages so rapidly that I feel I no longer have to be envious of your speed." The great battle raging through the winter around Stalingrad had been on his mind as he worked on the story: "The curse at the end, against the present-day wretches to whom power was given to profane his work, the Tables of the Law, came from my heart and at least at the end leaves no doubt of the militant intent of this otherwise frivolous little thing."

The morning after completing this story, Mann cleared his desk of all the mythological materials he had been using for the past sixteen years. Everything was packed away, and by the following day he was already digging up forty-year-old jottings on plans for a novel about "Dr. Faust." By the beginning of June he could inform Agnes Meyer, at the end of a highly emotional letter, after a quarrel that had tried their friendship: "I am writing again—on the novel for which the war in Europe, alas, will probably give me time. The thing is difficult, weird, uncanny, sad as life. . . ." Mann himself has pointed out in *The Story of a Novel* that whereas all his other major works had grown to monumental size unexpectedly, in the case of *Doctor Faustus* he knew what he was setting out to do: "to write nothing less than the novel of my era, disguised as the story of an artist's life."

Throughout the war years, Mann continued to work on what he called his "terrible novel"—with his narrator, Serenus Zeitblom, keeping a running account of the slow turn in the fortunes of war and Germany's movement toward inevitable collapse. Mann heard the news of the long-awaited invasion of Europe by the Allied forces on the morning of his sixty-ninth birthday. "It was a moment of great emotion, and looking back upon the adventures of these eleven years I could not help but see a meaningful dispensation, one of the harmonies of my life," he later wrote. Less than three weeks later came another "memorable day in this span of eleven years," when Katia and Thomas Mann became American citizens. And in another month the attempt on Hitler's life and the abortive generals' revolt of July 20, 1944, raised hopes that were quickly dashed. But the war was clearly approaching its end; the German Christmas offensive that resulted in the Battle of the Bulge proved to be only a temporary setback in the steady advance of the Allied armies.

In spite of recurrent bouts of ill health, Mann made progress on *Doctor Faustus* during this period. By the end of February 1945 he had concluded the crucial dialogue with the devil which marked the midpoint of the book. Here he stopped for a while to work on his Library of Congress lecture, "Germany and the Germans." He argued against the distinction, so often made, between good and bad Germans. The evils Germany had brought upon the world sprang from her good qualities, he maintained. In speaking of Germany, he spoke about himself as a German, about his "feeling of solidarity almost bordering on the hypochondriac" with the German people. This was a position to which many of the German exiles indignantly objected; they responded with public attacks on Mann that hurt him deeply. The misunderstandings, both inside and outside Germany, of his complex attitude toward his native land were to preoccupy him for the next several years, and in fact to trouble him for the remainder of his life. They form the subject of many of his letters.

Germany had capitulated by the time Mann set out for the East at the end of May 1945. He went partly to lecture, partly to participate in the celebrations of his seventieth birthday. Fiftieth, sixtieth, and seventieth birthdays of literary figures had not usually been public occasions in America. But by the end of the war the exiles had made enough impact on the cultural scene for Americans to give themselves enthusiastically to this new custom. There was an outpouring of private and printed appreciations. The first issue of the resurrected *Neue Rundschau* was dedicated to Mann. *The Nation* gave him a testimonial dinner that was attended by men in the highest ranks of government and the literary establishment. There were innumerable private celebrations. Mann, already weakened by the first signs of an approaching serious illness, found it all rather exhausting, although he also thoroughly enjoyed it. "God have mercy on me, what a brouhaha it is, but this is the way I wanted it, after all (*did* I want it? Sometimes I tell myself I didn't. It's just turned out that way.) And then again, it's pure escape and restfulness, this living outwardly, doing nothing, and facing the world with a smile day after day. Only I simply can no longer bear to hear and read my name, and am glad that now in all likelihood the world will have done with me until I shuffle off. On which occasion it will make some fuss again, but then I won't have to play my part,[5] but will perform my public duties merely as a bust."

That reminder of mortality was reinforced in the following months by the deaths of his close friends and fellow writers, Bruno Frank and Franz Werfel. Mann himself had half seriously predicted in *A Sketch of My Life* that he expected to die in 1945, at the same age as his mother. At the end of the year a *Time* reporter called on him to challenge him for

[5] Here Mann whimsically puns on his own name; the German phrase is "meinen Mann zu stehen."

failing to be a true prophet. Mann whimsically explained, quoting his own Joseph, that prophecies often "did not come true literally, but suggestively. Fulfillment might be a bit wide of the mark, open to question, and yet unmistakable." At any rate, he pointed out, "in the year I had set for it, my life had—biologically speaking—reached a low such as I had never known before."

The crisis came three months later. Mann's health had steadily deteriorated during the early months of 1946. X-rays had revealed a possibly serious abscess of the lungs, and although the new drug penicillin helped his condition considerably, an operation proved necessary. With some delight he discovered that he was to undergo preparatory pneumothorax—"it was after all curious to experience, upon my own body, a technique of which I had so often spoken in bygone days, when I was working on *The Magic Mountain*."

The difficult and dangerous surgery was performed by Doctor William Adams at Billings Hospital in Chicago. To judge by Mann's cheerful account in *The Story of a Novel*, he luxuriated in the whole harrowing experience. It fitted in with his theories about the relationship between *Krankheit* and *Geist*; he gladly accepted the pain and physical risks as the toll which had to be paid in his creative struggle with *Doctor Faustus*. "Like no other of my books, this one consumed . . . my innermost forces," he later wrote.

By the end of May he was back home in Pacific Palisades, and although he was still convalescing, he immediately resumed work on the novel. Throughout the remainder of the year he labored steadily on it, often turning to Erika Mann for advice on where to cut what he himself considered "infernally long passages." In the aftermath of his illness, he noted, he was inclined to leave such decisions to others; it was as if he felt that the novel would not be published during his lifetime.

But such forebodings proved unjustified. By the end of January 1947 *Doctor Faustus* was finished and the manuscript sent to Switzerland for printing, since conditions in Germany were still too chaotic for normal publication there. The Manns themselves soon made their first postwar visit to Europe; Katia and Thomas Mann and their daughter Erika sailed on the *Queen Elizabeth* in May 1947. They went first to London, where Mann was received like visiting royalty. He lectured, gave endless interviews and press conferences, attended receptions, and spoke over the B.B.C. But in spite of insistent demands from writers and politicians in Germany that he return "home," he could not bring himself to face the spiritual ordeal that even a brief stay in Germany would have meant for him.

Introduction

Since the end of the war Germans had been showering him with appeals, requests, and denunciations. There were Germans who wanted him to certify that they had never been Nazis, Germans who expected him to use his prestige to secure them or their country better treatment from the Allies, Germans who proposed him for the next president of Germany, and Germans who blamed him for having lived securely in Switzerland and America while they had suffered bombing and invasion. He had wrestled with the problem of Germany, and his own attitude toward it, throughout the writing of *Doctor Faustus*; he wrestled with it again in letters to Germans such as Walter von Molo (see page 478) and Hans Blunck (see page 505). Now, in London, he tried once more. He refused to set foot inside Germany, but in lieu of a personal visit he wrote a "Message" which was published in the German newspapers. It aroused a storm of criticism and provoked a number of unsavory slanders of Mann (see page 526).

In Switzerland, however, Mann was greeted with a warmth that deeply moved him. In Zurich he addressed the International PEN Congress. Returning to Zurich, the city of his first exile, was a highly emotional experience: "One June morning—and it was like a dream—I sat on the stage of the Schauspielhaus in Zurich, where eight years ago I had bidden farewell to Europe by reading from *The Beloved Returns*. Happy and animated by the reunion with this dear city, I performed Fitelberg's Riccaut scene for an audience that helped me celebrate the occasion in the friendliest fashion."

He traveled about Switzerland a good deal that summer, lecturing and reading, and then vacationed at Flims in the Grisons, where he corrected the proofs of *Doctor Faustus*. The book had nearly cost him his life, he felt, and perhaps for that reason he brooded more over its fate in the world than he had done for any of his other works. He could hardly wait for the reviews; every comment concerned and agitated him. Into this novel he had poured all that he knew and sensed about the situation of modern art and of the artist; and at the same time he had succeeded in making that situation a parable for the fate of German and Western civilization. The technique he had adopted for this most autobiographical of his novels demanded the frankest of fictional confessions—and required also that he spare neither his family nor his friends. In *Doctor Faustus* living persons appeared in only the thinnest of disguises, sometimes even under their own names. Mann had burned his fingers in the past by depicting mere outward traits of his contemporaries—notably in the case of Gerhart Hauptmann. But now past unpleasantness did not keep him from making free use of close friends and even of his favorite grandson within the gallery of his novel.

For the most part the various "victims" accepted their equivocal immortality with good grace. Ironically, the one person who violently protested had not been portrayed at all. The composer Arnold Schoenberg became convinced before he even read the novel that Mann had used him as the model for his fictional composer, Adrian Leverkühn, and had stolen his "intellectual property," the twelve-tone system. The course of the dispute can be traced in the letters; Mann ultimately placed a disclaimer at the end of *Doctor Faustus* stating what he had thought the whole world knew: that Arnold Schoenberg, not Adrian Leverkühn, had invented the twelve-tone technique of composing.

By the time the German edition of *Doctor Faustus* was published in the fall of 1947, the Manns had returned to Pacific Palisades. Since completing the novel Mann had busied himself with essays and occasional pieces, but by October he was already considering "all sorts of writing projects: a medieval legend novella . . . ; a working up of the Felix Krull fragment into a modern picaresque novel set in the hansom cab era. Comedy, laughter, humor, seem to me more and more the soul's salvation."

He chose the medieval legend, which provided opportunities both for comedy and for talking about salvation. After several months of Middle High German studies he began, in January, the actual writing of the book that was to be *The Holy Sinner*. But Faustus continued to obsess him; he read the reviews avidly, and was on the whole disappointed by their shallowness. (The one piece of criticism that gave him satisfaction was Erich Kahler's magnificent essay, "Secularization of the Devil.") In an attempt to set the record straight and to provide hints for future critics, he dropped *The Holy Sinner* for a time and set to work on an account of the circumstances under which *Doctor Faustus* had been written. *The Story of a Novel* was begun in the latter part of July and completed within four months. Drawing upon the unusually full diaries he had kept during the years 1943 to 1947, Mann skillfully interwove two planes of reality: life lived and life distilled in fiction. He told much and hinted more, both revealed and concealed the mainsprings of the novel, and produced in the end one of his most charming works: a sizable fragment of autobiography which was also carefully "composed" in its own right as a kind of variation on themes from *Doctor Faustus*.

He finished writing *The Story of a Novel* just before the English translation of *Faustus* was published. The novel was a Book of the Month

Club selection, but Mann's pleasure in this commercial success was somewhat spoiled by the response of the reviewers. "I have good cause to be bitter about the largely miserable press *Faustus* has been having here," he wrote to his son Klaus. Nevertheless, he promptly added: "But I am too cheerful to feel that way, first of all because I am back at work on the little legend novel, and then because of the highly amusing outcome of the elections." Mann had been much concerned over what he regarded as the growing reactionary trend in America, and Truman's upset victory over Dewey delighted him, although he himself had given his support to Henry Wallace's third party.

He was far more concerned about Klaus himself, who had only recently attempted suicide. All his life Mann had written about the morbid attraction of death; and behind the easy, chatty tone of this letter to Klaus (page 564) can be seen a desperate effort to strengthen his gifted son's hold on life. In this he failed. In May of the following year, while Mann was on an extended lecture tour in Scandinavia, the news reached him that Klaus had taken his own life. Only a short time before, Mann had learned of his brother Viktor's death. Despite these sorrows, he decided to continue his lecture tour. "I believe this was the right thing to do," he wrote to Alfred Knopf. In the circumstances, the distractions of travel and lecturing were welcome. Moreover, he was unwilling to use personal grief as an excuse for evading the visit to Germany which he had promised to undertake at last.

His mixed feelings about that visit, and the mixed reception he was given, can be seen in his letters. Germany was then celebrating the two hundredth anniversary of Goethe's birth, and Mann agreed to deliver an "Address for the Goethe Year" both in West and East Germany: in Frankfurt, Goethe's birthplace, and in Weimar, the city where Goethe spent most of his mature life. Such a decision could please no one amid the mounting tensions of the Cold War. In West Germany there were angry protests against his going to Weimar; in the United States there were charges that he had become a Communist or a fellow-traveler. But Mann kept to his resolve to remain above the parties. "I recognize no zones," he declared in his address. Who else could represent Germany as a whole, he asked, if not the writer who used the common German language?

Charges of being "soft on Communism" now began to be made against him. Mann defended himself in a letter to the Swedish journalist Paul Olberg (see page 581) in which he declared: "I refuse to participate in the hysterical persecution of Communists and the incitement to war."

Introduction

Afterwards, he regretted some of the other things he had said in the letter: "It was pure cockiness." When he returned home, he found himself the object of repeated attacks by rightists; and with that sense of balance which has been referred to earlier, he leaned a little farther to the left. Nevertheless, he was stung by the denunciations. The political atmosphere in America now seemed to him "more and more unbreathable." His renewed contact with Europe, moreover, reminded him of the pleasure of being surrounded by people who spoke his own language, both literally and figuratively. For the first time in years he began seriously to consider returning to Europe permanently—not to Germany, where he felt he could never be at ease again, and where he would have been forced to choose between the two Germanys, but to Switzerland, and particularly to Zurich, the city he had loved.

The death of his brother Heinrich in March 1950 severed one more of his ties with California, where so many friends in his circle had recently died. He was now seventy-five and feeling his age and the increasing emptiness around him. "Left behind and alone, one must try to keep going for a while longer, until permission comes, as people say here, 'to join the majority.' "

Much of his time was taken up in answering the irresponsible charges of Communism or fellow-traveling. Nevertheless, Mann continued to work on his novels, although with "my energies plainly dwindling and a sense of depression growing." He completed *The Holy Sinner* and, as he had long planned, took up *Felix Krull* again, resuming work on the very page where he had left off forty years before in Munich. But political events repeatedly distracted him. In the rise of Joseph McCarthy to a peculiar kind of power in America he saw parallels to the rise of Hitler, and he alternated between confidence in the soundness of American democracy and fear that under the pressures of the Korean War in Asia and the confrontations with Communism in Europe, America would go far in the direction of Fascism.

During those years of the early fifties the Manns formed the habit of spending each summer in Europe, and with every visit his longing to stay there grew stronger. By the summer of 1952 he had made up his mind. The unusual success of *The Holy Sinner* in America—the novel had been taken by the Book of the Month Club and printed in an edition of more than 100,000 copies—provided the money which made the decision easier. At the end of June 1952 the Manns flew from New York to Zurich with the intention of remaining. After months of travel and living in hotels, they rented a house in Erlenbach, near Zurich. They had

Introduction

their furniture shipped from Pacific Palisades, sold the house there, and began looking around for a place of their own. "I am an inveterate homeowner," Mann commented. After a prolonged search, they found a house in Kilchberg, on the narrow, winding old highway that runs along the steep slope above the lake. Mann bought the house in January 1954, but it was not until April that he was able to move into what he rightly called "my definitively last address."

He had completed *Felix Krull*—or rather, written as much of that modern picaresque novel as he wished, for in his heart he knew he would never finish it. In spite of spells of melancholia and illness, he had contrived to maintain a consistently humorous tone in this last of his novels. But he was troubled by his lack of energy—"my productive powers seem exhausted." *Krull*, he felt, had been somewhat too light. "I really would like to do something entirely different, more dignified, more suitable to my years," he wrote, perhaps with tongue in cheek.

Once more, however, he summoned up the strength to do exactly that. For the 150th anniversary of Schiller's death in 1955 he had promised to deliver the festival oration in Stuttgart and Weimar. He threw himself into studies of Schiller with something of his old zest, and the intended address turned into a major critical article, the "Essay on Schiller." There was an autobiographical element in this essay: in paying tribute to Schiller, Mann was also trying to secure for his brother Heinrich his rightful place in the history of German literature. Not for nothing did he quote Schiller as saying of Goethe: "Critics will, I promise myself in my most courageous moments, point out our differences, but will not rank our genres one below the other, but one alongside the other as specimens of a higher idealistic species."

In May 1955 Mann spoke on Schiller in Stuttgart, along with President Heuss of Germany. Then—consistent to the last in his policy of treating the two Germanys as one—he went on to Weimar to repeat his address at the East German Schiller celebration. A visit to Lübeck followed. "Home at last, he stood in the Council Chamber in Lübeck, on the very spot where his father had been elected a senator and where he had worked and ruled. The last head of the ancient firm of Mann, who in matters of discipline had always been a model to his son, would surely have appreciated with joyful wonder the recognition this deserter from business to the kindgom of art was now enjoying."[6] It was an emotional week, in which he was made an Honored Citizen of Lübeck and walked

---

[6] Erika Mann: *The Last Year of Thomas Mann* (New York: Farrar, Straus & Cudahy; 1958), p. 59.

Introduction

for the last time along the beach at Travemünde. Then he returned home to Zurich to prepare for the "tumult" of his eightieth birthday.

The festivities proved tumultuous beyond anything he had anticipated. There were dinners given by the city of Zurich and the township of Kilchberg, and special performances of his works were offered at the Schauspielhaus in Zurich. Bruno Walter flew over from the United States to conduct the music for the occasion. Alfred Knopf had also come, as well as friends from all over Europe and official emissaries from both East and West Germany. A public reception at home was followed by a private party for friends and for his children and grandchildren. The house filled with flowers and presents. Every half hour the mailman brought fresh bundles of telegrams and letters, and finally congratulations from the hard-pressed but cheerful post office employees themselves.

Through it all, the octogenarian stood up manfully but he was totally exhausted when it was over. He tried to answer some of the innumerable messages from his intimates, at least, but the task of responding to all proved impossible; a card of thanks had to be printed and sent out. Yet his adventures in the public realm—which he regarded as obeying the call of duty—were not yet over. He had agreed to deliver his Schiller address as his contribution to the Festival of Holland being held that year, and at the end of June he flew to Amsterdam. There fresh honors were heaped upon him, in spite of the postwar anti-German sentiment among the Dutch. He was awarded the Commander Cross of the Order of Orange-Nassau and granted an audience with the Queen. This particularly delighted him, for only recently he had created such a royal audience in imagination when he described Felix Krull's reception by the King of Portugal. The conversation went somewhat differently, however; they talked about the queen's children and the Manns' grandchildren: "Her eldest daughter is not a good student, and the queen is anxious about her final examinations. We refrained from saying that we hardly thought there was any cause for worry. Moreover, this might really be the wrong attitude. The princesses' studies at school are treated with most democratic seriousness."

After the exertions of travel, the Manns spent two weeks at the seashore in Noordwijk. There, sitting in a beach hut, Mann wrote an introduction to *Fiorenza* couched as a letter to the director, who was putting on a performance of the play in Bremen (see page 683). Alert, as always, to the current situation, he pointed out that "the dialogues on the day of Lorenzo the Magnificent's death can serve as parables and parallels for these times."

Introduction

On July 18th he complained of a pain in his leg. Nevertheless he continued working, and two days later finished another introduction, this time to a book of stories. But he reported to his wife that he had had difficulty walking back from the beach to the hotel. "This stupid rheumatism."

A doctor was consulted, and it was discovered that he was suffering not from rheumatism but a thrombosis. After treatment, it was decided to fly him back to the Cantonal Hospital in Zurich.

He withstood the trip well, and after two weeks at the hospital seemed on the road to recovery. Then came a sudden relapse, followed by a complete collapse; he was suffering from advanced sclerosis of the entire arterial system. He died on August 12, 1955, and was buried in the cemetery at Kilchberg, near the grave of the great Swiss poet Conrad Ferdinand Meyer, in whose house the community of Kilchberg had honored him only two months before.

RICHARD WINSTON

LETTERS OF THOMAS MANN

1889-1955

1889

---•---

Lübeck
October 14, 1889

Dear Fried,

(The old name for you.) I shall begin our correspondence with a quotation from "Aischa" by a certain T.... M... "Still no news!" I am referring to the so far total absence of any sign of life from you. All of us are waiting with *fervent* longing for a letter from Ölznitz. We've already had several letters from Heinrich[2] in Dresden—he seems to like it very much there. —Have you heard again from Fridele, who was supposed to have a life-or-death (?) operation, or from Herminele, who can be nice when she wants to—or from Grandmoth—? Oh no, I suppose she's dead.

Here in Lübeck everything is going on as usual again. School has started, and lately I've had rather a lot of homework.—How did you like the farewell scene at the railroad station? Touching, wasn't it?—but I still have a long letter to write to Heinrich, so I'll close. Many regards from Mama,[3] Papa,[4] Lula,[5] and Carla,[6] all of whom—including myself—think of you often. Write very soon to your friend, admirer, and adorer

Th. Mann
Lyric-dramatic author.

---

[1] Frieda Laurentine Hartenstein (1860–1931), probably at one time a "nanny" in the Mann household.
[2] Heinrich Mann, Thomas Mann's brother. See page 17.
[3] Julia da Silva Bruhns Mann (1851–1923).
[4] Senator Thomas Johann Heinrich Mann (1840–91), last head of the venerable grain firm of Mann, which was liquidated after his death.
[5] Julia Elisabeth Mann Löhr (1877–1927), Thomas Mann's sister.
[6] Carla Mann (1881–1910), the older sister.

1890

———————— • ————————

TO FRIEDA HARTENSTEIN

Lübeck
January 2, 1890

Dear Fried,

(This is what I shall call you.) My warmest, although somewhat belated, greetings for the new year.

If you are no longer in Ölznitz, I hope this letter will be forwarded to you and that you'll kindly let me know your address, so our correspondence won't suffer a sudden death.

Here in Lübeck we have had a very jolly Christmas and all received fine presents, both from Mama and Papa and from Grandma[1] too. On Christmas Eve Papa had influenza, but it was awfully nice anyhow. I hope you too had a very merry Christmas.

Did you too receive a written greeting from Fridele for New Year's? Do you know what I mean? With eight seals. Princely! All of us here had a touch of influenza. Thank God it never lasts long. Is it going around Ölznitz too? It would be a pity for that fine little town. I am now diligently reading Schiller's works, which I got for Christmas, and when I came to the poem, "Hector's Parting from Andromache," I thought of the parting at your train the morning you left. That was really a dramatically touching scene, as though the good ladies wanted to say with Schiller: "Hector's love shall not be drowned in Lethe." School starts again on Saturday. Think of it, Saturday! How dopey!! I think, though, that I can handle the work pretty well from here on. But now I must close, dear Fried. Many regards from Papa, Mama, Lula, and Carla. God keep you as well as I hope you are.

Your grateful
Th. Mann

1 Thomas Mann's paternal grandmother, Elisabeth Marty Mann (1811–90).

4

1894

———————•———————

TO RICHARD DEHMEL[1]

Rambergstrasse 2
Munich
November 9, 1894

Dear Sir:

Please accept my warmest gratitude for your gracious letter and your exceptionally kind words about my novella "Gefallen."[2] I cannot tell you how pleased I was to receive praise from the author of "Aber die Liebe" and those wonderful poems in Bierbaum's *Musenalmanach*, and how grateful for your advice concerning my little story.

I had of course heard with great pleasure about the new art magazine *Pan*.[3] The good influence that such a free, independent, and materially sound enterprise can exert upon modern literature—which we all too often see wallowing in compromises with the *misera plebs*—can scarcely be measured.

As for your kind offer, I regret that at the moment I have nothing finished, but as soon as something suitable is ready I shall certainly send it to you.

Respectfully yours,

[1] Richard Dehmel (1863–1920), poet.

[2] *Fallen*, Thomas Mann's first published story, appeared in the October 1894 issue of the Leipzig magazine *Die Gesellschaft*.

[3] *Pan*, a magazine of art and literature, founded in 1895, ceased publication in 1900. During its brief existence it published the work of some of the most prominent painters and writers of the period.

1895

---•---

TO RICHARD DEHMEL

Rambergstrasse 2
Munich
May 15, 1895

Dear Sir:

In sending this manuscript to you after all—although I know that you do not have time to instruct and encourage every timid beginner—I should at least like to say explicitly that I am not casting a longing eye at *Pan*. All I hope is that you can sooner or later look through the story and let me know whether you think it is worth anything. That is more than enough to hope for, if it is not, indeed, asking too much; but when I recall your letter of last year which rewarded me for "Fallen," I think I may almost assume that you have some interest in my further progress. Then you also read the "Little Professor,"[1] which *Gesellschaft* is probably going to publish one of these days, and wrote me an extremely kind letter about it. May I take this opportunity to thank you for that!

I am not at all sure whether this new story represents an advance over "Fallen." Some people say it does; others think that "Fallen" is far superior to it. May I ask you to decide? Do you think that "Walter Weiler" is more unsuitable to my age of nineteen than "Fallen"?

If you do find time to send me a reply, please accept my warmest thanks.

Most respectfully yours,

---

[1] Probably the preliminary title for "Little Herr Friedemann," 1897.

1896

---•---

TO KORFIZ HOLM[1]

[Postcard]

Naples
November 6, 1896

Dear Holm:

Why haven't I heard anything from you? Didn't you receive my card from Venice? I am staying at Via S. Lucia 28II—too expensive, but with a very fine view of the sea and Vesuvius. I spent about three weeks in Venice, then went by boat to Ancona and then directly here via Rome. Here I feel very much at ease. Only now do I feel that I am really in the southland; that's because of the audible note of the Orient that forms part of the medley. It is very amusing.

I have not yet received the last issue of your fine periodical. Has the decision been made on the story-without-love?[2] Who has received the golden laurel? For my part I am forever ashamed of the dastardly plagiarism I committed upon Jakob Wassermann.[3] Certainly unwittingly; but I suppose his influence is generally in the air.

Please write me how things stand in Munich. I thought Wedekind's[4]

---

[1] Korfiz Holm (1872–1942), schoolmate of Thomas Mann, and joint editor with him of the schoolboy magazine *Frühlingssturm*, "a monthly for art, literature and philosophy," which Thomas Mann published at the age of eighteen. (Only two issues appeared.) Holm subsequently became editor of the satirical magazine *Simplicissimus* and a partner in the publishing house of Albert Langen.

[2] *Simplicissimus* had offered a prize of three hundred marks "for the best novella in which sexual love plays no part." The prize was won by Jakob Wassermann.

[3] Jakob Wassermann (1873–1934), novelist. Mann and Wassermann became good friends. Someone had apparently accused Mann of having plagiarized Wassermann.

[4] Frank Wedekind (1864–1918), playwright, founder and member of the famous Munich variety theater *Die elf Scharfrichter* (The Eleven Executioners), where he accompanied his own chansons on the guitar and frequently acted in his own plays. His erotic and "leftist" productions brought down the wrath of the censors. In 1899–1900 he was imprisoned for lese majesty.

defense (Rogoschin)[5] much too emotional, didn't you?

Cordial greetings, and my regards to your mother. Has she forgiven me for not paying a farewell call?

T. M.

---

[5] Rogoschin, an "eminent Russian writer" fabricated by Wedekind to satirize the authorities for banning one of his stories.

1898

———————•———————

TO KORFIZ HOLM

Theresienstrasse 82 gr. fl.
Munich
May 1, 1898

Dear Herr Holm:

I write this to *Simplicissimus*, although I do not know whether you are still there, and do not even assume that you are. But ever since I returned to the united Fatherland a few days ago I have been eager to see you and totally ignorant of your address, so the safest way seems to turn to Schackstrasse.[1] I would be delighted if you would drop in on me some fine afternoon around four o'clock. I will then slip a copy of my volume of stories into your pocket, so that at least one person reads it.

On the first day of my return I had the pleasure of seeing your mother in the street, I think. But perhaps I merely doffed my hat to an unknown lady.

Give my best regards to your mother.

[1] The editorial offices of *Simplicissimus*, where Mann worked as a reader during 1898–9.

1899

───────── • ─────────

TO KORFIZ HOLM

4 Schackstrasse
Munich
November 20, 1899

Dear Herr Holm:

Yesterday, Sunday, I was at the office from eleven to twelve, but as you know, without being vouchsafed a look at you, for you were probably still lying in the arms of love. Was there anything you wanted to tell me?

I enclose the original text of a translation offered to us. (On request. If it is nothing for us, please return it soon.) Furthermore, since you were able to handle the first ones so quickly, here are three more little manuscripts.

I read in *das Literarische Echo*[1] *that Resurrection (Rebirth) by* Tolstoy is being published in German by Diederichs. I must not keep this news from you.

TO KURT MARTENS[1]

Feilitzschstrasse 5 III
Munich
Saturday evening
July 8, 1899

Dear Herr Martens:

You must be most displeased that I have not kept my word to call on you,

---

[1] *The Literary Echo*, a biweekly Berlin periodical.
[1] Kurt Martens (1870–1945), writer, subsequently feature editor of the *Münchner Neueste Nachrichten*, was Thomas Mann's most intimate friend for about five years. He was one of the few persons whom Mann addressed as "Du." Five years older than Mann, from a good Leipzig bourgeois family, Martens stood out among Munich's bohemians for his breeding and "aristocratic" manner. These qualities attracted the young Thomas Mann.

but I simply could not. For if in addition to the stupid editorial work (you would not believe how time-consuming such nonsense is!) I am to have as much as two hours a day to roll my novel[2] a little way along, I must forgo even the pleasantest distractions.

Tomorrow I am sending your book[3] back by mail, because I cannot justifiably keep it any longer. For the present, warm thanks; I'll tell you more the first chance we have to get together. It is the first German novel in a long time that has made a powerful impression on me.

Since you liked my "Wardrobe,"[4] it may interest you that the New York *Volkszeitung* has reprinted it. Apparently this can be done over there without any more ado. At any rate the American people are to be sincerely congratulated.

Have you already gone to the country? If so, I trust these tired lines will be forwarded to you. Do send me something else for *Simplicissimus* very soon.

Incidentally, I always address you simply as "Herr Martens"—are you by any chance Doctor Martens? If so, please set me right. As for myself, I am nothing but

Your cordial well-wisher,

TO RICHARD DEHMEL

4 Schackstrasse
Munich
August 31, 1899

Dear Dr. Dehmel:

Permit me, in the name of the editorial board of *Simplicissimus*, to ask you to honor us with a prose contribution after this long interval. As you have no doubt noticed, the periodical is in desperate straits in this respect (please regard such stories as "Gerächt"[1] only as evidence of that!).

I hear that a small difference arose at some time in the past between you and one of our editors; but surely that cannot be sufficient reason for you to withdraw your sympathy permanently from *Simplicissimus*, can it?

A number of years ago you had the kindness to encourage my very

---

[2] *Buddenbrooks* (1901).

[3] *Roman aus der Décadence* (1898).

[4] "Der Kleiderschrank—Eine Geschichte voller Rätsel." Published in the *Neue Deutsche Rundschau*, June 1899. Translation: "The Wardrobe" in *Stories of Three Decades* (New York: Alfred A. Knopf; 1936).

[1] "Avenged," short story by Thomas Mann, 1899.

first literary efforts; since then we have met only in magazines. But if your interest of those days (perhaps you have retained a remnant of it) might now help persuade you to resume your association with *Simplicissimus*, I would be delighted.

Sincerely, and as ever respectfully,

1900

————————————•————————————

TO PAUL EHRENBERG[1]

Feilitzschstrasse 5 III
Munich
June 29, 1900

Dear Paulus:

Now will I raise my voice in praise and gratitude to you for your dear, nice letter from Wituchomo. It's really horrid of me that I am only beginning to do so today, isn't it? Fie! 'tis a fault to heaven. But the thing is that right at the end these past weeks, my superiors in Schackstrasse loaded me up with a heap of boring work. So much so that if I also wanted to pay a little attention to justly beloved posterity, letter writing became virtually impossible. I say "right at the end" because my activities for the Langen publishing house will shortly be over and done with. Hear now a pretty little tale.

At the beginning of this month, on the 6th to be precise, their lordships of the Higher Reserve Commission, to whom I had the honor of presenting myself, classified me as fit for all branches of the services, whence it follows that on October 1, to the consternation of all enemies of the Fatherland, I shall shoulder a gun. . . . What do you say to that? As for me, I am completely acquiescent (believe it or not), and assure you that the spiteful and mocking expression with which you have been reading since the second line of this paragraph is out of place. First of all, I recognize that in the long run the German army could not possibly manage without me. Secondly, arrogant *décadent* that I am, I imagine that it will be extraordinarily refreshing to be bawled out ruthlessly and vigorously for a year. Which I shall no doubt deserve—

[1] Paul Ehrenberg (1878–1949), impressionist painter, brother of Carl Ehrenberg and half-brother of Hilde Distel. He and his brother Carl were close friends of Thomas Mann in his youth. Paul Ehrenberg was an excellent violinist who frequently played chamber music with Mann.

No, joking aside, I am sincerely glad that I have not been sent away again. I really felt humiliated the time I was rejected at the barracks on medical grounds, and the sense of satisfaction when I returned from the "hot seat" with the certificate of fitness in my pocket is still with me. It is certainly providential. Only in this way can those nervous crotchets of mine be exorcised, and if I forfeit a year from my civilian work, it will undoubtedly add ten more to my life. Of course it is possible that I won't be able to stand up to it, and that they will have to release me again after a few weeks; but I hope for the best.

In short, you must kindly make allowances if you return to Munich and find me a romantically costumed and brutalized mercenary who steals the silver at Lula's[2] wedding, drinks immoderately, spits on the floor, and altogether behaves in the best style of a landsknecht.

What else is new in Munich? I'm trying hard to think what to tell you, though somewhat distracted by the glee club in the tavern downstairs, whose maudlin song is wafting upward. I might mention the art shows, although so far I have seen only the Secession, because I am always a little afraid of entering the Glass Palace. To my feeble lay intelligence the Secession has been more interesting in the past, but it is still very good-looking. Granted, the real big shots are not very happily represented except for Klinger,[3] who has some splendid sculptures there, a few in vari-colored marble. Stuck[4] has provided a new edition of his *Guilty Cons-cience* which I find no less clumsy and uninspired than the first version— (may I take another sheet of paper? If you don't mind!). Uhde's[5] *Moment of Leisure at the Studio* gives the impression of an intermezzo even from the subject alone; for my taste the material element is too important in his work. And Böcklin's[6] little *Madonna Enthroned on Clouds*, curious, primitive, and ugly to the point of being comic, seems to me simply a joke on the old gentleman's part. My favorite painting in the whole show is *The Heart* by Martin Brandenburg,[7] a Berliner. I must give you some sort of description of it. Here goes. In a forest rendered in a strange moody way, a girl stands leaning against a tree trunk and holding in her hand a heart, with which she is playing pertly and gracefully; while at her

---

[2] The marriage of Mann's sister Julia to the director of the Bavarian Bank of Commerce, Dr. Joseph Löhr (1862–1922).

[3] Max Klinger (1857–1920), painter and sculptor.

[4] Franz von Stuck (1848–1911), painter and sculptor in bronze; cofounder of the Secession.

[5] Fritz von Uhde (1848–1911), painter.

[6] Arnold Böcklin (1827–1901), Swiss painter.

[7] Martin Brandenburg (1870–1919), painter, noted for his illustrations of fairy tales.

feet kneels a young man, a knife in hand, a great gash in his chest, his eyes—fanatic, ecstatic, and suffering—directed upward. The picture made a great impression upon me, from which it probably follows that it is not worth two cents as a painting. Yet it *cannot* be altogether bad. I should have liked to hear your precocious professional opinion of it. I am now willing to turn Richard Pietzsch[8] over to your tender mercies. You are right, he is just an idjut after all. I did find his things in the spring show witty, but this time he is simply boring. On the other hand, Schramm-Zittau's[9] fowl are again very competent. L. v. Hofmann[10] is unfortunately represented by only a few drawings. Liebermann,[11] Leistikow,[12] Jank[13]—oh well, what is the use of my running down the list of names for you. I hope you will have a chance to see it all for yourself.

What else? Oh yes, recently Carla and I went to *Götterdämmerung*, and moreover, to ingratiate ourselves with the common folk (only for that reason, of course) took seats in the gallery. We didn't see very much, but the orchestra sounded magnificent up there, and Gerhäuser[14] was really splendid. His voice could be more brilliant, of course, but his acting is preeminent. What I particularly like is the force and devotion with which he goes at it, and the way he combines a distinct sense of style with great feeling for handsome sculptural tableaus. I am looking forward to his *Tristan*, which I shall be going to on Monday. You are missing a good deal. Kainz[15] will also be coming here soon, and I absolutely must see his Hamlet.

The family are well and send their regards. Mama is very pleased because we now have an extremely good cook (I hope her cooking will benefit you too!), and Lula and Löhr have come closer to one another in the most gratifying way. Lula only recently told me how you virtually fell on your knees that time, imploring her to say No to him. Really, was that so sensible of you? In these matters one must not fetch up too much

---

[8] Richard Pietzsch (1872–1960), realistic landscape painter with a preference for subjects from the Munich region.

[9] Rudolf Schramm-Zittau (1874–1950), animal and landscape painter; professor of art.

[10] Ludwig von Hofmann (1861–1945), painter. In 1914 Thomas Mann purchased his *The Spring*, which now hangs in the Thomas Mann Archives, Zurich.

[11] Max Liebermann (1847–1945), painter and graphic artist, and president of the Prussian Academy of Arts until Hitler came to power. He did many portraits of Thomas Mann, but none in oil.

[12] Walter Leistikow (1865–1908), painter, cofounder of the Berlin Secession.

[13] Angelo Jank (1868–1940), painter and illustrator.

[14] Emil Gerhäuser (1868–1917), celebrated Wagnerian tenor, later operatic director; in 1911 he staged the first version of *Ariadne auf Naxos* by Richard Strauss and Hugo von Hofmannsthal.

[15] Josef Kainz (1858–1910), Austrian actor.

idealism. With all due respect for "love," one does get further without it. A truism, by the way, that is rather repugnant to me personally. But what can one do on this inferior planet? And Löhr really is a good, kind, cultivated person, you know. Already I can no longer think of anyone else for Lula. —As for Carla, she has recently taken it into her head to become an actress. But I suppose that is normal at her age, and since she is otherwise mentally stable, I suppose we should be reassured. Don't let on!

My novel (naturally that has to come up again!) will be finished next month, whereupon I shall probably have to throw it into my publisher's maw for a song. Money and mass applause are not to be won with such books; but even if it should again turn out to be only a small literary success, I'll be proud and grateful. (May I take still another page? If you don't mind. But don't worry, I won't fill this one up completely.)

The violin is giving me great pleasure now, unquestionably thanks to you. I practice a little every day and play regularly with Ilse Martens once a week, as well as whenever she comes to visit us at Herzogstrasse.[16]

To leave the most important thing for the end: Both of us know a certain person, a writer, single, eligible for conscription for military service, a native of Lübeck, residing here, who would be *very* pleased if in the course of the summer he were actually to receive the promised *drawing* from you. It would be assured of an honorable place in one art folder or on one of his four walls.

Good Lord, what a letter! You see, it takes a while, but once I begin gossiping away, I go on and on.

Best regards! And do make sure that you spend next winter here.

Yours,

T. M.

TO KURT MARTENS

Garrison Hospital
Munich
November 1900

Dear Herr Martens:

Through my loyal friend Grautoff,[1] who in these hard days has been Love's messenger between me and freedom, I received the contents of my

---

[16] Number 3 Herzogstrasse, the house of Frau Julia Mann.

[1] Otto Grautoff (1876–1937), classmate of Thomas Mann, coeditor of *Der Frühlingssturm*, later art historian. His *Nicolas Poussin* is still highly regarded as a standard work on the French painter.

mailbox yesterday, with your kind note. Many thanks, especially for your compliments on "The Way to the Churchyard."[2]

As you see, I am already invalided—spent a week in bed in the barracks and was transferred here day before yesterday. The trouble is in my right foot, which is so poorly endowed by Nature for parade marching that it will possibly cause my release. The stupid person who pronounced me fit for service overlooked this infirmity.

Your account of the séance actually depressed me! Was the fraud really so blatant? Then I am almost glad not to have been present.

I still have heard *nothing* about my novel. I would like to present Herr Fischer[3] with a copy of *Simplicissimus* and take the occasion to ask for news; but I have no chance to do that now.

Do write again some time—here. But don't visit me—I'd rather you didn't. I hope you won't see me in uniform at all.

With warm regards, to your charming wife as well.

TO HEINRICH MANN[1]

Munich
November 25, 1900
Sunday

Dear Heinrich:

Today at last I can get around to sending you a word, although it must be brief and provisional, for I am dead tired.

I received your last letter at Herzogstrasse just when I was temporarily on my feet again. Discharged from the hospital, I soon found myself back on the sick list once more, because my foot relapsed after the first few steps. After another week on my back under the most repugnant circumstances, I drilled for a few days and then reported sick again, partly because I really was, partly to make them release me. But nothing

[2] "Der Weg zum Friedhof," story, 1900. In *Stories of Three Decades*, 1936.

[3] Samuel Fischer (1859–1934) was the founder and owner of one of Germany's great publishing houses, S. Fischer Verlag. He remained Thomas Mann's publisher and fatherly friend throughout his life.

[1] Heinrich Mann (1871–1950), Thomas Mann's elder brother. Author of many novels. During the First World War and afterwards, Heinrich Mann was regarded as one of the intellectual leaders of the pacifistic left. From 1931–3 he was president of the section for fiction of the Prussian Academy of Arts in Berlin. In 1933 he emigrated to southern France. There he worked on his noted historical novels, *Young Henry of Navarre* (1937) and *Henry, King of France* (1939). In 1940 he escaped to the United States and took up residence in California near Thomas Mann.

happened, and since Wednesday I have been back on duty. This has its pleasant side, since today is the first Sunday in a long while that I've spent outside the infirmary, the most unhealthful and abhorrent place I have ever seen in my life. What will happen now is uncertain. Through Mama's intervention I have consulted her doctor, Hofrat May. He has examined my foot and does not think I will be able to do my military service. Moreover, he knows both my captain and the chief medical officer personally, and when I have to report sick again—which will probably happen sooner or later, possibly as early as next week—he is going to intercede for me. I am firmly convinced that I will not serve out the year; but nobody knows how long the matter will drag on. Perhaps I shall be free next week, perhaps by New Year's, perhaps later. You see that with the best will in the world I can't tell you anything definite about my trip to Florence. Besides, I think that after my discharge I'll need a while to rest and recuperate; the way I feel now, I wouldn't like to climb aboard an express train. I wish I could make promises and give you clearer, more pleasing answers. But things are obscure and uncertain, and I have neither time nor strength to arrange them more satisfactorily. You will have to see how you make out with Florence, Riva, and your funds; I can't promise anything. But of course I'll send word the instant any change whatsoever takes place.

They are really giving your *Schlaraffenland*[2] a grand sendoff. Grautoff told me about a new squib that links it to *Sternberg*.[3]

Schaukal[4] is a queer bird. He has also sent his works to me, and his portrait with them: probably the result of his becoming acquainted with Praisegod Piepsam.[5] Weisskirchen is in Moravia, and I hear that Schaukal, who married rich, occupies some government post there. God knows what he sees in me, for it is obvious that he is much closer to you. Just leafing casually through his books, I found a good deal that was appealing; but in general I am a poor reader of verse, and my Tolstoyism already predisposes me to feel that rhyme and rhythm are wicked.

Nothing new yet about *Buddenbrooks*. The *King of Florence*[6] is quiescent, of course; but I have received the *Civilization of the Renais-*

---

[2] *Im Schlaraffenland*, Heinrich Mann's first novel.
[3] Probably Leo Sternberg (1876–1937), a writer and judge. His first volume of poems had recently been published.
[4] Richard von Schaukal (1874–1942), theater critic and poet.
[5] The protagonist in "The Way to the Churchyard."
[6] Title originally intended for Thomas Mann's only play, *Fiorenza* (1906). In *Stories of Three Decades*, 1936.

sance[7] and see that the two volumes contain some magnificent material. How is your *Duchess*[8] going?

I hope I can soon give you good news about all pending questions.

Warmly,   T.

TO HEINRICH MANN

Munich
December 17, 1900

Dear Heinrich:

You see, all has turned out well—at least for the moment, and such problematical creatures as I am are prone to stick to the moment.

All that was needed, of course, was the establishment of a private and social relationship to the medical powers-that-be; I owe it to Mama's doctor, whom you know. He is friendly with the Medical Corps major and worked on him, so that now I have been declared unfit for infantry service and have been given a furlough in anticipation of my deferment's being confirmed by the highest authorities. I am allowed to wear civilian dress, and until my official departure from the regiment I need only show myself in the barracks every so often, in order to have my presence in Munich certified and the furlough extended. It is, as I say, merely a declaration of unfitness for the infantry and a deferment. What will happen next year—whether I shall then continue the gay and glorious soldier's life in the supply wains or the artillery—is in God's hands. I keep thinking I should be able to avoid it one way or the other. Couldn't I withdraw at the right moment to some medicinal baths or similar refuge? We'll have to talk about it. For in these two and a half months I have really had enough of the flurry of barracks and infirmary.

Good luck can never be complete, so just at this time the painful business of paying taxes had to come along and give me some temporary anxiety about my trip to Florence. But it will have to be managed and so it will be, as Fontane would say.[1] I still don't know when, exactly. My deferment might come through by the year's end, but might also drag on to the middle or even end of January. So perhaps I shall not start out

---

[7] *Civilization of the Renaissance in Italy*, by Jakob Burckhardt (1818–97), the Swiss historian and art critic.

[8] Heinrich Mann's trilogy, *Die Göttinnen oder die drei Romane der Herzogin von Assy* (1902–3), translated as *The Goddess* (1918) and *Diana* (1929).

[1] Theodor Fontane, German novelist (1819–98).

before the beginning of February, and I imagine that two months, February and March, will do me quite well for Florence.

So you plan to do something else later on along the lines of *Schlaraffenland*? I believe Grautoff will tell you all about Sternberg. I know almost nothing—only that he is very fond of children and has set in motion one of those proliferating corruption trials Berlin is so proud of. Yes, I received Ewers's[2] article, "A New Social Novel." A bit sloppily written, but it certainly must have gained buyers for your book. In general I imagine that its success is even greater than we know. Engels recently included the novel in his Christmas book list in the *Münchener Zeitung* among the books every self-respecting person must own. At any rate, the way has been beautifully smoothed for the *Duchess*.

If I only knew what is to become of *Buddenbrooks*! I feel certain that it has some chapters not everyone can write nowadays, yet I fear that it will be left on my hands. So far there is nothing of the *King of Florence* but the psychological points and a formless dream: the rest is yet to come. The ambiguity of the title is of course intentional. Christ and Fra Girolamo are one: weakness become genius dominating life. Supreme moment: the *cruciamento delle vanità*. —Incidentally, all sorts of materials for novellas are running through my mind now, so it is very possible that a volume of tales will be ready before the drama I have set my heart on.

I've forgotten two things: First, Grautoff asks me to tell you that the brochure on Sternberg he promised you *may* be out of print or banned. Otherwise you will receive it. Second: My Burckhardt is the seventh revised edition and it cost, in an elegant format, twelve marks. "Revised" scarcely implies new material, and six lire is at any rate temptingly cheap.

I am tenderly cherishing my freedom. It will, of course, be even better when the day comes that I am finally and fully free. But one must be grateful, and in this sense: Dear God, hurray, hurray, hurray.

Yours,   T.

---

[2] Ludwig Ewers (1870–1946), a Lübeck journalist and critic. A classmate of Heinrich Mann, he long maintained friendly relations with both Mann brothers.

1901

———————•———————

TO HEINRICH MANN

Munich
January 8, 1901

Dear Heinrich:

I find nothing by Ewers. If the *Berliner Tageblatt* has gone and lost a manuscript of his, he can at least claim compensation, can't he? But *that* isn't what matters; rather, we must now settle my Florentine project. I sat down between two candles to work it out and am still pale from the effort. Here in Munich, you know, figures are largely meaningless to me, and so I managed hitherto to deceive myself hopefully and frivolously about the facts. Compelled to look them squarely in the eye, I find I must say with Vicco:[1] "I'm all a-tremble!" The truth in its horrid nakedness is that after cashing what remains of my fifth, ignoring my civilian tailoring debts, ignoring the rent, and even apart from the allowance for Mama (which I cannot ignore), I shall have some 240 marks. "You ask—Oh do not ask me why!" Enough; that's how it is. The sheet of paper with its irrefutable sums lies beside me. To repeat them here sickens me. No extras in sight for the near future. What I am writing now will be too long for *Simplicissimus*, and won't be finished overnight in any case, and Fischer is silent about *Buddenbrooks*. The situation remains: 240 marks for a quarter of a year, and to try and travel on that would be insanity. Not only can I not come on the 15th or the 20th; I cannot come to Florence before April. I've had to come to terms with that these past few days, and I'm only sorry that I strung you along in a pleasant hope that completely lacked a solid basis. I could eventually swallow the postponement if it weren't for the awkward fact that spring is just when you want to

---

[1] Viktor Mann (1890–1949), the youngest of the three brothers, adviser to a land bank, author of *Wir waren fünf, Bildnis der Familie Mann* ("We Were Five"), 1949, 2nd ed. 1964.

come back up here again. I rather enjoy being in Munich in the winter, and would miss a good deal if I left now. There are all sorts of premieres; Richard Strauss is coming, Wüllner[2] is coming; the programs of the Literary Society are in the offing; I can write stories and for the present read Burckhardt and Villari.[3] So I'll get through the winter all right. Are you absolutely set on coming back by the beginning of April? I don't quite see what you want to be here for, and why you can't stay down there at least until May. If I had to spend two weeks or so alone in Florence after you left, I wouldn't mind. The moment you tell me that we can be together in Florence for the month of April, *I* shall be comforted, and you after all will manage to spend your time quite well in the company of the Hartungens[4] and the *Duchess*. Incidentally, I realize that I ought to give you a more detailed explanation of my money problems, but it would be humiliating and pointless. Please, let me have your comments only on the possibilities for April.

Certainly, *Schlaraffenland* was highly praised by Leo Greiner in the *Münchner Zeitung*, and so was Holitscher's[5] latest. Don't you receive the clippings from Langen? Dr. F. Grautoff[6] sends you his regards. He likes your book *very* much, he says, but the publisher of the *Leipziger Neueste Nachrichten* won't permit an article on it. —Incidentally, the advertising is magnificent. I heard recently that there were notices about the book on the Variété's programs. —Does Langen[7] mean to underwrite your studying in Paris? You certainly could manage that if you wanted to. How well looked-after you are, and how brightly your star is beginning to shine. Fischer is silent, as I said, and if I send him an inquiry I'll probably have the changeling shot right back to me. Suppose nobody wants the novel? I think I would become a bank clerk. These fits come over me sometimes.

Warmly yours,   T.

---

[2] Ludwig Wüllner (1858–1938), actor, singer.

[3] Pasquale Villari (1827–1917), Italian historian and statesman. His *Savonarola ed i suoi tempi* was published in German for the first time in 1886, and represented one of the sources for Thomas Mann's *Fiorenza*.

[4] Dr. von Hartungen, proprietor of a sanatorium on Lake Garda and a friend of both Mann brothers.

[5] Arthur Holitscher (1869–1941), author of novels and travel books. He and Thomas Mann frequently played music together.

[6] Dr. F. Grautoff, father of Otto Grautoff and a bookseller in Lübeck.

[7] Albert Langen (1869–1909), the Munich publisher.

TO HEINRICH MANN

Dear Heinrich:

I hope you have received the art book. Holitscher has sent it to you with his greetings and best wishes for the progress of the *Duchess.*

Unfortunately I still cannot give you any information about the French books, the reason being that for the present I cannot show my face in Rieger's bookshop. You see, some time ago, on impulse and whatever the cost, I ordered the German edition of Vasari, and only afterwards learned from Grautoff that it is a book of so and so many volumes priced at easily a hundred marks, and moreover terribly dull. Whereupon I naturally did not call on Rieger again. I hope you will find out what you need some other way, and I shall have to look at Vasari in the library, if I find it necessary.

Is all well with you? I go through ups and downs. When spring comes, I shall have behind me a terribly turbulent winter. Really dreadful depressions with quite serious plans for self-elimination have alternated with an indescribable, pure, and unexpected inner joy, with experiences that cannot be told and the mere hint of which would naturally sound like boasting. But these highly unliterary, very simple and vital experiences have proved one thing to me: that there is something sincere, warm, and good in me after all, and not just "irony"; that after all everything in me is not blasted, overrefined, and corroded by the accursed scribbling. Ah, literature is death! I shall never understand how anyone can be dominated by it *without* bitterly hating it. Its ultimate and best lesson is this: to see death as a way of achieving its antithesis, *life.* I dread the day, and it is not far off, when I shall again be shut up alone with my work, and I fear that the egotistic inner desiccation and overrefinement will then make rapid progress. —But enough! Amid all these alternations of heat and frost, exaltation and suicidal self-disgust, a letter from S. Fischer blew in telling me that come spring he wanted, first, to bring out a second small volume of my stories and then, in October, *Buddenbrooks,* uncut, probably in three volumes. I shall have my picture taken, right hand tucked into the vest of my dinner jacket, the left resting on the three volumes. Then I might really go down happy to my grave. —But no, it is good that the book is going to see the light after all. So much of what is characteristically my own is there that it really will define my profile for the first time—for our esteemed colleagues in particular. Incidentally, I have heard nothing about Fischer's terms, which will probably consist of cautious codicils in respect to remuneration. —As for the volume of stories, it will be a thin one meant to yield no more than a quick refreshening of my name and some pocket money. The contents will be: (1) "The Way to the Churchyard" (as the title piece), (2) "Little Lizzy," (3) "The Wardrobe," (4) "Avenged," (5) a burlesque that I am working on at the moment and that will probably be called "Tristan." (Isn't that something! A burlesque named *Tristan?*) And possibly also (6) A long-planned novella with the ugly but thrilling title "Literature."[1] (*Illae* lacrimae!)

As of this moment it seems I shall leave for Florence on the 15th of March. It depends on whether I can finish up the things I must get done before that date, for I am quite sure I can raise the money, especially since I have Fischer's explicit assurance that he is "altogether not of a mind to drop" me. Of course I will let you know in good time. Let me hear how you are doing, for a change.

Warmly yours,   T.

TO HEINRICH MANN

Munich
March 7, 1901

Dear Heinrich:

I would naturally have answered at once, but for about a week all the incoming letters got wedged in my mailbox so that when I peered through the grating, I saw nothing. Today when I opened it by chance, a heap of letters tumbled out at me, some of them important, including yours.

No, you can leave for Italy without the slightest worry that for the present I shall commit any "follies." There is a good passage in *Buddenbrooks* when the news comes that the ruined aristocrat landowner has shot himself, and Thomas Buddenbrook, with a mixture of thoughtfulness, mockery, envy, and contempt mutters under his breath: "There's the nobility for you!"[1] This is highly characteristic, not only of Thomas Buddenbrook, and should serve to reassure you for the present. At the moment, too, I don't want to hear anything about the typhus. It is all metaphysics, music, and adolescent sexuality—adolescence hangs on with me. Grautoff, too, was deeply concerned; but it is hardly acute and is

---

[1] Probably *Tonio Kröger*. With the exception of "Avenged," all the stories named appeared in *Stories of Three Decades*, 1936.

[1] *Buddenbrooks*, Part Ten, end of Chapter 1.

taking root so slowly; at the moment there is so little practical reason to go through with it, that you may rest easy. Of course I cannot vouch for what may happen some day; and whether, for example, with that obsession for the "wondrous realm of night" in my heart I could go through the next bout of military service, is a question that disturbs me myself. But meanwhile a good deal of water will be flowing to the sea, and we will be here together again. —First I'll spare myself any more detailed confessions because writing and analysis only deepen and exaggerate these things. And they are things that should not be exaggerated. What is involved is not a love affair, at least not in the ordinary sense, but a friendship, a friendship—how amazing!—understood, reciprocated, and rewarded—which (I candidly admit) at certain times, especially in hours of depression and loneliness, takes on a character of somewhat excessive suffering.[2] According to Grautoff, I am simply going through an adolescent infatuation; but that is putting it in his own terms. My nervous constitution and philosophical inclination has incredibly complicated the affair; it has a hundred aspects from the plainest to the spiritually wildest. But on the whole, the dominant feeling is one of profoundly joyful astonishment over a responsiveness no longer to be expected in this life. Let that be enough. Perhaps one of these days I'll say somewhat more when we are talking.

I have just received your postcard too. Genoa is a good idea. If I should reach Florence before you go south, you will come there for a while, won't you?

I'll write about the book of fairy tales.

Warmly,

Yours,   T.

TO HEINRICH MANN

Munich
April 1, 1901

Dear Heinrich:

No, I absolutely cannot come right away, although the *cinque-lire pension* is very tempting indeed. But, first, I have no money at all, secondly my new story and my portrait must be finished, and thirdly I am feeling much too good here at the moment. I go on being "negative" and ironical in my writing largely out of habit, but for the rest I laud, love, and live,

---

[2] Mann is referring to his briefly intense friendship with Paul Ehrenberg.

and since spring has come besides, everything is simply one grand festival. If I leave, it will be over for the present and won't come again *this* way; we know how that is. I want to hold on to it to the last moment. —I am being painted, of course, by the good fellow to whom (assuming that one should not talk about fate all the time, but may also thank specific persons) I owe such an incalculable debt of gratitude. He is doing it because it's fun for both of us. When I'm in the mood sometime I'll tell you more about him, face to face. Incidentally, I shall dedicate to him either the volume of stories or a section of *Buddenbrooks*, which he has read and likes very well—whichever comes out first.[1] I feel such boundless gratitude. My sentimental need, my need for enthusiasm, devotion, trust, a handclasp, loyalty, which has had to fast to the point of wasting away and atrophying, now is feasting—

But do you absolutely have to go to Naples? Can't you let that wait for another few weeks, or even drop it entirely for the present, especially since you don't even feel like going? It would be so fine if I could find you in Florence shortly after the middle of the month and we could spend a little while together there. Do let me know whether you can't simply remain there for the present, since you're enjoying it. I'll postpone sending the Baedeker until I hear.

As for Fischer's conditions, you must consider that after all you received quite a lot of cash right at the outset, whereas I shall see nothing at all until September 1902; only then (a year after publication) is the first statement due. If the edition sells out, I grant you, I shall be receiving two thousand, for the bookstore price will probably have to be around ten marks. But who is to say that even as many as 100 copies will be sold? Incidentally, I expected nothing better, and in fact nothing so good.

My postcard about the fairy-tale book has no doubt reached you from Levanto.

Today I again received a new book of Schaukal's. You too?

I'll get the money.

But once again: My plea is that you simply stay calmly in Florence for an indefinite time. I'll arrive there around the 20th. After all, you do know Naples, and if you need it for a setting you can easily refresh your memory from photographs. Spare yourself the trip, and write that you are going to await my arrival in Florence.

Warmly,

Yours,   T.

---

[1] Part Nine of *Buddenbrooks* was dedicated to Paul Ehrenberg.

1902

———————————•———————————

TO HILDE DISTEL[1]

Ungererstrasse 24 I
Munich
March 14, 1902

My dear Fräulein Hilde,

You must permit me to add mine to the endless parade of birthday greetings. What prompts this? Aha, you see, through the influence of your brothers[2] (who now are almost mine as well) I have already become a half Dresdener, know all of you outwardly and inwardly, am kept up to date on all important events affecting you, and feel it my right and duty to participate in them. Moreover, I shall sooner or later come to Dresden without fail, if only for the sake of at last witnessing a performance of *Tristan* in your Court Opera. Of course it would be even better if you were to visit us here in Munich some day—seriously, you must do that! I assure you that we would get on very well with one another, especially in view of the fact that since the last time we met I have grown and straightened out somewhat, humanly speaking—for example, sociability no longer makes me completely melancholic. —You remember the confession I made to you that time. Undoubtedly the influence of your brothers can be felt in the change—chiefly that of Paul. I have made him a little more literary and he has made me a little more human. Both changes were necessary!

But once again, my heartiest good wishes for the 16th of March.

And will you be so kind as to accept on this occasion the copy of my first novel which I am sending separately? Not that you have to read it. God forbid! The first volume is dull, the second unwholesome. But I

---

[1] Hilde Distel (1880–1917), a half-sister of the Ehrenbergs, a girlhood friend of Thomas Mann's sister Julia, and later a singer in Dresden.
[2] Paul and Carl Ehrenberg.

don't know what other way I can find to ingratiate myself with you somewhat, for I have (now it comes) a great favor to ask, the same one I prepared you for a while back on a greeting card. To put it briefly then and without demur, Madame—as King Philip used to say!

Some time ago a sad story went the rounds of the journals—an episode in Dresden between a young musician, a member of the court orchestra, and a society lady. It involved an unrequited love of many years' standing on the part of the woman, and one evening after the theater, the affair came to a bad end in a streetcar. You knew both parties personally and at the time took a lively interest in the matter. For reasons of a partly technical, partly psychological nature, it made a remarkably strong impression upon me, and it is not impossible that one of these days I shall use it as the factual and plot framework for a wonderfully melancholic love story.[3] (The "plot," you know, is infinitely unimportant, but we do have to have one of some sort, don't we?)

In short, would you do me the favor of using some hour of leisure one of these days to recount the whole story from its very beginnings to the final explosive and sensational end? To tell it precisely, carefully, in great detail? May I observe that the details are what matter most to me. They are so stimulating. What was her, what his, previous history? What did she look like? Who was her husband, and under what circumstances had she married him? How did she meet the musician; how had he happened to enter her house? What were the relations of husband and wife, and of the husband to the musician? What was the character of the lady in general? Did she have children? Hadn't her unhappy passion gone on for some ten years? Did anything special happen during those years? Were the two parted from time to time, or were they always together in Dresden? How did he behave toward her, and vice versa? What is the story behind the presents he is said to have accepted from her, wittingly or unwittingly? What was the nature of their association with one another? Musical? Social? What finally precipitated the catastrophe— a love affair or an engagement on his part? Just how exactly did the business in the streetcar take place, and had any noteworthy circumstances preceded it? And so on. —Of course, I could work it all out for myself, and when I have the facts I shall probably deal with them in my own way. The facts interest me only for their stimulating effect and their possible usability. If I really should do anything with the incident, the chances are it will be hardly recognizable in my version.

[3] More than forty-three years later Thomas Mann made use of this "melancholic love story" for the narrative of Schwerdtfeger's death in *Doctor Faustus*.

I wonder whether your altruism goes far enough so that you will do this for me. I know it is asking a great deal and that your time is no doubt completely taken up with many good and lofty things, so that I am over-bold in making such claims upon it. But we artists are all alike: when our work is involved, we are possessed of an altogether Renaissance-like lack of consideration. So please, please, please! And once again: *details*!

We have had a most eventful winter, or to be more exact, we are still in the midst of it. New impressions come thick and fast, as in the past few days: day before yesterday Burmeister fiddled at the Bayerischer Hof (it was phenomenal, truly terrifying); today in the Odeon there was an Academy Concert under Zumpe with *Zarathustra* as the principal attraction; and tomorrow in the Künstlerhaus Fischer will be giving one of his Wagner piano evenings—among other things, the entire second act of *Tristan*! It is almost too much, but one doesn't like to miss any of it.

And now farewell, dear Fräulein Hilde—I have already kept you too long. Take care not to eat too much cake on your birthday—I know what it's like, it ends in extreme discomfort—and keep in friendly remembrance

Your sincerely devoted   Thomas Mann

TO KURT MARTENS

Munich
June 2, 1902

Dear Herr Martens:

Many thanks for your notes. I am sorry that now nothing will come of our meeting, but it is certainly my fault that nothing came of it sooner. There is scarcely any explanation. I haven't worked this winter, I have merely lived, simply as a human being, and assuaged my conscience by filling my notebook with observations. —A thousand good wishes for the completion of your first act, and as many more for the continuation. Where you are concerned I fear no disappointment. We can rely on your taste. I too am working again, finishing the volume of stories[1] which is to be published in the fall. Fischer has sent me unexpectedly good news about *Buddenbrooks*: it is not only a literary but also a sales success. I won't be receiving the statement until autumn, as you know, but he is offering me 1,000 marks in advance. That is quite something.

On July 1 I am going to Starnberg, where I have rented a place for

[1] *Tristan, Sechs Novellen*, 1903.

three months. Who knows, I may pay you a surprise visit one of these days.

Please give my regards to your good wife.

TO KURT MARTENS

Munich
July 12, 1902

Dear Herr Martens:

Back at my accustomed place at the desk, I must give way to the impulse to express my warmest thanks once more to you and your wife for your hospitality. I shall not easily forget those few peaceful summer days I was privileged to spend with you and yours. Yours is a very good life, my dear fellow—do not ever be ungrateful! I wonder whether any "salvation" like yours will some day be granted to me, Flying Dutchman that I am:

The ride home proved very pleasant. I found rainy weather here, but today it seems to be brightening, an event I greet with loud applause.

I see that I left about half of my possessions in your house: a nightshirt, a pair of slippers (very worn), and a bottle of mouthwash. Please do *not* go to the trouble of sending them after me! I am accustomed to such losses; they happen on every journey, and the things are easily replaced.

Greetings from Uncle Thomas to Hertha[2]—and once again many, many thanks.

---

[1] Richard Wagner, *The Flying Dutchman*, Act 2.
[2] Martens's daughter.

1903

———————•———————

TO S. FISCHER

Munich
October 29, 1903

Dear Herr Fischer:

Today three of your new books arrived—thank you very much. May I again express my warmest thanks to you and your wife for your kind hospitality this time, too. I particularly appreciate your having arranged for me to meet Gerhart Hauptmann[1] —a momentous experience for me. I only wish I had been able to make a somewhat more favorable impression than he probably received. He, in his glory, must have had an impression of confusion, conflict, tension, and extreme torpor—and that would be accurate. Perhaps he also sensed some element of good; his own ultimate essence is, after all, goodness. The others, who may have looked forward with some curiosity to meeting me, will simply have been keenly disappointed. So be it. Perhaps I shall continue to compensate them by the diligently forged symbols of my life, which is less uninteresting than my mustachioed personality.

Cordially yours,

[1] Gerhart Hauptmann (1852–1946), dramatist and novelist, who received the Nobel Prize in 1912. The character of Mynheer Peeperkorn in *The Magic Mountain* was in part based on Hauptmann's idiosyncrasies.

1904

———————— • ————————

TO KATIA PRINGSHEIM[1]

[*Early April 1904*]

My headache recently, when I had supper with your family after the theater, was trivial; it was only a side effect of my sore throat, which I've now cured beautifully, thanks to your father. Naturally you don't understand that, being unaware how deeply concerned your father is for my welfare. You see, I let it be known that I had a sore throat, that I was all swollen up. "Then you must make a damp compress," your mother said. "Yes, I suppose I must," I said in my conciliatory fashion. "Do you have gutta percha?" your father asked. . . . . "No," I replied with masterly repartee. Whereupon your father stood up—he stood up, I say, although because of his stomach he was lying on the sofa, went to his closet, and brought me a piece of gutta percha, his last and only piece of gutta percha, which was in fact already somewhat brittle. He gave it to me and carefully instructed me how I must use it in order to get the most out of it. —What do you say to that? What conclusion follows? *At least* the conclusion that he does not desire my death. But *more* follows from it. You will say again that your father knows how to control himself. But this is

———

[1] Katia Pringsheim (b. July 24, 1883), was educated at home, since there was no humanistic secondary school for girls in Munich. She was the first young woman of Munich to take the *Abitur*, and went on to study mathematics under her father and Professor Ferdinand Lindemann and physics with Professor Wilhelm Röntgen, the discoverer of X-rays. She and Thomas Mann were married on February 11, 1905. At the time of their courtship her father, Alfred Pringsheim (1850–1941), was professor of mathematics at the University of Munich. A passionate Wagnerian early in his life, he knew Wagner personally and once fought a duel on his account. Alfred Pringsheim was also an ardent art collector; his collection of Renaissance majolicas was world famous. In November 1939 he and his wife went into exile in Switzerland. Hedwig Pringsheim (1855–1942), his wife, was the daughter of Ernst Dohm, journalist, satirical writer, and editor, and Hedwig Dohm, a writer, noted suffragette, and member of a circle which included Franz Liszt and Ferdinand Lasalle. Thomas Mann described the Pringsheim house in Munich in *A Sketch of My Life* (1930).

more than self-control—say what you will. You're always telling me of your father's tigerish temper only because you don't like me. . . . .

TO KATIA

[Late April 1904]

You must not make me wait like that again, Katia. Waiting is horrible. One must not abet fate in its evil propensity for letting all good things arrive only after we are so benumbed from sheer waiting that we can scarcely rejoice in them——

I also wholly approve of your not giving too much attention to your tomes on mathematics and physics. For though I usually don't like to admit it, I will confess to you just this once that underneath I am a little jealous of the sciences and secretly experience a diabolic joy when you thoroughly neglect them. That is old-fashioned, sentimental, and base, I know, and I promise that I'll never again voice such feelings. . . . .

TO KATIA

[Late April 1904]

. . . and *even though* you say so, I think you mean it halfway seriously.

TO KATIA

[Mid-May 1904]

. . . that I am quite conscious of not being the sort of man to arouse plain and uncomplicated feelings. I add today that I do not exactly regard this as an objection to myself. To prompt mixed emotions, "perplexity," is after all, if you will forgive me, a sign of personality. The man who never awakens doubts, never causes troubled surprise, never, *sit venia verbo*, excites a touch of *horror*, the man who is always simply loved, is a fool, a phantom, a ludicrous figure. I have no ambitions in that direction——

TO KATIA

. . . Recently I read the following note in Hebbel's diaries: "For the total release of what lies within, man always needs something from without; what we merely conceive intellectually (even if it should be a person) is a part of ourselves and has no bounds; it can scarcely be distinguished from a product of the fancy and no longer seems free and definite. An image, on the other hand, lives an independent life, speaks in its silent language to all psychic states and intellectual experiences, serves as proxy to the extent that the altogether irreplaceable can have one." I underlined that passage and thought, as usual, of you. But it seems to me —impertinently opposing my experience to that of the great Hebbel— not really quite right. For there does exist a kind of fancy so intense, a form of conceptualization so fervent, that it attains to the absolute sense of life and the independent self-sufficiency of hallucination. Hebbel was probably too robust to recognize that; for I imagine he too must have loved. At times—it has to be perfectly quiet and perfectly dark for this— I see you, Katia, I really see you so luminously, so vividly alive in magically fine detail such as the most successful portrait could not attain; at such times I am shaken with joy. Curiously enough, it is almost always in the Kaimsaal that I see you, for I often watched you there through my opera glasses before we knew each other. I see you coming in from the left, up front, with your mother and your brothers, see you going to your seat in one of the front rows, see the silver shawl around your shoulders, your black hair, the pearly pallor of your face, your expression as you try to seem unaware that people's eyes are on you—it is impossible to say how perfectly and how wonderfully in detail I see you! . . . .

TO KATIA

. . . and that moreover your eyes can flash with such wonderful artfulness the while. . . . All these little amusements that fill the evening mean wasted time, an almost wicked waste of time, while we—you and I— would have so many more important things to talk about. You must know, must see from my face, how intensely, how painfully, that keeps coming back into my mind. If only we were alone more! Or if I knew how to make better use of the brief minutes that are sometimes given to me! I've already told you with what gladness I read what you wrote about "coming closer"—and how poignantly it affected me at the same time. I know, know only too terribly well, how guilty *I* am of causing that "kind of awkwardness or something" (this touching "or something"!) which you feel toward me, how my "lack of innocuousness," of unconstraint, of un-self-consciousness, all the nervousness, artificiality, and difficulty of my nature, hampers everyone, even those who are most well-meaning, from coming closer to me or in fact from dealing with me in any tolerably comfortable way. And that depresses me all the more when I sense in people's attitudes toward me (as, all things considered, happens with really incredible frequency) that warmer concern which expresses liking. . . .

So it is my fault; and that is the reason for my incessant craving to analyze, to explain, to justify myself to you. It may be that this craving is altogether superfluous. You are intelligent, after all; you are perceptive out of kindness—and out of just a little fondness. You know that I could not develop myself personally, humanly, as other young people do; that a [talent] can act like a vampire: bloodsucking, absorbing. You know what a cold, impoverished existence mine has been, organized purely to display art, to represent life; you know that for many years, *important* years, I regarded myself as nothing, humanly speaking, and wished to be considered only as an artist. . . . You also realize that this is no easy, no merry life and, even given strong sympathy from the outside world, cannot lead to any relaxed and bold self-confidence. Only one thing can cure me of the disease of representation and art that clings to me, of my lack of trust in my personal and human side. Only happiness can cure me; only *you*, my clever, sweet, kind, beloved little queen! . . . . What I beg of you, hope for, long for, is trust, is for you to stay by me without doubting me—it is something like belief—in short, is *love*. . . . This plea and this longing. . . . Be my affirmation, my justification, my fulfillment, my savior, my— wife! And never let yourself be put off by that "awkwardness or something"! Laugh at me and yourself if I awaken such a feeling in you, and stay by me! . . . .

TO KATIA

[*June 6, 1904*]

Alas, Katia—between the inexpressible bliss of the seconds in the dark garden when I felt your sweet, sweet head against my cheek, and the mortal sadness with which I left you today (on my birthday!)—what a fearful gulf! This is no reproach. Perhaps it is some weakness of mine, but I have no reproaches for you. Only love! Only love!

TO KURT MARTENS

Konradstrasse 11
Munich
June 9, 1904

Dear Martens:

Do believe that I too have thought frequently of our Brenner plan in recent days; but you know how strong are the chains that hold me here, and how they cut into the flesh whenever I attempt to escape. "I cannot go; a spell has bound me here. . . ."[1] Although I really should pull myself together and for a few days at least breathe different air, rather than the mild, entrancing perfume that emanates from her letters and her hands. Perhaps I would come to myself again somewhat, whereas I am altogether stuck fast and lost now. Anyhow, I do not complain and have nothing to complain about. I suffer a great deal, but also enjoy quarter hours of unimaginable happiness; and when I of all people chose K. P. of all people for love and marriage, I could not expect that everything would run as smoothly as between Hans Müller and Käthchen Schulze. So do not be surprised and don't ask too many questions. In the end everything will have to turn out well.

As regards our outing, I am totally undecided, as you can see. When will you be leaving with Keyserling?[2] Perhaps we'll manage to set out for a day or two together before that, anyhow. I imagine we'll see each other shortly—possibly tonight at the premiere in the theater?

I am sending the accompanying collection sheet to you because I don't know whom else to send it to. Naturally you are not obligated to pledge anything. If you don't feel like it, simply pass the sheet on to an acquaintance.

You still have 16 marks 50 pfennigs coming to you from me—I've even neglected that, although I'm usually fairly punctilious about such things! Well—at the next opportunity.

---

[1] Richard Wagner, *Lohengrin*, Act 2, Scene 1.
[2] Count Eduard Keyserling (1855–1918), novelist, then living in Munich.

1904

TO KURT MARTENS

Munich
June 13, 1904

Dear Martens:

Rest assured that I am grateful for your friendly comments. The way you see the matter is the way every impartial person must see it, and those who are most concerned about me have been urging the same thing. Nevertheless, you are not right. To manifest manly strength by confronting the girl with the decision would mean forcing her to say No, to the sorrow of both of us; for right now, due to the unusual nature of her whole development, she cannot yet persuade herself to say Yes. To play the vexed lord and master on that account and with dignity throw the whole thing up, must strike me as the height of folly as long as I have reason to believe that it would be doing her an ill service. And she has given me reason for believing that. As far as people are concerned—well, they are entitled at last to have some reason for gossiping about me. I've been a reserved eccentric long enough and not very generous about feeding people's craving for sensation. Their talk can scarcely harm us, after all, for since when has it been a disgrace for a man to pay court openly to a girl? We had scarcely danced together once or twice before the word "engagement" could be read on everyone's face. But that does not bother me; on the contrary, it proves the enormous plausibility and probability of the outcome. Just to make sure, I have shown "At the Prophet's"[1] to Frau Professor P., and cannot imagine that she will be angry with me over this harmless tribute.

Shall we talk more about this face to face? Won't you pick me up some time soon and we'll have dinner together?

Cordially,   T. M.

TO KATIA

[*Late June 1904*]

. . . You see, I thought that you had taken offense at certain possessive pronouns and nouns I let slip in my last letter, and did not want to answer me, and that I was not to be allowed to come on Monday, and you never wanted to see me again—and all sorts of similar dreadful fancies.

---

[1] See *Stories of Three Decades*, pp. 283–9.

All day long I waited for a letter, "anguishing, languishing in painful suspense."[1] At last at six o'clock I could stand it no longer, mounted the bicycle, and set off on a desperate ride at an insane pace. I went on for two hours, have no idea where—pedaled through altogether unknown villages, one of which was named ———, I think, and where I had a skirmish with a butcher's dog that obviously thirsted for my young life. And then when I returned home, totally disheveled and covered with dust, your letter was in the box. Your dear, dear, blessed letter; in it you are sweeter and more confiding than you have ever been in speaking to me. Infinite thanks for it, my happiness, my star, my wonderful little queen!

—What does patience mean! I love you! A friend wrote to me: "What kind of weakling are you anyhow? Everyone knows that you are wooing her, everyone is talking about it. And she continually sets you trials of patience, puts you off, plays with you. Is that a proper part for you? Show yourself a man! Give her an ultimatum! You cannot help seeming less and less desirable to her, the longer the thing drags on. . . ." That last phrase annoyed me, and so I answered plainly: "Don't interfere in matters you do not understand. Confronting her with a decision now would mean forcing her to say No, to the sorrow of both of us, because by her whole nature she cannot yet persuade herself to say Yes. That is why to play the vexed lord and master and with manly dignity throw it all up cannot help striking me as the height of folly, as long as I have reason to believe that it would be doing her an ill service; and she has given me reason for believing that."

—Silly little Katia, still going on with that nonsense about "overestimating" and still maintaining that she cannot "be" to me what I "expect" of her. But I love you—good Lord, don't you understand what that means? What more is there to expect and to be? I want you to "be" my wife and by being so make me madly proud and happy. . . . What I "make of you," the meaning I attribute to you, which you have and will have for my life, is my affair, after all, and imposes no trouble and obligation on you. Silly little Katia! Babbling on quite seriously as if she —now, really!—were not worthy of me—of me who asks timorously each time after we see each other: "Do I come up to her? Can she possibly want me? Am I not too clumsy for her, too unworldly, too much a 'writer'?" . . .

---

[1] A quotation from Goethe's poem, *Freudvoll und Leidvoll.*

1904

TO KATIA

[*Late June 1904*]

Twice last night I ran to the barometer and tapped it as if for a cardiac examination.[1] But it did not rise and did not fall, remained in a state of insidious motionlessness. What that meant is now apparent. Everything is dripping. And I am staring into the leaden gray drizzle outside with a kind of despairing satisfaction at the baseness of the universe. Alas, the refractoriness of life, of substance, of matter, could sometimes drive us to "frenzy" or to apathy. We would like to dash our visions down rapidly with a big brush, as fresh and perfect as we first saw them; but everything resists, blocks, checks, intrudes difficult details, demands compromises and renunciations. Everything is so hard, hard and obstinate, and must be mastered slowly, slowly, with superhuman patience and tenacity. And you, who maintain that "it" is happening too quickly, has happened too quickly! Do you know that since the day I told you in plain words how much I love you, two whole months have passed!

TO KURT MARTENS

Konradstrasse 11
Munich
July 14, 1904

Dear Martens:

Many thanks for your card with its sympathetic inquiry. How do I feel? Thoroughly miserable. She is gone, left to join her gravely ill father in Bad Kissingen, where her mother is also. These last days have been wonderful. I saw her every other day. Then, on the afternoon before her departure, her good little twin brother[1] actually left me alone with her for half an hour. There was an inexpressibly sweet and painful parting which has left all my nerves and senses still quivering, but again without any definite result. Impossible. She cannot, cannot "imagine it," cannot decide. As long as the decision does not directly confront her, she feels that everything—in her own words—is easy, natural and uncomplicated; but when the issue comes up, she looks at me like a hunted doe and is

[1] During this period Thomas Mann and Katia occasionally went on bicycle excursions; hence his concern with the weather.

[1] Klaus Pringsheim (b. July 24, 1883), later a musician, pupil of Gustav Mahler, at one time musical director of the Reinhardt theaters in Berlin; also a journalist and conductor in Tokyo.

incapable. . . . Dr. Seif, a neurologist and good psychologist who knows all about the affair, like everybody else, has discussed the matter in detail with me. He confirmed (what I have long suspected) that this fear of coming to a decision has a decidedly morbid element. If I do not proceed with much more tact and restraint, he said, he would predict from experience that nothing will come of the engagement. Tuesday morning I went to the train, brought her flowers, and since Klaus took a touchingly long time to pay the porter, I had the opportunity to tell her how sad I felt. Did she, too, feel a little sadness? A little, yes. Very careful. But at any rate she pressed my hand for a long time, and looked only at me while the train pulled out of the station. I feel like death. This is a parting for an almost indefinite time. She will stay three weeks in Kissingen, then stop only briefly in Munich on her way back; and she is going to Switzerland with her mother for the rest of the summer. In the autumn she will be with relatives in north Germany. Isn't it enough to drive one to despair? On the 21st of this month I am supposed to read to the Göttingen Literary Society, and I wanted to be in Bayreuth on the 31st for *Parsifal*, but I'll give that up if I can see her here for fifteen minutes. From August 1 on I intend to spend six weeks with my mother in Utting on the Ammersee, and hope to be able to work there—right now working is still absolutely impossible for me. How happy, how strong and enterprising I could feel, if she had given me some assurance at parting. You cannot imagine how I love this creature. I dream of her every night, and wake with my heart all sore. I have tasted too much of her to be able to surrender now. Death seems to me far less a surrender than living without her.

So long. Have a good rest.

TO KATIA

[Mid-July 1904]

And since the weather has turned lovely, B[erchtesgaden] is really magnificent. Mornings in the garden before breakfast, when the snow-covered peaks of the Watzmann float above the mists against the blue sky—you should be with me. I am not one of your nature fanatics; but there are still some sights that move me.

1904

TO KATIA

[*Mid-July 1904*]

I live without a vest and read Rousseau.

TO KATIA

[*Mid-August 1904*]

That is love. We imagine that we need only allow our feelings to speak
in order for everything to turn to happiness. But that is not the right thing
at all, certainly not between *us*—I recognize that quite clearly now.
Between us, reason must have its say: its full say. We must talk with one
another, talk everything over without reserve, calmly, circumspectly,
and sensibly. . . .

TO KATIA

[*Mid-August 1904*]

That old whimper about coldheartedness with which Carl Busse[1] began,
the one who writes such singularly trivial poems. I am coldhearted, you
must know—of course you can confirm that out of your own experience.
In all seriousness, there are no more than five or six persons in Germany
who know what irony is, and understand that it need not necessarily stem
from a desolate inner life. If a writer knows how to make his work
pungent, and to be economical with his means, he is dismissed as an
emotionless trickster. I always wonder that Wagner has not been declared
an ice-cold *contriver* because he put the *Liebestod* at the end of the act. . . .
But I should like to send all these blockheads to you, Katia, so that you
can tell them whether or not I am "cold." What would you answer?

. . . You know that I am indescribably fond of you and that I believe
in our union as I believe in myself and the future: without this belief it
would be best to go straight to the grave. That is very simple. But you,
who do not feel and think so simply on this matter as I, you who are still
in doubt and bothered by scruples . . .

Incredible! In Munich, two or three days that I had to spend without you seemed to me an insuperable eternity, and now I manage to do

---

[1] Carl Busse (1872–1918), poet and novelist.

without you for almost three months in a tolerably good state of mind. Man is a remarkably tough vertebrate!

TO KATIA

Katia, dear beloved little Katia, never have I been more filled with you than in these past days. I imagine I hear the strange and elusive sound of your voice, see before me the dark gleam of your eyes, the pearly pallor of your sweet, clever, mutable face—and a burning admiration seizes me, a tenderness swells in me, for which there are no signs and symbols! And you? And you?

TO KATIA

[*Late August 1904*]

. . . In you I saw a minor miracle of harmonious education, a realized cultural ideal, an altogether rare and lucky chance of a creature, artistic and demure, free and full of grace. But what was my delight in all this by comparison with my rapture at the knowledge granted me gradually, and which I could not have acquired at first sight. For you were *good*, were *kind*. If you understood what that meant to me! The feeling for you, which until then had stirred only hesitantly and uncertainly in me, was suddenly released; I took heart, saw wonderful hopes. Up to then, where I had loved I had always at the same time despised. The mingling of longing and contempt, ironic love, had been my most characteristic emotion. Tonio Kröger loved "life," blue-eyed commonness, nostalgically, mockingly, and hopelessly. And now? A being sweet as the world— and also good, and also uncommon, and also able (though perhaps not willing) to meet me with intelligence and kindness: something absolutely and incredibly new! This love, the strongest there can be, is from this point of view—*whatever may happen*—my first and only *happy* love.

TO KATIA

[*Late August 1904*]

. . . because my work is causing me much trouble. This is of course quite in order and in itself not a bad sign. It has never yet "effervesced," and would make me suspicious if it did. It effervesces only for ladies and dilettantes, for the easily satisfied and the ignorant who do not live under the pressure and the discipline of talent. For talent is nothing easy, nothing playful; it is not an ability to perform without more ado. At the root it is *necessity*, a critical knowledge of the ideal, an insatiability which creates and intensifies the ability it requires, and does so at the cost of some torment. For the greatest, the most insatiable, their talent is the harshest scourge. Once when I was much younger I came on an inconspicuous sentence in Flaubert's letters that I lingered over a long time. He wrote to a friend, at the time he was working on *Salammbô*, I think: *"Mon livre me fait beaucoup de douleurs!" "Beaucoup de douleurs!"* Even then I understood that, and since then I have done nothing without repeating this sentence to myself a hundred times, for consolation. . . .

TO KATIA

[End of August 1904]

. . . Stupid? If you like. You are so utterly enchanting a creature, my Katia, that for all I care you could be "a little stupid." That you aren't, you yourself know best. But if by "stupid" you mean the opposite of "smart" (and I suppose that is it), by all means be so. I am the same way and am pleased to be so. For "smartness" is something deeply nasty. The "smart" person confines himself to eating no more than two rolls every day, lives cautiously, loves cautiously, and is too cautious to resolutely bind his life to his love. Everything naïve, noble, and devout is "stupid," all intrepid devotion on this earth. *Let us be* "stupid," my Katia!

TO KATIA

[End of August 1904]

Your letter, your last letter, these few deliciously sly, evasive, promising ambiguous phrases—can you really guess what a Grail miracle and sign of salvation this little sheet of paper covered with its somewhat childlike scrawl was for me? . . . A storm of rapture! And then, by way of reaction, an almost sluggish sinking down in happiness. —And then came our meeting—without moonlight, at six o'clock on a dully bright afternoon, the time when one is sick and tired of the day and dusk simply will not come yet, a superfluous and nervous hour—at the tea table. . . . .

Amuse yourself—oh, you may amuse yourself! I do it myself. I shall never forget a certain moment in the performance of *The Inspector-General*. One of Gogol's officials, about to try his luck at bribery, falls in his nervousness into a kind of trembling that probably only happens on the stage. And you (I see *everything*), you turned your head toward me to see what kind of look I would have on my face at this sight. I don't know whether you expected me to sink into the floor along with my folding chair; but I assure you I suddenly felt filled with a wholly liberated, objective, and artistic merriment. Your turning your head at this moment was so thoroughly genuine, it so wonderfully brought out the girlish curiosity, the *gamine* quality that is in you along with so much else and that I certainly would not want otherwise, that I instantly hailed it as the real *petit fait*, the affirmative result of the evening. . . . Once in the good old days, when you still had great respect for me, when you were simply my reader and who knows, perhaps even "admirer," I told you that in associating with people I almost never was consciously aware of my own worth. That is true. But if I do not have this awareness, I have instead the confidence *that others have it for me*. And arrogant as it may sound, I regard a person's conduct toward me as a criterion of his inner cultivation. . . . People say that a strong emotion elevates and animates a man, must make him bold, joyous, and active; but that is only what people say, though it may be right enough for the common run. Not for me. I am distracted, derailed, alienated from myself. . . . But you must not be misled by this, but keep in mind that I am, by my origins and personal merit, fully entitled to hope for you. No matter what kind of faces I may make, you should never forget that you absolutely will not be stooping, absolutely will not be performing an act of condescension, if someday you publicly take the hand that I so beseechingly extend.

TO KATIA

[Early September 1904]

With your letter in hand I wept like a child. . . . No doubt I would damage myself by this candor if I were dealing with an ordinary young girl; but you are not ordinary. If you were, the joys—and sorrows—you give me would be less extraordinary.

Do you remember what I once wrote you: A primitive and vital instinct tells me, in a kind of colloquial and unsophisticated language, that emotions of the sort I have for you cannot be in vain? They cannot!

Someday, since nothing really hostile, no dislike and no *other* liking, opposes them, someday you must reach out and draw to yourself what you long for.

TO KATIA

[Early September 1904]

Today is such a fine day . . . the sky a festive blue as it has not been for weeks, and I feel young and strong in feeling as never before in my life. I can only think that everything must turn out well and happily after all; for I love you, Katia, I love you beyond all creatures and all virtues!

TO KATIA

[Mid-September 1904]

Do you know why we suit each other so well? Because you belong to neither the bourgeois nor the Junker class; because you, in your way, are something extraordinary—because you are, as I understand the word, *a princess*. And I—you may laugh now, but you must understand me—I have always seen myself as a kind of prince, and in you I have found, with absolute certainty, my predestined bride and companion.

TO KATIA

[Late September 1904]

I think you feel as well as I that it is high time this interim state was ended. Once we belong together publicly . . . won't that be a much cleaner and cozier relationship?

TO KATIA

[Late September 1904]

. . . that you—immortal phrase—showed me your books.

TO KATIA

[End of September 1904]

Oh, you amazing, painfully sweet, painfully tangy creature! Longing— *Sehnsucht!* You don't know how I love the word. It is my favorite word, my holy word, my magic formula, my key to the mystery of the world. . . .

1904

TO KURT MARTENS

Ainmillerstrasse 21 III
Munich
October 4, 1904

Dear Martens:

Along with expressing regret for having missed you yesterday, I can now inform you that *I became engaged to Katia Pringsheim* yesterday. I would be delighted to see you soon.

Yours,

TO PHILIPP WITKOP [1]

Munich
October 30, 1904

Dear Doctor Witkop:

Many thanks at last for your friendly lines. I wish I could have written sooner to say how pleased I was that for once you broke your silence (which, by the way, I perfectly understand); but you can imagine that I am very taken up right now. [. . .] Moreover my conscience will not come to rest, for my fear of "happiness" is by no means small, and I am still caught up in doubt as to whether my surrender to "life" is really something highly moral or a kind of dissoluteness. You with your Workmen's Welfare would probably vote for the former; and your fine poems show me how well you know how to combine life and art.

My Berlin reading had to be postponed because I must finish my dramatic poem [2] next month. The evening has now been fixed for November 30.

Perhaps my fiancée and her mother will come too.

I am looking forward to seeing you again.

Yours,

---

[1] Philipp Witkop (1880–1942), poet, professor of modern German literature in Freiburg. Among his works: *Das Wesen der Lyrik, Die neuere deutsche Lyrik, Deutsche Dichtung der Gegenwart.*
[2] *Fiorenza.*

1905

————————•————————

Franz Joseph Strasse 2
Munich
November 11, 1905

Dear Martens:

I announce to you the happy arrival of a well-formed little girl.[1] The day of the arrival was a fearful one; but now everything is idyll and peace, and to see the infant at the mother's breast is a sight that transfigures and sanctifies the atrocious agonies of the birth. A mystery! A great thing! I had a notion of life and one of death, but I did not yet know what birth is. Contemplation of it has shaken me through and through.

---

[1] Erika Julia Hedwig Mann, born November 9, 1905. Erika Mann became an actress, journalist, and writer. She was briefly married to the actor and later director, Gustaf Gründgens; in 1935 she married the poet W. H. Auden. Among her works are texts for her cabaret, *The Peppermill*; *School for Barbarians* (New York, 1938), a study of education under Hitler; *The Lights Go Down* (New York, 1940), and *The Last Year of Thomas Mann* (New York, 1958). With her brother Klaus she wrote *Runderhum, ein heiteres Reisebuch*, an account of their travels around the world, *Escape to Life* (Boston, 1939), and *The Other Germany* (New York, 1940). For many years Thomas Mann relied upon her for editorial and practical advice. She died in 1969.

1906

———————•———————

TO KURT MARTENS

Franz Joseph Strasse 2
Munich
March 28, 1906

Dear Martens:

Many thanks for your kindness in sending your essay.[1] A fine dual portrait that testifies to your talent as a critic. Certainly it contains minor distortions, exaggerations, misunderstandings, premature judgments—but the important thing is that you say something definite. And after all, what does "a likeness" matter? Everything is viewed interestingly and said interestingly; that is the main point.

Nevertheless, I should like to note for you personally a few things that I shook my head over.

It won't do to attribute to me "icy misanthropy" and "lovelessness toward everything of flesh and blood" which is "replaced" by a fanatic worship of art. Both *Tonio Kröger* and *Fiorenza* are full of irony toward art, and written into *Tonio Kröger* is a confession of love for life which verges on the inartistic in its overtness and directness. Isn't that confession believable? Is it only rhetoric?? It won't do to call *Buddenbrooks* a "destructive" book. "Critical" and "sardonic"—that may be. But not destructive. It is too affirmatively artistic, too lovingly graphic, at its core too cheerful. Must one write dithyrambs to establish oneself as an affirmer of life? Every good book that is written against life is actually tempting its readers on behalf of life. —I am sorry to have to confuse you; but the matter is not as simple as you say. It's a good point that *Buddenbrooks* is not exactly "regional art," but it does not do to call it an essentially un-German book. How much of Wagner, Schopenhauer, even

[1] "Die Gebrüder Mann" ("The Mann Brothers"), *Leipziger Tageblatt* No. 151, 1906.

Fritz Reuter is in it! Simply ask yourself in what national atmosphere other than the German it could have been written. In none, you must admit. And then consider whether you are right in saying that I feel myself an outcast among my own people.

It won't do to say that I "would like to put creative imagination on the same level with dime-novel ingenuity." In fact I do not regard the gift of inventing characters and plots as the essence of the art of writing. Every lyric poet who can do nothing but directly express his own soul proves that I am right. And I am, after all, a lyric poet (fundamentally). I say that writers who have nothing but "inventiveness" are not far from the dime novels. I say that very great writers did not invent anything in their whole lives, but merely poured their souls into traditional materials and reshaped them. I say that Tolstoy's work is at least as strictly auto-biographical as my humbler product. "Imagination?" You will admit that I have some gift for detail, some liveliness and contemporaneity, some keenness of vision and *energy of conception*. And what does all that amount to if not imagination? (I say nothing of linguistic, stylistic imagination.) "*Creative* imagination"? But I have created, you know! Terribly little as yet—four medium-good books—but they do *exist*. What are you asking for?

You speak slightingly of "Bilse und Ich."[2] Why? It's strange: people always think they have to take a stand on this essay. What in the world for? An assertion can be confirmed or contested. But—do read it right!—I haven't really made any assertions at all, you know. I don't say: The novelist has the right to do portraits of people. Such a right cannot be proved. I do say: Important writers through the ages have assumed that right. I should like to present a few reasons for this. I should like to point out the error inherent in making a literal identifi-cation between reality and its artistic image. I should like to have a work of art regarded as something absolute, not subject to everyday ques-tions of right and wrong. I note a misunderstanding and I undertake to analyze its origins; if possible to decrease its harmful effects. That is all. Is this unworthy, useless, megalomaniacal? Have I not acted in the interests of society as well as those of art? I had counted on plain grati-

---

[2] "Bilse and I," an essay first published in the *Münchner Neueste Nachrichten* (February 1906). The essay took issue with the reading public's tendency to look for a real person behind every character a writer creates. The essay was prompted by a libel suit in Lübeck, in which a Lieutenant Bilse, author of a novel, "The Little Garrison," was accused of having vilified the little garrison in which he had served. The prosecution lawyer persistently linked Bilse's book, which had no literary merit, with *Buddenbrooks*, and thus provoked Thomas Mann's rejoinder.

tude and I hear people shouting: Yes, yes! or No, no! The world is odd.

"Thomas Mann would like to extract some glory from mere resistance to *physical* complaints." You say that with such astonishment, with an undertone of "What nonsense!" —You apparently think I want to confer immortality on everyone who smiles when he has a stomachache. That is how one's remarks are understood at the Odeon Bar. No wonder I prefer to stay home. What I mean has been fairly well expressed in a few words by my Lorenzo: "No greatness comes effortlessly. . . . Hindrance is the will's best friend. . . ." (In the words of Lorenzo, the lord of pleasure, whom I did not draw without a measure of sympathy, after all, And yet when you consider him you assert that I "on principle impress the stamp of baseness upon every kind of lust for life.") So you think I regard men like Heracles or Siegfried as fine popular idols, but not as heroes! For men, heroism is an achievement "in spite of"; it is weakness overcome; *tenderness* is part of it. Klinger's weak little Beethoven[3] who has taken his seat upon the great throne of the gods and clenches his fists in passionate concentration—there you have a hero. Physical suffering seems to me an almost necessary concomitant of greatness, and this seems to me psychologically reasonable. I do not think that Caesar would have become Caesar without his sickly constitution and his epilepsy, and if he had he would have been less a hero in my eyes. After all, isn't there a great deal of heroism in Thomas Buddenbrook, worn out as he is, forcing himself to play his role? Can it be you have no feeling for that?

"T. M. by his whole nature condemned to be an ascetic"—that is not wrong, but it is extreme. (I repeat: You did have to say something resolute.) I am an ascetic insofar as my *conscience* directs me toward *achievement* in contrast to pleasure and to "happiness." So much the worse for me, since I have no great aptitude for achievement. I am, then, hardly an ascetic except in the sense: "Do I strive for happiness? I strive for my work!" I distrust pleasure, I distrust happiness, which I regard as unproductive. I think that nowadays one cannot serve both masters, pleasure and art; that man is not strong and perfect enough to do so. I don't believe that anyone today can be a *bon vivant* and at the same time an artist. One must decide, and my conscience decides for achievement. If that is "Quakerish," then *Fiorenza* preaches a Quakerish mode of living—insofar as such a mode fosters achievement. *But otherwise not.* You really ought to know that I am too skeptical or, putting it more proudly, too *free* to preach anything in my books—let alone preaching

[3] Max Klinger's Beethoven monument in Leipzig.

Quakerism! *Fiorenza* is a dream of greatness and spiritual power. "At stake are souls, at stake is the realm"—that is all. It is the representation of a heroic struggle between the senses and the spirit—and this representation is completely impartial. The fact that Fiore treats the artist-children condescendingly does not imply any doctrine. The book would have a doctrine only if *I* treated Lorenzo condescendingly. I have treated him as a hero. I have permitted an almost excessive justice to prevail. At moments the prior is not given his due. And didn't you feel that I gave at *least* as much of my own self to Lorenzo as to the prior, that Lorenzo is at least as subjective and lyrical a figure?—Incidentally, the fine things you found to say about the language of *Fiorenza* warmed my heart. In *Zeitgeist* recently a different note was struck. There were all sorts of remarks about the "tortured language of modernity such as adolescent snobs cultivate everywhere nowadays" and about *"crude infractions of the rules of grammar."* That was the way the whole thing went, and it was by none other than Richard Schaukal. Naturally he had *reasons* for this criticism, or as you would put it, "he felt obliged to. . . ."

And now just one more thing. You say that one of these days, if I am ever to become somebody, I will receive more cool respect than heartfelt affection. Dear friend, that is simply not true. Granted, if you say it to people a few more times, they will accept it. If you represent me a few more times as embittered, icy, mocking, and rootless, your prediction will probably come true. So far it has been otherwise. It is not true that *Buddenbrooks* and *Tonio Kröger* have been foisted on the public by essays and that they are coolly appreciated. These expressions of my self are *loved*, believe me, and to such an extent that I might well feel disturbed. "Am I so soft, so insipid, so mediocre," I have more than once asked myself, "that I should be loved like this?" No matter. Since I am neither frivolous nor crotchety nor tart nor stiff, I do not see, if I should somehow prove lasting, why Germans should refuse me love in the future. What aspects of my humanity would they take exception to? I was a quiet, well-behaved person, who won a measure of prosperity by the work of his hands, took a wife, begot children, attended first nights, and was so good a German that I could not stand being abroad for more than four weeks. Is it absolutely necessary to go bowling and drinking on top of that?

These are the sorts of things I objected to in your essay. I am pretty sure that my brother too would have similar reservations—this Heinrich Mann whom you describe as so egoistically solitary and who right now, in the most expansive way, is doing battle in the newspapers for Professor Murri.[4] But let everyone sweep his own doorstep.

I hope you won't find this reply ungrateful or preposterous. But I thought: Why shouldn't I gently steer right my most intelligent and best-informed critic where he seems to be going wrong or distorting?

Forgive me this long piece.

TO KURT MARTENS

Munich
November 19, 1906

Dear Martens:

With great joy I announce the happy birth of a well-formed boy.[1]

---

[4] On May 5, 1906, an essay by Heinrich Mann appeared in *Die Zukunft* (a magazine of politics and the arts) in which he espoused the cause of Professor Murri, the defendant in a much discussed murder trial.

[1] Klaus Heinrich Thomas Mann, born November 18, 1906. Klaus Mann published his first book at the age of twenty. Among his works are *Der fromme Tanz* (1926) and *Alexander, Roman der Utopie* (1929; English edition, 1930). Written in exile were *Journey into Freedom* (1936), *Symphonie Pathétique* (1936; English edition 1948), *The Turning Point* (1942), *André Gide and the Crisis of Modern Thought* (1943). He edited the magazines *Die Sammlung* in Amsterdam and *Decision* in New York, and collaborated with his sister Erika on a number of books, including *Escape to Life* (1939) and *The Other Germany* (1940). During the Second World War he served in the American Army. He committed suicide in Cannes on May 22, 1949.

1909

---•---

TO HUGO VON HOFMANNSTHAL

Dear Herr von Hofmannsthal:

I have no intention of letting you go unthanked for the friendly letter that accompanied *Die Zukunft*. But it arrived when our move here was already impending; first we had to dismantle our household in Munich and then cope with the chaos here. Order is only now emerging, gradually, very gradually.

It makes me very happy that you take such a kindly interest in my pair of lovers in the *Rundschau*.[2] When we met, I was glad to see by your remarks that you can judge the story in terms of its intentions. You also used the word *allegory*, which, as we both know, is in extreme disrepute in contemporary aesthetics. Nevertheless, poetic allegory on the grand scale seems to me a noble form, and I believe there is no better way to ennoble the novel than by making it idealized and constructivistic. The effort to do so is my sole excuse for oddities such as the ones you point out. The conversation about the countess's husband is certainly impossible socially; but you have to consider that the two are "probing" one another for knowledge and "clues." Of course, the prince's ignorance is not intended realistically but is decoratively exaggerated, and one must cling to the humorous assumption that his knowledge has not progressed beyond the revelations of the shoemaker Hinnerke. Isn't it forgivable that he somewhat neglects the social graces in conversation with the little "sister" he has found, and with whom he will find the way out of

---

[1] In 1909 Thomas Mann bought a small country house in Bad Tölz. He and his family spent their summers in it, and Mann occasionally went there in winter to work in quiet. The house was sold in 1917.

[2] *Royal Highness*, first printed in the *Neue Rundschau* between January and September, 1909.

majesty into life—especially since the matter is most cautiously expressed? Frankly, there is another passage which to me seems more dubious than this one, and whose perils my brother Heinrich has pointed out. I mean the scene between the prince and the poet Martini. Here reality suddenly appears and converses with its own symbol. That is at best amusing. During the writing, I referred back to the dialogue in *The Pretenders*[3] between Skule and the skald—perhaps wrongly so. It would mean a great deal to me to hear whether you let the scene pass.

I read *Peints par eux-mêmes*[4] about ten years ago and recall it as a highly virtuoso variation on the epistolary novel. This genre, of course, usually deals in direct confessions, whereas Hervieu's book entertains by the art of indirect characterization. (I hear there are still people who claim "indirect characterization" as an advantage of the drama—is it true?)

The Reinhardt[5] theater has impressed me very much; it has at times seemed to me the most interesting project of our day. In any case, I believe that if it is critically enjoyed in its typical and intrepid modernity, it has a good deal of reassurance and encouragement to offer to every modern artist. I have not missed a single premiere, and I am looking forward to all the new ones, including *Elektra*,[6] which I have already seen in Berlin but with an inadequate cast.

With all good wishes and greetings.

---

[3] Drama (1864) by Henrik Ibsen (1828–1906).

[4] Novel (1893) by Paul Hervieu (1857–1915).

[5] The *Deutsches Theater* in Berlin, under the direction of Max Reinhardt (1873–1943). Reinhardt was also the founder, with Hugo von Hofmannsthal, of the Salzburg Festspiele (1920). He emigrated to Austria in 1933 and in 1938 went to the United States, where he profoundly influenced both the theater and the film.

[6] *Elektra* (1903), drama by Hugo von Hofmannsthal; first performed as an opera with music by Richard Strauss in Dresden in 1909.

1910

---•---

TO KURT MARTENS

Franz Joseph Strasse 2
Munich
January 11, 1910

Dear Martens:

Thanks so much for your article. It is very fine, and probably needed to be written since Hermann Bahr's "doctrines" can sow confusion because of their entertaining style.[1] I don't really believe though, that he takes them or himself very seriously, and feel sure that like all Viennese he basically far prefers my brother to me—Heinrich no doubt belongs rather more to the "sword-swallowers." Bahr demonstrated that recently by sending Heinrich his *Dalmatinische Reise* "with great respect." At the moment his taste does not quite harmonize with his theories, for the latter are always the result of his eternal nervousness about remaining modern and not missing out on the newest of the new. He was the first in Germany to utter the *dernier cri de Paris*. Now he has nimbly changed over to Walt Whitman's Indian Rousseauism and the democratic movement in Germany, which of course is only one among many "movements," but which in fact may have a considerable future—in literary terms too. But instead of clarifying it as a critic, as by rights he should, Bahr has to set himself up as its *gonfaloniere* merely because it's the latest and barely arrived fashion. Nevertheless, it's in the air, for as you too may point out, I was not entirely untouched by it myself while I was writing *Royal Highness*. I hinted as much when we were talking about it in Dresden. A certain didactically anti-individualistic note in the book cannot be denied, and my brother, a passionate democrat of the newest stamp (his latest novel is extremely interesting as a topical work) was *delighted* with

---

[1] Hermann Bahr (1863–1934), Austrian dramatist, essayist, and theater critic.

55

Bahr's interpretation of *Royal Highness*. Doesn't that strike you as significant? Politically, democracy is certainly on the march in this country, and belles lettres are unmistakably taking some part in it. Haven't you noticed that almost all our "intellectuals" signed the appeal of the *Berliner Tageblatt* in favor of electoral reform in Prussia? Granted, they'll write their names on practically anything that's put in front of them; but it's still a sign of the times that the politicians are trying to recruit them. The increasing interest is mutual. The politicians on their part are concerned about us! The *Frankfurter Zeitung* recently carried an article on the education of princes in which my novel was discussed at length! It is certainly a misunderstanding to regard *Royal Highness* as a book of social criticism; and what you call the "altruistic"—and Bahr and my brother the "democratic"—element in it is only one of its implications. Although its artistic merit is not based on that, perhaps its intellectual or ethical merit is, and if the book is read at all in the future it may possibly be for the sake of this element.

Forgive my verbosity. I only wanted to defend Bahr, so far as he deserves it. At any rate you are perfectly right in saying that henceforth "democratic" books cannot seriously be expected from me. As you know, an artist can give certain trends of the times their due in one work and then show himself entirely independent of them afterwards. Insofar as I can foresee my future work, it certainly will have nothing whatever to do with democracy. I am now collecting, noting, making studies for something long planned, something quite unusual: *The Confessions of the Confidence Man.*[2] [. . .] And what are you up to? How is your book of criticism going? I'm looking forward to it with great curiosity. Let me hear from you before too long.

Do, please, give Herr v. d. Gabelentz[3] my regards when you see him, and best regards to yourself.

---

[2] Thomas Mann began writing *Confessions of Felix Krull, Confidence Man* in 1910, but dropped the project in the summer of 1911 in favor of *Death in Venice*. Not until 1951 did Mann turn to *Felix Krull* again. He had carried the fragmentary manuscript with him through all the years, and resumed on the same page and line where he had ended in 1911.

[3] A Munich writer.

TO HEINRICH MANN

Landhaus Thomas Mann
Bad Tölz
August 7, 1910

Dear Heinrich:

After writing you a long letter, I set it aside because I realized that in your present state of nerves[1] it would do more harm than good. And so I simply let you know that we are expecting you. Your letter contains much that is feverish and reprehensible, much that must be strictly and firmly dismissed. I hope that talking it over will be more profitable than further correspondence, which with us always tends to take too literary a turn. Mama is not returning here until Tuesday or Wednesday. It would be a kindness if you made the trip with her.

With warm greetings from us both,   T.

TO PAUL EHRENBERG

Bad Tölz
August 12, 1910

Dear Paul:

Many, many thanks for your sympathetic lines. Yes, poor Carla. There is hardly any satisfactory explanation for her death; at least none that can be couched in a few words. You probably knew that she was engaged to a young manufacturer from Mühlhausen, and quite happily so. Nevertheless there were inner conflicts which made it impossible—subjectively —for her to go on living. She imagined she saw her hopes collapsing, thought her chances for life were exhausted. And so she took some of the potassium cyanide which she had had around for a long time. She must originally have bought it as a sort of aesthetic caprice and idiosyncrasy— you know, the way she kept a skull on the dresser as a young girl. But then she played too long with the idea, grew used to the thought of taking it at the first provocation. She once boasted to Liane Pricken that she had poison enough for a whole regiment. And then she swallowed enough for a company, so that she died very quickly and, unless all appearances were deceptive, without pain. What she would do to all of us, what a blow it would be to our lives when she smashed her own life, apparently never entered the poor child's mind. You can imagine our Mama's grief. It

---

[1] Thomas and Heinrich Mann's sister Carla had committed suicide on July 30.

happened in Polling—in Mama's apartment. She is here with us now and is gradually returning to a tolerable state of mind. I would be very glad to tell you more of the story face to face, would be altogether very glad to see you again. Won't you visit us with your wife one of these days? Mama asks me to send you her warm regards and to thank you for the handsome wreath. My wife sends her greetings too, as do I.

Ever yours,

TO PAUL EHRENBERG

Bad Tölz
September 3, 1910

Dear Paul:

Many thanks for your kind letter, which really made me feel what a loyal good friend you are. Of course I understand the reasons you cannot come here now. I have just been in Munich, and in a week or so must go back for a prize jury conference (I want to take in the Mahler symphony as well). To make still another trip in between would be too much for me, especially as I badly need rest. Well, winter is not far away, and let us hope we see each other often then—in spite of urban distances. (We are moving to 13 Mauerkircherstrasse, Herzogpark.)

Yesterday we very pleasantly celebrated my father-in-law's sixtieth birthday here. A vast number of telegrams arrived, in the morning the band from the baths gave a concert in our garden, at dinner I managed to deliver a speech, and in the evening there was a torchlight procession and singing by the schoolchildren. Yes, life goes on, and as long as one is not also lying in a black, rectangular pit in the ground, interlaced by tree roots, one must go along with it a little.

My feelings have been in sad disorder all this while. If Carla had been able to imagine what her deed would do to the rest of us, I think she would not have committed it. But gradually we regain our balance, and already I can think without disgust of the toilsome and passionate playing that is called artistic work.

So, then, I look forward to seeing you again in about two months. We'll talk it all over and try, although it isn't easy, to come to some terms with poor Carla's action.

With cordial greetings from house to house.

1912

---•---

Mauerkircherstrasse 13
Munich
April 2, 1912

Dear Heinrich:

[. . .]

I have conveyed your greetings and good wishes to Katia. She writes cheerful letters and already feels better. The doctors up there say that her case is not serious but tedious. She will have to stay in the mountains six months—and should certainly have gone up long ago. The injection treatment (which Dr. Ebenhausen advised against) caused extensive nervous damage. I couldn't stop her because the idea was that it would avoid the long separation from the children.

Things are rather hard for me now, but aside from a few days of illness I have never entirely stopped working, and I hope *Death in Venice* will be finished before I go to Davos (beginning of May). It is something very singular at the least, and although you won't approve of it as a whole, you won't be able to deny certain felicities. An archaizing chapter in particular seems to me successful. The story will be published first in a limited edition by Hans von Weber,[1] in a deluxe format.

I am looking forward to your drama with extraordinary eagerness. Dr. von Jakobi,[2] who visited recently, told me something about it.

Warmly,   T.

---

[1] Hans von Weber (1872–1924), Munich publisher and editor.
[2] Bernhard von Jakobi, actor at the Royal Bavarian Court Theaters.

TO HEINRICH MANN

Munich
April 27, 1912

Dear Heinrich:

Forgive me for not answering your letter until today. I could not get to it at once. In addition to the usual afternoon correspondence I now have the regular reports to Katia.

Congratulations on the completion of the play! I wish I could say the same for my novella, but I can't find the conclusion. Perhaps I'll have to wait for the change of air in Davos in mid-May to help me along. My vitality is extremely low right now.

The military: My recollections of it are quite dreamy and hazy, mostly intangibles, matters of atmosphere that can't really be transmitted as facts, although I shall be able to bring it all into the penitentiary episode in *The Confidence Man*. My chief memory is the sensation of being hopelessly cut off from the civilized world, subject to a terrible, overpowering external pressure; and in connection with that, feeling an extraordinarily enhanced enjoyment of inner freedom—when, for example, in the barracks, while cleaning my rifle (which I never learned how to do properly) I whistled something from Tristan. But I suppose the patrioteer[1] would not react that way. Even if he is averse to bourgeois attitudes, he would necessarily succumb completely to the spirit of this isolated world, as I saw the other conscripts doing. Does he *want* to be freed? Then let him do as I did and from the start seek a connection with the bourgeois world, with whose help he can free himself. I took refuge behind Mama's doctor, Hofrat May (whom I have used in *The Confidence Man* as Health Councilor Düsing), an ambitious ass who was friendly with my chief medical officer. In the regiment you scarcely come into contact with the chief medical officer; you're dependent on his subordinate, the junior medical officer, who examines you and sends you to the "infirmary" (the barracks sickroom for light cases) or to the hospital, or else orders you back to duty, etc. This medical officer was extremely rough to me. "Who are you, what do you want," was his tone. During examinations, which I respectfully held out for, he made outrageous speeches and would say, for example, that he had to light a cigar or else he would faint (from disgust). The result was "Back to duty. Enough. Dismissed." Dr. May, however, talked with the chief medical officer,

---

[1] A reference to Heinrich Mann's projected novel, *Der Untertan*, ultimately published in English as *The Patrioteer*.

who sent for me right on the drill ground and had me up to his room for examination. He seemed unable to find anything definite, but declared that I was to continue on duty only "for the present"; he would see what could be done. "With *that* foot . . ." After a few days an infirmary aide took a print of my foot on charcoaled paper. I had been treated in the hospital for "inflamed flatfoot," but the print showed that there could be no question of a flatfoot. Now, however, the chief medical officer came paper in hand to the infirmary where I was waiting, and where the medical officer was also present. The scene was marvelous and most appropriate for your novel. The chief medical officer, cap on his head, enters with aplomb, plants himself in front of the medical officer, and gazes bleakly and severely at the latter's cap. The medical officer, who is used to associating with him as a colleague, snatches off his cap in astonishment and stands at attention. Thereupon the chief medical officer shows him the paper, speaks to him in a low voice, and commands him to see something that isn't there. The medical officer blinks alternately at his superior, at me and at the paper, and agrees, clicking his heels. From that moment on he was exceedingly polite to me and treated me as a gentleman. He knew that I had higher connections. A few weeks passed because of official formalities; then I was on the "outside." Most amusing example of corruption. Generally it is considered extremely difficult to get out once you're in.

In contrast, there was a case of idiotic severity which made a great impression on me right at the start. In other companies of one-year volunteers, infirmary cases (not hospital cases, that is) were allowed to take to their beds at home after the first fourteen days of illness (which are spent entirely in the barracks). Our captain forbade this. One soldier fell sick in the evening and next morning ran a temperature of 104°, so that he was quite unable to make it to the barracks. He went through the illness at home and when he recovered brought a certificate from his doctor. For "punishment" he was confined to the barracks for a very long time—months, I think, which is very hard on these one-year volunteers. He had to sleep in the squad room, etc. Crazy. But the captain wore an expression of immense pride on such occasions. "My company," he used to say, "is going to be a company of *soldiers*." And as a matter of fact the company was called the Iron Eleventh. Another item for you. In connection with "squad room," I just remembered an incident: Someone was actually released as unfit because he announced to the Chief Reserve Commission that he was homosexual. Couldn't you weave that in?

But now with the best will in the world I can't write further. I leave for Davos in the middle of May.

Warmly,   T.

TO FRANK WEDEKIND

Munich
December 7, 1912

Dear Herr Wedekind:

Upon receiving your letter I naturally asked the office of the police commissioner how a talk such as you describe could have taken place. I was informed that none whatsoever took place.

If it should cause you any difficulties to explain the contradiction between this definite statement on the part of the authorities and your letter, I will gladly let the riddle go unsolved.

At all events, you can rest assured that I am not the sort of person who would find your works "offensive" and prompt the authorities to take "measures" against them. This idea is absurd, and I regret that you have held it at all. On the contrary, I consider it my task as a member of the censorship advisory board to warn the superintendents of public order against infringing on works of literary status. Since we do have these censorship authorities, I prize this opportunity of letting them know my opinion from case to case, and I hardly intend to give it up. Today, too, I took the opportunity to recommend to the commissioner of police that the sentence he objected to in your play be allowed to pass; unfortunately, he did not feel that he could accept my recommendation.

Let me add, incidentally, that the line of dialogue in question may be among the most effective theatrically but certainly is not one of the most important lines in your Mystery.[1] In fact, it seemed to me at the first performance as if the public's gleeful response to this passage unnerved you yourself and as if you turned away, waiting with some impatience for the laughter to stop.

With unchanged, unchangeable esteem, my dear Herr Wedekind.

---

[1] Wedekind's *Franziska, ein modernes Mysterium* (1911).

1913

<hr>

TO HUGO VON HOFMANNSTHAL

Munich
January 9, 1913

Dear Herr von Hofmannsthal:

My thanks for your kind gift[1] come very late—but I was in Berlin, involved in a theatrical matter: My poor *Fiorenza* was being performed— that problem child which cannot live and cannot die. The performance was inadequate, everyone agrees, and since the play nevertheless pre- served a tolerable coherence and held the attention of the audience for three and a half hours, I can take a certain pride in that. Reinhardt, who had kept his hands off the whole business, prudently took off for the Hungarian mountains. But in spite of all disappointments, fruitless ex- citements, and pangs which the theater holds for the likes of me, it is still an exceedingly strange and intoxicating experience for a solitary novelist to see his dreams going about in the flesh. There was something so festive about it, for all the flaws. But the best of all was Kerr,[2] writing in the *Tag* two days after the performance. I had known more or less what was going to come, but it surpassed all expectations. A venomous snarling. Even the most innocent outsider couldn't help noticing the almost murderous personal animosity and thinking, What a character! For very few people would know how much it was his *character* that was on display. . . . But this must bore you.

Your selection is splendid. With the finest tact you have found what is of permanent interest: authentic narration. And the little foreword made me admire once again the winning tone, the intellectual music of

<hr>

[1] *Deutsche Erzähler*, a collection of German stories edited with an introduction by Hofmannsthal.

[2] Alfred Kerr (1867–1948), one of Germany's leading theater critics.

your prose. I need not say how eagerly I am looking forward to your own story. I hear that the *Rundschau* will be publishing it. When?

All good wishes. My respects to your wife.

TO THE ROYAL BAVARIAN
COMMISSIONER OF POLICE, MUNICH

Landhaus Thomas Mann
Bad Tölz
April 30, 1913

My Dear Commissioner:

After taking note of the deletions and emendations which the management of the Artists' Theater has made in Wedekind's tragedy *Lulu*, I herewith respectfully return the play with the following observations:

It is an unusually responsible task to have to pass judgment on this play as literary adviser of the censorship board. But I would nevertheless rather assume responsibility for advocating release of the play than advise that public performance be forbidden. I urgently request you to consider that it is not a worthless piece of hackwork aimed at sensationalism, sensual titillation, and glorification of vice, but a modern work of art whose importance, profundity, seriousness, and value have long been acknowledged among literary experts. It will always hold an honorable place in the history of the German drama, in spite of all the grotesque and dubious elements it contains. I have attended both private performances of the second part (*Pandora's Box*). In 1904 the audience was thoroughly outraged, repelled, and inclined to angry protests, and the evening ended with an out-and-out theatrical scandal. In 1910, at the Artists' Theater, the same play enjoyed a serious and unqualified triumph. This shows that superior public opinion has changed greatly in favor of Wedekind the artist in the last decade; in fact, this change is not confined to "superior" audiences, as was demonstrated by the surprising success with the wider middle-class public of his *Franziska*, which to my mind is artistically weaker. There is no longer any need to fear that public performances of Wedekind will scandalize audiences; and anyone who desires that the actions of the board will not unnecessarily infringe on the best interests of culture must in this case recommend prudent broad-mindedness.

I have already said that the proposed cuts are equivalent to substantial alterations. The boldest dialogue has actually been eliminated. And as for the last act, which you have called "brutal"—undoubtedly with some justice—it nevertheless carries such somber ethical weight that to my mind there can be no moral objection to it, quite aside from its dramatic indispensability.

I have not the slightest personal reason for advocating Herr Wedekind's cause. Ever since I joined the censorship advisory board he has behaved with extreme hostility and has irresponsibly and indeed insanely picked quarrels with me. I completely agree with you in your opinion of his dubious character. But as history teaches, dubious characters can make significant cultural contributions. I, and many other people, believe that this is such a case. And I believe, finally, that one should not feed Herr Wedekind's delusions of martyrdom by a new act of "suppression."

For all these reasons I vote for the release of *Lulu* in the version proposed by the Artists' Theater.

With all respect I am, sir,

Yours sincerely,

TO KURT MARTENS

Bad Tölz
May 26, 1913

Dear Martens:

I have thought it over and decided that the problem will best be solved by my resigning both from the censorship advisory board and from the League [of German Writers]. I entered the former as well as the latter for honorable reasons, out of a desire to be active in social and professional affairs. But one is not thanked for that sort of thing, and the conduct of the League disturbs me. It's what I told you recently: As long as I belonged to the censorship advisory board and the executive committee of the League simultaneously, as long as I thought it possible to hold both these positions, it was gross tactlessness on the part of the League to place "discussion and *resolutions* on the relationship of the League and the censorship advisory board" on the agenda—assuming that the League even took notice of my presence on the executive committee. But that seems not to have been the case—to judge from the highhandedness with which the honorable membership meeting passed over me with a "unanimous resolution." I would have been ready to back any action in favor of Wedekind's tragedy, but that did not suffice; my membership on the censorship advisory board had to be elevated into "the most important question facing writers today." That is the limit. I will not have the

Mühsams,[1] Lilienthals, or whatever the names of the radical loudmouths are, telling me what I am to do or not do. I have had my fill of the League of German Writers. Right at the start the bickerings with Berlin, then the sessions over Herr Daja, and now "discussion and resolutions" about me. So let there be an end of my social activity and the pretty fiction of solidarity among writers—I am only curious to see how long you'll be able to stand it. I am of course resigning from the censorship advisory board because I do not wish to be exposed to the amiable imputation that I took the side of the police against freedom fellowship, and the things of the spirit After all, I feel most at my ease unorganized and unburdened by office. And now I am going to read your novel.

TO FRANK WEDEKIND

Bad Tölz
May 29, 1913

My dear Herr Wedekind:

Your letter has given me real pleasure and compensated me for the vexations of the last few weeks.

You misunderstood me—but one who is so little understood himself is under no obligation to understand others.

If a bourgeois element in my work, in my whole sense of life and my attitude toward it (an element which discredits me neither as a human being nor as an artist, for it was present in some very great artists)—if, I say, this element inspired the bourgeois authorities with a crude confidence in me, why should I not have utilized this confidence to mediate politically between genius and authority? This mode of making myself publicly useful amused me, and I imagined that now and then I could claim a victory. . . . No matter. Since my resigning as an "arm of the police" has reinstated me in your good will, I am delighted to have resigned. The suppression of your greatest work was in any case a prime reason for resigning. Aside from the odium of this particular public office, I feel most at my ease entirely without any official position whatever.

---

[1] Erich Mühsam (1878–1934), revolutionary poet, playwright, editor. Belonged to the extreme left in Germany, although he was never a Communist. An anarchist member of the short-lived Munich Soviet Republic (1919), he developed steadily in the direction of humanitarian pacifism. He was murdered by the Nazis in 1934.

1914

———————•———————

TO STEFAN ZWEIG[1]

Munich
May 5, 1914

My Dear Herr Zweig:

I understand your view quite well. It wasn't my idea either.[2] I joined the committee after everything had been decided. But after all, what can we do? Wedekind is hardly the right subject for a public cult. No one is going to give him a villa, and his works are not the sort to attain mass circulation. Nor will he ever receive the Nobel Prize. Strindberg, who didn't receive it either, was compensated by a national donation which amounted I think, to some 60,000 crowns. In W.'s case, however, there can be no question of that. He is exceedingly German, although in such a way that the nation will take a long time to realize it. But why should not those who love and honor this profound, tormented man in all his deeply moving absurdity join to present him with a testimonial which he will be able to use in any way he pleases? No doubt he has already thought up something devilish. If it amounts to 10,000 marks, the money can be given to him. If it comes to less, something will have to be bought for him, perhaps a gold punch bowl or loving cup—he can appreciate that

[1] Stefan Zweig (1881–1942), Austrian novelist, biographer, essayist. A strong pacifist, he belonged, with Romain Rolland and others, to that group of European intellectuals who ostentatiously spent the years of the First World War in Switzerland. With the coming of Hitler, Zweig went into exile in Brazil, where in 1942 he and his severely ill second wife both committed suicide. In his memorial essay on the tenth anniversary of Stefan Zweig's death ("Stefan Zweig zum zehnten Todestag," *Altes und Neues*, 1953) Thomas Mann wrote: "Never was world fame worn with deeper modesty, finer shyness, more unfeigned humility. . . . Propagation of the good was his deep concern, and he probably devoted half of his life to translating, disseminating, serving, and helping."

[2] It had been proposed to make Wedekind a gift in honor of his fiftieth birthday, July 24, 1914.

sort of thing, too. Though I am afraid it may have to be something of silver. Prince Ernst of Sachsen-Meiningen has already turned me down. Wedekind's works afford him no pleasure at all, he writes; on the contrary they actually arouse his repugnance. I should think so! In addition to the gift, there is to be a volume in his honor published by Müller and a banquet—so that he has the feeling: Just as for Gerhart Hauptmann. I think this is primarily what matters to him.

With sincere esteem,

TO LUDWIG VON HOFMANN

Munich
June 27, 1914

My dear Sir:

I am writing about a picture of yours which I fell madly in love with this winter. It was one of the group which was exhibited at Caspari's[1] for a few weeks. I was on the point of buying it, but did not dare. My affairs at the moment are too disordered—like a typical modern German, I am living *beyond* my means. Building a house has stripped me clean— excuse my bluntness—and so I must listen to the voice of prudence, at least for the moment.

I have loved the elevated, new, solemn humanity of your art from the time I was young; I saw it and loved it in every canvas, every sheet and scrap of yours that ever came my way. But I had never before had the privilege of viewing so many of your works all together as are now on exhibit in the gallery on Briennerstrasse. I returned to *The Wave* and to the mourning women more than once. It happened that I gave a reading from my works in the midst of your dreams and figures—and I think I did better than usual.

But the painting that appealed to me above all—lastingly, as you see—is called *The Spring*.[2] You will know immediately which one I mean. Where is it now? Has it already been sold? But it might be sold at any time—before I could find out about it and snatch it up at the last moment! May I ask just one thing of you—and this request is the purpose of my letter. For the sake of the deep affection I have so long felt for your

[1] Georg Caspari (1879–1930), owner of the foremost private gallery for modern painting. Caspari often used his large exhibition room for readings and lectures. Thomas Mann gave many talks and readings there.

[2] *The Spring*—an oil painting representing bathing youths. Mann bought it shortly afterwards, and contrived to save it when he went into exile. It is now in the Thomas Mann Archives in Zurich, along with the entire contents of his study.

paintings, do me the honor of granting me first refusal on this picture. Would you please let me know if another buyer asks for it? I know the price. It is low, relatively, but I cannot raise it at the moment. But the instant I run the risk of losing the painting to another admirer, I shall probably raise it some way or other.

With my good wishes, dear sir, and my cordial admiration.

TO HEINRICH MANN

Landhaus Thomas Mann
Bad Tölz
August 7, 1914

Dear Heinrich:

If you stick to your plan of being married in Munich on the 12th, you'll have to forgive my not coming. For the present, it appears, there is no question of calling up the older classes of the landsturm. So after having acted as witness for good old Vicco at his wedding[1] and bidden him goodbye (we sent Katia's brother[2] off to war as well), we have returned here and for the present want to await developments. The train connection with Munich is extremely bad; the ride takes four hours, and presumably this will go on for weeks. In these circumstances, and since any friend or acquaintance, Brantl,[3] Herzog,[4] or anyone else can replace me (Klaus Pringsheim would also be happy to fill in), I would be grateful if you will excuse me from the witnessing. But perhaps you will postpone the wedding for a little while?

I still feel as if I'm dreaming—and yet I suppose I should be ashamed that I didn't think it possible and didn't see that the catastrophe was bound to come. What a visitation! What will Europe look like, inwardly and outwardly, when it is over? I personally have to prepare for a total change in our material circumstances. It is fairly certain that if the war lasts long, I shall be what is called "ruined." So be it! What would that signify compared with the upheavals, especially the large-scale psychic upheavals, which war must necessarily bring? Shouldn't we

[1] Viktor Mann hastily married Magdalena (Nelly) Kilian before leaving for the front.
[2] Heinz Pringsheim (born 1882), who became first an archaeologist, then a musicologist and a well-known music critic in Munich.
[3] Maximilian Brantl (1881–1959), a lawyer by vocation, a writer by avocation. He was Heinrich Mann's lawyer and also a good friend of Thomas Mann.
[4] Wilhelm Herzog (1884–1960), writer, pacifistic socialist, for many decades Heinrich Mann's closest friend.

be grateful for the totally unexpected chance to experience such mighty things? My chief feeling is a tremendous curiosity—and, I admit it, the deepest sympathy for this execrated, indecipherable, fateful Germany which, if she has hitherto not unqualifiedly held "civilization" as the highest good, is at any rate preparing to smash the most despicable police state in the world.

Meanwhile I am trying to work. What luck for you that you have just finished. I must take comfort from the fact that my project,[5] too, is not completely divorced from what is happening.

Warm greetings—to your wife also,   T.

TO HEINRICH MANN

Poschingerstrasse 1
Munich
September 18, 1914

Dear Heinrich:

[. . .] I don't share your pessimism about your work and its future in Germany. Rather, I think you are being most unfair to German culture. Your fame has been climbing steadily these past ten years. Can you really think that as a result of this great, fundamentally decent, and in fact stirring peoples' war, Germany would be so set back in her cultivation or ethos that she could permanently reject your gifts?

Warmly,   T.

TO PHILIPP WITKOP

Munich
November 11, 1914

Dear Professor:

Thanks so much for your friendly letter and the pamphlet. Ah yes, who would have thought that along with my reading in Freiburg, Europe's era of peace would end in a last transfiguration! But seriously, shouldn't we be ashamed of having failed to sense anything at all? Even after the Archduke's death I did not have a glimmering, and when war was declared I went on saying that it would not come to anything serious. It really is ridiculous that I simply no longer believed in war—just because I happened to be born four years after the last peace treaty. But in the end

---

[5] *The Magic Mountain*, which he had already begun.

it is *good* to have been taught this lesson—I feel it so at any rate, without in the least wishing to pose as a strong man, although the physical and spiritual atrocities the war brings with it at times give me a nasty turn. But it is not good when people no longer believe in war. Pretty soon they no longer believe in many other things which they absolutely must believe if they are to be decent men.

My military situation is like yours, except that I am not at all indispensable, and if the thing goes on long, which it will certainly do (the General Staff here is now reckoning on two years), my turn will no doubt come somehow. A younger brother[1] of mine was in the field as an artillery sergeant, but he promptly came down with rheumatism of the joints, which still afflicts him. One of my wife's brothers is in Flanders as a cavalry lieutenant[2] and has already been awarded the Iron Cross; another[3] is held as a prisoner of war in Australia. He has the hardest time of it, although not physically.

What you saw in the *Frankfurter Zeitung* was a fragment. As a whole it looks less egocentric. What you did *not* (I hope) see in the *Rundschau*[4] is pure journalism. Now I am writing something essayistic again on the great coalition of 1756,[5] but afterward I think I shall be able to go on quite well with *The Magic Mountain*.

One wonders how it will come out. The anxiety, curiosity, suspense are tremendous. The logic of history certainly seems to favor our victory but Germany's paths and destinies are not like others—it could once again prove a dreadful disaster—though certainly things don't look that way at the moment.

Many greetings to your charming wife and your brave Harold.

TO RICHARD DEHMEL

Munich
December 14, 1914

Dear Sir and Warrior:

It is a long time since anything has given me so much pleasure as your card. I rejoice at *every* line I receive from the front. You can imagine that when a man must stay at home (heart and brain would not make the

---

[1] Viktor Mann.
[2] Heinz Pringsheim.
[3] Peter Pringsheim.
[4] "Gedanken im Kriege" ("Thoughts in Wartime") in the November 1914 issue of the *Neue Rundschau*.
[5] "Friedrich und die grosse Koalition" ("Frederick and the Great Coalition").

grade), his relationship to the war quickly becomes somewhat senti-mental. But of course a greeting from you was special anyhow. I felt heartily ashamed when I heard that you were marching off, and in the end it was this shame that gave rise to my little essay in the *Rundschau*— that made me feel the need to put my mind, at least, directly in the service of the German cause. Not that I deluded myself that writing it was any special achievement. I am not one of those who think that the German intelligentsia "failed" in the face of events. On the contrary, it seems to me that some extremely important work is being done in spelling out, ennobling, and giving meaning to events, and I feared that my little piece of journalism would make a miserable showing alongside these other things. Now I am beginning to believe that it was not entirely superfluous after all.

One wonders how it will all turn out. The anxiety and curiosity are tremendous. But it is a joyful curiosity, isn't it? It's a feeling that every-thing will have to be *new* after this profound, mighty visitation, and that the German soul will emerge from it stronger, prouder, freer, happier. May it be so.

Hail and victory, dear Herr Doktor; and may you have a strangely lovely Christmas under such harsh circumstances. I cordially clasp your hand and remain

> Yours gratefully,

TO KURT MARTENS

Landhaus Thomas Mann
Bad Tölz
December 30, 1914

Dear Martens:

I was busy with the move here when I received your *Verses* and therefore couldn't thank you at once, although I read through the little volume immediately. They are all exquisite, filled with a lovely, artistic sensu-ality. Only the blasphemous "Fervent Prayer" makes me uneasy. The most important, of course, is "Grave in the Countryside." Is this its first publication? You can imagine that it took me aback. But I am as I am and as an artist shall never be able to obey the admonition to take the side of life against death. I cannot take sides on anything—I would feel that to do so robbed me of my freedom. What is more *distinguished*, life or death? I do not know. What is more repulsive, death or life? That, too, seems to me still open to question, in spite of your poem. It seems to me that one must raise these questions and vivify them in artistic freedom and unconstraint, without deciding them. After all, it is only in an aesthetic sense that death and life are antitheses. In religious terms they are one—the same mystery.

I am expecting copies of my book of stories from Berlin and will send you one as soon as they come. It is a very modest little publication—mostly old stuff that Fischer has gathered together in this format because the "cheap book" is trumps now. A copy is your due anyhow, since the casino story which I owe to you is in it.[1]

I reported for the landsturm muster right away. Where did you hear that we are to be called up in April? I too think our turn will come. The war is certain to go on a long while.

Before we left Munich I wrote a rather bulky historical sketch on the prehistory of the Seven Years' War—quite an occupation. The *Neue Merkur* will probably publish it. I shall be staying here for about a month, and want to try to work my way back into *The Magic Mountain*. . . . You could easily be a great magician.

[1] "A Gleam," 1904. In *Stories of Three Decades*, 1936.

1915

---•---

TO FRANK WEDEKIND

Bad Tölz
January 11, 1915

Dear Herr Wedekind:

I was shocked to hear from Kurt Martens that you have been very ill and probably still are—have had to have an operation and all. May I say how sorry I am and how intensely I wish that you may soon recover completely.

We also have had a rather bad time these last months. The children have been sick, one of them dangerously; my wife's health suffered from the nursing; I too have been much affected by the shocks and anxieties of the times. And so we have sought refuge here for a few weeks, and I am trying to find my way back to my current work, after I squandered the first months of the war on all sorts of political and historical oddments. I hope I will have another chance soon to see you in Munich and talk over events—on the whole they take a good deal out of us—we were not prepared to experience history on the grand scale. For after all, these things must be acknowledged as history on the grand scale, although a certain radical intellectual, humanitarian-pacifist group represents the war pretty much as a swindle.

On Martens's recommendation I am at last reading Kubin's[1] novel *Die andere Seite*, which came out quite a few years ago. I find it highly entertaining. I shall be finished with it in two or three days, and if the book interests you I'd be glad to send it on.

Best wishes for a rapid and perfect recovery.

---

[1] Alfred Kubin (1877–1959), a highly imaginative artist and illustrator, given to grotesquerie and weirdness.

1915

TO S. FISCHER

Poschingerstrasse 1
Munich
June 7, 1915

Warmest thanks to you and your wife for your friendly birthday greetings.

The day was a hard and anxious one for us: Our oldest boy has been in the hospital for two weeks, severely ill. Ruptured appendix, peritonitis, recurrent abscesses which have required repeated operations. Yesterday was the third, and the child already has two drains in his abdomen. One night his life hung on the thinnest of threads, and there is still grave danger. You can imagine what this is doing to my poor wife. She places her faith in the doctors; they have assured her they can pull the boy through. As long as I was allowed to see him (at present I may not) my impressions were such that I can hardly believe in a happy outcome. Let's hope I am mistaken. It would hit me very hard, but what would become of my wife I cannot bear to imagine.

TO PAUL AMANN[1]

Munich
June 13, 1915

My dear Herr Doktor:

Many thanks for your letter from Budapest (where I spent several most enjoyable, stimulating days last year). You put me to shame with what you say about our correspondence. I know only too well that you are the giver, and in the final analysis perhaps that is quite in order. Is the artist an intellectual being at all? Is he not, perhaps, too much involved in both shaping and willing to be a man of intellect? I doubt that the stock of human thought has ever been enriched by artists. In fact, Nietzsche contends that artists have always been merely the lackeys of some morality or other and firmly refuses to take them seriously as thinkers. A great many things might be said concerning the relationship of intellect to art. At best the two will supplement one another, but even so, the debt will not be on the side of intellect.

I sincerely hope that our contact will never again be completely

---

[1] Paul Amann (1884–1958), Austrian philologist and cultural historian. Amann was a humanist, pacifist, and pan-European even during the war. Although in the beginning he and Thomas Mann held diametrically opposed views, they carried on an extensive correspondence. See *Letters to Paul Amann*, Wesleyan University Press, 1960.

broken off, and would be most grateful (as I think I have already said) if you would keep me up to date, when you are in the field too, by dropping me a few lines from time to time.

My best wishes go with you. That you are confident of a happy return is to me an excellent augury. On that assumption, too, I gladly promise to do my utmost to further the publication of your writings. But if fate should hold something else in store for you, I shall consider myself honor-bound to be the guardian of your work.

Once more, all good wishes![2]

TO ELISABETH ZIMMER[1]

Bad Tölz
September 6, 1915

Dear Fräulein Zimmer:

Many thanks for your kind letter of the 2nd.

Yes, I read Professor Heilborn's[2] review at the time, and with pleasure. Of course it was not exhaustive, either in pros or cons, but I suppose a review never is. Each critic sees only certain aspects of the matter, certain intentions of the author, and the picture he gives will always need supplementing. But it would probably be much the same if the author himself attempted to criticize his work—at least, after the piece has been out in the world some time and has, as it were, won its independence. Today I am scarcely a competent interpreter of *Death in Venice*; I have almost forgotten the writing of it. Certainly it is in the main a story of death, death as a seductive antimoral power—a story of the voluptuousness of doom. But the problem I especially had in mind was that of the artist's dignity—I wanted to show something like the tragedy of supreme achievement. This seems to have been clear to you, since you regard the address to Phaedrus as the core of the whole story. I had originally planned nothing less than to tell the story of Goethe's last love, the love of the seventy-year-old for that little girl he insisted he wanted to marry, though neither she nor her family would hear of it—an ugly, beautiful, grotesque, stirring story. Perhaps I shall tell it some day, but for the time being it has turned into *Death in Venice*. I think that this particular

---

[2] Translation (by Richard and Clara Winston) copyright by Wesleyan University Press. Reprinted by permission.

[1] Elisabeth Zimmer, born 1892, later the wife of the art critic Heinrich Jacobi.

[2] Ernst Heilborn (1867–1941), editor (1911) of the semimonthly *Das literarische Echo*. His review of Thomas Mann's volume of stories, *Das Wunderkind*, was published in the February 1915 issue.

genesis is also a guide to the original intention of the novella. But after all, any such work of art is hard to reduce to a single formula; it represents a dense webwork of intentions and relationships which has something organic about it, and therefore something thoroughly ambiguous.

With kindest regards,

TO MAXIMILIAN BRANTL

Munich
December 31, 1915

Dear Herr Doktor:

I forgot to ask you a favor today. I know you have the issue of *Die Weissen Blätter*[1] which contains my brother's Zola essay.[2] Would you lend it to me for a while? If so, please send it. If there is time before you join up.

[1] *Die Weissen Blätter*, a monthly with a pacifist and expressionist tone. Like all publications of this sort, it was banned during the war. From 1916 to 1920 the magazine was published in Zurich under the editorship of René Schickele.

[2] Heinrich Mann's essay contained what Thomas Mann regarded as thinly veiled malicious attacks upon everything he believed and stood for. Thomas Mann planned an indirect "treatise" in reply. But as so often happened with him, it took its own way and grew enormously. The distinctly political *Betrachtungen eines Unpolitischen* ("Reflections of a Nonpolitical Man") was not finished until the autumn of 1918, by which time the cause the book espoused was thoroughly finished. Nevertheless, the author had it printed unabridged.

1916

---•---

Bad Tölz
August 28, 1916

Dear Dr. Bertram:

It must have seemed awful my not writing you for so long, as if I were thinking: "Let everyone stand on his own two feet!" and leaving you to fend for yourself. But that would only be the way it seemed. I keep thinking about your unexpected fate,[2] although it is common these days ("Ay, madam, it is common!"). But writing letters comes harder lately, and you can imagine why: When a writer has done something halfway three-dimensional in the morning, he turns to his correspondence gladly and easily in the afternoon. But if he has spent the morning acting the man of letters and engaging in "direct discourse," the same kind of activity is repellent later. Or at any rate, the inhibitions are stronger. There have been a good many other factors too; the purely intellectual work tires my nerves and head exceedingly ("sticking it out," if the word can still be used *these* days, is much harder with an undertaking of this kind than with a creative task). Moreover, I have been out of sorts because I'm not making the progress I had hoped for on this work. And finally there have been distracting visits and socializing.

Your fine, brave letter is dated the 20th. I wonder how things have gone with you this past week. Is it possible that you are already somewhat "adjusted," at least have "found your bearings" and are tolerably re-

---

[1] Ernst Bertram (1884–1957), professor of the history of literature, author of *Nietzsche* (1918) and other books. Bertram and Mann had met only after some two years of intensive correspondence. For many years the two were very close intellectually. They had also played chamber music together until Mann gave up playing the violin, for lack of time, shortly before the war.

[2] Bertram had been called up, although he had apparently expected to be passed over.

assured from knowing where you stand and having some idea of which way the wind is blowing? Or has something new already developed and are you in the hospital thanks to some foot ailment? Scribble me a few lines very soon about your situation in general. And when I am back in Munich, which will be from September 16 on, you must let me know when you'll be on furlough, so that I can visit you during your rest cure and hear your story. Certainly tramps in Herzogpark (where, incidentally, I hear an "open-air theater" is about to open—the things people have time and inclination for!) are absolutely not for weary warriors.

The brave composure of your letter has given me, if not reassurance (no, I feel anything but reassured on your account) considerable pleasure; and still more the mental energy demonstrated in your witty, free-wheeling observations on the military system. Reading that sort of thing, one is almost irresistibly tempted to believe it sprang from a state of good cheer; it's easy to forget that understanding, as always, is conditioned by experience and is the product of suffering. But how much of what you say, for example, about the typical waste of time in the army, called to mind my own experiences of fifteen years ago. As I forewarned you, one gathers previously unsuspected impressions. That such things as the military system still exist today in our civilized world is fantastic; to take a positive view of it, once one is thrust into it, demands either the most vulgar apathy toward experience or unusual strength of mind.

What *is* there to tell about myself? The little intermezzi punctuating my rural summer won't interest you. It always comes back to the work, in which you do indeed take an interest that is a blessing to me. Which I need, because the project has already cost far too much time and strength to be abandoned and must somehow be carried through. Well then, I've made some progress, in fact have pretty well finished with the part that really had to be worked up from scratch, and what remains is more a matter of arrangement. But when I think of all I still have to talk about! I have a great many fine things, dear to my heart, to say about the aesthete, and the politician, about the Jacobin, about politics and art, about irony, about virtue, about *humanitas* and freedom, about political aestheticism, about democracy, about conservatism as a counterforce. But will anyone thank me for saying them? The literati will scold and the public will yawn. I am writing a big fat book for a few *friends* like you. But I confess that my feeling for friendship, my gratitude for it, has been very much awakened lately, and I feel that after the war, which has turned the world into an intellectual witch's cauldron, the value of friendship will have risen very high.

Surely I've said this to you once before. But in the spirit of friend-ship, then, my dear Herr Doktor . . .! To bid you *Lebewohl* sounds like irony, but is sincerely meant. Stay brave and in good spirits!

TO PETER PRINGSHEIM

Munich
October 10, 1916

My dear Peter!

Halloh old boy, what is the matter, are you down-hearted? I hope you are quite well, and I hope you will return as a merry old hommele, and so I am going to write my second war-letter to you. . . .[1]

But after having led you to think all sorts of fine things about my fluency and range in English, I shall not risk my reputation any further but will fall back into our mother tongue, which is also much subtler (the censor may black that remark out if he doesn't like it, without making it a reason for quashing the entire letter).

It is not quite a full year since I first wrote to you in the land of Australia.[2] I assure you that I would do so more often if it weren't for the *conditio sine qua non* of Latin script, which for me is a very hard conditio. The finger rapidly grows numb, and thoughts too become numb in the process. *"Car il est plus Allemand et moins Latin que vous ne pourriez le croire de premier abord. C'est là son originalité."* That was once written about me in a French periodical before the war, and it has been demon-strated and confirmed in the course of the war—to the embitterment of our radical literati, who naturally are doing everything in their power to contribute to Germanophobia and arouse sympathy for the Roman West, and with whom I have extremely tense relations. . . . But no politics! Except that nowadays the question is What else? —Poor Andreas![3] His wretched death touched me very closely too—for it must surely have been wretched—inwardly, for what inner resources could have helped him?— and outwardly, as a common soldier in hand-to-hand combat with muzhiks. His comrades have written; they left out the details so that his mother wouldn't feel still worse. Faulty psychology. Now Aunt Else can picture the most harrowing things. But she probably has enough sense

[1] In English in the original.
[2] Professor Pringsheim had been attending an international congress of physicists at the outbreak of the war, and had been interned.
[3] Andreas Rosenberg, Katia Mann's cousin, had been killed on the Russian front at the age of twenty.

not to. Fink[4] finds her calm and composed. Fink being in Berlin right now because Urmimchen[5] has a nasty cough. . . . But you know all that.

Klaus will shortly be coming here for a concert, with his friend, a mellifluous baritone who has already delighted us in Tölz. I too recently made a public appearance, in which I read from the *Confidence Man*. By this time there is the liveliest demand for "detached" subjects, and the greatest gratitude for them. I can't say that I feel the same way. I am caught up in the mental stresses of the times, and my *Betrachtungen eines Unpolitischen* has grown into a fairly fat book. A sizable section of it is to appear in the January issue of the *Neue Rundschau*. I admit that at times I feel cravings for what is called "free creative work"—*you know*—but now I have to stick it out with this book of direct discourse, and it also interests me enormously.

Dear *Babüschlein*,[6] I tell you again what I told you last time: Not a day passes that I don't think warmly of you and wonder how you are. Be of good cheer. It will be an extraordinary reunion, as it has been an extraordinary separation.

Your brother-in-law,   T.

TO ERNST BERTRAM

Munich
November 25, 1916

Dear Herr Doktor:

I hasten to thank you for your charming letter so that I won't be hopelessly in arrears, as I am with my other correspondence because of my Berlin expedition.

The Reichstag seems to be in a highly critical mood with regard to the civilian service bill, and far from inclined to grant *plein pouvoir*. Besides, I scarcely think that the administration really means to go very far. The chief purpose of the bill probably is to put the workers in the war goods industries, who might someday strike, under the thumb of the military. But strange things can still happen, and our being drafted into a news agency would not be the strangest.

What you say about the fate of Germany is only too true. Not

---

[4] Fink was the Pringsheim children's nickname for their mother.

[5] Nickname for Hedwig Dohm (1833–1919), writer and suffragette, Katia Mann's grandmother.

[6] For unknown reasons Peter Pringsheim bore this nickname in the family circle from childhood on.

megalomania, merely the need to regard things in intimate terms, long ago led me to see this fate symbolized and personified in my brother and myself. I have long believed that it is impossible, for internal more than for external reasons, to create an authentic political life in Germany. I feel deeply that I shall forfeit any chance to influence German current events, as my brother has done, but in a different way. It all comes from the fact that we are not a nation. Rather, we are something like the quintessence of Europe, so that we are subject to the clash of Europe's spiritual contradictions without having a national synthesis. There is no German solidarity and ultimate unity. European wars will no longer be waged on German soil, you say? Oh yes, they will be! There will always be German civil wars, in fact.

I found the essay on Stifter again very stimulating.

Have you read about Hofmannsthal's lecture in Christiania, "We Europeans"? The account of it makes me uneasy and jealous. This Mercury has already passed far beyond the kind of broodings that I am fettered to; he speaks freely and conciliatorily about a synthesis of the ideas of 1792 and 1914. Time is swift, and I am slow. I must think everything out minutely and pedantically, and I fear I am growing old and tired in the process.

Auf Wiedersehen, my dear Herr Doktor.

1917

——————— • ———————

Munich
May 19, 1917

Dear Herr Professor:

Last night I finished reading your *Palestrina* and want to thank you wholeheartedly for the privilege of seeing the book before the performance—which I now look forward to in quite a different way, with joy and solemn suspense. It will certainly be nothing less than an apotheosis of music itself—the libretto is that, and at the same time it is, as Nietzsche said of the text of *Parsifal*, "a supreme challenge to music, but also a supreme challenge to the composer's mastery." What fearless, high-hearted awareness of your own abilities you must have felt when you wrote this text. It would be impossible to reach any higher, but remarkably, it also inspires absolute confidence in me that on June 12 we shall see the laurel wreath in your hand.

Forgive me for speaking of confidence when I should be expressing gratitude for what I have already received. But of course an outline like this is nothing complete, nothing that may properly be regarded as we are accustomed to regard self-contained literary works. From such a standpoint it undeniably has elements of harshness, crudity, seeming dilettantism; but in conjunction with the music these will doubtless be vindicated—I mean bits of philosophical prosiness which have not been poetically "absorbed," such as "individual existence" and similar phrases. But the significant thing is that wherever the language seems

---

[1] Hans Pfitzner (1869–1949), composer, late romantic. His *Palestrina*, first performed by Bruno Walter in Munich on June 12, 1917, made a deeper impression on Thomas Mann than any opera since he had first heard Wagner. The beginning of Mann's novel *The Holy Sinner*, describing the bells miraculously ringing out over Rome, corresponds to the finale of the first act of *Palestrina*.

83

inadequate, it is always in those passages which one is tempted to take as something absolute, as direct literary communication—never where the words are, shall I say, not so much written *for* the music as born *out of* the music and in themselves are really already music, as in the magnificent sixth scene of the first act—this glorious page 33 of the text, which I, at least, cannot read without a surging sense of musical happiness.

You forebore to place the name of the drama on the title page; and in fact it scarcely has a plot in the ordinary sense of involvement, suspense, solution, or catastrophe. But as a structure originating in and designed for music, it produces an extremely dramatic effect: the colorful and grotesque reality of Act II comes in wonderfully between the seraphic metaphysics of Act I and the exalted mildness of the conclusion. And how is it that the hero, without having had to prove himself in any actually dramatic action, nevertheless seems so totally tragic? It is the effect of sheer lyric immediacy.

Your whole spirit is in this work, your high-principled conservatism, your devotion to art, your authentic native Germanism. Walter[2] spoke to me with the greatest respect of the mature mastery you have displayed in the musical part of the work, which is equaled, he said, only by the supreme composers of the past. I believe him implicitly, for this very mastery is inherent, as a natural requirement in the libretto itself. . . . Incidentally, I clearly see the threads that run from this work to your polemic against those Italian absurdities. "Since from great masters' days the firm-formed heritage . . ." etc.

No more for today—except, once again, my gratitude. Do you need the book? Or may I keep it a while longer? Also, would you, when the weather is fine enough to take the sting out of the distance, favor my wife and me with an afternoon or evening out here? Since all the things that used to be at most "interesting" have now become urgent, I find that the need for discussion has grown enormously.

---

[2] Bruno Walter (1876–1962), the conductor, became a close friend of Mann's during the period 1912–22, when Walter served as general director of musical activities in Munich. In later life he was a neighbor of the Manns in Beverly Hills.

1917

TO BRUNO WALTER

Munich
June 24, 1917

Dear Herr Walter:

There was an impassioned curtain call for you last night, strongly endorsed by the Schillingses,[1] husband and wife, who were sitting behind me; and everyone was most unwilling to accept the fact of your absence, which Pfitzner indicated with eloquent gestures. He was hailed with as much enthusiasm as at the premiere and could well be satisfied, I think, with the obstinacy of the applause after Act II, which went on even though the house remained dark almost to the beginning of the prelude to Act III. I thought this third prelude in particular, with its fine repetition of the Ighino theme, altogether wonderful yesterday. All in all, I enjoyed this performance intellectually and musically more keenly than any other. My seat had much to do with it: the distance from the stage and the isolation from the mass of the audience, which in this theater is so finely coherent and a pleasure in itself to survey, significantly sustain the mood for me; and the orchestra sounds gloriously soft and clear back there. But the position alone did not do it, of course. This was my third performance, and it became clear that I have simply advanced a good deal in the conquest, penetration, understanding of this work. It is dear, congenial, and—there is no arrogance in my saying so—*akin* to me, in its feeling toward life and attitude toward art. That was borne out by the sense I had yesterday of the work's sublime *brevity*—there was not a trace of the prolixities that some people have referred to in order to have an opinion to express. On the contrary, every moment stirred the wish: "Linger awhile."[2] Though it may sound hysterical, I must say that the idea of having to wait six weeks till the next performance gives me a veritable pang.

I cannot express how close to my heart this *Palestrina* is. My affirmative response to it comes from love and embraces all the things which might be considered questionable in the artistic sense. With its metaphysical mood, its ethos of "cross, death, and tomb,"[3] its union of

---

[1] Max von Schillings (1868–1933), composer and opera conductor; during 1919–25, director of the State Opera in Berlin; from 1932 to his death, president of the Prussian Academy of Arts in Berlin. He was much influenced by Wagner. His chief work is the opera *Mona Lisa* (1915).

[2] An allusion to Goethe's *Faust*, line 1,700.

[3] A quotation from Nietzsche (letter to Erwin Rohde, October 8, 1868), who used the words of Richard Wagner.

music, pessimism, and humor (I use this combination to define "humanity"), it meets my own deepest needs. In fact, its appearance at just this moment has been a great piece of good fortune for me; it has made me affirmative, released me from polemicism, and offered to my emotional life a great object to which it can cling, and from this viewpoint all that is repugnant—I mean everything that runs counter to my concept of humanity, and there are such things!—is revealed as flimsy semblance.[4]

The Pfitzners recently spent an evening with us. I don't think he felt at ease, although he downed at least five glasses of Moselle wine and put away a sizable quantity of home-baked pastries, so that at least in this respect he was receptive to our offerings. For the rest, I suppose he was not born to feel at ease; he is a difficult, sore, ambivalent person, I think, who for all his love of the saving power of "intellect" undoubtedly holds within himself much of the malevolent voluntaristic world of the second act of his *Palestrina*. But he said a few tremendously moving things about the *Palestrina*—I'll tell you when we talk. For I see that the fifth page is almost filled and realize that you will find this epistolographic assault a little strange. So be it! as the older dramatists liked to say. As for myself, I have a sense of putting this midnight hour to good use in thanking you for everything you have given us this winter. When I look back on it— the *Euryanthe*, the *Winterreise*, the *Kindertotenlieder*, the *Heiling*, just to mention a few, and finally the *Palestrina*. It has really been a cornucopia of benefactions that you, in your ardent kindness as mediator, have poured out upon the just and the *unjust*; and in our quick goodbye yesterday in front of the theater I could not adequately express my gratitude.

Have a good vacation, all of you, and if you should someday feel inclined to come over to Tölz, where we shall be from July 15 on, it would give us great pleasure. Cordial greetings to you and your wife from both of us.

With sincere respect and friendship,

TO PHILIPP WITKOP

Munich
October 4, 1917

Dear Herr Professor:

Many thanks for the Hindenburg festival issues. They served as sickbed reading, for I have been laid up this past week: a dysenteric intestinal

---

[4] An allusion to Goethe's *Epilogue to The Bell*. Cf. Mann's *Last Essays* (New York: Alfred A. Knopf; 1959), p. 84.

ailment which is going the rounds has familiarized me once again with the invalid's existence, which is not without its attractions and advantages, you know. It always reminds me of C. L. Philippe's fine aphorism: "*Les maladies sont les voyages des pauvres.*" A favorite quotation of mine. One does not have to be among the poor to be struck by it.

A few days were abominable, but now the fever has gone and I am on the mend. I read a great deal and have been going through Tolstoy's *War and Peace*—which is fundamentally new to me, since I had read it only once when I was quite young. What a mighty work! Its like will not be done again. And how I love the Russian spirit. How its contrast to and contempt for Gallicism amuses me—one finds this throughout Russian literature. How much closer the Russian and German temperaments are. For years my heart's desire has been reconciliation and alliance with Russia.

By now the political situation is running to farce. The Central Powers as the spokesmen of "the human race" and Eternal Peace, berated by the Entente for uttering unctuous generalities—the world turned upside down. In any case, democracy is now official among us; perhaps that will render it impossible in literature.

For the winter I am planning an extensive journey: I will give readings in ten cities scattered the length and the breadth of the Reich. I begin in Strassburg and end in Bromberg. I hope to God that my large intestine doesn't keep me from finishing my book before I leave. I am looking forward with such eagerness to *narration*. Incidentally, there is an essay of mine on Pfitzner's *Palestrina* in the October issue of the *Neue Rundschau*. It, too, has been taken from the *Betrachtungen*.

I have recently become acquainted with Adalbert Stifter[1]—can you imagine, I hadn't read anything of his. He was a find—I felt profoundly at home with him. These past years I have learned to think of myself, irrespective of all international coloration, as a belated offshoot of the German bourgeois art of fiction.

> Yours,

---

[1] Adalbert Stifter (1805–68), a major German novelist, little known in English-speaking countries.

1918

TO HEINRICH MANN

Munich
January 3, 1918

Dear Heinrich:

Your letter comes at a moment when it is physically impossible for me to reply properly. I must start on a fourteen-day journey which I curse and for which I am scarcely in the mood, but I have to go through with it. However, I wonder whether there would be any sense in trying to compress the mental torment of two years into a letter which would have to be much longer than yours. I believe you implicitly when you say that you feel no hatred for me. After the eruptive release of the Zola essay, and considering the way everything stands with you and for you at the moment, you have no reason to. The phrase about fraternal hatred was in any case rather a symbol for more general discrepancies in the psychology of the Rousseauite.

If I troubled you, you naturally troubled me a great deal more; that was in the nature of the thing, and I, too, honestly did what I could. To this day I praise at least two of your books, in the teeth of everyone else, as masterpieces. You forget or conceal how often you, with the "justification of passion," mercilessly abused my simplest and strongest feelings before I reacted with so much as a sentence. Of course, that statement is not meant just personally, any more than any one of yours. The fraternal constellation does indeed color everything personally. But the things you permitted yourself in your Zola essay and expected me to take—no, I have never done or expected a living soul to take. And when after the truly French spitefulness, slanders, and slurs of this brilliant piece of hackwork, whose very second sentence was already monstrously excessive, you imagined you could "seek a rapprochement" although it "seemed hopeless"—this demonstrates the frivolity of a man who has "sought to

88

embrace the world." At the time, incidentally, my wife wrote at length to yours, a delicate and warm letter, and received effronteries in reply.

It is not true that my conduct during the war has been "extreme." Yours was, and moreover to the point of being wholly detestable. But I did not suffer and struggle for two years, neglect my dearest projects, sentence myself to silence as an artist, probe, compare, and manage to keep going, just to answer a letter which (understandably) exudes triumph, sees me at the head of "a few desperate men" searching for last-ditch arguments, and concludes that I need not regard you as an enemy. Every line of your letter was dictated by moral smugness and self-righteousness. Don't expect me to fall sobbing upon your breast. What lies behind me was a galley-slave's work; all the same, I thank you for the knowledge that I now stand less helplessly exposed to your zealot's sophism than in the days when you could hurt me to the quick with it.

You and yours may call me a parasite if you like. The truth, *my* truth, is that I am none. A great bourgeois artist, Adalbert Stifter, said in a letter: "My books are not poetic creations alone; as moral revelations, as human dignity preserved with austere seriousness, they have a value which will last longer than their poetry." I feel I have the right to repeat those words after him, and thousands whom I helped to live—although I did not recite the *contrat social*, one hand on my heart and the other in the air—*recognize* that I have this right.

Not you. You cannot see the right and the ethos of my life, because you are my brother. How was it that no one, not Hauptmann nor Dehmel nor Harden, that advocate of preventive war to whom you now pay visits of homage, referred the invectives of the Zola article to himself? Why was all of its rending polemic aimed at me? The fraternal constellation drove you to this. Take Dehmel, who sent me thanks and congratulations from the trenches for my first war articles in the *Neue Rundschau*. You can be as cordial and intimate with him as you please at dress rehearsals and he with you in return, for though you are radically different intellectually you are not brothers and therefore there's room enough in the world for both of you. —Let the tragedy of our brotherhood unfold.

Sorrow? It is bearable. One grows hard and apathetic. Ever since Carla killed herself and you broke with Lula[1] for life, such ruptures are

---

[1] The reference is to a sudden quarrel on political and ideological matters between Heinrich Mann and his extremely conservative sister Julia (Lula) Löhr.

nothing new in our family circle. This is not the kind of life I care for. I despise it. But one must live it to the end, as well as one can.

Farewell.   T.

TO PHILIPP WITKOP

Munich
May 23, 1918

Dear Herr Professor:

I rejoiced to hear from you again, to hear of your achievements and your adventures. Congratulations on the Iron Cross. It will mean something to you in spite of everything.

Rolland[1] has given me a rough going-over in his war book with its self-deceiving title, *Au dessus de la mêlée.* So I suppose I am not in a position to pass judgment on him. But he is decidedly not a creator, although he would like to be one. On the other hand, at least in the Paris volume of *Jean Christophe,* he proves himself an excellent critic and writer. This volume, especially where it deals with art and literature, is well worth a German's reading. Hauptmann is incomparably the greater creative writer, I should think. But you and I agree fairly well on the *Heretic.*[2] It certainly offers beautiful landscapes, but is distinctly impoverished in the spiritual and intellectual sense. And it does not become Hauptmann, that extremely Christian writer, to deal so "humoristically" with Christianity.

But it becomes me even less to go on with literary shoptalk when first and foremost I should tell you that four weeks ago my wife presented me with a fine little girl—the third—I mean the third girl.[3] For in addition there are two boys, you know, and one might imagine that we had reached our full complement by now. But as Philip II used to say: "Oh, who knows what slumbers in the reaches of time." Incidentally, I

---

[1] Romain Rolland (1866–1944), French writer, pacifist, later pro-Communist. Nobel Prize, 1915. Perhaps best known in the English-speaking world for his *Above the Battle* and *Jean Christophe.*

[2] *The Heretic of Soana* (1918), a short novel by Gerhart Hauptmann that celebrates pagan eroticism in opposition to the restrictions of Christianity.

[3] Elisabeth Veronika, born April 24, 1918. The birth and early childhood of this latecomer was a great joy to Mann. For her he wrote his idyll in verse, *Gesang vom Kindchen.* She married Antonio Borgese in 1939. Among her books are *To Whom It May Concern* (New York, 1960), *Ascent of Woman* (New York, 1963), and *The Language Barrier: Beasts and Men* (1968). She is a consultant to the Center for the Study of Democratic Institutions in Santa Barbara, California.

am very fond of the patriarchal full complement. We have engaged a governess again, and so I preside at table over seven settings.

I have told you, haven't I, about my trip to Brussels, etc.? You are right, one "swallows a great deal in silence." Although I have now written a book of more than 600 pages about "the whole thing" (I am in the midst of reading proof), I still have the feeling that I have swallowed most of what I had to say in silence. What will come? Will Western Europe be spared the Bolshevist phase? It doesn't look as though we shall escape it. And yet belief in "freedom" is also impossible for humanity today. Then what shall we believe?

1919

·

TO JOSEF PONTEN[1]

Munich
March 29, 1919

My dear Herr Ponten:

It's hard to say why it took me so long to get around to reading your novella[2]—and therefore to writing you again. Other things kept coming up: my own work demanded special reading; and the politics, the newspapers, the constant shocks and distractions of these times! One postpones and postpones, and the result is that a thing begins to seem as if it will be duty and work, when originally it promised pure pleasure—and then it becomes pleasure once again the moment it is really taken up. When your letter arrived I had just begun on your story, and God knows I finished quickly enough, at two or three sittings; a few hours were enough. It was certainly no labor but an utter delight; it has supplemented my picture of your literary personality in a remarkable way and made me even more curious about all that is to follow. What beautiful grotesquerie! A scene like that of the black-robed monks on the mountain in their dance of exorcism around the sinful lovers in the morbid night is not easily forgotten. And your intonation, the quality of your recital, appeals enormously to me. It has something conservative about it, though it also offers the attractions of modernity. In short, I am glad to have "come upon" you again.

As for myself, after the *Betrachtungen* I have turned to the sphere of the idyllically intimate for a change, and have written two little things which, after magazine publication, will probably be brought out by Fischer as a small book in the autumn or winter. . . .

---

[1] Josef Ponten (1883–1940), novelist. His chief work was *Volk auf dem Wege. Roman der deutschen Unruhe* (1934–42), six vols., unfinished.
[2] *Die Insel* (1919).

I prefer not to start on politics. I share your feelings and scarcely even *hope* that the disgusting "virtuous" democracy over there may still learn a lesson from the events in Hungary, which I find deeply stirring. Let them go on and bring things to a head. In our country too, the fusion of nationalist sentiment and Bolshevism might happen any day. "Communism," as I understand it, contains much that is good and human. Its goal is ultimately the total dissolution of the state (which will always be dedicated to power), the humanization and purification of the world by de-politicalizing it. At bottom, who would be against that? To be sure, I too cross myself twice and thrice at the prospect of "proletarian culture."

TO KARL STRECKER[1]

Munich
April 18, 1919

Dear Herr Doktor Strecker:

Today the *Monatsheft* reached me—presumably very belatedly—with your review of the *Betrachtungen*, and I hasten to thank you. I have read your fine analysis with all the pleasure I knew I would have from the moment I saw it announced; I appreciate and admire the result of your friendly, sympathetic efforts in behalf of my work all the more because I realize how hard it is for a critic to give any impression of this terribly strange book. Such strong support by your periodical will of course do a great deal for the book's distribution, and in this respect, too, I am greatly obliged to you.

I cannot thank you without some embarrassment, and as is so often the case, embarrassment prompts me to offer a few objections. You judge between my brother and myself, placing one above the other. As a critic, you have the right to do so. But this is neither the intention nor the meaning of the book, and the antithesis itself strikes me as too important and symbolic for me really to welcome the intrusion of this question of rank and worth. I frankly do not believe in my superior rank and worth; I believe only in differences of temperament, character, morality, experience, which have led to an antagonism that may be regarded as "significant" in the Goethean sense, an opposition of principles—but based upon a deeply felt brotherliness. In me the nordic-Protestant element is uppermost, in my brother the Romanic-Catholic element. With me, accordingly, the emphasis is more on conscience, with him more

[1] Karl Strecker (1862–1933), writer, essayist, theater critic of the Berlin *Tägliche Rundschau*. Among his works: *Totentanz, Goethes Faust, Nietzsche und Strindberg*.

on the activistic will. I am an ethical individualist, he is a socialist. However this antithesis might be further defined and formulated, it reveals itself in the realms of intellect, art, politics—in short, in every relationship. Any assignment of rank must be purely subjective, depending on personal affinity and sympathy. Indeed, in the end I give myself the benefit of the doubt in declaring that the matter cannot be determined objectively.

Once again, many thanks and my best regards.

TO PHILIPP WITKOP

Munich
May 12, 1919

Dear Herr Professor:

Many thanks for your kind inquiry. I did receive your letter (of the 3rd) day before yesterday, and wished I could have answered immediately, just as I wish I could write today at greater length than I shall be able to manage. But during the period of blockade the mail has piled up, and now I am overburdened.

Well, then, it was wild, but we are well and have passed through all the storms virtually unaffected.[1] In fact, when I count heads in my family, I find them actually increased by one. On Easter Monday (with the heavy artillery blasting away) my wife brought into the world an infant boy who is to be named Michael.[2]

I read the announcement in the university catalog with a good deal of self-congratulation. When you have the chance, do let me know about the attendance and the effect. As to the chronology of the novellas, the chief thing to note is that *Tonio Kröger* comes *after Buddenbrooks*, not before, as is often assumed. The next thing after *Buddenbrooks*, written right on its heels, was "The Way to the Churchyard." "Little Lizzy,"

---

[1] Kurt Eisner, the Bavarian Premier, an independent socialist and well-known man of letters, had been murdered by Count Arco-Valley on February 21, 1919. During the subsequent disturbances a mixed group of leftist radicals formed the short-lived Bavarian Soviet Republic. Bourgeois circles feared the worst, and because of what he had written in the *Betrachtungen* Thomas Mann had particular reason to expect serious trouble. "The Reds" went through the neighborhood confiscating so-called hoarded food supplies—but carefully avoided Mann's house. Ernst Toller and other revolutionary writers were members of the government and had evidently issued orders that Mann was not to be molested.

[2] Michael Thomas Mann, born April 21, 1919. After a considerable career as a violinist and violist, he became professor of German at Berkeley. He is the author of *Heinrich Heine's "Zeitungsberichte über Musik und Malerei"* (1964) and *Das Thomas Mann Buch* (1965).

which was included in the *Tristan* volume, actually belongs in point of time in the volume *Little Herr Friedemann*, that is, in the first edition. The current edition of this early book of mine contains two stories ("The Hungry" and "Railway Accident") which were written later and really belonged in *The Infant Prodigy* volume.[3] [. . .]

Your work in Freiburg is markedly affecting wider and wider circles. I hope they are grateful to you!

The *Jaákob*[4] has also made a great impression on me. I am not yet acquainted with Spengler,[5] but have put him down on my reading list. As the best book in at least five years I solemnly nominate Ernst Bertram's *Nietzsche*, which you absolutely must read at once if you have not done so.

I have the pleasantest memory of the reading in Freiburg, and would gladly repeat it. But travel conditions! We must wait and see how things turn out.

I—and I am not alone—have had our good Munich up to here. The mixture of apathy, frivolity, and bohemianism is disgusting and, as we have seen, capable of sprouting the bloodiest absurdities. Now the bourgeoisie has come to the top again with outside aid, but totally deceives itself about the lasting danger of the situation. Once the federal troops are gone, the Bavarian soldiers will be undermined in a month, and what then? No government will have an unpolitical, dependable military force behind it. I am considering moving away.

Not a word about the Entente's peace. The blindness of the victors is revealed—whom the gods would destroy . . . The venomous old man[6] who concocted this peace in the insomniac nights of old age has *slant* eyes. Perhaps he has a blood right to dig the grave of Western culture and bring on *Kirghisdom*.

TO KURT MARTENS

Munich
June 26, 1919

Dear Martens:

I know you will believe me when I say that it is hard to refuse your

---

[3] All these stories are included in *Stories of Three Decades* (New York: Alfred A. Knopf; 1936).

[4] *Jadkob's Traum* (1918), a play by Richard Beer-Hofmann (1866–1936).

[5] Oswald Spengler (1880–1936), philosopher of history. It was his sensational *The Decline of the West* (New York: Alfred A. Knopf; 1926–8), published in German between 1918 and 1922, that Mann intended to read.

[6] Georges Clemenceau (1841–1929), French premier from 1906–9 and 1917–20, chief architect of the Versailles Treaty.

request, which moreover does me honor. But at the moment with the best will in the world I really cannot do it. Everything is still so much in flux, the peace treaty has not even been signed yet, and when it is signed that won't end the confusion either; the wildest things are still possible at home and abroad, and whatever we say today is still outdated by tomorrow. After finishing the *Betrachtungen* I swore off journalism (I was and am terribly weary of it) and firmly resolved to concentrate strictly on my artistic plans. For I am forty-four years old, and by the time I am fifty I want to be finished with the two novels I began before the long interruption, so that my Collected Works will be safely tucked away. But if meanwhile I should have something to say on political and moral questions, then it must be a proper, conscientious accounting of how things seem to the author of the *Betrachtungen*. Not only is my mind not clear for that now (I am absorbed in spinning my way back into *The Magic Mountain*), but also this is not the moment for it. What could I possibly say? "Fellows, cheer up, it isn't so bad?" I can't, for I find it as bad and repulsive as it possibly could be. In short, don't be angry with me, I am simply in no state to comfort and encourage people; I don't feel very much like the man of the hour who is called upon to speak, and will decidedly do better to tend quietly to my own affairs.

TO GUSTAV BLUME[1]

Munich
July 5, 1919

My dear Sir:

Letters like yours should be answered at once, without the least delay. I am ashamed that I have had to postpone this inadequate reply and expression of gratitude by several days, meanwhile giving you time to wonder whether you had wasted your confidence on a fool. But there was no help for it; I am a harried man. I don't want to complain; I would probably be sorry if it were otherwise. But the world does not leave me sufficiently alone and in its myriad urgencies and importunities forgets that I have, in Bruckner's words, "imposed on myself composition as the chief task in life, which likewise places great demands on the nerves."

But please do not think that I count you and your letter as part of "the world." On the contrary, it touched me directly and deeply; I read it again and again with emotion and thank you from the bottom of my

---

[1] Gustav Blume (b. 1882), Berlin neurologist.

heart for deciding to write. I cannot remotely repay you in kind, but I do want to tell you that the physiognomic kinship of our existences has made a mysterious impression upon me. Once again it appears that "vocation," though apparently so personal, is actually more or less a matter of chance. Certainly the life of a physician was always among my inner potentialities, as that of the writer—to judge by your letter—is obviously among yours.

Some of the things you say about our national destiny have an intensity that I have scarcely ever found in public or private observations on these matters—no wonder, considering the seemingly insane frivolity with which historical events are taken among us. What was Canossa compared to the spectacle the German Emperor will present before the tribunal of the Entente! Perhaps it won't come to that, but the possibility is enough to make it a reality for us. "Our entire national existence to be condemned as guilty and erroneous"—that is what my *Betrachtungen* would not concede, long before people imagined that we might ever come to such a pass. That the great tradition of Germanism from Luther to Bismarck and Nietzsche should be refuted and discredited—this is the fact which is *hailed* by many among us, the fact which is laid down in many a carefully considered paragraph of the peace conditions, and the fact which I was opposing in my fight against the "civilization literatus."[2] It lay in the nature of things that my opponents would triumph; I recognized that early and said as much. One must take a contemplative, even a resignedly cheerful view, read Spengler and understand that the victory of England and America seals and completes the civilizing, rationalizing, pragmatizing of the West which is the fate of every aging culture. More and more I see this war (insofar as it was not social revolution from the start; that is the other side of the matter) as a vast quixotism, a last mighty effort to rear up and strike a blow on the part of the Germanic Middle Ages, which remained astoundingly well preserved before collapsing with a rattle of bones. What's coming now is Anglo-Saxon dominance of the world, that is, perfected civilization. Why not? We will discover that it is quite comfortable to live under. The German spirit need not even die—on the contrary, there are signs that under the pressure of unparalleled dishonor this spirit will recollect itself and want to keep alive. The denigration of the great tradition of Germanism will diminish as conditions improve—the whole thing may even turn out to be highly interesting. But Germanism will probably play a

---

[2] *Zivilisationsliterat*, a term invented by Mann to characterize the pro-Entente, pro-democratic German writer whose spiritual homeland was France. "France is his country, the Revolution his great age," Mann wrote in the *Betrachtungen*.

predominantly romantic role—representing the nostalgia of an old, clever civilization for its youth, when it had been a true culture and that culture had been German.

These things can never be fully expressed, or well expressed even in part. But this is more or less how it all looks to me at the moment.

Again, my gratitude for your letter, which I shall continue to prize.

TO JOSEF PONTEN

Munich
July 8, 1919

Dear Herr Ponten:

Just a few lines in answer to your friendly letter of June 20. I am on the point of leaving for a few weeks at the seashore, which by now I badly need. But it's possible that the railroad workers, in pursuit of their economic interests, may still cross up my plans.

I have been able to find out virtually nothing about Sinclair.[1] He wraps himself in mystery. Fischer, whom I asked, reports that he received the manuscript through Hermann Hesse, who said it was by a young writer, ill, living in Switzerland. That is all. I am glad that you so strongly agree with my opinion of *Demian*. If the author had not made clear that he doesn't want to be bothered, I think I would write to him as I wrote to you after reading your *Turm*,[2] which gave me the same kind of pleasure. The other things you have been so good as to tell me about yourself have interested me greatly and have increased my respectful sympathy. My ignorance is vast; I really have learned nothing but—at best—how to write German; and only the thought that there is more to this than the phrase seems to say consoles me most of the time for my other inadequacies.

May I supplement these scanty lines by an enclosure—the photograph of a bronze bust made by Professor Schwegerle, a countryman of mine living here in Munich. Even in this reproduction it is a remarkable likeness, which, however, by no means exhausts its virtues.

---

[1] Emil Sinclair, the pseudonym under which Hermann Hesse published his novel *Demian*, which Mann greatly admired.
[2] Ponten's novel *Der babylonische Turm* (1918).

TO KURT MARTENS

Dear Martens:

I must trouble you again with a small request. A younger brother of mine, Viktor, by occupation agriculturalist and for five years an army lieutenant, has published a small book entitled *Aufruhr* (Delphin Verlag). It is a collection of all sorts of stories and episodes of revolution. My brother Heinrich and I are also in it. I would like to put in a good word for it so that the book (it has already been sent to your offices) is reviewed in the *Münchner Neueste Nachrichten*—best of all, of course, by you. Forgive the importunity of a solicitous brother.

With many greetings,

I'm here renewing memories of youth and enjoying truly *naïve* food—the region is untouched, in every respect.

TO ERIKA MANN

Dear Eri:

Many thanks for your lively little letter. It amused me very much. I hope your trip to Starnberg turned out well and no one fell into the ditch—an easy way to tear pants, as once happened to me. But before the outing there was Mielein's[1] birthday, of course, which I shall doubtless hear something about from the boys. You certainly described the preparations very excitingly. But it takes me baack when you write that "unfortunately" Aunt Lula will be coming. Such a fine lady, finer even than your Pielein[2] himself, and you say "unfortunately"! I should like to have heard that eight-handed Arcissi concert.[3] If only you were all here, you would dance and rejoice at the heaps and heaps of good food. Last night we again

---

[1] Family pet name for Katia Mann.

[2] This nickname for Thomas Mann was used for a time in the family.

[3] The concert hall on Arcisstrasse had two concert grands. Professor Pringsheim, who had arranged almost all the Wagner operas for two pianos, frequently played there, and on the occasion mentioned had played with three friends.

had some of those marvelous, firm North German scrambled eggs and baked potatoes shining with butter, followed by excellent cold cuts. It is a Garden of Eden. I had been in Herr Schellberg's fruit garden before-hand and eaten everything my heart desired from bushes and trees: red, black, and yellow currants, cherries and raspberries as big as cultivated strawberries. But now I'll stop or your mouth will be watering streams. I'll write extra and specially to Moni.[4] Be a good help to Mama.

Your   P.

[4] Monika Mann (b. 1910), the Manns' fourth child. Author of *Past and Present* (1960), a memoir of her childhood and later life.

1920

———————•———————

TO COUNT HERMANN KEYSERLING[1]

Munich
January 18, 1920

Dear Count Keyserling:

Thank you for your friendly letter of the 12th and for sending me your article in the *Kreuzzeitung*.[2] I have read it with great pleasure and profit. It is a fine reformulation of the creative doctrine which at present engrosses you and which you have so well succeeded in bringing to the fore. The lecture takes a popular turn—which presumably shows up more strongly in the written than in the spoken form. Nevertheless I am decidedly in favor of its not being restricted to this single—and incidentally, very sensibly and correctly chosen—mode of publication. You should include the article later in a volume of shorter pieces. It is quite up to that standard.

I was very much interested in your remark that before too long the conservatives will again have the greatest say in Germany. I too believe that; in the end nature restores the balance somehow, and "the German *is* conservative"—Wagner will prove to have been forever right in that regard. For this very reason nothing is more important than the infusion of intelligence into German conservatism—and all your activity, after all, comes down to that in the end. For what is at stake is nothing other than the celebrated "reunion of intellect and *soul*."

In accordance with an old promise, I have sent my "Open Letter"[3]

---

[1] Count Hermann Keyserling (1880–1946), writer, philosopher, founder of the "School of Wisdom" in Darmstadt, 1920.

[2] The newspaper of the radical right wing of the Prussian conservatives.

[3] "Letter to Count Hermann Keyserling." Thomas Mann had been asked to participate in Keyserling's plan for a "School of Wisdom" in Darmstadt, and had used the occasion to defend himself against actual and potential reproaches directed against the *Betrachtungen eines Unpolitischen*.

first to Stefan Grossmann,[4] the editor of the *Tagebuch*. It is a question whether this weekly will have room for it. So far I have not heard. The article is just being set. My *Betrachtungen* is already provided with an overlong preface. Whether the letter to you should be added to it in a new edition, perhaps as an appendix, is certainly worth considering.

With the kindest regards,

TO CARL MARIA WEBER[1]

Munich
July 4, 1920

My dear Herr Weber:

W. Seidel's[2] friendly offices have brought me such a moved and moving letter and so fine a poetic gift from you—both were a joy to me, and I thank you warmly for them.

I have read a great many of your poems and found much I liked and much to admire. It is certainly not by chance that you achieve your best effects where your emotion attains the highest degree of freedom and unselfconsciousness, as in the "Swimmers," which contains much of the humaneness of the younger generation, and in "Voluptuousness of Words," a poem of incontestable beauty. I say this although I have written *Death in Venice*, for which you have such kind words of defense in your letter—against objections and rebukes which may well be only too familiar to you yourself. I wish you had taken part in the conversation I had about these matters recently, one evening that stretched on and on, with Willy Seidel and another colleague, Kurt Martens. For I should not want you and others to have the impression that a mode of feeling which I respect because it is almost necessarily infused with *mind* (far more necessarily so, at any rate, than the "normal" mode) should be something that I would want to deny or, insofar as it is accessible to me (and I may say, with few reservations, that it is), wish to disavow.

You cleverly and clearly recognized the *artistic* reason why this might seem to be the case. It is inherent in the difference between the Dionysian spirit of lyricism, whose outpouring is irresponsible and individualistic, and the Apollonian, objectively controlled, morally and

[4] Stefan Grossmann (1875–1935), publicist, essayist, founder and editor of the Berlin weekly *Das Tagebuch*. Author of political novels and an autobiography, *Ich war begeistert*.

[1] Carl Maria Weber (b. 1890), critic, essayist, teacher.

[2] Willy Seidel (1887–1934), novelist.

socially responsible epic. What I was after was an equilibrium of sensuality and morality such as I found perfected in the *Elective Affinities,* which I read five times, if I remember rightly, while working on *Death in Venice.* But that the novella is at its core of a hymnic type, indeed of hymnic origin, cannot have escaped you. The painful process of objectivation, imposed on me by the inner necessities of my nature, is described in the introduction to the otherwise miscarried *Gesang vom Kindchen.*

> Do you recall? Higher frenzy, extraordinary emotion
> Once may have come over you too, casting you down
> So that you lay, brow in hands, your soul rising
> In hymnic praise. Amid tears the struggling spirit
> Pressed forward to speak in song. But alas there was no change.
> For a sobering effort began then, a chilling command to control.
> Behold, *the intoxicate song turned into a moral fable.*

But the artistic reason for the misunderstanding is just one among others; the purely intellectual reasons are actually more important. For example, there is the naturalistic bent of my generation (so foreign to you young people), which compelled me to see the "case" *also* in a pathological light, and to alternate this motif (the climacterium) with the symbolic motif (Tadzio as Hermes Psychopompos). Something still more a matter of intellect, because more personal, was added: the altogether non-"Greek" but rather Protestant, Puritan ("bourgeois") basic state of mind not only of the story's protagonists but also of myself; in other words, our fundamentally mistrustful, fundamentally pessimistic relationship to passion in general. Hans Blüher,[3] whose writings fascinate me (certainly the idea of his "Role of the Erotic," etc., is greatly and profoundly Germanic), once defined eros as the "affirmation of a human being, irrespective of his worth." This definition comprehends all the irony of eros. But a moralist—whose point of view, to be sure, can be only taken *ironice*—would have to comment: "That's a fine kind of affirmation, 'irrespective of worth.' No thanks!"

But more seriously: Passion as confusion and as a stripping of dignity was really the subject of my tale—what I originally wanted to deal with was not anything homoerotic at all. It was the story—seen grotesquely— of the aged Goethe and that little girl in Marienbad whom he was absolutely determined to marry, with the acquiescence of her social-climbing procuress of a mother and despite the outraged horror of his

---

[3] Hans Blüher (1888–1955), a writer who exerted considerable influence on the German youth movement. Mann had read with close attention his *Die Rolle der Erotik in der männlichen Gesellschaft* (1917–19).

own family, with the girl not wanting it at all—this story with all its terribly comic, shameful, awesomely ridiculous situations, this embarrassing, touching, and grandiose story which I may someday write after all. What was added to the amalgam at the time was a personal, lyrical travel experience that determined me to carry things to an extreme by introducing the motif of "forbidden" love. . . .

I have had to put this letter aside for a while. I did not want to close without having said something further about my relationship to that emotional tendency. You will not demand of me that I place it absolutely above the more common variety. There could be only one reason to place it absolutely *below*: that of its "unnaturalness," a term which Goethe long ago rejected on good grounds. Obviously the law of polarity does not hold unconditionally; the male need not necessarily be attracted by the female. Experience refutes the idea that an attraction to the same sex is necessarily allied to "effeminacy." Experience also teaches, to be sure, that degeneracy, hermaphroditism, intermediate creatures, in short, repulsively pathological elements may be and frequently are involved. That is the medical side of it, which is important but has nothing to do with the intellectual and cultural side of it. On the other hand, it can scarcely be suggested that, say, Michelangelo, Frederick the Great, Winckelmann, Platen, Stefan George were or are unmanly or feminine men. In such cases we see the polarity simply failing, and we observe a masculinity so pronounced that even in erotic matters only the masculine has importance and interest. It does not surprise me for a moment that a natural law (that of polarity) ceases to operate in a realm that in spite of its sensuality has very little to do with nature, far more to do with mind. I see nothing unnatural and a good deal of instructive significance, a good deal of high humanity, in the tenderness of mature masculinity for lovelier and frailer masculinity. In matters of culture, incidentally, homoerotic love is obviously as neutral as the other kind. In both, the individual case is everything; both can generate vulgarity and trash, and both are capable of highest achievement. King Ludwig II of Bavaria is no doubt a type, but the typicality of his instincts seems to me amply balanced by the noble austerity and dignity of such a phenomenon as Stefan George.

As for myself, my interest is somewhat divided between Blüher's two basic forms of social organization, the family and associations of men. I am a family founder and a father by instinct and conviction. I love my

children, deepest of all a little girl who very much resembles my wife—
to a point that a Frenchman would call idolatry. There you have the
"bourgeois." But if we were to speak of eroticism, of unbourgeois intellectually sensual adventures, things would have to be viewed a little
differently. The problem of eroticism, indeed the problem of beauty,
seems to me comprehended in the tension of life and mind. I have inti-
mated as much in an unexpected context. "The relationship of life and
mind," I say in the *Betrachtungen*, "is an extremely delicate, difficult,
agitating, painful relation charged *with irony and eroticism*." And I go
on to speak of a "covert" yearning which perhaps constitutes the truly
philosophical and poetical relationship of mind to life. "For yearning
passes back and forth between mind and life. Life, too, longs for mind.
Two worlds whose relation is erotic *without clarification of the sexual
polarity*, without the one representing the male and the other the female
principle: such are life and mind. *Therefore there is no union between
them, but only the brief, inebriating illusion of union and understanding,
an eternal tension without resolution. . . . It is the problem of beauty* that
the mind feels life and life feels mind as 'beautiful.' . . . The mind that
loves is not fanatical; it is ingenious, political; it woos, and its wooing is
erotic irony. . . ."

Tell me whether one can "betray" oneself any better than that. My
idea of eroticism, my *experience* of it, is completely expressed in those
lines. But finally, what else have we here if not the translation of one of
the world's most beautiful love poems into the language of criticism and
prose, the poem whose final stanza begins: "Wer das Tiefste *gedacht*,
liebt das *Lebendigste*."[4]

This wonderful poem contains the whole justification of the emotional tendency in question, and the whole explanation of it, which is
mine also. To be sure, Stefan George has said that in *Death in Venice* the
highest is drawn down into the realm of decadence—and he is right; I
did not pass unscathed through the naturalistic school. But disavowal,
denunciation? No.

I am glad to hear that K. Hiller[5] likes the story, for I respect Hiller;
he is overintellectual, but his sharpness has no insolence; he is not
malicious; his attacks upon me have remained honorable. The special
erotic disposition is obviously just as neutral in regard to philosophy as to

[4] "He whose thought has plumbed deepest, loves life at its height." The beginning
of the second stanza of Friedrich Hölderlin's poem *Sokrates und Alkibiades*.

[5] Kurt Hiller (b. 1885), writer and revolutionary pacifist, sent to concentration
camp in 1933, went into exile in 1934, first in Prague, then London. He returned to
Germany in the fifties.

aesthetics and culture: the widest variety of attitudes can come out of it. The humanitarian activism which Hiller derives from the roots of his sexuality is alien to me, and often repellent. It is of course not so steeped in chandalaism as Dr. Hirschfeld's[6] ghastly "committee"—but it has a tinge of that. Blüher's conclusions are far more congenial to me, and also far more interesting. Not to speak of George's personality and noble leadership. Hiller's hostility toward me is that of the Enlightenment toward romanticism. "Conservatism as erotic irony of the mind"—that, to be sure, is a somewhat audacious romantic formulation.

I have had to write hastily, inadequately, and scrappily. Make the best of it. To do justice to the subject I should have had to write a treatise —which, I grant, it is high time for.

With the kindest greetings,

TO STEFAN ZWEIG

Munich
July 28, 1920

Dear Stefan Zweig:
My cordial thanks for your fine, valuable gift, your book[1] which I have looked forward to for so long, and which I now possess with pride in the sympathy your dedication expresses. My pleasure in this sympathy has intensified as I read on. That the author of these artistic critical essays sets store by my life and writing is bound to make me happy. People like me judge the value of analysis and criticism by their direct benefit to us—I mean their encouraging, stimulating, tonic effect. I confess that great criticism sometimes does this for me almost more powerfully than work of a primary nature. In the case of your *Three Masters* I feel that effect very strongly indeed. Your "Dostoevsky" is certainly the boldest and most knowledgeable thing that has been written since Mereshkovsky about this great son of the nineteenth century (the century that is often so insolently despised nowadays). As you know, Tolstoy comes closer to my epic ideal. (You speak of the "great secret" of this ideal and this tradition on page 173.) Tolstoy, the seer of the body, belongs in the Homeric line of ancestors to which my frail modernity looks back with reverence but with a certain—pardon the word—familiarity. In Dos-

---

[6] Magnus Hirschfeld (1868–1935), physician and sexologist, founder and head of the Institute for Sexual Science in Berlin. Hirschfeld fought for abolition of the special laws governing homosexuality. He died in exile in France.
[1] *Three Masters* (1930).

toevsky I have scarcely ever been able to see anything but a totally extraordinary, wild, monstrous, and tremendous phenomenon outside all epic tradition—which, however, has not kept me from recognizing in him an incomparably deeper and more experienced moralist than Tolstoy. "Experience in Christianity"—the phrase has remained with me from the time of my studies on Savonarola. Nietzsche, who had that experience and consciously shared it with Pascal, loved it in Dostoevsky. His is a totally different world from the organically formed world of epic; Tolstoy, whose moralistic bent had a childlike, naïvely sensual quality, did not know much about that world. Dear God no, he was no great sinner, for all that he tried with such excessive contrition to convince himself that he was. Dostoevsky was one. I think I shall always prefer to call him a great sinner rather than a great artist. But at any rate he certainly was something very great, terribly and shockingly great; and I thank you with sincere admiration because your essay has once more made me feel, with rare intensity, this greatness of his.

TO PAUL STEEGEMANN[1]

Fürstenhof
Garmisch
August 18, 1920

Dear Sir:

I have read the poems of Verlaine you so kindly sent me—both *Femmes* and the proofs of *Hommes*, which are even worse. Let me say first that I find the translation by Kurt Moreck a most adequate one. I will add that the indecency of the poems has shaken me. For this is the effect which indecency and voluptuousness usually have upon me when their real abysses become visible. The sniggering reaction seems to me as stupid and incomprehensible as that of "moral indignation." What morals or morality really involve—purity and self-preservation, or abandon, that is, abandonment to sin, to what is harmful and consuming—is a problem that occupied me early in life. Great moralists have mostly been great sinners also. Dostoevsky is said to have been a debaucher of children. Moreover he was an epileptic, and nowadays medicine is inclined to explain this mystic disease as a form of indecency. At any rate, the chasms of voluptuousness are constantly gaping wide in the works of this religious man. It is the same in many a great, noble, and inviolable work, at which

---

[1] Paul Steegemann (1894–1956), publisher.

fools, even if they noticed anything, would not dare snigger or wax indignant. Wagner's *Tristan* is an extremely indecent work. Nietzsche in *Ecce Homo* applies to it the phrase "voluptuousness of hell," an expression from the mystics which he says is not only permissible but requisite in this case. It is worth noting that certain phrases in the text of *Tristan* come from a *notorious* book, Schlegel's *Lucinde*. Other elements are taken from Novalis's *Hymns to Night*, or at any rate from that realm of romanticism which is likewise exceedingly voluptuous, although the philistines never "noticed."

> Dullards, what do you think is pure? I have heard
> That no guilt is so deeply profaning as dullness itself.

That is from Count August von Platen, an austere spirit who, however, precisely because he loved only young men, understood the mysteries of the flesh in a more than "moral" manner. "Abysses," he says,

> Abysses lie in the heart
> Deeper than any inferno.

The realm of morality is wide; it includes that of immorality. Great moralists, men of broad-ranging experience, traverse the whole realm. Verlaine, who has felt what is frailest, expressed what is most sublime, presents in these verses "dissolute pictures and accursed scenes." That is his own characterization of the poems, and it sounds a most unpagan and moralistic note. It would be ridiculous to deny the indecent character of these pages, as ridiculous as for some liberal-minded literary expert to attempt to gloss it over by pleading "the grace of form." I certify bluntly to you that the poems are shockingly indecent. Perhaps this was not what you wanted to hear from me, but I say it in a sense that justifies you as against those who might condemn you for publishing such intimate material.

1921

---•---

TO WOLFGANG BORN[1]

Munich
March 18, 1921

Dear Herr Born:

It has given me great pleasure to study your graphic fantasies on my story *Death in Venice*. For the writer it is always a flattering and moving experience to have a product of his mind taken up, reproduced, celebrated, glorified by an art that appeals more directly to the senses— graphic art or the theater, say. In this case, however, your illustrations seem in fact to have produced a spiritualization of the subject, or at any rate a strong emphasis on and summoning up of its spiritual elements— which surely is the happiest thing that can be said about an illustrative work or a theatrical performance. Truly, it would be ungrateful if I were to complain about the degree of sympathetic interest that my story has aroused and continues to arouse in the German public. And yet I have frequently been bothered by an element of sensationalism which attached to this interest, and which was connected with the pathological character of the subject matter.

I do not deny that the pathological element exerts a powerful intellectual attraction upon me, and always has. But I have always disliked it when critics hammer away at that aspect of my work alone, seeing only this one side of it. For example, only yesterday I came upon the statement that my *Buddenbrooks* was really the story of a uric-acid diathesis extending over four generations—which is going pretty far. The attraction that morbidity has exerted upon me has always been intellectual,

---

[1] Wolfgang Born (?1894–1949), painter, graphic artist, illustrator, professor of art and art history. Emigrated to the United States. Taught at Maryville College, St. Louis, and Queens and City Colleges in New York City. His nine colored lithographs for *Death in Venice* were published as a bibliophilic item in Munich in 1921. This letter served as a foreword to the book.

and for that very reason I was concerned with intellectualizing it, removing it from the realm of instinct, well knowing that only crass naturalism practices the cult of the pathological for its own sake. Pathology can enter the realm of literary art only if it is used as a means for intellectual, poetic, symbolical ends.

What I like best about your lithographs is that they remove the novella entirely from the naturalistic sphere, purging it of pathological and sensational elements and leaving only the poetic quality. This comes about, first of all, by the intelligent choice of situations or psychological factors. For example, it would not have occurred to the average "illustrator" to make the figure of the graceful martyr, which appears seemingly as only a fleeting reference in the story, the subject of a special lithograph.[2] But your effect is also accomplished by a certain spiritual and symbolic tone in the pictures themselves, something atmospheric, which I can only call good and right, leaving it to the experts to produce critical judgments on the artistic value of these works.

One word more on the last picture, entitled "Death," which strikes me as almost uncanny because of a certain resemblance. The conception of my story, which occurred in the early summer of 1911, was influenced by news of the death of Gustav Mahler, whose acquaintance I had been privileged to make in Munich and whose intense personality left the strongest impression upon me. I was on the island of Brioni at the time of his passing and followed the story of his last hours in the Viennese press bulletins, which were cast in royal style. Later, these shocks fused with the impressions and ideas from which the novella sprang. So that when I conceived my hero who succumbs to lascivious dissolution, I not only gave him the great musician's Christian name, but also in describing his appearance conferred Mahler's mask upon him. I felt quite sure that given so loose and hidden a connection there could be no question of recognition by readers. Nor was it likely in your case as illustrator. For you had not known Mahler, nor had I confided anything to you about that secret, personal connection. Nevertheless—and this is what startled me at first glance—Aschenbach's head in your picture unmistakably reveals the Mahler type. That is certainly curious. Has it not been said by Goethe, for one, that language cannot express individuality and specificity, so that it cannot be comprehensible unless the other person shares

---

[2] In *Death in Venice* Thomas Mann writes: "The new type of hero favored by Aschenbach, and recurring many times in his works, had early been analyzed by a shrewd critic: The conception of an intellectual and virginal manliness which clenches its teeth and stands in modest defiance of the swords and spears that pierce its side." Wolfgang Born's lithograph for this brief passage represents a St. Sebastian.

the same kind of perception? This other person, it is said, must look more to the speaker's intention than his words. But since you, the artist, hit on the secret behind my words, language must operate not only in direct communication from one human being to another, but must also, as a literary form, possess powers of "induction," powers of suggestion capable of transmitting direct perception. This seems to me so interesting that I cannot forbear taking this opportunity to comment on it. With that, good luck as your work goes forth into the world, and my thanks for your noble efforts on behalf of mine!

TO GEORG MÜLLER VERLAG

Munich
October 8, 1921

My dear Sir:

I have received and carefully read Oskar A. H. Schmitz's[1] *Das rätselhafte Deutschland* ["Mysterious Germany"]. I am astonished at the reception this work seems to have had from the public. If I understand you aright, a misunderstanding exists which is threatening to separate this exceptionally intelligent writer from his hitherto loyal audience. I myself have sincerely admired him ever since his excellent book on Disraeli.

This misunderstanding is probably due solely to the excessive vulnerability of a nation that a few years ago felt itself to be one of the foremost, perhaps the foremost, and which today feels boundlessly humiliated. The book seems to have been taken for a lampoon in the style of those leftist radical scribblers whose "European" effusions Germany has understandably had quite enough of for the time being. It has been taken for a denunciation of Germanism, which by now has certainly been reviled and slandered to the extreme limits of justice. I trust you will believe me when I say that if this were what it is, I should be the last to speak in its favor. There have been enough such books; no one should be singing their praises. But I cannot possibly see anything of the sort in Schmitz's work; at its core it has no more to do with any such point of view than, say, Keyserling's essay, "Deutschlands wahre Politische Mission" ["Germany's True Political Mission"] with which it shares many an idea and conviction, or than my own *Betrachtungen eines Unpolitischen*. Its comment on the latter is: "Here the German essence has been formulated in a manner valid for Europe, without in the least compromising any of its content."

[1] Oskar A. H. Schmitz (1873–1931), novelist and writer on topical subjects.

As a matter of fact Schmitz's book itself represents such an attempt at German self-formulation. Moreover, the attempt strikes a highly affirmative note because of its earnestness, its honest and persistent striving for truth, in spite of all the criticism it offers.

Granted that errors, biases, and dubious statements occur. After all, it is only metaphor and hyperbole for Schmitz to say that in 1914 the Germans were "the people of sergeants and traveling salesmen." Nonsense; we were no more that than we were "the people of poets and thinkers." What does the phrase "traveling salesmen and sergeants" mean if not that alliance of industry and the military which is called imperialism? But that was and is a completely international passion. Today we see French captains of industry in the Saar conspiring with Marshal Foch, or the American steel association cleverly joining with Schneider-Creusot to buy up the Hungarian steel plants. Certainly the author's dream of a united Europe under the leadership of England is questionable, for this extra-European empire is not enough interested in the welfare of the Continent to persuade the nations once and for all that its leadership is divinely appointed. And Schmitz, who so clearly recognizes those elements in the German nature and destiny which are dangerous to the world, shows himself blind to the fact that *every* nation, every single one, England by no means least, has in one way or another by character and destiny become dangerous to mankind.

For all this, the book contains a great many clear and true, sympathetic and well-turned insights. German self-examination is of great importance to the world today. To my mind, therefore, it would be a real loss to suppress this book (and something of the sort seems to be going on). I need only point out the excellent sections (pages 111–16) which deal with the law of polarity in world history, with true and false antitheses. Here we see how the finest virtue of this little book becomes its own menace. For when the author, having considered and discarded our current sham antitheses, tries to look at it all in a vital new way, he necessarily offends both parties, "right" and "left," is denounced by the one as a revolutionary and by the other as a reactionary, and has nowhere to lay his head. This is a plight that I feel quite at home with. To negate everything in order to build anew out of nothingness—this Bolshevist principle is sterile madness in the outer world but profoundest truth in the world of the inner self. For there we seek not the vacuous nothingness of the negating intellect, which gives birth only to revolution and reaction, but the spontaneously creative ground of being. Operating from that ground, one is free to negate the revolutionary negation of the present day, without thereby selling his soul to bourgeois affirmation. It is essential to break with all so-called idealism of the kind that broods over how the world ought to be and would lovelessly impose on the world the results of its thinking, whatever the name—communism or nationalism. A labor of Sisyphus, for the antimonies of this world are inherent in existence itself; they are existence, the very fullness thereof. The pacifism of the West thus had to give rise to militarism, the militarism of Central Europe to socialism, the socialism of the East to dictatorship. You intellectual Germans, go find the contradiction to all contradictions in yourselves! . . . An intellectual leader may be expected, precisely, to step outside the interplay of contraries, recognize the inherent polarities, and find their equilibrium, but not to postpone attainment of the equilibrium by putting more weight on the one pole than the other. . . . Salvation can come only from those who, without being rigid conservatives, have something to preserve, and who at times in the past would have tried a flippant blast or two on the revolutionary trumpet, not out of genuine conviction, but out of dissatisfaction with the existing state of things. . . . I can only hope that a book containing such sentiments as these will be read. And I can only hope for the author's sake that his life will not be made miserable by a perverse misreading of his real intention. Hence this letter of mine, which you may use in whatever way you think fit.

1922

———•———

TO ANDRÉ GIDE

Dear Sir:

Back only a few hours from one of those art tours which in the last years have become the fashion in "Central Europe," I am at last able to thank you for the fine, rich gift of your book,[1] which reached me three weeks ago, on the day I left for Austria-Hungary. To receive it, and to receive it from you yourself, was a great surprise and great joy to me, and my gratitude, or rather my admiration, arises first from the handsomeness of the act—the proof of broad humanity implicit in your words of dedication—and secondly from the high merits of the book itself—the rare sense of intellectual well-being that leafing through it and reading it gave me.

The volume is almost inexhaustible. I dare not say that I have fully absorbed it; I have not yet had the leisure. But I promptly picked out what is closest and most important to me—above all the astonishing letter on Nietzsche,[2] this little masterpiece whose insights remind one of the shameful fact that by far the cleverest criticism of Wagner, too, has been done in France. German Wagnerian criticism can be found only in one place: the works of Nietzsche. The rest is prattle. And where is Nietzsche criticism now? In Paris, so it seems. (However, let me call your attention to the Nietzsche book, published by Bondi in Berlin, written by my friend Ernst Bertram, incidentally also a friend of Herr E. R. Curtius,[3] with

---

[1] *Prétextes.* Translations appeared in London, 1959, New York, 1964, under the same title.

[2] *Lettres à Angéle*, December 10, 1899.

[3] Ernst Robert Curtius (1886–1956), professor of Romance languages and literature at Marburg, Heidelberg, and Bonn. Among his works: *Maurice Barrés, European Literature and the Latin Middle Ages.*

whom you have just had such an interesting literary dialogue on Franco-German relations.)

You say moving things in that letter, and I am by blood enough of a German to be charmed to the point of rapture by such statements as, say, "*L'important, c'est que ces choses-là soient dites; car maintenant, il n'est plus besoin d'être fou pour les penser.*"[4] Also your conclusion—"*Je préfère dire que Nietzsche s'est fait fou*"[5] shook me with delight; and the word *dévouement* in this connection seems to me a finer example of Franco-German "reconciliation" than any political gesture could be. In an essay[6] that started from your dialogue with Curtius and that has appeared in the January issue of the *Neue Merkur*, I recently called Nietzsche's life a "holy spectacle of *sacrifice.*"

I also involuntarily thought of this essay, which you may have seen (I at once wish and fear that you have) when I read with intense interest and almost total agreement your "Reflections on Germany"—which, indeed, are no less reflections on France and its intellectual situation today. You made a remarkably keen observation that the great instrument of culture is not music but drawing, and that German culture came to grief for lack of the latter. [End of letter missing.]

TO HEINRICH MANN

Munich
January 31, 1922

Dear Heinrich:

With these flowers accept my warm greetings and best wishes—I was not allowed to send them to you earlier.[1]

Those were difficult days that lie behind us, but now we are over the hill and will go on better—together, if you feel as I do.

T.

---

[4] "The important thing is that these things should be said; for nowadays one does not have to be mad to think them."

[5] "I prefer to say that Nietzsche made himself mad."

[6] "Das Problem der deutsch-französischen Beziehungen" ("The Problem of Franco-German Relations"), an essay dealing with French criticism of the *Betrachtungen eines Unpolitischen*, in *Der Neue Merkur*, January 1922.

[1] See the following letter.

TO ERNST BERTRAM

Munich
February 2, 1922

Dear Bertram:

Along with my thanks for your good letter of January 27, accept once more our hearty congratulations on your appointment.[1] I suppose we all have reason to regard the event with one glad and one sad eye; but in the end the satisfaction, the pleasure at your exceptionally rapid academic rise outweighs our regrets. And Litzmann[2] assures us, as he has you, that the teaching will soon go along smoothly, so that your higher work will certainly not suffer for long. We are still grieved about your being tied down away from Munich. But in the first place you certainly won't be wholly lost to us for the present; and in the second place we tell ourselves cheerfully, for we trust in your stars: "After all, he won't stay in Cologne forever"—and our "not forever" is highly ironic. If things go on as they have been with the Eastern Nietzsche in the Auditorium Maximum, they are sure to begin throwing covetous glances at you from here before long. A highly topical theme, incidentally! Have you seen what I quoted from Suarès[3] in the *Neue Merkur* on Germany's secret Orientalism?

For all that, how I wish you were nearby just at this time. Vitally important things are happening, and I miss talking them over with you. My brother (in the higher sense I have only one brother, you know; the other is a good fellow no one could quarrel with) became severely ill several days ago: grippe, appendicitis, and peritonitis; he underwent an operation while suffering from a bronchial catarrh which made the doctors fear lung complications. His heart, too, worried us, and for three or four days the situation was about as grave as it could be. You can imagine how wrought-up we were. My wife visited his wife. He was told of my concern, my daily inquiries, and I was told of his delight. This delight, it seemed, reached its climax when I sent flowers and a few lines as soon as there was no more risk that such a gesture might do harm. I said we had passed through difficult days but now we were over the hill and would go better—together, if he felt as I did. He sent back his thanks, and said that

---

[1] Bertram had been appointed full professor at the University of Cologne.

[2] Berthold Litzmann (1857–1926), professor of the history of literature in Bonn. Bertram wrote his dissertation on Stifter under Litzmann. After his retirement Litzmann and his wife moved to Munich, and there was a lively neighborly exchange between his house and Thomas Mann's.

[3] André Suarès (1866–1948), French writer and essayist. Principal work: *Sur la vie.*

from now on—whatever our opinions—"let us never lose each other again."

Joyful, in fact wildly shaken with emotion though I am, I have no illusions about the fragility and difficulty of the revived relationship. A decently human modus vivendi will be all that it can come to. Real friendship is scarcely conceivable. The monuments of our dispute still stand—incidentally, people tell me that he has never read the *Betrachtungen*. That is good, and then again it is not; for it means that he has no idea what I have gone through. It wrenches my heart when I hear that after reading a few sentences in the *Berliner Tageblatt* in which I refer to those who proclaim the love of God and hate their brother, he sat down and wept. But my long struggle for everything I value, waged moreover for years in a state of physical undernourishment, left me no time for tears. He knows nothing of that, nothing of how time has forged me into a man, how I have grown in the process and even become the support and leader of others. Perhaps he will feel it somehow when we actually meet. As yet he is not allowed to see anyone.

He is said to have become softer, kindlier in these past years. It is impossible that his views have not undergone some rectification. Perhaps we may after all speak of a certain evolution toward one another: I feel this may have happened when I realize that the thought which truly dominates my mind these days is of a new, personal fulfillment of the idea of humanity—in contrast, to be sure, to the humanitarian world of Rousseau. I shall speak on that topic at the end of the month, in the Frankfurt Opera House, before the performance of *The Magic Flute*. The occasion is Goethe Week; you must certainly have read about its program. It is taking an official turn. The president of the Reich has promised to take part. Hauptmann will speak before the performance of *Egmont*.

You had far too many forebodings about our eastward trip. All in all, it went splendidly, except for the initial stage, the journey to Prague, which because of cancellations of trains took thirty-six hours (our overnight quarters in a place named Kirchenlaibach were fantastic)—and up to the criminal episode in Vienna's Hotel Imperial, which on the other hand also contributed to the greater glory of the whole thing, especially since our losses were trifling. The *gentleman* lingered too long over my small treasures: my pearl cufflinks, wristwatch, leather toilet kits, neckties, handkerchiefs, and so on are gone. But he must have been disturbed, for he did not find the main things, my wife's diamonds and the cash. Incidentally, the reception in Vienna was overwhelming. We lived like princes, nary a bill sent.

Till we see each other again, dear Bertram! Come as soon as you can and stay with us as long as you can! I shall be going to Frankfurt, only for a few days, at the end of February, beginning of March.

TO JACK[1]

Munich
May 10, 1922

Alas my good Jack, poor Bashan,[2] to whom you so cordially and nicely wrote, has long been dead—gone to the happy hunting grounds, to put it in consoling terms. A severe distemper, combined with pneumonia, carried him off very soon after I had told people about him; in other words, after he had come to life on another plane, so to speak, and sometimes I cannot repress the thought that there might be a connection and that perhaps what I did to the poor creature was not well done, but sinful. Who knows? In any case he had a very fine obituary in the newspaper here, entitled *Bashan* with a heavy cross after the name; so much he had, but it did him no good. There can be no doubt, given his temperament, that he would have been delighted by your letter. Thank you.

TO ARTHUR SCHNITZLER

Munich
September 4, 1922

Dear Herr Dr. Schnitzler:

I still owe you thanks for the kind lines which Mr. Thayer,[1] truly a most likable young man, brought from you. Out of this acquaintanceship have sprung business relations which are necessarily welcome to me as a multiple paterfamilias.

It was a great pleasure to testify, on the occasion of your sixtieth birthday, to my devotion to your beguiling life work. I have just been reading *Casanova's Homecoming*—oddly enough, my first encounter

---

[1] The reply to a pretended letter from a dog named Jack, written by a reader, Luise Pagenstecher.

[2] Bashan, the name of the dog in the novella *A Man and His Dog* (1919); actually Bauschan in its original form, the name was taken from the novel *Ut mine Stromtid* by Fritz Reuter.

[1] Editor of *The Dial*, for which Thomas Mann wrote regularly for a while. Because of the inflation, the fees from *The Dial* were vitally important to the Mann family at this time.

with this novella—and can't describe my immense delight as I let myself be carried along by your narrative art.

In the October issue of the *Neue Rundschau* you will find an essay of mine entitled "The German Republic," which may have to be continued through two issues. In it I urge the intransigent elements of our youth and middle class that it is time to place themselves wholeheartedly at the service of the Republic and of humanism—an injunction which may astonish you. But precisely as the author of the *Betrachtungen eines Unpolitischen* I believed I owed my country such a manifesto at this moment. As for my infatuation with the idea of humanism, which I have noted in myself for some time, it may be connected with the novel on which I have been working for all too long, a kind of *Bildungsroman* and Wilhelm Meisteriade in which a young man (before the war) is led by the experience of sickness and death to the idea of man and the state. — Forgive the uninvited confidence!

In October I shall be following in your tracks in Holland. In January I am to visit Vienna again and so, I hope, you as well. I am looking forward to seeing you.

TO HEINRICH MANN

[Postcard]

Amsterdam
October 20, 1922

Greetings from the land of Spinoza. I am staying with friendly people and resting at last here; thanks to the amiable smallness of the country, most of the cities I must visit can be reached from my headquarters in Amsterdam. Have experienced a world of things in these ten days. After the great Berlin adventure (they consider me some sort of campaign speaker for Ebert;[1] politics is foaming around me) came an episode in Hanover, then Düsseldorf; Duisberg with an impressive tour of the Rhine port; then Cleve, where I visited the big insane asylum. In Nymwegen, on the border, I had a curious literary conversation with a young Chinese who with great delicacy advocated the social ethics of Confucius against European individualism. He is studying phonetics in Leipzig and was about to leave for London over the holidays. I have not yet seen much of

---

[1] Friedrich Ebert (1871–1925), president of the German Reich.

Amsterdam, shall be visiting the Rijksmuseum in the afternoon and taking the train to Utrecht for the evening lecture.

T.

TO IDA BOY-ED[1]

Munich
December 5, 1922

My dear Madam:

I want to thank you for your letter, whose concern and solicitude I respect. But I cannot help thinking that you, too, would have read the essay with different eyes if the bungling newspaper accounts had not preceded it. The axe-grinding Wolff Bureau[2] reported me as asserting that the Republic was not the result of disgrace and defeat, but of exaltation and honor, period. Thus I was affirming the revolution. You have seen what I actually did say. I dated the Republic not from 1918 but from 1914. It came into being in the hearts of the youth at that time, as they faced death on the field of honor. In saying this I contributed something toward a definition of the Republic I mean—I certainly did not hail the Republic until I said what I meant by it. How do I define it? Approximately as the opposite of what *exists* today. But for that very reason, the attempt to infuse something like an idea, a soul, a vital spirit into this grievous state without citizens seemed to me no mean undertaking; it appeared to me something approaching a good deed. And in your letter you frequently come so close to me that I truly do not understand your sorrow. You see it my way, for you speak of a union of the concepts of humanitarianism and democracy. You call my democracy "the ideal of all mature creative people who believe in the future." And yet you speak of apostasy, self-betrayal, want of character, disavowal of my own acts. I disavow nothing. This essay is the direct continuation of the essential line of the *Betrachtungen*, I assure you! In the name of German humanitarianism I took arms against the revolution when it was starting. Today, out of the same impulse, I take arms against the reactionary wave which is sweeping over Europe just as one did after the Napoleonic wars (for I am not thinking of Germany alone), and which seems to me not a whit more agreeable where it takes a fascistic-expressionistic form. I feel that the great danger and fascination for a human race weary of relativism

---

[1] Ida Boy-Ed (1852–1928), Lübeck writer.
[2] The Wolff Telegraph Bureau, semiofficial German news agency.

and craving absolutes is obscurantism in one form or another (see the successes of the Roman Church); and I hold with the great teachers of Germany—Goethe and Nietzsche—who knew how to be antiliberal without making the slightest concession to any kind of obscurantism, without abandoning an iota of human rationality and dignity. You see, I have not turned away from Nietzsche, although I do turn away from his clever imitator, Herr Spengler. But I should think that my being twice in opposition in this period rather expresses a certain instinctive steadfastness and independence of conscience instead of a capitulation to "influences" and "connections."

Be charitable, please, with this woefully incomplete attempt at justification, and with me in general.

Yours,   T. M.

1923

―――――――――●―――――――――

TO HEINRICH MANN

Munich
February 17, 1923

Dear Heinrich:

I needn't tell you that German lecture tours scarcely pay nowadays. I have just been in Dresden for 50,000 marks, which the impoverished association had received as an ad hoc gift, and I would have come out in the red if I hadn't stayed in a private house and hadn't needed to go to Berlin anyhow, so that the lecture at least covered the cost of the trip. If you ask 30,000 marks per evening for a cluster of cities, you won't make enough to compensate for the fatigue. On the other hand, I hardly think that the clubs can afford more. Ask 40,000 per evening for a start. I am going to Augsburg in the near future for 25,000, the arrangement having been made some time ago.

Our Frenchmen are behaving brilliantly. They seem determined to give the lie to everyone in Germany who urges moderation. One hears that the details about the Ruhr are not exaggerated but rather lag behind the truth.[1] The anger is terrible—deeper and more united than that which brought on Napoleon's fall. There is no predicting the outcome. And the unfortunate part of it is that a French retreat, desirable though that would be, would signify the triumph of nationalism in domestic politics. Must the better side of Germany really be forced into this dilemma? Germany was completely malleable in 1918, but the others, who were convinced that they were so much better, have shown little capacity to learn.

―――――――

[1] The French had just extended their area of occupation of the Ruhr in punishment for Germany's refusing the Paris reparation proposals. The Germans retaliated by cutting off all reparation deliveries and beginning a campaign of civil disobedience inside the occupied district.

TO FELIX BERTAUX [1]

Munich
March 1, 1923

Dear Sir:

I want to thank you immediately for your kind letter, which has given me great pleasure. Truly, it would be impossible to go on living in this Europe of vicious misunderstandings between nations if we did not still have an individual and intellectual realm of sympathy, of exchange and friendly concord.

Your many and various communications by no means "alarm" me; on the contrary they have pleased me very much, and I am sincerely obliged to you for the sympathy with my work that they express. *Death in Venice* has met with good fortune in the wide world. It recently became available in Polish, after having already been translated into Hungarian, Russian, Swedish, and, I think, Italian. It will be a special satisfaction to me to see it also in the language of Flaubert. This story is really *Tonio Kröger* retold at a later stage of life. If the latter has the virtue of greater freshness, of youthful feeling, *Death in Venice* is undoubtedly more mature as a work of art and more successful as a composition. I shall not forget the sense of satisfaction, not to say happiness, that swept me momentarily in the course of its writing. For once everything went right, came together with a rush, and the crystal was pure.

You ask for some biographical facts for your portrait in the *Revue Européenne*. Your request is quickly met, for my life so far, that is, to my forty-seventh year, has passed very quietly indeed—although not quite quietly enough for my taste; it is increasingly disturbed and distracted by demands from the world, which I try to meet out of a kind of pedantic sense of duty, although the real craving of my heart is directed entirely toward concentration and not at all toward distraction. My origins, as you know, are described in *Buddenbrooks* with excessive precision, and *Tonio Kröger* is in a sense the autobiographical continuation of that work. I was born in Lübeck in 1875, the second son of a senator of the Free City. He was the heir of an ancient commercial house that was liquidated after his death. My mother, who is still living, was born in Rio de Janeiro; her father, however, was a German; only her mother was a native Brazilian. Thus there is a Latin admixture in our blood which

---

[1] Felix Bertaux (1881–1948), French specialist in German literature; translator of *Death in Venice* (1925) and *Sufferings and Greatness of Richard Wagner* (1933), author of *Panorama de la Littérature Allemande.*

emerges artistically much more strongly in my brother Heinrich, but doubtless can also be observed in me—reason enough for our literary Teutons to reject me. Nevertheless, the nordic element preponderates in me in one respect: I have never really felt spiritually at home in Munich, to which my brothers and sisters and I were transplanted when I was barely out of boyhood. The Catholic, communal sphere is not mine. Speaking in terms of social categories, my world is rather that of patrician burgherdom; speaking intellectually, that of individualism molded by Protestant inwardness in which, in the past, the *Bildungsroman* flourished. I have dealt with these things at length in the *Betrachtungen eines Unpolitischen*, a wartime project that contains a good many peripheral matters which today seem untenable even to me. But only crude misunderstanding can convert the book's apolitical humanism into political reaction. A certain antiliberal tendency in its profession of beliefs can be explained by my relationship to Goethe and Nietzsche, whom I view as my supreme masters—if it is not impertinent to call oneself the disciple of such higher beings. I have tried to convey my idea of humanity in the essay "The German Republic," which has been denounced as apostasy from Germanism and as contradicting the *Betrachtungen*, whereas inwardly it constitutes the linear continuation of that work.

In brief, although the Munich of peasant sensuality and the baroque is in some respects scarcely "my" city at all, I have struck civic roots here. I married here, fairly young; built a house right on the bank of the Isar, whose rushing waters provide me with a substitute for the surf of the Baltic Sea. I see a surprisingly large number of children around me, six in fact, and I shall probably remain here to the end of my life. One pleasant little high point of that life occurred last year in Lübeck, when, surrounded by my fellow townsmen and the chief officials of the city, I presided over the opening of the so-called Buddenbrooks Bookstore, which has been established on the lower floor of our old family house. For the local citizenry had been forced to observe that tourists inquired after the house, and whereas in earlier years I was considered a black sheep of that worthy community, today I have been promoted to a "son of the city." This is comic, and if it nevertheless pleases me, the fact is an indication of the deeper relations which will always bind me to that region.

I am all too frequently diverted from my major literary enterprises by lecture tours and essayistic flights forced on me by current events. Even before the war I had begun writing two novels. One of these, entitled *The Magic Mountain*, I am now trying to finish, after prolonged interruptions. It is a far-ranging composition with political, philosophical, and pedagogical elements, representing an attempt to revive the *Bildungsroman*. The other, a persiflage of the Rousseauan and Goethean type of autobiography, presents the memoirs of a confidence man and hotel thief.

I have asked my publisher to send you *Tonio Kröger*. For my part, I am adding a copy of the essay "The German Republic," which has now been published as a pamphlet; for this edition I have provided a foreword.

Please let me see your piece about me for your countrymen, and be good enough to keep me up to date on the fortunes of the French *Death in Venice*.

1924

---•---

TO KARL BOHM[1]

Munich
January 4, 1924

My dear Sir:

If you indeed agree with Fontane that the most important thing is to be able to stand up to one's own criticism, it is hard to understand why you insist on knowing whether you can also stand up to my criticism, which should be a matter of complete indifference, since there is nothing at all authoritative in one writer's opinion of another. But because I should not like to live in anyone's imagination as a person who "sits at table and relishes what he has behind the fence of success" (a foolish image; no one who accomplishes anything sits and relishes what he has; everyone who accomplishes anything works like a dog and doesn't get much out of life), I gladly give you leave to send me samples of your poetry and shall bravely tell you my personal opinion of it, although that seems to be not without its risks.

TO ANDRÉ GIDE

[Original in French]

Ahlbeck on the Baltic Sea
August 22, 1924

Dear Sir:

Because I have been moving about, your remarkable gifts[1] reached me belatedly, and so my thanks are also belated. Please forgive me and rest assured that I received and studied your books with extraordinary

---

[1] Karl Bohm (1893–1933; suicide), physician. See also Mann's letter of September 27, 1925.
[1] *Corydon* (1924) and *Incidences* (1924).

pleasure: the spiritual apology for an area of feeling which I too hold can be despised and condemned only by barbarians and ignoramuses; and that admirable volume of political and literary studies, many of which I have already read in French or in German, such as the "Reflections on Germany" and the "Preface to *Armance*." It is truly a great pleasure for me to possess these excellent pieces, along with others of equal value.

I shall perhaps be able to reciprocate shortly, around November, by sending you my new novel, which I am just finishing and which is called *The Magic Mountain*. But I assure you that I do not in the least expect you to read it. It is a highly problematical and "German" work, and of such monstrous dimensions that I know perfectly well it won't do for the rest of Europe.

TO JOSEF PONTEN

Munich
September 12, 1924

Well, well, my dear Ponten, so I am a corrupter of youth and deserve the cup of hemlock. Read the enclosed letter which I received one day after yours and ask yourself whether you have not misread my little article. For all that, your treatise may still be excellent, and I am sure you are not supporting any outworn tendencies. But what I write comes from obedience to edicts of practical reason, or let us say, of intellectual policy, which has a certain bearing on pedagogy. It is an expression of good will and feelings of amity toward life. To take issue with that, no matter how cleverly, is hardly proper, I assure you. It seems to me you would have done better to keep your treatise independent and not relate it to me. Perhaps (I recently discussed this with Martens and he said I was right) you should not relate yourself to me so much, in general. There are more things in the world than you and I. I see no necessary "either-or," not even a necessary "and"—no necessary comparison at all. You are quite absolutely an unusual fellow, and all relative thinking in this regard is superfluous ambition.

We had very little bad weather at the seaside. The two weeks in Bansin were actually ideal. But when I am "finished" here, in a few days, I shall take off again for a little while, and probably will be getting to Lugano also. Will you still be there?

To a good reunion, in any case!

1924

TO ERIKA MANN

Munich
September 19, 1924

Dear Eri:

Be my child
"Faithful" styled.

It was a perfick, simply nifty idea to write straight off to me, disregarding tradition and prejudices—a bold, simple, original inspiration, Columbus's egg. Say what you will, that sort of thing takes mother-wit.

Mielein has just telephoned from Dr. Ach's[1] clinic. Imagine, the beaver[2] had a fever and no movement at all despite all laxatives and was thoroughly wretched. Heiermanns[3] at first didn't know what to make of it, since the poor boy was quite insensitive to pressure in the region of the appendix, but in the end there could be no other possible diagnosis. At four Mielein took him to Ach in the car, and just now—at half past five—I heard from her that the operation is already over and went well and really proved to be altogether indicated. It was a regular inflammation with exudation. But in eight or ten days the beaver will probably be well again.

What sort of nice letter have I written to Rosen?[4] I don't know a thing about it. On the other hand, I did actually write to Daniel[5] suggesting that for reasons of artistic fellow-feeling he come down somewhat, for fifteen marks per lesson is really steep. I said he needn't bother answering me. He will tell you his decision.

I am glad you are so hard-working. The Joan part[6] was not a bad idea, but of course somewhat premature. I think that you personally would have been just right, and if you always practice your lines carefully but most spitefully, everything will come to you.

That Kraus[7] sends his regards is generous of him. He isn't exactly

[1] Alwin von Ach, a well-known Munich surgeon.

[2] Michael Mann ("Bibi").

[3] Dr. Hermanns, the family doctor, whom the younger children, Elisabeth and Michael, called Heiermanns.

[4] At that time Rosen was the business head of the Reinhardt theaters in Berlin, where Erika had been engaged as an apprentice actress.

[5] Oscar Daniel, a then famous voice teacher from whom Erika took lessons for a short time.

[6] Reinhardt was staging the first German performance of Shaw's *St. Joan*, with Elisabeth Bergner in the lead. Erika, who longed to play the role herself, had a walk-on part.

[7] Karl Kraus (:874–1956), Austrian writer, humorist, polemicist. He was editor and largely the sole contributor to *Die Fackel* ("The Torch"), and Thomas Mann refers to him as "der Fackelkraus."

carrying a torch for me, because I have not spoken of him with the requisite unstinting praise. He no doubt distinguishes sharply between social regard and any higher respect. Incidentally, I consider him the most decent of his type (Harden, Kerr). He is just as vain as they are, but cleaner, and his total nihilism is probably more apparent than real, I suspect. At bottom he must be soft and good-natured.

Today that swine R. Hoffmann[8] had the cheek to write and invite me to Ansbach. What should I say to that? Mielein tells me I must not answer him at all, but has he really behaved like what he is?

The duel[9] seems finished and I am at the very last and final conclusion, but that is giving me wholly unexpected troubles and the brain-pan feels numbed. It is sheer nervousness. In any case, by the end of next week I must and will be done.

Old Yeats writes amusingly in *The Dial* about Stockholm and how it was not until November that *"a journalist called to show me a Reuter paragraph that the Nobel Prize would probably be conferred upon Herr Mann, the distinguished novelist, or upon myself."* The good fellow thought it highly improbable that he would receive the prize. *"For Herr Mann is in every way fitted for such an honour,"* etc. In short, *üsis*.[10]

Auf Wiedersehen. Greetings to the famous big-city critic.

Z.[11]

TO HEDWIG BULLER[1]

Munich
December 24, 1924

My dear Frau Buller:

A thousand thanks for the pair of heroes.[2] I have just returned from Denmark, in time for the Christmas presents—I spent a while there taking the wind out of the sails of the Alliance Française. A pleasant little country. And what smörbröd!

---

[8] Professor Rolf Josef Hoffmann, founder and at that time head of an academy for philosophy and literature in Erlangen.

[9] The duel between Naphta and Settembrini in *The Magic Mountain*.

[10] A word coined by Erika and Klaus when they were small, which remained in the family vocabulary. It combined the meaning of touching, innocent, naïvely helpless.

[11] Z. stands for *Zauberer* (Magician), a nickname first conferred on Thomas Mann by his children and later also used by close friends.

[1] Hedwig Buller (b. 1893), wife of an industrialist; Thomas Mann's hostess in Duisburg.

[2] Figurines made by Frau Buller out of dried prunes, pears, hazelnuts, etc. (*Kletzenmanndln*), representing the characters Naphta and Settembrini from *The Magic Mountain*.

Hans Castorp is finding friends in the world, it seems. Ah well, he is a good young man; I was sorry to let him go.

Imagine, we are building a garage and getting an automobile! I won't be able to believe it when I am sitting in it. A plain person like me!

Many holiday greetings to you and your husband. My wife joins me in them.

TO FELIX BERTAUX

Munich
December 28, 1924

Dear Monsieur Bertaux:

Many thanks for your letter of the 7th, which I am answering so late because it came while I was on a trip abroad; I have just returned in time for the holidays.

I have written out a few lines from *Death in Venice* for you, for the facsimile reproduction. I hope the sample is narrow enough. Any narrower and it would not look well, I think.

I have instructed Fischer to send you a copy of *Buddenbrooks*. I gladly give you permission to reprint some sections of it in your anthologies.

To the *Journal littéraire* my reply is:

How could I fail to regard a fruitful exchange between French and German writers as possible and desirable? I feel more and more that *admiration* is man's best faculty, and just as in individuals' lives nothing is more natural and human than for one person to admire in another what he himself is *not*, cannot do, and does not have, so it should be in the life of nations. If mutual admiration were the fundamental passion of international life, how different the world would be! I shall not enter into a discussion of what German minds have to learn from the French, and vice versa. The mixture of humility and boasting which can easily follow from such disquisitions is distasteful to me. But I know theoretically and in general that only mutual complementing of differences yields what is essentially human; and I know from extremely personal and practical experience how necessary it is to absorb the alien with love and admiration, and to learn from it.

1925

———————— • ————————

TO HERBERT EULENBERG[1]

Munich
January 6, 1925

Dear Herr Eulenberg:

What do you want to do: Write about the Peeperkorn case? Cry it from
the rooftops? Rub the public's nose in it? Create a scandal? For whose
benefit? Hauptmann's? Impossible! For the public's benefit? But you will
only be providing it with a sensation, a false, outrageous sensation; and
I should have to defend myself indignantly against the charge of having
portrayed Gerhart Hauptmann in the character of the Dutchman. I did
nothing of the kind. But in saying this I certainly want to tell the truth.
At the time the character became a pressing matter for me, in the fall of
last year, in Bozen, I was under the impress of the great writer's powerful
and touching personality. This experience gave a certain stamp to the
characterization of Peeperkorn, to some of his outward features. I cannot
and would not deny it. But I won't go a step further in my concessions.
What other similarity is there between Hauptmann's life and that of the
former coffee trader from Java who comes to Davos with his malaria and
his mistress and by way of abdication kills himself with Asiatic drugs?
None, and it is inevitable that any resemblances which insiders may
possibly see at the beginning of the episode fade away the further they
read. Perhaps 50,000 persons have read the novel by now. Of that
number two dozen, by a generous reckoning, will be in a position to see
resemblances, because they happen to have shared that experience with
me. The others are as unsuspecting as they properly should be. And you
want to enlighten them? I beg you, as warmly and strongly as I can, to
abstain.

[1] Herbert Eulenberg (1876–1949), writer; author of many plays, novels, and
essays.

As in other cities, I recently gave a public reading of the beginning of the Peeperkorn episode in Stuttgart, a few days after Hauptmann had appeared there. I shall say nothing about the audience at large, but even among those who spent some time socially with the Master after the recitation, not one so much as blinked an eyelash—it was obvious that no one had even been brushed by a reminiscence. Close acquaintances and friends of Hauptmann; Loerke,[2] Reisiger,[3] his "Eckermann" Chapiro,[4] who has turned in a quite enthusiastic piece on *The Magic Mountain*, Dr. Eloesser,[5] to whom I am likewise indebted for a singularly favorable review—all these have had, I will not say the slightest association, but not the slightest compunctions about letting the character affect them as such. Wassermann, who likewise knows H., wrote to me on this subject: "When the dialectical voices of your orchestra at last raise up a figure like Peeperkorn (an enviably seen and delineated picture), one is simply confronted with the irrational and a product of the imagination on the grand scale." That is what it is, a product of the imagination which was involuntarily and half unconsciously colored by a powerful real experience. *The idea and the essential features of the character, as a contrasting figure to the self-dwarfing "talkers," was of course established long before I met Hauptmann.* To that meeting, two weeks spent together, the character owes a few living traits. Does that mean that I have profaned Germany's foremost writer by making a caricature of him? Are not you as a poet, is not G. H. himself, familiar with the process I am speaking of? Michael Kramer was an actual person, they say. Kollege Crampton, the drinker, was an actual person. Gabriel Schilling's story is a "true" one.[6] But Pieter Peeperkorn's story is *not* a true story and only a few furrows on the forehead are borrowed from reality.

Needless to say, none of the many newspaper reviews of the book contains the slightest hint of a relationship. Out of discretion? No, because the reviewers naturally had no suspicion. To disturb this innocence would be harmful to everyone concerned. But it is not quite irrelevant that not a single printed or epistolary comment fails to recognize this Peeperkorn,

---

[2] Oskar Loerke (1884–1941), poet, editor at S. Fischer Verlag.

[3] Hans Reisiger (b. 1884), novelist, poet, translator of Walt Whitman, among others. Reisiger was one of Mann's closest friends.

[4] Joseph Chapiro (b. 1893), writer, author of *Gespräche mit Gerhart Hauptmann* ("Conversations with Gerhart Hauptmann"), among other works.

[5] Arthur Eloesser (1870–1937), critic and historian of literature and the theater. For Mann's fiftieth birthday he published a monograph, *Thomas Mann. Sein Leben und Werk*, which was the first book devoted exclusively to him.

[6] *Michael Kramer, Kollege Crampton, Gabriel Schillings Flucht*—dramas by Gerhart Hauptmann.

along with Joachim Ziemssen, as the most successful and lovable character in the book. Wassermann, for example, continues: "Your secret love belongs, of course to him, Peeperkorn." Your secret love! I did not think it was all that secret. And now I am to defend myself against the charge of cold-blooded betrayal.

Believe me, my dear Herr Eulenberg, it would be a painful thing to me, humanly speaking, if the thought of treachery, malicious spying, disrespectful exploitation—a seed which I cannot but suspect has been nurtured by others—should strike root in Hauptmann's mind. In any case, that would be a matter between him and me—and not a hopeless one, I venture to think. His greatness, kindness, and serenity cause me to trust that we would arrive at mutual understanding. But I beg you again, for heaven's sake: Don't "write" about it. Write to him, write to me, as your heart prompts you. But don't spoil everything by bringing the question before a public which, you must know as well as I, is not able to cope with it and not worthy of it.

TO JOSEF PONTEN

Munich
January 21, 1925

Dear Ponten:

Thank you for your letter, which I have read attentively, and for sending me Binding's[1] excellent account. I am almost certain that I would have been as moved as he by the consecration to death and life of those fine young men. If it is true that they feel antipathy toward me, that is sad for both sides. But since it is sad for both, there is the hope of change.

I must reject your proposals. I feel no compulsion to offer reassuring explanations to close the picturesque breach which you have evidently had an irresistible compulsion to open up publicly between us. If you feel yourself somehow corrected by publication of *The Magic Mountain*; if in addition you find that your remarks are being distorted and misused, it is your business to make statements about the matter. I have nothing to say, not publicly. Anyone who has read the *Betrachtungen eines Unpolitischen* knows that your polemical work[2] contained no shattering revelations for

---

[1] Rudolf G. Binding (1867–1938), writer. Among his works: *Opfergang, Unsterblichkeit, Moselfahrt aus Liebeskummer, Erlebtes Leben, Selbstbildnis und Bild der Zeit.*

[2] Ponten had published an "Open Letter to Thomas Mann" in the *Deutsche Rundschau*, sharply attacking Mann for a passage in his essay "Zum sechzigsten Geburt-

me. Anyone acquainted with the musical dialectic of *The Magic Mountain* likewise knows that, and also knows that I would be quite capable of answering you. Every sensible person understands why today it seems right to me—to keep to the terminology that you have taken over from our conversations—to come down on the side of "intelligence"—without at all worrying that "nature" in our Germany can ever be so overbalanced that it will go flying off into the blue sky. If in your zealous friendship you have succeeded in mobilizing the nationalistic youth against me—well, the new novel has, as I have heard, aroused feelings of shame and contrition toward me in a good many young hearts. Besides, I am so used to being seen in a bad light, the illumination that falls upon me has already changed so frequently, that I have renounced the thankless and scarcely dignified nuisance of self-defense and self-justification. I am resolved to leave everything to time and to whatever slow, continuous influence my character may exert.

I could really close at this point, but I'll go on a little because I don't want you to think I am taking the matter too lightly.

Do you know the fine, strong words that Varnhagen von Ense[3] wrote in 1813, when Goethe had contrived to have himself denounced as an unpatriotic scoundrel? I want to set them down here, whether you know them or not. "Goethe not a German patriot?" Varnhagen exclaimed. "All the freedom of Germania was early gathered together in his heart and became, to the never sufficiently acknowledged benefit of us all, the pattern, the model, the sturdy trunk of our cultivation. All of us walk in the shadow of this tree. Never before did roots penetrate harder and deeper into the soil of our fatherland, never did veins draw more mightily and steadily upon the hearty interior of that soil. Our fighting youth with their noble ideals truly have a closer relatedness to this great spirit than to many another who claims to have been so forceful in the fray."

Fine, strong words. They come down to the truth which I should gladly uphold publicly, that in national affairs the intention and words of a man count very little, but his being and his actions are all-important. If a man has written *Goetz von Berlichingen*, *Faust*, the *Proverbs in Rhyme*, and *Hermann and Dorothea* (the latter a poem that Schlegel honored with the adjective "patriotic"), he can be the greatest humanist,

stag Ricarda Huchs." Ponten denounced the "hostile fools [i.e., Mann] who with heads in the sand go on repeating the dreary rot about the German creative writer (*Dichter*) and the un-German man of letters (*Schriftsteller*)."

[3] Karl August Varnhagen von Ense (1785–1858), poet, critic, biographer, soldier, and diplomat, who with his wife, Rahel Varnhagen, was largely responsible for the rise of what may be called the "Goethe cult" in Germany.

can take the most treasonable stance for "civilization" and cosmopolitanism, and still be and remain the purest wine of great Germanism. And if one—forgive this parallel in a purely private letter—has in his youth written *Buddenbrooks* and *Tonio Kröger*, in maturity *The Magic Mountain*, a book that is possible only in Germany, and that could not conceivably be more German—then he is genuine enough, has enough of a national "nature," to be permitted to say a word or two, with specific and carefully considered motives, as spokesman for the "world of the intellect"—without tumbling into "literary" vacuity. And our good nationalistic youth may perhaps "have a richer relatedness" to such a spokesman than, in their impetuosity, they imagine today.

Let us stay with Goethe for a moment. You know that the old humanist could not tolerate "the Cross." Nevertheless he made frequent and eloquent confessions of reverence for the idea of Christianity. "The human spirit," he said, "will not go beyond the nobility and *ethical culture* of Christianity as it glimmers and shines in the Gospels." Words which suggest a sympathy, a feeling of alliance, that is worth pondering upon. Goethe bows down before the "ethical culture" of Christianity, i.e., before its humanity, its civilizing, antibarbarian tendency. This was his own tendency; and such occasional tributes undoubtedly spring from insight into the kinship between his own mission and that of Christianity within the racially Germanic world (which, again confidentially in a personal letter) is always but three steps from barbarism, insofar as it is not plumb in the middle of barbarism. He conceived his task, his national calling, as essentially one of civilizing; therein lay the deepest and most German meaning of his "renunciation." For do you doubt that in Goethe there were potentialities for a more savage, more rank, more dangerous, more "natural" greatness which was only reined in by his instinct for self-restraint? Instead he fostered the highly pedagogical image of his personality that stands before us today. In his *Iphigenia* the idea of humanity as the antithesis of barbarism bears the marks of civilization—not in the polemical, and indeed, already political sense in which the word "civilization" is commonly used today, but in the sense of "ethical culture." It was a Frenchman, Maurice Barrès,[4] who called *Iphigenia* a "civilizing work." Perhaps the phrase is even more apt for that other work of self-discipline and self-castigation which is so readily disdained because of its atmosphere of cultivation,

---

[4] Maurice Barrès (1862–1923), French writer. Originally a preacher of virulent decadence, he became a foremost advocate of chauvinistic nationalism. Among his works: *Roman de l'energie nationale.*

courtliness, and prudery: *Tasso*. Those are works of "renunciation," works which are intended to educate the Germans and which deliberately eschew the advantages of barbarism that the thoroughly voluptuous Richard Wagner permitted himself with such enormous effectiveness—and with the inevitable penalty that his lushly ethnic works daily appeal to an ever coarser popular taste. Truly, the inevitability of law operates here. For is not the didactic duty of renunciation, which Goethe imposed upon himself, something more than personal? Is it not prescribed by fate? Is it not the innate imperative, to be violated only at the cost of severe penalties to the spirit, of any Germanism that has ever been destined to grow somehow and to some extent into a principle of formative responsibility?

These are large trends, my dear Herr Ponten, which today are not without relation to the problem of Germany's reconciliation with Europe and to the salvation of Europe in general. You have bumbled into the matter quite naïvely, and it might profit you to know that there are people who do not think it at all naïve and will not forgive me for the good nature with which I have received it. I think otherwise, however. But since I have already ruined my relations with the dear young people, I cannot on top of that ruin my relations with my friends by appearing together with you as a fellow pamphleteer. I must undertake sooner or later to "reach the youth" on my own account, and I believe you too should prefer to reach them in another fashion, rather than by polemics against me: namely, through your creative work.

TO JOSEF PONTEN

Munich
February 5, 1925

Dear Ponten:

Your last *Magic Mountain* letter, dated the 2nd, reached me today—a document that can truly in the finest and purest sense of the word be called "naïve." I sincerely thank you for it. Of course I don't doubt your explanation that you wrote it *before* reading my reply to your last letter, whose naïveté was of a somewhat less fine character. But my faith goes a step further: I believe you would have written no differently even *after* reading that letter. Take this statement as the moral compliment it is. Today I have given a good deal of thought to the things you say, in sadness and admonition, about the inner nature of the book. We must take this nature, the alliance with death that you scent, the melancholy that depressed you (although betweenwhiles you had to laugh aloud—a strange complication and confusion!), the skepticism and nihilism which is (or so I think) the final effect of the disputes—we must take all this as something imposed by destiny, I suppose, a personal fatality which evidently emerges from my work. Hardly likely that anything can be done about it. You now know better than before how, where, in what sphere, under what humanly not wholly secret inner circumstances, this well-balanced and not humorless, though sometimes irritable and fatiguable Herr T. M., honorary doctor and paterfamilias, really dwells, and henceforth you will subject your relations with him, if you continue them at all, perhaps somewhat more than previously to the rule of discreet forbearance.

But let's be just in the matter of hostility toward life. Is not my book, despite its own inner fatality, a book of *good will?* In saying this I leave aside the question of whether the kind of nihilism that pokes fun at extremist theories and manages to counter them with such characters as the brave Joachim and the high and mighty stammerer Peeperkorn (the age provides nothing better)—is really such dyed-in-the-wool nihilism, after all. This is just by the way. But where in all the history of art and literature have you ever before encountered the attempt *to make death a comic figure?* That is literally done in *The Magic Mountain,* and our good Hans, though by nature inclined to consider death as the most noble and superior principle, is systematically disillusioned on that score, however piously he fights against it. Is that hostility to life? I feel that it at least testifies to the intention of denying such hostility. Nor is it accurate to say that Hans Castorp learns nothing at all, arrives at no resolution and no decision in his sorry place. In his dream in the snow he sees this: Man is, to be sure, too superior for life; let him therefore be good and attached to death in his heart. But man is also and especially too superior for death; let him therefore be free and kind in his thoughts. This insight into the human incompatibility of aristocratic alliance with death (history, romanticism) and of democratic amity toward life is not something that Hans bears "triumphantly home on the point of his hunting spear," as Wandrey[1] (who in other respects also is not so sound) writes. On the contrary, Hans promptly forgets it again; in general he is not personally able to cope with his higher thoughts. But how does he come to be concerned about "man" and man's "standing and status" at all? Primarily not through Naphta and Settembrini, but rather in a far

---

[1] Conrad Wandrey (b. 1887), Munich literary critic, author of books on Stefan George, Hans Pfitzner, and others.

more sensual way which is suggested in the lyrical and *enamored* treatise on the organic in nature. You found the section too long, but it is not an arbitrary digression. Rather, it shows how there grows in the young man, out of the experience of sickness, death, and decay, the idea of man, the "sublime structure" of organic life, whose destiny then becomes a real and urgent concern of his simple heart. He is sensuously and intellectually infatuated with death (mysticism, romanticism); but his dire love is purified, at least in moments of illumination, into an inkling of a new humanity whose germ he bears in his heart as the bayonet attack carries him along. His author, who there takes leave of him, is the same who emerged from the novel to write the manifesto "The German Republic." He is no Settembrini in his heart. But he desires to be free, reasonable, and kindly in his thoughts. That is what I would like to call good will, and do not like to hear branded as hostility to life.

Wandrey is priceless. He denies me creativeness, music, sculptural quality, in short everything, and does so with the greatest deference. It is difficult to take any kind of attitude toward that sort of thing. And how he treats me as a kind of shuffling old wizard. "The pastmaster." "Oh, that cunning old puppetmaster." I had to laugh aloud. But I shall thank him nicely; he has taken great pains.

Early in March I am going traveling [. . .]: Venice, Corfu, Constantinople, Port Said, Naples, Algiers. On invitation from the Stinnes Line. Perhaps we can see each other some time before then. Frau Hallgarten[2] recently spoke of inviting us together.

TO JULIUS BAB[1]

Munich
February 22, 1925

Dear Herr Bab:

Your letter is perhaps the finest I have received on this occasion[2]—at least so it seems to me now, when its impression upon me is fresh. Many, many thanks!

---

[2] Constance Hallgarten (b. 1881), wife of the scholar, philanthropist, and patron of the arts Dr. Robert Hallgarten, whose house was near Mann's. It was one of the most cultivated intellectual centers of Munich. Frau Hallgarten was a cofounder of the Women's International League for Peace and Freedom. Richard Hallgarten, the younger son, was an intimate friend of Erika and Klaus.

[1] Julius Bab (1880–1955), noted critic of drama and literature. Left Germany in 1933 and remained in America after the war.

[2] The publication of *The Magic Mountain*.

Admittedly the séance scene is highly questionable. I embarked on it because it fits so well, just as Peeperkorn does, into the design of the book, which repeatedly refers back to the mysticism of the body, the organic mystery. With the reprehensible reckless curiosity of the cultural tourist, I had looked in on some of these devilish doings, and even falteringly touched them (for what I related in the *Neue Rundschau* was not the last of my experiences). As a result—let me confess this to you—I do not regard them in principle as entirely impossible. This was my other reason. In the novel, I grant, the future uniform[3] introduces a metaphysical or rather temporal-telepathic element which goes beyond my experience not just in degree but in essence. Thus it is something that I probably should not have permitted myself. But once again, it fits well into the structure, in which the idea of time constantly plays its implicit or explicit part. And then, has one no right to play with metaphysics, provided one goes about it in a tolerably meaningful way? The war is slowly gathering in the background, and it will be filthy enough to be heralded in a filthy manner. For I have surely left no doubt that Hans Castorp, like the characters of Dehmel's *Zwei Menschen*,[4] feels the spooky business to be thoroughly indecent. Only he has a greater affinity for vice than they, and has far more trouble achieving, even momentarily, a pure concept of human potentiality.

It is hardly proper to defend oneself against the criticism and pocket the praise. But the above is meant to be more an explanation and apology than a defense, and the novel—even *as* a novel, I hear you saying— retains enough questionable material, even if the most questionable thing of all were tenable. As for the praise, you are the only person so far— aside from Ernst Bertram, who mentioned the same feeling—who has been as moved by the recurrence of that song at the end as I was when I put it into the mouth of our good Hans. I do after all have a little of the poet in me, in spite of the intellectualism with which I have "ruined the novel."

Isn't it curious, incidentally, that Scheler[5] is said to have spoken of the book in terms of the strongest praise (against Bertram)? Schnitzler has said he would enjoy reading four more such volumes.

---

[3] In the séance described in *The Magic Mountain*, Hans Castorp has a vision of his cousin Joachim dressed in the uniform of a war that lies in the future.

[4] A verse epic by Richard Dehmel, strongly influenced by Nietzsche's idea of the superman, published in 1903.

[5] Max Scheler (1874–1928), philosopher and sociologist, who for a time had strong leanings toward Catholicism. He was particularly influential because of his revival of philosophical anthropology, the stark intellectuality of which Mann found uncongenial.

1925

I am going traveling at the beginning of March: a Mediterranean voyage of five weeks. But do be sure to send anything you may have written about the M. M.

TO GERHART HAUPTMANN

Munich
April 11, 1925

Dear, great, revered Gerhart Hauptmann:

Let me write to you at last! I have long wanted to, but have not dared. As you know, I have a guilty conscience; I know that I have sinned. I say "sinned" because the word has a dual import: it is strong and severe, as is fitting, and then again it is, in a certain usage, a somewhat genial, confidential, and tentatively humorous word which would not be applied to acts of real baseness. I may say: I have sinned, as children sin. For believe me (I believe you do believe it), I have much more of the artist-child in me than is suspected by those who rattle on about my "intellectualism"; and since you too are an artist-child, a noble, understanding, and forbearing child of art, I hope that by these lines, inadequate though they may turn out, I shall win your *full* forgiveness which—let me believe—I have already *half* had all along.

I have sinned against you. I was in need, was led into temptation, and yielded to it. The need was artistic: I was seeking a character vital to my novel and long since provided for in its scheme, but whom I did not see, did not hear, did not hold. Uneasy, anxious, and perplexed, I came to Bozen—and there, over wine, was unwittingly offered what I should never, never have allowed myself to accept, speaking in human and personal terms, but which in a state of lowered human responsibility I did accept, imagined I had the right to accept. I did so blinded by the passionate conviction, foreknowledge, certainty, that in my transmutation (for, of course, it was not a question of a portrait but of a transmutation and stylization into a totally foreign element, in which even the externals were barely akin to reality) I should be able to create the most remarkable character of a book which, I no longer doubt, is itself remarkable.

That was no delusion; I was right. I did wrong, but I was right. I do not say that the end justifies the means. But were these means, was the spirit in which I made use of those human externals, infamous, perfidious, loveless, disrespectful? Dear, venerated Gerhart Hauptmann, it was not.

If I committed a betrayal, it was certainly not against my feelings for you, which are clearly and distinctly expressed in the treatment I gave my intrinsically nonrealistic giant puppet who dwarfs all babblers; which are also expressed in the reverence I make my dear son, little Hans Castorp, feel from the first moment he encounters that mighty personality who has supplanted him in the possession of his beloved. No perceptive person will be deceived on that score by the, let us say, ironic and grotesque artistic means which it is my wont to manipulate. I leave aside what you know: that no one who does not know you closely and intimately has "noticed" anything at all; in a word, that the matter is not public. That does not serve to exonerate me. I have always known and said that it is a matter between you and me. But your closest friends, disciples, and admirers, the Reisigers, Chapiros, Loerkes, Heimanns,[1] Eulenbergs, and others who could have "noticed" something and did—are they affronted by the character? Have they taken offense and expressed indignation? The fact is that they have not; some of them have done just the opposite, and this phenomenon should also, I think, moderate your anger.

Dear, revered man! Is a bad prank, an artist's sin, to wipe out all memory of things I have said on the theme of Gerhart Hauptmann when it was *you* I was describing, and not a magnificent mask? That essay, for example, which won me your friendship, and in which I called you the nation's king? In time of need I may be permitted to remind you of it. And perhaps your wife,[2] who judges me more severely, may be reminded of it also—I already venture to ask you to put in a good word for me with her, so strongly do I believe by now in your own forgiveness.

Rest assured that I shall make no excessive demands upon your kindness if life should lead us together once more—which, as you know, is not unlikely. I am well aware that my prank—for some time to come, at least—has ruled out a good many things that otherwise might have been possible. But if the moment comes, then I beg you, do not deny me your hand, which in my mind I venture to clasp with all the true feeling that at no hour of my life and work, in your company or far from you, has ever left me.

---

[1] Moritz Heimann (1868–1925), essayist, critic, editor at S. Fischer Verlag and of the *Neue Rundschau*.

[2] Frau Margarethe Hauptmann assured Thomas Mann after Hauptmann's death that the character of Mynheer Peeperkorn was the finest monument that anyone had erected to the departed great dramatist.

1925

TO JOSEF PONTEN

Dear Ponten:

Your long letter has moved me deeply. It makes a clean breast of something I have seen for a long time without wanting to name: that you are suffering from a fixation, which might almost be called morbid, upon my literary personality. I have never done anything whatsoever, wittingly and willingly, at any rate, to produce or perpetuate this fixation, and as your friend, which I am, I wholeheartedly hope you will be cured of it. Really, there must be an end of this staring at me, this comparing yourself with me and measuring yourself against me, this perverse brooding on how I can possibly amount to something when it's plain as day that in order to legitimately amount to something I ought to be completely different, to wit, like you. Good God, it seems as if nothing in the world exists but you and me and the problem of our relationship to each other. That is not a sound way to feel. And good Lord, how wrongly you see certain things about me. My work, you think, makes mock of competence. According to you that mockery, for instance, is represented in the character of Hofrat Behrens, that devil's henchman and sovereign of bodies who conceals his melancholy behind a *Korps* student's bluster. And I have even made mock of greatness in Peeperkorn—whereas, for example, the by no means stupid Julius Bab concludes in a long essay that Peeperkorn is probably the finest creative character in the book and that he is enveloped by the dignity of nature. Bab regards it as a very pretty sign of the young hero's moral development that instead of hatred, he feels admiration for this rival. And Bab calls the scene in which Peeperkorn delivers his last speech at the edge of the thundering waterfall the finest literary conception in the book. Scarcely anyone has ever responded to my much-discussed irony as you do when you call it destructive, nihilistic, and diabolic. On the contrary, my literary antagonists tend to see it as the expression of a mild and unradical bourgeois temper, and those who take a more affirmative attitude toward me customarily speak of kindliness. I do not know who is right; I don't see myself; no one does. But the mirror image that you hold up to me must be somehow distorted. And one might expect so a priori, given your exceedingly impassioned, which is to say pathological, attitude toward me. Certainly I must hope it is distorted. It's difficult to understand why my existence and character should have become more and more of a problem and *crève coeur* for you.

Thomas Mann in 1900 and 1904.

Katia with Erika and Klaus in 1907 (opposite).
The Manns with baby Golo, Erika, and Klaus at their country house
in Tölz, 1909 (above); and, below, left to right: Erika with Elisabeth,
Klaus, Katia holding Michael, Golo, Monika, in Munich, 1919.

Thomas Mann with the cast of his play Fiorenza *(above)
and in 1925 portrait (opposite).*

Thomas Mann with Hermann Hesse (opposite)
and with Katia in Chantarella, Switzerland, 1932 (above).
Bruno Walter, Thomas Mann, and Arturo Toscanini
at the Salzburg Music Festival, 1935 (below).

With Dorothy Thompson in New York, May 1938 (above),
and with Katia and Erika on the Île de France, April 1937 (below).

*At Princeton, November 1938 (above), and at the
home of Alfred A. Knopf in Purchase, New York, May 1940 (below).*

About 1938.

With grandson Frido, 1942.

Heinrich Mann in New York, 1940.

With Erika and Katia at home,
Pacific Palisades, California, 1944.

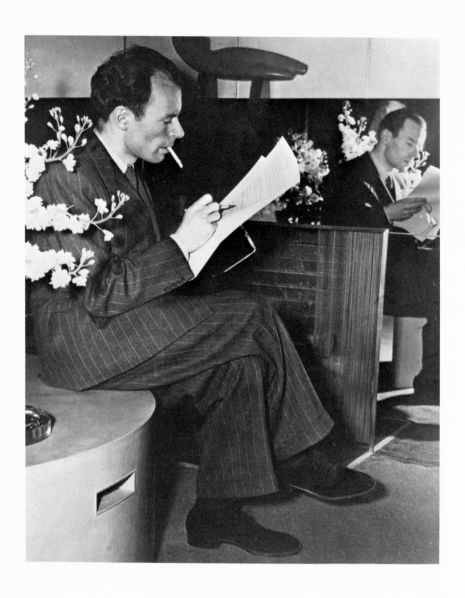

Klaus Mann in Cannes, May 1949.

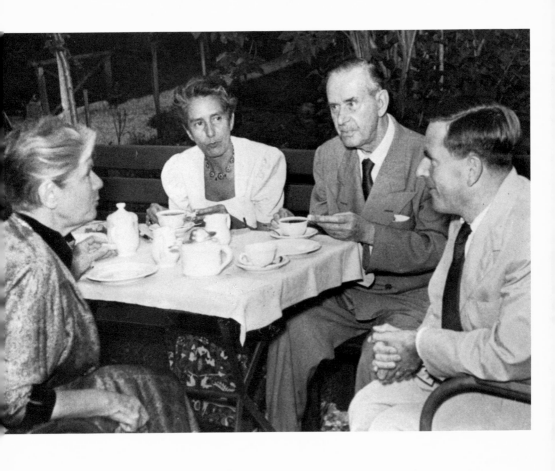

Thomas with Katia, Erika, and Golo, about 1952.

Erika and Thomas in Munich, October 1952 (opposite).
Zurich, June 6, 1950: party for Thomas Mann's seventy-fifth birthday.
Left to right: Gret Moser Mann, Thomas, Katia, Erika,
Elisabeth Mann Borgese, Michael (above).

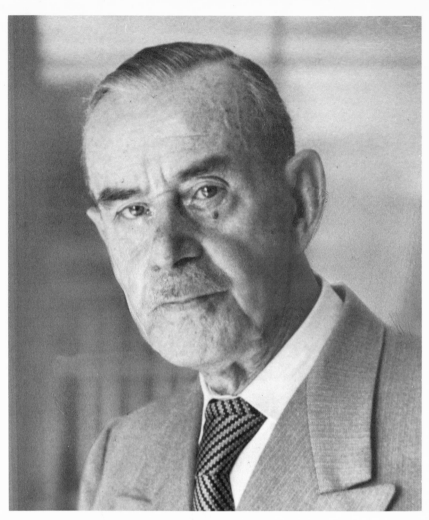

On his eightieth birthday, June 6, 1955, in Zurich.

For since you yourself feel that we are so different, there is no competition and scarcely any comparison, and you might peacefully let me be as I am and thus remain at peace with what you are. Really, as I said above, peace is what I wholeheartedly wish you, out of friendship. You must free yourself from this mania which has begun to upset your productivity, for I see with alarm from your remarks that this brooding and bondage are what keep you from creatively shaping the wonderful material you told me about that time we were tramping together. I have always believed in your special and strong gift, which is so different from mine and at the same time so great. The *Studenten* will certainly turn out to be remarkable if you are wholly yourself in the course of the work. I hear you want to go traveling. I am obliged to hail the idea almost with relief. I would say, be a man, if I did not know that you are one, and in a certain sense more so than I. Manliness, too, is not a simple matter; the pros and cons of it are highly complicated. We shall certainly talk more about this before we each set out on further traveling adventures. Thank you for having poured out your heart to me. With many warm greetings,

TO JULIUS BAB

Munich
April 23, 1925

Dear Herr Bab:

I must thank you for your magnificent essay. I have read it with deep emotion. I am very much aware that social problems are my weak point and I also know that this puts me to some extent at odds with my art form itself, the novel, which is propitious to the examination of social problems. But the lure—I put it frivolously—of individuality and metaphysics simply happens to be ever so much stronger for me. Certainly the very concept of the novel implies "novel of society," and the *Magic Mountain* did become this to a certain extent, quite of its own accord. Some criticism of prewar capitalism comes into it, along with other things. But I grant you that the "other things," such as music and the meaningful interweaving of life and death, were much, much more important to me. I am German—don't think I use the word in the sense of unreserved self-praise and without some national self-doubt. The Zola-esque streak is feeble in me, and that I should have had to discuss the eight-hour day strikes me as almost a parody of the social viewpoint. But there you are; that's the crux of it. I am starting to dabble in such matters now, but suspect in advance that the principle of division of labor will be preserved between my brother and myself.

Incidentally, you're quite right: Hans Castorp is in the end a proto-type and forerunner, a little prewar German who by "intensification" is brought to the point of anticipating the future. This is as good as said in the author's final words of dismissal, and in the course of the work I was constantly telling myself: "I am writing about a young German who before the war has already reached beyond the war."

The candidacy of Hindenburg is "Linden Tree"—to put it mildly. An article of mine in the *Neue Freie Presse* denounces this shameful exploitation of the German people's romantic impulses. In it I say that I "shall be proud of our nation's political discipline and instinct for life and for the future if on Sunday it refrains from electing an antediluvian valiant as its chief of state." Little Hans has come that far!

TO ERIKA MANN

Munich
May 7, 1925

Dear Erikind:[1]

Many thanks for your beautiful gift! The picture is somewhat too much in shadow, but the expression is completely lovable.

Yesterday we accompanied the Hauptmanns to the dress rehearsal of his festival play; we drove them and Benevenuto[2] in our car. We clasped hands a great deal, and everything is in order again. Such stature; I love him dearly. And the festival play is such a heartwarming piece of nonsense.

I read Klaus's book[3] with sympathy. A good deal of it is remarkable. But our gallant boy has a sizable Z.[4] complex, among other things. Day after tomorrow we are off to Florence. Till we see each other!

Z.

---

[1] Eri-child, Mann's pet name for his daughter.
[2] Benevenuto Hauptmann (b. 1900), Gerhart Hauptmann's youngest son.
[3] Klaus Mann's first book, *Vor dem Leben* ("Before Life"), 1925.
[4] See note 11, p. 129.

TO HANS PFITZNER

Dear Maestro:

I had not felt your silence during those days[1] to be golden—and therefore feel your present letter to be all the finer. I thank you from the bottom of my heart for its congratulations and frank expression of your beliefs.

Of course I realized that my recent intellectual stand must be repugnant to you. Do believe at least that it sprang from good will—and from a sense of responsibility which may be sharper than that which a musician needs to feel. You rapturously obeyed the power of love.[2] . . . Not everyone may do so, and there are cases of a conscious and by no means painless self-disciplining which earn a man the name of Judas. Our play, dear Maestro, speaking in the grand and representational sense of intellectual history, has long ago finished its run; we are only a latter-day, journalistic acting-out of the case of Nietzsche versus Wagner. Nietzsche's conscience made him free himself from Wagner, but he loved him unto death. And Nietzsche, like Wagner, was a late-born son of romanticism. But Wagner was a great and greatly fortunate self-glorifier and self-consummator, whereas Nietzsche was a revolutionary self-conqueror and "became a Judas." With the result that Wagner remained only the last glorifier and supremely effective consummator of an epoch, whereas Nietzsche became a seer and the leader for mankind toward a new future.

The modest hero of my last novel is occasionally called a "problem child of life." All of us artists are life's problem children, but we are children of life all the same, and whatever the romantic license of the musician may be, a literary artist who in such a moment of European history as the present did not choose the party of life and the future as against the fascination of death would truly be an unprofitable servant.

This is what I meant by "good will" and also by "responsibility." But what has moved me most deeply in your letter is the allusion to your loneliness in the midst of fame, and your comment that for all the swarms of admirers, you do not have many true, superior friends to lose. No, you do not, and I do not either. We both know the solemn misunderstanding, the fakery of fame, the shallowness of those who make it for us. What

---

[1] The grand official celebration of Thomas Mann's fiftieth birthday on June 6, 1925.

[2] Richard Wagner, *Walküre*, Act 3, Scene 3: Wotan to Brünnhilde.

stands or hovers between us joins us at least as much as it separates us. There can be no better reader than you for much of what I have written, and in turn my essay on *Palestrina*, to be blunt, is the only thing that is approximately worthy of its subject, no matter what the asses among your friends, such as Ehlers,[3] may say. In these times the position of each of us reveals curious kinships. We are at liberty to fall out with one another, but we shall not be able to prevent future ages from often mentioning our names in one breath. Perhaps, therefore, we should regard our relationship a little *sub specie aeterni* and, however much we dissent on some things, recognize a fraternity which posterity is likely to insist on.

Once more, my thanks for the honesty of your letter.[4]

TO STEFAN ZWEIG

Munich
July 26, 1925

Dear Stefan Zweig:

I did not want to thank you for your splendid, eloquent birthday congratulations in the June issue of the *Rundschau* as long as I would have had to do so on an assembly-line basis, as it were, together with so much else. But now that things are quieter, thank God, let me tell you with what rejoicing I read your prose paean to a tutelary genius[1] whom I certainly revere without flattering myself that I can live up to him. But I do really love him. He is truly the spirit of the golden mean, which I believe to be my destiny: the mean between the demonic and the bourgeois mentality, between act and conscience. This mean is not a bad region, and my life seems to me to demonstrate that an art which speaks to ordinary humanity can thrive there. I am happy that the tokens of good feeling came from so many different quarters, from oldsters such as Bahr, Hauptmann, and Schnitzler, and also from the newer generation, whom I might have expected to show estrangement and rejection. But your serious and impressive words, dear Herr Zweig, were among those that most honored and reassured me, and I thank you for them from my heart.

[3] Paul Ehlers (1881–1942), music critic for various newspapers; from 1916 on, music editor of the *Münchner Neueste Nachrichten*.

[4] In 1933 Pfitzner published this letter without authorization in order to defame Thomas Mann.

[1] Stefan Zweig's essay was entitled "The Genius of Responsibility: dedicated to Thomas Mann."

My wife and I intend to come to Salzburg around the 20th of August, to spend a few days at the festival. Will you be there about that time? It would be a great pleasure to meet you again.

TO KARL BOHM

Casamicciola
Ischia
September 27, 1925

Dear Sir:

Your letter of the 17th has just reached me here. I consider it impermissible to impose upon a stranger the task of deciding whether you are to be or not to be. But as things now stand, I must of course do my best to restrain you from acts of violence against yourself. I cannot understand why you regard your artistic and literary ambitions as so opposed to your profession as a doctor that they must cancel out your life. One of our foremost novelists, Alfred Döblin, is a welfare doctor on Berlin's North Side. You say that you feel your life has miscarried and ask me to suggest some possible way of putting it to good use after all. For the person with medical training especially, such ways exist. If, as you say, your lack of vocation for artistic creation has been proved to you, resign yourself like a man and turn to other forms of ethical action and self-realization. Everything transitory is only a parable, and it does not matter in the least whether a person makes pots or bowls, writes novels, or cures the sick. Leave your present surroundings, where evidently no spirit of mutual confidence is developing; go to Leipzig, Berlin, or some other big city, and practice your profession of healer, even if it should yield little in the way of outward honors, in order to regain your moral grip. If Europe won't do, there is always America. If you are destroyed, it will not be because of objectively oppressive circumstances, but only because of hypochondria and weakness of will. Your destiny is decided within yourself; what I say can be of little help, but may possibly summon you somewhat to manliness.

With my best wishes,

1925

TO ERIKA MANN

Munich
November 6, 1925

Dear Erikind:

Many happy returns on your birthday, and also forgive us generously for our enormous levity in having brought you into the world. I promise it won't happen again, and after all, we weren't treated any better. It will always be a pity that Mielein was not at the Hamburg festival.[1] On the other hand, I wouldn't have thought it wise for her to travel all the way back there when she had just barely returned. On the whole, you seem to have come out of the affair best of all, as far as the press is concerned. I found many comments to the effect that you would no doubt make your way as an actress. As for the playlet itself, I was lucky to have seen the second performance here, in a relatively clean, pleasant, and benevolent atmosphere, so that I could appreciate its particular youthful-super-youthful charm. This the play does have, and I have upheld that aspect against everyone. I suppose the rejection, with varying degrees of gentleness, by the press can really be called general, and I might add that it often takes a thoroughly unintelligent note. Certainly some strong objections could be raised to Tim Klein's[2] virtually judging all recent writing from the viewpoint of whether it strengthens youth for the coming war of *revanche*. I too, of course, have been thoroughly belabored, in print as well as in rough and incredible anonymous letters. But these don't bother me in the least. I think that although it may not have been absolutely essential to put on the play, as a maiden effort it is by no means so bad as most people pretend. This view of mine is occasionally confirmed, as, for example, by a card today from Wilhelm Michel[3] (the Hölderlin Michel) in Darmstadt. He informs me that on Saturday an article of his on *Anja und Esther* will be published, and that he will send it to me so I can pass it on to Klaus. He said that the play and performance gave him *great pleasure* (his underlining) and that he wished to defend a work of genuine literary art against the largely uncomprehending criticism in Germany. So there. Klaus may well be gratified by such an advocate. He

---

[1] The premiere of Klaus Mann's first play, *Anja und Esther*, in which Pamela Wedekind and Erika and Klaus Mann played the leading roles. Although not well received by the Hamburg newspaper critics, the play remained in the repertory for a run of many months.

[2] Tim Klein, feature editor and theater critic of the *Münchner Neueste Nachrichten*.

[3] Wilhelm Michel (1877–1942), essayist, lyric poet, and literary critic who specialized in Hölderlin.

surely counts for more than all the Tim Kleins, who is basically a crude bigot.

Mielein has bought some nice gifts for you, and opened her purse wide. In January she will probably go with me to Paris, for chances are that I am to deliver a lecture there for the Carnegie Institute.

All the best, my girl! Aren't you finished playing Jessica and Käthi[4] by this time?

Your loving   Z.

TO ROBERT FAESI[1]

Munich
November 21, 1925

Dear Professor:

Many thanks for the fine article. Truly, I would have missed your voice if it had not spoken up. The parallel with Hesse, whom at the moment I was feeling close to in his "Badegast,"[2] is very much to my liking. You say many things that are wise and penetrating about *The Magic Mountain*. I can't, and wouldn't want to, refute your objections. In general, however, I wish to say (and have already done so publicly) that I am reluctant to see myself cast as a relativist and nihilist. The novel, although it deals with death, is distinctly "friendly to life," an inner quality which is expressed outwardly by humor. Perhaps it is the only humorous novel of our day—a proud claim when we consider how closely the humorous vein is connected with the epic; but it is true, I think.

Hans Castorp is a victim, a little, artificially forced forerunner. His ethos is the experiment. He "resists not evil." But in this way he senses, before he is wrenched into the war, some glimmering of "truth," of future *humanitas*.

---

[4] Erika Mann played Jessica in *The Merchant of Venice*. The planned performance of *Old Heidelberg*, in which she was to play Käthi, did not take place.

[1] Robert Faesi (b. 1883), literary critic, novelist, poet, professor at the University of Zurich. Among his works: *Thomas Mann, ein Meister der Erzählkunst* and a trilogy of historical novels: *Die Stadt der Väter, Die Stadt der Freiheit, Die Stadt des Friedens*.

[2] An article by Hesse published in the *Basler Nachrichten*, actually entitled "Kurgäste."

1926

---•---

Waldsanatorium
Arosa
May 24, 1926

Dear Ponten:

Greetings and thanks first of all. I have read,[1] but prefer not to take up the red pencil, for the same reason that old Voss declined when Goethe sent him *Hermann and Dorothea* for correction of the hexameters: "I would have to mark up the whole of it." It hardly behoves me, who have the *Gesang vom Kindchen* on my conscience, to act as critic for another's verse. And yet I think my case was different. It involved only a half-humorous hint of hexameter; it was enough that here and there an actual verse turned up, while the rest really remained prose. But your ambition is a different one. You meant to offer us something really Roman, to attempt a veritably classicistic poem; so your distiches should have turned out fuller and purer if the whole were to be stylistically satisfactory. There are many lame verses and examples of prosaic harshness. The chief fault seems to me to lie in the mistreatment of the second half-line of the pentameter, which much too often in your verse—in fact, almost on principle—runs to thin trochees instead of sprightly dactyls. A proper pentameter, you know, should go as in Goethe's epigram: "Still will the stranger be gulled, *do* what he *will* to es*cape.*" The omission of two un-accented syllables from the second half of the line ("*though* he *try* to *flee*") makes it dull and empty, and this kind of thing is repeated in your poem with such consistency that it almost looks as if you thought that was the proper way; for sometimes only a very small change is needed, such

---

[1] The manuscript of Ponten's collection of poems, which was published in 1927 under the title *Römisches Idyll.*

as the substitution of an "although" for a "though," to fill out the line rhythmically.

That is, as I have said, far from the sum total of things calling out for criticism, but it is so pervasive, and this weakness in form so hurts the poem, that I should like to urge you to undertake a thorough revision of the language. It would really be worthwhile. For in spite of these deficiencies the idyll has so much atmosphere, and is filled with such a hearty and sturdy human quality, that it would be a pity to present it in this half-crippled shape and not to tighten up the form. The right spirit is there. You should first work your way much more deeply into the right form, which to my mind is indispensable in your case, by reading and then by going over the whole, correcting, purifying, reshaping. If you did, a perfectly delightful and durable work might well result.

A hesitant breath of spring is beginning to make itself felt here. My wife's bed can be rolled out on the balcony for hours at a time. Her health is slowly improving. Her appetite and sleep are better, and by the beginning of June she will probably be getting up. My own days here are numbered. On the 28th I am going to Zurich for a reading to students, will be in Munich from the 30th to the 2nd, and then will set out for Lübeck and Hamburg. On the 9th I will be back in Munich. And when will you be back there?

My wife is still reading and withholds her opinion, but already shares my pleasure in the human charm and wholesomeness of your poem.

TO ERNST FISCHER[1]

Arosa
Switzerland
May 25, 1926

Dear Sir:

I must apologize for not having thanked you sooner for your important letter, all the more so since even today I cannot express my thanks by a thorough discussion, a worthy response. I am coming to the end of a brief stay here (caused by the illness of one of my family) which was filled with

---

[1] Ernst Fischer (b. 1899), Austrian Social Democrat, at that time editor of the Graz newspaper *Arbeiterwille*, later a Communist. Essayist, literary and cultural historian. Fischer returned from a sojourn in Moscow after the Second World War and for a time held the office of State Secretary for Education and People's Instruction in the temporary East German Renner government.

work on occasional pieces, of the kind that the inexorable world repeatedly demands of a man who imprudently let it be known that he had a conscience, thereby sowing the misunderstanding that he was a born preceptor. I am on the point of departing for Zurich, then for my native Lübeck and Hamburg, and unless I do now in a makeshift way what I really cannot do adequately, more weeks would pass before I could tell you how your letter affected me, touching as it did on problems so familiar to me, and how profoundly I have taken it to heart.

It virtually challenges me to justify and excuse what I have done, but I have no desire at all—no courage, if you will—to undertake anything of the sort. I might argue that *The Magic Mountain* is explicitly characterized as a historical novel, that its action takes place before the war, and thus in an essentially aesthetic or aestheticizing era in which the choice of "art or socialism" was not, or did not seem to be, nearly as sharp as it is today. This era of prewar capitalism, I might say, is symbolically reflected in the images of the magic mountain's world, and there is no lack of socio-critical sidelights, of moral repudiations of that world, which was to meet its end in the tempests of the war. I might say such things, but they would strike me as more or less alibis. In the final analysis the novel is not historical, but I myself am. My roots lie in the cultural world of Goethe's autobiography, in the bourgeois atmosphere, in romanticism. Astute as you are, you must have noticed that *Tonio Kröger* (a young man's work), *Death in Venice*, and *The Magic Mountain* are extremely romantic conceptions. Wagner was my strongest and most formative artistic experience. However, there is another element that links me with modernity and alone gives my work some validity on the intellectual plane: my experience with romanticism's self-transcendence in Nietzsche. What you feel to be fascinating (in the bad sense) in my works is a critical distortion of fundamental instincts: irony. *The Magic Mountain* is a completely authentic expression of my character, especially in its parodistic conservatism, by means of which I as an artist hold myself in suspense between eras. The very revival of the German *Bildungsroman* on the basis of tuberculosis is a parody. It seems to me that the crisis in art as form or even as idea, a crisis which your letter so intelligently describes, also finds expression in my books, and that is quite enough for me. To my mind an artist is not obligated to know a great deal or to solve problems, to be a teacher and leader. I have already said that an artist is occasionally pushed into this role, and then he must play it as well as he can, and meet its demands. But his vocation, his nature, consists not in teaching, judging, pointing directions, but in being, doing, expressing states of the soul. Only in doing this is he "significant," a word that in relation to art and artists can have only this meaning.

Please accept this inadequate answer, and thank you for your thoughtful concern with a work whose problematical nature the author would be the last to deny.

TO COUNT RICHARD COUDENHOVE-KALERGI[1]

Munich
September 17, 1926

Dear Count Coudenhove:

May I once again express my deep regret at being unable to participate in person at the First Pan-Europa Congress in Vienna, and permit me to add my most sincere and earnest good wishes for the proceedings at this great conclave.

I was privileged to affirm my sense of identity with the idea whose servant and spokesman you are by joining the committee of the Pan-European Union. I honor you personally as an emissary of the aims of our times. Tirelessly, staking your whole spiritual existence in this cause, vigorously marshaling and gathering support, with prudent pliancy and the clearest dedication, you have propagated this idea that the world so stands in need of. I believe that you will prevail, that the idea of life will prevail.

Hasty thinkers too easily forget all the obstacles still ranged against this victory. They tend to regard the hatred and resistance of those who adhere with godforsaken loyalty to traditional ways as merely pitiable. That would be dangerous, for the power of this hatred and resistance, this godforsaken piety, is terrible indeed, and it may prove the victor. If thinking men do not arm themselves with that patience which a great philosopher equated with fortitude; if, surrendering to their aesthetic impulse and repelled by the intransigence of the material world, they grow prematurely bored with the idea and choose to scrap reality, all would be lost and what is needed will not be accomplished—which means death. Thinking men must understand that what matters today is the realization of the dream—or else they themselves will no longer matter.

[1] Count Richard Coudenhove-Kalergi (b. 1894), of Japanese-Austrian birth, writer and politician, founder of the Pan-Europa Movement (Vienna, 1923). He conceived of a European League of Nations excluding England and Russia. In 1938 he went into exile in Switzerland, in 1940 moved to New York. Since 1952 he has been honorary president of the Pan-European Union. He now lives in Switzerland.

They must not grow bored. Let their freedom of thought be inalienable, but this freedom demands that they resist boredom until the conditions for life are fulfilled. That is what their "politicalization" means.

What is at stake are the conditions of life for our children. It is hardly likely that we men of fifty will see the Europe in which our children ought to live, would want to live. But we can foresee it, and by the pressure of our wills and words help to bring it about. That is a question of solicitude, and also in a way a question of honor. We owe something to our children, taken as a generation; to some degree we stand guilty before them. May they recognize that they are not entirely alone, and that the gulf between the generations is not quite so deep and hopeless as they may imagine. May they see that we, although less free of dogmas than they, although richer in tradition and more burdened by the past than they, have not entirely lost contact with present and future, are not without sympathy for life, are not without love. That we seek the peace of our souls not in the sloughs of the past and of death, but in knowing ourselves to be men of good will.

TO ERIKA MANN

Munich
December 23, 1926

Dear Erikind:

I must thank you for all your love and loyalty, and write you a Christmas letter, thank you also for the Negro record as a token of good intentions, although, as I must alas, alas confess to you, it arrived broken clean down the middle. But the children's records are whole, and the sweets very refreshing, ginger chocolate, like figs.

We will only hope that our liquor did not meet the same fate as your record; for in that case the other little items in Mielein's package would have been reduced to a sad state. The shippers simply toss parcels around brutally. I scarcely deserved your letter of thanks for the Coll. Works, for it was Mielein who ordered them from Fischer for you, and of course they too were meant as a Christmas gift, so that G. G.[1] (I hope he made eyes at the sight of his bathrobe!) should really have kept them from you for the time being and not displayed them to you until tomorrow evening.

---

[1] Gustaf Gründgens (1899–1963), actor and director, to whom Erika Mann was briefly married.

And now you have already laughed tears in advance. But then again I'm not exactly displeased about that either.

For Mielein I have a beautiful pocketbook, a platinum wristwatch, some Murano vases, warmly lined gloves, and a flashlight so she can look in on the little ones late at night without waking Kürzl.[2] The recipient of these gifts has for some days been chasing restlessly through streets and shops, for there is much to get for so many, which, of course, she knew perfectly well in advance without being impelled by this knowledge to begin the work in good time. By tomorrow evening she will probably be totally exhausted, but nevertheless we are all looking forward to the festival, which promises to strike a particularly sociable note. In addition to the old Fays[3] and Babüschleins,[4] the Fränkchens[5] will also probably come to dinner (with turkey and sparkling wine), and also your friend Speyer,[6] who otherwise would be lonely.

I am very glad that I am writing again. I really feel like myself and know something about myself only when I am doing something; the intervals are gruesome. *Joseph* is growing, page by page, although for the present it is only a kind of essayistic or humorously pseudoscientific laying of the foundation, just for my own amusement. For the thing is more fun than anything else I have ever done. It is for once something new and quite remarkable in spirit, in that with these people, meaning and being, myth and reality, are constantly passing into one another. And Joseph is a kind of mythic confidence man.

I'm also doing something for my advancing years: early every other morning receiving Herr Silberhorn, the masseur and gymnastics teacher (recommended by Lampé[7]). Among other things he makes me hop forty times and finally rubs me down with cologne water. He drives up in his car and takes eight marks for his visit each time, the thief. But after all he was a captain in the war, and he also massages Gustl Waldau.[8]

Well, enough, my girl. This evening we are to see *Gneisenau,*[9] a

[2] Marie Kurz, housekeeper and for a time governess to Elisabeth and Michael. Fräulein Kurz stayed on in the Mann house on Poschingerstrasse after the family went into exile, and she succeeded in saving some small but important items of family property.

[3] Katia Mann's parents.

[4] Professor Peter Pringsheim and his wife.

[5] Bruno Frank (1887–1945) and his wife Liesl. Frank, poet, novelist, and playwright, was Mann's close friend and neighbor, both in Munich and in California.

[6] Wilhelm Speyer (1887–1952), novelist and playwright, a friend of Bruno Frank and the Mann household, likewise in Munich and California.

[7] Arno E. Lampé, a famous physician specializing in internal medicine.

[8] Gustl Waldau (1871–1957), a nobleman and army officer who became Munich's favorite actor.

[9] *Gneisenau* (1925), a play by Wolfgang Goetz (1885–1955).

ridiculous imposition, but we are yielding to it. I wish you, your good husband, and Klaus very happy holidays!

Z.

TO ERNST BERTRAM

Munich
December 28, 1926

Dear Bertram:

The houseful of German professors in Herzogpark is unanimously distressed and disappointed because the long-cherished hope of seeing you here now, after Christmas, is apparently not going to be fulfilled after all. And why not? You prefer visiting your relatives? Incomprehensible! Having meals four or five times a day and lounging around with the family during the holidays is truly ghastly—I've just tried it again, and have this very day excused myself from tea at my younger brother's—a very good fellow, incidentally—on the grounds of a chest congestion which unfortunately isn't invented and this morning simply stopped me from writing something about paradise, which must not happen, for if you claim to to be a poet[1] . . . etc. Only this reprieve lets me convey to you the gratitude of our house for all your faithful, rich, thoughtful remembrances: we are all touched by them, grown-ups and little ones. [. . .] The comparative mythology is exceedingly welcome and valuable. I have already been consulting it and finding just what I need. It confirms my view that Joseph is a Typhonic Tammuz-Osiris-Adonis-Dionysus figure, which, however, by no means signifies that he was not a real person. The whole existing religious culture was subsequently carried over into the life of Jesus, too, so that his life also seems only a solar myth. I think I am on the right track in making Joseph a kind of mythic confidence man who early begins to "identify" himself as a man-god figure and is reinforced in this sense of himself by the people around him, who have a tendency to draw no sharp distinctions between being and meaning. It took some 3,000 years for the world to become "mature" enough to dispute over this difference. What attracts me, and what I should like to express, is the transformation of Tradition into Present as a timeless mystery, or the experiencing of the self as myth. But the thing must be handled in a light, humorously intellectual manner; I don't intend to go in for pathos and religious fervor. Incidentally, what I am working on at the moment

---

[1] A quotation from Goethe's *Faust*, Prelude in the Theater, line 188.

is only laying a kind of pseudoscientific foundation for the story; I have scarcely come to the real beginning yet, although there are constant allusions to Joseph. My real and secret text is in the Bible, at the end of the story. It is the blessing the dying Jacob pronounces upon Joseph: "The Almighty shall bless thee *with blessings of heaven above, blessings of the deep that lieth under.*" When one chooses a subject there has to be, in the material, a point somewhere that regularly stirs the heart every time it is touched. This is that potent point.—

Forgive me. I should have told you about other things instead of running off at the mouth about this. But I know you take an interest, and then again too many of those other things have accumulated for them to be dealt with by letter. Won't you come after all? We are thinking of going to the mountains for a while in January, if the weather permits. How would it be if you joined us there?—Among the things for which I should have thanked you at greater length is your fine Stifter fragment. It again aroused the strongest desire for the *whole*. But I hardly have the right to complain about others being slow!

Greetings from all of us to you and your dear mother.

1927

———•———

Munich
June 11, 1927

Dear Rabbi:

May I thank you warmly for your kindness and courtesy. I am reading
your book with that burning interest which a person in my situation feels
for everything that is "pertinent." It is a welcome supplement to the
scholarly material which I have been consulting for my novelistic evocation of the beloved, beautiful old story. Your expositions are always
helpful, and I shall certainly be following them in most cases. I wonder,
however, whether I can bring myself to abandon the idea that the
brothers themselves sold the boy and sent the bloodstained coat to their
father to convince him that a wild beast had torn Joseph to pieces. (As
you yourself say, that idea has entered everyone's bloodstream and has
been fortified a hundred times over by graphic art.) I have always
assumed that the "Midianites" were one and the same as the "Ishmaelites," considering the second term merely a tribal name: the troop
accordingly consists of sons of Ishmael, half-Egyptians, in other words.
As for the "stolen," may it not be said that he was perfidiously snatched
away, stolen from the emotional old man? Moreover, I tend to go along
with Jeremiah, though I grant that he is too obsessed by mythology, in
seeing that "stolen" as a mythic-underworldly motif. I do not quite
understand the determination with which you fend off any thought of
such an influence upon the story and try to isolate it as a literary work.
Whether we take the events as historical or legendary, the form in which
we have the narrative is a late version whose author was working in the
ancient Oriental literary tradition. It would therefore hardly be astonish-

---

[1] Jakob Horovitz (1874–1939), rabbi in Frankfurt am Main, author of *Die
Josepherzählung* (1921), among other books.

ing for him to have tricked it out with all sorts of mythic allusions and smuggled into it a whole body of traditional ideas. My fondness for the history of religions, which accounts for a good part of my pleasure in the story, inclines me to believe that; but I long ago decided to turn things topsy-turvy and allow the characters themselves to make the allusions. The Amurru boy Joseph with his Babylonian and Egyptian culture naturally knows about Gilgamesh, Tammuz, Osiris, and he acts out an *imitatio* of them. We may impute to him a somewhat fraudulent identification of his ego with the egos of these heroes, and as I see it, the re-realization of the essentially timeless myth would have been a major psychological trait in all the people of that world. You will shake your head, but inside mine all this is developing in a most charming manner, and I hope that it won't lose too much of its charm in the process of being set down on paper.

It would lead too far afield for me to outline my intentions in full. But may I continue to count on the benevolent interest in my curious undertaking of a man so experienced and deeply versed in this field as you are? May I come to you with questions when I find myself stuck through ignorance of some fact? There will be no lack of such moments; already there is no lack of them. What, for example, is the etymology of the name Josef (and what about the proper spelling? Is *f* or *ph* more correct? I suppose the *ph* does not exist in Hebrew, does it?) Is *Jo* really or presumably *Jeho* and a name for God, and is the second part *sefer* in the sense of "book," "writing implement," as in the name of the city *Kirjath Sefer*? Then again, Joseph must have used another name in Egypt, or at any rate distorted his own into an almost unrecognizable Egyptian form. For it will take some juggling to explain the fact that old Jacob in Hebron should hear nothing about the life and glorious rise of his son down there. This must somehow have been by Joseph's design, for otherwise, given the conditions of lively traffic at the time (even if one places the story in an earlier period than I do when I set it in the New Kingdom, during which Asiatics repeatedly rose to high honors in Egypt), such ignorance would be absolutely inconceivable. After all, Joseph would only have had to write to Hebron. That he did not do so implies motivation, which will be my concern. But is there a theory about the name he bore in Egypt? This seems to be discussed on pages 124–125 of your book, but I can't quite follow. Can *Osarsiph* be considered? I would rather forgo the possibility of identifying Joseph with the historical *Janhamu*. And how is a divine name contained in the name *Peteseph* (page 124, note 1)?

Further, I am worried about the Babylonian, Canaanitish, and Egyptian names of the *months*. The fragments of calendars that have come down to us give no precise information. I should like to assume that in pre-Israelite Palestine the Babylonian terms for the months predominated, or at any rate were in use alongside the West Semitic names. To which of our months, for example, does the month *Tammuz* correspond? May? I suppose *Iyar* is West Semitic. I believe it means April/May. My story begins in the spring, March, and I have displaced the sale of Joseph to May. In that case, which ancient Oriental names of months are involved? In Erman-Ranke[2] numerous Egyptian months are mentioned, but I have the impression that the authors themselves are not quite clear about their meanings, that is, their relationships to our own months. It would interest me to know what reasons H. J. Heyer gives for saying that Joseph's coat "almost necessarily had to remain in the woman's hand" (page 103 of your work). Likewise, what misdeeds of the brothers, according to the later commentators, did Joseph's tale-bearing to their father refer to? There is a passage of your book that deals with this, but now the place eludes me.

Which is the better spelling, "Ruben" or "Reuben"?

So now you have a host of questions all at once. No doubt more will occur to me, if you take these in good part. The whole project involves entering a realm so alien, remote, and perilous for one who has always been accustomed to move about in the world of middle-class stability. Hence my craving to make sure of my ground by obtaining scholarly assistance.

Enough for today. Let me repeat my deepest thanks for your interest and beg your pardon for the immoderateness of this epistle, which reflects my passion for my task.

TO HEINRICH MANN

Kampen z/Sylt
August 29, 1927

Dear Heinrich:

Your splendid letter has made me see quite clearly how wrong I was to carelessly accept Schäfer[1] and Ponten's proposal. Soon after I said yes,

---

[2] *Ägypten und das ägyptische Leben im Altertum* by Adolf Erman, edited by Hermann Ranke, 1923.
[1] Wilhelm Schäfer (1868–1952), writer. Among his works: *Die dreizehn Bücher der deutschen Seele*.

which was more of a "Well, if I must," than anything else, this carelessness struck me as a mistake, if only because this move comes hard on the heels of the one I subscribed to, exactly as if the first had been the planned prelude for the present one. But I easily let myself be taken by surprise on the telephone, if only to shake free, and Ponten is a follower who is perpetually troubled by my literary existence and overcompensates by a blindly zealous friendship. In one respect, to be sure, the aims of these gentlemen are not so remote from yours: A more significant name at the head of the Academy, even if placed there only for decorative purposes, might help the cause—even financially. For this reason it was regrettable that Hauptmann dropped out of consideration from the start, due to the clumsiness of the Ministry, although he wouldn't have been the man you are looking for, either. But I wonder whether this man exists at all among German writers. You would be the one, if you had the time. Fulda[2] probably would have the time; he has no quality, but he shows a certain competence. The only trouble is that his kind of competence corresponds to his quality: his point of view is unspeakably trivial compared with yours. He thinks of representing professional interests and no more—which seems to indicate that after all, the question of quality in this appointment had better not be entirely excluded. In any case my candidacy is nonsense, for the reasons you have cogently set forth. I shall write as much to Ponten and Schäfer and ask them to withdraw their nomination. What prompted me to agree temporarily and conditionally was not ambition, not at all, but rather the habit of putting myself at the disposal of others, "If you think so, fellows"; in other words, it was a kind of modesty. Our mutual professional standing, the relationship of yours to mine, is a ticklish matter in itself—"ticklish" being another one of those careless expressions. But in spite of your joke that sometimes you pick up a crumb or two from my successes, you know me well enough, I think, to know that I don't let myself be fooled. With me it always comes down to that "If you think so, fellows"; but many fellows don't think so at all, and I am only too inclined to regard them as right and to be contemptuous of the others. I won't go into the question of hypochondria, and to what extent it opens one's eyes to the truth.

This is a uniquely beautiful and exciting place. I can't work at anything major, but there is always something to do, of course. We too shall be returning to Munich toward the middle of September. Then we

---

[2] Ludwig Fulda (1862–1939), poet, dramatist, translator of many plays by Molière and Rostand's *Cyrano de Bergerac*. Fulda left Germany in 1933, but returned and ended his life by suicide.

can confer again, and primarily I must hand over to you 150 marks, a fee from the *Tagebuch* which I accepted for you because it was addressed to Poschingerstrasse.

Warm greetings—see you soon. T.

1928

———————•———————

TO WILLY HAAS[1]

Munich
March 11, 1928

Dear Herr Haas:

Many thanks for your letter. Privately, I have received a good deal of approval and applause for my article,[2] directly and indirectly. For example, Georg Bernhard[3] is reported to have said that he would gladly have published the reply himself. For the rest, it would not surprise me if the leftist press gave me poor support. That is its wont in such cases. We can rely on it much less than the enemy can on their press. I have seen only two newspaper comments, both from the nationalist side. The *Völkischer Beobachter*[4] itself sent me its counterblast, which I glanced at and sent back marked "inept." I hardly think there is any sense in wasting words on it. On the other hand, I might call your attention to the article published in the entertainment section of the *Tag* on March 7. The thunder and lightning hurled down on me by a young dynamiter and fascist "revolutionary" in an article entitled "The Disenchanted Mountain" is well worth reading as expressive of the state of mind of a certain type of political or pseudopolitical youth, and I have the feeling that it would be very good if you, you in particular, were to comment critically on it in the *Literarische Welt*. As a boyish and personal outburst of temperament it is even rather charming, but the absolute lack of a sense

[1] Willy Haas (b. 1891), writer, editor of *Die literarische Welt*. Went into exile in India, then England. At present he is associated with leading newspapers in Germany.
[2] An open letter to Willy Haas, "Thomas Mann versus the *Berliner Nachtausgabe*," had been published in *Die literarische Welt* as a sharp reply to an attack entitled "Thomas Mann's Kowtow to Paris."
[3] Georg Bernhard (1875–1944), journalist, editor-in-chief of the *Vossische Zeitung*. After his emigration in 1933 he edited the newspapers-in-exile *Pariser Tageszeitung* and *Pariser Tageblatt*. He died in New York City.
[4] The organ of the German Nazi Party.

163

of responsibility which it reveals is certainly thought-provoking. Does this so-called nationalism have anything to do with patriotism or any idea of patriotism? It seems to me that it does not. It is pure dynamistic romanticism, pure glorification of catastrophe for its own sake. Basically it is popular culture, and this is the sort of thing that an organ of the bourgeois restoration presents to its readers nowadays as entertainment. These are curious times.

It seems I am universally lambasted for pluming myself on my "fame," when as a matter of fact I can vouch that it leaves my heart and mind extremely cool. I have not leaned on my fame but on the genuine national quality of my life work, as against people whose sole evidence for being German is their loud shouting. Furthermore, I scarcely understand how my comments on the difference between German and French nationalism could provoke such bitterness, as if what I said were outrageous. I have just been leafing through Hermann Keyserling's new book, *Europe*; the chapter on Germany contains sentences which I would like you to read in connection with this affair: "For there does not exist a German accepted throughout Europe who is not universal in scope. The nationalistic German, *in contrast to the nationalistic Frenchman*, is of no consequence culturally and humanly; he belongs in the private purview of Pomerania and Bavaria, if not of clubs." As I have said, you would not do badly to revert to the incident once again, with a postscript in which you cite this quotation.

TO ARTHUR HÜBSCHER[1]

Munich
June 27, 1928

My dear Herr Doktor:

I do not think you are acting rightly. My letter to the *Süddeutsche Monatshefte* is outdated and superfluous, and your reply, if you will forgive me, is not very impressive. In your personal letters you express what you mean much better and with more warmth. You should print my statement from the M.N.N.[2] *in extenso*—it doesn't take much room—and then reply to it as you feel inclined, that is, in terms similar to the

---

[1] Arthur Hübscher (b. 1897), writer, at this time coeditor of the *Süddeutsche Monatshefte*.

[2] Thomas Mann had replied in the *Münchner Neueste Nachrichten* to a massive assault in the *Süddeutsche Monatshefte*, written by Arthur Hübscher, which denounced Mann for his deletions in the second edition of *Betrachtungen eines Unpolitischen*.

ones you use in your letter to me. This, it seems to me, would be the correct procedure.

You regard me as a party person and a party writer, and conclude that "the circle of my publications has been compressed in the years after the war into an ever-narrowing space." I don't exactly know what you mean by that, but I have the impression that the same essential part of our people goes on taking an interest in my work, even if only out of old habit, as did so in the time of *Buddenbrooks*: namely, the cultivated middle class. And I scarcely think that they regard me as a politician or party person. In any case, I am neither. Nor do I have much leaning toward politics by nature, nor do I subscribe to any party doctrine. In political matters I aim for and desire nothing but the things that are sensible, necessary, favorable to life, concerned with human dignity— what one might be allowed to call "German," I should think. In general, to use Nietzsche's language, I regard myself as "very German," and although I am of course subject to international influences in literary matters, I am personally as little international as possible. But I live in this new, shrunken Europe which is striving for unity; I have some contact with its spiritual forces and a very general insight into the conditions of its life. My intelligence and my character are repelled by certain stupidities and malignancies. I do not hide the fact that I want to have nothing to do with people who said of Rathenau's[3] assassination: "Bravo, one less!" (Munich University professors!), and that I find the Munich bourgeois press dreadful. And since I happen to be writing to you on the very day that our good but misguided city is performing a nationalistic headstand in honor of the two flying dunces,[4] I admit that this kind of nonsense strikes me as worse than *Johnny spielt auf*.[5] A party man? *You too* want me to be one in the sense that *everyone* is today. Only you would have me join the party which during the war called itself the Fatherland Party and which was a *very* political party, outwardly and inwardly. That, I grant you, I cannot do. If that is the redeeming word you expect from me, I cannot speak it. I would not have the arrogance to speak it. Who could today? The life of the mind is difficult, and perhaps it has never been a greater feat to be pleasing in the eyes of God than today. A

[3] Walter Rathenau (1867–1922), statesman, industrialist, prolific writer and idealist, was foreign minister of Germany when he was assassinated by a band of young conservatives in June 1922.

[4] The aviators Köhl, von Hünefeld, and Fitzmaurice had in April 1928 made the first flight across the Atlantic Ocean from east to west. When Köhl and von Hünefeld returned home they were hailed throughout Germany as national heroes.

[5] *Johnny spielt auf* (1925–6), a jazz opera by Ernst Křenek (b. 1900).

leader? I have never had the slightest ambition to be one. All that writers like myself can possibly aspire to might be to act as exemplars to the thoroughly confused young people—but even that we can only do by modesty, circumspection, and good will.

TO STEFAN GROSSMANN

Kampen auf Sylt
August 5, 1928

Dear Herr Grossmann:

In regard to the insignificant little affair to which you have called my attention, for several days I groped about totally in the dark, asking myself in vain how a passage from a private letter which I wrote four weeks ago could have reached the daily press. From the astonished queries that were directed to me here and from blurred reports of newspaper attacks, then from the approving and indignant letters from the public that are usual on such occasions, it became clear that this had actually happened. But as late as yesterday I could not have told you how it had come about. Now I have been enlightened; I am still shaking my head over it, but I know. An article in the *Münchner Zeitung* has been sent to me; it bears my name as the headline, and it informs me of the circumstances at last.

I had good-naturedly lent my hand to a debate between Hübscher, the editor of the *Süddeutsche Monatshefte*, and myself over my book *Betrachtungen eines Unpolitischen*. Behind my back a pamphlet[1] was put together out of the various documents of the debate. Not content with including already printed material, the authors of the pamphlet underhandedly and spitefully included a private correspondence linked with the controversy. I wanted to give this correspondence a tolerably friendly conclusion. Accordingly, I answered Hübscher's lengthy expatiations, representations, and charges about my political or intellectual attitudes, in a handwritten letter, spontaneously dashed off, from man to man. I briefly explained the attitude of mine which is so offensive to Munich literati. Those true-blue Germans of the *Süddeutsche Monatshefte* included this letter in their pamphlet (whose existence they concealed from me) because it contained a sentence that they thought could be twisted

---

[1] The pamphlet contained a reprint of Hübscher's attack on Mann for deliberately falsifying the *Betrachtungen* by cuts, and five personal letters to Hübscher and Paul Nikolaus Cossmann (see next note), accompanied by extremely hostile commentary.

into a noose to hang me by. It was a casual and irritable remark about the stormy, excessive, black-white-and-red reception, turning the city topsy-turvy, which Munich was giving to the transoceanic flyers, Hünefeld and his comrade, on the very day I wrote my letter. Naturally I would have said it differently if I had intended it for the public. But it was not in the least directed against the brave aviators, whose achievement of course inspires me with a wholesome respect. Rather, it sprang from a fleeting annoyance at the fashionably extreme and anticultural over-valuation of sports records and the nationalistic exploitation of the same— an annoyance that, I am sure, a good many better Germans have also felt. Nevertheless, the sentence contained the expression "flying dunces," and it did not escape Herr Cossmann's[3] bleak perspicuity that I was thereby revealing a weakness which could be used against me. Granted, they had to act a little unscrupulously, but that could always be justified in the name of politics. Thus they printed the pamphlet, which I shall be the last to see, but which the *Münchner Zeitung* promptly received, whereupon it informed me that I had finally separated myself from the German people, from their love and their pride.

Messrs. Cossmann and Hübscher of course know as well as I that the misuse of private letters is dishonorable. Desperate patriotism prompted them to ignore honor, a *sacrificium* whose moral value remains uncertain because it cannot be determined how hard or easy it was for them. I suspect, however, that their conduct is not even legally permissible and have taken steps to inform myself, and then no doubt them, on this question.

TO STEFAN ZWEIG

Munich
September 1, 1928

Dear Stefan Zweig:

Thank you for your card. It arrives almost at the moment of my return from the North Sea (Kampen) where I spent weeks in love with this mild wilderness. To Moscow? Travel with God! I haven't been invited, which doesn't surprise me, for since *The Magic Mountain* has been refused the *placet* because of bourgeois principles, I know that I am not *reçu* there. The children are problematical, but charming, I grant you. We are expecting them Monday, and as usual I cannot help rejoicing.

---

[3] Paul Nikolaus Cossmann (1869–1941), writer, editor of the *Süddeutsche Monats-hefte*, early advocate of Hans Pfitzner, passionate German nationalist; he died in the Theresienstadt concentration camp.

1929

———————•———————

Dear Herr Landgerichtsrat:[1]

Your letter of the 8th has reached me here, with some delay. Since it is a personal letter, permit me to answer it personally.

I am sorry that you feel offended by my statement on the Frieders[2] case. It was never my intention to arouse any such feeling, and could not have been. For I do not have the honor of your acquaintance; until today I knew no more about your existence than I knew of any of the other participants in the affair. How then in composing my letter should I have meant to insult any individual? It is one thing to accuse a judge of perverting the law, deliberately and maliciously; it is something else again to protest against a verdict which has been called a miscarriage of justice by many groups, including some who are diametrically opposed to one another. In my lay judgment it was just that. Undoubtedly the verdict was delivered in good faith, subjectively speaking; but I feel that it was the product of influences which have nothing to do with the will and the interest of the individual, but with the times, with the general intellectual and psychic circumstances of these times—influences which have aroused widespread uneasiness and opposition.

You, your Honor, know as well as I the phrase in which this uneasiness and opposition is generally summed up: "Crisis of confidence in justice." You know as well as I (who can help knowing?) that for at least

[1] *Landgerichtsrat* is the title of a judge who presides over a district court in a German state.
[2] Urged by the defense attorney, as described in the letter, Thomas Mann had published an article on the sensational "Frieders case" in the *Berliner Tageblatt*. Later, as a result of further correspondence with the judge, he partially retracted his statements.

ten years we have been living in an atmosphere in which the idea of pure justice threatens to atrophy. The disrupted state of the nation, the exacerbation and exposure of all political and ideological antagonisms, the unprecedented hatred, the depraving consequences of the war—all that (and what is implied by it) operates against the nobility of justice, operates to demean justice to an instrument of power in the struggle of the "affirmative" credos of class, of race, of political decision making, etc. Explicitly anti-human and anti-idealistic intellectual tendencies, those tendencies which are generally subsumed under the political formula of "fascism," meet that trend halfway and merge into it, with the result that a great many people today regard the perversion of justice by ideology and emotions as natural, divinely willed, and humanly right.

But there are minds and hearts who see it as nothing of the kind, who are tormented by these symptoms of illness and feel impelled to resist them. I belong in that group, and my letter to the Viennese lawyer is one statement among others that I have made along these lines. If I speak of "corruption" (I do not have the letter by me here and am not certain whether and how I applied the word), I am not thereby accusing any individual or impugning anyone's personal honor; rather, I am commenting on the nature of the times. And when I speak of "national feeling" it is not to boast of my Germanism, but rather to communicate what I have communicated in the letter: that "no nation's face is more disfigured by repudiation of ideals than Germany's, and that what Russians and Italians may be able to afford we are far from being able to afford." This is *my* national feeling, I stressed; and I repeat the words because this letter may make you see them in a different light from that of your first reading.

So much in general. Let me now come to our case in point. Dr. Pressburger sent me his pamphlet with the urgent request that I give him a statement of my opinion. He added that the unfortunate man involved in the case would, along with his wife and three children, be faced with utter destitution after the disciplinary procedure. A letter from the Vienna League for Culture was enclosed, to the effect that a declaration from me on the disturbing case would be desirable. For some time I had no opportunity to look into the pamphlet. At last I read it on a journey—not once, but three times. I was deeply shocked by the incomprehensibility of what had happened (and was threatening to happen further) to this man. To be sure, I would not venture to say that his personality particularly attracted me. On the contrary, in spite of all the representations of his champions, this personality struck me as ambiguous and not at all engaging. But I felt strongly that he was the victim of an injustice.

You reproach me for having acted in an un-German manner by neglecting to query the other side. The proverb "Give the other fellow a chance to be heard" is not especially German. The *audiatur et altera pars* is older, is Latin. I had that *altera pars* before me in the form of the verdict and its justification, and it alone was being heard; it had the power to destroy all that a man had made of his life—unless public criticism and the word of a writer proved to have a *little* power. I did indeed take into account the tricks of lighting with which a lawyer endeavors to transfigure his cause and his client. But even discounting the effects of this art, the fact remains that a legal clause which in any case many highly qualified jurists consider senseless, impracticable, and superfluous has been applied with a rigor which stands in alarming contrast to the dubiousness and more-than-dubiousness of the case. How was this rigor to be explained, if not by disturbances in the general atmosphere of the times, by influences which lie outside the desire for pure justice? You strongly object to my criticism of the judicial opinion. This opinion stated that the penalty had to be set so high because Frieders had been a chief prosecuting attorney. What can one say to this, or think of it? That Frieders had been a chief prosecutor should rather have been a strong argument for his acquittal. A prosecutor who would testify under oath that a document had not been presented to him, when it has been filed away with his signature on it, belongs in a sanatorium, not in prison.

In my letter to the Viennese lawyer I based my comments on specific facts which he presented in his pamphlet, and which he certainly would not have falsified. If my letter is offensive to you, the pamphlet itself must have been, and you would have felt compelled to register your objections to it, even though it does not mention your name either. Was the defense lawyer acting legitimately in writing and publishing his pamphlet? Then legitimacy must also be allowed to the writer who is concerned with the moral state of the times and of his nation.

Finally, your assumption that the letter was published in the daily press with my consent is not quite accurate. I wrote the letter with the intention of offering moral support to the defense attorney in a cause which had also been taken up by the League for Human Rights, and I was prepared for it to be reproduced. I did not count on having the letter actually published in the press, and therefore I could not advise against such a step. In this respect, too, Dr. Pressburger undoubtedly believed he was acting to further his legitimate interests. I am not complaining that those interests were not exactly the same as my own; for after all, what I have written I have written.

I have made an effort to clarify for you, your Honor, the circumstances that gave rise to my letter, and the principles underlying it. These principles are not directed against anyone's probity. Surely you did not believe for a moment that at your mere command I would retract my words as "lacking all foundation"—in other words, as empty babble. But I would indeed welcome factual information (which unfortunately is wholly absent from your letter) which might lead me to a better interpretation of the case.

TO GERHART HAUPTMANN

Munich
October 15, 1929

Dear Gerhart Hauptmann:

Georg Hirschfeld[1] has informed me—and I sincerely appreciate the confidence—of the letter he has just addressed to you, in which he speaks of his difficult situation and refers to the Gerhart Hauptmann Foundation and the Gerhart Hauptmann Prize. It is perhaps odd of him, but he would like me to support his reference, and I am heartily glad to do so, for the harshness of life that this fine, quiet human being and serious artist has to endure moves me, and I would gladly help him. I know nothing of the funds at the disposal of the Hauptmann Foundation, nor who awards the Hauptmann Prize. But I certainly don't need to persuade you that a tribute to Hirschfeld's life work in the form of a subsidy, a testimonial gift, such as he requests, would be justified. And I think that if there are no funds available from this source, some friends should get together to make up a testimonial which might provide him with relief and freedom to work, at least for a while. I would propose that you and I start the collection with, say, 300 marks apiece, and I am convinced that Fischer, too, would participate, and then perhaps Wassermann also, and whoever else you may think of. May I ask you to pass this proposal on to Fischer? I could talk to Wassermann myself, since I am meeting him at the end of the month in Berlin. Do let me know that you approve!

Since we are on the subject of prizes, what do you say to the lively rumor that, thanks to the promotion of a clique of headmasters who have

---

[1] Georg Hirschfeld (1873–1942), naturalistic dramatist.

been pushing him, Arno Holz[2] is to receive the Nobel Prize? Let me say quite candidly to you, although otherwise I am perhaps not quite in a position to do so, that I would regard such an award as absurd and scandalous, and I am convinced that all Europe would greet the announcement with stunned incomprehension. I am speaking objectively, believe me; I have enough to live on and would, for example, be overjoyed if our clever and important Ricarda Huch[3] received the prize. But Holz? It would be a real vexation, and truly something ought to be done about it. But all the activity is, as usual, on the wrong side.

May I hope to hear from you?

With the most cordial respect and greetings to you and your wife,

[2] Arno Holz (1863–1929), dramatist, poet, one of the cofounders and theoreticians of naturalism.

[3] Ricarda Huch (1864–1947), writer, historian. In 1933 she resigned from the Prussian Academy of Arts in protest against National Socialism. She is considered one of the few important women writers that Germany has produced.

1930

———————————•———————————

TO SIGMUND FREUD

Munich
January 3, 1930

Dear Herr Professor:

Amid the turmoil of a correspondence swollen disastrously by the world's herd instinct,[1] I can thank you only in the scantiest manner for the extraordinary gift of your book, whose range so formidably surpasses its outer dimensions. I read it at one sitting, deeply moved by a courageous search for truth which, the older I grow, I see more and more as the source of all genius. Please also accept my thanks for your magnificent letter of November. Between the time I received it and the present hour lie all sorts of momentous changes in my life, but they cannot reduce the importance of that event for me. Your correction of certain suppositions in my article,[2] your insight into the supramedical implications of your discoveries, is enormously interesting to me, and makes me think that it might have been better to address you directly before writing the essay. On the other hand, one seems as a writer better able to deal freely with a person who has not yet become a concrete reality, but remains something of a myth.

I could not help feeling profound emotion upon reading of your years of isolation and ostracism. This may sound odd to you, but I can somewhat gauge what you experienced by the reactions my essay has aroused—now, in this present day, after the triumphal victory of your theory—among people who represent various types of German piety and "complex" conservatism. The things I have been forced to listen to were

---

[1] The reference is to the announcement that Thomas Mann had received the Nobel Prize.

[2] *Die Stellung Freud's in der modernen Geistesgeschichte* ("The Position of Freud in the History of Modern Thought").

not exactly mellifluous—but alas, I have little reason to be proud of that. I came to you shamefully late—I am altogether and in all respects *slow* by nature. Everything must be extremely ripe within me before I can communicate it.

You love the poets? But chiefly, I suppose, as objects for your investigations; with a few boring exceptions we are all born to that end—myself in the van, I would say, if it did not sound conceited. It would be good to talk with you about this and kindred themes. I have been asked to come to Vienna this month to attend the Halsmann[3] appeal to the Supreme Court, and I rather like the idea. If I do decide to go (I might not; I've had a bit too much of this traveling about), may I call on you?

With most respectful greetings,

TO MAXIMILIAN BRANTL

Ettal
Oberbayern
January 7, 1930

Dear Dr. Brantl:

Your fine congratulations on that significant picture postcard moved me deeply. Many thanks for it! I think of you often as a good and uncorrupted person. I hope that you also read Heinrich's radio address on the award, a simple, splendid gesture, intelligent and seemly. For the rest, I am not the sort of person who lets something like Stockholm go to his head. The truth is that everything has remained the same, and the ludicrous danger of vanity is something one might at worst encounter in retirement. Work keeps one modest.

All the best for the New Year.

TO ANDRÉ GIDE

Munich
January 20, 1930

Dear Monsieur Gide:

Yes, I most certainly did receive your kind and flattering letter of December 5, and have ever since been feeling so much in debt to you

---

[3] The Halsmann murder trial caused a great sensation at this time, and many persons in public life took up the cause of the defendant. Young Halsmann was accused of having pushed his father so that he fell to his death on a mountain-climbing tour. The young man was acquitted and later went to America as a photographer.

that your second letter of January 13 embarrasses as much as it delights me. I see now that I should have sent you the issue of *Literatur* with my article.[1] But I took it for granted that either the publisher or your translator would do so. Then again, I did not visit you personally with this little study because I was extremely uncertain that it would please you; uncertain not because of the minor criticisms that I made (and which in spite of your graciousness remain questionable), but because I was not really satisfied with the piece. Since I was speaking publicly about you for the first time, I really ought to have widened the scope and gone deeper.

I take considerable pride in the good and perceptive things you say about *The Magic Mountain*. Beyond the pleasure it gives me that the author of *The Counterfeiters* should be receptive to this novel, it is another vindication of my feeling that the book can arouse particular interest in France; and for this reason I have been impatient for the appearance of a French translation. One is now to be done at last. Fayard & Co. have decided to publish an unabridged edition in two volumes, and I am eager to see what the response will be. I have had a strange experience with this book. As usual I had few hopes for its reception by the public and was totally surprised by the warm sympathy it met with in Germany, as reflected by the big printings, and then in America also. On the other hand, I repeatedly hear the most scathing judgments of it, mostly to the effect that it is not a novel, not a creative work, but a product of intellect and criticism. The most amusing part of it is that the Stockholm critic and professor of literature Böök, who usually has a decisive influence upon the choice of the Nobel Prize winner, publicly proclaimed the book an artistic monstrosity and said I was receiving the prize exclusively, or at any rate chiefly, for my early novel *Buddenbrooks*. At least, that is the view of the Academy, but it is patently wrong. *Buddenbrooks* alone would never have won me the status which prompted the Academy to confer the prize on me. This reputation was in fact first created by the execrated novel, whose purely narrative elements, I think, balance its analytical qualities so that the whole remains tenable as structure and work of art.

I am talking too much about myself. Once again, I wish I could have gone into your autobiographical book and your life work in general at much more length, but I accepted the editors' request in a time of great turmoil and had no leisure for anything better. Your autobiography

---

[1] Review of André Gide's *Si le grain ne meurt* in *Die Literatur*, December 1929.

made a profound impression upon me, both for what you set out to do and for the way your intention was realized, and I think that this impression will one day prove fruitful in my own life. A certain type of writer is in the long run not content with the stylized and symbolically clothed confession, and since reading your book I dream more distinctly than I did before of an autobiographical account of my own.

I would dearly like to meet you personally some time. My brother and my son Klaus both know you, and I do not. What inhibits me is my lack of conversational French, but then you understand German, and so we would manage. At present there are no definite prospects for my coming to Paris again, but whether I travel there or whether your ways again lead you to Germany, I hope for and look forward to such a meeting.

Cordially and with special esteem,

TO MAXIMILIAN BRANTL

[Postcard]

Munich
April 29, 1930

Dear Herr Doktor, many thanks for your greeting! It was a significant trip, far up the Nile into Nubia, then slowly via Assuan, Luxor, Cairo, and across the Canal into Asia. How I took notice!

Yours,   T. M.

TO OTTO HOERTH[1]

Munich
June 12, 1930

My dear Herr Doktor:

My heartfelt thanks for the sympathy with which you have responded to my little story,[2] and which you express in the well-wrought "Gespräch auf hoher See" ["Dialogue on the High Seas"]. Although you have distributed the roles, one and the same subtlety and perceptiveness—yours—is present in the replies of both interlocutors, and gave me great pleasure as I read.

---

[1] Otto Hoerth (b. 1879), head of a private school in Freiburg in Breisgau, writer and critic.

[2] *Mario and the Magician.* In *Stories of Three Decades* (New York: Alfred A. Knopf; 1936).

I am particularly grateful to you for recognizing the justice of my intention and for seeing that the story contains no slur on Italy and the Italian spirit. Elements of critical idealism and political morality did indeed crop up from the personal sphere in the course of the story and give it a further meaning; these elements call forth a certain distaste and bring what is initially an atmosphere of mere irritability to the uncanny and explosive climax. Since it interests you, the "magician" existed and behaved exactly as I have described. Only the lethal outcome is invented. In reality, after the kiss Mario ran away in foolish embarrassment and next day, when he waited on us at tea again, was extremely well pleased with himself and full of matter-of-fact appreciation for "Cipolla's" work. You see, what took place in life was a good deal less passionate than I subsequently made it. Mario was not really in love, and the bellicose young man in the standing-room section was not his more fortunate rival. But not even the shots are my own invention. Back here, when I described the evening, my eldest daughter said: "I wouldn't have been surprised if he had shot him down." It was only from this moment that the experience became a novella, and in order to carry it through I needed the previous anecdotal details that provided the atmosphere— otherwise I would have had no impulse to tell the story. When you say that without the hotel manager I would have let Cipolla live, the truth is really the reverse: in order to kill Cipolla I needed the hotel manager— and the other preparatory annoyances. Neither Fuggiero nor the angry gentleman on the beach nor the Principessa would otherwise have entered the world of literature.

You say I should have identified myself in the hotel? But what then? After all, I had corresponded with the management, had filled out the registration form; my name was known. What good would it have done for me to insist on it explicitly and tastelessly? I had no reason at all to defend myself. We were dissatisfied with the food and the favoritism shown to aristocracy, and found the tone at the Pension Regina much more to our liking. Why flash my credentials at the risk of having the idiot ask: "So what?"

These are a few passages with which I cannot agree. For the rest, it would of course be nice if the elegant essay were to be printed. The only halfway promising place to try would be *Velhagen und Klasing*.[3] But it seems to me rather doubtful that they would take it. The story itself really did not quite belong there, and I wonder whether the editors

[3] *Velhagen und Klasings Monatshefte*, the magazine in which *Mario and the Magician* appeared.

would impose on their readers another and so thorough an elucidation of the case. I suspect the answer would be: "The contribution does not meet the requirements of our magazine."

In any case, you have found a grateful reader in me. Nothing could have impressed me more vividly than this reflection of my story from someone so knowledgeable.

1931

———————————•———————————

Munich
March 18, 1931

My dear Herr von Kahler:

Your letter honors me and has given me great pleasure. What you have
to say about your work, and the invitations you extend, so fascinate and
move me that I am more than ever ashamed of the objections I raised in
my conversation with Preetorius,[2] in which I spoke of how overburdened
I am with work and how severely subject to fatigue. But what's to be
done? These factors remain and I must rationally take them into account,
even if a momentary indisposition were not depressing me and specially
reminding me of them. That will pass, but my general situation remains:
this concern for a many-layered, problematical, refractory task, alongside
of which run a hundred other affairs and trivialities—the result of a
perhaps too conscientious compliance with the desires and demands of the
world. In any case I feel myself painfully in arrears with those matters.
"Trials," says Goethe, "increase with the years." Since we make them
for ourselves, we are allowed to be proud of them; but the trouble is that
in the purely athletic sense we ourselves are not always in top form when
they reach the top of their curve. Although at first we find it extremely
unwonted and repugnant, given a certain ready willingness of character,
we must "learn to conserve our strength." A disagreeable, insipid, and
disconcerting phrase, but one day it simply becomes more than just an

---

[1] Erich von Kahler (b. 1885), writer, historian, philosopher, now at Princeton.
Author of *Man the Measure, The Tower and the Abyss, Der deutsche Charakter in der Geschichte Europas, Out of the Labyrinth.* Kahler and Mann became intimate friends in later
life.
[2] Emil Preetorius (b. 1883), president of the Bavarian Academy of Fine Arts in
Munich, stage designer, artist, writer, book designer, collector of Asiatic art. He was
responsible for epoch-making reforms in the presentation of Wagnerian operas.

empty phrase; it becomes an expression of the need to know what we want. On the 25th I am going to Berlin for the celebration of my brother's sixtieth birthday. This is a matter of both emotion and honor. I must speak in the name of the Prussian Academy and participate in other formal affairs. All this was arranged long ago. It will cost me four or five days, not including the preparations and aftermath. In May a trip to Paris is impending, for a lecture long since agreed to out of God knows what sense of duty. I would certainly have read your letter poorly if I thought these obligations more important than the visit to Wolfratshausen and a joint reading of your work in days that could well be a wonderful festival of friendship and ideas. I am aware of the important bearing this work has on mine, I am truly grateful that you yourself have considered it. But those other commitments do happen to be older and I cannot, without falling into conflict with myself, add to them new undertakings, absences, irregularities, and festivities. It may sound ridiculously boastful, but I have responded to five or six such temptations with plain refusals before exercising the severest self-discipline of all and saying no to you too, as I must.

I am not being vain when I say that you would have found me a good listener. So much the worse. My consolation is that I shall not be any less attentive a reader. I should like to be one soon; but this is not the only reason that I venture to advise: Give the times their due and publish what you have written. I understand your inhibitions, but we believe until almost at the end that the decisive word remains to be written, and yet we have always set down far more of the decisive words than we ourselves can possibly appreciate. Go into print and permit us to read! I can think of no more important gift to us Germans than the book your letter describes to me, and I have no doubt that the first volume alone will be such a gift.

TO JENÖ TAMÁS GÖMÖRI[1]

Munich
May 28, 1931

Of all things, the most dangerous, destructive, and stupid is vaulting ambition. We should not be trundling around gigantic plans, but holding

---

[1] Jenö Tamás Gömöri (b. 1900), Hungarian writer and translator of Mann's stories, among other things. This letter is a reply to Gömöri's questionnaire to a number of writers asking them to "sum up" their lives. Mann's accompanying letter has been lost. The symposium went unpublished for political reasons.

to modest intentions and carrying out to the best of our ability what we have unpretentiously undertaken, trusting that qualities and forces from realms we are not masters of, from our unconscious lives, will lend it validity and importance. Blessing's all. "One has it or one does not have it." But anyone who has it, or even merely has some knowledge of it, is modest—a quality which by no means excludes discontent, but is akin to it.

1932

————————•————————

TO [UNKNOWN]

January 8, 1932

Dear Sir:

I have received your questionnaire, and I took pleasure in the graceful precision with which you describe the literary situation and the prospects it may or may not offer. Your comments strike a note deeply familiar to me. That, and my immediate feeling of agreement with them, make me keenly aware of how little political boundaries count in the life of the mind nowadays, and how effectively Europe already forms an intellectual unity.

Your question is formulated so fully that there is scarcely room for anything except simple agreement. I might perhaps add the following supplementary comments:

The sufferings and adventures through which Europeans have passed in recent times have stirred a new and peculiarly intense interest in the problem of man himself—in his nature, his position in the cosmos, his past, his future. The universal urgency of this interest, which so far has manifested itself most effectively and distinctly in science, did not exist before. The concern with man has inspired a new anthropology, perhaps especially here in Germany: a singular reanimation in the fields of archaeology, mythology, and the history of religions; remarkable efforts to penetrate into man's prehistory. In those efforts speculation has been passionately mingled with exact science in a way somewhat like the psychoanalytic investigation of primitive life. Physiognomy, characterology, linguistics have undergone revivals.

Works such as those of Max Scheler (snatched away all too soon before he could finish his great book,[1] so helpful to an understanding of

---

[1] Max Scheler's *Philosophische Anthropologie.*

182

our times) are especially characteristic of this new, humane interest which seems to me to constitute our period's chief intellectual tendency. I call it a humane interest because it seems to me that such researches contain the germs of a new humanism in the sense of the Goethean maxim: "The proper study of mankind is man."[2] I am sure that this neo-humanistic tendency is bound to have artistic consequences. And as you rightly suggest, in works of art the humane mode will have to preserve its natural spiritual relationship to the classic mode. In literature I expect to see a turning away from all extremes, experiments, sensational and exotic materials back to original and simple human matters; I see a trend toward purity and the underlying myths of humanity, in other words a new classicism, recurring on a different plane. It will naturally assume another cast from that of earlier forms, since art has meanwhile passed through a good deal. I am more or less speaking from experience here, for when I consider the fundamental instinct that was at work when I conceived the biblical-mythological novel which has been occupying me for some years, I clearly see the link between this conception and the general tendencies I have been trying to describe. Once more I find that man, and especially the artist, is much less of an individual than he hoped or feared to be.

I must ask you to make do with this inadequate reply, which is really only a slight extension of your own words.

With sincere good wishes for the success of your young magazine,

TO B. FUCIK[1]

April 15, 1932

Dear Herr Doktor Fucik:

Many thanks for your kind letter.

I have also received the handsome and bountiful package of books and am delighted to own these tasteful editions. The sheets have come along too, and I will be signing them as soon as I can get to it.

I can best show my appreciation for your friendly words and fine gifts by answering your questions as well as I can.

(1) To profess European thoughts and feelings nowadays easily exposes one to the petty charge of being unpatriotic. Perhaps it is well, therefore, that I feel myself to be a better German than a good many of

[2] One of the rare occasions on which Mann misassigns a quotation. The line, of course, is from Alexander Pope's *Essay on Man.*
[1] Unidentifiable.

those who denounce me for my Europeanism. What I owe to the German tradition of thought, and how deeply rooted I am in that tradition, is perfectly clear to me, and will not escape any sensible person. But my belief in a higher unity of Western culture is less a faith than a clear and simple insight. The two basic elements of this Western culture are classical antiquity and Christianity. Right now, when we are celebrating the memory of a great Western figure, Goethe,[2] these two elements stand out in the course of our review of his life work. I completely share the opinion of Ortega y Gasset, as set forth in his book *The Revolt of the Masses*: "Should we by way of experiment imagine that we are to live solely with what is 'native' to us, should we for example try to strip the average German of all the aspects, thoughts and feelings he has taken over from other countries of the globe, we will be astonished to see how impossible such an existence is; four fifths of what we possess is European common property."[3] Incidentally, there is another experiment by which we can assure ourselves of the unity of Occidental man. We need only go to Asia or Africa, where at once we feel that every European—whether German, French, Italian, or whatever—is unqualifiedly a brother.

(2) As a young man I absorbed a great deal of the intellectual and artistic world of the Russian East, and could not help but come under the tremendous influence that Dostoevsky exerted upon all Europe. But there, too, I was more strongly drawn toward minds influenced by the West, such as Tolstoy and Turgenev. Moreover, a Latin admixture of blood from my mother's side makes it understandable that the Latin mentality, which as you know cares more for form than any other, has always attracted me and perhaps attracts me even more powerfully with the passing years. I do not in the slightest share the belief in the decline of the European West, which only recently has produced so prodigious a literary phenomenon as Marcel Proust, and I have always received some of my strongest and happiest stimuli from the spiritual achievements of the Romanic-Celtic West.

(3) I would certainly hesitate to label the Slavic element as anarchic and disruptive, if only for the reason that the concept of the disruptive is

[2] The year 1932 was the centenary of Goethe's death.

[3] This passage is given here in a translation from the German. The anonymous English translation from the Spanish, authorized by Ortega y Gasset (New York: W. W. Norton & Company, 1932, p. 194), reads as follows: "If we were to make in imagination the experiment of limiting ourselves to living by what is 'national' in us, and if in fancy we could deprive the average Frenchman of all that he uses, thinks, feels, by reason of the influence of other sections of the Continent, he would be terror-stricken at the result. He would see that it was not possible to live merely on his own; that four-fifths of his spiritual wealth is the common property of Europe."

very vague and has a ring of unacceptable bourgeois timidity. Often what is called disruptive is not something directed against life, but rather a reinvigoration and renewal of life. Goethe's desire for order, moderation, and form was an expression of his determination to control that potentially dangerous and demonically intense nature of his. This determination, moreover, had a conscious pedagogical purpose; Goethe meant it as a lesson for his whole people. But if we wish to regard the spirit of criticism, say, as inherently disruptive, then there is certainly just as much of it in the German character as in that of any other race. The "pulverizing" life work of Kant is a celebrated example of that. And surely people are aware of how much lyrical self-portraiture is concealed in the figure of Goethe's Mephistopheles, who so magnificently and amusingly personifies the principle of rationalistic disruptiveness.

(4) I regard art as a primal phenomenon that in no conceivable circumstances can be banished from the world, and I consider the figure of the artist to be immortal. Self-examination teaches me that artistic representation is a natural and indispensable mode of vital expression. Therefore I cannot believe that even the most utilitarian and mechanized society could ever permit the general type I modestly represent to become extinct. There was a time when a great man, Schiller, could say: Man is only wholly man when he plays. In grave and distressed times like ours the statement sounds frivolous, and yet I am convinced that man will always need the holy and liberating form of play that is called art in order to feel himself as properly human.

(5) Probably no artist surveys the plan of his life in advance and knows the materials which he will utilize in the course of time. But frequently he can see a connection between each of his productions, can observe that germs of his newest work were already present in the preceding one; and he grows more and more aware that each element comes out of a personal center so that a natural unity forms of its own accord.

(6) When asked in the French interview which of my works I have the most faith in, I named *Tonio Kröger* and *Death in Venice*, because I suspect that the coherent and pregnant form of the novella has more durability than the loose, expansive form of the novel. My most popular book in Germany is undoubtedly *Buddenbrooks*, and it may be that there my name will always be linked with this novel. In America, *The Magic Mountain* has had a much stronger effect because of its more modern complex of problems. As for *Mario and the Magician*, I hardly like to have this story considered a political satire. To do so is to put it in a category

to which it hardly belongs. I would not deny that minor political high-lights and topical allusions are tucked away in it, but politics is a broad concept that passes without a sharp boundary into the problem and area of ethics; and leaving aside the artistic aspects of this little story, I should prefer to see its significance in the realm of ethics rather than politics.

(7) I think that the experiences of childhood, which are so crucial for a person's attitude toward life, play a great part in the life of every artist and are certainly a major source of motifs and impressions in a writer's life work. In any case, those who believe they have observed something of the sort in me are quite right. In autobiographies and auto-biographical novels, too, the parts dealing with childhood usually are poetically the densest and freshest. —I have always passionately loved music and regard it as the paradigm of all art. I have always considered my talent a kind of displaced musicianship, and I see the novel as a kind of symphony—a tissue of ideas and a musical construction. In these terms *The Magic Mountain* is probably more like a musical score than any of my other books. In music, German romanticism has always been closest to me, but an early love for Chopin has never faded, and I have a decided fondness for the Slav Tschaikovsky. From him, it seems to me, a clear line leads to so modern a phenomenon as Stravinsky, in whose art I take a keen interest.

(8) With regard to Czech national culture, I must candidly admit that in music I have encountered it only through Smetana, whose work of course is part of European culture; and in literature through some of the most recent writers, such as the famous author of [*The Good Soldier*] *Schweik*, Hašek, Karel Čapek, whose prose I highly respect, and the dramatist Langer,[4] whose plays are put on a great deal in Germany. That is very little, but unfortunately the language is too great a barrier so that I am not able to come any closer to Czech cultural achievements.

(9) My relations with Bohemian-German literature, on the other hand, are lively and wide-ranging. As the chief representative of that literature you mention Rilke, whom I too, of course, acknowledge as a poet of the highest rank. The specifically Prague note in modern prose has always fascinated me. I need only mention the names of Werfel,[5]

[4] František Langer (b. 1888), playwright, author of psychological stories. Langer emigrated to London in 1939 and returned to Prague after 1945. Among his successful plays are *The Camel Goes through the Eye of the Needle, Grand Hotel Nevada, Periphery*.

[5] Franz Werfel (1890–1945), Austrian novelist, poet, playwright. Fled from Austria to France in 1938 and in 1940 to the United States, where he settled in Beverly Hills, close to Thomas Mann's California home. Among Werfel's many works, perhaps the best known in the English-speaking world are *The Forty Days of Musa Dagh, Verdi, The Song of Bernadette*, and the posthumous *Star of the Unborn*.

Franz Kafka, Max Brod, Hermann Ungar,[6] Ludwig Winder[7] to suggest the importance of these men for modern prose in general.

(10) The new book I have been working on for a number of years, which will require some time to complete, is a biblical and mythological novel entitled *Joseph and His Brothers*. I had never imagined that religious history and even theology could gain such a hold over me. This tendency seems to me a result of age, and I am surrendering to it with the readiness proper to everything that life organically brings with it.

[Conclusion missing]

TO ERIKA AND KLAUS MANN

Munich
May 25, 1932

Dear Erikind:

Now that you are at the Bains[1] I want to write you both a letter, because the place is so important to me and I am glad to think of your being there. In spirit I am with you leading that unique life between the warm sea in the morning and the "ambiguous" city in the afternoon. Ambiguous is really the humblest adjective that can be applied (Simmel[2] used it), but it is wonderfully relevant in all its meanings, and for all the city's modern silliness and corruptness, which you two also object to, this musical magic of ambiguity still lives, or at least has hours in which it is victorious. You mention that it must have been lovely in the middle of the last century. But Platen[3] was already saying: "All that is left of Venice lies in the land of dreams." Nevertheless, he passionately loved it the way is was, even as Byron did, as Nietzsche did later, and still later your insignificant honorable sire. For certain people, there is a special melancholia associated with the name of Venice. It is full of the home atmosphere—nowadays a spiritually rather corrupt and staled atmosphere, I grant (Godfather Bertram has been unable to get that out of his head); but still my heart would be pounding were I there again.

[6] Hermann Ungar (1893–1928), novelist and playwright. Among his works: *Knaben und Mörder* (novellas), *Die Verstümmelten* (novel), *Die Gartenlaube* (drama).

[7] Ludwig Winder (1889–1946), writer. Emigrated to England in 1939. Among his works: *Hugo, Tragödie eines Knaben*; *Der Thronfolger, der Kammerdiener*.

[1] The Grand Hotel des Bains on the Lido in Venice.

[2] Georg Simmel (1858–1918), philosopher and sociologist. Among his works: *Einleitung in die Moralwissenschaft, Philosophie des Geldes, Zur Philosophie der Kunst.*

[3] August Graf von Platen-Hallermünde (1796–1835), late romantic poet with many classical overtones.

Very sensible of you to take only half pension on the Lido and to dine in town evenings. We always had to be back for dinner and then frequently found ourselves taking the vaporetto once more. Is the theater going at this time? It is so nice to go to the theater in Venice! Are you seeing churches, pictures? There are charming Bellini madonnas. . . .

I am writing not only on account of Venice, dear Eri, but also because of what you wrote to Mielein about your guilt and agonizing night thoughts over Rikki's immense naughtiness[4] and that you keep brooding over the "possibilities" there might have been for keeping him alive—chances that were missed. It is my conviction that they did not exist. You did all that is in the power of a friend (and not every friend) to support him and cure him of his fad for death. Without you and your authority over him he would surely have yielded to his perverse whim long ago and made use of the freedom to die which in the end you could not deprive him of. . . .

Since day before yesterday Keke[5] has been here and will be entertaining with theatrical and radio performances and readings from Joseph.

The Little Ones are happy because I had Knappi[6] sign their photographs of him. They also have his baton, you know, because it flew from his hand while he was conducting *Siegfried* and fell right between them. But perhaps that happened while you two were still here.

The *Neue Freie Presse* recently carried an extremely skillful article on Parisian films by you, Klaus Heinrich. In regard to journalism I have mentioned you to L. Schwarzschild,[7] who came to see me recently because he is taking soundings; just think, he is considering transplanting the *Tagebuch* to Munich. We discussed the question at length; it is certainly an important and highly interesting topic. He has reason to fear that in Berlin the paper will be banned by the generals. But I wonder whether it will thrive in the Munich atmosphere.

I have just heard that there has been a horrible brawl in the Prussian Landtag, with many persons injured and knocked unconscious. The

---

[4] Richard Hallgarten had shot himself.

[5] Elisabeth's and Michael's childhood name for Käthe Rosenberg, Katia Mann's cousin.

[6] Hans Knappertsbusch (b. 1888), at that time conductor and general music director of the Munich State Opera.

[7] Leopold Schwarzschild (1891–1950), writer and publicist, at this time editor of the weekly *Das Tagebuch* in Berlin. A keen political and economic analyst, he was one of the best-informed and most widely read of anti-Hitler journalists. After going into exile, he edited *Das Neue Tagebuch* in Paris. He also wrote a biography of Karl Marx, *The Red Prussian*.

Nazis, singing songs, took over the chamber. Here the Corpus Christi Day procession has been canceled for fear of rioting. That, too, has never happened before and scarcely speaks well for Schwarzschild's plan.

All good things and *auf Wiedersehen.* Z.

TO WALTER PERL[1]

Munich 27
June 22, 1932

Dear Herr Perl:

I was glad to read your essay,[2] but it seems to me to beg the question. It is a poor consolation that the International of nationalism is everywhere sprinkled with good-hearted, promising young people if these young people simply do not understand that nationalism has left its heroic age behind it, that it entirely attained its ends in the nineteenth century, drained itself in achieving this fulfillment, and today is nothing more than an unfortunate mass passion which is hampering progress and blighting life. Goethe wrote in 1798: "Patriotism, like resolute personal striving, has outlived itself, along with clericalism and aristocratism." In those days it took a great man to see that. Today it can be perceived more easily, but those good-hearted, promising youths do not see it—from which it follows that to be good-hearted and promising is not enough. They also do not see that nowadays all the forces of brutality and reaction, all the antispiritual and anticultural elements of the past, are allied with nationalism. They think themselves future-oriented, courageous, revolutionary. That is a hopeless misunderstanding—which an essay such as yours should have exposed.

It should also have deplored the fact that a nation like Germany, which certainly might have the capacity to lead the way, to place itself at the vanguard of the world, today wants nothing but restoration. It looks backward toward a past that cannot help it; and one must shudder

---

[1] Walter H. Perl (b. 1909), professor of German at Marshall College, Huntington, West Virginia. Specialist in studies of Austrian symbolism. Literary executor of Leopold Andrian, a friend of Hugo von Hofmannsthal. Author of *Das lyrische Jugendwerk Hofmannsthals* ("Hofmannsthal's Early Lyric Poetry"), 1936; *Thomas Mann 1933–1945: Vom deutschen Humanisten zum amerikanischen Weltbürger* ("Thomas Mann 1933–1945: From German Humanist to American Citizen of the World"), 1954; *Leopold von Andrian und die "Blätter für die Kunst,"* 1950; editor of the Hofmannsthal-Andrian correspondence (*Briefwechsel Hofmannsthal-Andrian*), 1968.

[2] "Zur Psychologie der nationalistischen Jugend." This essay, written while Dr. Perl was in his senior year at Berlin University, was an attempt to analyze the psychology of the nationalistic young people with whom he had held many discussions.

at the prospect of the defeats that still await it, which of course will be accompanied by desperate self-laceration.

Reactionary patriotism is today sweeping all before it. We shall see what it makes of Germany, outwardly and inwardly (with which last it is chiefly or exclusively concerned). May it have its fill. Then at least it will become clear where the "opposition" lies, and what the real role of courage and honor is nowadays.

TO COUNT HERMANN KEYSERLING

Thomas Mann Haus
Nidden
Kurische Nehrung
July 30, 1932

Dear Count Keyserling:

Since your essay was badly delayed by repeated forwarding, I read it at once and with all the satisfaction that good and right things bring us nowadays in recompense for the bitter vexation of so much evil and falsity. I regret only that my young people are not here with me; they would also have been grateful readers, and will be soon, I hope.

It has surely never been truer than today that we begin to err as soon as we speak. I myself am forever conscious of this truism, and am willing to offer only a very general defense of the public statements I have made on these questions in moments of urgency. Even your observations might well call for a marginal question mark here and there. Thus it does not seem quite self-evident that the nineteenth century was so completely adverse to Germanism and denied the Germans their chance to be themselves. After all, throughout whole decades of that century they exerted a genuine and legitimate hegemony in Europe. Renan exclaimed: "There's no help for it, the Germans are a superior race." Nowadays, alas, they do not impress us as being anything of the kind, persuasive though your arguments are for the thesis that the global hour of the Germans has struck. Ah, it could be so, should be so. In the past fourteen years Germany could have accumulated tremendous moral prestige, if she had consciously and resolutely, as a social-minded republic dedicated to peace, taken the lead and shown the way toward a new and better age on this continent. She was unable to decide. Panicky fear of the nationalist leaders proved stronger; she truckled to them daily, and today we see her practicing the grossest nationalistic excesses without seeming to realize that God is disgusted by staleness, that he wants to lead us on to new things and in spirit has long since passed beyond the musty old things. You are a kindly prophet. With me, grief is the stronger, grief for this exceptional nation whose behavior is so much beneath her and who is so little aware that, along with France, she is responsible for the continent, and not only for this continent.

All this does not prevent your essay from being in the main the best and the soundest statement that can be made on these burning questions. Especially your comments on and against so-called National Socialism strike to the heart of the matter, in my opinion. Germany reduced to the notion these idiots have of it—what an absurdity! What a ludicrous impossibility! We owe you a debt of gratitude for saying as much, though you do so in philosophically unemotional words; and also for opposing to their childishly brutal threats the richness, multifariousness, and universality of Germany. Incidentally, what is that feeling for balance and tolerance which you praise in Germany if it is not a democratic feeling? Can it be that the Germans only imagine they are antidemocratic?

No, I did not let the *South American Meditations* pass me by, and without wishing to belittle the famous travel diary I am glad that you too assign a higher place to this most recent book. It is surely your most vivid, most animated, most poetic work. Your prose in the past had something technological and philosophical about it, full of "nows" and "fors" which gave it a logical but not a musical flow. Schopenhauer long ago wrote more poetically, and your friends were grieved that Spengler, the detestable parodist of Nietzsche, could surpass you stylistically. But the situation seems to me greatly changed by the *Meditations*, which show a fine artistic buoyancy.

With cordial respects I am, my dear Count,

TO KÄTE HAMBURGER[1]

Munich 27
October 12, 1932

Dear Fräulein Hamburger:

Thank you once again for your fine parcel. I was right: I had already read the essay[2] in *Der Morgen*, but it was a renewed pleasure to see the

---

[1] Käte Hamburger (b. 1896), teacher of German literature; emigrated to Sweden in the thirties, taught at the University of Göteborg. Author of a number of essays on Thomas Mann.

[2] "Romantische Politik bei Thomas Mann."

intelligence with which you recognize and express the organic unity of my political statements.

The essay on Novalis was new to me, and I was astonished not only by your mathematical accomplishments but especially by Novalis's visionary anticipation of Einstein's theories. It is curious enough to see how he advances from Kantian epistemology to physics. I had never noticed that. But is is evident that the musings on time in *The Magic Mountain* are of an entirely different character from Proust's—that is, their origin is romantic, as are the "biological" elements in that book. In the past I too truly grasped (through Schopenhauer) only the "ideality" of time and space, and arrived at their physical relations without having properly read Novalis, let alone Einstein.

On the whole I am once again surprised to see my participation in the German idealistic-classical-romantic tradition so convincingly demonstrated. To think that something so genuinely national is denounced as "international"!

I am on the brink of leaving for a week in Vienna. There, among other things, I shall be violating romantic traditions by speaking to socialist workers. Once I am back we would be delighted to see you at our house again.

1933

———————•———————

TO WALTER OPITZ[1]

Munich 27
January 20, 1933

Dear Herr Opitz:

I was delighted to receive your letter—many thanks for it.

I was forced to cancel my participation in the meeting of the Socialist League for Culture because my health at the moment is not all it should be, and even so, I am burdened with an assignment connected with the forthcoming fiftieth anniversary of Wagner's death. By an arrangement of still longer standing, I am to deliver the festival address at the Wagner celebration in Amsterdam on February 13, and then to repeat it in French in Brussels and Paris. You will understand that for me to have let myself in for the theme of Wagner was dangerous from the beginning, for there is quite a bit to say, especially for me, and it is something of a feat not to write a book. Under these circumstances it was impossible for me to undertake the political journey as well, and I had to withdraw from an occasion in which I would have been truly glad to participate in order to stand up for my convictions, as I have already done several times in speech and in writing. It gave me great pleasure to see from your letter that you and I agree in these convictions and feelings. Sympathy and understanding come high these days, amid so much hatred and dissension; one often feels completely isolated, although that is probably an illusion, for Germany is big and a love of freedom and rationality are basically more widespread and more powerful than the screaming of the ruffians and know-nothings allow one to think. The Kyffhäuser celebration in the Sportspalast which you mention must have been priceless. I did not listen because that sort of thing makes me ill from grief and

---

[1] Walter Opitz (b. 1879), writer; in his youth a member of the circle comprising Martens, the Ehrenberg brothers, and Thomas Mann.

disgust. Yes, things look bad in Germany, but, once again, they are surely not so bad as they look.

Thank you again and with cordial regards,

Sincerely,

Ten days after Mann wrote this letter, Adolf Hitler became Chancellor of Germany. Heinrich Mann, warned by friends that his life was in danger, immediately left the country. On February 11 Thomas Mann departed for his lecture in Amsterdam, never suspecting that he would not see Germany again for sixteen years.

TO PAUL ZSOLNAY, PUBLISHERS[1]

Neues Waldhotel
Arosa, Switzerland
March 4, 1933

Dear Sirs:

I am especially grateful to you for sending me the page proofs of Wilhelm Herzog's *Dreyfus Case*.[2] I am reading the book—have almost finished it already—with a degree of violent emotion it would scarcely have aroused in me in my unpolitical middle-class German youth. In this very respect I think I am representative of millions of Germans who have traveled the same path and who, like me, will be profoundly stirred as they read by the feeling of *Tua res agitur*. By *Tua res* I mean: This is also the cause of your nation, your country, your own conscience. You remark that the author shows present conditions in Germany symbolically reflected in the Dreyfus drama. But that is almost going too far. A stylizing jog to the reader's mind is scarcely necessary or effective. The eternal symbolism, the universal validity, is contained in the powerful story itself; it need only be told—told as powerfully and with such deep feeling as Herzog tells it. Certain passages, in fact whole paragraphs, from Zola's polemics have merely to be quoted to sound staggeringly topical.

And alas, what shame, what *envy* overcomes us when we read them.

[1] The fact that Franz Werfel was looking for a publisher for his almost completed novel *Verdi* prompted Paul von Zsolnay (1895–1961), a young gentleman farmer and rose fancier, to establish a publishing house in Vienna in 1923. Within a few years the list included such writers as Pearl Buck, Theodore Dreiser, Heinrich Mann, Arthur Schnitzler, and H. G. Wells. After the *Anschluss*, Zsolnay emigrated to England, where the firm of Heinemann and Zsolnay was founded. After the war the publishing house was reestablished in Vienna.

[2] *Der Kampf einer Republik. Die Affaire Dreyfus, Dokumente und Tatsachen.*

For it is disgraceful that such outcries are impossible among us today. They were impossible in the Germany of my youth because of the nature of the middle-class mentality; they are impossible today because violence smothers the word, because the German language is under a ban. Indeed, all guilts are avenged upon this earth.

No matter what the state of affairs was then in France, among the French youth and the French bourgeoisie, it was possible to speak, to write, to fight like this for truth, for intellectual honor. Freedom existed. There was not yet the suffocating silence of dictatorship, in which character can no longer be tested, courage can no longer act, ethical life is throttled. The whole abominable immorality of repression becomes tangible as one reads this book, which along with our own immediate experience can teach us Germans what freedom is, and that it was a stupid, ugly folly of the mind to make a mockery of it.

TO LAVINIA MAZZUCCHETTI[1]

Arosa
March 13, 1933

Dear Miss Mazzucchetti:

Many thanks for your lines of the 3rd; their sympathetic concern has done me good, for my heart is very heavy indeed, and horror and disgust my prevailing emotions.

When you wrote, we were still enjoying comparatively hopeful days. Since then the worst misfortunes have occurred, and the future for me and mine is totally uncertain.

It is only by sheer chance that I am outside Germany. On February 10 I set out with my wife for the Wagner celebration in Amsterdam, and from there according to schedule went on to Brussels and Paris. A great deal of socializing accompanied the lectures, and since I had worked strenuously beforehand we thought it well to come here directly from Paris for a few weeks of recuperation. Medi joined us for skiing.

Well, nothing has come of the recuperation, or rather just the opposite, and our stay here is being protracted by force of circumstance. We had counted on Bavaria and expected that, thanks to the strength of its Catholic People's Party, everything would remain pretty much

---

[1] Lavinia Mazzucchetti (b. 1889), essayist, critic, Thomas Mann's Italian translator, editor of his first foreign collected works (*Opera Omnia*, Mondadori, Milan). Author of *Novecento in Germania* and many essays on Thomas Mann. Thomas Mann's last letter was addressed to her (see p. 689).

unchanged. Such an electoral outcome as actually occurred there, there of all places, was something that informed people never remotely dreamed of. The news affected us like a senseless natural disaster. We found ourselves deceived in all our hopes, but our very apprehension tugged us to return home, and our bags were already packed. Then from all sides came friendly admonitions and warnings that at present my personal safety could not be guaranteed and that I absolutely must wait out the next few weeks and remain where I fortunately was.

And so we have stayed on, willy-nilly. As long as individual acts of terrorism persist throughout the whole country, acts that the new holders of power have probably had to concede to their people within certain limits, after all the promises they had made, it really would be foolish to return home. For the victors' newspapers have violently denounced me, and I am on the list of those who have committed "pacifistic excesses" and "intellectual high treason." At any rate it is possible that within the near future some kind of law and order, a tolerably decent way of life, may be restored in Bavaria, so that I can return with my family. If the reign of terror goes on, I personally will have to remain abroad—I don't yet know where; in the Tyrol, perhaps, or Zurich.

Moreover, the question arises whether from now on there will be any room at all in Germany for the likes of me, whether the air there will be breathable for me. I am much too good a German, far too closely linked with the cultural traditions and the language of my country, for the thought of an exile lasting years, if not a lifetime, not to have a grave, a fateful significance to me. Nevertheless, we have had to begin looking around for a new base, if possible in the German-language area. At the age of fifty-seven *such* a loss of settled life and livelihood, to which I had become adjusted and in which I was already growing a bit stiff, is no small matter. But I think my being an artist has kept me elastic enough for such a new beginning on an entirely different footing, and as long as I have my brave wife at my side I am afraid of nothing. We must only take care that they do not separate us by trickery, say by keeping her in the country while I am outside it.

Tomorrow our eldest children intend to join us up here for a few days. There is much to discuss.

With all good wishes,

Please do confirm the receipt of these lines!

1933

TO RENÉ SCHICKELE[1]

Villa Castagnola
Lugano
April 21, 1933

Dear Herr Schickele:

Your charming letter has given both of us great pleasure. Thank you so much for it. It has confirmed our intention to join you, especially because of your and your wife's friendly offer to help us make arrangements for settling down for the rest of the spring and summer. We are not yet sure whether we shall come at the beginning or the middle of May. We must first stop in Basel and straighten out the matter of my passport.

Our grown children, who have just visited us, today started back for Le Lavandou, where they have been staying for the past few weeks. They have taken the two youngest with them. They intend to get in touch with you in the next few days, or perhaps will call on you, in order to begin looking for suitable quarters for us. Since they know exactly what we want and need, it may even be possible at this point for them to find something suitable to rent. Otherwise we shall follow your suggestion and stay at the Grand Hotel in Bandol with the idea that we will continue to look from there.

We would prefer a cottage similar to yours rather than an apartment. We need about six rooms, so that we can have the two youngest with us and if possible put up the two eldest as well. The bathroom and decent plumbing are quite important.

Excuse me if I say nothing about events and the situation we are all in. We understand one another without need for words, and in any case shall soon be able to talk over the whole thing.

TO PHILIPP WITKOP

Lugano
April 27, 1933

Dear Professor Witkop:

Your card reached me here without trouble. There have been a good many essays on Flaubert and myself, but no larger study as yet to my

---

[1] René Schickele (1883–1940), writer. An Alsatian with a German father and French mother, Schickele edited the pacifist and expressionist journal *Die weissen Blätter* in Zurich during the First World War. In 1933 he voluntarily emigrated to France, where he died. Among his works: *Das Erbe am Rhein, Symphonie für Jazz, Heimkehr.* Long acquainted with Thomas Mann, Schickele became a close friend from 1933 on.

knowledge. I made the acquaintance of Flaubert, and incidentally of Balzac and Zola also, fairly late, and am scarcely conscious of any real influence from them. However, Flaubert's austere artist's temperament must have impressed me and can be counted among the educational experiences of my later youth.

I hope you are in good spirits and, as far as that is possible, untouched by the recent events. I cannot say the same for myself. I shall probably have to place my own life, and the lives of my family, on an entirely new basis. You will not find me in Munich.

TO ALBERT EINSTEIN[1]

Grand Hotel
Bandol (Var)
May 15, 1933

Dear Professor:

Frequent changes of scene are to blame for my having put off thanking you for your kind letter until today.

It was the greatest honor that has come my way, not only in these evil months, but perhaps in my entire life; but it praises me for conduct that was natural to me and therefore scarcely calls for praise. Less natural, to be sure, is the situation into which I have fallen as a result; for at bottom I am much too good a German for the thought of permanent exile not to weigh heavily indeed, and the breach with my country, which is almost unavoidable, fills me with depression and dread—a sign that it does not fit my nature, which has been formed by elements of the Goethean tradition of representation, so that I cannot feel I was destined for martyrdom. For me to have been forced into this role, something thoroughly wrong and evil must surely have taken place. And it is my deepest conviction that this whole "German Revolution" is indeed wrong and evil. It lacks all the characteristics which have won the sympathy of the world for genuine revolutions, however bloody they may have been. In its essence it is not a "rising," no matter how its proponents rant on, but a terrible fall into hatred, vengeance, lust for killing, and petit-bourgeois mean-spiritedness. I shall never believe that any good can come of it, for either Germany or the world. And to have warned as earnestly as possible against the elements which have brought about this moral

---

[1] Albert Einstein (1879–1955). From 1938 to 1940 the great physicist was Mann's near neighbor in Princeton, New Jersey, and the two became close friends.

and spiritual misery will some day certainly accrue to the honor of all of us, although we may possibly be destroyed in the process.

TO ALEXANDER M. FREY[1]

Bandol (Var)
June 12, 1933

Dear Herr Frey:

In haste—I am once again on the point of moving. Actually moving in this time—into a small house we have rented for the summer in a neighborhood called La Tranquille and located in Sanary-sur-mer. But I want to thank you for your friendly lines of the 4th and for the enclosure. I can't blame old Hauptmann for keeping silent. Why talk himself out of all his possessions and his country as well? I am silent too—simply because I am used to carrying things around inside me for a long time and to working them up, that is, to objectifying them—although in my case there would be many reasons for subjectivity. My situation is difficult and my bitterness great over the decisions I must make, for the only solutions are perilous to life itself. I saw this merely in reply to your friendly inquiries about my welfare. I should rather ask you about yourself and your plans and hopes, your work. I continue to try to do mine, and hope it will be easier now that we have set up our private and domestic mode of life, which I have greatly missed for four months.

TO ALEXANDER FREY

Sanary
July 27, 1933

Dear Herr Frey:

Many thanks for your two letters. I found it touching that you were afraid of upsetting me by passing on G's news and thought to reassure me by your postscript. The situation is perfectly clear, of course; it is obvious that there should be enormous ferment when it turns out that the capitalists were right to finance the "revolution." I am not afraid of the revolt; rather, I desire it, for anything is better than this. But your informant's expectations seem to me far too sanguine. Moreover, I feel sure that communism, too, would never be able to sustain itself in

---

[1] Alexander M. Frey (1881–1957), writer, chiefly of comic and imaginative short novels. Among his works: *The Stout-Hearted Cat, Kastan und die Dirnen, Spuk des Alltags.* After 1933 Frey lived in Switzerland.

Germany; it would have to remain an episode, a transition to something more suitable. Incidentally, preventive measures have already been taken by changes in the conscription law. The dissatisfied, who are undoubtedly numerous, are impotent, and not much is likely to happen in the near future. The present regime must in time and of its own accord lead *ad absurdum* and prove to have been a horribly superfluous detour to rationality. Nevertheless, it does look more and more improbable to me that I, who am already fifty-eight, shall ever see Germany again.

At present the summer heat is at its height here, but it never really becomes oppressive, since there is almost always a little wind and the evenings are refreshing. I frequently sit up late on the small veranda outside my study, smoke my cigar, gaze at the stars; and ponder the strangeness of life.

We have been offered a fine house near Nice for the winter, and I am considering accepting it. It seems a good idea to keep at a distance for a while. In the long run, I suppose, I shall be drawn back to the German cultural sphere, which means either Zurich or Basel.

Best wishes for your well-being and your work!

TO GOTTFRIED BERMANN FISCHER [1]

Sanary
August 19, 1933

Dear Dr. Bermann:

Thank you for your friendly lines of the 15th. I have just finished revising the page proofs and felt as moved by Rachel's death as I was when I wrote it. Say what you will, there are a good many fine and remarkable things in the volume—for instance, the deception over the blessing and Jacob's wedding. I recently read that chapter aloud in the garden; my audience consisted of some twenty persons, and the little terrace outside my room served as a platform. Everyone seemed much taken with it. Even the dreaded "essayistic" prelude is not so bad, in its

[1] Gottfried Bermann Fischer (b. 1897), M.D., publisher, son-in-law of S. Fischer. From 1928 on he was manager of S. Fischer Verlag and became head of the firm after S. Fischer's death in 1934. He remained in Berlin until 1936, then evacuated what he could save of his stock and moved the firm to Vienna. From there, after the *Anschluss*, it was moved again to Stockholm (this time without any stock of books). Expelled from Sweden in 1940 for anti-Nazi activity, Fischer moved to the United States, where he helped found L. B. Fischer Corp. In 1950 he managed to reestablish the venerable firm of S. Fischer Verlag in Frankfurt and Berlin.

fashion. The sore spot is at the end of the first chapter. But I do not know how to improve it.

Habent sua fata—I am afraid that the fate of this *libellus* will be stormy, and sometimes I am astonished at the apparent calm and confidence with which you await it. Calm, very well. But confidence? At times I ask myself: What is he really thinking of? But then I too go back to acting as if everything were normal and, for example, start considering questions of format and binding that I wished to ask you about. Shall we simply go on including it within the Complete Works—which are "complete" only by virtue of the ten numbered volumes, but which also exist as an open series? In our discussions we considered a special form for this novel, but only in case the whole should be published at once. Nevertheless, even now I keep telling myself that it would almost be a pity to forgo the decorative possibilities that the subject offers. Have you considered a special format? For an illustrator with imagination and a feeling for symbolism, that would certainly have its charms. A good deal could be done with Hebrew script alone— יוסף is roughly the name Joseph, and יעקב is Jacob, clumsily written. Only I am afraid it will look at first glance like a kosher restaurant. Nevertheless, perhaps you will give the matter careful consideration once more and tell me whether you too are inclined to deviate from the lyre and bow[2] for once.

Has Herr Loerke been kind enough to take over the task of writing the advertising copy? Best regards!

TO JULIUS MEIER-GRAEFE[1]

Schiedhaldenstrasse 33
Küsnacht-Zurich
December 23, 1933

My dear Herr Meier-Graefe:

You have heaped coals of fire on my head. Long ago—in fact, ever since our departure—I have been meaning to write and thank you for all the pleasant times in Sanary and St. Cyr, for your friendliness, concern, and patience as a listener. It was only due to weakness, sluggishness, inadequacy, that I did not get around to it. Now you have anticipated me— and how generously! What you say about my book "sits smiling to my

---

[2] The lyre and bow design are stamped in gold on the covers of all Thomas Mann's works in the German editions published by S. Fischer.

[1] Julius Meier-Graefe (1867–1935), noted art historian; prepared the ground for Impressionism in Germany. Emigrated to Southern France in 1933. Meier-Graefe was an intimate friend of René Schickele and a good friend of Thomas Mann also.

heart," as Hamlet has it. It has done my soul good—for all of us who have "talent" need a great deal of comforting and encouragement. There's something to that line about "satisfying the best minds of his time." The others scarcely count, and would not count at all if one did not need a livelihood. The likely prospects in that regard are highly dubious at the moment. I too thought that the matter of the Berlin compulsory organization[2] was settled after I had written to Blunck[3] that I assumed I would go on being included among German writers and that I did not think any further formalities were necessary. Bermann, after telephoning the Propaganda Ministry, wrote to me that that would suffice. But yesterday ominous forms arrived from the "Reich Association," with a notice that they absolutely must be signed. I will not do that, and if Bermann, whom it greatly concerns, doesn't find some other way out, my exclusion is sealed.

I still can't really grasp it. At bottom I am aware that my books are not written for Prague and New York, but for Germans. The rest of the world has always been merely an "extra," and I still don't see how I am to manage with it alone. But on the other hand, what sense is there in working for a country where people are ashamed and afraid to show my name, and brazenly and impudently cut out the dedication in your essay? I thank you warmly for your intention. Do replace the dedication when the essay eventually appears in book form. I shall be proud of it.

I heard from Schickele that you would like to enter into closer and more definite relations with the *Neue Zürcher Zeitung* instead of the *Frankfurter Zeitung*. In connection with that I have written to Dr. Korrodi, whom I know. He replies that it is difficult these days to work in new associates, even when they have names like yours. The art department reports that if you want to make use of the N.Z.Z. from time to time, you will of course be welcome, but that at present they unfortunately cannot enter into any fixed arrangement. Incidentally, Korrodi says, Dr. Hans Graber is the man in charge there, and he will certainly be extremely receptive if you wish to approach him. Of course this news is not very satisfying; it contains only what might be taken for granted anyhow. But I imagine that once a start is made there, the N.Z.Z. will develop a taste for your things and a settled relationship will emerge, after all.

[2] The *Reichsschrifttumskammer*, the Nazi writers' organization.
[3] Hans Friedrich Blunck (1888–1961), writer; from 1933–43 president of the *Reichsschrifttumskammer*. Blunck pleaded with Thomas Mann to help in his rehabilitation after the war. See letter of July 22, 1946, pp. 505–7.

We are content to stay here chiefly because of the children, who are extremely happy in their conservatory and the free gymnasium. The house here, overlooking the lake, is also very pretty, but it is much too dear in the long run and available to us only until April. What will become of us then, we do not know, and oddly enough rarely consider. [. . .]

Give the Schickeles our warm regards, and my special thanks to René for his last letter. Please give him the enclosed clipping also.

We remember Sanary often and gratefully. I often think that I ought to build a cottage and round out my life there.

I hope your dear wife brings a nice little car back. We are now driving a very neat and efficient little Fiat sedan.

TO ALEXANDER M. FREY

Küsnacht-Zurich
December 30, 1933

Dear Herr Frey:

I want to thank you at least before the end of the year for your friendly letter of the 16th and for your heartwarming words about *Joseph and His Brothers*. I have put this off long enough. In any case I am not in the best of form (for one does feel these ten months; with the passage of time, it seems to me, everything becomes not easier but harder, and in fact a quiet grief perpetually gnaws), and I have devoted too much energy to the artistic and social distractions that a city such as this offers, especially when one is a new arrival. As a result I have frequently been in a state of ineffectuality which I hate like the plague, without always being able to avoid it.

Once more, your good opinion of the novel gave me great joy. I stand in need of it psychologically; for although the sympathetic interest of thinking and feeling men—Werfel, say, or Schickele, or my brother—does make me happy, the critical echo in the press at home has for the most part been so miserable, permeated with such blatant indifference, that I often feel wounded and repelled to the depths of my soul. The whole atmosphere inside Germany is ghastly—be glad you are outside. Almost every comment I come across inspires a horror of the base submissiveness and emasculation—by this time no longer even conscious—of those people.

What a pity no review of the book by A. M. F. has been published.

My son's *Sammlung*[1] would have been the right place for it. For I assume that you have stopped worrying about the sublime sensibilities of the German holders of power and are writing where you please. It is rank negligence on the editor's part that he did not turn to you. Ephraim [sic] Frisch[2] wrote a highly intelligent article; but since he still has interests in Germany, his work can be published only under a pseudonym, and that takes away half the pleasure.

January 1, 1934

The New Year came in before I could complete these lines, and I send you my best wishes for it. We, my wife and I, will soon be reaching the anniversary of our unsuspecting departure from Munich—it was on the 12th of February. What a year! And we are by no means out of the mess. Our affairs in Munich continue in suspension. The Political Police have kindly permitted us to pay our "desertion of the Fatherland" tax. [. . .]

Appeasement of the Munich Tax Office, incidentally, has not kept the rest of my property from being confiscated in a wholly senseless and illegal fashion, namely my house and its contents, while on the other hand they have stopped blocking royalties, so that Bermann was able to pay for *Joseph and His Brothers*. There is no logic or sense to any of it. It is "irrational," or "irnational,"[3] as a typographical error in a German newspaper recently had it. They are already confusing the two ideas and can no longer pronounce the word.

It is quite likely that the fragment from the second volume of the *Joseph* which has just appeared in the *Neue Rundschau* will prove to be my literary swan song for Germany. I absolutely will not sign the entrance forms for the Berlin compulsory organization of writers. I submitted my application by writing: As an honorary member of the League of German Writers, now absorbed in the Reich League, I assume that I shall continue to be regarded as a member of the German literary profession, and that further formalities are unnecessary. At first it looked as though they intended to close an eye, but then they sent the papers to me after all, stating that it was indispensable for them to be filled out. I shall, as I have said, absolutely not consent. Perhaps I can circumvent

---

[1] *Die Sammlung*, a literary monthly sponsored by André Gide, Aldous Huxley, Heinrich Mann, and others, edited by Klaus Mann. The magazine became a representative organ of the German writers in exile.

[2] Ephraim Frisch (1873–1942), essayist, critic, translator, last editor of *Der Neue Merkur* before this magazine was Nazified.

[3] The implication of this typographical error in German is "crazy nationalistic."

all this by entering the Swiss Writers League. If that should prove impossible, or if it should do no good, then that's the end of it, and the responsibility will have to be borne by those who wanted to extort from me the pledge to serve literature in the spirit of the "nationalist government."

May I take it that you are beyond these problems? Do you intend to remain in Italy? If so, that scarcely casts a hopeful light on the prospects for the future in Austria. But would the annexation of Austria really be tolerated internationally? Granted, the weakness and perplexity is vast, and I fear that this gang may put Europe into its pocket by "legal," "democratic" methods—without war, that is. The fact is that their present propagandistic claims of pacifism are a complete fraud—simply the counterpart in foreign policy of the pose of legality which they used on the domestic front in order to come to power. We had better arm ourselves with the equanimity of the cynic in the event that they succeed.

Best regards, and best wishes for your work.

1934

———————•———————

TO ERNST BERTRAM

Küsnacht-Zurich
January 9, 1934

Dear Bertram:

The Year II must not go any further without my having paid you due
and overdue thanks for your great epistolary effort of November—that
generous sacrifice of time and energy which you made to our old friendship. As a personal gesture it must not go unacknowledged, alien and
depressing though I find the point of view, not to say the state of mind,
from which it sprang. I shall not embark on a reply and an attempt at
correction, for it would necessarily be endless and hopeless. We have
moved too far apart, and arguing back and forth can only cause more
sadness on both sides. There is only one thing I ask you to believe: My
attitude, my verdict, are not determined or influenced by the spirit of
exiles. I stand for myself and have no contact at all with the German
emigration scattered over the world. Moreover, this German emigration
has no existence whatsoever as an intellectual and political entity. There
is total individualistic splintering; and if the whole world has not yet
reached a proper understanding of the grace and dignity of your Germany,
the wholly uninfluential exiles are not to be blamed or credited for that.
The widespread notion to the contrary among your fellow countrymen is
totally benighted, and it would be a good thing if you opposed it.

No, I do not regard the new Germany (but can it be called new? it
is simply that the same forces which have oppressed and threatened us
for more than ten years have now achieved absolute autocracy) through
any distorting medium. Rather, I see it as I am accustomed to see things,
with my own eyes. I know its thoughts and works, its style of speaking
and writing, its bad—in every sense of the word—German, its base
moral and intellectual level proclaimed with astonishing frankness. I

know all this, and it suffices. I am sure that you too occasionally find this level an embarrassment, however fiercely you may deny it. But I use far too facile a word for things that are ultimately mortally serious. I hope to become a Swiss, by an abbreviated procedure, and desire to be buried in Switzerland, as Stefan George desired it—George who in the light of his "last will and testament" hardly deserved the gigantic government wreath that adorns his grave.

Enough. It was my intention to keep this reply as calm and restrained as possible. If we should see each other again (but will you risk exposing yourself to fresh air?) we will be able to talk about the "landslide of a century" with the requisite manly self-control. I shall then stem your fiery torrent of words with a mild gesture, and answer: "My friend, I too believe in Germany's future . . ." In all seriousness, I wish I resembled Goethe as much as you resemble Luden.[1]

I can strongly recommend that you accept the invitation from the Zurich students. They are nice, open-minded young people, and I have the most pleasant memory of the two evenings they arranged in the large auditorium of the Polytechnical Institute, where I read from the *Joseph*. At the beginning of February I shall be touring this whole little country —ten cities; it is quite a lot for my somewhat flagging energy, but psychically good for me. For this occasion I shall also fetch out the Wagner lecture with which I said goodbye to Munich—before very long it will be a full year since I delivered it for the first time in Munich's Auditorium Maximum, to warm applause. Vossler[2] and Brecht[3] were there at the time, and Vossler said that it was the best lecture he had ever heard in that hall. Next day we set out on our tour. . . . I must shake my head when I think of it.

We spent Christmas Eve with the children and a few friends, really quite in the old fashion. Now the elder sons have returned to their work in Amsterdam and St. Cloud, the little ones are going to school in the city, and Moni, who had stayed on in Sanary until Christmas, wants to

[1] Heinrich Luden (1780–1847), professor of history at the University of Jena. In November 1813 Luden attempted to persuade Goethe to collaborate with him on his new anti-Napoleonic periodical *Nemesis*. In conversation with Luden, Goethe expressed his irritation and commented: "Only the thought of Germany's future offers consolation; I hold this belief as firmly as you do." It is to this remark that Thomas Mann alludes. In conversation with his secretary, Riemer, about the magazine, Goethe said: "The Germans are ruminants."

[2] Karl Vossler (1872–1949), professor of Romance languages in Heidelberg, Würzburg, and Munich, translator of—and author of critical works on—Dante and \cine, among others.

[3] Walter Brecht (1876–1950), Munich professor of literature.

make her home in Florence, where she has friends. Erika remains with us—a child for whom my admiration and love has steadily grown. She has reopened her literary cabaret[4] with a success that for Zurich conditions is quite unprecedented. The cabaret is founded solely upon her energy and imagination, her delicately melancholic and nevertheless courageously aggressive mind and spirit. The little restaurant *Zum Hirschen*, otherwise an insignificant bistro, is jammed night after night; the cars of Zurich high society park in front of it; the audiences rejoice and the press is unanimously delighted. The mixture of brashness and innocence that pervades it has proved effective in Bern, Basel, and other Swiss cities, and will soon be trying its wings in the wide world. I take more pleasure in this success than in the applause that *Joseph and His Brothers* has received. That is the imperceptible and painless creeping abdication of advancing age in favor of the young folks.

Your newspapers will have informed you in two lines of the death of our friend Wassermann. A certain empty pomp and solemn verbosity in his works sometimes forced a smile from me, although I recognized that as a fashioner of plots he was far greater than I am. [. . .] In any case, his life constituted a tremendous and internationally effective effort in behalf of the German novel, and the curve of that life, rising brilliantly and very high out of wretchedness and darkness and then setting again in night and poverty, has the grandiose novelistic style of his dreams. The news of his death did not come unexpectedly, for we had seen him here a few weeks before and were forced to recognize that he was failing; but in my present state of nerves it was a severe shock. Naturally his death is not unconnected with the landslide of the century. Who are we to grumble? One cannot make an omelet without breaking eggs. Isn't that what you say?

Do read the little excavation with which a Prague literary journal is amusing itself! (See enclosure.[5]) On the other side are two remarks by me about my experience with *Witiko*,[6] which might interest you, since it was you who led me to Adalbert Stifter. If I should ever again write a long essay, it would be devoted to this writer, whose nature, as the years

---

[4] The Peppermill.

[5] The enclosure was a passage from Thomas Mann's *Pariser Rechenschaft* concerning the Russian writer-in-exile Ivan Bunin (1870–1953; Nobel Prize, 1933). "Here," Thomas Mann had written prophetically in 1926, "I feel sympathy, solidarity, a kind of potential comradeship; for we in Germany have not yet come to the point where a writer of the approximate character of Bunin must shake the dust of the Fatherland from his feet and eat the bread of the West. But I have no doubt that in some circumstances my fate would be his."

[6] A historical novel by Stifter.

go by, seems to me more and more remarkable. Unless, that is, you should at last give us your work on him—in which case I should certainly keep my hands off.

With earnest good wishes, and regards to your mother,

TO ALFRED KNOPF

Küsnacht-Zurich
January 20, 1934

Dear Mr. Knopf:

That luxurious volume of Willa Cather was a handsome New Year's remembrance; please accept my cordial thanks for it and my own and my wife's very best wishes for the year that has begun.

We have not heard from one another for a long time, but my wife and I speak often of you and would be delighted to see you here in Switzerland some time. I have just had word from Mrs. Lowe[1] that she is occupied with the proofs of the English edition of *Joseph and His Brothers*. I am all the more pleased that the English edition is so close to publication because the translations into Italian, Danish, Polish, and Hungarian have been ready for some time. The novel has had a success in Germany that surpasses my expectations. So far almost 25,000 copies have been sold, which—given the rather high price of the book, the depressed state of German purchasing power, and the demands the novel makes upon the reader, quite aside from political conditions—is fantastic. In keeping with those same political conditions, the German press has been friendly only in part. The response of the German-language press outside Germany itself, as well as the foreign press, is all the more gratifying. For example, may I recommend for advertising purposes the review by Marcelle Brion in the *Nouvelles Littéraires*. The Austrian, the Czech, and above all, the Swiss press have also been very appreciative. You undoubtedly saw the good review by Gabriele Reuter in the *New York Times*; it too may be useful for your announcements.

Our stay in Sanary-sur-mer, where we were very content, was protracted until the autumn; then we moved to Switzerland because I felt the need to live once more in the atmosphere of German culture and language. We have been given a very friendly reception here and are enjoying the many cultural stimuli that this intellectually lively city offers. The only difficulty is that the climate in winter is not altogether

---

[1] Helen Lowe-Porter (1877–1963), the English translator of most of Mann's works.

healthful; it is very dark and the *föhn* wind affects the nerves. Moreover, Switzerland is the most expensive country in Europe, if not in the world, and this makes us doubtful that we shall be able to stay here permanently. Return to Germany is and will remain, as far as such things are predictable, out of the question as long as the repulsive regime lasts. It is of course a great pity about our fine house in Munich, but how could we possibly enjoy it given the present state of that city? It is difficult to decide to regard this condition, as well as that of Germany in general, as anything definite, and so we simply await events.

Cordial regards to you and your wife from both of us, and do let us hear from you again.

TO KATIA MANN

Hotel Bellevue
Bern
February 3, 1934

Dearest,

Thank you for the mail. The letter from Lindley[1] truly gladdened me. Here is an altogether upstanding, pure, and manly type of homage that means something, and if Reisi[2] sees any possibility of making the letter known in Germany, he ought to follow it up. The letter might also be sent to Bermann.

I shall worry no more about Andrea's information. The matter is scarcely pressing now, you know, and we can first of all try to have the passport renewed by the consul.

Yesterday noon Strich[3] had me to lunch in a restaurant with a couple named Faburg or Faberg[4]—friends of his (the man specializes in Romance languages and literature and was *Rektor* of the university when I met him two years ago). Today Strich is in Zurich with Singer. We join each other again tomorrow evening.

Toward evening yesterday I went on to Thun and had dinner with the chairman, a Dr. Sauer,[5] who has an Adler convertible, and his

[1] Denver Lindley (b. 1904), editor, translator of Mann's last novel *Confessions of Felix Krull*, as well as works of Maurois, Remarque, and others.

[2] Hans Reisiger.

[3] Fritz Strich (1882–1963), historian of literature, professor in Munich and Bern. Author of many critical works and a number of essays on Thomas Mann.

[4] Karl Jaberg (1876–1958), professor of Romance philology and Italian language and literature at the University of Bern; *Rektor* of the university 1931–2.

[5] Helmut Anton Adolf Sauer (1894–1936), chemist.

German wife. The reading in the auditorium of the junior high school before about 200 persons was innocuous and no strain. The audience was polite and perfectly quiet, but obviously stupid. Afterwards I promptly returned to Bern on an international train full of Americans and on the way read the review I enclose, which would be quite the thing to add to Knappi's repentance.[6]

It's good that you didn't make any commitment to . . . . But I suppose she will have to come some time between the 10th and the 26th, won't she? Or should we put her off until the middle of March?

Today I am my own master until evening and then have only the half-hour Bashan reading. Day after tomorrow I am due in Glarus.

Greet Reisi and the children for me!

T.

TO DENVER LINDLEY

Küsnacht-Zurich
February 12, 1934

Dear Mr. Lindley:

I am very much afraid that you will be unable to read my handwriting, but I don't want to dictate my thanks for your letter to any intermediary. I should like to tell you directly and in my own hand how much joy your words gave me when they reached me a few days ago, while I happened to be on a lecture tour that was taking me through the whole of this small country. Your letter is one of the most engaging documents ever addressed to me, and of all the comments on *Joseph*, both written and printed, that have come my way, it is the one I like best. If that gladdens you, so much the better. It is an objective observation. A friend who is living with us at the moment because he likewise finds things in Germany distasteful—Hans Reisiger, the translator of Walt Whitman—was as moved by it as I was. "What a breed of men over there!" he said. Moreover, he urged that the letter be published in Germany, apparently with the idea that it would do our countrymen—at the moment so hostile toward me—no harm to find out about this opinion from abroad—for at bottom they have a great deal of respect for foreign parts. However, to me this is the less important matter. It is enough for me that your letter was written. This is a reality in the realm of the spirit which remains

[6] Hans Knappertsbusch had been one of the initiators of a "protest of Munich, the Wagner city" against Mann's lecture on Wagner. He was later rumored to have regretted this action.

alive and significant whether or not others beside you and me know of it.

I am very happy to hear that those lines with which I replied to your first letter long ago could speak to you in human, spiritual terms, and that you received from them, in your situation at the time, a certain encouragement in the struggle of life. What I wrote was certainly unpretentious; but you "made something of it," and that is a creative artist's trait. For to be a creative artist does not mean to think up all sorts of things; it means to make something out of the things that are.

My best wishes to you! I have just had a visit from an American agent who proposed that I go on a lecture tour of the States. I dare not think of such an undertaking while the engrossing burden of these biblical novels still rests upon me. But let us hope that one of these days, in a few years, life will bring the two of us, who have exchanged this symbolic handclasp across land and sea, together for an actual meeting.

TO KARL KERÉNYI[1]

Küsnacht-Zurich
February 20, 1934

My dear Herr Professor:

It was a great pleasure to me, and a lively stimulus, to receive your important letter and the two remarkable essays with it. Now that I have become acquainted with these smaller examples of your perceptiveness in matters of religious history and mythology, I mean to turn as soon as I can to your major work on Greek-Oriental Romance literature. I must see whether I can cope with it receptively. It will probably make me shamefully aware of how little I know about this beautiful and profound realm. But there must be some basis within myself for extending this knowledge—or so I am encouraged to believe by your statement that *The Magic Mountain* and *Joseph and His Brothers* had something to say to you, could serve to corroborate the ideas of a scholar like yourself. At the same time this is evidence to me—or a reminder—of the extent to which concerns and motifs touched on in *The Magic Mountain* (whose foreground themes alone have been the object of attention) subsequently became the explicit subject of the narrative in the Joseph novel. In other words, I realize how precisely the "sanatorium novel" forms the connect-

---

[1] Karl Kerényi (b. 1897), Austrian philologist and student of comparative religions. Among his works: *The Gods of the Greeks, The Heroes of the Greeks.*

ing link between the realistic novel of my youth, *Buddenbrooks*, and the manifestly mythological work of my very nearly sixty years.

In my case this growing interest in myth and religious history is actually a phenomenon of aging; it is in keeping with a taste that has been turning, with advancing years, from bourgeois individuality to what is typically and generally human. In my youth I would certainly not have enjoyed a scene such as you mention: Jacob's dream of Anup, a reply such as that of the jackal-headed god: "I shall one day be rid of my head too." It is almost a private joke that everyone passes over in reading. But it deals with the career of a god. This Anubis, at the moment still half animal and satyr-like, is of course the future Hermes Psychopompos. Did you notice that I placed him on his stone exactly in the pose of the Hermes of Lysippus in Naples? I particularly love this statue, of which there is a fine copy in the Old Museum in Berlin, and the passage is a secret tribute.

Of the English writers you mention, I know two quite well. I admire Aldous Huxley, who represents one of the finest flowerings of West European intellectualism, especially in his essays. I prefer him to D. H. Lawrence, who is no doubt a significant phenomenon and characteristic of our times, but whose fevered sensuality has little appeal for me. My attention was called to Powys at the same time as your letter by an article in the *Neue Zürcher Zeitung* which dealt with his books *Defense of Sensuality* and *The Meaning of Culture.* The article was entitled, moreover, "Back to the Ichthyosaurus." That is to be sure a coarse and coarsening heading, but the sneer implicit in it is not entirely without justification. One finds in European literature of the present day a kind of rancor against the development of the human cerebrum, a rancor which has always struck me as a snobbish and ridiculous form of self-negation. Permit me the confession that I am no friend of the anti-intellectual movement represented in Germany, particularly by Klages.[2] I feared and fought it early, because I saw through all its brutally anti-human consequences before they became apparent.

The "return of the European mind to the highest, the mythic realities," of which you speak so impressively, is truly a great and good cause in the history of thought, and I may claim to have contributed something to it by my work. But I trust you will understand when I say that the *fad* of irrationalism frequently involves a sacrifice and a callow

---

[2] Ludwig Klages (1872–1956), graphologist and philosopher. Among his books: *Handschrift und Charakter, Grundlegung einer Wissenschaft vom Ausdruck, Der Geist als Widersacher der Seele.*

throwing over of achievements and principles which not only make the European a European, but the human being human. That sort of thing is a "back to nature" movement of a far more ignoble sort, in human terms, than the movement which prepared the way for the French Revolution.

But enough. You will understand perfectly. I am a man of balance. I instinctively lean to the left when the boat threatens to capsize on the right, and vice versa. . . . After this digression it can do no harm if I again turn to the extraordinary stimulation I received from your study on the figure of the little Telesphoros with "cucullus"[3] and book scroll. What an enchanting creature, this little god of death. And in particular, what enchantment streams from the history of the capuchin hood down the millennia. How strange. I had no inkling of these things, and yet I have provided my Joseph—after his resurrection from the well, when the Ishmaelites are leading him through Egypt—with a capuchin hood and a scroll. These are mysterious sportings of the mind which can lead one to a high appreciation of scholarly knowledge.

TO JULIUS BAB

Küsnacht-Zurich
March 25, 1934

Dear Herr Bab:

Many thanks for your letter of the 20th. I am particularly glad that this second volume also held you. It begins a little laboriously, but later on there are all sorts of things in it that I too feel are remarkable and captivating. Incidentally, it really shouldn't be regarded as an entirely independent book. Later it will have to form a whole with the first, and the entire work is to be in two volumes.

Your question about Leah is of course completely justified. My wife was the first to point out this gap, which seems the product of forgetfulness, and to demand that it be filled. A compound of laziness and conviction prevented me from taking her advice. The fact is that a measure of artistic intention underlies the silence about Leah; she is meant simply to drop into oblivion. If she does not, as in your case, and if the question of what happens to her is asked, then I am afraid I must decline to answer. I had the feeling that the narrative can pass over this "wrong one" after she has played her part and we have been told that she "sat

[3] A hood.

ever disdained in the tent with her inflamed eyes," that her unimportant further destiny can be wrapped in silence. Purely from the storytelling point of view, there was no urge to relate her death; and if the reader should feel that as a lack, I must accept the blame, only suggesting that a callous account of Leah's death might have seemed, by contrast with the account of Rachel's passing, even more loveless than complete silence.

The Bruno Franks have not yet carried out their plan to move to England. As I have only recently learned, they are staying in Sanary-sur-mer (Var), sur-la-Colline, Villa Fayet.

I am not at all pleased that *Young Joseph* was sent to you for reading in galley proofs; quite aside from the typographical errors, the proofs did not at all provide a correct picture of the book. An entire unnecessary chapter was subsequently deleted, and in addition all the section headings, which are so important to the whole picture, were not yet entirely straightened out. If your impression was nevertheless favorable, so much the better. I am looking forward keenly to your review.

With all good wishes and regards,

TO RENÉ SCHICKELE

Küsnacht-Zurich
April 2, 1934

Dear René Schickele:

On this lovely Easter morning (with, I think, the bluest sky I have ever seen at Easter time), I want to send you greetings once more and ask how things are with you and yours in the new home, which I hope is pleasant for you and favorable to your work. We often speak of our regret that we aren't able to see it, and our regret also that the sociable life of neighbors which we led last summer should have been only an episode, with scarcely any prospects for renewing it. Recently the same subject came up between me and my brother, who wrote deploring the fact that now of all times we are not living in the same city or even in the same country; I answered with an explanation of what holds us here. It is chiefly the children who attach us to Switzerland, for the next few years at least. They are installed here in their school and conservatory; they are obviously happy, and it would be unjust to transplant them once again, moreover to an area where another language is spoken. For the boy in particular, who is making good progress with his music, still another change of teachers would be decidedly harmful. Ultimately we could leave him here; but we want at least to wait for Medi, who will be taking her *Abitur* in a year and a half. Further than that we do not think—who thinks beyond a year and a half these days? For that long, at any rate, we shall continue to pay the horrendous rent for our house above the lake, and shall see what the future holds. Incidentally, I don't deny that I should like to maintain the state of demi- or not entirely stark exile which is represented by life in eastern Switzerland—at the gates of Germany, so to speak. In fact, I would be glad if I could eventually give it a looser shape, with more freedom of movement. I often envy Hesse, who has been out of Germany for so many years, but for whom Germany is not closed. My abhorrence of the conditions there, and my ardent desire to see the gang in control there go to hell one way or another in the shortest possible time, has not changed in the slightest. But I less and less see why I should be excluded from Germany for the sake of these idiots, or should leave them my belongings, house, and property. I am continuing my efforts to wrest these things from the hands of the Munich hoodlums; and since, to the disappointment of these same hoodlums, I was not expatriated during the latest deportations, there actually is some chance that I will regain possession in the foreseeable future. To have our own furniture would mean a great saving in rent for us, and it would also be a psychic reassurance to be surrounded by the objects of our previous life. But the chief point is that recovering them would be a triumph over the present tyrants of Munich and would willy-nilly have to be accompanied by the renewal of my passport. Then I could at least travel to the Memel area to see to our house there. I claim the right of such freedom of movement; I feel their denying me that freedom is an outrage. Isn't that a possible attitude *too*? Do tell me whether you regard it as treasonous and unprincipled.

On the other hand, you needn't bother, for my attitude, my plans, and my resolves are wavering and ambivalent. As soon as I look up from my curious epic, in which I have now come as far as the first talk between Joseph and Potiphar in the date garden, I begin to think about a book-length discussion of German affairs, highly personal and unsparing. One of these days I shall no doubt have to set to work on it, and that, of course, would mean the final breach with Germany until the end of the present regime, which in all probability means to the end of my days. Or do you believe in the likelihood of a collapse in my lifetime or in yours? The discontent is vast; there is a great deal of vigorous and open grumbling; the outlook for the economy is bad (although certain industries are thriving); a fall of the mark and ersatz goods are in the offing; further-more, there will be no lack of setbacks in foreign policy, and so on. But the German people are great at taking what comes, and since they do not love freedom but feel it rather as a form of neglect (for which reason it actually does become a kind of negligence for them), they will in spite of harsh disillusionments feel even better and happier under the new grimly disciplinarian constitution than under the Republic. Added to that is the regime's vast apparatus for deceiving, stupefying, and brutalizing them. The intellectual and moral level long ago sank so low that the spirit necessary for a real uprising simply cannot be summoned up. And at the same time they have, in that debased state, the heady sense of representing a new world—which indeed it is; a world of debasement. We are aliens in it, and ultimately can do nothing but resign ourselves. I, at any rate, have long since begun to regard myself as a historical relic, a leftover from a different cultural era which I as an individual will carry on to its end, although in reality it is dead and buried. Eduard Korrodi of the *Neue Zürcher Zeitung* is no great critic, but I was really moved by his calling the *Joseph* "the swan song of the German literature of individual development." Ferdinand Lion,[1] with whom I have many a pleasant chat here, has an even more solemn term for the book. He calls it "les adieux de l'Europe." It is a somber but honorable appellation which I quite accept, and in pessimistic moments, at least, I think that everything we are doing these days deserves that name. Your plan for a magazine, and its title "Defense of the West," show me that you are more belligerently disposed than I. I know I advised you against it, but at the bottom of my heart I hope you will be able to carry out the plan. There is nothing finer than gallant rearguard actions, and besides, we may not know how strong we still are.

I would send you the newly published *Young Joseph* if I were not sure a copy will be reaching you anyway. I hope soon to have the opportunity to inscribe it to you personally. Bermann has brought it out with somewhat peculiar haste. The second pause will therefore be all the longer. The serenity indispensable to productive work has to be labori-ously won from my troubled broodings on current events. Moreover, a certain fatigue after the first thousand pages is also inevitable.

I can't remember so blue a spring as this year's. How wonderful it must be where you are! Tomorrow I shall see how far along it is in the

---

[1] Ferdinand Lion (1883–1965), Alsatian essayist and cultural critic. Among his works: *Cardillac* (an opera with music by Paul Hindemith), *Romantik als deutsches Schicksal*, *Thomas Mann, Leben und Werk*.

Ticino, for I am going to a lecture in Locarno. Four hours—about the longest journey one can take in this country.

This evening Annette[2] is having dinner with us. So we shall talk about you. Incidentally, since this letter wasn't mailed for a while, the date is now the 4th.

My regards to your family, and also to my brother should you see him. And greetings to you yourself.

TO RENÉ SCHICKELE

Küsnacht-Zurich
May 16, 1934

Dear René Schickele:

I thank you from the heart for your good words about the *Joseph* and for your precise and sensitive concern with the book. I am deeply moved and feel it to be no small blessing and encouragement, to hear such things about the problematical piece of work from one who matters. It is to your French sensibility in matters of prose that I owe the pleasure of this letter; for we may as well face the fact that all the things you so kindly note and quote are simply shouted to the wind as far as German ears are concerned. They don't even notice. The Mediterranean and universalistic subject alone makes present-day Germans shut their minds off (except, of course, for the Jews, whose joy and gratitude are affecting). The Germans want to know nothing; all they have in their heads is "the German people"—at the wrong moment, as usual. The fact that my novel loses out inside Germany is truly the least of it. The same is happening to a good many other things; but a fair certainty is that first and last the Germans themselves will lose out.

I am especially glad that you so strongly emphasize the pictorial elements in the book. It has been said that although the conception is great, it is far too intellectual, that a sensuous counterpoise is missing. But isn't it there somehow—in the language, in the way things are approached, in the atmosphere, and in the people too—who in spite of being bound to type and tradition are three-dimensional? I must hope so —and hope above all to bring off the third volume, for I am ambitious for us in the outside world. You and I and my brother, from whose *Henri IV* I expect a great deal, must do our jobs very well; then

---

[2] Annette Kolb (1875–1967), novelist, biographer, essayist, musician. Went into voluntary exile in Paris in 1933 and to the United States in 1940, returning to Paris after the war. She was an old friend of the Pringsheim family and very close to René Schickele.

someday people will say that during this period we were the real Germany.

Excellent—your remark about the novel as a total work of art. It has long been a pet idea of mine. The Wagnerian concept was ridiculously mechanical.

I must say adieu. Tomorrow we are leaving for Paris, day after tomorrow for Boulogne, where we embark for America. It's only a quick trip; we have been invited there by Knopf, who wants me to help celebrate the publication of *Joseph and His Brothers* in English right on the spot. There will be a public dinner and other affairs—ten days of it, which will be no easy matter. But we can build up strength on the crossing, assuming that the ocean is peaceful, which it ought to be at this season. In the middle of June we shall be back here, and in the autumn we hope to see you. We have southern France very much in mind for that time.

Greetings to your whole household. I was overjoyed to hear that you are sprightly and well, that the asthma is gone, and that you go walking.

TO IDA HERZ[1]

Holland-America Line
R.M.S. Volendam
May 25, 1934

Dear Fräulein Herz:

Since there's no knowing when I will be able to find time in New York, I want to thank you here and now for your friendly farewell letter and the delicious travel provisions that accompanied it, and send you our best wishes from this sea voyage now coming to an end. At the start we had distinctly bad weather; the foghorn hooted for days and we made slow progress, with the result that we shall set foot on the soil of the New World not on the 28th but on the morning of the 29th. But what does that matter? Since then the weather has become fine and summery—it happened very quickly under the influence of the Gulf Stream—the ship has been cutting its path through the horizons almost without rocking, every trace of seasickness has gone, and it is good living on the decks and in the salons of this fine, cozy vessel, so that we are in no hurry to arrive

---

[1] Ida Herz (b. 1894), originally a bookseller. In the thirties she emigrated to London, where she has lived since. An early admirer of Thomas Mann, she became a passionate collector of Manniana. Her collection, to which she continues to add, is now in the possession of the Thomas Mann Archives in Zurich.

and at bottom are already looking beyond the whole visit and its experiences to the pleasures of the return voyage. It is like being in a top-notch sanatorium that offers a free choice of fabulously good food and maximum comfort in every respect, and has the advantage, as well, of floating in a circular horizon of violet-colored ocean. The total emptiness all around is amazing. This "track," after all, is plied by ships of every nation, but in these days at sea we have not seen even the smoke of another steamer. There is simply too much room; there is something cosmic about such conditions. The stars in space lose themselves like ships on these waters, and for two to meet is obviously an exception. The feeling of elemental solitude between worlds is in itself remarkable and contrasts curiously with the elegance and comfort that surround us. Say what you will, it is different from traveling by land. For all the physical ease, an element of primitiveness and adventurousness is preserved; that is implicit in the uncertainty of the hour or even the day of arrival, and I find myself liking this element in the same way I like the kind of motion: this dignified gliding through vast expanses differs pleasantly from the way the train tears around curves.

Today we saw a flock of birds on the waves—gulls. They had ventured far out, but all the same they were a sign to us that land is no longer so distant.

Incidentally, the ship is very empty; there are only ten of us in first class, so that it is like traveling on one's own yacht. For our return voyage the *Rotterdam* will probably be somewhat more populated, since June is when Americans begin to travel to Europe.

We are playing nice deck games with a young Dutchman and a businessman from Philadelphia who has a passion for champagne. We especially like a kind of polo in which we have already acquired some skill.

Word has got around that I am a "German author"; but no one knows any more about me than that, except for a little steward from Hamburg who has even read the *Joseph*, as he informed my wife. One evening, before the motion picture, Mrs. King, an American mushroom, asked me to write down the English titles of my books and promised to read them all in the winter. I advised her not to.

Auf Wiedersehen.

1934

TO GOTTFRIED BERMANN FISCHER

Küsnacht-Zurich
June 21, 1934

Dear Dr. Bermann:

To my surprise I find myself back in my Küsnacht study—the adventure has been lived through and now seems only a dream. A rather confused but very pleasant one. I had many agreeable experiences and harvested what had been sowed over the years. The testimonial dinner on June 6 was a great success: 300 persons headed by the mayor of New York. And the whole thing was dreamlike to other people as well: I shook hands with many who said that it was "like a dream" to have me actually there before them. More about all this some other time, preferably face to face. Above all, many thanks for your friendly telegram and for the one from the oldsters. Sinclair Lewis telegraphed: "As long as T. M. writes in the German language the world will not forget its debt to the people and the culture that produced him." His wife, Dorothy Thompson, wrote most skillfully and favorably about the *Joseph* in the *New York Herald Tribune*.

I am writing today chiefly in regard to another review. I hear that Brion has once again praised the second volume in the *Nouvelles Littéraires*. That would interest me, and if you have the review do send it, please.

F. Lion's comments on the two volumes in the *Neue Zürcher Zeitung* were intelligent and subtle. Have you seen them?

I found the proofs of the essay volume on my return, and am setting to work on them at once. To be honest, the Hauptmann address worries me somewhat; it undeniably comes at the wrong time and I shall be criticized in the outside world for including it. But after all, what I have written, I have written.

Many regards.

TO ERNST BERTRAM

July 30, 1934

Dear Bertram:

From the dedication of your *Deutsche Gestalten* I see with sorrow that you have lost your friend[1]—weeks have already passed. I had not heard, and none of the serious differences of opinion and principles that stand

---

[1] Ernst Glöckner, calligrapher, a member of the Stefan George circle.

between us today can prevent me from offering you my sympathy for the bitter grief this parting must have brought. My nature will not properly accept the Indian consolations to which another of your dedicatory pages alludes. In the spirit of that brave nineteenth-century pessimism which I have always prized, I hold with Storm's: "Then you will never be again/Just as you never were before." But in your devoted heart your friend will live on, as he will in the mind of everyone who had the privilege of encountering him in his noble youthfulness.

I have been reading your essays with all the response that your upright and judiciously intelligent Germanism has always aroused in me. That you are capable of confounding this Germanism with its basest travesty and taking the most repulsive scarecrow begotten by world history for the "savior" of whom your poet speaks—this is a constant grief to me, a grief that often enough all but converts into its opposite the feeling of which it ultimately is an expression. I am surely not speaking with exaggerated solemnity when I remind you that if I had followed your well-meant and insistent advice I would today—the probability is so great that it may just as well be called a certainty—no longer be alive. What would that matter, you will say, compared with the "historical creativity" now in progress? Of course it would not matter. And yet I sometimes think that this certainty, simply in view of your nature, should slightly modify your credulous support of the powers from whose grasp a merciful fate has preserved me.

"We shall see," I wrote to you a good while back, and you replied defiantly: "Of course we shall." Have you begun to see? No, for they are holding your eyes closed with bloody hands, and you accept the "protection" only too gladly. The German intellectuals—forgive the word, it is intended as a purely objective term—will in fact be the very last to begin to see, for they have too deeply, too shamefully collaborated and exposed themselves.

Unhappy, unhappy nation! I have long ago reached the point of begging the World Spirit to liberate this nation from political life, to dissolve it and disperse it in a new world like the Jews, with whom so much kindred tragic destiny links it.

I reciprocate your regards and, truly, your good wishes also.

1934

TO KARL KERÉNYI

Dear Professor:

It troubles me that I have not yet thanked you for sending your last critical essay, and I should like to make amends as best I can at the moment. I have been a poor correspondent recently, not only to you but to everybody. You know the chief reason: our trip to America, which cost me a month of time, and has wrought some havoc in my whole small economy. It was really nothing but a grand spree—a term which covers both the impressive and the unnecessary aspects of the whole thing. I do not want to regret such gamboling, for there is something right and good about harvesting sympathies that have been sowed and have grown over the years, especially when the harvest has been blasted by hail in one's native land.

The unfortunate part was that soon after our return, when I had barely begun regular work again, new travels intervened: to Venice, to an incidentally quite superfluous International Congress of the Arts. The good aspect was to return to that city which I have always loved for deep and complex reasons, and the Lido where a certain story now twenty years old takes place. Throughout half of that period I had not revisited the city, but this chance trip has opened the way and I hope that next spring, if we live and the condition of Europe permits, I shall spend a few weeks there without fruitless chatter about such subjects as *l'art et l'état* or *l'art et la réalité*.

When I mention that perplexing "state of Europe," which involves such a complex of problems for the future, I have come to the chief disturbance, from which my tranquillity, my peace of mind, my need for concentration, my psychic and even physical health, and in short my productivity, have been suffering. I do not know how you as a scholar react to the developments of the day, to political events, so-called "world history," but I suspect that you know how to keep yourself inwardly freer in regard to them than I can. This is to my shame, I suppose I ought to add, were it not for my excuse that the chief scene of these events nowadays is my Fatherland, from which I am excluded, and therefore my relationship to the events is necessarily far more direct and, to speak with Goethe, more "pathological" than yours. The fate of my country—which also threatens to become the fate of the continent—never ceases to grieve me. Throughout this year and a half I have attempted honestly, though not with consistent success, to carry through my personal tasks in spite of that grief. But I cannot say how much I have been affected by the atrocities of June 30,[1] the Austrian horrors,[2] and then the *coup d'état* of that creature, his further elevation,[3] which undoubtedly represents a new consolidation of his tottering regime. I cannot say how much they agitate me and alienate me from the work that, if my heart were firmer and colder, I ought to regard as the only important thing. What concern is "world history" to me, I suppose I ought to think, so long as it lets me live and work? But I cannot think that way. My moral-critical conscience is in a state of constant exacerbation, and it is becoming more and more impossible for me to continue pursuing the, it may be, sublime game of novel writing until I have "rendered an accounting" and unburdened my heart of its concern, its perceptions, its pain, as well as its freight of hatred and contempt.

Therefore I shall probably turn from narration to another such profession of beliefs as I undertook at the time of the *Betrachtungen eines Unpolitschen*, and the completion of my third volume will be postponed to the distant future. So be it. A man and a writer can only do what his fingers are itching to attack. It is logical that the crisis of the world should also be a crisis in life and work for me, and I must regard that as a sign that I am alive. The time seems ripe for such a statement as I have in mind, and the moment might soon come when I would repent having delayed too long in silence.

I wanted to tell you this to fill in the picture. Once again thank you for your essay. Once again, what new and surprising interrelationships! Inwardly, I can assure you, I shall not abandon the realm of interests we have in common.

TO RENÉ SCHICKELE

Küsnacht - Zurich
August 10, 1934

Dear René Schickele:

After all we forgot the 4th of August and feel deeply ashamed. Forgive us. The cause was simply politics, the death of Hindenburg, so untimely,

---

[1] The purge of June 30, 1934, in the course of which Hitler killed some of his oldest followers, including Ernst Röhm, the founder of the Storm Troopers, and in which many innocent persons also died.

[2] The bloody confrontation in February 1934 between the Dollfuss regime and the Social Democrats, followed on July 25, 1934, by the Nazis' assassination of Dollfuss and unsuccessful putsch.

[3] Hitler's assumption of the office of president of the Reich.

so blasting to many overly sanguine hopes. Its consequences preoccupied us, especially me, so that our firm intention of writing you on your birthday dropped right out of our minds. Please accept our hearty though ridiculously belated congratulations. I hope you spent the day in good health and cheerful spirits.

As for myself, at the moment I have neither one nor the other. Ever since we returned from Venice (and what a joy it was to see the city again), my work has been in a beastly crisis, which robs me of sleep and good humor. Again, the reason for this is politics. Daily events in Germany so sharply irritate my moral, critical conscience that work on my third volume has come to a total halt; I am on the point of setting it aside in order to devote myself to a political credo and polemic in which I relieve my heart and take revenge for all the spiritual injury inflicted on me during this year and a half. Maybe I can deliver a blow that the regime will feel. Of course I am miserable about the novel, which in any case has been delayed, and I know very well how many arguments there are against such an investment of time and energy. Is there even any sense in neglecting finer duties to argue against this rot? On the other hand, isn't it also a duty which the world would thank me for? In short, I vacillate and don't know what to put my hand to—a horrible condition. I have long since stopped caring about the breach with "Germany"; I want that breach and would much rather have my books issued outside.

You never told me about your essay on Lawrence—I heard of it from Klaus and feel very curious to see it. I would guess that you incorporated all sorts of things in it besides literature. My brother's novel[1] will be coming along soon, and one by Neumann,[2] and I must not forget Frank's[3] *Cervantes*. So there will be no lack of reading matter. And all these are being published outside Germany. After all, I too should like to be among them.

[1] *The Youth of King Henry IV.*
[2] Alfred Neumann (1895–1952), novelist, noted for historical novels of high literary quality. Both in Munich and in exile in California, Neumann and Thomas Mann were close friends.
[3] Bruno Frank.

1934

TO FERDINAND LION

Dear Lion:

Thank you for your letter. When I "give expression to my horror" I hope that it will be a positive benefit, a personal contribution toward improving matters; but we cannot and must not, even to that end, play into the hands of the present masters and corruptors of the country. This vile excrescence must first be removed, so that something decent and possible for the world and human beings can arise. Listen to Serbs, Hungarians, Italians talk about the German regime. The abhorrence is unanimous, and it reveals the gulf between that regime and even the very political attitudes and ideologies which are termed fascistic and dictatorial. So-called National Socialism has no place at all within any European and ethical framework. It stands in opposition not only to "liberalism" and "Western democracy," but also to civilization in general —using the word in a sense that not even German *Kultur* mysticism can ignore. I am often ashamed of engaging in follies and not doing what is probably my duty—to say some pertinent words on the subject to the world. Or of not yet doing it, at any rate. However, I could not go on with the novel, and so for the time being am writing a light essay called *Voyage with Don Quixote*, a chatty, associative thing which serves to gain me time and, moreover, will complete the volume of essays.

A copy of *Joseph* is on its way to you. (It is being filmed in London.)[1] I am looking forward eagerly to your expanded study in the *Antologia*. That should remain my chief interest, and at bottom I imagine it is. And how do things stand with your offer to Fischer? No answer yet? Bermann, who is staying with the old man in Freudenstadt in the Black Forest, recently telephoned that he would be coming to see us. He wants to discuss rights because he feels that I am disposed to break away. But he informed us that Fischer's condition did not permit his departing. I imagine the end is approaching for my old friend. He sleeps most of the time and scarcely takes any nourishment.

We have an absurdly large number of visitors now, chiefly from Germany. Even people who have moved very far from us, such as our guest of today, Emil Preetorius, are coming again—aged, speaking low, and shaken by what they learn in the outside world about their country.

---

[1] This project came to nothing.

1934

TO HEDWIG FISCHER

Küsnacht-Zurich
November 2, 1934

Dear Frau Fischer:

I should like to send you only a greeting, nothing more. Since we heard the sad news in Basel on the way back from Lugano, not a single day has passed, I think, that we have not talked about your husband; and the shock we felt then still reverberates and will go on for a long time. One had to be prepared for this parting, and in the end almost to consent to it; yet I cannot say how deeply it affected me when it came at last. Almost four decades of association! I was extremely attached to him. There was a serene cordiality between us, of a kind I have rarely experienced in relations with people, and we had almost no superficial discord and disagreement. Our characters were complementary, so that I always felt that I was the born author for him and he my born publisher. I have suggested something of this in the obituary which you have probably seen in the Sunday supplement of the *Basler Nachrichten*. Strange how on such occasions I rein in my feelings, involuntarily repress them and replace them by chillier psychology and characterization. But after all I am not a lyric poet; objectifying and distancing are my normal mode. I would not be surprised if you found the piece in some way painful. I did better, I think, in the two short pages I have just sent to Suhrkamp for the memorial issue of the *Rundschau*. I hope this issue turns out to be a truly fine memorial.

We heard from Reisiger, who will be coming to visit us in a few days, that the end was gentle and without consciousness. So it should be. And yourself? How have you withstood the parting? After going side by side for so long and sharing everything! As soon as one reflects on life, the tears come.

Your house has published many fine and interesting things lately. The book on Charlemagne[1] is extraordinarily interesting. Döblin[2] wants to do an essay on it for the *Sammlung*, so I hear, although the exiles ordinarily don't like to mention German books—that is, books published in Germany. But the one I recently read from beginning to end with

---

[1] *Karl der Grosse*, by Rudolf Wahl.
[2] Alfred Döblin (1878–1957), novelist and for a long time a practicing neurologist as well. Cofounder of the expressionist magazine *Der Sturm* (1910). Emigrated to France in 1933, to the United States in 1940; returned to Germany in 1945 as a colonel in the French army. His *Berlin Alexanderplatz* was the most successful of his many novels.

unusual sympathy is Gumpert's[3] *Hahnemann*—whose life I knew scarcely anything about and which has deeply stirred me. Keep well, and be consoled! Regards from us to your children and grandchildren.

[3] Martin Gumpert (1897–1955), physician and writer, close friend of the Mann family, one of the founders of geriatrics.

1935

———————— • ————————

TO ERICH VON KAHLER

Küsnacht-Zurich
March 19, 1935

Dear Herr von Kahler:

I read your proofs to the end day before yesterday and am fascinated to the depths of my soul. The book[1] is far and away the most elevating and penetrating thing I have seen on these problems. Reading it, in fact, I had the feeling that it is precisely your characteristic fusion of Judaism and Georgian Germanism, and no other combination existing today, which establishes your right and vocation to speak validly on all this—and by "all this" I mean not only the German-Jewish question, but also the problem of Europe itself. The extended chapter on Germanism and Judaism is incontestably the truest and the psychologically keenest statement ever made on the subject—and I say that as a German with an overseas Latin admixture who in the course of time has grown more and more disgruntled with living among Germans, and who cannot wholly forgive certain generous extenuations in your estimate of them. I felt closest to you in the passages which arouse a kind of tragic cheerfulness, such as the one about "vain knowledge" of the inevitable disillusionment of a "mighty faith." In a few truly poetic lines, you make us feel the painfulness of such a symbiosis: on the one hand, the ironic mother-wit of old cosmopolitan blood, on the other hand, the credulity of a crude psyche bound to the flesh.

I hope the book does come out at last—it almost doesn't matter where anymore. Is there any chance at all for it in Germany now, after the recent threats to the Jewish publishing houses? On the other hand, I well understand that it is intended for Germany, even written with a

---

[1] *Israel unter den Völkern.* Completed at the end of 1932, it was destroyed several times by the Nazis while being set. It was finally published in Zurich in 1936.

great deal of concern for Germany, and perhaps it could come out there. But what do we really know about the situation? And what Swiss or Dutch publisher would not be delighted!

After this, there is scarcely need for my little memorandum.[2] Would you just mail the text back to me, printed matter, sometime?

I hope we shall be seeing you soon. Regards to you and your wife.

TO ANDRÉ GIDE

Küsnacht-Zurich
May 5, 1935

Dear André Gide:

Your kind letter gave me a glimpse, as through a crack, into certain preparations and conspiracies[1] of S. Fischer Verlag which rather alarm me. Your friendliness makes me very happy, and your letter will probably be the best thing that comes out of these conspiracies for me. It is enough to know personally of your good-hearted concern for me and my work; public announcement of it is by no means necessary, deeply gratifying though it would be for me if something of the sort should come out in France. That you cannot today be a contributor to a German magazine is self-evident, and rest assured, I fully understand.

On my bookshelf the splendid row of your collected writings grows steadily, and I want to thank you once again for making such a precious gift available to me. It is a lasting joy to see this life work gradually building up in such admirable outward dress. It is truly life even more than works, the condensation of a pure and proud life lived in the spirit, a trace of earthly days that "in eons can never pass away."[2]

Thank you once more my dear friend, and I hope that we shall see one another again.

TO LOUISE SERVICEN[1]

Küsnacht-Zurich
May 23, 1935

My dear Madame:

I received your friendly letter of the 16th while still in Nice, but un-

[2] An opinion that Thomas Mann had written for Bermann Fischer on *Israel unter den Völkern*. In view of the political situation, the memorandum had become unnecessary.
[1] The publisher was preparing a special issue of the *Neue Rundschau* for Thomas Mann's sixtieth birthday on June 6, and had asked André Gide for a contribution.
[2] Goethe, *Faust II*.
[1] Louise Servicen (b. 1896), Thomas Mann's French translator.

fortunately I had to neglect my correspondence there because of personal commitments. I very much hope that the following information does not arrive too late.

In Nice, too, I received the first copy of the *Histoires de Jacob*. Since then I have spent a great deal of time on the translation, and it impresses me as being of the highest quality. You seem to have overcome the difficulties of this translation with extraordinary tact, and I hope that the French public will show appropriate gratitude. I myself feel sincerely indebted to you for your dedication to this complicated and demanding task, whose difficulty I can well estimate. As a small token of appreciation I am taking the liberty of sending you my photograph, with the request that you keep it as a memento of your fine work on my book.

I am delighted to hear that Monsieur Maurice Noël plans a study on the novel for the *Figaro*. You say that he needs some information on the origins and intentions of the book. I shall have to be brief, for a reasonably complete statement of the psychological conditions from which such a work arises would lead me far afield and demand a great deal of space and time. A variety of tendencies and moods coincided to shape this strange book. Purely in terms of subject matter it has rather deep and old roots in my intellectual life, for I recall that even as a boy I had a pronounced interest in ancient Oriental, and particularly ancient Egyptian, life and read a good deal about it. My interest in religious history and religious psychology, which formed one of the motive forces for the undertaking, came later. In my youth I never dreamed of such concerns. In general I may say that with this novel I have entered a new stage of my literary life, in that I have broken with the milieu of the middle class and the individual, at least this once, and have moved over to the realm of the typical and the mythic. What really underlies the whole work is an insight into the identity of these two concepts of typicality and mythicality. Connected with that is my feeling about basic human factors, a feeling which accounts for my pleasure in the sprawling narrative. Basically it is once again, like *Buddenbrooks*, the story of a family's development; in a certain sense it is even again a story of decadence and refinement. Young Joseph, an *artistic* personality living in a religious sphere, has approximately the same relationship to his forefathers as Hanno Buddenbrook to his—except that, as I have said, in this mythic book the familial and middle-class element is lifted into the realm of general humanity. At bottom the book aspires to be, so to speak, an *abbreviated history of mankind*. The long introduction entitled *Descent into Hell* which precedes the first volume (but, of course, is not meant to be applied to that volume alone, but rather to the whole work) hints at such intentions.

The feeling for basic human factors of which I have spoken enters into the novel in still another fashion. It seems to me that the hard and turbulent experiences through which Western man, at least, has passed in recent decades have inspired a wholly new interest in man's destiny in general, in his origins, his position in the cosmos, and his future—a new *humane interest*, I should like to call it, which is not mine alone. This interest is undoubtedly stirring in many minds today and was operating in me when the narrative was conceived. If the idiosyncratic work is striking chords of sympathy, I attribute that to precisely such a meeting of emotions between myself and my contemporaries and fellow victims.

I trust that these remarks have suggested the essential motifs from which the book proceeded and is still proceeding. I hope that the critic of *Figaro* will find in them some usable psychological material. Please give Monsieur Noël my regards and express to him my appreciation for his interest. I am enclosing a postcard picture for him.

With best wishes and the hope that I shall one of these days have the opportunity to talk with you personally in Paris.

TO ALFRED NEUMANN

Küsnacht-Zurich
June 7, 1935

Dear Alfred Neumann:

What shall I say? I feel so grateful for all these good, lovingly conceived signs and symbols of your loyalty, affection, attachment. In the tempest of good wishes that has raged around me (to my confusion) for the past several days,[1] I recall your words and your thoughtful, magnificent gift with deep emotion, and thank you a thousand times. The manuscript of your great work in its luxurious binder will be a solemn and precious possession to me, and my children too will one day hold it in honor.

I can scarcely say more. The turmoil is enormous, and when I can read, let alone answer, all the mail that has come, the gods alone know. But the hundreds of letters from Germany—yes, yes, from Germany, even from labor service camps—have done my heart good, I don't deny it.

Yesterday was a jovial and festive day, spent among children and friends from morning till night. You and your dear wife were not there,

---

[1] During the celebrations for Thomas Mann's sixtieth birthday.

which saddened us, but we understood. As your thoughts were with us, ours went out to you, and your present came in for much attention when the house was full that evening. Once again thank you, my friend.

TO RENÉ SCHICKELE

Küsnacht-Zurich
June 7, 1935

Dear René Schickele:

How kind you are to think of me in friendship even while you are deep in grief over the loss of your best friend.[1] I thank you for that, but a dark shadow fell even upon our festivities here, and in the midst of the gay turmoil of yesterday our thoughts sobered repeatedly and turned toward you and Vevey. That is life's "game"; should we call it wanton or stupid? We too were attached to the man and mourn with you. . . . Your card has just come. It is a relief that your wife and Hans haven't had to leave, not to speak of you yourself, for certainly you should be spared taking on the world's work just now. My warm wishes for your health, peace, and good spirits.

Here the waves are surging high. [. . .] The children make a merry company, but in a few days they will be scattering in all directions once more, and we too are embarking on the 10th (after a visit with Annette) in Le Havre. On board the *Lafayette* I suppose I can sift through the torrent of mail that has descended, but I want you to have a word right away. Keep up your courage, dear René. We all love you, and our good wishes surround you.

TO GOTTFRIED BERMANN FISCHER

On board
Cunard White Star Berengaria
July 10, 1935

Dear Dr. Bermann:

I can send you and yours only a brief greeting on our return voyage, for in America we were kept too breathless even to think of writing, and now that I suddenly have time and repose, the ship is rolling too heavily, has been for days—it is too great a strain on the head to write under such conditions. Incidentally, I have had to accept bankruptcy as a correspondent since the birthday. With the best will in the world I could not

---

[1] Julius Meier-Graefe had died on June 5.

cope with it, in spite of the two hundred printed thank-yous which we did up on board the *Lafayette* in the sweat of our brows and mailed, of all places, in Riverside, Connecticut, where we spent a few days at the country house of the Dutch-American writer Hendrik van Loon.

Before that there was the awarding of the doctorates at Harvard University, and the audience of five or six thousand converted the ceremony into an impressive demonstration by the mighty ovation they gave us two Germans, Einstein and myself.

I heard that the choice of us—of me in particular—did not come about without some influence on the part of President Roosevelt. He invited my wife and myself privately, without involving the ambassador, of course, to the White House in Washington. We traveled there from New York by airplane in one hour and twenty minutes. It was my first flight, a technical adventure, not very significant otherwise, except for a stretch above illuminated clouds, with a view like that from the Rigi. Washington is an astonishingly beautiful, representative city, but at this season is afflicted by a completely tropical, enervating damp heat. [. . .]

After this expedition came several days in New York, which also has its points. Now we are once again nearing the old Continent; day after tomorrow, very early in the morning, we shall be in Cherbourg and mean to travel straight through to Zurich, since my wife's aged parents will be there to celebrate her mother's eightieth birthday.

It will be good to be back home, to return to normality and to work. Only at Riverside, in the country, was I able to push my chapter on a little. I left Zurich reluctantly after the 6th. I would rather have let the pleasant excitement of the birthday gently subside. I thought it better not to take your casket[1] with me and scarcely had a chance to study the contents. That, too, is something I must make up for now. But I read your own handsome words at once, and I thank you again for them, and for everything you did, including your coming personally to the celebration —which all in all gave me so much to be grateful for. I have already said that the accents in which the world saw fit to speak to me this time were quite different from those I heard at my fiftieth birthday, or at the time of the Nobel Prize. Since I am blessed with some imagination, as well as modesty, I could not help being tremendously moved, and I can only hope that posterity will partially agree with the opinion of the present.

Well, this has turned into a kind of letter after all. I hope to be seeing you before too long.

---

[1] The casket contained congratulations from a number of important writers and was presented to Mann as a birthday gift.

1935

TO RENÉ SCHICKELE

Küsnacht-Zurich
July 25, 1935

Dear Schickele:

I'm horrified to learn that you have had to suffer so much—among all disagreeable things, that kind of blood poisoning must be the worst. It reminds me of Mahler, who had streptococci, and when Bruno Walter asked whether he was in great pain replied with a groan: "No, not pain, but it is so *unpleasant.*" Unpleasantness intensified seems to me the worst thing of all. But I hear that you are also in pain, especially now as the disease recedes with suppuration. May you get well quickly! St. Cyr and the sea will do their part, I am sure. It was very clever and energetic of you to endure the ride there. Moreover, I imagine the life of your small community of fellow patients is not without its attractions. Certainly it would not be bad to be one of your party.

My life has scarcely been tranquil lately. Have I written you about the travels which began immediately after the unexpected hubbub at the beginning of June? If I did not, I would have liked to. But my bankruptcy as a correspondent is total. America, for which I set out reluctantly, was impressive after all. When Einstein and I received honorary doctorates at Harvard, the huge audience created a demonstration with their prolonged applause, which I trust was heard far away. For that reason alone it is good that I didn't cross up the university's well-thought-out plans by refusing to go. Incidentally, I've heard that the President had some share in the choices. And indeed he gave us a very friendly invitation to visit him, and we had an interesting private dinner at the White House with him and Mrs. Roosevelt (as a meal, very bad). He impressed me. Completely paralyzed for ten years, and yet this energy and experimental, not to say revolutionary, boldness. He has made enemies among the rich, whom he hurts, and among the guardians of the Constitution because of his dictatorial traits. But can one raise much objection nowadays to an *enlightened* dictatorship? It's true that he spoke rather contemptuously of the Congress, made fun of the French habit of overthrowing governments, and boasted of his own position in comparison: "I am Prime Minister and President at the same time and before four years [are up] they can't get me out."[1] Followed by a broad American smile. But he is a very cultivated person.

---

[1] Roosevelt's remark quoted in English in the original letter.

We spent a week in the country, at Riverside on the Sound, in the home of a Dutch-American writer, Hendrik van Loon, and there I actually worked a little. The third volume is indescribably difficult. I am now launched on a grand scene between Potiphar and his wife; Klaus commented that it had something of Proust. But then I must once again rework and compress the beginning of the volume; the approach is wrong there. Have a quick recovery, dear Schickele. My wife was overjoyed and moved by all your letters.

TO HARRY SLOCHOWER [1]

Küsnacht-Zurich
September 1, 1935

Dear Mr. Slochower:

I am embarrassed that I have kept your manuscript so long and must ask your forbearance. [. . .] I have studied the extensive chapter from *Three Ways of Modern Man* with understandable interest. My impression is that the entire book will be an extremely interesting analysis of the situation of modern man, and I am proud that my work could be of service to you in defining that situation. It is naturally rather stirring for a writer to see himself integrated in this way into a critique of our times and their evolution, and your intelligent and knowledgeable approach has given me real pleasure.

There is, however, one element in your characterization of my life work which takes me aback and, I must admit, even saddens me. That is your notion of a certain liberal wavering and indecisiveness in my thinking. As you see, I have in mind the last pages of your paper, where this view emerges most bluntly. There you attributed to me a kind of liberalism incapable of defying irrationality and anti-intellectuality, and a certain misuse is made of statements taken from "Goethe and Tolstoy." It never occurred to me that the ironic reserve which I speak of there, my dislike for any rash choice in favor of nature or intellectuality, could be viewed as liberalistic anemia and weakness. In those passages my thought was focused on the idea of humanity itself as I understand it; namely, the idea that the essence of man simultaneously embraces nature and mind and is only completed in both. What I stand for is the idea of balance, which determines what I may call my tactical partisanship and my

---

[1] Harry Slochower (b. 1900), American literary critic and psychoanalyst, author of *Three Ways of Modern Man*, *Thomas Mann's Joseph Story*, *No Voice Is Wholly Lost*, etc., editor of *American Imago*.

position on the problems of the times. For about a decade I have struck a strongly rationalistic and idealistic note in my essays and cultural criticism; but I arrived at this attitude only under pressure of the irrationalism and political antihumanism which has been spreading throughout Europe, and especially in Germany, making a mockery of humanistic balance. Do you recall Antigone? This maiden initially honors equally both kinds of divinity, the chthonic and the Olympian gods; but her antagonist Creon's shallow overestimation of the powers above leads her to exaggerate her reverence for the powers of Hades. The case with me is the reverse, and nevertheless related. But it is significant that my rationalistic, idealistic humanism is expressed almost exclusively in my critical essays and polemical pieces, scarcely at all in my creative work—in which my original disposition, which requires balance in the human realm, is brought out with far greater purity.

Almost alone among German writers, I have with all my might assailed the forces that have been emerging in Germany for years and have now attained absolute power, and my present exile, half voluntary, half involuntary, simply represents the outcome of that struggle. I have sacrificed two thirds of my worldly possessions in order to be able to live in freedom outside the German frontiers. And even without engaging in furious polemics against the Third Reich, by being outside I am perpetually demonstrating against what is being done in Germany and to Germany today. It has seemed to me worthwhile to remain in contact with my German public, which by character and culture is in opposition to Hitler's system today and from which someday the countermovement against it can emerge. This contact would be immediately destroyed—that is, my books, which the Germans can still read, would have been banned at once—if I had drawn my sword more plainly than I have in any case done in my statements of recent years. To conclude from this deliberate and carefully considered reserve and self-restraint that I lack the moral capacity to call baseness base and to abominate abominations signifies a critical offense which, coming from so congenial a mind as yours otherwise is, has saddened me.

I had to say this, and I do so in the hope that you may yet decide on some slight revision of your book. It would be for the sake of truth, for I certainly am not asking you to spare my real weaknesses.

Once more, I am sincerely delighted with the whole work and send you my best wishes for its happy completion. With many regards and the hope that I may meet you again.

1935

TO RENÉ SCHICKELE

Küsnacht-Zurich
October 31, 1935

Dear Schickele:

In thanks for your good letter I am enclosing a memo which I recently sent to the Peace Prize Committee in Oslo and which may amuse you.[1] Much more than this I cannot manage at the moment—I am thoroughly done in by a gastric attack which probably (one seeks the most innocuous reasons) has been precipitated by the disagreeable *föhns* and storms of the past several days. This indisposition does not diminish my pleasure at your continuing recovery, which is so charmingly indicated by your lively letter. Keep it up! The man who wrote those two pages already has an appetite for work and will soon be scudding along under full sail again.

Travel? Aside from the outing to Salzburg, which was pure amusement and festivity, we have done nothing since the visit to America, except for short Swiss trips from city to city. It was delightful to witness the tremendous success of the Salzburg season—politically delightful, for the vexation over it in Germany was enormous and the *Völkischer Beobachter*[2] asserted that the Austrian government chartered 300 automobiles and had them driven around with foreign license plates. Nothing of the kind. Austria, not only Salzburg, really had a wonderful season; a good thing, too. The fact is that everything smacking of happiness and prosperity immediately hurts Nazism. It has to be night where Hitler's stars shine. We went to *Faust, Fidelio, Don Giovanni, Falstaff*, and two concerts. Everyone was astonished at our youthful stamina. The best of all was *Fidelio*, under Toscanini and with Lotte Lehmann. People have a feeling for that opera now, and we all agreed that it would be perfect as the festival opera for a certain day.[3] I also read in the Mozarteum, something from my third volume—a death. Deaths happen to be one of my strong points. But since that sort of thing is not in the cards every day, I am making only slow progress, although it is always progress. A long conversation between Potiphar and his wife, a somewhat uncanny scene, is to appear in the December issue of the *Neue Rundschau*. At the moment the poor lady has a great deal to suffer; psychologically she seems to be slightly influenced by Proust, whom I find suddenly fascinating.

---

[1] Mann's memo urged that Carl von Ossietzky be given the Peace Prize. The former editor of the *Weltbühne*, afterwards martyred in a German concentration camp, did receive the 1935 Peace Prize.

[2] The official Nazi Party newspaper.

[3] Mann means the day of Hitler's overthrow.

He has a fantastic leisureliness which astonishes and attracts me. And things like "my grandmother's death" in *The Guermantes Way* with the leeches in her hair are really unforgettable.

All honor to France, but I do not share your opinion of England and the Abyssinian affair. The English, whatever mistakes they commit and however much classical cant they may spout (the leopard cannot change his spots), were ready to overthrow Mussolini and do away with Fascism, which would have been a great thing—indeed, the main thing. The Berliners already wanted to have no more to do with Fascism. If Fascism remains unshaken in Europe, only Laval[4] is to blame. He is a thoroughly noisome creature, an incipient Fascist, who is negotiating with Berlin and now has even issued an ordinance for the protection of foreign heads of state and government chiefs. For my part I hail old Churchill and his golden words in the *Strand Magazine*. A pure gleam of light.

I have the highest admiration for Heinrich's novel.[5] Unquestionably it is great literature, and I do not think Europe has anything better to offer today, to say nothing of the towering heights to which mediocrity has risen within Germany. Writing to Heinrich, I too have remarked that his frequent pointing up of contemporary parallels to historical situations verges on journalism. But after all, why not? One feels rather pitiable and at any rate much too "German" when one acts as the preserver of Pure Literature. Besides, there is no lack of the literary element in his novel; I am thinking not only of the chapter "Death and the Nursemaid," but also of the pervasive wisdom, irony, moral beauty, and straightforwardness of the book. It moves me as the synthesis of all the gifts of the author, as a magnificent personal summation of his late and early thought, and also as the intellectual summation of the epoch from Montaigne to Goethe (see the little *Faust* quotations scattered throughout). The conjunction of the German and the French spirit is nothing less than the Faustian spirit of Germany and Greece; in essence these two spirits are perhaps the same. And the *moralités*, which Bertaux declares are written in classical French, could be amply justified as homage to that beloved realm to which he owes the greater part of his education, and which should show him a certain gratitude, too. By rights he should long ago have received the Legion of Honor, not just the ribbon, the

---

[4] Pierre Laval (1883–1945), French politician; 1934–6 Foreign Minister, in which capacity he frustrated the sanctions imposed on Italy by the League of Nations because of the Italian attack on Ethiopia. After serving under Pétain in 1940, Laval was French Premier after 1942. In 1945 he was condemned to death and executed for collaboration with the Germans.

[5] Heinrich Mann's *The Youth of King Henry IV*.

rosette, instead of having to do battle like an ordinary exile with the Nice government offices—to which, just to make things more difficult, he unfortunately also sends his mistress.

Now you see, something like a letter has emerged after all! Please send the carbon copy of my memo back at your convenience, give my regards to your wife and child, and keep a friendly thought for

Your   Thomas Mann

TO ALFRED KNOPF

Küsnacht-Zurich
November 8, 1935

Dear Alfred:

It is some time since we have heard from one another, but our thoughts often cross the ocean to you and we remember the time we spent together. Quite some time has also passed since we saw Blanche[1] in Salzburg. Those were glorious impressions, especially the *Fidelio* (with Toscanini conducting; I don't know whether Blanche heard him). Today there is something particularly stirring about the humanity of this work, and we all agreed that *Fidelio* is virtually made to be the festival opera for the day of liberation from the second-rate Pizarros under whom we now groan.

At the moment we have the majority of our children with us—five, to be exact. Erika is preparing for a Swiss guest tour of *The Peppermill*, and Klaus (whose *Tschaikowsky* is having a considerable, and I feel deserved, success) is busy with preliminary work on a new novel. Golo will shortly assume his new professorship in Rennes in Brittany, and the two youngest live for their music.

I have a problem of literary business to discuss with you. Recently I once again read aloud a chapter from the third Joseph novel, *Joseph in Egypt*, and the occasion prompted me to do something which I have so far avoided out of timidity: calculate what manuscript page I have arrived at. It is the *six hundredth*! This is something of a disaster, for I am not much beyond the middle of the narrative, and it's obvious that in bulk this third novel will equal the first two put together. Because of the sheer number of pages, its appearance in a single volume will probably be impossible, and the question now arises whether, since the principle of

---

[1] Wife of Alfred A. Knopf and associated with him in directing the publishing house from its founding in 1915 until her death in 1966.

successive publication is already established, we ought not to bring out the first part of this third novel in the near future, perhaps in spring. I am speaking, of course, of the German edition; the American editon could still wait some time, in keeping with the later publication of *Young Joseph*. Right now I only wanted to hear your general opinion on the matter. Is it or is it not advisable to divide up this final novel? As far as substance goes, I think the first half can stand on its own, and the public, which would otherwise have to wait quite a long time, would get a kind of installment payment and find it easier to purchase the entire work, since this could be done in stages. There is also a natural break in the material, since the first part of the third novel could conclude with the disastrous outcome of the love story in Potiphar's house. These are the arguments *for* successive publication. Against it, of course, is a certain weakening of the momentary effectiveness, which naturally would be stronger if we waited patiently and brought out the entire work at once. As far as America is concerned, we must also consider that publication of the collected stories is planned for next year, so that a new Joseph volume alongside it might be too much. In any case, I would be very interested to hear what you and your wife think about this question, which naturally concerns me deeply.

Enough for today; many regards from house to house.

TO RENÉ SCHICKELE

Küsnacht-Zurich
December 16, 1935

Dear Schickele:

I want to thank you at once for your friendly letter. "Letters into the Darkness" is a beautiful title—may I make a note of it?

The Hamsun case, or shall I say Hamsun's decline, has upset me too. What incomprehensible crudity! By this beastly step[1] he has certainly damaged his reputation both with his contemporaries and with posterity. His sympathy for the regime may be partly caused by his confounding it with Germany in general, for like all great Scandinavians he is deeply indebted to Germany. But besides that, we know quite well what kind of political ideology has always attracted him, with his apostate's attitude toward liberalism. In his *Mysteries* long ago he mocked Gladstone and

---

[1] Knut Hamsun, the great Norwegian writer and Nobel Prize winner, in 1935 joined Quisling's National Socialist Party of Norway.

said that Victor Hugo's pen resembled "a ham dripping flaming red drops"—a bad image, an ugly image, and stupid to boot. After all, Hamsun's art too was strongly influenced by Paris; but later he began to introduce peasant blood-and-soil, antiliterary, anticivilization elements; and today he has arrived at comradeship with the Nazis. I was much tempted to write him, for he has always been friendly to me and even congratulated me on my birthday. I thought I owed him a warning; but it would lead too far; I have given up the idea, and it reassures me that, as you say, comments in his own country have been keeping his ears burning.

The review of *Henri IV* was a typical prank on the part of the "Züri Zittig";[2] it fitted the newspaper only too well. You have guessed the author of the review almost to a hair, except that it is not the father, Hermann Kesser, but his silly son Armin. He was on good terms with my son Klaus and we have even had him to our house, but I have written Herr Korrodi[3] that after this performance I no longer wish to see the young man.

I feel touched that you promptly read the chapter in the *Rundschau*. I have about made up my mind to publish a new volume in the spring. It will not take the book to its conclusion, but goes as far as Joseph's stay in Egypt up to the disaster with Potiphar's wife and the second descent into the pit. It has turned out that the Egyptian novel cannot be compressed into one volume, and since the new batch is substantial enough to stand alone, I shall offer an installment payment and thus gain more peace for the final section.

Bermann had just left when your letter arrived. He was negotiating and making efforts to obtain the work permit, but there are difficulties, here as well as in Berlin. For the form that the sale will take can be predicted; he alone still has illusions. I had not thought of Strasbourg. But if he established himself there of all places, wouldn't it involve absolute loss of the German market that he is still counting on? Anyhow, I shall suggest it to him. Lately he has been thinking seriously about Vienna, in view of the obstacles he has been encountering here. I suppose the clerical mustiness is better than the National Socialist pestilence, but who can say how long Vienna can hold out?

Greetings to you and yours from me and mine.

[2] Nickname of the *Neue Zürcher Zeitung*.
[3] Eduard Korrodi (1885–1955), Swiss literary historian and critic. From 1914 to 1950 he was feature editor of the *Neue Zürcher Zeitung*.

TO ANDRÉ GIDE

Küsnacht-Zurich
December 21, 1935

Cher André Gide:

Je viens de terminer vos *Nouvelles nourritures* et je suis incapable de vous dire, combien j'admire cette petite merveille de livre qui ressemble à une cassette de bijoux. Vous n'étiez jamais, dans un de vos ouvrages principaux, plus grand et plus aimable que dans ce petit. "C'est votre coeur qui se raconte" ici—un coeur grand, tendre et sage, souffrant et gai en même temps. Il y a tant de poésie dans ce petit volume, une gratitude douloureuse vers la vie, une bonté plaisantante qui est d'une extraordinaire profoundeur humaine. Nous nous amusons souvent, à table, en famille, sur cette mère qui trouve son enfant "insupportable" et à qui vous répondez: "Ah! Madame, pas tant que vous." Et quelle belle et forte simplicité dans les conseils moraux de la dernière page! Ce serait quelque chose pour nos jeunes gens!—Je sens bien que je m'exprime très mal. Mais en lisant j'etais saisi de l'ambition de vous rendre grâce dans la langue de ce charmant livre.[1]

---

[1] I have just finished your *Nouvelles nourritures* and cannot tell you how much I admire this little marvel of a book, which is like a jewel box. In your major works you have never been greater and more endearing than you are in this little one. "It is your heart that speaks" here—a great heart, at once compassionate and wise, suffering and gay. There is much poetry in this little book, a melancholy gratitude toward life, a bantering kindness in which there is an extraordinary depth of humanity. Around our family table we often joke about that mother who finds her child "insufferable" and to whom you reply: "Ah, Madame, not as much as you are." And what fine and strong simplicity there is in the moral counsels on the last page. That would be something for our young people. I feel that I am expressing myself very badly. But while I was reading, the ambition seized me to thank you in the language of this charming book.

1936

————————•————————

TO EDUARD KORRODI [1]

Küsnacht-Zurich
February 3, 1936

Dear Dr. Korrodi:

Your article, "German Literature in the Exile's Mirror," which appeared in the Second Sunday Edition of the *Neue Zürcher Zeitung* of January 26 has been much noticed, much discussed, and much quoted—not to say exploited—by the press of various political opinions. Moreover, there was a connection, though a rather loose one, between it and the statement which a few friends and I issued in behalf of our old literary home, the S. Fischer Publishing House. May I therefore now make a few comments, perhaps even raise a few objections?

You are right; it was a distinct polemical error on the part of the editor of the *Neue Tagebuch* to assert that all or virtually all of contemporary literature has left Germany, or as he puts it, "has transferred abroad." I fully understand that such an exaggeration would arouse the ire of a neutral such as yourself. Leopold Schwarzschild is a brilliant political publicist, a good hater, a forceful stylist; but literature is not his field, and I suspect that he—perhaps rightly—regards the current political struggle as far more important, honorable, and decisive than all the realms of gold. In any case, his statement demonstrated a lack of knowledge of the field and a lack of artistic fairness which provoked you as a literary critic to object, and the fact that some of the writers you named are still inside Germany indubitably refutes him.

It remains to be asked, however, whether some of these writers would not prefer to be outside if it were possible. I do not want to call anyone to the Gestapo's attention, but in many cases purely mechanical rather than

---

[1] This was published as an Open Letter in the *Neue Zürcher Zeitung* and led directly to Thomas Mann's "expatriation" by the Nazi authorities.

intellectual reasons may be decisive, and thus the boundary between exiled and nonexiled German literature is not so easy to draw; it does not coincide so precisely with the boundaries of the Reich. It seems to me that the German writers living outside those boundaries should not indiscriminately look down on those who have chosen or have had to remain at home. The exiles should not tie their artistic judgments to the question of "inside" or "outside." They are suffering, but there is suffering inside as well; and they ought to guard against that self-righteousness which is often a product of suffering. Let them be more charitable also to colleagues whose belief in Europeanism and conception of Germanism have prompted them to renounce home and country, prestige and property; who have ignored broad hints that they would be welcomed back and their transgressions overlooked for the sake of their incomprehensible but after all existing world reputations; who have remained where they were, preferring to wait out the zenith and nadir of the Third Reich in freedom; but who still, whether the present German regime is to hold on or to pass away, do not wish to destroy all bridges to their country and all possibility of their influencing it. Let the exiled writers refrain from instantly denouncing such a colleague as a scoundrel and renegade as soon as he disagrees with them about the relocation of German intellectual life, perhaps for good reasons they cannot fully see.

But enough of that. It is impossible to equate exile with German literature if only because Austrian and Swiss writing also belong to German literature. Of living men writing in German, two are especially dear to me personally: Hermann Hesse and Franz Werfel, both of whom are poets as well as novelists. They are not exiles, for the one is Swiss, the other a Czech Jew. But neutrality remains a difficult art even for people who have such long practice in it as you Swiss! How easily the neutral, in combating one injustice, falls into another. The moment that you raise objections to the identification of exile literature with the whole of German literature, you yourself set up an untenable equation. For, curiously, it is not the error itself that angers you, but the fact that a Jewish writer commits it; and even as you conclude from this fact that once again literature of Jewish origin is being confounded with German literature (the old complaint of the Fatherland fanatics), you yourself confound exile with Jewish literature.

Must I say that this will not do? My brother Heinrich and I are not Jews. Nor are Leonhard Frank,[2] René Schickele, the soldier Fritz von

---

[2] Leonhard Frank (1882–1961), novelist, short story writer, playwright, early expressionist. An ardent pacifist, Frank went into voluntary exile in 1933. He remained

Unruh,[3] that authentic Bavarian Oskar Maria Graf,[4] Annette Kolb, A. M. Frey, or talented younger writers such as Gustav Regler,[5] Bernhard von Brentano,[6] and Ernst Glaeser.[7]

It is in the nature of things that the Jewish contingent should be numerically strong in the exile movement; that fact follows both from the sweeping nature of National Socialist racial philosophy and from the revulsion which the Jewish spirit feels for certain state institutions of our times. But my list of writers (which I would never have thought of compiling of my own accord and which does not pretend to be complete, any more than yours does) shows that one cannot speak of the literary exiles as being even predominantly Jewish.

I add to it the names of Bertolt Brecht[8] and Johannes R. Becher,[9]

in the United States until 1950, then returned to Germany. Many of his works have appeared in English: *The Cause of Crime, The Robber Band, Carl and Anna, Brother and Sister, In the Last Coach and Other Stories.*

[3] Fritz von Unruh (b. 1885), writer, most notably of historical dramas. Scion of an old Prussian family of army officers, Unruh's experiences in the First World War made him an active pacifist. He emigrated to France in 1932, to America in 1940. Among his works: *Ein Geschlecht; Louis Ferdinand, Prinz von Preussen; Opfergang; The End Is Not Yet; Der Sohn des Generals.*

[4] Oskar Maria Graf (1894–1967), novelist. Though deeply rooted in the Bavarian peasantry, Graf became a revolutionary toward the end of the First World War and joined the Munich rebels around Kurt Eisner. Emigrated to the United States in 1933. He is noted for his humorous and robust peasant stories and his autobiographical novel, *Prisoners All.*

[5] Gustav Regler (b. 1898), novelist and short story writer. His life of adventure and constant political metamorphoses carried him from Jesuitism to Communism and halfway back. Emigrated in 1933, fought in the International Brigade in the Spanish Civil War, fled to Mexico after the collapse of the Spanish republic. His early novel *Der Sohn* was something of a sensation. Later books: *Aretino*, and his autobiography, *Das Ohr des Malchus.*

[6] Bernhard von Brentano (b. 1901), novelist and essayist. Emigrated to Switzerland in 1933. Among his works: *Theodor Chindler, Franziska Scheler, Die Schwestern Usedom*, novels; *Du Land der Liebe*, autobiography.

[7] Ernst Glaeser (b. 1902), novelist and journalist. Best known for his novel of the First World War, *Jahrgang 1902*, and its less successful sequel *Frieden*. Although he went into voluntary exile in Switzerland in 1933, Glaeser returned to Germany in 1939 and subsequently became editor of the military newspaper *Adler im Süden.*

[8] Bertolt Brecht (1898–1956), playwright, novelist, poet, director, songwriter. Beginning as an expressionist with anarchistic political views, Brecht soon became convinced of the absolute correctness of Marxist doctrine. Without ever entering the Communist Party, he wrote Communist didactic plays and verses. In 1933 he emigrated to Denmark and Sweden, then went to the United States; in 1945 he returned home and became head of the German Theater in East Berlin. He is regarded as one of the foremost German writers of the twentieth century.

[9] Johannes R. Becher (1891–1958), poet and playwright. His early development closely resembled that of Brecht. A youthful expressionist, he later placed his talents completely at the service of the Communist Party. In 1933 he emigrated first to France, then to Moscow, where from 1935 to 1945 he edited the German edition of *International Literature*. He returned to Germany after the war and served from 1954 until his death as Minister of Culture in the German Democratic Republic (East Germany).

who are poets, because you say that you cannot name a single emigrant poet. How can you make such a statement, since I know that you regard Else Lasker-Schüler[10] as a true poet? You say that those who have emigrated are chiefly in the "novel industry," along with "a few novelists of real creative talent." Well, industry implies industriousness, and certainly uprooted people, who are everywhere barely tolerated by an economically fearful and distinctly ungenerous world, must be industrious if they are to earn their bread. It would be harsh indeed to find fault with them for that. But it is harsh enough to ask them whether they imagine that they represent the national wealth of German literature. Truly, it occurs to none of us, neither the industrialists nor the creators, to think so.

Of course there is a historical treasury of German national literature which is precious to all of us. And I grant that little of what is produced today will be considered worth including in that treasury. In comparison with earlier ages, many current works, the products of living human beings, may be unimpressive. This is true everywhere in the world. But again, as throughout the world, the *novel* plays a special and indeed a dominant part in German writing today—a part to which you are not entirely just when you say that it is not poetry but at best prose, the novel, which has emigrated. This in itself would not be surprising. Pure poetry—"pure" insofar as it holds itself handsomely aloof from social and political problems (which, by the way, poetry has not always done)—is governed by different laws from those of the modern prose epic. The novel, because of its analytical spirit, its consciousness, its innate critical attitude, is forced to flee social and political conditions in which poetry may continue to flower quietly on the fringes, undisturbed and sweetly oblivious of the world. But these very prosaic qualities of consciousness and critical attitude, along with the wealth of means at the novel's disposal—its free and flexible control of creation and investigation, music and knowledge, myth and science, its human scope, its objectivity and irony—make it what it has become in our stage of history: the representative and dominant form of literature. Compared with the novel, drama and poetry are archaic genres. It takes the lead everywhere in both Europe and America. It has done so for some time in Germany; and therefore, my dear sir, your statement that the novel has emigrated was somewhat incautious. If this were true—and you are saying it, not I— then the political commentator Schwarzschild would surprisingly prove to have been right and you, the literary critic, wrong; for it would mean

[10] Else Lasker-Schüler (1876–1945), poet and playwright. She emigrated to Switzerland in 1933 and to Palestine in 1936.

that the principal branch of German literary life has been transferred abroad.

Recently, in connection with the Karlweis[11] biography of Wassermann, you discussed the process of Europeanization of the German novel with your customary perceptiveness and subtlety. You spoke of the change in the type of German novelist wrought by such gifted writers as Jakob Wassermann, and you remarked that by virtue of the international qualities of Jews the German novel had become international. But look here: my brother and I have had as much share in this "change," this "internationalization," as Wassermann, and we are not Jews. Perhaps it was the drop of Latin blood (and Swiss blood from our grandmother) which enabled us to do that. The "international" qualities of Jews are nothing more nor less than their Mediterranean-European qualities. And these are at the same time *German*; without them, Germanism would not be Germanism, but a totally useless sluggishness. That is precisely what the Catholic Church—which today is in straits that make her revered once again even by a product of Protestant culture—is defending inside Germany when she declares that only after the Germans accepted Christianity did they enter the company of civilized nations. Being *völkisch* is not being German. But the Germans', or the German rulers', hatred of the Jews is in the higher sense not directed toward the Jews at all, or not toward them alone: it is directed against Europe and all loftier Germanism; it is directed, as becomes increasingly apparent, against the Christian and classical foundations of Western morality. It is the attempt (symbolized by the withdrawal from the League of Nations) to shake off the ties of civilization. That attempt threatens to bring about a terrible alienation, fraught with evil potentialities, between the land of Goethe and the rest of the world.

Countless human, moral, and aesthetic observations support my profound conviction that nothing good can possibly come of the present German regime, not for Germany and not for the world. This conviction has made me shun the country in whose spiritual traditions I am more deeply rooted than the present rulers who for three years have vacillated, not quite daring to deny me my Germanism before the eyes of the world. And I am certain down to the bottom of my conscience that I have acted rightly in the eyes of my contemporaries and posterity to join with those to whom the words of a truly noble German poet apply:[12]

[11] Marta Karlweis (b. 1889), maiden name of Martha Wassermann, writer and psychoanalyst; Jakob Wassermann's second wife.
[12] August von Platen.

But one who baseness in his heart despises
From hearth and home by baseness will be banned
Whenever a servile nation baseness prizes.
Far wiser to renounce the Fatherland
Than to endure in all its childish guises
Blind hatred and the rabble's heavy hand.

TO HERMANN HESSE

Küsnacht-Zurich
February 9, 1936

Dear friend Hesse:

Don't be distressed by my action. Consider the great difference between your situation and mine. That difference has existed from the start and has assured you freedom, perspective, immunity. Sooner or later I had to declare myself in clear language, both for the sake of the world, in which a good many highly ambiguous, half-and-half notions of my relationship to the Third Reich prevail, and for my own sake as well. Something of the sort has been a psychic necessity to me for a long time. After Korrodi's nasty trick of using my name to attack the exiles, I owed them some compensation, a profession of solidarity. The torrent of letters shows that I have warmed the hearts of many sufferers. I have also demonstrated to many neutrals that there are such things as character and conviction. Some regret my decision along with you, and in the same sense that you do. But I believe I did the right thing at the right moment, "and feel better ever since," as the song has it. Moreover, I am not even sure yet that the ruling gang will strike back. The Olympics, as well as considerations of foreign policy, will hinder them, and I think it quite possible that nothing at all will happen—although I shall never recover my property, of course. On the other hand, I may well be expatriated and my books banned. But if that should happen, I can at least tell myself that either there will be war, or else within a few years the situation inside Germany will change so that my books may once again be distributed.

I never thought of my action as a parting of our ways; otherwise I would not have taken it, or at any rate it would have been considerably harder for me. Now that the letter is written, my attitude remains exactly the same as before. I shall continue to do my work and leave it to time to verify my prediction (which has been very belated) that nothing good can come out of National Socialism. But my conscience would not be at ease toward my own age if I had left this unsaid.

Cordially and faithfully,

1936

TO RENÉ SCHICKELE

Küsnacht-Zurich
February 19, 1936

Dear Schickele:

Just a short note. I must manage to finish the final part of my new book, the adventure between Joseph and Potiphar's wife, which in a literary sense is quite an adventure in small—as the whole book is an adventure. In addition, my remarks in the *Neue Zürcher Zeitung* have caused an enormously swollen correspondence. So please bear with me.

The point is simply this: I was taking my chances and was aware of the probable consequences. I was not afraid of them. Only afterwards did I learn that they might be regarded as improbable, for Valeriu Marcu[1] is not the only one who assumes there will be no repercussions. I have heard this opinion frequently in the past several weeks, especially from Germans who called here and were utterly delighted about my letter. It was certainly not a wise move, in the sense that it puts an end forever to any hope that my money and property might be released or a passport granted. I'll simply have to wait and see what more happens. Bermann, who has just been here, maintains that my books will certainly be banned immediately, even if I am not officially expatriated. Very well; I simply do not believe that it will be for long. Sooner or later I had to speak out, and I chose a moment when someone was insidiously attempting to draw a line between me and the exiles, and with the feeling moreover that unpleasant half-and-half notions of my relations to the Third Reich prevail in some parts of the world. But in addition, simply from inner, psychic reasons. It was in good part a temperamental act, a natural reaction to all the insults and outrages that daily come raining down upon us all. It was also the real and deep conviction that this mischief will mean the doom of the whole continent if it continues, and that I must oppose it here and now, so far as my feeble strength permits, as I have already opposed it at home. But in saying all this I'm not telling you anything new. [. . .]

Everyone from Germany whom I speak to seems to feel that the National Socialist adventure is in its final stage and that general disintegration is at hand. But no one knows what will come; people who report

---

[1] Valeriu Marcu (1899–1942), a writer of popular historical works. Emigrated to Southern France in 1933, then to the United States. Author of biographies of Lenin and Scharnhorst, *The Expulsion of the Jews from Spain, Accent on Power: The Life and Times of Machiavelli.*

these things are themselves constantly changing their theories, and a good deal of what they say may be mere wish-fulfillment. Such wishes, however, are gradually becoming general and no doubt must ultimately produce some changes. I tell myself that either the war will come in a year and a half or two years, or conditions within this period will change so much that our books, too, will again be permitted in Germany.

But that's enough for today. My wife will be writing your wife shortly. Warm regards, and our best wishes for your health and your work. It would be good to see each other again. But unfortunately we're not likely to go to Nice for quite a while. We are toying with various fantastic travel plans and are making half-to-whole arrangements even for visiting Argentina and Russia.

TO HEINRICH MANN

Küsnacht-Zurich
July 2, 1936

Dear Heinrich:

Thanks for your card. It must be lovely up there, and I hope you are thoroughly enjoying your hard-earned rest. I myself have unfortunately taken too much time off, not for rest but for distraction. Our last trip to Budapest and Vienna was great fun, especially the stay in Budapest, with the sessions of the "Coopération,"[1] the Freud lecture, a second lecture in the Inner City Theater, and much gala opera and banqueting. The Hungarian government took pains to show itself as civilized, but we refused the invitations from government ministers which arrived in spite of our staying with Hatvany.[2] The prettiest touch was that the German ambassador telephoned the Minister of the Interior to ask that the press pay less attention to me. For I had delivered a speech at the Coopération on "militant humanism" which was much talked about. Everyone ignored his request. But isn't it delightful to think of the German ambassador protesting against publicity given to the only German participant in a meeting of European intellectuals?

Festivities went on much the same in Vienna for a while. After my reading, we went to hear *Tristan* under Walter, arriving in time for the

[1] Comité International pour la Coopération Intellectuelle.
[2] Lajos Hatvany (1880–1961), Hungarian writer who also published in German. A leader of the Radical Party after the First World War, he fled from the Fascistic Horthy regime, suffered acutely from homesickness, and returned only to be jailed. After his release he fled again, this time from Hitler. He lived in Oxford, returning to Budapest after the war.

third act and entering a vile-smelling house. The Nazis had thrown stink bombs, but the performance was continued—ultimately with just the orchestra, for the Isolde, who had thrown up throughout the intermission, made only a lovely gesture of incapacity and did not rise from Tristan's corpse. Incidentally, the same thing had been done punctually to the minute in the Burgtheater and three cinemas—a blow against the summer festival. That, too, is an experience worth having; now at least I know exactly what Nazism smells like: sweaty feet to a high power.

Now I must pay for the holiday by taking up my neglected affairs. *Joseph in Egypt*, which is to be published in Vienna in October and is already being printed, is not yet finished, and I am very much afraid of getting into a jam with it. Just a few final important chapters must be done, and tired as I am, I doubt whether I can manage them this month. But I simply have to. Afterwards I shall badly need a rest and have been considering Majorca, which our eldest children visited not long ago and strongly recommend. What do you think about it? Toward the autumn it might well be nicest.

For France one can feel only love and admiration.

The response of the respectable world press [. . .] toward such events is unspeakably base. As for the German press, it of course revels in hopes of general collapse.

Warmly,   T.

TO MR. KOLTSOV [1]

August 1, 1936

My dear Mr. Koltsov:

I have learned from German friends and fellow exiles of an occurrence in Russia which causes them the deepest concern and which I myself find hard to believe. May I ask you to give me information about it?

It concerns the widow of the German writer Erich Mühsam, who was killed in a German concentration camp. His wife stayed in Prague for a while and then went on to Russia, where she has been imprisoned for "anarchistic" statements—statements which, it seems, were made before she ever came there.

You will understand my astonishment at this news. For decades Frau Mühsam was married to an intellectual who held anarchistic ideas, ideas that I do not mean to discuss here, and that at best inspire sympathy

---

[1] Chairman of the League of Russian Writers.

in me only to the extent that the man suffered martyrdom and death for them in Hitler's Germany. It seems quite natural that his wife lived in her husband's intellectual atmosphere and spoke the same political language. But it would also be natural to think that a harried fugitive, who for years had to look on at the sufferings that Hitler's henchmen inflicted upon her husband, and who finally witnessed his cruel death at their hands, would be met with sympathy and kindness and would be honored when she sought refuge in the new Russia. I do not know Frau Mühsam; from what I have heard about her she is a native of Munich with deep roots in the populace, with no intellectual pretensions, harmless as a person, and definitely not dangerous politically. I shall never, never believe that her imprisonment could be essential to the safety of the state; I can only explain such an action as excessive zeal on the part of subordinate officials. Upon hearing this news I once again looked through the draft of the new Soviet Constitution. Article 127 states: "The citizens of the USSR are assured personal inviolability. No one may be arrested without the order of a court or without the approval of the state prosecutor." If Frau Mühsam has really been thrown into prison, was this done on the basis of a court order and with the approval of the state prosecutor? Article 129 says: "The USSR grants the right of asylum to foreign citizens who have been persecuted for advocating the interests of the working class, or for scientific activity, or for engaging in the struggle for national liberation." What bitterness for all of us who would like to regard the new Russian Constitution as the instrument of an authoritarian democracy, if this asylum should actually take the form of a prison cell.

But I am becoming heated and have already said what I would repeat here: that I cannot believe the story at all. All that I should really like to hear from you is that it is founded on an error and that my [end of letter missing]

TO GOTTFRIED BERMANN FISCHER

Küsnacht-Zurich
October 31, 1936

Dear Dr. Bermann:

Many thanks for your interesting, detailed report. I was very eager to know about it and am delighted by your success, which is also mine; for no matter what I may seem to do to hinder it, at bottom I always want my books to reach Germany—and not for material reasons alone. We must brace ourselves for the moment when this will no longer be possible.

For the present I am glad and grateful that it can still be done as well as is feasible under the circumstances. In all likelihood this volume[1] will receive no attention at all from the press in Germany, unless the *Frankfurter Zeitung* should summon up courage for a review. Dr. Diebold,[2] who paid me a visit today, intends to put in a request to do one. Perhaps an article that pretends, so to speak, to be a piece of foreign correspondence may still be possible.

The past few weeks must have been strenuous and agitating for you. But apparently you have acted with circumspection and energy, and in doing so have also served the common good. Here in Zurich I see your books, including the *Joseph*, everywhere, even in the book sections of the department stores. The notices from Vienna, Prague, and Budapest were decidedly favorable, as you know; and I can at least tell myself this much: that there probably is something to a book which has called forth the praise which our friend Reisiger has expressed to me and others. Ernst Weiss,[3] whom I think more highly of than ever since his *Der Arme Verschwender*, wrote me: "To my mind, here we have a perfectly integrated and self-sufficient microcosm—for the first time in the German language since *Faust*." He will review the book for the *Prager Presse*.

If nothing else, such tributes strengthen my resolve to finish what I have begun. And I may hope that the fourth volume will surpass the third in human warmth (the reunion scene!). Once done, the whole will at least be a memorable curiosity, if nothing more. For one thing, it is astonishing that anything of the sort could have been carried out in these times, and for another, it is strange that something so characteristically and incomparably German had to be written in exile. At the moment I am going to try, as a change of pace, to do something different: the Goethe story, *Lotte in Weimar*. I am spending my mornings, and actually all my days and nights, spying out the terrain, without having fully clarified the form for myself. In any case this too will be something special—I already feel that—and will make a pretty little volume.

I must, as I told you, ask for a number of additional copies of Joseph III. Please send twenty all at once, for in the long run, what with Christmas, I shall certainly need that many.

---

[1] *Joseph in Egypt.*

[2] Bernhard Diebold (1886–1945), Swiss theater critic. For many years associated with the *Frankfurter Zeitung*, he returned to Switzerland after 1933 and served as theater critic of *Die Tat* until his death.

[3] Ernst Weiss (1884–1940), physician and writer. A friend of Kafka, Weiss was a fine novelist with an undeservedly small reputation. He committed suicide as the Germans were marching into Paris.

I also wanted to ask you whether this volume too will appear in the customary half-calf edition. Certainly there are others besides myself who own the first two volumes in this binding.

P.S. A Stuttgart bookseller has declared, so I hear, that as soon as the *Joseph* comes in, he will instantly send copies to the customers who have placed orders, for he is convinced the book will be promptly banned. Let's hope he takes too gloomy a view. But as I have said, we must be prepared for everything.

TO ALEXANDER M. FREY

Küsnacht-Zurich
November 10, 1936

Dear Herr Frey:

What a magnificent letter about the *Joseph*! Even though the important thing is that *I* should have these reassuring, indeed exhilarating words, I feel very sorry that you have not published or will not publish them—it seems a pity if only on grounds of economy, since I am fully aware what a luxury such a letter is for a professional writer. [. . .]

I know only too well that the book is burdened by pedantic pro-lixities which, I suppose, are scarcely or just barely sustained and swept along by the whole. The simple fact is that one has to carry on such a work through a good many different states of being, including lassitude; and the odd case with me is that subsequently I do not wish to deny the existence of these states. Of course I eliminate a good many things which I wrote yesterday and today recognize as misguided. But on the whole I am a man of the *scripsi* and feel a kind of piety toward the daily stint performed under specific personal circumstances. This gives me a probably inartistic tendency to see in such a book not so much the objective work of art which must be brought to the highest possible perfection, but a track of my life which it would be almost dishonest to retouch. This by way of explanation, if not excuse. On the other hand, I would not want you to imagine that I lack the urge to perfection. I always do my best. But precisely because I know that, I let stand some things which are not of the best.

TO STEFAN ZWEIG

Küsnacht-Zurich
December 8, 1939

Dear Herr Stefan Zweig:

Cordial thanks! I have been receiving many friendly letters these days, but your note especially soothed my spirit and did me good. I cannot deny that I provoked the action.[1] It was inevitable. But that does not make it any less nonsensical. There is a truly pretty irony in the fact that I am at the moment writing a novella on Goethe. For the rest, Czechoslovakia has given me citizenship, so that once again I have behind me a government I respect. —Special thanks for suggesting the book by Martin du Gard.[2] I certainly will read it.

TO SIGMUND FREUD

Küsnacht-Zurich
December 13, 1936

Dear Herr Professor:

Your splendid letter has given me great pleasure and was a particular kindness during these days which have been somewhat clouded, although I am foolish to let them be so, by the Berlin decree pronouncing me an outcast. How vividly your letter has recalled to me the afternoon with you, which belongs among the finest memories of my life, when I had the privilege of reading my festival lecture to you. Your daughter is quite right: on this occasion you outlined to me and the other guests those remarkable, those fascinating ideas about Napoleon and the unconscious fixations of his life which you express in this memorable letter.[1] Thus they were no longer new to me, but they retain their quality of surprise and striking probability, so that the question of their actuality is of secondary importance to me. At any rate, this letter is a stirring example of your genius, your incredible perspicacity in matters of the unconscious psychic life and the effects produced from its depths, and I take pride in being the recipient.

[1] Thomas Mann's expatriation by the Nazi regime.
[2] Roger Martin du Gard (1881–1958), French novelist, Nobel Prize, 1937. His principal work is *Les Thibault*.
[1] Freud commented that the life of the biblical Joseph had been a kind of "mythic model" for Napoleon "so that we may sense the Joseph fantasy as the secret demonic motive force behind his complex biography." [Freud to Thomas Mann, November 29, 1936; see Sigmund Freud, *Briefe 1873–1939* (S. Fischer Verlag; 1960)].

It is likely that my wife and I will be in Vienna around the middle of January, and of course we hope to see you again. Please give your wife and your children our most cordial regards.

TO KONRAD ENGELMANN[1]

Küsnacht-Zurich
December 15, 1936

Dear Herr Engelmann:

Many thanks for your kind words. I am well, I live and work as before and truly do not need to envy those who have remained at home. The better spirits among them probably have a harder time of it. But my rage at all the heartache and suffering that those infamous rulers have caused and continue to cause forced me to the words and acts which brought about my "expatriation." I would be a scoundrel like the authors of that ukase if I were to regret anything. God knows, I was not born for hatred, but I hate those bloodthirsty fools and corrupters of humanity from the bottom of my heart and fervently wish them the dreadful end they deserve.

---

[1] Konrad Engelmann (b. 1892), government official and political economist; left Germany in 1936 and went first to Turkey, then to the United States.

1937

---•---

TO OTTO BASLER[1]

[*Picture postcard*]

Arosa
January 22, 1937

Dear Herr Basler:

Thank you for your warm words, and greetings from the blue-white heights. *You* have a Fatherland![2] Astoundingly beautiful.

Cordially yours,　　　　　T. M.

TO LAVINIA MAZZUCCHETTI

Küsnacht-Zurich
February 20, 1937

Dear friend:

Believe me when I say that you are a *tesoro*. Toscanini's crescendo gave me great pleasure, and I cannot thank you enough for going to the trouble of making the translation[1] specially for the maestro. Perhaps one or another use may be found for it sub rosa.

The effect is spreading rather rapidly. The fifteenth thousand of the German edition has already been dispatched; Swedish, Dutch, and Czech translations are ready, the American translation, which is to be widely circulated, is in preparation or already out. Even the Hungarian press

---

[1] Otto Basler (b. 1902), Swiss teacher and essayist, friend of both Hermann Hesse and Thomas Mann. Essays of his on Mann appeared often in various Swiss publications.

[2] This bitter exclamation refers to Mann's recent exchange of letters with the dean of the philosophical faculty of Bonn University, whose notification that he had been deprived of his honorary doctorate prompted Mann's famous rejoinder. See *An Exchange of Letters*, translated by H. T. Lowe-Porter (New York: Alfred A. Knopf; 1937).

[1] Of the Bonn letter.

has published long extracts and good articles on it, and in Paris *Marianne* will be publishing the exchange of letters in a few days. Only London is being troublesome—it is always like that. To be sure, the *Manchester Guardian* and the *Times* have published extracts; but as a whole the letter simply cannot be placed. Which would annoy me less if it were not so typical.

Congratulations on the capture of Malaga.[2] Italy's glory is certainly growing steadily.

We spent three fine weeks in Arosa, which decidedly did me good. A rather longish Goethe novella *Lotte in Weimar*, which I am slipping in before the fourth Joseph, is making excellent progress.

Greetings and best wishes from me and my family.

TO HERMANN HESSE

Küsnacht-Zurich
February 23, 1937

Dear and revered Hermann Hesse:

Let me confide the following bit of news—who should be told first, if not you? The longed-for free German journal seems on the point of becoming a reality; in fact, the matter is already settled. A wealthy lady, a friend of literature who incidentally wishes to remain completely in the background,[1] has supplied the necessary funds. She and her confidential agent in Paris have just finished a round of negotiations with me, who am to be the editor-in-chief, with Oprecht,[2] the publisher, and with Ferdinand Lion, who is being considered for managing editor. For a start it will be a bimonthly, to be called *Mass und Wert*. The name says something of the spirit in which the magazine is to be conducted, the direction and meaning we shall try to give it. It is intended not to be polemical but constructive,

---

[2] This ironic reference is to the part played by Italian Fascist troops in the Spanish Civil War.

[1] Madame Aline Mayrisch de St. Hubert, widow of the Luxembourg steel magnate Emile Mayrisch.

[2] Emil Oprecht (1895–1952), Swiss bookseller and publisher. For many years an active Social Democrat, Oprecht ultimately abandoned all political activity because of his widening cultural interests. Among his numerous offices were those of president of the Zurich theater organization (Neue Schauspiel AG), vice president of the Swiss UNESCO commission, president of the Swiss Theater Association. In 1924 he founded the bookstore in Zurich which bears his name, and in 1933 went into publishing as an answer to Hitler. His Europa Verlag first published *An Exchange of Letters* and also put out the magazine *Mass und Wert*. He and his wife Emmie were among Thomas Mann's closest friends in Zurich.

productive; it will seek to conserve and at the same time to be forward-looking, and will aim at winning confidence and authority as a refuge of the highest contemporary German culture for the duration of the inter-regnum inside Germany. The desirability, not to say the necessity, of such a medium for the German spirit outside the Reich is undeniable, I think, and universally felt. I must say that I am delighted with the project; I look forward to what may come of it and have thrown myself into it wholeheartedly.

How good if you could do so too. I do not know how you now stand toward Germany and in Germany, what considerations you still have to take into account, but I need not say that your cooperation in this, it seems to me, well-conceived undertaking would be of the highest symbolic and practical importance. I am writing these lines to prepare the ground somewhat for the proposal the future editor is going to make to you. Lion will explain matters in more detail and, I imagine, make more specific requests, unless you should tell me at once that you cannot consider any collaboration. I am a little afraid that this will be your answer, but I hope for a prompt word of general consent.

Greetings to you and Frau Ninon from me and mine.

TO THE SOVIET WRITERS' LEAGUE

Küsnacht-Zurich
April 5, 1937

Dear Sirs:

In calling upon "the writers of the world" to send you contributions for a collection celebrating the twentieth anniversary of the Soviet Union, you do not fully realize what a precarious thing you are asking of us, your Western colleagues. The merest hint of communistic—what am I saying? of any sort of socialistic sympathies—in Europe today entails nothing more nor less than martyrdom. It means unleashing a hatred, a homicidal mania, a fury of persecution which you can scarcely conceive —for if you could, you would not have had the naïve cruelty to issue your call to me also, a writer who still has something to lose in the way of bourgeois-conservative reputation.

As it happens, my attitude toward this reputation somewhat resembles that of Goethe toward the title "friend of the existing order," a title which in conversation he angrily repudiated. "If the existing order were excellent, just, and good," he said, "I should certainly have no objection to it; but since alongside much good it also contains much that is bad, unjust, and imperfect, to be a friend of the existing order usually means nothing better than friend of what is outmoded and bad." This strikes me as very right. And on the other hand, I have never been able to convince myself that Russian socialism is so radically hostile to tradition, or that it intends "to destroy our Western culture"—with which, after all, more than one of the great representatives of Russian thought have been closely linked. The nationwide enthusiasm with which the memory of Alexander Pushkin was recently celebrated in Russia did not suggest hatred of tradition; it did not sound "bolshevistic" in the sense of sweeping destructiveness (the sense in which the West takes that word to this day).

"The figure of Pushkin," I wrote at the time, "the Europeanism of his form, his classicism, assume a higher contemporaneity at this moment when Russia takes her seat in the League of Nations beside the peaceful powers of the West, and when in the realm of thought new relationships of tolerance, attention, and amity are being established between the socialism of the Soviet world and the humanism of still-bourgeois Europe. The name of Alexander Sergeievich Pushkin, the Russian classic, might become the symbol for much that lies in the future."

What I said about new relations of tolerance and friendship between Eastern socialism and Western humanism, wherein the synthesis of the future may lie, did not come solely from general observations of the world situation, but also from my own most personal experience. It belongs, however, among the statements which here and there in my native West have already earned me the epithet of a communistic writer. "The communistic writer T. M."—I have seen this phrase, intended as an annihilating indictment, in black and white. I regard it with a mixture of amusement and alarm which you, my Soviet colleagues, will have to forgive me for. Truly, I am not a communistic or any other kind of -istic writer; I am plainly and simply a writer, which is to say a human being who contemplates things in terms of freedom and the life of the mind. I happen also to cherish a fondness for truth, a feeling which is calmly intense rather than doctrinaire, and which has led me to an incurable hostility to the world of lies constructed by Fascistic nationalism. Who knows, perhaps that is enough to make a mere writer into a *communistic* writer.

But to my mind it is not enough. I must reject the label—for one reason, because if I were ever to take on a political mission over and above my artistic task on this earth, it would only be to prepare the way for what must some day follow the present horror in my country, in Germany. The subjugated and spiritually humiliated German people are deeply, agonizingly longing for some alternative—and it is certainly not communistic dictatorship.

Don't misunderstand me. I do not lightly lump all dictatorships together. I myself know how to make distinctions. Dictatorship in the name of man and the future, in the name of freedom, truth, and justice is quite conceivable—as opposed to a dictatorship of lies and crimes. The political profile of the American Franklin D. Roosevelt, whom I greatly admire, also has dictatorial features, and yet he is a sincere servant of democracy. Probably freedom without dictatorial features and elements is no longer possible or conceivable on earth. Liberty's mortal enemies have knocked the liberalism out of her; in the future she will have to know what she wants, will have to maintain that quantum of intolerance and resolution vital to her survival—if we have not learned this, we have learned nothing in the last twenty years. And yet I fear I would be meeting my political obligations clumsily indeed, and committing a serious breach of tact, if I as a German writer were to accept the communistic label and thus indirectly imply to my nation that it exchange one dictatorship for another. At every performance of Schiller's *Don Carlos* in Germany the audience answers the Marquis Posa's cry for "freedom of thought" with frenzied applause, intended as a demonstration against the present repression. In such a country nothing can be accomplished with slogans which negate, if only in appearance and only temporarily, its unrecognized thirst for freedom, legal rights, and individual dignity. These principles—freedom, justice, and humanity—are the only ones on which a future German government can be based.

Although my sense of this governs my attitude toward the Soviet world, it does not in the least diminish my awe for the tremendous social experiment that the Russian revolution represents, an awe that, as is only proper, is accompanied by shuddering. "The cruelties of the revolution were too close to me," Goethe said thirty years after 1789. "They outraged me every day and every hour, since I could not yet see the beneficent consequences of the revolution." Won't we contemporaries of the Russian revolution have to apologize in similar terms some day? That it has achieved and continues to achieve great things for the cultural elevation of the Russian people is already beyond doubt, and it may well be that its effect in reshaping human life will one day be regarded as no less than that of the French revolution. Moreover, for all the fear it has inspired, the world has from the beginning shown far more respect and sympathy for it than for the Fascistic pseudorevolutions. Most people have always profoundly despised the latter. It can be said without exaggerated optimism that the base temptations which these pseudorevolutions offer are already vanishing. Thoughtful young people throughout the world are already disabused of the Fascist fad. Young intellectuals of all countries are fighting on the Loyalist front in Spain; the "left" is everywhere undergoing a moral upsurge; the best minds feel that what lies in the future, what must be won by hard work, is a new humanism. Word of the imminent doom of freedom, which prophets who were nothing but perverse scribblers have dinned into our ears for ten years and longer, is being exposed as empty chatter.

No idea today is so bursting with youthfulness, so vibrant with longing, so promising for the future, as that of freedom. But it is a wider freedom, conscious of its dignity, that must prevail, a virile self-reliant humanism—the kind of social and vigorous democracy which the recent Soviet Constitution outlines. May the Russian people and all peoples succeed in making it a reality.

TO SIGMUND FREUD

Küsnacht-Zurich
May 4, 1937

Dear Herr Professor:

Returning from New York, where I indulged somewhat to excess for my age in *lectures, dinner speeches,* and *meetings,*[1] I find your Moses essay here and hasten to offer at least the barest thanks for such a precious gift, every word of which reminds me in the most poignant way of our conversation—or more properly of your lecture—during my last visit. And how much else it reminds me of! All kinds of things are called "stimulating reading." But this is exactly that.

All my devotion to you and yours.

---

[1] Here, and in subsequent letters, italics indicate that Mann used English words in his original.

1937

TO RENÉ SCHICKELE

Küsnacht-Zurich
May 31, 1937

Dear René Schickele:

Thank you. It did me so much good, bowed down as I am with pain,[1] to have your friendly words. I knew that Glaeser's miserable twaddle[2] would be painful to you. "Behind him stands the breath of a born poet." This was the laudatory part. After that, what could be expected of the critical part? It comes down to: What can be expected of a writer who lives in an unforested country?[3] Heaven knows, not tragedy. The École de Zurich is a Nazi school, stylistically and intellectually. Its way of holding aloof from the "ordinary refugees" scarcely encourages one to share its isolation. I have had to invent a special isolation for myself, and how reassuring to gather from your letter that I have somewhat succeeded in this by taking the position I have. Korrodi, to be sure, does not think so. According to these people, we are compromised by being outside at all— whereas aloofness from this Germany seems to me considerably more important than aloofness from the "ordinary" exiles. After all, we two are in little danger of being confounded with them, even if we do not try to prove our status by keeping our noses in the air and using Nazi German. *You* could very well be the one to write an excellent, clarifying essay which would put the whole problem of the exiles in the proper light. It would be something for the new magazine, for whose first issue I have written the enclosed foreword—please mail it back after you read it. Lion writes that it is the only good piece he has received so far. I knew from the start that   would have to do the whole thing alone, and it may well come to grief because of that.

You guess rightly: I am trying to push on with my work, and it is an inexpressible reassurance to me that after the interruption of the silly triumphal tour—which incidentally actually produced a donation of $100,000 for the University in Exile[4] (if only a bit of that fell to me!)— the Goethe novella is at least moving forward again by a page every day.

---

[1] Mann was suffering from sciatica.
[2] Ernst Glaeser's review of Schickele's novel *Die Flaschenpost* in the *Neue Zürcher Zeitung* (May 24, 1937).
[3] René Schickele was living on the "unforested" French Riviera.
[4] The University in Exile was set up in connection with the New York School for Social Research as a center of antifascist and exiled scholars. A patron had promised to contribute the large sum if Thomas Mann would come to America to rally support for the institution.

It is just barely going, for I have been limited to an extremely inadequate ration of sleep. Toward midnight I take phanodorm and sleep until three. Then the pains start and I dissolve two alonal tablets in camomile tea. That lasts me until five. Then it's finished, and I can no longer find any position that is endurable even for a few minutes. And what do you do then with a morning that has already started so early?

I intend to go to Ragaz for the cure. We are waiting for Erika, who is coming on a visit from New York, because we would like to spend another few days with her here. Then I shall seriously make a start with the radium waters on which I am placing all my hopes, since so far every therapy, including shortwave heat treatment, has failed completely.

You have been through some physical ordeals while I was well. May your health steadily improve, despite the German naval war in Spain and all the other things that try our hearts. Warm regards to your dear wife. The foreword is intended, if possible, to tempt you into writing something for "us" one of these days.

TO HERMANN J. WEIGAND[1]

Küsnacht-Zurich
October 28, 1937

My dear Professor:

Today your friendly letter of the seventeenth arrived. I want to thank you for it immediately and to apologize for my long delay in answering your previous letter. This postponement or inhibition was connected, I frankly confess, with some remarks in that letter which rather put me out of sorts. The *Exchange of Letters* has touched the hearts of thousands of spiritually and morally tormented persons, especially in Germany, where it is more widely circulated in various guises than any other militant statement against the so-called Third Reich. I did not and could not like the way you spoke of it. It is better, and can prevent misunderstandings, if I say openly to you that I am deadly serious about all matters concerning the regime that burdens Germany today and that has driven me from house and home. Any expression of the slightest sympathy for this corrupt and corrupting monstrosity is enough to make me turn my back upon the speaker.

With this clarified, let us speak of my coming visit to America. It is

---

[1] Hermann J. Weigand (b. 1892), professor emeritus of German, Yale University, author of numerous books and articles on literature, including *The Modern Ibsen, Thomas Mann's Novel "Der Zauberberg."*

going to be very demanding; I am rather afraid of it, for my health has not been at its best for some time, but on the other hand I have discovered that productive work is always more consuming than anything else; I am capable of surprising performances and feats of endurance when my life is wholly directed outward. My program, however, is so heavy that I am exceedingly doubtful whether I shall be able to work in the requested lecture at Yale. A few days ago I wrote Mr. Angell[2] to let him know that our departure from here is being advanced and to propose that our little Library celebration be held not after the end but before the beginning of my lecture tour. February 24 or 25 would be suitable. I hear that in conjunction with the opening ceremony, at which I shall probably have to give a brief talk, there will be various social affairs. Since I shall be spending only a day and a half at Yale, it seems to me scarcely possible to add a lecture to this program—quite aside from the fact that in addition to the big lecture[3] and various minor dinner speeches, I would have to work out an additional address. I think, therefore, that we had better give up the plan, for I am afraid I would be overtaxing myself. I certainly hope there will be a chance during those days for some friendly get-together.

Your kind words about the beginning of *Lotte in Weimar* delighted me. I am curious to see what you will say about the conversation with Riemer in the second issue of the magazine. And I am eagerly looking forward to your study of the *Joseph*, for I am certain that in artistic and psychological insight into my intentions it will far surpass the generally rather trivial things that I have seen on this subject so far.

With best regards, from my wife as well.

TO KAREL ČAPEK[1]

Küsnacht-Zurich
October 10, 1937

Dear and revered Herr Čapek:

Privately and confidentially I should like to turn to you about a matter

[2] Joseph W. Angell (b. 1908), professor of English at Yale University during this period, subsequently military historian, editor of *The Thomas Mann Reader* (New York: Alfred A. Knopf; 1950). The Thomas Mann Collection at Yale University was started on his initiative.

[3] "The Coming Victory of Democracy" in *Order of the Day: Political Essays and Speeches of Two Decades* (New York: Alfred A. Knopf; 1942).

[1] Karel Čapek (1890–1938), Czech novelist, playwright, essayist, close to Masaryk and Beneš. He died a few months after Munich, unable to face the prospect of leaving his country or witnessing its impending destruction by Hitler. Most of his works have been translated into English; but he is perhaps best known for coining the word "robot" in his play *R.U.R.*

that has come to my attention often lately. It concerns the predicament of the German exiles in Czechoslovakia and the measures which, it appears, the Prague government has taken or is threatening to take concerning them. You will understand both that this question deeply affects me and that I am most reluctant, precisely in my capacity as a very recently accepted citizen of the Republic, to make any public statement about it. I should like to know your opinion of the situation, and whether you think that the German exiles are truly threatened by these measures which I am told of in piteous and frightened terms. The gist of it is that the exiles residing in the major cities, Prague, Brno, and Bratislava, are no longer to be issued residence permits; instead they are due to be re-settled in a number of small districts on the Bohemian-Moravian border. Although the refugees are not allowed to work at their professions, the big cities do offer at least some opportunity for making small livelihoods within permissible bounds. Moreover, here there are more congenial working conditions and cultural stimuli (libraries, lectures, etc.). Finally, they are within reach of a number of charitable organizations which have somewhat eased their lot by providing free meals, free lodging, and so on —things which would be sorely missed. One may gather how bad a blow the projected measures would be to the exiles by the desperate efforts being made by the Comité Central pour les Réfugiés en Tchecoslovaquie to avert this threat and keep them where contact can be maintained and help provided. For simplicity's sake I enclose the memorandum that I have received from this committee; everything I could tell you is in it.

You must not imagine that I underestimate the complexity of the question and judge it one-sidedly. I can understand the reasons for such measures. But on the other hand you can understand not only that I am deeply concerned about the fate of my hard-pressed fellow countrymen who have been expelled and persecuted by the despicable government of their native land, but also that it would be painful to me if the country to which I now belong, and whose exemplary democratic spirit has always filled me with pride—if the country that was headed by the great exile Masaryk[2] and that today is presided over by the former exile Beneš[3]—

[2] Thomas G. Masaryk (1850–1937), Czech sociologist and statesman, first president of Czechoslovakia, 1918–35.

[3] Eduard Beneš (1884–1948), Czech political economist and statesman. In 1915 Beneš became secretary general of the Czech National Council; 1918–35 foreign minister of Czechoslovakia, then president until his resignation in 1938 and exile in the United States. In 1939 he became a professor in Chicago, in 1940 president of the Czech government-in-exile in London. After his return home in May 1945 he once more became president of Czechoslovakia. Practically stripped of power by the Communists in February 1948, he resigned his office in May of that year and died soon afterwards.

should in this very realm exhibit a harshness which, granted all the need for caution, scarcely any other country has so far regarded as necessary.

Once again, I ask for your opinion on the problem and whether you believe that the authorities can be persuaded to follow a more lenient policy. If there is anyone who could exert influence, certainly it is you. It would be a great joy to me if you could respond to this suggestion in some way. But if you think it might be in the least useful for me to take any action on my own by way of writing letters, I would be grateful if you would suggest someone I could turn to. I imagine you will agree that a public appeal on my part would be most inappropriate.

TO ERIKA MANN

Küsnacht-Zurich
December 4, 1937

Dear Eri:

Please find encased the *Message* for the *artists*. Couldn't do it any better in my hurry. But well translated and read aloud with warmth, it should more or less do the trick.

It grieves me to hear that you've been sick again and had to stay in bed for several days. That New York life, although you find it so much to your liking, is nevertheless strenuous and iron-hard. In the struggle for success over there, one can hardly pay the necessary attention to one's health. Do it anyhow!

I am now scribbling so much about politics for my lecture that half the stuff will have to be discarded—which is terribly wasteful, but once let loose I can't be reined in. I must also prepare a half-hour speech for Yale and the speech for the Christian Refugee Dinner. Once these are out of the way, I intend, since it can be all polished off in one session, as it were, to write the introduction to an American condensed Schopenhauer,[1] for which they are offering $750. Can I cast that to the winds in order to devote myself to my fictional works? People had better not ask me about them. By the middle of May, when we are back from the horrible lecture trip, I shall at least be able to think of them again—insofar as the Prague Pen Club Congress will permit, for by then that will be looming. The wish to live to an enormous age is simply forced on one.

With love,   Z.

---

[1] This introduction was published in *The Living Thoughts of Schopenhauer*, presented by Thomas Mann (New York: Longmans, Green & Co.; 1939).

1937

TO IDA HERZ

Dear Fräulein Herz:

Thank you for the interesting clipping, which makes me homesick for the *Joseph*.

You must not worry on my account. My health is good and my life flies along without any remarkable or newsworthy events. I have kept you informed by sending small batches of things now and then. But I am absurdly busy, working away at high pressure on the things that have to be done now in order to put them behind me. I must meet a hundred incidental demands on my time, and in any case I have often mentioned that I am a poor correspondent. Please don't make complaints and demands; they add to the nervousness that plagues me anyhow, because I have had to neglect my fictional work for so long that I won't be able to think of it again until May, and even then only continue with *Lotte in Weimar*; Joseph does not even come into the question. If I had anything against you, I would tell you. But there is nothing except what I have just mentioned.

Today our youngest arrives from Paris, and Moni too will probably join him, Golo, and Medi for the holidays. Alas, we shall probably have to do without the two eldest for Christmas, but will see them in America in February. The American tour weighs me down in advance, but that's probably nothing compared with what it will do afterwards. Incidentally, there is great interest in it; Chicago, for example, was sold out long ago (for the beginning of March!). The manager is brazenly taking $1,000 for the evening, of which I receive only half. That is a great deal, but if I am going to have the reputation for brazenness anyhow, I'd like to get a great deal out of it.

Let me wish you a pleasant Xmas and a happy New Year.

TO HERMANN HESSE

Dear Herr Hesse:

This is wonderful. Warmest thanks. Your magnificent poems will be a great adornment and help to the magazine. They are to appear as soon as possible—that is, in the fourth number.

All the best to you and your dear wife.

1937

TO ERNST WEISS

Küsnacht-Zurich
December 22, 1937

Dear Herr Ernst Weiss:

What with the many demands the days bring, I have been reading your novel at night before going to sleep (and it has often kept me up quite late—last night, during the final sprint, until 1.30 A.M.). The result was that it has taken longer than I thought; but now that I have really absorbed this bountiful book, have "striven for it in order to possess it," I can thank you once more in a fuller sense than I did before. I cannot say that I am surprised, for I have long been familiar with your special gifts as a novelist and knew in general what I could look forward to. But *Der Verführer* is so new and so remarkable a demonstration and "objectivation" of these gifts that I am inclined to speak of a surprise, simply in the sense that good and original work is always surprising—for the very simple reason that it is rare. We deal with so much mediocre and unauthentic stuff that in the end we almost forget what good and remarkable things are like. Well, they are like this book of yours. And the book teaches us again what is interesting. To be interesting is certainly the first and perhaps the only demand to be made of a storyteller, *the* criterion of his talent, far more than in the case of a poet or playwright. For if we are to listen to someone, and to listen for a long time, he has to be interesting—though I grant you it is a mysterious and almost indefinable quality; but you possess this mystery and this indefinableness, and that makes you a—shall I say great? but what is the point of the adjective?— it makes you quite simply a storyteller.

The book is one of the most interesting that has come my way in years, and as I read I frequently looked back at the dedication and rejoiced that it was to me. But the quality of being interesting, mysterious in itself, seems to cast its mystery over the factual contents of the book. One ponders and wonders: what kind of book is this, what kind of author, what kind of hero; how does the author arrive at this cool, bold, successful hero; to what extent is he identical with him? Evidently to a great extent, for the narrator too is cool, bold, and successful, inwardly successful— this narrator who causes a story to be told but then tells it again himself, relating a life, a youth, which can scarcely be his in this particular form: a wish-life and a life of pain which he brings into being with so much coolness, boldness, and success that it is his own—his second life, his second youth.

The success, the achievement, is really extraordinary. It is astonishing the way everything is made real, decisively autobiographical, concretely lifelike. For a long time the father's story appears to be the best, but by and by the mother becomes even more wonderfully lifelike and interesting. And episodes such as the mountain climbing, learning to ride, the chamois hunt, and oddities of reality such as "Postillon" and "Marty," and the love affair with A.v.W., and the keenly realized male rivalries, Maxi, the duel—one more fictional duel and yet not just a fictional duel, but something entirely novel and vitally unique, something of which one says, "That was how it was." It is exquisite.

I am filled with impressions, stirred and preoccupied with strange but unforgettably vivid images, people, events. Moreover, the whole thing is very Austrian, at least in its air of sociability, sophistication. At the same time there is this loneliness—to the point of coldness. Very, very thought-provoking and moving.

With my congratulations and greetings for Christmas.

TO WILLEM DE BOER [1]

Küsnacht-Zurich
December 30, 1937

My dear Herr de Boer:

After the beautiful concert at your home last night I want to thank you and your wife once more and to tell you how interesting and moving your playing of the viola d'amore was for me, what an extraordinary and novel impression it made.

When I say "playing" I mean the player and the little-known instrument which has so undeservedly gone out of fashion. For the two belong together, and one has no notion of the capabilities of that amazing instrument until one has heard what it can do in the hands of a player like yourself. That is why the majority of people have feeble and inadequate notions about it, and until now I was one of the majority. Your art and virtuosity have converted me entirely to the viola d'amore. What potentialities for solo performance in its multiple strings! What encompassing sonority; what delicacy and power; and what a tonal range—which you drew on so splendidly that the phrase "string organ" at once

[1] Willem de Boer (1885–1962), Dutch violinist, composer, and music teacher. As concertmaster of the Zurich Tonhalle orchestra he exerted a decisive influence on Zurich musical life, especially in promoting contemporary music. His own compositions were largely for the violin and viola d'amore.

occurred to me. It is truly something of the sort in your hands, and I would imagine that your example will produce not only pupils and disciples, but also a viola d'amore literature, which unfortunately does not seem to exist. However, the Ariosti sonata that you played is a lovely piece, and you yourself have composed some admirable things which brilliantly demonstrate the virtues of the viola d'amore.

I hear that you are going on a concert tour to Holland with your instrument. I am sure that for many listeners your performances will be a revelation, and that I can congratulate you in advance on the great success which you will have with the music-loving public in your native land.

1938

―――――――・―――――――

Küsnacht-Zurich
January 4, 1938

Dear Monsieur Bertaux:

Your friendly New Year's wishes touched me and shamed me too, for my greetings are late by several days, although the year is still young. [. . .] We often think of you and your family, and regret that so much time has passed since our last visit in Sèvres. A trip to Paris is long overdue, and given the short distance between us it is ridiculous that we have not managed it. But I am, to quote Schopenhauer, "a mushroom that sits tight," and if I did not insist on regularity and instead went gallivanting, I would get nothing done at all, given the slowness of my natural tempo. My wife and I are all the more pleased that a reunion appears virtually certain this coming spring. [. . .]

I am very happy to hear of the warm reception that my little political pamphlet[1] with Gide's friendly introduction has had in your country. But although our friend Desjardins[2] may regard it as a sign that "something has changed in Europe," this seems to me rather too optimistic on the part of that old fighter for freedom and humanism. If we consider the trend in its rough and general outline, the change is moving in a completely inimical and repellent direction. And though counterforces are presumably forming under the pressure of evil, it is hard to measure how strong or how conscious these are. The general spiritual state of the world, current events as we see them in the newspapers, are scarcely consoling. Indeed, they are psychic toxins. The sole encouragement comes from our sense of belonging to an elite of better, freer, and more well-

―――――――――――

[1] *An Exchange of Letters.*
[2] Paul Desjardins (1859–1940), French philosopher and philologist. Among his works: *Le devoir présent* (1892), *La méthode des classiques français.*

disposed minds who despise the insanity of that blind and self-imprisoned trend. The decision-making potentiality of this elite will in the end probably determine the future. Let us sustain our association in this sense, dear friend, and rejoice in our friendship! [. . .]

I must close, for it's time to turn on the radio to hear Pierre.[3] Give him my thanks for this active demonstration of his interest.

With warmest regards to you, him, and your wife from me and my household.

P.S. It was hard to follow; there was a great deal of static; I think Goebbels[4] was jamming the broadcast. But to be truthful, Pierre also spoke too low, too rapidly, too much *a la légère*. This time, moreover, he didn't get as far as the *Avertissement*,[5] or at any rate he only gave the title. I hope that next time he treats his words with greater rhetorical respect. They deserve it. (My handwriting in Latin script is that of a seven-year-old.)

TO COUNTESS MERCATI

[*Telegram in English*]

April 18, 1938

I am very happy at the news of the great Carnegie Hall concert.[1] The brilliant artists associated with it—Jascha Heifetz, the NBC Symphony Orchestra and Dr. Artur Rodzinski—guarantee that it will be a success. It will constitute a tremendous help to hundreds of victims in a dark and gruesome time. The concert is inspired by the spirit of the most beautiful American tradition. It serves as a consolation and a hope that American democracy is alert and alive.

[3] Pierre Bertaux (b. 1907), specialist in German literature, a writer and a politician; son of Félix Bertaux. During the war he organized a resistance group in southern France. On the occasion mentioned above, he was to deliver a radio address on Mann's new book (see note 5 below).

[4] Joseph Goebbels (1897–1945), Hitler's propaganda minister.

[5] Thomas Mann's collection of political essays, *Achtung Europa!* was published in French under the title of *Avertissement à l'Europe*.

[1] Countess Mercati was the sponsor of this concert for the benefit of Austrian refugees. The new tide of refugees had begun after Hitler's annexation of Austria in March, while Thomas Mann was in the midst of his American lecture tour. The telegram above was printed in *The New York Times* (April 20, 1938).

1938

The Bedford
118 East 40th Street, New York
May 21, 1938

Dear Madam:

I can thank you only briefly for your letter, which I read with understanding and emotion. The crime against Austria—that it was possible, that it was tolerated—has hit me so hard that I have decided for the present not to return to Europe from this trip to America, which I began in February as a mere lecture tour. I am dissolving my Swiss household and mean to locate in a university town in the eastern part of the United States. No longer young, I must continue my work as well as possible and at the same time adjust to entirely new conditions. That places quite a strain on my energies. Any halfway adequate reply to your questions would lead me very far. I can only advise you: Be thankful that you are able to live in a still free, not fascist, country, to be a citizen of it by marriage; take care not to give vent to your understandable longing for reprisal by calling loudly for military intervention by the democratic powers, to *écraser l'infâme*. The Austrian refugees will discover what the German refugees have long since found out: that the world is unreceptive to such exhortations from us and either takes offense or shrugs. The world's patience with Fascism, however painful for us, and the world's endeavors to come to an arrangement with it, have their good, or at any rate cogent, reasons. But as I have said, analysis of those reasons would lead me too far. To put it concisely, National Socialism and Fascism are expedients against the threat of social revolution everywhere in the world; they are methods for suppressing, whitewashing, postponing, checking that revolution by taking some of it over in a false and deceptive spirit. In other words, they are brutal quack medicines for which the respectable world everywhere, despite its distaste for the attendant humbug, has a secret weakness. This explains why we find it so hard to mobilize the world against Fascism and why our warnings are taken as agitation for our own selfish ends. My one remaining desire is to live within the shelter of a society that still loves and honors what I do not so much advocate as represent, and to carry my life's work to its end. If you ask me, I would recommend to you a similar resolute but tranquil attitude of trust in the future.

TO ERICH VON KAHLER

Dear Erich von Kahler:

Tomorrow, Friday, Erika will be in Paris, and at the beginning of next week in Zurich. She will bring you and other friends our greetings and our tidings. But I don't want to leave it entirely up to her; I want to tell you myself how often we think of you, and with how much sadness, and how acutely we will miss you in our future life. You do understand our decision, don't you? We very much hope and wish that people in Zurich and in Prague also will understand it. The shock of the crime against Austria was severe; the parallel with 1933 forced itself upon us; we felt it as a "seizure of power" on the continental scale, and again we had the sensation of being cut off, as in 1933. All this may prove to be exaggerated or premature. Nevertheless we cannot regret our decision and our act of "immigration"; there are too many good reasons, in Europe and here, for making this country our residence at least for a time, although we shall keep in touch with the old continent as much as possible. The reception of *Joseph in Egypt* here, and my tour from East to West and back again (which, in spite of all the strains connected with it, might have been a merry harvest festival had it not been for the anxieties and alarms over Europe), have shown me how much trust, sympathy, and friendship is given us here. And how can I help feeling attracted by this atmosphere of warmth and friendliness, when these are so totally lacking in Europe? I also believe that more and more of the better "Europe" will be moving here, including German publishing; so that perhaps the German editions of my books may even appear here. In short, it seems to me that my place is here now. The thought that by leaving Europe at this point we shall very possibly escape the war is actually of secondary importance. My reason cannot believe in the war. No one wants it or can possibly want it because of the unforeseeable consequences. But on the other hand, reason also tells me that nothing but war can be the result of what is brewing in Europe now.

Our little country in the East[1] is behaving wonderfully. I prefer not to express the feelings that the behavior of the Germans arouse in me.

After the wanderings of the past three months, we have come to a temporary resting place here at the seaside in a borrowed cottage, and

---

[1] Czechoslovakia.

I am taking up the thread of *Lotte in Weimar* as I would have done in Küsnacht. For the autumn I am making an arrangement with Princeton for a kind of honorary professorship which will not impose an excessive burden upon me and will provide a basic livelihood. We will therefore settle there around September. The place has the advantage of being rural, with very good connections to New York.

And what about you? And your mother? What plans do you have? Or rather, what wishes? Naturally I was thinking of you when I said that the better Europe will gradually be moving over here to join "us." *Auf Wiedersehen!* Here or in Switzerland, where we shall almost certainly be coming on a visit soon—perhaps as soon as next winter.

TO AGNES E. MEYER [1]

Jamestown, R.I.
June 19, 1938

Dear Mrs. Meyer:

Many thanks for your lines of Saturday. It is reassuring to us that you approve of our summer-in-Europe plan. We are hurrying to find a suitable house in Princeton. My wife has just been there for two days, but has not yet found anything really attractive, and the prices seem quite high. But at any rate there are already a few to choose from, and when we have the Yale celebration behind us we will go to Princeton once more to make a final decision. This is why we have postponed our departure from the 24th to the 29th, which is the sailing date for both the *Washington* and the *Normandie*. It depends on which of the two boats has cabin space for us.

My wife is now copying the Schopenhauer essay, since no one but her in this whole great continent can read my handwriting. But she was so burdened by arrears of correspondence that she has not yet made much progress and will have to finish the job on board ship and in Küsnacht. As soon as the carbon copies are available, of course you will receive one.

Yesterday the first copies of the democracy speech[2] arrived. My

---

[1] Agnes E. Meyer (b. 1887), the wife of Eugene Meyer, publisher of the *Washington Post*, journalist and writer, occasional translator of Thomas Mann's articles. Among her books: *Journey Through Chaos*, *Out of These Roots*. During the latter part of his life Thomas Mann corresponded with her more frequently than with anyone else. The letters in their totality—some 300 which Mrs. Meyer has given to the Thomas Mann Collection of Yale University—constitute a running autobiography of his later years. Of the 110 letters printed in volumes 2 and 3 of the German *Briefe*, 58 are translated here.

[2] See note 3, p. 266.

impression is that the translation is masterly, and I am very pleased with the tasteful format.

Best regards and *auf Wiedersehen.*

TO AGNES E. MEYER

Schiedhaldenstrasse 33
Küsnacht-Zurich
July 18, 1938

Dear Friend:

We both want to tell you something about what has been happening to us since we parted. I am dictating this to my wife, so please regard it as coming from both of us.

As I think we wrote you en route, we had a fine crossing on the *Washington,* a most agreeable boat. The life on board was pleasant—I have scarcely found the like on ships of other nationalities—and we also had unusually good weather during most of the voyage. Only in the Irish Sea was there a real storm, and that held the boat up for quite some time. We had to abandon our plan of visiting a friend[1] in Paris and took a sleeping car straight through. Spirited along that way, it felt all the more like a dream to find ourselves back in the old environment, which we had hardly imagined we would ever see again. Our decision, which you encouragingly approved, was decidedly right. It is doing both of us good to breathe once more the air which has become like home in these past five years, and to take our old, beautiful walks in the woods. Our enjoyment of it all is heightened by the knowledge that we have a new home in Princeton. We scarcely feel threatened by the political situation, although there is no denying that more critical days are in the offing. The fall of Austria has turned the general mood in Switzerland more against Germany; that is, against the Hitler regime. However, this reaction to Hitler's outrage, although in itself gratifying, is accompanied by growing intellectual and political tendencies toward autarchy. We plan to stay here for the next few weeks enjoying the house, which has great charm, especially in the summer; after that we shall go to a spa in the Valais, and we already have our tickets for the *Nieuw Amsterdam* for September 17. I am working well on *Lotte in Weimar.* Old Zurich friends visit, there is much good conversation, and we have a great many things to discuss in connection with the magazine and the publication of my American lecture in it.

[1] Félix Bertaux.

May I add to this little report a question in the interest of a third party? I have received a letter from the German writer and journalist Werner Türk,[2] now a refugee in Scandinavia. I am indebted to him for his work on behalf of the Thomas Mann Gesellschaft and its fund to assist German and Austrian refugees, for which he has raised impressive sums. I know him as a competent and skillful journalist and can therefore support his request with good conscience. He would like to write about Norway for an American newspaper; he thinks there is a great deal in that country which the United States is not yet aware of. He is also counting on America's special interest in the Scandinavian democracies. He wants to write some articles on Norway describing the strange beauties of the landscape and presenting the present-day economic and social development of the country, as well as giving some notion of the intellectual life in the captial. I thought that the *Washington Post* might be interested in such a contribution, or several; in which case I give you the author's address: Werner Türk, Schouterrassen 36, Oslo.

Today or tomorrow we are expecting our eldest children back from Spain, where they have been on newspaper assignments. They were in Madrid and Barcelona and have, so I hear, reached Valencia by a singular mode of transportation: a submarine.[3] We are eager to hear their accounts and at the same time greatly relieved to know that they are safely back in France.

Keep well, and our best regards to your husband and your children from both of us. We are already looking forward to seeing you again.

TO BOLKO VON HAHN[1]

Küsnacht-Zurich
July 24, 1938

My dear Herr von Hahn:

Your fine letter belongs among those documents which a writer takes joy in adding to his small stock of personal trophies, because it gives him more

---

[2] Werner Türk (b. 1901), author of *Der Arbeitslöwe* (1932), *Kleiner Mann in Uniform* (Prague, 1934), *Die Zauberflöte* (a biography of Mozart; Copenhagen, 1939), and articles on Thomas Mann.

[3] The report was incorrect. Klaus Mann escaped from Valencia on a small Loyalist boat, while Erika Mann, a British subject through her marriage to W. H. Auden, was evacuated by a British destroyer.

[1] Bolko von Hahn (b. 1904), businessman; journalist by avocation. In South America, 1925–58; author of *Das Herz des Gaucho* and studies in South American history, among others.

of a sense of the living effect of his work than any printed critique. Thank you very much.

It seems to me that in our time people take the things of the mind for granted as part of life, rather than, as they did in our fathers' days, setting them apart in a special category of literature—alongside, but aloof from, reality and active life. So I rejoice when my books have something to say to bold and practical men of wide-ranging activities such as yourself, and share after their fashion in the shaping and fulfillment of such a life.

Your differing views of the events in Spain cannot lessen this pleasure. But I cannot help wondering that you approve of my other political opinions and insist on making an exception of the Spanish question. All these opinions, it seems to me, necessarily belong within the same logical and moral framework. I assure you, the incitement and prolongation of this civil war is one of the greatest crimes in history. If you were to fight there, what folly if you did not do so on the side of the people, who for two years have defended their freedom with the courage of lions. My eldest children have just come from Spain. They are full of admiration for the morale of the Republican troops, which far surpasses the fighting spirit of the other side, though it is much better equipped. And they are also surprised at their own fearlessness in the trenches and under bombing and shelling. They explain it on grounds of the indescribable satisfaction they feel at being in the one place where that vile corruption of the world called Fascism is being *shot* at. [. . .]

Once more, my thanks and earnest good wishes.

TO HEINRICH MANN

Küsnacht-Zurich
August 6, 1938

Dear Heinrich:

I hear your great work is finished. If so, that would be glorious—and the time is particularly favorable for a visit. The thing is that, realizing that we would otherwise not finish up here and would be pressed in making final arrangements, we have decided to give up the idea of a longish vacation. Actually we are rather pleased, for we are fully enjoying our way of life here and need nothing better. At most we want to spend a week in the Engadine, at Sils Maria or Sils Baseglia, where Erika already is. That will be too high for you (1,800 meters); but Leuk in the

Valais would not really suit you either. We are starting our "homeward" journey to Princeton on September 15. Would you be our house guest here in Küsnacht toward the end of the month and into September? The woods and lake shore, an easy drive, are so beautiful, and you would be coming to a country whose attitude toward *l'infâme* has turned into the most gratifying resoluteness since Austria. I have never felt endangered for as much as a moment, and no one need even know that you are here. What do you think? Around August 26 would be the right time, from the point of view of our own convenience. I am counting on your being free when I offer this date. At the moment we have Moni, Medi, and Golo, who has developed wonderfully and is writing excellent things for *Mass und Wert*. Have you sent off your Nietzsche introduction? I have written not twenty but sixty pages on Schopenhauer. Why was I ever set on that track? Now the foreword has had to be carved out of the surplus again. —Golo has already attended to that, too.

You have time to think over the visit, for which I hope you'll have cooler weather. We were pleased when it turned hot at last, but the pleasure is already proving a calamity.

Warmly,   T.

TO HERMANN HESSE

Küsnacht-Zurich
September 8, 1938

Dear Herr Hesse:

I was delighted to hear from you. Thank you for your lines, and accept my admiring respect for your helpful work in these abominable times. In Switzerland you can do more than I, but once or twice I too have been able to help a little; thus we were able to provide tolerably well for Robert Musil,[1] at least for his first months abroad.

Poor Amann. I haven't much hope that I can do anything for his manuscript. At the moment I had best follow your suggestion and pass it on to Welti,[2] since he is interested in it. I shall suggest that he return it to me in Princeton, for we are moving in the next few days. It is painful not to be seeing you and your wife before we go. But if the "grand

---

[1] Robert Musil (1880–1942), Austrian novelist; emigrated from Berlin to Vienna in 1933, to Switzerland in 1938. Among his works: *Young Törless* and the vast, unfinished novel *The Man Without Qualities*. Musil's reputation has grown steadily since the war.

[2] Jakob Rudolf Welti (b. 1893), writer. Together with Eduard Korrodi, feature editor of the *Neue Zürcher Zeitung*, 1919–55.

accounting" does not come, I shall certainly be back for a few months next May.

TO ERICH VON KAHLER

65 Stockton Street
Princeton, N.J.
October 19, 1938

Dear Kahler:

I would gladly have written to you long ago—I have thought of you so often during these weeks, felt anxious about you and yours, and wished that I could talk with you about the common misfortunes. But you can imagine how I have been living: first the disturbing days of uncertainty in Paris, then the week of depression along with the painfully inadequate news aboard ship, then the hours of tense hope after arrival here, culminating in a gigantic mass meeting in Madison Square Garden, at which I spoke and witnessed tremendous demonstrations; then Munich, and the realization at last of the filthy play which was being performed all along. The denouement came when the "democratic" governments transmitted Hitler's blackmail threats of war to their own peoples. . . . The shame, the disgust, the shattering of all hopes. For days I was literally sick at heart, and in these circumstances we had to install ourselves here. Now I am over the worst of it, have accepted the facts, whose meaning and logic is only too despicably clear. And now, I am tempted to think by magic, my desk stands in my study with every item arranged on it exactly as in Küsnacht, and even in Munich. I am determined to continue my life and work with maximum persistence, exactly as I have always done, unaltered by events which injure me but cannot humiliate me or turn me from my purposes. The way that history has taken has been so filthy, such a carrion-strewn path of lies and baseness, that no one need be ashamed of refusing to travel along it, even if it should lead to goals we might commend if reached by other paths. But who knows what further atrocities this trail may still pass through? Yet that Hitler will die as a transfigured prince of peace and chancellor of a Fascistic United States of Europe remains improbable.

I have made similar remarks in a preface to the small collection of political essays that Bermann meant to publish (whether he still wants to and can, I do not know). I felt the need to bring these outmoded things up to date, so the essay is also called "Up to Date." I like the title. But whether anything of the sort can still be printed in Europe is now extremely doubtful. People here are already highly suspicious of all European sources of information and believe that the censorship is widening. Naturally the peoples of Europe must not be allowed to realize too quickly how they are being hoodwinked and bullied.

I read a few lines of yours, a letter to Lion that he sent to me. The happiest news I gathered from it was your growing resolution to come over here. Do so! What's the sense of staying now? And how fine it would be to live as neighbors. Our house, which belongs to an Englishman, is very comfortable and an improvement over all those of the past. I think it important always to fall upstairs. The people are well-meaning through and through, filled with what seems to me an unshakable affability. You would breathe easier among them, would be touched and happy. The landscape is parklike, well suited to walks, with amazingly beautiful trees which now, in Indian summer, glow in the most magnificent colors. At night, to be sure, we already hear the leaves trickling down like rain, but people say that the clear, serene autumn often continues until nearly Christmas, and the winter is short.

The youngest children are with us; Erika is arriving tomorrow, probably with Golo, whose Czech military obligation doubtless need no longer be a problem, thanks to Chamberlain's[1] deep love of peace. Erika was in Prague. . . . I am curious to see what kind of European atmosphere the children will bring with them.

TO CORDELL HULL[1]

Princeton
October 25, 1938

Dear Mr. Secretary of State:

Letters and telegrams from Prague which are veritable cries of distress impel me to address the following plea to you.

In Prague there was a society bearing my name[2] which had been

[1] Arthur Neville Chamberlain (1869–1940), Prime Minister and author of the British foreign policy that led to Munich. Thomas Mann commented on him in "This Peace" [*Order of the Day* (New York: Alfred A. Knopf; 1942), p. 175]: "It is uncanny to see how the wretched figure of von Papen, the conservative who delivered up Germany to Hitler, recurs again in the English Chamberlain. Everything is the same: the treachery, the underlying motives, above all the fundamental self-deception. . . ."

[1] Cordell Hull (1871–1955), U.S. Secretary of State 1933–44. Roosevelt's adviser at the Moscow and Teheran conferences. Nobel Peace Prize, 1945.

[2] The Thomas Mann Gesellschaft of Prague.

aiding exiled German intellectuals. It received encouragement from the highest governmental authorities in the country; President Beneš was particularly well disposed toward it and gave it generous financial support. It was not primarily a charitable enterprise; it was concerned with those independent German intellectuals who had escaped from the present totalitarian regime to the safety of the Czechoslovak Republic and its purpose was to help them continue their work.

It is obvious that a society of this sort could not go on existing after the recent turn of events in Europe and in Czechoslovakia. Moreover, its leading members are directly endangered by the new situation, so that they must leave Prague as quickly as possible. Unfortunately there are formal obstacles to their doing so, and my question and plea is this: Could not you, Mr. Secretary of State, do something to see that in this emergency, which appeals so strongly to our humanitarianism, these obstacles may be removed? For example, the American consul in Prague is certainly only doing his duty when he demands that those concerned present birth certificates and evidence of good character from Germany, but under the circumstances such documents simply cannot be obtained. Would it be possible for higher authorities to give the consulate in Prague power to facilitate entry to America for these imperiled and extremely worthy persons? Herewith is a list of the persons in question.

Professor Leo Kestenberg[3] and wife

Joachim Werner Cohn,[4] sociologist, his wife and two small children

Dr. Wilhelm Necker,[5] wife and child

Dr. Alexander Bessmertny[6]

Egon Lehrburger[7]

---

[3] Leo Kestenberg (1882–1962), pianist (pupil of Busoni), music consultant in the Prussian ministry of education 1919–32. Exiled to Prague in 1933 and Palestine in 1938, where he contributed greatly to musical life in the Mandate and later in Israel. Author of many books on music.

[4] Joachim Werner Cohn (later Conway) (1906–55), journalist. Fled to Czechoslovakia in 1933, to England in 1938. Wrote for the *Spectator*, the *Manchester Guardian*, the *Daily Telegraph*, and other journals.

[5] Wilhelm Necker (b. 1897), writer. Emigrated to Prague in 1934 and in 1938 to England, where he remained. Among his works: *Nazi Germany Can't Win* (London, 1939), *This Bewildering War* (London, 1940), *Invasion Tactics* (London, 1944), *Es war doch so schön*, autobiography (1947). Correspondent for the *Evening Star* and *Daily Mail*, among others.

[6] Alexander Bessmertny (1888–1943), writer. Fled to France in 1933, then to Czechoslovakia. Arrested by the Gestapo in Prague in 1939, executed in Berlin in 1943. Among his works: *L'Atlantide* (Paris, 1949).

[7] Egon Lehrburger (b. 1904), writer, photographer. Emigrated to France, later to Czechoslovakia, in 1938 to England; London correspondent of the Bavarian Radio. Among his works: *Chase across Europe* (London, 1940), *Inventors' Cavalcade* (London, 1943), *Abenteuer der Technik* (1950), *Mensch und Meerestiefe* (1957).

Ursula Hönig[8]
Wilhelm Sternfeld[9]
Friedrich Burschell[10]
Frau Fritta Brod[11]

I am well aware, sir, that in these tragic times you are overwhelmed with petitions of this sort, and I should have hesitated to add to your burdens were it not that it so pains my conscience and my feelings, while I myself am fortunate enough to enjoy the protection of American democracy,[12] to abandon these people who helped others as long as they could and who now appeal to me in their need.

Most respectfully and sincerely yours,

TO J. GEORGE FREDERICK[1]

[Original in English]

Princeton

Dear Mr. Frederick:

I am flattered that you attribute to me the ability to evaluate properly the gourmet standard.

Your invitation to attend the November meeting of the Gourmet Society is especially attractive since I have a thoroughly sympathetic understanding of your aims, both gastronomical and social. However, I very much regret that my work makes it necessary for me to refuse your kind invitation at this time.

I was delighted with your statement that even the peoples of the East traditionally suspend hostilities while dining together, for this opens

---

[8] Ursula Hönig, stepdaughter of Friedrich Burschell, the then secretary of the Thomas Mann Gesellschaft in Prague. Later married to Egon Lehrburger.

[9] Wilhelm Sternfeld (b. 1888), journalist. Emigrated to Paris in 1933, to Prague in 1935, to London in 1939. Secretary of a Thomas Mann Group in London for aid to Czechoslovak exiles and a key figure in the Self Aid of Refugees from Germany. Himself impoverished, Sternfeld performed prodigies for his fellow unfortunates. Author of, among others: *Deutsche Exil-Literatur 1933–1945* (1962).

[10] Friedrich Burschell (b. 1889), writer, translator, journalist, associated with such important journals as the *Frankfurter Zeitung, Neue Rundschau, Weisse Blätter*. Fled to France in 1933, then Spain, Czechoslovakia; to England in 1938; has lived in Munich since 1954. Among his books: *Jean Paul, Entwicklung eines Dichters*.

[11] Fritta Brod, actress, wife of Friedrich Burschell. Emigrated from Prague to London in 1939; there she worked sporadically for the German section of the BBC (1940–7) and gave many lectures to students of German at Oxford.

[12] This protection was not granted to the persons on the list, but with two exceptions they escaped to England.

[1] President of the Gourmet Society.

up the possibility of a considerable extension of the scope of work of your Society in places not so remote as the East.

With many thanks for your kindness,

TO OSKAR MARIA GRAF

Princeton
November 1, 1938

Dear Herr Graf:

How right you are that the various committees ought to be consolidated. That is evident from the fact that I did not even know of the existence of the Hollywood Committee. Otherwise I would have gotten in touch with [Bruno] Frank about Burschell's list of persons. It did not coincide with the names you list, with the exception of Burschell and Fritta Brod, but dealt exclusively with the principal members of the Thomas Mann Gesellschaft; in other words, persons for whose weal and woe—in this case woe —I cannot help feeling especially responsible. What I have done is to address an extremely urgent letter to Secretary of State Hull pleading with him to instruct the American representatives in Prague that the persons mentioned by Burschell be granted clearance for entry into the United States—above all, be spared the need to supply documents that cannot be obtained. I wrote some days ago and have not yet received an answer from Hull—perhaps should not expect any. The chief thing would be for him to have actually sent instructions to Prague.

Naturally I will do all in my power to arrange this vital discussion among Manfred George,[1] Bruckner,[2] and Dorothy Thompson.[3] I am writing to her immediately. Will you and the others please set an hour for the meeting.

Let me add that I am deeply touched by your devoted work for our

---

[1] Manfred George (1893–1965), writer, editor, translator. Until 1933 editor-in-chief of the large Berlin afternoon newspaper *Tempo*. Emigrated to Czechoslovakia in 1933, to the United States in 1938. Founder and editor-in-chief of the New York German-Jewish newspaper *Aufbau*, which continues to flourish. Author of, among others, *Männer, Frauen, Waffen* (Locarno, 1934); *Wunder Israel* (1949).

[2] Ferdinand Bruckner (1891–1958), Austrian playwright and director. Founder of the Berlin Renaissance Theater (1923). Emigrated to Austria in 1933, to the United States in 1936. Author of *Krankheit der Jugend* (1929), *Die Verbrecher* (1929), *Elisabeth von England* (1930), *Simon Bolivar* (1945), *Gesammelte Dramen* I & II (1947).

[3] Dorothy Thompson (1894–1961), noted American journalist, at that time the wife of Sinclair Lewis. As a foreign correspondent she was the first American citizen to be deported by the Nazis after their seizure of power. Throughout the years of Hitlerism she was one of the leaders in the fight against Fascism, befriended the German refugees, and never lost her faith in the German people.

colleagues. I also understand only too well the suffering that brings home to all of us our impotence, or at any rate our extremely limited ability to help.

TO OSKAR MARIA GRAF

Princeton
November 22, 1938

Dear Herr Graf:

I did want to show you Hull's reply. It doesn't amount to much, but at least it is something that a copy has gone to the consul in Prague.

The storm of indignation at the most recent German bestialities[1] may also help the cause of the refugees somewhat. Unfortunately there is the clear danger that the loathing of all that is German will be extended to everyone without distinction, including us.

TO ANNA JACOBSON[1]

Princeton
November 30, 1938

Dear Professor Jacobson:

Your news of the situation in the German Department of Hunter College has deeply impressed me, in both an affirmative and a negative sense. You write that the students have been disturbed and embittered by the appalling events in Germany, that they have begun to doubt the humanistic value of their studies in German and to question whether there is any sense in their concerning themselves with the language and culture of a nation where such despicable things take place, apparently without resistance. I understand their feeling only too well, and more than that, I approve of it, rejoice in it. It is proof of a moral sensibility and a hatred of evil which have become all too rare in a world steeped in moral apathy. It is to America's credit that this abhorrence and indignation are so strong and widespread here.

[1] On November 9 Goebbels had organized the notorious Crystal Night, during which synagogues were burned, Jewish homes and shops were wrecked all over Germany, and their inhabitants and owners beaten and dragged off to concentration camps.

[1] Anna Jacobson (b. 1888), professor of German at Hunter College, New York, 1924–56. Author of numerous studies on Walt Whitman, Stefan George, Gerhart Hauptmann, Franz Werfel, Herman Hesse, and Thomas Mann. This letter was published in English, in a different translation, in the *Hunter College Bulletin* and made the rounds of other colleges and universities. The threatened elimination of German at Hunter College did not take place.

Unfortunately, however, this is not the first time that I have encountered the tendency here to extend such justified repugnance toward the present German regime and its crimes to things German in general—the tendency to reject German culture, which has nothing to do with the regime. One must not forget that a large part of the German people live in necessarily mute and suffering opposition to National Socialism and that the horrors and crimes perpetrated in Germany in recent weeks are by no means acts of the people, despite all the efforts of the government to pretend that they are. The arson and the campaign of annihilation directed against the Jews are exclusively the work of the rulers. The claim that these outbreaks represent a spontaneous reaction of the people to the regrettable event in Paris is a propaganda lie, like all the rest. It is established that the "Bolshevistic" acts throughout Germany were organized by the government and carried out by its gangster crews. The German people have been forced to look on, as at so many other things, in outrage and silent horror.

The shortsighted, feeble, and uncomprehending policy of the Western powers in Europe has conferred upon the National Socialist regime a plenitude of power, which enables these creatures to fulfil their wishes and evil instincts to the utmost, without fear or consideration for anyone. What they are doing certainly sets a stain upon the honor of Germany which time will not erase without great difficulty. Nevertheless, the German spirit has made noble contributions to the culture of mankind in the past, and we all hope that it will do so again in the future, when the unhappy nation has routed these rulers who disgrace it. German culture in music, art, and intellectual life was and remains one of the richest and most important in the world, and no atrocities of our distracted present age justify turning away from the study of this culture and the language in which it has manifested itself. I think that the students of your college ought to see that, and should even take pride in cultivating and keeping alive these values in America during a dark time in which they are trampled underfoot in Germany itself. To my mind, it is a morally upright but immature action to abandon the study of German because usurping rulers have for the moment brought public discredit upon it. May I ask you to convey this modest and well-meant view of mine to the ladies of the German department? Perhaps my comments may help prevent high-minded but nevertheless superficial and overhasty decisions.

1938

Princeton
December 6, 1938

Dear Professor:

Yesterday, on a train ride to New York, I read your fine essay on the birth of Helen. I cannot tell you how much this paper, like your other work, stimulated, enriched, and moved me. The world of your studies has a magical allure for me, and the relationships you uncover, this mysterious oneness of Helen, Nemesis, and Aphrodite, have preoccupied me and given me the keenest intellectual pleasure, ever since you introduced me to them. After such reading I always wish I were back with the *Joseph*, where it could bear fruit more directly than it can for my present undertaking. But then it may be that your essay will also leave its mark on my Goethe novel, in which Helen will surely have to turn up sooner or later. That would be a project for you someday: to write about Goethe's version of Helen—the way he united the classical tradition with rococo and galanterie is in itself quite unique and charmingly impermissible, and has never, so far as I know, been analyzed with the tools that you have at your disposal.

In reading your essay I recalled Goethe's meetings with a predecessor of yours, the mythologist Creuzer, which are recounted in Biedermann's *Conversations*. In Heidelberg in 1815 Creuzer had a discussion with Goethe on the symbolic interpretation of the Greek mythological figures and stories, for Goethe had shown an intense interest in these matters. Goethe's use of mythology, especially in the "Classical Walpurgis Night," has always seemed to me the bridge between him and Wagner, who particularly loved this part of *Faust* and during his last years in Venice would read it aloud to his family with many exclamations of admiration.

We have adjusted well to our new surroundings. Outward conditions have been good, but our minds troubled, for I need not say that the events in Europe have been a great burden and source of anxiety. I shall not go into that; I have aired my feelings in a small essay, "This Peace," which has also been published in English and widely distributed in many thousands of copies. I find the situation in Hungary opaque. Perhaps you can tell me something about that—at least a few hints? When will we see each other again? The way to Budapest is cut off for me, the way to Europe in general not quite yet, I hope, and Switzerland in the summer would be the right place for a meeting, assuming that your ways do not actually lead you across the ocean to us one of these days.

Keep well; and thank you again for the intellectual delight you have given me; and please continue to keep me up to date on your work.

P.S. Recently I gave my first two public lectures here. They dealt with Goethe's *Faust* and were well received by young and old.

TO ERIKA AND KLAUS MANN[1]

(December 1938)

Dear children:

You, my two eldest, have written a book after my own heart. You know that; for you know that I have thwarted all attempts to separate me from the German emigrants and to give me a separate, ambiguous position among them; that I have emphasized my relationship to them—did so years ago because I did not want the rulers of Germany to hesitate any longer to "expatriate" me too, as they had already "expatriated" you and my brother. And they did not hesitate any longer.

Your book is a book of that solidarity on which I then insisted. Let it be a solidarity not alone in suffering and in pride, but in guilt as well. German freedom and the Weimar Republic have been destroyed; we, you and I, are not altogether guiltless in that matter—though surely we may disclaim any part in the degradation and shame which ensued. Mistakes were made, of omission and commission; that we cannot deny. The spiritual leaders of the Republic did not err, perhaps, on the side of the spirit; but they did so in the matter of leadership and the conscious-ness of their responsibility. Freedom was sometimes compromised; often it was not treated with the care and concern which the circumstances in Germany demanded. But was that to be wondered at? Freedom is a more complex and delicate thing than force. It is not so simple to live under as force is. And we German intellectuals were new to freedom; we were politically very young and inexperienced—as young as you were then in actual years.

Why should I not admit that I am father enough to see in your development during these six hard years an example of the maturity

---

[1] This letter was published as the preface to Chapter V, "Portrait of Our Father," in *Escape to Life*, by Erika and Klaus Mann (Boston: Houghton Mifflin Company; 1939). Translation (slightly amended) by Erika and Klaus Mann.

which freedom can reach in exile? Knowing the deep soundness of your natures, I have always interpreted the hatred displayed toward you, my children, as a sign (if indeed one was needed) of the malignant mindlessness of the rising tide of brutality in Germany. Now, in your growing strength to will and to achieve, in your increasing abilities, I can see a parable and guarantee of the political and social advancement the German spirit has undergone by virtue of its very banishment.

We may be certain that the same process is going on inside our country. The German people are going to a hard school. For they have long needed such a discipline, and one thing they are certain to learn in it—indeed, unless all signs deceive, they have already learned it—is what freedom means. They have never really known this. If some day, by God's mercy, they are granted it again, truly I believe they will know how to guard it.

Your book on the German refugees appears at a favorable moment, at a crisis whose only good side is that it reveals to the world the mental state of the German people, their yearning for peace, freedom, and justice. A whole world, immeasurably threatened, has had its attention called to the unofficial feelings of the German people; and it now regards the refugees with increasing interest and sympathy. People outside Germany have begun to wonder whether our warnings were really actuated by mere resentment and desire for revenge, or simply by better knowledge of the kind of men who have acquired power in Germany; to wonder whether the world might not have learned from us what to expect of them, if only the world had been willing to learn earlier. Your book gives us, in a sequence of vivid portraits, a clear idea of the rich individual value and content of the German emigration. I think it will be welcome.

Your Father

1939

---•---

TO EMIL OPRECHT

Dear Herr Oprecht:

The fate of our magazine is always on my mind, and since Golo has been here I have talked a great deal with him about it and conferred with others. His ambition to take over the editorship in the spring is very strong, and his confidence that he can conduct the magazine in a spirit that will win it the new friends it needs has impressed me and strengthened my own confidence in his ability. I do believe, however, that he must have an adviser for the belletristic part of the magazine. His judgment in this field is probably not clear and sure enough. He himself seems to feel that. We must therefore consider what reliable person, who nevertheless will not be too demanding, we can secure—if, as may be assumed, Lion will not be available.

But all this, of course, is secondary to the major question: whether the magazine can be kept going without the kind of financial backing it has had up to now. I am well aware that unless new funds can be raised, we shall have to cease publication. That would be painful for me, for I set great store by this undertaking. It is, after all, the only free German periodical of major importance that still exists, and its suspension would be tragic in every way. I keep trying to think where interest might be aroused in this country. The problem is to find someone willing to make a financial sacrifice for an idealistic cause, so that the magazine's future can at least be assured for another year or so. I even have someone in mind, and have appealed to him with all the intensity that I feel. But in order to be able to discuss the matter without sounding vague, I need documentation of the magazine's previous business history. Would you please send me data on the following points as soon as possible:

I need a list of the funds that have been at our disposal, an accounting of the sum total of capital that we have received. I must also know the income from copies sold, the income from advertising, and, for example, even from pulping—in short, the total assets. And against that the costs, in as much detail as possible: editorial, fees, distribution, setting, printing, binding, paper, advertising, and general expenses.

Furthermore, could you please tell me: Is the magazine's budget balanced at a certain level of circulation, and would it be self-sustaining if it reached that level? What would the figure be?

Golo often speaks of the need to make economies. He is only too right about that. For I haven't any hope of a subsidy of the size provided by Frau Mayrisch; I would be lucky if I could raise $2,000 per year. To cut back on expenses I am prepared to waive payment for my contributions, both future ones and those still due (Yale speech and August chapter). Also, Golo would surely be cheaper for the magazine than Lion, and would take care of the editing without a paid secretary, as Klaus has done for *Die Sammlung*, so that this rather considerable item could be eliminated. These, at any rate, are a few suggestions; and in general we would have to seek the most rational and economical manner of conducting the magazine's affairs.

In addition to the balance sheet, it will also be necessary to set up a budget for the magazine, considering all conceivable savings, and based on realistic circulation figures. In other words, let's arrive at an estimate of the minimum subsidy per issue.

There is also the hope that Madame M. may be persuaded to give a small additional subsidy if we can raise a really significant sum here, or that other funds may possibly be collected elsewhere in Europe.

In addition, Golo spoke of a considerable deficit that you yourself have been bearing. The amount will no doubt be apparent from the statement I have asked for. You can imagine that this news distresses me and makes me most reluctant to liquidate the magazine right now. But if that should be the outcome, we would naturally have to make sure that the entire loss does not rest on your shoulders.

So much for today. I would be extremely grateful if you could reply by return post, and will cable you if my efforts here meet with success.

Regards to you and your wife from me and all of us.

TO AGNES E. MEYER

Princeton
February 1, 1939

My dear friend:

Your letter today made me very happy, and I hasten to thank you for it. I promise not to hope for too much and not to rejoice prematurely, but your and your husband's agreement in principle was in itself comforting and encouraging. Please give him my best regards and tell him how much I appreciate the effort he intends to make.

Meanwhile I have done what I should have done before writing to you: I have asked the Zurich publisher for a detailed balance sheet of the magazine in case prospective donors should, as is only reasonable, want to examine its financial affairs.

Thank you also for your kindness in taking care of the Swiss matter. I would be glad to show my appreciation to the country that granted me hospitality for five years, and the article would be a good beginning.

We must talk as soon as possible—about the lecture, too, which I have already laid aside with probably unwarranted feelings that it is satisfactory. But should one really make further concessions to popular understanding? It is a pedagogical question, and my principle has been that one should not descend too far toward one's audiences, but rather tempt them upwards. They are actually grateful for that.

Since you are in New York, we feel drawn to the city. But will I be able to break loose from here this week? There has been a great deal of distraction from visits lately, and I am passionately eager at least to finish off the monologue chapter, which of course I have made as hard as possible for myself, before the lecture tour begins—it starts in a few weeks, and will hardly be a time for work. It will be April before I can begin again, and I ought to have the book done before our summer trip, so that another German oddity of the better sort will once more be brought into the world. . . . Such are my inner conflicts, but if you telephone, they will be swiftly resolved.

TO AGNES E. MEYER

Princeton
February 7, 1939

My dear friend:

Many thanks for your letter and the clipping, which will certainly please Falke[1] *quand même,* in spite of the omissions, I mean. I have written him that "my liaison man" in Washington (that's you) will speak with the Swiss ambassador. Do so, please! Switzerland is terribly menaced, and everything depends on the country's being economically strengthened.

Now, of course, I shall set my mind completely at rest about the lectures. Should there be any objections, I shall reply: Approved by Agnes E. Meyer.

The letter about Erika delighted my paternal heart. But the child worries me. She is alarmingly thin, coughs, and is visibly overworked. Success is a stern god in America, almost as stern as failure. I am glad not only for my own sake that she will come along again on my trip West. It will be a vacation for her and a chance to recuperate. I am deeply grateful for the sisterly concern you have for her, for I love this child immensely. The mixture, or the existence side by side of a vein of comedy and a vein of dark ardency in her nature has something deeply touching and appealing to me.

TO KARL KERÉNYI

Princeton
February 16, 1939

Dear Professor Kerényi:

I have received your Christmas letter twice and twice read your essay on the festival—are you pleased? I need scarcely say, and scarcely could, how much at home I felt with this essay of yours, which I consider among the finest things you have ever done—perhaps I should say the very finest, seduced as I am by the way it falls in with the things I use to refresh and restore myself against the miserable stupidities and vileness of the public scene. My opinion therefore has a personal cast, but I seriously think that the essay's literary qualities, the grace with which its ideas are expounded, deserve special acknowledgement and represent a loftier, freer stage of your work. No doubt this has to do with the "breakthrough into a higher and wider realm of scholarship" you speak of. But I can scarcely see it as a breakthrough, since I have long accepted you as a full-fledged master of that realm which I can enter only as a dilettante equipped with a bit of artistic intuition.

You can imagine how often my thoughts turned to *Joseph* as I read

---

[1] Konrad Falke (1880–1942), Swiss writer, coeditor of *Mass und Wert.* Among his works: Translation of Dante's *Divina Commedia* (1921), *Der Kinderkreuzzug* (1924), *Dramatische Werke* (5 vols., 1930–3).

you. "Festival" in the sense of mythic ceremony and the playful solemn repetition of primal events is, after all, virtually *the* fundamental motif of my novel; in fact, its hero is once directly called *Joseph em heb*: "Joseph in the festival." I might have felt homesick for the book, as so often happens when I read anything pertinent to it; but that feeling was checked because you also sounded the notes of a good many ideas which pertain to my present work, the Goethe novel. Has this one, too, turned out to be "mythology"? Enough; I was strangely stirred to all sorts of recollections by your remarks on the draining away of vitality through recurrence, and on the lingering of creativity in recurrence; furthermore, on the marked compatibility of life and mind, of vitality and awareness. Recurrence enhanced by awareness, though at the sacrifice of some vitality, is a major theme of *Lotte in Weimar*; for the "Hatem"[1] affair with Marianne Willemer is just such a recurrence. To make it stronger, she is even called Jung. The beloved is forever young; but the matter is slightly confused, because together with the timeless sweetheart the now aged Lotte also puts in an appearance. —That is more or less how it goes.

I wish I could do something about your longing for America, to have you invited somewhere. If you would give me some suggestion about whom I might turn to, I would gladly try. Do you speak English? The very best to you and your wife.

TO H. M. LYDENBERG[1]

[*Original in English*]

Princeton
February 27, 1939

Dear Mr. Lydenberg:

I have been told that the Astor and Lenox Foundations of the New York Public Library have endowment funds for the purchase of books which are quite separate from the annual appropriations made by the City of New York for the maintenance of the library and its various branches. Also that in the "reference collections" there is a special German section. I am writing to ask whether you and your board of directors would be interested in acquiring a valuable collection of the books and manuscripts of Franz Kafka, the German novelist, who died in 1924.

Dr. Max Brod, the German-Czechoslovakian novelist and dramatist,

---

[1] Goethe's whimsical name for himself in the poem written on this occasion. See Thomas Mann, *Last Essays* (New York: Alfred A. Knopf; 1959), pp. 98f.

[1] H. M. Lydenberg (1874–1960), director of the New York Public Library until 1941.

who is probably well known to the chief of your Jewish section of the library, Dr. Joshua Bloch, has recently written me from Prague. I have known and admired Dr. Brod for many years. He is now 54. For the past twenty years and more he has worked for his country, not simply as a writer, but as a civil servant and also as editor of the *Prager Tagblatt*. He is a gifted and cultured man; but now, because he is a Jew, he is no longer permitted to write what he thinks and believes, and is being ridiculed and vilified in the German press.

As a young man Dr. Brod became an intimate friend of Franz Kafka. When Kafka died, leaving his work unfinished and incomplete, Dr. Brod, as executor, undertook the editing of his friend's books. His scholarly and devoted work led to the publication of many of Kafka's books, such as the novels *The Castle*, *The Trial*, etc., which have been translated into English.

Dr. Brod is anxious to leave Czechoslovakia and come to the United States. He fears he will not survive the period of fifteen months to two years which he would have to wait to enter this country as an ordinary immigrant. If any institution here would invite him to take up a position at a minimum salary of $2,000 (the amount the American consuls abroad require guaranteed to prospective immigrants before granting visas), he thinks he could come at once as a nonquota alien. He writes that he is willing to give his collection of the books and manuscripts of Franz Kafka to any institution of repute which would accept it and in return offer him a position to act as assistant or curator of the collection, and so make possible his entry into this country.

If you and your board of directors will consider this offer I shall be profoundly grateful. I have no hesitation in recommending Dr. Brod for any position requiring the highest degree of scholarship and integrity. For your information I am attaching a copy of the letter I received from Dr. Brod. Should you wish to write to him directly, may I suggest that, for his protection, no reference be made either to his difficult position or to the fact that he is a Jew. The Nazi penetration of Czechoslovakia, since Munich, has proceeded with a rapidity hardly as yet appreciated in this country, and the lives and situations of Jewish men and women in the Czechoslovak republic are desperate in the extreme. For this reason it would be of inestimable help if you could arrive at a decision at an early date. I am shortly leaving Princeton to go to the West, but will be glad at any time to give you any other particulars I can, if they are needed, though I realize that should you be in any way interested, you will probably prefer to communicate with Dr. Brod directly.

I am deeply appreciative of the generous and humane consideration which the American public is giving to the very difficult problem of the refugees from the fascist countries. Had it not been that Dr. Brod is a man who is well known and who would add to the distinction of any institution attaching him to its staff, I would have hesitated to trouble you as I know that there must be many demands made upon you. Perhaps you will agree with me that the possibility of acquiring the manuscripts and books of so well known a writer as Franz Kafka is an opportunity deserving of consideration quite apart from the human tragedy of the individual for whom the collection represents the one real chance of escape from an intolerable situation.

TO HEINRICH MANN

Princeton
March 2, 1939

Dear Heinrich:

Your novel[1] arrived at last a few days ago. And I can truly say that I am reading it day and night, by day in every free half hour, and at night in the quiet before I switch off the lamp—which, thanks to you, happens late. As I read I am never without the sense of an exciting uniqueness, the sense of having to do with the best, the proudest, the highest this age has to offer. Certainly people will wonder someday how our debased times could bring forth anything of the sort—and will realize that all the blatant idiocy and crimes are not so very important after all and that the human spirit, fundamentally undisturbed, meanwhile goes its way and creates its works. The book is great in love, in art, boldness, freedom, wisdom, kindness, exceedingly rich in intelligence, wit, imagination, and feeling—a great and beautiful thing, synthesis and résumé of your life and your personality. It must be said that such growth—such transformation of the static to the dynamic, such perseverance, and such a harvesting —is peculiarly European. Here in America the writers are short-lived; they write one good book, follow it with two poor ones, and then are finished. "Life" in the Goethean sense is in our tradition alone; it is less a matter of vitality than of intelligence and will. Kesten,[2] in the essay we were fortunate enough to be able to publish in the last issue of *Mass und*

---

[1] *Henry, King of Navarre.*

[2] Hermann Kesten (b. 1900), writer and novelist. Kesten emigrated to France and then to the United States, where he became very involved in the affairs of the Emergency Rescue Committee. Through this work he became friends for a time with Thomas Mann. In 1949 he returned to Europe and now lives in Rome.

Wert, took many of the words right out of my mouth; in this case, one must admit, enthusiasm helped him surpass himself. I imagine you too were affected by it; it is virtually a model of a favorable review, and since he sees the whole, it also forms a kind of homage to a life. I can imagine that the German exiles as a group feel proud of this monument! And ultimately, for don't we know how such things go, Germany too will take pride in it. "For he was ours." Well, yes, in a manner of speaking.

There's another matter I want to mention, not the most pleasant: the affair with your son-in-law, my nephew, Dr. A. He was here, paid a short visit to his uncle, as he is wont to call me, then departed for a long stay in the West (he said "South" but meant California). What he had to say about the transfer of the business (a chemical factory is, after all, not transportable, and I doubt that there is anything at all to be transferred) and about the guaranty sum for Goschi[3] (a man who has entered this country as an immigrant and is settled here can bring his wife over without more ado, as I have already told you), was all rather vague and indefinite. Nor was it clear what he intended to do in California. A few days later an American, Morton W. Lieberman of South Orange, New Jersey, came to see us to warn us. He said that there is an indictment pending against Dr. A. for embezzlement of objects of value, jewels and the like, which a Jewish lady had given to him to spirit out of Germany. The Jewish lady had succeeded in getting out herself, and so she was able to institute proceedings against him, while many other Jewish people of substance, for whom he had also taken out valuables, can do nothing because they are still in Germany or Austria. Mr. Lieberman impressed me as being sensible and well-meaning; and we had previously heard from people in Prague that they wished Mimi[4] and Goschi the best of everything, but that someone seemed to have been acting too precipitately. In view of all this, we have begun to worry about what you have done about your furniture, which I suppose A. also brought out and which, he made haste to say, might be delayed for months. And indeed, we wonder what you have done about this whole connection. God knows whether the young man is being unjustly suspected. People may be maligning him to us. But I can't really see why they should bother, and sorry as I am to trouble you, I thought you had better know about it. Golo thinks so too and has written to Mimi, though not so bluntly as I am doing here. These

---

[3] Henriette Leonie Mann (b. 1916), the daughter of Heinrich Mann's first marriage, his only child.

[4] Mimi Mann, née Kanowa, Heinrich Mann's first wife. She died in 1946 from the consequences of her internment in the Theresienstadt concentration camp.

rumors and charges are going the rounds; the suspicion that A.'s marriage to Goschi might be a dishonest person's exploitation of your name and mine cannot be rejected out of hand; and for good or ill you should both govern your attitude accordingly, not send Goschi over here prematurely, and in general be somewhat on your guard. I hope it all turns out to be sheer nonsense.

Another week and my lecture tour starts in Boston, then leads to the Middle West and West—five weeks of it. There will be three of us; Erika will come along as secretary and assistant. It will be strenuous, but I know how it goes now, and the American sleeping-car beds in private compartments are excellent.

With hearty congratulations,   T.

TO SIGMUND FREUD
[*Telegram*]

Princeton
May 7, 1939

With memories of the lovely celebration of your eightieth birthday in Vienna, in unalterable loyalty and veneration,

Thomas and Katia Mann

TO AGNES E. MEYER

Princeton
May 13, 1939

Dear friend:

I am happy to have your lecture[1] so handsomely printed, and relieved that the lecture manuscript I sent you has turned up. Whether 18 or 16, the post office is certainly lazy! I should think that "Crescent Place," in fact "Washington," in fact "America," would be enough for your address.

Your comments on my *Magic Mountain* piece[2] could not have been finer. Of course such a light, chatty article didn't tell you anything new. But purity, *Reinheit*, is not really what Hans Castorp is "seeking."

---

[1] "Freedom of the Press, Freedom of Speech and Religious Tolerance."

[2] "Introduction to *The Magic Mountain* for the students of Princeton," printed as an introduction to the one-volume edition of *The Magic Mountain* (New York: Alfred A. Knopf; 1962) under the title "The Making of The Magic Mountain." It was originally published in the *Atlantic*, January 1953.

Neither he nor I have ascetic inclinations. What stirs him is the problem of man in general, the question of man's "standing and status." It is a matter of his humanistic instruction, and *Erziehungsromane* customarily contain both education and seduction. Madame Chauchat is seductive first of all in a sense that I should not like to object to, and secondly, as Settembrini sees it, a little in an intellectual sense as well. But she is no more so than Settembrini himself with his horn of reason, or Naphta, or other overpowering temptations of the novel, and I should not like to be saddled with the reputation of regarding woman as the one and only seducer. Mérimée, too, certainly did not look at things that way, in spite of *Carmen*. After all, my portrait of Potiphar's wife is clearly a *vindication* of a woman who has always been regarded as a licentious seductress. And the deep emotion stemming from the character of Rachel, for others as well as for me, has nothing to do with seduction. I admit that I am more concerned with delineating what is generally human than what is specifically feminine. But I am in total agreement with the charming homage Goethe paid to femininity in the lines:

> For a woman's disposition
> Is so close akin to art.

My very best wishes for the progress of your work.

TO AGNES E. MEYER

Princeton
May 20, 1939

My dear friend:

A few more stations of the cross have been passed since I received your nice note of the 15th. The doctoral ceremony here was very fine and dignified; my words of thanks were pleasantly received and most sincerely meant. For it is a blessing to me to sink roots into this soil, and every new tie confirms me in my feeling of being at home. I am glad of that, for Europe, where things looked somewhat more hopeful for a few weeks, once again seems to be in a bad way. Isn't there a new Munich in the offing? But let's drop that.

The booksellers' affair is also over; we combined it with a visit to the World's Fair for the opening of the Russian pavilion. Yesterday Einstein and I spoke in the chapel here to the divinity students, but duties of this sort are about over. On June 2 I have to address American writers, and before that, on the 29th, there is a degree and a talk at a college some distance from here, an overnight journey. I promised to come when the date was still far off, and at least there is a fee connected with it. After that I am in the clear, and next year shall have cards printed stating that I am a writer and must write.

One job which I have taken on is to write an introduction for a large illustrated edition of *Anna Karenina,* to be published by Random House. This will be a pleasure. Incidentally, there is also a request for a foreword to a new edition of *Royal Highness,* a task I would prefer to transfer to you. Furthermore, President Dodds,[1] who in a recent speech here gave my academic activities rather fulsome praise, has proposed a new arrangement with Princeton for the *second half* of next winter. [The] Rockefeller [Foundation] seems to be in difficulties. . . . But there is the possibility of a supplementary arrangement with the Flexner Institute.[2] I shall probably accept. What do you think?

For the present we are looking forward to our European holiday—with plenty of time for work, I hope. First Switzerland, then a Swedish seaside resort. On June 6, my birthday, the *Ile de France* is sailing, and it now seems to be settled that we shall board it with Erika. Can we manage to see you before we go? Alas, it's doubtful. Yet I wish I could tell you about my parents, so as to neglect nothing that might help your project. I can only say that except for May 28 and 29 and June 2, I shall be here.

In Zurich the future of *Mass und Wert* will have to be discussed. The situation is this: If we count on an edition of 2,000 copies, the printing costs for six issues will come to about 12,000 Swiss francs. Editorial costs for the year will be about 3,000 francs. If at all possible, the fee for contributions should not be lowered—I personally have waived my own and merely have it credited. Perhaps one or two other writers will follow my example; we could then reckon with an average fee of 6 francs per page, or about 1,000 francs per issue and 6,000 per year. If we add, say, 3,000 francs for unforeseen expenses, the budget for the next year would come to about 24,000 Swiss francs; and if we assume that half of this will be covered by sales, there remains a deficit of 12,000 francs—approximately $3,000. I have given my word to raise $2,000 of that sum here; the remaining $1,000 would *then,* in all likelihood, be contributed from European sources. Question: Is that generous soul whom you and your husband have encouraged me to place my hopes in prepared to let me

---

[1] Harold W. Dodds (b. 1889), professor of political science; president of Princeton University 1933–57.

[2] Mann probably meant the Institute for Advanced Study, then headed by Abraham Flexner.

have the providential check for $2,000, so that I can take it to Europe? My neat balance sheet should surely please the person involved.

What better way to conclude my letter than by speaking of that generous person? The warmest regards to you and your whole household.

TO FRANZ WERFEL

Dear Franz Werfel:

In the midst of turmoil and uncertainty, of threats of war and fresh danger of appeasement, one thing is becoming increasingly clear: the decision must and will be made in Germany. Until the German people have liberated themselves from this "leadership" there will not be lasting world peace. We have long known that, and the world is beginning to grasp it. We also know that the Germans basically hate their regime and that the only thing they fear more than Hitler is war. The suspicion and frightened disgust that the Germans feel toward the Nazi government is not primarily "political" in character. What horrifies the better Germans is the moral abyss into which they are sinking—the abominable depravity in morals and culture. We know that within the past six months a considerable number of Germans have left their country who could not be considered "tainted" either "politically" or "racially." They left simply because the November pogroms and the propaganda campaign against Czechoslovakia have been too much for them. They speak of the avidity with which they snatched at statements from outside, from the world of freedom. Dangerous though it was, nothing could quench their thirst for truth, for decency, above all for dignity, for quiet recollection. They describe their longing for the voices of intelligence and civilization. And while the books of the prizewinning government writers no longer find any readers in Germany, however much they are trumpeted, translations are what "sell." Works of the few "permitted" foreign authors are devoured. But our friends in Germany are yearning intensely, urgently, to hear from us. In the course of the campaign against the intelligentsia, the *Schwarze Korps*[1] denounced the booksellers only a few weeks ago, declaring that if it were up to them nothing but exile literature would be sold. On this point we have every reason to believe the *Schwarze Korps*.

It is imperative for the Germans inside the country, and for us, the

---

[1] *Das Schwarze Korps*, the weekly newspaper of Hitler's SS.

representatives of intellectual Germany on the outside, to make contact with one another. There must be an end to the unnatural situation in which we who might teach the Germans to remember their better selves are cut off from them. For if we speak insistently enough, our voices will be heard at home. This is my plan:

In the course of a year some twenty-four pamphlets, written by representatives of the German intelligentsia *for the Germans,* will be sent into the country. The series will not be narrowly political. It is meant to appeal to the better instincts of our fellow countrymen, whereas Hitler can arouse only their most dangerous impulses. A committee of American friends (under the chairmanship of Dr. Frank Kingdon,[2] president of Newark University) will undertake the financing of the project. In the next few months I shall approach some twenty-four German writers, scholars, theologians, and artists with definite proposals. For the moment I am asking you for nothing more than your agreement in principle. I should like permission to add your name, which carries weight and persuasiveness in Germany and the world, to the roster of my German committee. If you consent, you will soon hear more details.

I am writing similar letters to the following friends and colleagues: Wilhelm Dieterle,[3] Dr. Bruno Frank, Professor James Franck,[4] Leonhard Frank, Lotte Lehmann,[5] Heinrich Mann, Dr. Hermann Rauschning,[6] Professor Max Reinhardt, Ludwig Renn,[7] René Schickele, Professor

[2] Frank Kingdon (b. 1894), originally a minister, later university professor and radio commentator. From 1936–40 president of Newark University. Chairman of the International Rescue and Relief Committee and many other organizations. Author of *That Man in the White House: You and Your President* (a biography of Roosevelt; 1944), *An Uncommon Man: Henry Wallace and 60 Million Jobs* (1945), *Architects of the Republic* (1947).

[3] Wilhelm Dieterle (b. 1893), actor and director. Among his major films: *The Life of Emile Zola* (1937), *Dr. Ehrlich's Magic Bullet, Portrait of Jennie.*

[4] James Franck (1882–1961), physicist. Nobel Prize 1925. Until 1935 at the Kaiser Wilhelm Institute, Berlin. Emigrated to the United States, where he taught at Johns Hopkins University and the University of Chicago.

[5] Lotte Lehmann (b. 1888), singer, particularly celebrated as an operatic soprano and singer of *Lieder*. Refused to appear in Germany after the Nazis seized power; moved to the United States, where she enjoyed triumphant concert tours and Metropolitan Opera appearances.

[6] Hermann Rauschning (b. 1887), president of the senate of the Free City of Danzig until 1936. He then broke with Hitler, fled through Poland to Switzerland, made his way to France in 1938, to England in 1940, and to the United States in 1941. In his writings he unmasked the nature of National Socialism. His books, among them *The Revolution of Nihilism, Conversations with Hitler,* and *Time of Delirium,* created a sensation throughout the world and were translated into many languages. Rauschning was also associated with *Mass und Wert.*

[7] Ludwig Renn, pen name of Arnold Vieth von Golssenau (b. 1889), writer. Following the Reichstag fire, Renn was imprisoned for two years on charges of "high treason." After his release he escaped to Switzerland, then went by way of Spain, France, and the United States to Mexico. Professor of modern European history at the University

Erwin Schrödinger,[8] Professor Paul Tillich,[9] Fritz von Unruh, Stefan Zweig.

In the next few weeks I myself will begin one of the articles.

As for methods of distribution, these are numerous—they might even be sent through the mails. We are counting on printing at least 5,000 copies per pamphlet, and every copy will be read many times over. The articles are to be paid for, modestly, at about the rate offered by American magazines such as *The Nation* or *The New Republic*.

Let me sum up: Together with our own proper and personal tasks, together with the "demands of the hour" and beyond them, we are duty-bound to use our influence on the Germans. War can be averted only if the Germans make an end of Hitler. If it is not averted, any hope for a peace that will not once again contain the seeds of a new war depends upon the Germans repudiating the regime *before the defeat*. The Germans must be brought to their senses; and who will do it if we remain silent?

Let me hear from you soon. With my best regards,

TO HEINRICH MANN

Grand Hotel & Kurhaus
Huis Ter Duin
Noordwijk am Zee
The Netherlands
June 19, 1939

Dear Heinrich:

You must be back home by now, and we have installed ourselves here, together with Erika, for the first stage of our European summer. Let me say once again how happily Paris fitted in, and how exhilarated all three of us were by this first meeting with you. We feel that from now on we must meet fate halfway in arranging such happy accidents, and if it's at all possible we hope to pay you a visit in Nice before our holidays are over,

of Morelia and president of the Free Germany movement. In East Berlin since 1947. Among his works: *Krieg* (1928), *Vor grossen Wandlungen* (Zurich; 1936), *Adel im Untergang* (Mexico; 1944).

[8] Erwin Schrödinger (1887–1961), physicist; professor in Stuttgart, Breslau, Zurich, Berlin. Emigrated to Oxford in 1933, to Austria in 1936, then to Dublin in 1939. Nobel Prize (shared with Dirac) in 1933.

[9] Paul J. Tillich (1886–1965), theologian and philosopher; taught in German universities until 1933, then emigrated to the United States, where he taught at Union Theological Seminary and Harvard Divinity School. A prolific writer; among his many works: *The Protestant Era* (1948), *The New Being* (1955).

so that we can see your new home and continue our Paris conversation in a domestic atmosphere. For there's no saying when we shall see each other again. [. . .]

It seems we have done well after all to choose this place. The hotel is excellent, the beach glorious, and the air has something like the effect of the Engadine. So we hope to strengthen ourselves after a winter in which I, at least, have asked a little too much of myself. Incidentally, in spite of our American background it was not at all easy for us to enter the country on our Czech passports. But a visit to the Dutch ambassador and a letter of recommendation from him have worked miracles, and secured for us not only the Belgian transit visa, but also special respect and expedited treatment at the border. Nevertheless, Europe with its military customs officials and passport scrutinizers seems to us narrow, overcrowded, and ill-tempered. At least, it did during the journey. Here one still has a sense of emptiness and space—except for Sundays, when the place fills up with people whom Idachen Springer[1] in Travemünde used to call "day-flies." There are Germans among them too; one looks at them as one glances at a German newspaper. Rhineland industrialists sat behind us on the grand terrace of the hotel, and I gathered from their conversation that they often cannot make deliveries for weeks because of the shortage of raw materials. From time to time they dropped into whispers. It was fascinating.

This is also meant as thanks for your birthday letter, which has not yet reached me here. It will be in the first batch of mail from Princeton, which is being forwarded by Dr. Meisel, my secretary.

Keep well! And let's hope to see each other once more this summer.

Warmly,   T.

TO FERDINAND LION

Noordwijk am Zee
The Netherlands
July 12, 1939

Dear Lion:

Your last letter was very bitter—I say "was" deliberately, for these are moods—you were bitter, [. . .] too, toward me for having written you only three letters in five months. That is certainly very few—too few; I

---

[1] Governess to Thomas Mann and his brothers and sisters. She remained attached to the family all her life.

had the impression I wrote more often. But in any case, I apologized every time for my remissness. If you knew how I spent last winter, you would be forgiving. I had somewhat more to do with *Mass und Wert* than you and have grown older in the process. When I did write you, however, I said how pleased I was with the development of the magazine and congratulated you on the high level you have been able to give it. If you have really been under attack, I had absolutely no part in it; I would not and could not want to attack you. I have far too much appreciation of your literary acumen, which is gracefully combined with a measure of venom. And after all, has it been so bad? You certainly have enjoyed running the magazine; you've had power and used it; you were able to publish fine aesthetic articles which you might otherwise not have written; and materially you have not come out so badly either, for in these two years you made a round sum of 17,000 francs, including the fees for your contributions. That's quite decent—insofar as payment for us writers can be decent in any sense.

I would very much like to coax you out of your bitterness, for I earnestly hope that come what may, you will remain a friend of the magazine and will continue to collaborate on it; that you will think of the cause—good, necessary, and important as it is. [. . .] The cause is necessary—we are all agreed on that, I imagine—and perhaps its necessity can be made even clearer henceforth by your not getting involved with ambiguous mythologists and then permitting them out of delicate spitefulness to write nasty reviews that compromise me in regard to a great man whom I wholeheartedly revere.

The cause is necessary and at the same time materially almost impossible—that is the problem. By pulling strings, Golo has secured his French visa and thus can come over. I have confidence in his earnestness and eagerness, though these are by no means proof of his ability; and he has helpful friends and advisers (you among them, I hope!). But the magazine's financial predicament is such that it cannot survive unless it is placed upon a different and broader basis. As I see it, the new league of the exile publishing houses might best prove its value by taking the magazine under its wing. I have urgently invited a number of people to discuss this idea with me.

Meanwhile, my dear Lion, I am tremendously grateful to you for having brought Volume III, Number 1 as far as you have, so that Golo can finish it up once he is here without having to prove his editorial powers too precipitately. I confine myself to this expression of gratitude; for something in me revolts against bidding you goodbye with thanks, dismissing you as though all were over between you and the magazine. No, you belong to us and to the cause.

TO KLAUS MANN

Noordwijk am Zee
The Netherlands
July 22, 1939

Dear Eissi:

The point is to start this letter sometime. I don't know how far I'll come, for it is after dinner, when I am tired here, with this curious air which is at once dense and wild. The afternoons are usually stolen from me by visitors. But the time is long overdue for me to report to you on your novel.[1] Mielein for her part has already done so in detail, after holding on to our copy for a long while. But since I have had it, I have written various people to call their attention to the book seriously and to ask them to do something for it because it is really a first-rate thing which is only too naturally being neglected by a world caught up in stupidity and malice. I've written Alfred Neumann, Uncle Heinrich, Fränkchen,[2] and others. I am convinced that everyone who gives it a chance, even in a skeptical frame of mind, will read to the end, fascinated, entertained, touched, and moved. That's what I did; and in saying this I will confess that I had the secret intention of taking only a look at it, though a closer one than the ordinary reader. But nothing came of that intention. The book held, amused, and stirred me so that for several days I read until long after Mielein had put out her lamp—read it through word for word.

The 23rd. As you see, I did not get very far yesterday. I had to go downstairs after all for my evening beer. Well, then: I read it through all the way, with emotion and gaiety, enjoyment and satisfaction, and more than once with deep sympathy. For a long time people did not take you seriously, regarded you as a spoiled brat and a humbug; there was nothing I could do about that. But by now it cannot be denied that you are capable of more than most—this is the reason for my satisfaction as I read; and my other feelings had their good reasons also. Before I was finished I was completely reassured that the book as an enterprise, as an exile novel, is totally without a rival because of its personal qualities, and that you

[1] *Der Vulkan.*
[2] Bruno Frank.

needn't fear any other book of its kind, not even by Werfel. As time goes on, a good many writers are going to take up this great and painful but also poignant theme; but no one will be able to match the easy, faithful, corrupt Kikjou[3] melody as you sing it. That is your preserve, and anyone who has a feeling for this manner of expressing the painfulness and fantasticality and gracefulness and depth of life (for my part, I must say I have a feeling for it) will hold with your painting and panorama, a picture of German uprootedness and migration *a la* Jean Cocteau. Some, of course, will say: a strange approach, the painting is quite hopeless, these piqueurs, sodomites, and angel sighters would have found their easy, faithful, corrupt doom even without Hitler, that Germany had done quite rightly to expel them, and had lost nothing by doing so. But in the first place, a work of art is involved, which means primarily not a solid morality but a new, strong, curious, and colorful kind of experience; and then the unsuccessful withdrawal cure, to mention only this—so extraordinary a piece of narrative that we no longer think of Germany and morality, of politics and the struggle, but simply read because we have never before read anything like it. But secondly, the work—for that is what is it, a real work embracing a great deal and executed with a special kind of graceful energy—becomes in the second half more and more earnest, sound and healthy, thanks to a truly loved and admired, serious and strong and militant character who gives backbone to the whole, who stands in the center and to whom the whole weak swarm streams as if seeking help. It becomes a book of which the German refugees need not be ashamed after all, from the viewpoint of dignity, strength, and militancy; it is a book which they can gladly and gratefully endorse, provided they are not envious.

The atmosphere of cities and countries is magnificently rendered, has been experienced with the keenest senses and shows how everything after all is paid for with life and experience. This is in spite of the almost childlike naïveté with which the literary influences obtrude. In technical details and manipulations, your great uncle looms large. Toward the end, it seems to me, the old Magician comes out strongly; and what particularly struck me is the extreme distinctness with which Knut Hamsun speaks up a few times, although by all rights he shouldn't exist at all any more, you know. For you are also an heir who has assumed the right, one might say, to lie down in a made bed. But after all, one must also know how to inherit, for in the final analysis what is culture but an

---

[3] Name of a character in *Der Vulkan.*

inheriting? Not for nothing are the Bolsheviks always talking about the "bourgeois heritage." And then again, here is such an abundance of basic lyricism, cash payment, and a martyr's witness, that this remark about the made bed must be taken *cum grano salis*. And all your "heir-dom" would do you little good without your own great, supple talent, which masters difficult things with ease, which can be very funny and very sad and in a purely literary sense, in dialogue and direct analysis, has unfolded with astonishing strength.

In a word, I congratulate you heartily and with fatherly pride. As I hear, older colleagues and masters of the guild have also told you of their pleasure and their respect. No doubt many another encouraging rever-beration will be reaching you. But for the rest, don't take it to heart if your best is apparently passed over without public recognition. That is how it is nowadays, how it should be; and it is almost an honor. To quote Uncle Heinrich: "The day will come."

Warmly,   Z.

TO HEINRICH ROTHMUND[1]

Noordwijk am Zee
The Netherlands
July 28, 1939

Dear Herr Doktor Rothmund:

This is not the first time that I have appealed to your humanitarianism on behalf of a fellow countryman who is threatened by the difficulties of these times. I hope that you will receive my present plea with patience and kindness.

It concerns a writer of merit, Albert Ehrenstein—a Jew, of course, and one with a Czech passport. Since 1932—in other words, longer than the existence of the Third Reich—he has lived in one and the same home in Brissago, but now, because of the Czech disaster, he is threatened with expulsion from Switzerland. A French visa could be obtained for him if the Swiss authorities would grant him another six months' residence permit with the right of reentry. It seems to me that Switzerland would do itself no harm by extending the permit of a man who can well be called an old resident—all the more so because this would make it possible for him to leave for France, and because he has already, during his long stay,

---

[1] Heinrich Rothmund (1888–1961), chief of the Swiss Federal Alien Police, 1939–54.

proved to be a man of complete integrity and political probity. I value Ehrenstein as a gifted poet and subtle essayist, and amid all the hopeless misery which comes crowding in from all sides, it would be a satisfaction to me if my intercession could possibly spare him the disaster that expulsion would mean to him. His file in Berne is numbered 98098.

With respectful good wishes, my dear Herr Doktor,

TO LOUISE SERVICEN[1]

Hotel Waldhaus Dolder
Zurich
August 13, 1939

My dear Miss Servicen:

Now that you have the complete Seventh Chapter of *Lotte*, I feel the urge to say a few words to you—call them words of comfort—regarding what may seem to be the almost insuperable difficulties of this dreadful prose piece. I can imagine that you are depressed and rather perplexed by it. But I should like to ask you not to take the matter too hard, and first of all to go ahead and translate away boldly and ruthlessly. I myself think that in the foreign-language editions of *Lotte in Weimar* this chapter must be shortened and simplified, for certain allusions and literary reminiscences are probably possible only in German, and scarcely even in German nowadays. I think, however, that for us to have an overall view, the whole must first be translated at least in rough form. I have also recommended this procedure to my English translator. Once the text is available, we can see what to do next.

Furthermore, I think it would be good if the translations carried a few explanatory remarks in the form of a postscript, a short account of Goethe's work and love life, in order to help the reader. For the French edition I imagine that Félix Bertaux or even his son Pierre might be willing to undertake the task, which would be very simple for a specialist in German. What do you think?

Perhaps we will have a chance to discuss all this in September, since I am counting on our coming back to Switzerland once again from Sweden, and setting out for America by way of Paris. I have not stopped working on this whole trip, and I am approaching the end. I am already deep in the eighth chapter, which is again altogether social comedy, and the ninth is meant to be merely a downbeat; so that it seems fairly certain the German edition will come out this fall.

[1] Mann's French translator.

Since I feel somewhat uneasy, I would be grateful for a word from you that you are not too much annoyed with the Seventh Chapter. From a purely artistic point of view, the bits of dialogue incorporated into the interior monologue ought to give it some animation and change of pace. If you have anything to tell me or to ask me, your letters will reach me here until Friday morning; after that it would be best to write to Bermann-Fischer Verlag, Sureplan 19, Stockholm.

I must call your attention to a mistake of mine in dates. In the first chapter, Lotte's arrival in Weimar is given as an early October day. In fact it was September 22, and her stay extended into the beginning of October. So it must be in my story, and the information on her day of arrival in the first chapter must be corrected—in particular the dating of Lotte's ticket. This chould be given as precisely September 22; but in the first lines it is best to speak more vaguely of a day in the second half of September.

P.S. Please note also that it is First, Second, etc., Chapter, but "The Seventh Chapter."

TO JAMES T. FARRELL [1]

65 Stockton Street
Princeton
September 22, 1939

Dear Sir:

I have received your letter. I hardly feel obligated to reply to it. I tell you this because I think you may not be aware of the bad faith you showed some months ago, in connection with that anti-Nazi manifesto which I drew up at the request of some American friends. The manifesto was sent to you, among others, asking for your agreement in principle; if you disapproved of it, you could have refused your signature. Instead you thought it proper to launch a public polemic against a text still not available to the public, and thus set going a premature and senseless discussion which put a halt to an action initiated from the best of motives.

Now you write to me, call me to account for my relationship to the League of American Writers, and demand that I declare myself on the matter of the Russo-German pact. Well, although I could have withdrawn

---

[1] James T. Farrell (b. 1904), noted American novelist, essayist, and critic.

to my artistic work and·thus avoided giving offense, I have never refused to make my political professions, and to the best of my ability have tried to use my influence for the good. I intend to express my views on present problems, including that of Russia, at a time and in a form of my own choosing. I shall then amend whatever needs to be amended in those of my writings which belong to an era that the war has brought to a conclusion. I see no reason to do this merely in response to a letter from you.

As for the League of American Writers, I spoke at its Congress together with Eduard Beneš and a large number of other non-Communist writers. The members of this association, though far from united in their political convictions, are in fundamental agreement about freedom. I was gratified and took it as a sign of American generosity that they elected me, a foreigner, as their honorary chairman. At any rate, that election was certainly no token of the organization's being Communist.

TO GOLO MANN

Princeton
September 26, 1939

Dear Golo:

Your letters have been most welcome. Above all, they gave us the feeling that contact is not completely broken off. You received the cable reporting our safe arrival: "If only you were here." Really, that would be the best, most sensible thing. But we will have to take action without delay, for in all probability it will grow increasingly more difficult for you to return— more difficult from this side too; and it's a pity that on both sides we are divided and faltering in our wishes. Mielein does not believe that the magazine can continue. Kahler too is doubtful, and my own first thought after war was declared was that the magazine would have to be suspended for the present, if only for technical reasons. But at bottom it pleases me to hear that people in Zurich are more than ever in favor of keeping it going, and that Oprecht himself wants to. For I secretly desire it also, although the advantage of your editorship, namely my own closer tie, is all but wiped out by the circumstances, and although I am profoundly aware that it will be hard to find the right tone for the magazine under these circumstances. Just hów hard is apparent from the inhibitions that assail me every time I turn my mind to the prelude which, as you so properly point out, I must write for the war issues of *Mass und Wert*. After having said one's piece, one would prefer to keep silent now and leave everything to objective events which are taking their course.

Something of this sort is probably felt by the decent Germans, who I imagine are in a less revolutionary state than ever before; for now the old familiar war is here, in which a man can and must do his job well, and which puts an end to the burden of revolution by enforcing a degree of order. What should we say at this point, and in what way try to influence the Germans? Should we tell them to depose the Nazis and make peace? There is no prospect of their doing that as long as they can wage war, especially since they have no idea of what they could do of their own accord, and without the aid of objective events, to replace a regime that after a fashion has made them shape up. And is a rapid end to this war, which would leave everything essentially unchanged, even desirable? Doesn't the war have to go on long enough to produce fundamental changes *everywhere*, or at least bring forth ripeness for change? Yet in practice this ripeness could be a brutalization and misery which in God's name we would rather see averted. For Germany alone, however, one longs for that brutalization to proceed as far as is necessary for Brother Hitler to meet his merited end. It's unthinkable for this shameless abortion to wriggle out of the affair as he obviously would like to now, retiring to private life and spending his honorable declining days "as an artist."

The general talk is that there must not be "a new Versailles." But what does this mean? No one can say whether, since Russia's entry,[1] it is still possible for the war to end as it did in 1918. If we do assume that it is possible, and if the Germans let things go so far without shaking off Hitler and his henchmen in good time—which means *very* soon—then a devastating peace becomes inevitable. It will deprive Germany for a very long period, much longer than last time, of any chance of reverting to the power politics which are so gruesomely unnatural to her. Perhaps it will be long enough for a federated and denationalized Europe—even a planned world—to arise. The liquidation of the Reich would be a necessity, and from the point of view of cultural Germany—i.e., the only German point of view—is it not devoutly to be wished? The fear is that Germany would thereby lose her "great men," her Bismarcks and Friedrichs, and that the peace would once again have to be built upon the spiritual disorientation and homelessness of a major nation, which would be regrettable and dangerous. But can a nation which has plunged into such errors, which has so woefully misconceived politics as the Germans

---

[1] Mann is referring to the Russian invasion of Poland, which was officially partitioned by the treaty with Germany signed in Moscow two days after the date of this letter.

have, and whose "great men" have finally come down to a Hitler, expect anything else? And might not a more thorough "Versailles"— which is to say, the dissolution of Germany, above all the separate union of Bavaria with Austria—create conditions under which the Germans would find it psychologically easier to accept the annulment of their most recent history?

I am writing all this down only to suggest to you and to myself how difficult it is nowadays to speak to the Germans, or even to our own side. My American interviews are an optimistic makeshift. In the longer lectures I shall have to confront the issues in greater detail, but I don't have to deliver these until later in the winter, thank God. This reprieve, during which I can keep silent, is invaluable to me; for silence is preferable today, while one tries to digest matters inside oneself. I don't suppose it is a disgrace to confess that I am frightened by the task of writing a new foreword prescribing the magazine's attitude toward this war. The fronts are so confusing, give rise to so much distrust; the war is moving toward a perhaps miserably near, perhaps horrifyingly distant end. It is difficult to weigh the Russo-German reconciliation from the Russian side; from Hitler's viewpoint, his filthy talent for bewildering and weakening the world has once again proved its worth in the most repulsive way. One shrinks from even trying to imagine the effect of this upon the German working class or upon the now banned French Communists. Poland, since half of it is now Russia's, cannot be restored by Hitler's fall, and the act of violence which was not to be tolerated and will have to be tolerated can no longer be blamed on Hitler alone, since Russia took part in it. England and France will be powerless to prevent the "establishment of order" in the East, and the German query: For what moral or material goals are these countries continuing the war? has its outrageous and paralyzing justification.

. . . I could go on writing like this for days, but what's the use? Meanwhile there are rumors of the specter of ingenious peace proposals which would make the League of Nations blush. *Nascitur ridiculus mus*, but the mouse that has slipped out of his horrible liar's mouth is once again a bewilderingly pretty little thing, and it is not easy to treat it as the vermin it is. Will you tell me what should be done with Germany? She wants no war, she wants peace! Let the ruins of Warsaw serve as a warning to the wicked and insane men who want war. The situation in the West cannot be indefinitely prolonged; things are almost reaching the point where Saarbrücken will be shelled, and then the Germans would have to shell Mulhouse, just as if they had the misfortune to be at war with such a lovable and worthy country as France. What can one say? There is the word "disarming." If only it does not prove accurate.

Enough. Meanwhile I have received Oprecht's letter, for which I am deeply obliged, and which makes it clear that *Mass und Wert* is really to be continued. So I must push on with the foreword—and use it to express the wish that Europe will once more be vouchsafed peace and freedom and that these may long be preserved in order to fatten this goose. Well, it's both a hard and an easy assignment. I do not know how I am going to get it done. And can we continue to delay an issue that is already finished? I think you will have to draw on someone's expense account for a cable to bring me up to date on the situation. This will also tell me whether you have finally resolved to stay and whether we should stop thinking of steps toward your reimmigration.

Warmly,   Z.

TO MERVYN RATHBONE

[*Original in English*]

Princeton
September 29, 1939

Dear Mr. Rathbone:

I am very sorry that as I am not yet an American citizen I feel I must refuse your invitation to become a sponsor of a Committee seeking to defend what you feel are the lawful rights of the American telegraph messengers. My sympathies have always been with the just objectives of labor in all parts of the world, but in this case the problem is specifically an American one in which I feel I have no right to interpose.

I am grateful to you for having asked me to help, and hope that the outcome of your efforts will result in an equitable solution of the difficulty.

TO GOLO MANN

Princeton
November 3, 1939

Dear Golo:

I am sending you "Six Kings" by Borgi[1] from the *Atlantic Monthly*, an

[1] Giuseppe Antonio Borgese (1882–1952), Italian writer, historian, professor of German literature in Rome and Milan. Emigrated to the United States in 1931, taught at Smith College 1932–6. Married Elisabeth Mann in 1939. Editor of the magazine *Common Cause.* Professor of Italian literature and political science at the University of

essay that seems to me to have a fine historical perspective. Well translated, it would certainly be an excellent thing for *Mass und Wert*—unless you and the others think that its previous publication in English is a drawback. After all, Borgi ought to be represented in our magazine, and he himself considers this essay particularly important. He would also be prepared to write something new—the question is whether it would be as good.

It is a real misery that you have not received Mielein's letters. She has been writing you faithfully and at length. Has my own long letter reached you, the one in which I discussed the problems of the requested foreword? More important, have you received the foreword itself, and was it more or less the right sort of thing? Distance makes everything uncertain. Bermann, too, should have confirmed receipt of my final manuscript long ago, if he did receive it. Nowadays everything is sent into the void, and there are years ahead, I am afraid, in which we'll hardly be able to speak of living in the "age of communications."

But Bermann goes on bravely publishing. Yesterday I received *The Magic Mountain* in the Stockholm Collected Works, and I hear that *Lotte* is to appear before Christmas. It will be a quiet publication, but the report in the *Schwarze Korps*[2] that I have completely gone to the dogs and am knocking about half-starved in Paris cafés is somewhat wanting in accuracy. Ah, the poor rabble! They gloat over such images, hoping to see the greatness of their revolution and the proof of their own elevation. Perhaps soon not even a café will be left for them to knock about in.

Best regards to the ancients,[3] Oprechts, Leisis,[4] Barths,[5] Asso,[6] and the Maries.[7]

Warmly,   Z.

Chicago until 1947. From 1946 to 1951, secretary general of the Committee to Frame a World Constitution. From 1950 to his death, once again professor in Milan. Among his works: *Gabriele D'Annunzio* (1909), *La Vita e il Libro* (essays, 3 volumes, 1910–13), several novels, *Da Dante a Thomas Mann* (posthumous, 1958). In English, *Goliath, the March of Fascism* (1937), *Foundations of the World Republic* (posthumous, 1953), among others.

[2] The weekly newspaper of the SS.

[3] Mann's father-in-law and mother-in-law, who had taken refuge in Zurich.

[4] Dr. Leisinger, the Manns' dentist, and his wife.

[5] Professor Hans Barth and his wife.

[6] The Oprechts' Airedale terrier.

[7] The Mann family's cook and maid, who had followed them from Munich to Zurich and there married; both were named Marie.

1939

TO CAROLINE NEWTON[1]

Princeton
November 5, 1939

Dear Miss Lina:

Since the poodle has been with us a week now, I must tell you what a lovable gift you have made us. I say "us," for everyone in the house is daily delighted with him. But from the start I attempted to make him feel that he belongs especially to me, and it was not difficult to do, for his sentitive nature is touchingly susceptible to kindness and attention. During the first few days, of course, he was disconsolate, but his timidity has already given way to a wholly uninhibited and trustful personality. At first I was somewhat worried at the failure of his natural functions, for which the strange environment was obviously to blame. But that has long since straightened out. I am only sorry for him because he has so little freedom of movement and can't run about as he likes, for outside I don't dare let him off the leash, both because of the automobiles and because he does not yet respond well enough to being called and could easily stray. On the second or third day he actually did run away—we had a bad fright. In an unsupervised moment he jumped through one of the low windows of the dining room into the garden, and raced out through the gate—who knows with what in mind, perhaps on his way to you, perhaps to his original mistress. He could not be caught on foot, although I knew the direction he took and followed him for a long time. Finally he was caught, quite dirty and bedraggled, with the aid of two cars and of a woman (the original mistress!) to whom he had attached himself.

I imagine that by now he would not try any such escapades, and I hope we'll soon be able to allow him more freedom. In the house he is mostly with me in the library, where he likes to lie on my foot under the desk. But I don't think he can be allowed to spend the night there again, as he did recently when we were in New York; he chewed up a philosophical volume by Ernst Cassirer.

Incidentally, we have called him Nico, and he is beginning to respond to the name a little. "Guillard" was a misunderstanding. According to his papers he was called Gueulard, that is, "barker," and this did not strike us as fitting. He actually has a quite sonorous, low voice, as became apparent after a few days of muteness.

[1] Caroline Newton (b. 1893), psychoanalyst, translator of Wassermann. An early admirer of Thomas Mann, she was working on a Mann biography. Miss Newton had just presented the Manns with a black French poodle.

Herewith I conclude my report. You have added a charming member to our household, and I hope you will soon have the opportunity to convince yourself in person of his well-being.

TO CADETS J. P. MURRAY, L. E. HOLZMAN, A. M. VARNUM

[*Original in English*]

Princeton
November 21, 1939

Gentlemen:

Thank you for your joint very complimentary letter of November 16th. If you will come to my house here, which is at the corner of Liberty Place and Stockton Street, between five and six o'clock on the day you come to Princeton with the Corps of Cadets to the Navy-Princeton Football Game (Saturday, November 25th) I shall be very pleased to make your acquaintance.

TO HEINRICH MANN

Princeton
November 26, 1939

Dear Heinrich:

You know how we lost contact with you. After our happy meeting in Paris, the refreshing seven weeks in Holland, and trips to Switzerland and London, we went to Sweden for the PEN Club Congress—which didn't take place, as it turned out. The war began, and our intention of returning to Switzerland and from there arranging to see you again came to nothing. In the interest of our safety, people tried to persuade us "to spend the war period in Sweden." Thank God we did not. The return voyage had its problems, though. Precisely for reasons of safety, we could not use a Swedish ship. We had to fly to England in order to obtain an American ship that was bringing citizens home, and the flight from Malmö to Amsterdam, passing not far over Helgoland, was precarious. But everything turned out well, and from Southampton the American liner *Washington* brought us here—amid the throng of 2,000 persons who spent the nights on improvised cots in public rooms transformed into concentration camps.

We were happy—as happy as one can be nowadays—to have regained our base. But correspondence with Europe is hampered and complicated to the point of discouragement. Let's leave politics aside. I am writing you chiefly to congratulate the two of you, in Katia's name as well as mine, on your marriage.[1] We are both delighted. That is a good and fine, a reassuring act. It seals a well-tested relationship, which no longer stands in such urgent need of blessings as that of our little Medi with the man who has now become her husband, G. A. Borgese. Yes, we too have had a wedding: Medi has married her anti-Fascist professor, who at the age of fifty-seven probably no longer expected to win so much youth. But the child wanted it and brought it off. He is a brilliant, charming, and excellently preserved man, that must be granted, and the bitterest hater of his Duce, whom out of pure nationalism he regards as the worst of the worst. He castigates this nationalism of his with remarks such as: "Germany is an organ and Italy merely a violin." But the "merely" means nothing. Once he went so far as to say: "Europe—that is, Germany with fringes." Which might very well please Hitler. But at the same time he is an enthusiastic American, and although Medi knows Italian and he German, they speak only English to one another.

They will live in Chicago, where Borgese teaches. Thus we are left all alone in the big house, with a delightful black French poodle for company, a present from a patroness. Katia is reassured to know that her very old parents have at last actually reached Switzerland. It was finally managed with the help of House Wahnfried,[2] and for the time left to them the old couple, onetime millionaires, have enough to live on. But will they ever see their daughter again? That depends on what everything depends on.

I am well—that is to say, I am not sick, and at our age I suppose one must be content with that. The stay in Noordwijk happily gave the Goethe novel such a vigorous push that I was able to finish it here within the first few weeks after our return. The final manuscript reached Stockholm successfully (by way of Portugal, in Swiss diplomatic mail), and thus the German edition can be "published" before Christmas. I am curious to see how it will strike the tiny band of Swiss, Dutchmen, and Scandinavians who will make up its audience. And to hear how you like it!

It will be a good while before you receive this letter. I had better send you New Year's greetings right off. Let us hear from you, if you

[1] Heinrich Mann had married Nelly Kröger, his companion of many years standing.
[2] The family of Richard Wagner, with whom Alfred Pringsheim had been close in his early years.

can manage it. I have done all in my power for the interned German and Austrian writers. Giraudoux[3] has been very kind and has written to me in great detail, and Jules Romains[4] has also done his best. A large sum of money has been sent from here for the people involved.

Greetings and good wishes,

T.

TO THE LEAGUE
OF AMERICAN WRITERS

Princeton
(Early December, 1939)

Dear Sirs:

A friend has sent me the Bulletin of the League of American Writers of November 1939, Volume VI, No. 2, which contains the article "France Today" by Elliot Paul.

A note on the copy states that the Bulletin is intended "for League Members only"; but I must observe that it is not only in the hands of members; and since you have had the kindness to elect me your honorary president, I have reason to be astonished that I am the last to see it, and then only by chance.

Furthermore, I must say that I read the article with grave doubts—perhaps I should rather say, with considerable repugnance. This description of the hopeless state of France, of the Fascistic corruption to which she is supposed to have succumbed, is quite certainly as propagandistic, exaggerated, and misleading as it is offensive to the feelings of everyone who regards the fighting democracies—however great their sins—as the defenders of goodness and human decency and who desires their victory over the most abominable phenomenon that world history has produced, Nazism.

I can understand the feelings of a Communist in France today. That country, until yesterday deeply peace-loving, but now fighting for her life and liberty, has thought it necessary to suppress his party. But this very article proves the complete subservience of international Communism to Russian power politics and Russian alliances. The article does not provide objective information, but is an act of Stalinist wartime sabotage, a political assault upon the democracies in favor of Hitler and Stalin.

---

[3] Jean Giraudoux (1882–1944), French diplomat and novelist as well as world-famous playwright.
[4] Jules Romains (b. 1885), French novelist, playwright, poet. His chief work is the monumental *Men of Good Will* (1932–47).

It gave me real pleasure that a large organization of American colleagues such as the League of American Writers should have offered me, a foreigner only just in the process of becoming an American, the honorary presidency after the meeting at which I spoke together with Dr. Eduard Beneš. I took this as a sign of American liberality and generosity. But I was entitled to assume that it also expressed fundamental agreement on the large moral and political questions; for after all my public statements there could be no doubt about my antitotalitarian convictions. Obviously, however, an agreement no longer exists between my own principles and those of an association which produces such manifestos as the article "France Today," and I can no longer regard as justified the honorary position you were so kind as to confer upon me.

Noisy demonstrations are most repugnant to me. If at all possible I should like to avoid making a public announcement of the severing of my formal relationship with your association. We would do better to accomplish it by your removing my name from the place of honor you gave it, and in the future making no further use of it in connection with your organization.

TO HENRY BOGUE, JR.[1]

[Original in English]

Princeton
December 20, 1939

Dear Mr. Bogue:

Thank you for your letter of December 12th and for reminding me of the pamphlet which disgust and grief concerning the so-called Peace of Munich extorted from me. I am still conscious of the past offenses and defects of the Western democracies, but today these democracies are fighting what I hate most in all the world and in all history, and my heart is with them. I cannot forgive the Russian dictator his alliance with the most abject scoundrel history has ever produced.

I have never been a Communist, but I did have a certain belief in what is called The People's Front, in the international cooperation of the working classes, and in the Russian Revolution. I am deeply disappointed by the confusion and demoralization which the Nazi-Bolshevistic alliance has caused in all parts of the world. That I do not stand alone in this

---

[1] Henry Bogue, Jr., teacher at Baltimore Polytechnic Institute, had written to Thomas Mann asking him to speak up in defense of Russia and socialism as he had done in *This Peace*.

disillusion can be seen from the reaction against the Soviet Union which even such American sympathizers with communism as Mr. Vincent Sheean manifest.

I believe that the contention that Russia, still representing the idea of peace, has been ruthlessly attacked by the Finns at the behest of the democracies, is pure nonsense which sound reason can but reject outright. Nor do I think that a person who subscribes to the Russian ideal need accept this absurdity. A man of this creed may adhere to his fundamental belief while at the same time disagreeing with the bellicose undertakings of the Russian Government. Even if he declare that Communism, like Islam, has to be spread by fire and the sword, he should not descend to the low Fascist level of lies and the distortion of fact—Fascist methods which invert truth and play havoc with the ideas of peace and war.

The new situation caused by the failure of Communism is being seized upon as a most favorable opportunity for the reactionary elements; but for this the Russian dictator is solely to blame. It is his responsibility in the matter which is precisely, in my eyes, his greatest crime. I am sorry not to be able to give you any other answer.

TO MICHAEL SHENSTONE[1]
[Original in English]

Princeton
December 25, 1939

Dear Michael:

I must write you a letter in my best English (which is not just *the* best, but, after all, it is mine), in order to thank you very, very much for your splendid Christmas gift.[2] It was really a charming idea to give me this calendar covered with beautiful and witty symbols, the best and most impressive of which one finds on the back-side. The gay fury with which you spoiled and destroyed the emblem of our common enemy is the expression of a sound temperament and amused me in a very serious way.

I shall show your work to all my friends and to all the visitors of our house and will tell them that it came from our excellent young friend Michael Shenstone.

[1] Michael Shenstone (b. 1928), the son of Molly Shenstone and Professor Allen Shenstone, who was at this time professor of physics at Princeton. Mrs. Shenstone assisted with Thomas Mann's English correspondence from 1938–41.

[2] The Christmas gift consisted of a calendar mounted on cardboard under a picture of Goethe and surrounded by the flags of all the nations to which Mann and members of his family belonged. On the back was a heavily smeared and shattered swastika with the word "Soon!" in seven languages.

1940

TO STEFAN ZWEIG

Princeton
January 4, 1940

Dear Herr Zweig:

It is not my fault that my warm thanks for your letter about *Lotte* came so late. The letter is dated December 8, and arrived only *today*. If it takes as long for this note to reach you, you will scarcely remember what it is about. But since you did not let the present state of communications keep you from sending such a kind greeting, I won't hesitate to entrust my thanks to the sluggish mails.

Your lively concern with the novel made me very happy. The response to it, of course, is thin, coming not as a chorus but in driblets, at long intervals. One must be grateful for what there is—and I have always been. Shouldn't we be grateful and astonished at the mere fact that a German book can be published in such style nowadays? My son-in-law Borgese, when he saw it, at once began philosophizing about the forces of resistance in civilization. And the size of the edition! Bermann had 5,000 prepublication orders. In the course of time he may quite possibly dispose of the 10,000 he has printed. Isn't that an amazing audience under present conditions? Of course, when I consider that this of all books would promptly have had 100,000 readers if Germany still existed, a certain rancor concerning Hitler tends to creep over me. But I suspect that the present-day tenth is of greater importance.

It was very wrong of you not to say anything about yourself, your activities and your writing. I would even have been grateful for something political, for commentary on your surroundings. I have written a vigorously pro-British[1] piece that comes from the heart and from my convictions. It will be appearing over there shortly.

---

[1] The essay *This War* (New York: Alfred A. Knopf; 1940).

Do you see Harold Nicolson? If so, please give him my best regards and tell him that I read his political writings with great sympathy. My favorite sentence of his is: "The German character is one of the finest and most inconvenient developments of human nature."

TO HENRY SEIDEL CANBY[1]

[Original in English]

Princeton
January 8, 1940

Dear Mr. Canby:

It is very distressing to know that Hermann Broch appeared so exhausted when he was with you last Saturday. My wife and I have been anxious about him for some time, and now your letter confirms our fear that he is far less well than he will admit.

Your offer to have him live in comfort in your house in Connecticut is proof of such rare fellowship and friendship that it will touch him deeply, as it does us. Whether he would or could accept, however, one can hardly tell. When we saw him about a fortnight ago he said that he wanted to keep on with his work here. How important this is to him, both financially and psychologically, one can only surmise. Though he gave us the impression that he wants to stay here, it might well be that he could be persuaded otherwise on the grounds of his health, and I would, of course, be willing to urge the evident need of his taking greater care of himself.

I think that he gets a measure of comfort in Princeton from being near his fellow-countrymen, who, though unable to do very much for him, prevent his being too unbearably lonely. I would like your permission to talk to him about your generous proposal. If he feels he must stay here, then we will do all we can to find him better living quarters. On January 21st we are leaving to go on a lecture tour, and my wife has suggested that we invite him to stay in our house during our absence, if he would do so.

I have said little about Mrs. Canby's and your kindness, but permit me to tell you that our awareness of it is very real. I shall await word from you before speaking to Hermann Broch about your proposal.

With gratitude and kindest regards from us both.

[1] Henry Seidel Canby (1878–1961), author and editor; professor of English at Yale until his death. He was the editor of the *Saturday Review of Literature* from 1924 to 1936.

TO HEINRICH MANN

Dear Heinrich:

I received your good letter of January 17 somewhere deep in the land of Texas, on the lecture tour which I may have told you was impending. Before the trip back to New York, a matter of forty hours, we had a few days' rest in San Antonio, near the Gulf of Mexico, where it was already very summery. The population there has a strong Mexican admixture, a frequently most attractive type and a relief after the eternal Yankeedom. The city also has beautiful Spanish missions from the seventeenth century, the most picturesque things I have seen in America.

It touched me very much that you once again dealt so lovingly with my novel, and I am glad that it could hold you and move you. I don't know whether it is my finest, but it is dearest to me, because it contains the most about love and erotic union, in spite of all the mocking and ironically veristic aspects in which this love is clothed. Hence I see its weaknesses and pedantries with particular clarity. It would not be a novel at all, but something like a monograph in dialogue, were it not for an element of excitement belonging to the initial conception which seems to have been retained in the execution. Of course it is connected with the realization of myth, in which the *Joseph* has given me practice. The reader has the illusion of learning exactly what *he* [Goethe] was really like, as though he himself had been on the scene. That is something of an exploit, with the result that a critic in one Swiss journal wrote that he devoured the book as he had done the Indian tales of his boyhood.

What you say about the last chapter shows me that it was a happy invention, even more so than I knew. In reality no second meeting took place, and so I helped myself out by having Lotte, overwhelmed by the verse play as she is, bring about the meeting. It is the only really fictitious scene, although the conversations throughout are also imaginary enough.

After the summery days in San Antonio we are again back in the snow. I have much to do, must prepare lectures for the *boys* on the *art of the novel*, my major effort consisting in not doing the thing too well. I often wonder what you are doing and writing now. I cannot really believe you are content to be merely an onlooker, as you hint, because I myself must admit to being far from that, and often feel torn apart by hatred and the craving to see justice done. In the course of this tour I once again propagandized to the very limits permitted by "neutrality"

and also wrote a counterpart to *This Peace: This War,* which is shortly
to be published in London and, I hear, is also to be broadcast to Germany.

Keep well. Golo is doing his job splendidly in Zurich. Can you give
him a contribution sometime?

T.

TO VIKTOR POLZER[1]

Princeton
March 23, 1940

Dear Herr Polzer:

I should be very glad to help you with your work[2] as far as it concerns
me, but I must be brief and confine myself to objective facts, because this
happens to be the high season of my "academic" activity, and in any case
I have difficulty carrying on my personal work along with these obligations.

For many years I have done my serious writing, that intended for
publication, almost exclusively during the morning hours, from nine to
noon or half past twelve. I work by myself and write by hand, nowadays
using what is here called a *desk fountain pen* instead of the steel nib I
formerly used. About one and a half manuscript pages constitute my daily
stint. This slow method of working springs from severe self-criticism and
high requirements in matters of form, but also from the "symbolic
content" of style, in which every word and every phrase counts, for one
never knows what part one's present phraseology may have to play as a
motif within the total work.

I dictate (to my wife or secretary) only for correspondence, and sometimes for briefer improvisations: sections of lectures and speeches. I
find dictation repugnant; it is forced upon me solely by the necessity to
save time. I have become accustomed to it only in recent years, as the
result of a vastly swollen correspondence.

My handwriting has changed radically with time. That is to say,
with the development and hardening of personal idiosyncrasies, it has
gradually become more and more difficult to read. Before I actually
write my books, I think them through so thoroughly—usually on walks—

---

[1] Viktor Polzer (b. 1892), Austrian writer and journalist; reader and translator in
Paul Zsolnay Verlag. Emigrated to New York in 1938; worked for several years for
Hermann Broch; subsequently edited catalogs for a New York book firm.

[2] A lecture on creativity and the outward trappings of creation in contemporary
writers.

that the first draft of even my major works can be turned over for copying, and formerly could be sent out directly for printing. (Both *Buddenbrooks* and *The Magic Mountain* were sent to the printer in a single existing handwritten draft.) The number of corrections varies; some pages I rewrite completely—but in principle, the manuscript *"stands"* and undergoes no change's even for new editions.

For writing I must have a roof over my head, and since I enjoy working by the sea better than anywhere else, I need a tent or a wicker beach chair. Much of my composition, as I have said, has been conceived on walks; I also regard movement in the open air as the best means for reviving my energy for work. For a longer book I usually have a heap of preliminary papers close at hand during the writing: scribbled notes, memory props, in part purely objective—external details, colorful odds and ends—or else psychological formulations, fragmentary inspirations, which I use in their proper place.

Since in earlier days I restricted myself to subjects involving modern society, research began to play some part in my work only with the *Joseph*, though I used outside sources to some extent for *The Magic Mountain*: medical authorities for the earlier book and oriental studies for the later one. On the other hand, the *Joseph* is actually my first book without human "models." The characters are entirely "invented," whereas formerly I depended upon a known reality—although in the course of the work, that reality always underwent stylization.

The conceptions usually extend far back in my life; my subjects for the most part have very deep roots. My interest in the *Joseph* materials goes back to childhood.

Music is a constant influence on my writing, serving both as stimulus and as model to be rendered in terms of my own art. This is not to say that I conceived any particular ideas while listening to music.

As far as is physically possible, I try to keep myself independent of moods and of the influence of weather and seasons. Given my slow and step-by-step method of work, as well as the voluminous projects into which my books usually grow, I should never finish anything if I relied on moods. On the whole, I stick to the maxim: "If you claim to be poets, make poetry dance to your tune."[3]

Your last question, about the "real purpose" of my work, is hardest to answer. I say simply: *Joy*.

[3] Goethe, *Faust* ("Prelude in the Theater").

1940

TO CAROLINE NEWTON

Dear friend:

Really, it's not all that bad. If I looked at matters as you do, I grant you I too would be sorrowful. But I am taking it all much more casually; I regard the whole thing as temporary and experimental. Nothing has been finally decided—except that our Princeton house (whose lease can be terminated at any time) is needlessly large, and that there would not be much sense in paying rent for it all summer while we are away. We therefore intend to give notice for June 15 and pack our things before we travel. We are considering staying in Santa Monica for the summer, but that certainly does not mean that we will move to California for good. In fact, it is quite possible that we shall return to Princeton in the fall and take another house here. Just between the two of us, I even think we might take the same house again at a more reasonable price.

I admit there is a possibility that California may hold us beyond the autumn, possibly for the winter too. Why shouldn't we make a stab at spending a year there? It may well be that the climate and the greater isolation will prove helpful in speeding along the fourth volume of *Joseph*. It's certainly about time the project was finished. But even that would not signify anything like disloyalty toward the East and our friends here. We have become mobile in our declining years and no longer take settling down as seriously as we used to.

In any case we shall both miss our Caroline, even if the separation lasts only until October, and we always want to remain in touch with her. But surely we may also hope to see you now and then before June.

I hear you have questions for me in connection with the work you have already begun—is that right? I am ready at any time to answer them to the best of my ability, in writing or in person.

TO PETER VIERECK [1]

Dear Mr. Viereck:

I was delighted to receive your friendly letter and can thank you in

[1] Peter Viereck (b. 1916), American poet and political scientist; professor of history at Mount Holyoke College; one of the leading theoreticians of the "new conservatism."

German for saying that you would like to read my books in German if only they could be obtained. The sad part of it is that these books have vanished from the German market since the conquest of Vienna, and my German publisher in Stockholm is just gradually beginning to build up a German edition. But this is an undertaking which, of course, is once again gravely menaced.

Just recently I saw Mr. Knopf and heard about your book[2] which he will be bringing out shortly. It deals with an extraordinarily interesting subject, one little known here in America, I think, so that your book can provide vital clarifications. Your idea that the War of Liberation against Napoleon was the fatal period in which German romanticism became politicized seems to me entirely correct. One must also come out and admit that the German romantic counterrevolution against the world of Natural Rights, Enlightenment, and Progress originally had a legitimate intellectual basis. Unfortunately, the second half of the nineteenth century produced a dangerous degeneration of this romanticism, so that German thinking became disastrously estranged from those aspects of the Enlightenment which are indissolubly linked with the whole of life in the Christian West. In Nazism this estrangement has reached its culmination. The fall of Nazism must of necessity lead to a new reconciliation between the German mind and European thought.

TO PRINCE HUBERTUS ZU LÖWENSTEIN[1]

[*Edited version of an anonymous English translation. No German original available.*]

Princeton
April 21, 1940

Dear Prince Löwenstein:

Your article "The Dangers of the Policy of Destruction to the Entire Old World" in the *New York Staatszeitung* (an odd place for its publication in any case) is a remarkable piece of writing. It would be pointless to conceal the strong aversion it aroused in me. No Nazi—or Stalinist—agent in this country could have sown such evil propaganda against the democracies and the life-and-death struggle they are waging against the

---

[2] *Conservatism Revisited* (New York: Charles Scribner's Sons; 1949).
[1] Prince Hubertus zu Löwenstein (b. 1906), special adviser, West German Government Press and Information Office since 1960. Member of Parliament, 1953–7. Author of *The Tragedy of a Nation* (1934), *The German in History* (1945), *The Defense of the West* (1963), several volumes of autobiography; contributing editor to many publications in the United States and Germany.

German regime, as you do in this article which strengthens all the worst and most dangerous tendencies in America.

One would have to quote the whole in order to expose its distortions and misinterpretations. The bad conscience of the French and English concerning the treaty of Versailles is represented as "hatred of the Germans," as though this could be the only reason for the abhorrence felt by the civilized world for the Germany of today, and the only reason why nations long dedicated to peace, such as England and France, have at last resolved on war in order to put an end to an intolerable state of affairs.

Governments, you say, come and go: as though Nazism were a government which comes and goes like any other, as though this government would ever disappear unless a successful war freed an unfortunate people. A people which for seven long years has bowed to all that has befallen it, and which is now involved with Nazism more than ever because of the war.

You conclude from the shortwave broadcasts of the western powers and their propaganda that "a terrible spiritual degeneration is affecting political and international life." As you see it, then, the source of spiritual degeneration and political immorality lies in England and France.

You speak of the "forcible separation of Austria from the Reich"; you do not mention that she has been incorporated by force. No one, you say, should expect the Germans to start a revolution, for the price would be the destruction of the Fatherland. On the contrary, the world was entitled to hope, above all else, that the German people would not endure the boundless spiritual and moral dishonor which this regime has heaped on it, and would at least, at the outbreak of a general war, rise up against this accursed government. That did not happen; instead, the German people continue to share the responsibility of their leaders' crimes. All that is left now is to wish that the Germans should, through their terrible and decisive experiences, be cured and delivered from nationalism and the delusion of power. But you call anyone harboring this wish a traitor to his country.

The Allies, you say, discovered that the idea of federation was popular in the United States, and hence are calling for a European federation. I find this thesis singularly base. If someone said to you that you had written your article in order that you should become Hubertus I, President of the Republic in the next German Reich, or Comrade Number I, as the case may be—what would you think of such an insinuation? I, however, would find it a good deal more plausible than your interpretation of the Western Europeans' ideas of federation and union.

The deeds and misdeeds of the totalitarian state, you say, are only too well known, while too little is said of other no less horrible deeds, for instance, the English blockade! You dare to compare the unspeakable crimes committed by the Nazis in Poland, Czechoslovakia, or whatever luckless land they enter to England's using her sea power to cut Germany off from supplies of war goods and raw materials! I can have no dealings with a man who expresses and publishes such ideas. Nor am I mollified by your remarks concerning "the thousand-year-old concept of Christian community of the peoples" and "basic human rights." These very things are trodden underfoot in Germany today, and only by the defeat of that country can they be preserved.

To attribute plans to the Allies for the destruction and enslavement of Germany is stupid calumny. The threat of enslavement comes only from the side of National Socialism, not from those who are locked with it in a bitter struggle which is far from being decided. That the Reich of Bismarck is not the last word of German history has been proved by the Nazis themselves, who have deformed and dissolved the Reich to such a degree that one no longer knows today where the boundaries of Germany lie. A federation of independent German states within a European confederation, in an atmosphere of real peace and equality, would not mean degradation for its people. On the contrary, it would mean redemption— a deliverance from the illusion and curse of power politics.

To sum up: I cannot be reconciled to the repellent sentiments and ideas expressed in this article, and under no circumstances can I work with one who advocates them. You did not wish to accept my resignation from the American Guild for German Cultural Freedom. When I learned that the Guild was to be reorganized on a new financial basis, I reconsidered my decision, since I wanted to leave not because of fundamental differences but because of the organization's incompetence in practical matters. Simply on the grounds of fellowship I felt obliged to take part in the fund-raising effort supported by Dorothy Thompson and Mr. Kingdon. But now, in view of your political activity, I deeply regret my compliance and must correct it. I herewith dissociate myself completely from the organization, whose general secretary you are for life, it seems. I will inform the other persons concerned that I have taken this step.

I regret so harsh an end to relations which for years have been carried on so pleasantly, but we live in a world civil war in which everyone must choose sides, and you have chosen yours.

TO CORDELL HULL

[*Original in English*]

May 16, 1940

My dear Mr. Hull:

My wife and I have just learned from Washington with the deepest appreciation of the protection which you personally have arranged for our son, Gottfried Mann, in Zurich, Switzerland. Our sense of relief is beyond measure. We had tried unsuccessfully for four days to get in touch with our son, and had no possibility ourselves of being able to help him. Our knowledge that in the event of the invasion of Switzerland he would be in grave danger because of being my son, was causing us great distress.

We can never adequately repay you for what you have done, or for so generously giving us your personal assistance at a time when the critical affairs of State are making such heavy demands on you in every way, but we are profoundly grateful. My wife asks particularly that I should tell you that she thanks you from the bottom of her heart, but in this she is not alone.

TO AGNES E. MEYER

Chalfonte-Haddon Hall
Atlantic City, N.J.
May 25, 1940

Dear friend:

Many, many thanks. You know what I am feeling. All this, after all, is only the culmination of the sufferings of seven years, which were filled with foreknowledge and despair at others' lack of knowledge and refusal to know. But what is impending now is something I myself could not and would not imagine—even today it is still unthinkable. Nevertheless only a miracle can prevent it from becoming a reality. What can destiny have in mind when it grants so monstrous a triumph to the basest and most diabolic thing the world has ever seen? Time will tell.

Yours,
T. M.

P.S. Golo is in France, where he is presumably engaged in some kind of auxiliary military service. We can only concur.

TO WILBUR K. THOMAS[1]

[Original in English]

65 Stockton Street
Princeton
May 27, 1940

Dear Dr. Thomas:

I understand that the Boston Committee of Medical Emigrés has applied, on the basis of a recommendation from the Harvard Medical School (Dr. E. D. Churchill), for a grant from your Trust for Dr. R.[obert] Klopstock, Research Fellow in Surgery at the Harvard Medical School.

As I am a layman, I have no right to comment on Dr. Klopstock's professional qualifications and achievements, about which, in any case, you will have particulars already. But I do want to tell you that during the many years that I have been acquainted with Dr. Klopstock, I have had ample opportunity to know how unsparing he has been of himself in rendering, in study, in research and in practice, outstanding and unselfish service in keeping with the highest traditions of his profession.

I first met Dr. Klopstock through the gifted young German writer, Franz Kafka, for whom Dr. Klopstock did so much professionally and spiritually before he died. Since I have known Dr. Klopstock I have admired and respected him for his integrity, loyalty and idealism, as well as for his professional skill. I would be glad, indeed, if the necessary help could be provided to enable him to continue in the United States the work which he performed so brilliantly and devotedly in Europe.

TO BRUNO WALTER

Princeton
June 4, 1940

Dear Bruno Walter:

I have sent a general letter of thanks to the good *Neue Volkszeitung* for the wholly unexpected birthday symposium it provided for me, but I should still like to thank you personally for your dear letter of congratulations. [. . .] It introduces such a fine, natural and heartwarming note of friendship into a concert which otherwise did not sound entirely harmonious to my "musician's ear."

We shall soon be coming out to see you. Here the humid heat has

---

[1] The late Wilbur K. Thomas of the Philadelphia Oberlaender Trust.

already started. Last year at this time we were boldly sailing for Europe—and just barely made it back with whole skins. Shall we ever see the Continent again? I do not speak of Germany, for which I have little longing. "If Hitler wins," not a single country on the Continent will be accessible to us again, and I would be surprised if America too did not also become impossible for us. What do you think of Peking? It has already been recommended to me several times.

The word is that you live grandly in Beverly Hills. As yet we have no place in prospect. A house that seemed right was dangled before us but now cannot be had, and we are told that we ought to come out there first, that we would surely find something. But that would be too risky. We are placing our hopes in Liesl Frank's energy.

Moni and her husband in London are desperate to go to Canada, but we cannot succeed in bringing them over here. Golo is somewhere in France and apparently doing some kind of army service, which I certainly approve of. But we can so easily lose him.

Cordial regards and *auf Wiedersehen.*

TO ROBERT NATHAN[1]

[Original in English]

Princeton
June 9, 1940

Dear Mr. Nathan:

Although I realize that what I have to say does not fall within the PEN Club's normal tasks and responsibilities, I wish to present the following grave problem to you and to suggest a solution in which—I fervently hope—the PEN Club may be actively interested.

The fact is that the German Nazi Regime's notorious intention to eradicate the whole of the German intelligentsia has been carried out to a degree which will have the most horrible consequences for the future of the intellect as such. Wherever Mr. Hitler's soldiers march—wherever his "Gauleiters" take over, it is primarily the German exiles and among them first and foremost the men and women of spirit and character who are selected for immediate destruction. It is no exaggeration to state that we have lost more than half of our finest people within the past seven years.

---

[1] Robert Nathan (b. 1894), noted American author of *Portrait of Jennie* among many other novels, was at this time president of the PEN Club.

In Poland, Norway, Denmark, Holland, and Belgium an as yet untabulated number of our friends were either shot on the spot or took their own lives in order to escape the kind of death Hitler had in store for them. And although the lot of the invaded peoples themselves is certainly deplorable, it must be said that nobody can be considered in such deadly danger as those who, for seven years, have been the prophets of the disaster which has now befallen mankind.

No country has accepted as many German refugees, particularly writers, as France. And nowhere are they in a more dire situation. We do not protest against their being interned, since the safety of France requires the most drastic measures. But many refugees, whose nerves have been undermined by strain, hardship, and even starvation, will not survive this new ordeal. Yet even this—the possibility of many of our friends dying in prison—would not have caused me to write this letter to you. The real reason for this letter lies in the fact that some twenty of the *very best* representatives of the German intelligentsia *would have* the possibility of leaving France now, to escape the deadly Nazi persecution, and to save their lives for a future world in which they will be needed—if only some way can be found for their passage to be paid to any country overseas which will admit them. As the United States is definitely unwilling for the time being to admit any more visitors and as none of our friends would be in a position to obtain an immigration-visa for America, it seems to me that refuge in the DOMINICAN REPUBLIC would be their and our only chance. I understand that in order to be admitted to the Dominican Republic, nothing is needed but a trustworthy guarantor for the person seeking admission, as well as about one thousand dollars to cover the cost of his voyage and the first months of his stay there.

Would the PEN Club be willing and able to raise an amount of from twenty to twenty-five thousand dollars for such a purpose and would the PEN Club be willing and able to act as guarantors of these twenty or twenty-five writers now in France? I know the splendid work which the American PEN Club has been doing in collaboration with the French PEN Club, and I also know how many of our friends owe their lives and freedom to this very work. I realize that what I am asking now is quite exceptional and goes far beyond the limits of PEN's normal activities. But the circumstances are without parallel and therefore I feel obliged to make this most unusual request.

Could not the American PEN Club, which is so well known and has such influence and authority, approach persons of wealth and convince them that this task—the task of saving the slender remnant of the German intelligentsia from death and destruction—is one most worthy of their efforts and generosity. I would, of course, be happy to do everything within my power to support whatever action the PEN Club took in this connection.

Letters such as the one I enclose from Walter Mehring (who is one of our most gifted younger poets and satirical journalists) reach me daily. In addition to Mr. Mehring, people such as Alfred Neumann, Wilhelm Speyer, Hans Natoneck, Ernst Weiss, Hertha Pauli, Konrad Heiden, A. M. Frey, Leonhard Frank, Fritz von Unruh—and many others—are in dire need of immediate help. Mr. Jules Romains, President of the Paris PEN Club, would certainly be willing to collaborate fully with us. Both he and Mr. Cremieux have been extremely helpful already. Mr. James Rosenberg, President of the Dominican Settlement, would also give extensive cooperation. I would be glad to check the writers to be selected, so that we save the most talented, the most endangered, and the ones whose integrity, both political and moral, is most sure.

There is, of course, an all-important factor: speed. The race against time is desperate; with the German troops only forty miles from Paris, the fate of our friends will be decided within a terribly short time. I would be more than grateful, therefore, if you will give my plan your immediate consideration and if action could be taken without delay. Are there any people whom you would advise me to approach personally? Does the PEN Club possess any funds which might be made available at once and which we could refund as soon as money is raised? Dorothy Thompson may be willing to participate in our rescue work. It is also possible that the Rosenwalds in Philadelphia, as well as Mr. Bill Rosenwald in New York, might help.

I am sending a copy of this letter to Miss Bessie Beatty in order to avoid delay.

May I ask you to let me have your answer at the earliest possible moment? If we should succeed in rescuing these writers—all of them members of the PEN—from the Nazi group, it would be one of the most important and most magnificent services our organization could render its colleagues all over the world. No doubt one of the primary functions of the PEN Club is to defend and succor the creative mind; and now is the time we may prove whether or not we are able to protect some of our colleagues from the assault designed to destroy us all.

If you think that the publication of this letter or any part of it would be helpful, I would be glad for you to use it. Or if you wish me to write a special appeal, I will write whatever you consider will be of most assistance.

Believe me, dear Mr. Nathan,

Yours very sincerely,

TO AGNES E. MEYER

Princeton
June 14, 1940

Dear friend:

Thank you for your inquiry. The fate of France touches me very closely. She fought only to secure tranquillity—and what does she have now, what will she have? Tranquillity, certainly, but of a ghastly sort; and the shroud of silence will be spread over all Europe. If the monster now spends the night in the Tuileries, will that be the climax of his career, for which we all must bear the shame? Impossible to know. If all these woes and the whole catastrophe had a somewhat more honorable origin than in the putrid soul of that creature—it would be easier to bear. Golo is, as I wrote you, in France, where he seems to be serving as a driver for the Red Cross. Aside from a brief cable immediately after he reached there, we have had no news from him. It may well be that the maelstrom will silently engulf him. It is even worse to imagine his falling into the hands of the Germans.

But do not doubt my phlegmatic temperament, my doggedness, and the obstinacy of my habits. How should I not work? I know no other way, and shall go on as long as I live. I can tell you that the day before yesterday I read my family and a few friends a new chapter from *The Transposed Heads*[1] (a chapter involving an ascetic in the Indian jungle), and we all laughed until the tears came—not excepting the reader and author. Unfortunately I cannot read it aloud to you to prove my high spirits. It's somewhat indecent—the saint's fault.

We have rented a house for three months starting July 5, somewhere between Hollywood and Santa Monica. We shall go by train, having sent our blacks on ahead with the car. How would it be if, before we set out, we were to visit for three or four days at Mount Kisco, say on June 28? Would that be possible? You must tell me frankly whether or not it suits your plans.

In friendship,

[1] *The Transposed Heads: A Legend of India* (New York: Alfred A. Knopf; 1941).

1940

TO EMIL OPRECHT

Princeton
June 15, 1940

Dear Herr Oprecht:

Your letter of May 25 has reached me safely, and I can only hope that these lines of gratitude will reach you. You can imagine how moved we were by what you had to tell us about Golo and his farewell letter to you. It was an ill-starred decision he made, and what has since happened in France, much as it horrifies and depresses us in itself and in its ramifications, naturally increases our anxiety about the boy, who has obviously plunged into the midst of disaster. I am the last to condemn his decision, which I find humanly understandable and honorable. But the sense of the futility of his sacrifice would only make his loss the more painful. [. . .]

Your comment about continuing *Mass und Wert* if at all possible delighted me, but of course I wonder whether you can still cling to this idea after what has happened. Your feelings about the magazine give me so much pleasure because I completely share them and have always hoped we would be able to guide it through the storm. Moreover, if your decision holds, I could probably dig up another $2,000 this year. I could also offer you the longish Indian story which I shall be finishing this summer, and try to muster some essayistic contributions here. But alas, as things stand, all this seems extremely shaky, and we must probably wait out the post-Continental development of the war and its actual outcome before we resume the magazine. For the sake of the greater cause, may God grant that it will prove possible. Perhaps you have something more to say about this.

I won't comment further on the general situation, which leaves room only for an optimism of despair or, shall we say, of the very long view. We think of you all with intense concern and hope you will withstand the Deluge as well as possible. My wife and I, and the children also, send both of you our most affectionate greetings.

1940

TO EDWARD EDWARDS

[Original in English]

Princeton
June 23, 1940

Dear Mr. Edwards:

I feel that it is my duty to write and tell you that I believe you grossly underestimate the terrible danger of Nazism. When you tell me that our enemy is not Hitler but war hysteria, and that the Allies incite alarm to encourage intervention, then I—as a German who truly knows what this vile thing, Hitlerism, is—must in all sincerity protest against such views.

You say that wars and depressions are but dream manifestations of alarm and that remedy lies in more optimistic and less pessimistic views. Today there is room neither for optimism nor pessimism but only for courage and action.

Where there is Nazism, there is to be found the denial of every decent human attribute and a reversion to the pagan and barbaric state of life in which murder, corruption, and intrigue are not merely condoned but advocated. Truth, justice, dignity have been ideals cherished by free men through the ages, but under Hitlerism they are simply empty words. Hitler means to destroy every liberty and to keep the masses in peonage and docility so as to permit him and his friends to enjoy the fruits of power and conquest. Hitler *is* the enemy, the enemy of mankind, and he must be destroyed at all costs before it is too late if anyone anywhere is to have the security to enjoy life, liberty, and the pursuit of happiness.

TO ERICH VON KAHLER

441 North Rockingham
Los Angeles-Brentwood
July 8, 1940 [postmark]

Dear friend:

I feel the need to say how much we wish that we had you here together with us during this period of agonizing and numbing expectation. It is painful and constricting that we should be so far apart now of all times. The hour of decision is almost upon us, and there is little hope that the brainless fanatics will not succeed in attaining their every end. The world and the times show a distinct disposition to let them succeed, perhaps not only out of weakness and affinity to evil, but also out of the instinct to view these desperate fanatics, who nevertheless have a talent for victory, as an instrument for still unknown but necessary aims and purposes. The situation is ghastly, a torture to the mind and the emotions. Everything depends on England's capacity for resistance, which no one can estimate. If she falls in one way or another, the gates are thrown open to hell itself *everywhere*. We must prepare to face total defenselessness and homelessness, with eternity the only refuge. I have always believed that maintaining a kind of personal serenity can bring one safely through the darkest circumstances, and I have trusted to my capacity for adaptation. But these days I often feel hopelessly trapped.

We have had a few days in Mount Kisco—very pleasant outwardly, although somewhat too sociable; but then again that helped to distract the mind. The Busch quartet was there together with Serkin, and I heard for the first time a most magnificent quintet of Brahms, more like a symphony than chamber music—something to remember. The trip here was swift and comfortable, with a single day's stopover with the Borgeses' in Chicago. We have moved into a rather magnificent roomy house in a hilly landscape strikingly similar to Tuscany. I have what I wanted—the light; the dry, always refreshing warmth; the spaciousness compared with Princeton; the holm oak, eucalyptus, cedar, and palm vegetation; the walks by the ocean which we can reach by car in a few minutes. There are some good friends here, first of all the Walters and Franks, besides our two eldest children, and life might be enjoyable were it not that our spirits are too oppressed for pleasure—and for work also, as I discovered after some initial attempts. We know nothing about my brother, nothing about my wife's brother,[1] nothing about Golo. For the latter, diplomatic inquiries are in progress: San Domenico and Brazil, whose ambassadors we have had the good fortune to make friends of at Mount Kisco, are both trying. But the success of these efforts remains dubious. Erika has been called to England, and is capable of throwing herself into the turmoil there. At least she intends to wait another month.

Our warm regards to you and your wife and mother. Katia, too, means to write to you. Medi laughed herself to tears over the hermit. "Why he's so terribly sensual!" she cried again and again. She notices everything, you know.

---

[1] Peter Pringsheim, who had dropped out of sight somewhere in Belgium.

TO AGNES E. MEYER

Los Angeles-Brentwood
August 8, 1940

Dear friend:

We were both deeply touched by your prompt telegram and letter concerning Golo. Our warmest thanks once again for your energetic helpfulness. Thank you also for the fine picture; it delighted all of us, and we entirely agree with Eugene's opinion. Undoubtedly it is the best photograph of you I have seen, and I am saying too little when I declare that I like it better and find it a better likeness than that sculpture in Mount Kisco.

Our poor Golo is certainly in a grave situation. From what you say, it is not quite clear to us whether the Brazilian visa is ready or not. We have sent him word that it is ready, and that he should turn as soon as possible to the Brazilian representatives; and of course it would be dreadful if that should prove to have been an error. The new step you have taken in Washington almost suggests that Brazil has failed us completely, or at any rate is out of the question for the immediate future. Yet time is so terribly pressing, given the great danger of extradition, which has increased significantly now that Golo is once more in a camp. If the United States consul in Marseilles—with whom, as we know, Golo has already been in friendly contact—could intervene with the camp administration in Nîmes, that would of course be much more effective than any such step on the part of the Brazilian representative; but we can scarcely hope for this in the face of the mounting obstacles being placed in the way of people who are seeking entry into this country.

The Canadian government has shown surprising friendliness and obligingness about Monika and her husband. They say explicitly: "It was only your own exceptional and distinguished service to the causes for which this country is at war that allowed an exception to be made in the general rule in the case of your daughter and her husband."[1] It would be nice if similar considerations on the part of the United States could benefit my far more endangered [. . .] son!

So much for this depressing chapter. Meanwhile the grandchild[2] in Carmel has arrived—a healthy boy—and the young mother is well. A visit there is planned soon; that is, I am not yet certain whether I shall

---

[1] Quoted in English.
[2] Fridolin Mann (b. July 31, 1940), son of Gret (Moser) and Michael Mann. This child was the model for Echo in *Doctor Faustus*.

be able to accompany my wife, for the symptoms of fatigue which this climate creates, as people warned me, are really quite trying, and I rather shrink from such undertakings. On the other hand, everyone says that Carmel is so very attractive, and my curiosity about our Swiss-American grandson is so great, that I probably won't be able to resist.

Along with this letter a copy of the English *Lotte* is going off to you. The publication date is approaching, and thus the date of your review. That will be a real day of celebration for me.

The Indian story is still being copied; you will receive the carbon as soon as possible.

I worry about your peace of mind for work now that the invasion of England seems near, but after all you are used to carrying on your intellectual tasks despite a great deal of outward turmoil—which at the moment is certainly the major problem for us all.

TO A. M. FREY

Los Angeles-Brentwood
August 10, 1940

Dear Herr Frey:

I have received all three of your letters safely, and thank you heartily. At the moment I can answer them only very briefly. The third, concerning Switzerland and her no longer welcome guests, is being translated into English and will be sent to our Emergency Committee in New York, which collaborates with the officially appointed Roosevelt-McDonald-Warren Committee. The important thing is to draw up a list of those persons whom Switzerland wants to expel. In view of the affidavits and guarantees, the list must contain basic personal data on each individual, details about his work and about how, and how gravely, he is threatened. It would be best to send this list directly to: Miss Mildred Adams, Secretary of the Emergency Rescue Committee, 122 East 42nd Street, New York City.

I must restrict myself to this factual information for today. Our house has become a rescue bureau for people in danger, people crying for help, people going under. Our effectiveness does not match our efforts, and we seem fated not to be able to bring over my own brother and son.

All my good wishes.

1940

TO AGNES E. MEYER

Dear friend:

Only a word of thanks for your letter of the 10th with the enclosure from Washington. In the meantime you will have received our telegram. We were overjoyed to receive the first direct news from the boy since he went to France. It's obvious that several messages from him have been lost. The information we received from Switzerland about his being held in Nîmes was evidently wrong. He is at large, in Le Lavandou, near Toulon, staying in the house of a Mme Behr, and has already received his U.S. visa. That is a great deal, and we feel relieved. There is still the difficulty of departing from France. He says that he considers it *"surmontable,"* but will probably be in need of help to surmount it, and this is the point at which Count Chambrun[1] might possibly intervene and facilitate matters. That you have even given him travel money is especially moving. I indulge myself in the dream that two weeks from now, when the Count sets out for America again, he might simply take Golo with him.

Recovering this child would be all the more comforting to me because Erika, who has just left us to fly to New York, will be going to England in a few days. Her adventurous nature, her craving for activity, her serious desire to be of help, won out over our horror of this truly reckless undertaking. We cannot forbid such a step; ostensibly she is going for the *Nation* and other journals, but in reality, between you and me (and please say *nothing* about this), at the request and instigation of the British Ministry of Information [. . .]. And mustn't we help wherever we can? Send them destroyers! I am setting a good example and sending them my daughter.

Incidentally, you need not fear that one of these days you will have to exert yourself to pull Erika out of the morass by her forelock. She can of course be hurt, but with an English passport, first papers, and reentry permit, she will need no diplomatic intervention to bring her back.

What you tell me about the *Times* editor is splendid. He must be an excellent man, and I too shall more and more be acquiring a similar reputation.

---

[1] René de Chambrun (b. 1902), lawyer in Paris and New York, specializing in international law. He subsequently married the daughter of the French politician Pierre Laval (who was executed after the war for high treason) whereupon Mrs. Meyer broke off all relations with him.

I am writing on the *Joseph*, if that interests you. The beginning consists of a theological chapter.

TO HARRY SLOCHOWER

Brentwood
September 6, 1940

Dear Dr. Slochower:

I am very grateful to you for your two essays,[1] and look forward with pleasure to their publication. I scarcely know which I should prefer, for both manage to make the book decidedly interesting—which, after all, is the main thing. On the whole, I feel a little too much taken at my word. What you call "identification"—rightly so, for this Joseph-playfulness element is strong in the novel—does not, after all, exclude a good deal of skeptical criticism of the "Great Man," who is represented at once as a miracle and as a "public misfortune." Aristocratic satisfaction in the phenomenon is mingled with democratic pleasure—and from the latter point of view, the approval is by no means consistent. After all, what we have here is a German Great Man—and they are the most questionable kind. The criticism is partly from within the affinity and solidarity, and thus becomes a kind of intensified self-criticism. But partly it is also from outside, a quite objective bantering, so that all responsibility ceases. To be sure, the boundary tends to dissolve; I admit that the book is hard to get at. At any rate I am once again grateful to you for your good will and for the leniency and forbearance with which you try to get at it.

TO AGNES E. MEYER

Los Angeles-Brentwood
September 24, 1940

Dear friend:

Our second daughter, Moni, was with her husband, Dr. Lányi, on the torpedoed refugee ship.[1] Her husband is dead. The child was saved and is

---

[1] "Thomas Mann and Universal Culture: An Interpretation of his Joseph Cycle" (*Southern Review*, April 1939) and "Goethe as Mann's Nourisher" (*New Republic*, October 14, 1940).

[1] Although plainly marked, the British evacuation ship *City of Benares*, filled with children being sent to Canada, was torpedoed and sunk by a German U-boat. Among the evacuees were a few women and men unfit for military service.

in a hospital in Scotland. She seems in a condition to be moved, for Erika (how fortunate, after all, that she is there) has cabled us that she is going to fetch her. We had petitioned the Canadian government for an entry permit because Moni, who is psychologically a frail little thing, was suffering acutely from the bombings. And this is the outcome of the rescue. What the poor thing must have gone through. I assume that Erika will bring her over here in a few weeks. Nothing more, as yet, about Golo and my brother.

And all those children, your protégés, who went down in the waves. I cannot say how shocked and embittered I am. When will America's Flying Fortresses join with the R.A.F. to put an end to this bestiality?

Thank you for your telegram, your good letter, and the article on Santayana, whose excellent essays I am familiar with. Do believe that I consider *The Transposed Heads* of *no* importance, and don't feel obliged to say more about it to me than you already have. I am aware that it is an improvisation with a few droll moments, indifferently carried to its conclusion. The brief reminder of "human dignity" amid all the Hindu sensuality is rather touching. For the rest: "Not everything has to be surpassingly good."[2]

Auf Wiedersehen.

TO LUDWIG LEWISOHN[1]

Los Angeles-Brentwood
September 30, 1940

Dear Ludwig Lewisohn:

Your book[2] has arrived, has occupied me a good deal, and I would have written to you sooner were it not that my morbidly swollen correspondence, the product of these times, some days keeps me from my own writing. Today I received the news—or rather the confirmation of a report I had not yet brought myself to accept—that a good friend of mine, the Dutch writer and eminent critic, Menno ter Braak, took his own life when the Germans invaded. It's heartrending. Two other important Dutch writers have likewise fallen victim to this new variety

---

[2] Goethe, *Poetry and Truth*, Book XV. Goethe used this phrase to defend his play *Clavigo*, which he had written in a week to keep an overhasty promise.

[1] Ludwig Lewisohn (1883–1955), American novelist, literary critic, and translator. Among his works: *The Case of Mr. Crump, The Island Within, The Spirit of Modern German Literature, Story of American Literature, Anniversary.* Lewisohn was one of the first American critics to hail the work of Thomas Mann.

[2] *Haven* (1940).

of world history. The very best are those who are destroyed—which I suppose is only natural when ultimate baseness is victorious. Much trash has found refuge in America because such people raise a ruckus, while the nobler types go under silently.

Your book, now: I read it some time ago, very quickly, almost at one sitting, and understandably with keen interest, for American as it is, it breathes in, if not out, a most European atmosphere. In literary terms it is close to the French, English, German spirit, so that I felt at home with it. In addition there was the emotion aroused by the human document—a somewhat mixed emotion, I will have to add, inclining toward the side from which, evidently, there comes the opposition your book is encountering from the public, to judge by the hints in your letter. There is a sort of intimacy, a state of being filled with one's own ego, one's own fate, one's own errors and own happiness, one's own loving and being loved, which antagonizes people—not *only* out of ill-will and a petty insistence on discretion, but also out of an irritated pudeur. And at least in times of great public tribulations, when there is so much more reason to subdue the personal, it cannot be denied that there is a certain justification for that feeling. I might put it this way: The book really needs the shield and protection of posthumous publication. Let us assume that your considerable literary achievement were crowned and completed by a few more powerful works; that after you had become entirely what you are, you had departed this earth and friends had published these pages from your posthumous papers—in that case not only would there be nothing to be said against them, but they would be a real contribution. But as it is now, coming out of the midst of life, the book does constitute, if you will (I don't "will" at all, but others do, so it seems, and I cannot entirely blame them) a kind of imposition, an act of naïveté, which to be sure is probably a condition for your productivity and without which your *works* (for this is scarcely a work) probably would not have been written—and yet the nakedness does, after all, have something disturbing about it.

As you see: interested, moved, but not entirely in agreement—that is how I feel. A public statement of mine on *Haven* would necessarily turn out somewhat tortuous, and since I have reservations about the book's public existence, I have even more about my giving a public opinion on it. Thanks for something so personal had better remain personal. The occasion for my testifying once more to your literary gifts will come again—I prefer to wait for a new work cast more objectively, confident that you will not make us wait long.

TO LION FEUCHTWANGER[1]

6 5 Stockton Street
Princeton
October 21, 1940

Dear Herr Feuchtwanger:

There's no reason at all for thanks. But how gladly I take the opportunity to greet you and your wife on your arrival. May this country, which has been so friendly to you and your work, compensate you for what you have undergone.

My brother was exhausted and in need of rest the first few days. He means to go to California soon. Brave Erika, too, is safely back from England. Our widowed Monika is not here yet, but is on the way— once again. Her hands are numbed because she clung for twenty hours to the edge of a stove-in boat—without incurring so much as a bout of rheumatism or a cold. It is supernatural.

All the best.

TO AGNES E. MEYER

Hotel Windermere
Chicago
November 26, 1940

Dear Mrs. Agnes:

You will be surprised to see that we are still in Chicago. I have long since delivered my two lectures at Northwestern and Ch. University—very pleasantly, incidentally. We have seen Chaplin's somewhat weak, but in parts still very funny, travesty on dictators,[1] went to the opera (*Salome*, a musically rather coarse-grained festival performance on Thanksgiving Day, with Chicago dignitaries), have taken a look at the exceedingly innocuous hit, *Life with Father*, gone to the Oriental Museum, and have had a great deal of society, quite aside from the fact that the Borgeses and we have constantly alternated playing host to one another. Twelve days have passed, and the tardy grandchild whose arrival we so wanted to wait for is not yet here. God knows why the thing has been so protracted. The doctor's absolutely firm forecasts have been given the lie one after

---

[1] Lion Feuchtwanger (1884–1958), novelist and playwright, particularly noted for historical, biographical, and topical novels and revolutionary plays. Emigrated to southern France in 1933, to the United States in 1940. In 1941 he settled in California.
[1] *The Great Dictator* (1940). Chaplin and Thomas Mann were close friends.

the other. Lessing, Lichtenberg, or Schopenhauer would say that the little creature is quite sensibly in no hurry to turn up in such a progressive world. The little mother drags herself around patiently and cheerfully. She will be sad, and her husband also, when we actually leave tomorrow. But it has already gone on so long, and can just as well continue for another week, and the time has more than come for us to put an end to this expedition and reestablish our shaky order in Princeton once again. The poodle has already been lost once, and our blacks are going to pieces and doing too much entertaining. The one piece of good fortune is that our comfortable hotel apartment allows me to work as regularly as if we were at home. A new message to Germany for the London radio has been dispatched, a new chapter of *Joseph* is completed, and a still newer one has been begun. I have come to the two humorously mythological figures of the baker and the cupbearer (bread and wine).

The university here has been unsettled by the extremely arrogant attack upon the "positivistic" professors by Mortimer Adler, a Thomistic Jew who has influence with President Hutchins—and his wife. Adler is calling for a kind of theocratic democracy, categorically demands a return to the Middle Ages, and prophesies a fearful doom for this entire culture. He may be right about that last. But I have the feeling that this Savonarola is only an expression of the prevailing confusion. Nor do I like people who pretend they are swimming boldly against the stream, but who in reality are swimming with it.

This is just a sign of life.

TO AGNES E. MEYER

Princeton
December 3, 1940

Dear Mrs. Agnes:

The Chicago grandchild has been born—a girl, Angelica.[1] The matter went well, briefly and easily, and took place barely two days after we had lost patience. Apparently our presence exerted a certain inhibiting effect, and so it was all for the best that we discreetly turned our backs. The baby is vigorous and the little mother very well. She herself is still remarkably childish, although in intelligent ways, and the last time we took her for a walk with her great belly she asked me: "I wonder whether Mrs. Meyer will give me something for Christmas?" I said I scarcely

---

[1] Born November 30, 1940, eldest of the two daughters of Elisabeth Mann Borgese.

thought so, whatever would make Mrs. Meyer think of that? But if you should happen to do so, her pleasure would be as intense as a child's.

I read the Hutchins review with pleasure and agreement. Adler is obviously intelligent, although somewhat too deliberately sensational and bent on shocking. But this group's theories and demands also have something dangerous about them, I feel, and at bottom are closer to a kind of spiritual fascism than democracy. Adler's rancor toward Dewey is the clearest symptom of that. Authority is all very well, and is necessary for the future and a better world—I mean an ultimate, absolute authority, which rather limits than enlarges the concept. But we cannot and must not return to the Middle Ages, and that needful ultimate authority can probably scarcely be found in the transcendental any more. Rather, it must enter into the human realm itself and be based upon feeling for the human, for man's distinction, difficulty, dignity, and mystery. To inculcate this feeling in young people, and thus form the now lost sense of *decency*, should be the first and last task of education.

I read a great deal of Tolstoy while I was working on *Buddenbrooks*, and have mentioned before that *Anna Karenina* and *War and Peace* helped restore my flagging energy at the time. But I don't think I had read *Childhood, Boyhood, and Youth*; I became acquainted with it later. That, however, is unimportant, for Tolstoy is Tolstoy, and the splendid work of his youth is contained in the later monumental works, as these were already contained in it.

TO AGNES E. MEYER

Princeton
December 25, 1940

Dear friend:

We have exchanged telegrams like potentates, but now I must *write*, for what an illustrious article of clothing[1] it is that I found on my gift-table yesterday. There were other pleasing things as well (I am still as delighted with gifts as a child), but this outshone them all, and everyone agreed that it was the *pièce de résistance* of the Christmas room. Richard Wagner would have paled with envy at the sight of it. At the same time it has a restrained and dignified magnificence, fits perfectly, and there is only one fear: that traveling with it will increase my hotel bills. But even at the risk of that, my warmest thanks!

[1] A brocade dressing gown.

We had a pleasant Christmas Eve, with four children and German and British friends. When all is said and done, it is always charming to see the tree lighted and the presents spread out. After dinner we played some fine new records, and at last, like a proper paterfamilias, I read from the Bible—from my own, that is—about two courtiers who are sent to prison, and everyone had a little laugh. The book is a harmless distraction for me, exactly what I need; and it will certainly appear in a time when many people will stand in need of distraction.

On the 28th we are going to Chicago for a few days to visit our youngest, who was as enthusiastic over your present as I predicted. On January 11 we shall be coming to Washington. It is possible that Erika too will be with us.

So long!

1941

———————•———————

TO JOSEPH CAMPBELL [1]

Princeton
January 6, 1941

Dear Mr. Campbell:

Thank you for sending me your lecture, "Permanent Human Values." Naturally I read it with close attention. I should like to make the following comments.

As an American you must be better able to judge than I whether it is appropriate to recommend political indifference to young people in this country—which is just beginning slowly, slowly, against ponderous resistance (and, let us hope, not yet too late) to come to an understanding of the situation and the pressing necessities of the times.

The question as I see it is this: What will become of the five good things which you are defending, or think you are defending; what will become of the sociologist's critical objectivity, of the scientist's and historian's freedom, of the poet's and artist's independence; what will become of religion and humanistic education, in case Hitler wins? I know from experience exactly what would become of all these things everywhere in the world for the next generation, but a good many Americans do not know it yet, and therefore they believe that they must defend these good things by the method and in the spirit that you do.

It is curious: Since you are a friend of my books, you must think that they have something to do with the "permanent human values." Now these books are banned in Germany and in all the countries Germany at present dominates, and anyone who reads them, anyone who offers them for sale, anyone who even speaks well of me in public, would end in a

---

[1] Joseph Campbell (b. 1904), writer and teacher. Author of *The Hero with a Thousand Faces, The Masks of God* (three vols.: *Oriental Mythology, Primitive Mythology, Occidental Mythology*) and other works.

concentration camp, and his teeth would be knocked out, his kidneys bashed. You maintain that we must not allow ourselves to be excited by this, we must rather see to the preservation of the lasting human values. Once more, that is strange.

I do not doubt that your lecture has won you great applause. You should not, I think, be deceived by this applause. You have wittingly or unwittingly told young people already inclined toward moral indifference what they would like to hear; but that is not always what they need.

I know you mean well and desire the best. But whether you are right, and whether you may not be serving the cause of evil by such speeches, is a matter we had best not dispute further.

Once again, my thanks and sincere good wishes.

TO CAROLINE NEWTON

Princeton
January 20, 1941

Dear Miss Lina:

Now your mother too has departed from you—with my whole heart I can enter into the anguish of sudden loneliness that must fill you, with both your parents gone. I can still vividly remember how I felt when my mother died at the age of seventy: what an unexpectedly bitter grief the rending of this bond was. Certainly it is the common lot; but in your case the natural and dignified sorrow is troubled and intensified by cares and undignified discords which I will not mention, but which we want to talk about with you. We are so very sorry, Katia and I. Who would have thought, when you and your dear mother recently came to see us, that her days were so few.

Visit us soon! We feel the need to see you and comfort you. We also want to tell you about our most recent journeyings.

Keep up your courage, dear friend.

TO AGNES E. MEYER

The Bedford
118 East 40th Street
New York
January 24, 1941

Dear friend:

I call you that with special emphasis, for, as I fully understood only afterward, the fact that you suffered so severely over my Town Hall lecture[1] was precisely a sign of your friendship, closeness, and concern. I rejoice at that, and it makes me feel better even as I am pained that I have done something to hurt you.

I gave the lecture twice more, in Atlanta and Athens (Duke University in Durham was prudent enough to have me speak on *The Magic Mountain*), and each time the applause and the honors were great. But I was unable to take any pleasure in it, and whatever you may now think, the lecture has become insufferable to me because it made you suffer. If I could regret that I did not ask you to stay away entirely from it (but I couldn't do that, after all), I would regret it. I knew it all in advance, but had to let things take their course—a rather common predicament in life. The result is that I will never again repeat this speech in its present form. I no longer like it and will change it. The problem, however, is whether any revision at all could produce something you would find acceptable. We don't feel the same about this point, which for me is a life and death matter, and which you regard as mere "politics"—for which in your kindness you think me too good. *Je fais la guerre*—and you want to see me *au dessus de la mêlée*—in your kindness. But this *mêlée* is a decisive battle of mankind, and everything will be decided in it, including the fate of my life's work. For decades, at least, my books will not be allowed to return to Germany, into the tradition where they belong, if the wretched rabble should triumph, collecting those dividends of victory prepared for them over eight long years by a sluggish, craven, oblivious world. You don't know what I have suffered in these eight years, and how intensely I wish that the most repulsive baseness that has ever made "history" will be destroyed—and that I will live to see it happen. Have I behaved badly during these years and permitted hatred to degrade and paralyze me? I have written *Joseph in Egypt*, *The Beloved Returns*, and *The Transposed Heads*, works of freedom and gaiety and, if you will, of distinction. I am a bit proud that I have brought all that off, instead of joining the ranks of the melancholics, and I feel my friends should regard the fact that I also go on fighting as a sign of strength, not of weakness and humiliation. People's regard for my fiction is not complete and in the final analysis cannot make me happy if it is not partly governed by sympathy with this other cause. It is said, "Who is not for me is against me." But who is not against evil, passionately and with his whole soul, *is more or less for it.*

---

[1] Probably a version of the lecture subsequently published as "War and Democracy" (privately printed by Adcraft Press, Los Angeles, 1940) in which Mann speaks of the totality of the idea of humanism as comprising both art and politics. The "world civil war" mentioned at the end of the letter also figures in the lecture.

God forbid that this should have entered into your friendly suffering during my lecture. The decision remains: I shall not deliver it again.

What a lovely time you gave us in Washington, and how grateful I am for your responsiveness to my storyteller's jokes. The rest of our journey was interesting and tiring—interesting, of course, especially in its very next stage,[2] where we were granted astonishing honors. The dizzying height was the cocktail in the study—while the other dinner guests had to cool their heels below. And yet we had already had early breakfast with "him"! "He" once again made a strong impression upon me, or shall I say, again aroused my sympathetic interest: this mixture of craft, good nature, self-indulgence, desire to please, and sincere faith is hard to characterize. But there is something like a blessing upon him, and I am drawn to him as the born opponent, so it seems to me, of the creature that must be toppled. Here for once is a modern-style tamer of the masses who desires the good—or at any rate the better—and who takes our part as perhaps no one else in the world does. Why should I not take his part? I felt strengthened afterward. Let us hope that he has more influence upon the people than the aviator Lindbergh with his "stalemate" and his "unbeatable." "If only there were many such Americans!" the Nazi press cries out. Well, there are many; this is precisely the world civil war of which I spoke.

This letter was really intended only as a report of our happy return home. We then had to turn around and set out for New York, for the Federal Union Dinner at which I had to speak. That was day before yesterday. We stayed on yesterday to hear Walter conduct the *Lied von der Erde*—a *growing* work, it seems to me, whereas so much else from that period is fading and sinking. This noon we shall be going back to Princeton. Joseph has just been fetched to court by a breathless messenger.

Regards to Eugene.

TO ELEANOR ROOSEVELT

[*Original in English*]

Princeton
January 28, 1941

My dear Mrs. Roosevelt:

I am sending you a copy of *The City of Man*,[1] a little book which a group

---

[2] At the White House.

[1] A militant proclamation by leading liberals, stating the values and aims of democracy and arguing that these values must be defended against the menace of fascism.

of us prepared in all sincerity and humility as an attempt to outline the future world democracy and as a contribution to the solution of the fundamental problems facing all nations today. If the book appeals to you and you think it would interest the President, perhaps you will show it to him.

I cannot close this letter without reference to your recent charming and friendly hospitality. We regard it as a most gracious compliment that in these anxious and arduous days you and Mr. Roosevelt found the time to have us visit you.

TO AGNES E. MEYER

Princeton
March 12, 1941

Dear friend:

The people of Keme[1] called the precious transparent cloth of which these handkerchiefs are made "royal linen." They would no doubt have thought it a pity to use the fabric for this purpose. But although each single one of these ethereal squares would "add nothing in weight" to the egg of the phoenix, they seem by their size able to cope with even such a cold as I have just had and as I shall probably have again before long in California, because it is so easy out there to forget to put on a coat in the evenings. But no, if that should happen I shall make use of coarser kinds and merely let a corner of these delicate things peek coquettishly out of my breast pocket. Thank you for the wonderful gift.

And let me also thank you once again for your visit; it was good of you to come and a good token of your friendship. I had no idea that I seemed to be accessible the first day and abstracted the second. On both days I was equally glad of your animating presence, "filling the house with beauty" (that too is Egyptian). But what do we know about ourselves and how difficult we may be making things for those who are fond of us? It is bad and sad, what you tell me. If I make my friends suffer so, what must it mean to be married to me! You have churned up my conscience with regard to my poor wife, who for thirty-six years has had to put up with that. Ah well, I have burdened this earth for a very long time now, which is a good thing for me too, because, believe me, I am often thoroughly tired of myself and fondly look forward to the time when all

Among the contributors: G. A. Borgese, William Benton, Hermann Broch, William M. Hutchins, Thomas Mann, Lewis Mumford, Gaetano Salvemini.

[1] The ancient name for Egypt, meaning "the black" or "the fruitful soil."

that is left of me are the things with which I have tried to give people happiness and to "help them to live."

The day after you left, the dissolution began here. Downstairs everything already looks in a desperate state, and I have withdrawn to the bedroom, which for the present is still a wildlife sanctuary. The whole thing weighs heavily on my heart—homeless, confused weeks are coming, in which on top of everything I shall have to bear up at lectures and banquetings, all the while doubting whether what we are doing is right and sensible. We shall have to risk it and see. At any rate I can't and won't take this parting so very seriously. Are the distances from Washington to Princeton and Washington to Santa Monica so essentially different? It's America from sea to sea, and after all, we have already spent the entire summer out there. I shall have a letter from you now and then, and hear of the progress of your work, of your life, and so will you from me. When we come East once or twice a year, Washington will be our principal destination—and, moreover, not on behalf of "the man who is too superficial to be murdered."[2]

Auf Wiedersehen! And friendly greetings to Eugene.

TO ERICH VON KAHLER

Hotel Durant
Berkeley, California
March 30, 1941

Dear friend Kahler:

Let me send you melancholic and cordial greetings from the midst of a persisting wretched turmoil. Many adventures already lie between our parting and today, all stalwartly and bravely fought through. Chicago with Medi, Borgi, and the baby was peaceable and familial. Erika joined us there. The anti-Papist[1] read powerfully from his Mexican opera libretto[2] (in English), and I produced the dream-interpretation chapter,[3] which made the children laugh until they cried. Then came Colorado Springs and Denver—at the altitude of St. Moritz and therefore somewhat taxing. Colorado Springs must be a charming place in weather other than the kind we had almost all the time: rain and rain. Here too. The journey from Denver to Los Angeles took 36 hours. We found the Franks in the

[2] A remark by Mrs. Meyer concerning President Roosevelt.
[1] Mann's son-in-law, G. A. Borgese.
[2] *Montezuma*, a dramatic poem set to music by Roger Sessions; the premiere was given by the Berlin State Opera in the spring of 1964.
[3] In *Joseph the Provider*.

hotel; then my brother arrived, I having to change in the midst of all this to deliver my lecture. We stayed up late; we had to be up at five o'clock the next morning to catch the plane for San Francisco. The two-hour flight, with an excellent breakfast above the clouds and the magnificent mountains, was a remarkable experience. Another was being fetched from the airport by a police guard and being driven with sirens howling through all the lights. A new experience for me. Here, we are having fine, uproarious celebrations—too many of them. The ceremony on the campus, scenically perhaps the loveliest in the world, was for once favored by the weather; the sun shone and the big amphitheater, seen from the stage (where we again met Katia's brother), made a delightful, colorful picture. And so I have now become a doctor of law, again something new; but I don't notice the difference. The Freemason-like induction into the chapter of Phi Beta Kappa (*Philosophie Bioy Kybernetes*) was majestic; thereafter came a grand banquet, and then when sensible folk would have gone to bed, my lecture took place, in two overcrowded halls, one where I spoke and another that was served by a loudspeaker. I had made appropriate changes in the text and talked about the thinker's responsibility for life, which had been lacking in Germany, and also about Nietzsche, saying that were he alive he would be in America today and American tolerance would likewise have inducted him into the Phi Beta Kappa fraternity, in spite of his romantic sins. That brought laughter.

We are staying here a few days longer than planned. It is more sensible to go to Stanford University first and from there to Carmel. We shall be returning to Los Angeles on about the 8th or 9th and will then take refuge in the cottage at 740 Amalfi Drive, Brentwood.

The beast is not doing anything against the Serbs. He "will not let himself be provoked"[4]—too bad. The American confiscation of the ships[5] is certainly a cheering stroke—still barely *short of war*. But the British shipping losses must be dreadful, and although things go well in the Mediterranean and the "Axis" is by now no more than a name for the "maintenance of order" in Italy, we must arm ourselves against terrible blows still to come.

---

[4] The reference is to the military coup in Belgrade and the popular uprising throughout the country on March 27, 1941. The regent Paul, who had been subservient to the Germans, was deposed, and King Peter II was declared no longer a minor and given power to form a new government. On April 6 Hitler nevertheless allowed himself to be "provoked" and began his war against Yugoslavia.

[5] The Axis powers, Germany and Italy, had repeatedly violated American neutrality at sea. As a reprisal, and on suspicion of sabotage, German and Italian merchant vessels were detained in the ports of the United States.

TO JOSEPH ANGELL

740 Amalfi Drive
Pacific Palisades, California
April 19, 1941

Dear Doctor Angell:

I want to send you a greeting from our new temporary home in California, a pleasant, rustically situated, and practical little house in which we intend to remain for the present.

I must also thank you for having again attended my lecture in Los Angeles. I was sorry that I had nothing at all new to offer you. Since then, for Berkeley and Stanford, I have changed the lecture somewhat and improved it. I no longer liked the first parts.

There is a question troubling me, and immediately after our last meeting I thought of turning to you with it. It concerns my son Golo, who obtained his Ph.D. degree in Heidelberg and there prepared himself for an academic career. After our emigration he spent three years in France, teaching history and German literature in St. Cloud at the Ecole Normale Supérieure and at the University of Rennes. I enclose his credentials from St. Cloud; unfortunately he lost those from Rennes when he hastily left Switzerland to enter the French army.

He wishes intensely, as we do also, that he may somehow be able to resume his interrupted academic career in America. I am convinced that this is his vocation, for he has the temperament of a teacher as well as of a scholar. I have a high opinion of his academic qualifications, for he is thoroughly grounded in philosophy, history, and literature. In addition to German, history, and philosophy, he might also teach French, of which he has a complete command. Moreover, he no longer has any difficulty with English.

It has occurred to me that you might someday ask Dr. Story[1] whether there is any possibility of work for the young man, who is longing for a suitable occupation. His requirements at first would of course be minimal; he would be content with pocket money, since what matters to him most is to have a sphere of activity.

In recent years I have written so many letters in the interest of others that for once I can really permit myself to plead the case of a member of my own family, especially since I can do so with a good conscience and complete confidence that he is worthy of my recommendation.

---

[1] Russell M. Story (1883–1942), at this time professor of political science and president of Claremont College, Claremont, California.

I might also mention that Golo has just been asked to give a series of guest lectures at a college in the Middle West—which, however, has no permanent position open for him.

In the near future we mean to make up for the visit to Pomona which we missed last year. At the moment I am hindered by a painful dental crisis which came on just after the end of my lecture tour. But I am in good hands, and within twelve to fourteen days this will certainly be no reason to postpone the outing any longer.

Therefore I hope to be seeing you again very soon. With all good wishes to you and Mrs. Angell,

TO ERICH VON KAHLER

Pacific Palisades, California
May 25, 1941

Dear friend Kahler:

What is going on? Why haven't we heard anything from you for such a long time, literally since we parted? Something is wrong, and if you replied: "Why, I haven't heard from you," it would come to light that the letter I sent you en route, during our journey, has been lost, and that you had thought all along, "Out of sight, out of mind." It would be sad if you could possibly have taken this notion into your head. I no longer remember from what stage of the trip I wrote you. Perhaps from Colorado Springs, where I had a desk? But I did write—pages and pages, and we have often asked ourselves since: Why hasn't he written even once? [. . .]

Of course there may have been other reasons for your silence, e.g., the formidable burden of work with your lectures. The series[1] was concluded on a highly successful note, I hear. I have great respect for what you have accomplished, especially since you found you had to speak extemporaneously. You have given an example of fortitude that honorably differs from the complete incompetence of most refugee intellectuals faced with their new situation. None of them, I have the impression, is prepared to learn anything new; rather they all want to go on as they did in times now buried, and expect roasted squabs to fly into their mouths. Didn't Golo write that you have been invited to lecture in the Middle West? And what has been arranged with the New School for the next academic year?

---

[1] Lectures at the New School for Social Research in 1940–1, which later became the basis of Kahler's book *Man the Measure*.

Are you very depressed by events, i.e., by our constant defeats? That, too, would be sufficient reason for your silence. I often wonder at the phlegmatic disposition, a peculiar mixture of contempt and confidence, with which I take all this without especially allowing it to disturb my work. Perhaps the sunniness and vividness of this region, this easy living and somewhat slack oversized seaside resort, is helpful. Also we are inured—or numbed—to "taking" it, and a kind of permanent muscular contraction has developed so that we receive but don't really feel the successive blows. Enough; I live from day to day, and meantime pile one page of *Joseph* upon the other. I am in the middle of the grand dialogue —a whole series of chapters—between Joseph and Pharaoh Amenhotep, which will lead by roundabout and hermetically cunning ways to Joseph's elevation. You'd like it, I think. I recently read to Erika and my wife for hours, and once again "dear Erich" was very much missed.

As in the East, there is no lack of interruptions and episodes here. There was [. . .] a grand dinner and speech for the Federal Union in the Beverly Hills Hotel, and early in June I have to go to San Francisco for a meeting organized by the Emergency Rescue Committee, to which Kingdon will be coming also. My speech is ready and recounts quite bluntly what stupidity, baseness, and ignorance we exiles have had to endure from the world for eight long years. I must say, I am looking forward to getting this off my chest. [. . .]

Our plans for building have been subject to many vacillations—not only the plans, but even the very intention to build. That is to say, *we* were the ones who vacillated, which is understandable in these times, and given the uncertainty of the future. At one point we had definitely decided *not* to build, to pay off the architect and withdraw. But now it seems after all as if we will begin and from the autumn on live under our own—that is, under the Federal Loan's—roof. The thing appears more risky than it is. Rents will rise. Actually, we will live more cheaply than in the kind of rented house we would need in the long run, and the site is so beautiful that we can rent or sell at any time. The East is not lost to us. A lecture tour there for late fall is already being arranged. So we shall see you again!

Erika is with us and has been a real comfort—enlivening, entertaining, helpful—a dear, strong child. Only she is very anxious, as we are too, about Klaus, who is having ominous, exhausting problems with his magazine.[2] We have done everything possible to raise money to help him—with minimal success.

[2] *Decision: A Review of Free Culture.* The magazine, founded and edited by Klaus

How is your poor dear Fine?[3] My wife is very concerned about her too and would like to have her address.

TO ERICH VON KAHLER

Pacific Palisades
June 1, 1941

Dear Kahler:

All's well; the first and the second letter have arrived and I am once more up to date. Now that she has the address, my wife will write to Fine shortly.

Your notion of the townships here and their names is exactly right. We ourselves thought at first that we belonged to Brentwood, and added Los Angeles to our address for good measure. But we were repeatedly corrected by the post office until we resigned ourselves to living nowhere else but Pacific Palisades, California, although I did not consider that a town name at all—and in fact it probably isn't a township but a landscape with a few colonial homes and ocean view.

In this my favorite season of the year it is also lovely here, although I liked it better in Küsnacht and even in Princeton. Here everything blooms in violet and grape colors that look rather made of paper, and because one can't quite appraise them, one can't praise them. But I can appraise the oleander; it blooms very beautifully. Only I have a suspicion that it may do so all year round.

Day before yesterday we visited Claremont—Pomona College, to ingratiate ourselves there for Golo's sake. When he comes West he must also call there and put on his most polished manners. His French credentials made an impression after all. We heard and read the FDR speech with feelings similar to yours. This emphasis on the "Hemisphere" instead of on England and the English-speaking world was distasteful to me. Halifax[1] was not invited, but the ambassadors of those filthy Fascistic South American republics were, and Argentina has promptly disavowed the "Hemisphere" and declared her neutrality. Moreover, deeds are singularly lacking; and even under the *unlimited emergency* Lindbergh has been allowed to talk again, which I wouldn't have thought possible.

Mann (January 1941 to February 1942), was sponsored by Sherwood Anderson, W. H. Auden, Eduard Beneš, Julien Green, Somerset Maugham, Robert Sherwood, and Stefan Zweig, among others.

[3] Erich Kahler's wife, who was in ill health.

[1] Edward Frederick, Earl of Halifax (1881–1959) was British ambassador in Washington, 1941–6.

Twenty-five million dollars' worth of *supplies for Britain* go up in flames, and they say there must be no jumping to conclusions. No, things are in a bad way—unfortunately you are right about that. For the present England can expect only further defeats, and if America cannot be roused, we may well come to the point of asking ourselves whether we are not going to lose this campaign.

TO KLAUS MANN

Pacific Palisades
June 11, 1941

Dear Eissi:

Aside from your latest interesting letter concerning that cross and pleasure for all of us, *Decision*, and for your delightfully droll birthday telegram, I have also to thank you for your kind support for *The Transposed Heads*, which quite seriously the little book very much needs. The booksellers, as Knopf took the precaution of reporting to me, had reacted lukewarmly—wretchedly, in fact—and he was counting on advance orders of 7,000 at most, whereas he had printed 15,000. Now, however, the first *reviews*, especially those you sent me, look distinctly gratifying, not only from the literary but also from the business point of view. For they have sounded an enticing note. On the other hand, Fadiman[1] in the *New Yorker* has unfortunately failed us completely by taking an entirely negative view, which is a severe blow. It is too bad that he of all people could not read the thing in the original, where everything does make an entirely different impression. Nevertheless, the reception in general seems to be not bad, and I have helped it along somewhat by appearing on the radio with Professor Frederick.[2]

Now to your letter. I have made promises to all and sundry that I would actively collaborate on *Decision*, and I want to keep my word. At the moment the best I have to offer are the enclosed little things, two *messages* to Germany, a dinner speech for Federal Union, and the speech I delivered at Uncle Heinrich's birthday. These occasionally intersect one another, and I even fear that here and there they contain bits from things you have already printed. Still, you may be able either to use one of the

[1] Clifton Fadiman (b. 1904), critic, editor, author, master of ceremonies of the noted radio series *Information Please* (1938–48), one of the judges of the Book-of-the Month Club. Author of *I Believe* (1939), *Party of One* (1955), *The Lifetime Reading Plan* (1959), among others. See note 4 to the following letter.

[2] John T. Frederick (b. 1893), professor of English and modern literature at various universities. At this time head of the radio program *Of Men and Books* (1937–44).

lot, or by cutting and pasting to distill something you can bring out as a contribution from me. The prospectus does have to come out now, and I shall be happy to be listed as chairman of the editorial or the advisory board. Muriel Rukeyser[3] is unknown to me, of course, and I cannot judge how she will do as associate editor; that's something you must know better than I, and perhaps the practical side is more important than the decorative, namely that she can really be of help to you.

The news about Marshall Field[4] doesn't sound so bad; since he did not appear flabbergasted at the request for $25,000 but calmly replied that he could provide a part of that, we may probably count on his producing at least a fifth, and if Ascoli[5] then contributes another $5,000, our child of woe could be kept alive for a while. After all, you know, in the present situation we must tell ourselves that it would be honorable if the magazine can be sustained for a year. Only collapse midway between the start and the end of the year would really be disastrous.

The answer I received from the cotton king in response to my tactful letter is not so different from the other *showerbaths* I have been getting. I enclose it so you yourself can inform him that we all greatly appreciate his attitude and would be overjoyed if he would buy a $100 share.

We have many worries. There is our Eri. You know all about that. It's almost settled that she is going to England. Who wants to stop her? She insists it depends on our consent, but what is consent in a matter like this? She must go her way, and we can't take the responsibility for her state of mind if we were to stop her. Naturally it will be an anxious period, and we can only hope that her confidence in her star will prove justified.

Golo will probably be coming out here for a few weeks in the near future—that's good. Unfortunately it will probably be autumn before we see the East again. Is there any chance that you can take a breather and join us for a while?

Our best paternal and maternal wishes that you come through this happily, and at most with a black eye.

Your Z.

---

[3] Muriel Rukeyser (b. 1913), American poet. Among her works: *Theory of Flight* (1935), *A Turning Wind* (1940), *Willard Gibbs* (1942).
[4] Marshall Field (b. 1893), owner of Chicago's greatest department store, founder of the *Chicago Sun*.
[5] Max Ascoli (b. 1898), Italian writer, lawyer. Emigrated to the United States in 1931, taught (1933–42) at the New School for Social Research. Author of *Intelligence in Politics* (1936), *The Power of Freedom* (1948). Publisher of *The Reporter* until it ceased publication in 1968.

1941

TO AGNES E. MEYER

Dear Mrs. Agnes:

Thank you for the clippings. Your magnificent essay[1] looks even better in the *Post*—much more rounded than in the *Times*—and I really enjoyed the article by the Hindu gentleman or gentleman Hindu in the *Tribune*.[2] That such an expert accepts what is after all an extremely improvised India cannot help pleasing me, and that he didn't take offense at my Kamadamane[3] speaks for his sense of humor.

Time was also good, and useful for sales, and in general the press has been quite favorable, if the influential Fadiman in *The New Yorker*[4] had not failed us completely and written contemptuously of the book. It's really too bad. Had he been able to read it in the original, I think he would have come to a different conclusion. But he had already been left cold by *Lotte*—with whose hero he has in common an admitted distaste for Indian matters, though not much else.

Now for something "serious" and a matter of business, so to speak. It's a plea—not for myself. You once told me that if I needed money for refugee aid I should turn to you, that no better use could be made of available funds. I have not rushed to take you at your word, but now it seems to me that the moment has really come to do so—within limits. The funds of the Emergency Rescue Committee are virtually exhausted. I have repeatedly dipped into my own pocket, but today can no longer reasonably do so, although I know that in France, in Switzerland, in Amsterdam, in Lisbon the thoughts of all the refugees constantly circle around me and that each of the unfortunates there always thinks of my name first—God knows why. But it would be a great boon to me to have a small fund at my disposal, from which I could draw in actually urgent cases, a few of which have just come to my attention. I should like to send the publisher Oprecht in Zurich (he has just bravely brought out a good book on General Wavell[5]) a few hundred dollars for his support of the

---

[1] "Thomas Mann's Fable for Today: *The Transposed Heads*," *Washington Post* and *New York Times Book Review* (June 8, 1941).

[2] Krishnalal Shridharani: "Thomas Mann Spins a Fable of Brahmin India," *New York Herald Tribune Book Review* (June 8, 1941).

[3] The hermit who decides Sita's rightful husband in *The Transposed Heads*.

[4] The review in question, "Thomas Mann: *The Transposed Heads*" was actually written by F. O. Matthiessen, not Clifton Fadiman.

[5] Sir Archibald P. Wavell (b. 1883), organizer of the British offensive in Egypt during the Second World War (1940–1); Supreme Commander of all Allied troops in India, 1942. Editor of a highly praised anthology of poetry, *Other Men's Flowers* (1945).

destitute in Switzerland. Furthermore, in Holland there is Landauer,[6] former director of the gallant Querido Publishing House, who escaped from the Nazis rushing into his building by leaping out the window. Since then he has been in hiding somewhere, always in danger of death. With $350 he could probably be brought to America, and I would be happy to be able to contribute that amount. The third case that concerns me deeply is that of the well-known dramatist Georg Kaiser,[7] a genius in his fashion. He is stuck in Switzerland, where the air is getting thicker and thicker, and sighing for the opportunity to come over here; he also has the necessary papers but lacks the travel money. —In short, would you be willing to place $1,000 at my personal disposal? —I'd be glad to give you a point-for-point accounting of how it's spent. You would be providing me with some freedom of action and enabling me not to disappoint at least some of the hopes placed in me.

No more for today. The strange oceanic desert climate here still often tires me, but at the same time sharpens the appetite, which is a rather ridiculous combination.

TO AGNES E. MEYER

Pacific Palisades
June 18, 1941

Dear friend:

Thank you for the straightforward generosity with which you immediately fulfilled my request. A great deal of good can be done with this money, and some steps can be taken against the horrors of the times.

I was delighted by the letters you received about your *review*, all the more since you yourself had such scruples about it. They do you honor, certainly, but such grateful responses from totally impartial persons should finally settle your doubts about the value of your work. Incidentally, on the other hand I understand only too well your nervousness about a certain disproportion between the object under the critical microscope and such a troublesome organism as *The Transposed Heads*,

[6] Walter Landauer (1902–44). He was not, as Mann mistakenly writes, the former director of Querido Verlag, but head of the German exile department of the Allert de Lange Verlag of Amsterdam. Although Mann procured an American visa and travel money for him, Landauer died of starvation in 1944 in the Bergen-Belsen concentration camp.

[7] Georg Kaiser (1878–1945), one of the foremost Expressionist writers. Kaiser wrote some sixty plays. In 1933 all performances of his work were forbidden in Germany. He emigrated to Switzerland in 1938 and lived there in acute financial need.

which shimmers and squirms, never yields a clear meaning, and slips out of one's hand as soon as one tries to grasp it. How can anyone write about it? I couldn't. But you have done so with dignity and love, and have thereby won great praise.

Yes, Tonio, Hans, and Inge[1] are now united in the flaming pyre. Peace to their ashes! You might smilingly have drawn a cross over them in your review, but that you refrained is not in any sense a fault.

I am thoroughly sick at heart, for yesterday Erika left us, and unless something intervenes at the last moment—war, for example—will be flying to Lisbon on the Clipper on the 26th. The parting was as hard for her as for us; that much could be seen in her face. She is well aware that losing her would be about the worst that could happen to us, especially to me, since I feel more serene and happy the moment this animating child is about. But her sense of duty, her urge to activity, her fighter's honor, have been stronger, and I can't but respect her for all that. The Propaganda Ministry has called her; it has confidence in her and . . . she was more afraid of appearing cowardly than of causing us grief and anxiety, although her tears showed that the choice was terribly difficult. Heaven protect the dear, brave child! She has, incidentally, offered to set a time limit to her gambling with fate. Now *you* must promise not to undermine her resolution out of concern for me.

The warmest greetings! Mount Kisco will soon make well the winter's harms.

Yours,
T. M.

---

[1] Tonio, Hans, and Inge are the principal characters in Thomas Mann's novella *Tonio Kröger*. There is a certain kinship between them and the three "heroes" of *The Transposed Heads*: in both stories the simple, uncerebral, strong-bodied man (Hans, Nanda) is the object of the longings of the complex, intellectual, weaker man (Tonio, Shridaman). The female characters (Inge, Sita) are scarcely reminiscent of one another. Inge belongs to Hans, shares his nature, and is by no means attracted to Tonio, whereas Sita wishes to see her two lovers combined in one person: the clever, refined head of Shridaman and the vigorous, handsome body of Nanda. In the fable, her wish is fulfilled— but the fulfillment does not lead to happiness. The transposed heads alter the nature of the bodies they had formerly belonged to; the ultimate union of spirit and body takes place only in death, when Shridaman and Nanda kill one another by prearrangement in a deliberately suicidal duel, and the widow Sita, in accordance with Hindu custom, is burned alive with the bodies of both.

1941

TO AGNES E. MEYER

Pacific Palisades
July 26, 1941

Dear friend:

That's certainly great news![1] I fervently hope the young people won't keep after you too much in Wyoming,[2] so that you can have a little peace and rest and feel refreshed enough in August to come out here with Florence.[3] I am treating it as a certainty, and would be even more disappointed than Hitler by the Russians if nothing came of the visit. The life of a woman like you has something tragic about it. There is Washington—the exhausting great world. You flee to Mount Kisco, but the summer-palace life there is almost equally strenuous. You retreat to the ranch, but there the dear young people are on the go and again you have no chance to catch your breath. You might say with King Philip: "I find my peace in the Escorial." Perhaps you will find it *here* rather better than at all your far too hospitable properties. Joseph will take a vacation for the days of your visit and will have to see how he manages without me. At thirty, he is old enough to be on his own. Right now I am preparing a great deal of what is to follow—actually the whole second half of the book. An English commentary on the Torah has been very helpful. There will definitely be some highly dramatic, touching, and stirring scenes that are amusing at the same time. Crafty goodness will win out over stupid tyranny, over slave drivers who with ridiculous complacency admire their historical grandeur in the mirror.

You've made me curious about Hawthorne. I suppose I should read him, yet I doubt whether this civic virtue with an uneasy conscience, or this being an artist with an uneasy conscience toward respectability, has anything to say to me any longer. Those are worn-out shoes, and you are mistaken in addressing me as "Herr Tonio Kröger"—although on the other hand I should not like to repudiate the book. After all, it is my *Werther*—although it's hardly likely that Napoleon would have read T. K. seven times. Nevertheless, your choice of Hawthorne has considerable inner logic; he will serve to illustrate certain motifs of my youth to Americans in literary terms which are familiar to them.

[1] Kay (Katharine) Graham, Mrs. Meyer's daughter, was expecting her first child.
[2] At the Meyer ranch.
[3] Florence Meyer Homolka (1911–52), eldest daughter of Agnes and Eugene Meyer. A successful photographer; author of *Focus on Art*, with a preface by Aldous Huxley—a book containing many of her best photographs, including some of Thomas Mann.

1941

Last night we had a private performance of the new Dieterle film, *The Devil and Daniel Webster*—after a story by the same excellent man who did that nice biographical essay on me in the *Tribune*.[4] An excellent *picture*—an Americanized fairy tale and patriotic fantasy, brilliantly acted. Everybody was there, from Max Reinhardt to Krishnamurti.[5]

Well then, I am already looking forward to seeing you soon. Don't disappoint us. In another month the general outlines of Seven Palms House[6] will be visible, although only in a skeletal way.

TO ALBERT EINSTEIN

Pacific Palisades
August 4, 1941

Dear Professor Einstein:

May I make a request? Will you join me in putting in a good word with the State Department for the writer Wilhelm Herzog, whom you have probably heard of (he edited the magazine *Forum* and has written a good book on the Dreyfus case), so that his visa will be renewed? It has run out and he has been waiting many weeks in Trinidad for it to be revalidated.

It was his ill luck to be on his way to New York, well provided with all necessary papers and documents, when the *Winnipeg* on which he was sailing was seized by the British and taken to Trinidad. There his visa ran out, and as you know, Washington's immigration rules have been inhumanly stiffened. As they now stand, the Trinidad consul cannot renew the visa. One may well call it cruel that the summary procedures of the new immigration rules should bar entry to a writer who has so passionately fought Hitler gangsterism.

The consul in Trinidad, however, has assured him that if you and I vouch for his political and moral integrity to the State Department, it would undoubtedly authorize renewal of the visa. It would be a pity to refuse to try, and leave the man stranded in Trinidad.

Please do join me in signing the enclosed affidavit.

Our best regards. We hope to see you in the fall.

[4] "Thomas Mann, Honored by the Free World," *New York Herald Tribune Book Review* (June 29, 1941), by Stephen Vincent Benét (1898–1943).
[5] Jiddu Krishnamurti (b. 1897), Brahmin philosopher. Hailed by theosophist Annie Besant as the world's new teacher, he preached attainment of spiritual peace by meditation upon the unity of the soul and the universe.
[6] For a time Mann considered giving this name to his new house, in emulation of the Meyers's Seven Springs Farm.

TO COUNT CARLO SFORZA[1]

[*Original in French*]

Pacific Palisades
August 13, 1941

My dear Count:

I have read your book[2] on Italy and the Italians with the greatest pleasure. Let me thank you sincerely for having sent it to me, especially with so flattering a dedication. The subject could not have been treated with more wit, understanding, elegance, and authority. It is moreover a subject which has perpetually mystified the world, and which the world is most eager to penetrate.

You are fortunate. You can assert that for your country Fascism is something alien and against nature. It would be difficult to prove that National Socialism bears the same character for Germany. Your pages on Luther are profound and just. In a recent essay I too stated that *"the good old Germany of culture and learning"* is more or less an American fiction, and that one would have to drive pretty far upstream along the course of German history before one found no sign of that spirit which today has reached the last degree of baseness and threatens to barbarize and enslave the world. At least as far as the Middle Ages; for Luther, I said exactly as you do, already had decidedly Nazistic traits. And what horrors are to be found in Fichte! What menaces in the music, and even more in the writings, of Wagner! What a muddle of clarity and obscurity in Schopenhauer and Nietzsche!

Your conviction that "the long historical development of the Italians will make them fit easily into the larger framework that the future will provide for all the peoples of Europe" is far better founded than similar hopes for our country and our people. Yet it is perhaps permissible to believe that the Germany of Dürer, of Bach, of Kant, and of Goethe, the Germany that has created *Iphigenia* and *Fidelio* and the *Ninth Symphony*, has a continuity which will reach beyond Nazism or racism. We may even say that the German people, essentially nonpolitical as they are,

---

[1] Count Carlo Sforza (1873–1952), Italian statesman; foreign minister 1920–1; one of the leaders of the democratic opposition in Italy. Ambassador to Paris 1921–2; resigned in November 1922 after Mussolini seized power. Went into exile in Belgium in 1926, later to England and the United States. Returned to Italy in 1943 and became president of the Consultative Assembly, then deputy in the National Assembly. From 1947–51 he was foreign minister.

[2] *Les Italiens tels qu'ils sont* (Montreal, 1941). The dedication read: *A Thomas Mann—gran nome tedesco che non fa disperare dell'avvenire—cordialmente Sforza.*

seem predestined for the unified and depoliticalized world which should take shape after the abolition of national sovereignties. In such a situation they might well reveal their best qualities.

TO LOUIS B. MAYER[1]

Pacific Palisades
[October 1941]

Dear Mr. Mayer:

It is not my habit to meddle in affairs that do not concern me directly. Nevertheless I want to take the liberty of speaking to you confidentially about a matter which is a cause of anxiety to me as well as to many other persons of good will.

One of the finest and noblest episodes during these last turbulent years, which have destroyed the lives and happiness of so many—an episode that will certainly never be forgotten whenever the fantastic story of the emigration of European culture is told—has been the decision of two great film companies in Hollywood to give emergency contracts to a number of German and Austrian writers. The contracts not only enabled these men to immigrate to the United States, but also assured them of a basic livelihood at least for a time. For clarity's sake I am here setting down the names of the five authors in whose behalf M.G.M. has acted so generously, and I add the dates of their contracts.

Alfred Döblin	October 8, 1940, to October 7, 1941
Alfred Polgar[2]	October 24, 1940, to October 23, 1941
Hans Lustig[3]	December 10, 1940, to December 9, 1941
Wilhelm Speyer	March 10, 1940, to March 9, 1942
Walter Mehring[4]	April 5, 1941, to April 4, 1942

Perhaps I may say that it is not the writers alone who benefit from

---

[1] Louis B. Mayer (1885–1957), one of the pioneers of the movie industry, founder of L. B. Mayer Pictures, later to become Metro-Goldwyn-Mayer.

[2] Alfred Polgar (1875–1955), Austrian writer and theatrical critic, considered a master of the short prose piece. Emigrated to France in 1938, to the United States in 1940. From 1949 until his death he moved about Europe, with Zurich as his headquarters.

[3] Hans Lustig (b. 1902), editor and theater critic. Emigrated to France in 1933, fled from Paris in 1940, and reached the United States with the help of the Emergency Rescue Committee. A successful scriptwriter in France, Lustig remained under contract to M.G.M. from 1940–58.

[4] Walter Mehring (b. 1896), poet, satirist, novelist, memoirist. Escaped from France to the United States in 1940. A prolific writer, his *No Road Back* and *The Lost Library* have been published in English. At present he lives in Switzerland, continues to write and publish, and has recently been awarded the Fontane Prize for literature.

these agreements with M.G.M. Not only has the firm's reputation been enhanced by its connection with these distinguished European names, but in at least several cases there have been important practical rewards. I am assured that Hans Lustig, for example, has proved a most valuable *writer*, and I know that Gottfried Reinhardt[5] and Sam Behrman[6] have the highest opinion of Alfred Polgar's gift for dialogue, which he particularly demonstrated in the last Garbo film.[7]

As for Döblin, he has just handed in a *story* which Mr. Kenneth McKenna thinks very highly of. An American *junior writer* has been assigned to assist Döblin in developing his story. So in this case, too, the value of these contracts for the firm has been demonstrated.

I mention these matters, which you probably know as well as I, only to anticipate the criticism which might be made within the company if you renewed the contracts with the refugee writers: that money is being spent needlessly merely for humanitarian purposes. And in saying this I have already expressed my request, which is not mine alone. We are anxious about the future of these men, who in Europe had won high respect and earned their living by their writing; and my (our) plea to you, Mr. Mayer, is that you will use your influence in their favor and secure another year's engagement for them. Much can change in the course of this year, and shifts in the political situation may well produce new fields for employment and new economic opportunities for the refugees. If M.G.M. keeps them on until then, the policy could surely be justified in the face of any objection and from any point of view. For in the first place, there is the definite hope that writers such as Speyer and Mehring will in time also find ways to demonstrate their value to the studio. And in the second place, it seems to me beyond question that the salary for a man like Hans Lustig would be far higher if he had not come on a refugee contract, so that he is helping to support several colleagues.

I should like to mention another thing. At times it has been rumored that the Screen Writers' Guild is *opposed* to the engagement of foreign authors. This turns out to be completely false. I have before me a letter from Mr. Sheridan Gibney[8] in which he states that *"our organization*

[5] Gottfried Reinhardt (b. 1916), the son of Max Reinhardt. Emigrated to the United States in 1938. He became a successful film producer and director.

[6] S. N. Behrman (b. 1893), American writer and playwright. Among his successes: *The Second Muse* (1927), *End of Summer* (1936), *No Time for Comedy* (1939), *The Cold Wind and the Warm* (1958).

[7] *Two-Faced Woman* (1941).

[8] Secretary of the Screen Writers' Guild.

is open to writers of all nationalities who seek employment in the motion picture industry. We welcome new talent which serves to enrich the industry and would consider it highly improper if the Guild should discourage the employment of any of its members for other than lawful or contractual reasons."

Let me sum up: By supporting the re-engagement of the refugee writers, you would be doing a priceless service to men who have played an honorable part in the cultural life of our times and who presumably will do so again, if they are helped through this critical period. I would regard such a decision as a most praiseworthy act of kindness, as well as one that showed excellent sense. At the least it certainly would do the company no harm.

Forgive me for speaking so freely, but I thought it my duty to urge the cause of these endangered colleagues, and to commend them to your well-known goodness of heart.

P.S. Should you wish to discuss the matter further, I should be glad to call on you together with Mrs. Dieterle, who is very warmly concerned about it.

TO AGNES E. MEYER

Pacific Palisades
October 3, 1941

Dear friend:

I have just concluded the curious chapter of Joseph's marriage to Asnath, the daughter of the sun priest, and can best use the remainder of this hot desert morning to thank you for your good letter of September 26th. I am sorry that I haven't yet been able to send you the copy of the big dialogue with Pharaoh. My secretary is somewhat slow, and moreover really has a great deal to do in the way of dictated letters, *messages, statements,* and such trifles. It may be that I shall have to bring you the manuscript myself when I come to New York—that will be on November 8th or 9th, and I wish the time were already here. But before that comes the Calvary of the *lecture tour,* with its stops in Iowa, Alabama, South Carolina, and God knows where else. But what can I do? It is *business,* it brings a few thousand dollars into the house, and the father of a family must bestir himself. On the 17th we will set out. But I'll take Joseph with me. We want to give ourselves eight to ten days in New York and Princeton, and even on the train I have quite often done a bit of scribbling with pencil in the mornings.

Your letter was extremely interesting, especially the funny and embarrassing recollections of Rilke and Rodin. *"Un jeune Allemand qui écrit sur moi"*—that's how these great men are. Wagner's relationship to the young Nietzsche also had this quality. Do you think that a man who in *The Beloved Returns* has mustered all the irony at his command to portray this "grand" ingratitude in Goethe would have any inclination to imitate it? On this score one must raise oneself above these great men and have respect for the admiration that one arouses, even if one is too modest to share it.

The Rilke females must surely have been dreadful, and I am not excepting the princesses and countesses with whom the Austrian snob corresponded. Your opinion of him is harsh, but probably not too harsh, although there is no denying that he attained extraordinary heights in his poetry. I would not have said what you did about him, but I do not contradict it either. His poetic style was new, attractive, and evidently extremely seductive to those who sought the same ends. But his aestheticism, his aristocratic airs, his sanctimonious preciosity were always an embarrassment to me and made me feel that his prose was quite unbearable. Rilke or George—the choice is difficult. In purely cultural terms both are important phenomena, but the two of them certainly were arch-aesthetes—the one in a feminine, the other in homo-masculine-sadistic-dictatorial fashion. I suppose in the end he was the more dangerous, although he too ultimately refused the presidency of the Nazi Academy and had himself buried in Switzerland.

At the moment the children from San Francisco are with us for a visit, with little Fridolin, and the house is somewhat *overcrowded*. But I am utterly gone on the little boy, pretty as a picture, always sweet-natured, radiant with health. He will certainly have a good journey upon this earth. It's good to carry hopes and blessings for this young life in one's old heart.

See you soon!

Yours,
T. M.

1941

TO AGNES E. MEYER

Pacific Palisades
October 7, 1941

Dear friend:

The letter in which I commented on your Rilke recollections must
surely have reached you by now. I am afraid we shall each cut a poor
figure with posterity on the score of our critical confessions. For after all,
the man of the *Duino Elegies* was unquestionably a kind of lyric genius.
And both in the artistic and, I think, in the spiritual and religious sense
(I am repeating what I have heard rather than speaking from my own
deep understanding of his sensibility), he has had a great influence upon
a certain stratum of young people. Ah well, you and I don't have to be as
wise as posterity; they must pardon us, if as Rilke's contemporaries we
are somewhat irked by the weaknesses of—not his person, but his
personality. I mean the element of snobbery and preciosity in it, which
has always made me highly uncomfortable and formed a barrier to any
real affection. Incidentally, you probably don't know that Rilke wrote one
of the first and best reviews of *Buddenbrooks*. I forgot to mention that
last time. In those days he often wrote book reviews for a—if I am not
mistaken—Bremen newspaper, and he did a long study of my novel in
which he laid particular weight on the various deaths in the story—
there you see his religious strain, his feeling for "Cross, Death, and
Tomb,"[1] which he and I shared at the time. But in my case I imagine it
was all probably both more manly and more musical, although I am not
Tom the Rhymer. . . .

Since I began this, dear friend, your new letter (the "irrational" one)
arrived, and I was dismayed, in fact shaken, by these psychologically
very curious accesses of concern for my personal welfare which have
disturbingly intruded upon your intellectual involvement with my life
and work. I may say that my conscience is clear, for you know I have
never said a word to throw open the gates to these gloomy intruders. Not
even in response to your recital and your question do I wish to concede
any reality to these phantoms. *To begin with*, you call my life "hard,"
but I can't feel it so. In principle I feel it, with gratitude, to be a happy,

---

[1] A quotation from Nietzsche which Mann frequently cited. "I like in Wagner
what I like in Schopenhauer," Nietzsche wrote, "the moral fervor, the Faustian flavor,
the Cross, Death, and the Tomb."

blessed life. I say "in principle"; for the fact that in such a life all sorts of anguish, darkness, and perils quite naturally occur is not what really counts. What does count is that its foundation is serene, is so to speak sunny—and after all, a person's life is ultimately determined by the foundation. I often admire quite objectively, purely as a phenomenon, the way in which a gifted individual can win through and contrive to make the best of even the most adverse outer circumstances. In the beginning of the new Joseph volume there is a passage: "In any case the two, his ego and the world, in his view belonged together, they were in a way one, so that the world was not simply the world, by and in itself, but quite definitely his world and by virtue of the fact susceptible of being molded into a good and friendly one. Circumstances were powerful; but what Joseph believed in was their plasticity: he felt sure of the preponderant influence of the individual destiny upon the general force of circumstances. When like Gilgamesh he called himself a glad-sorry man, it was in the sense that he knew the happy side of his nature was capable of much suffering, but on the other hand did not believe in suffering so bad and so black that it would prove too dense for his own light, or the light of God in him, to penetrate."

This is a glimpse into the mind of a Sunday child, and there is some element of subjective experience at play there, as the dear reader no doubt realizes. Truly, when I consider the amount of blood and tears, misery and doom, that prevails on earth today, I have every reason to be grateful to my destiny; it has always tried to turn things well and favorably and aptly for me. Of course you must understand this in a relative sense; it's not that my life has been blissful. Of course there has been much loss and turmoil and difficult learning of new ways for me as well. But my work has advanced undisturbed; new opportunities have come my way to be of service to the human cause. I have continued to receive trust and to be shown honor, and my outward way of life has not been perceptibly demeaned. My position in this country is such that I ought to have only one anxiety: not to throw it away by lack of caution. Is it a small thing that in an alien land (but one that at bottom is no more alien than the world has always been for me) I should have found a friend and champion like yourself, who sees as much in my work as you see in it? I scarcely had that in Germany.

A hard life? I am an artist. That means a man who wishes to entertain himself—and this isn't a matter to pull a solemn face about. To be sure—and this is again a quotation from Joseph—what counts is how high one carries the entertainment: the higher it goes, the more absorbing the story becomes. In art one is dealing with the Absolute, which is not child's play. But then again, it is after all a form of child's play, and I shall never forget Goethe's impatient dictum: "In the making of art there can be no question of suffering." But later he said retrospectively: "It was eternally rolling a stone that forever had to be raised anew." Well observed. But let anyone take the accursed boulder away from us, and we would see how we missed it. No, in the making of art there can be no question of suffering. Anyone who has chosen so essentially amusing a job has no right to play the martyr in the presence of serious people.

Politics? The torment and shamefulness of world history? Yes, certainly, it lies like a ton of bricks on my heart. But then again it is interesting and suspenseful, and if having been right makes a man happy, then I may be very happy, for I have been completely right about where "National Socialism" would lead; my fellow countrymen and the world of appeasers have to admit that I was right, and as far as one can judge, I shall also be right about the outcome. I am absolutely convinced that Hitler's game is up and that he will be destroyed—no matter how many detours and how much unnecessary effort is required to complete the work. [. . .]

You ask about my health. It is the old familiar and rather vexatious story. I never really enjoyed strapping good health, but also scarcely ever have a serious illness; the organism is in good order, and basically I think that my constitution, by its whole tempo and character, tends to patience, endurance, a long pull; to carrying things to their end—not to say to perfection. It is this instinct that explains the urge toward a new establishment, toward building the house—a rather reckless and self-willed prank at my age, under today's conditions and given my present circumstances. But the decision is clearly founded on my habits, needs, demands —on the natural style of my life. If I may make the confession, I have often asked myself why a world so ready to pay tributes that cost nothing (I am thinking of the seven doctoral capes that have been draped around my shoulders in this country) does not concern itself in the least about such external matters, which after all are closely related to productivity. Actually, other people do sometimes concern themselves with these matters. Take the case of my friend Hermann Hesse, for whom a rich Swiss Maecenas of the Bodmer[2] family has built a handsome house in Montagnola in the Ticino. I have often visited him there. The dear man didn't even want to have it deeded to him, not caring to be involved with

[2] Hans C. Bodmer (1891–1956), physician, philanthropist, noted collector of Beethoveniana.

the obligations of ownership; the house belongs to his patron, and Hesse and his wife merely have lifelong use of it. —Why has a city or a university in this country never hit on the idea of proposing something similar, if only out of "ambition" to be able to say: "*We have him, he is ours*"? Is it because my books in the past made a great deal of money and I received the Nobel Prize? (This, of course, the Nazis swallowed up, along with all the rest, except for small sums that happened to be in Switzerland and to which I owe my freedom.) It must be due to the notion that "a person like that" does not need to be helped—or else it is pure thoughtlessness. This same thoughtlessness constantly takes my idealism for granted and makes honorary demands on me without honoraria because "a person like that," after all, mustn't think about money. I grant that it would be better and more dignified if he didn't have to think about it.

So now I am building the house myself—and of course not altogether frivolously. We can afford it; otherwise the Federal Loan wouldn't have approved the project—although perhaps it took more account of my position in general than of my circumstances at the moment. If so, that was right, for the difference should not be disregarded. Naturally my means have been severely reduced by the loss of the German and the European markets. My income in this country too has shrunk *since* the purchase of the property, for *The Beloved Returns* was not much more than a *succès d'éstime*, and *The Transposed Heads*, after all a slight thing, has had only a casual reception. There is no question of worry and distress, but certainly of inconvenience, constriction, having to be careful, so that in furnishing the house we must eye every chair closely—not for whether it pleases, but for whether it will fall within the budget. And yet all this does not quite correspond with the reality—I mean, the reality of my existence as a whole in contrast to momentary circumstances. I give the war another two, three, even four years—longer than that the *mess* can scarcely go on. With the victory of the cause of freedom, the position of those who called the inferno by its right name from the start and did what they could to combat it is bound to improve. [. . .] But let's leave war and victory aside. Let's only finish the Joseph, on which I am diligently working. There are plans for complete German and English editions; completion presumably will give a nice push to the whole work, and it is fairly certain that if public conditions are not too unsettled by then, a motion picture extravaganza will be made of the book—at least, people in the business, such as Dieterle, tell me it definitely will. That would help considerably to float my ship again, if one may speak this way of a ship which at the moment has not really run aground.

In short, "I" am an enterprise that can be considered a good credit risk and that shouldn't be treated with nerve-racking tact. If I speak this way (somewhat to my own amazement), ascribe it to the "Hermetic" commercial spirit that Joseph now personifies. Sometimes I *think* that way, and your letter inspired by feminine intuition has loosened the checks on my tongue—which it was meant to do, wasn't it?

I shall not reread this letter; I trust it has come out right. Something would have had to go wrong for it to have turned out either whimpering or lacking in frankness. And it also, I think, can be so read as to be completely reassuring.

Have you heard that all private building is going to be stopped? We really came in just under the wire! As it is, the house is making slow progress; the steel window and door casings were very long in arriving, and sometimes labor is short too. At best we shall be able to move in by the middle of December, but the architect advises us not to count on that. Oh well, patience is my strong point. Only it is vexing that all this time we have to pay double rent, so to speak.

Eugene has sent us a cheerful cable from Lisbon, where he has seen Erika. I wouldn't be surprised if they had both taken the Clipper flight today.

You asked about the probable date of my finishing Joseph. I am counting on May or June. In any case, given good health, it ought to be done in the course of the summer.

Yours,
T. M.

TO AGNES E. MEYER

Hotel Windermere
Chicago
November 3, 1941

Dear friend:

From this very first stop after Washington I want to tell you with what warm gratitude I look back on our visit with you and how happy I feel about the idea you disclosed. Your "distinguished"[1] ingenuity fills me with admiration. No finer solution was imaginable, and I am artist enough to delight almost more in the form you contrived to give it than in its

---

[1] A favorite word of Tony Buddenbrook.

"content."[2] Truly, this new symbolic connection with America and with Washington has about it something deeply gratifying to me, quite aside from the material reassurance which it brings. Please do tell MacLeish also what pleasure it has given me.[3] I look forward to the reading in the Library of Congress after the Joseph is finished as the celebration of a lifetime. I will be anticipating it throughout the work that lies before me.

I have a "symposium" here tonight with Norman Angell[4] and Borgese. Tomorrow we are going to Iowa, and after that we have one more brief stop in Indianapolis (Bloomingdale). On the 7th we will arrive in New York, Hotel Bedford.

Keep well. You have my esteem and gratitude.

Yours,
T. M.

TO AGNES E. MEYER

Pacific Palisades
December 16, 1941

Dear Mrs. Agnes:

I don't know whether you have seen the last issue of the *New Yorker*[1] with that embarrassing scribble about me and the people around me. If so, I assume that it left you unmoved. For my part, I cannot and will not conceal my indignation, although I too should be inured to the vexations of the literary life. What an insignificant piece of hackwork! It is truly a feat to be at once so cheeky and so boring. The combination is like the cross between indiscretion and false information which also distinguishes this piece of malice parading as biography. Every other fact is a falsehood. How brilliant, for example, that bit about Caroline Newton's having introduced me to the work of Freud—the poor dear lady. Also that under my aegis she intended to write a psychoanalytic elucidation "of him and his works." And linking three persons such light-years apart as you, Caroline Newton, and our good Lowe-Porter into a mutually jealous clique of bluestockings is really pretty strong—or rather no, not strong at all, but simply silly. Caricature is a good thing—in fact, I rather like the

---

[2] An untranslatable pun; the German word *Gehalt* means both "content" and "salary."

[3] Archibald MacLeish (b. 1892), poet, playwright, Librarian of Congress 1939–45.

[4] Sir Norman Angell (b. 1874), English economist and pacifist. His book *The Great Illusion* (1933) was translated into fifteen languages.

[1] Janet Flanner: "Goethe in Hollywood: Profile of Thomas Mann," *The New Yorker* (December 13 and 20, 1941).

accompanying drawing—although caricature should be a comic distortion of reality, not sheer nonsense. "All these women are useful to him." What a lovely set of principles that language reveals. Though how "useful" serious minds can be to one another is something this intellectual female has no notion of.

Very nice, too, that she calls your book reviews "lengthy." Her own gossip fills twenty columns, and there is to be as much again next week. I can only hope that in the next installment I alone and not my friends will have the pleasure of being the butt of her wit.

When I came into the living room with the issue, I commented that I had never laid eyes upon the author. My wife corrected me: I had forgotten that she once lunched with us in Princeton. At any rate, on that occasion, I was indeed as monstrously polite, stiff, and buttoned-up as she describes me. The only thing I regret about that is the politeness.

Forgive me for lingering so long in days like these over an annoying article in a humor magazine. Pearl Harbor hit me hard. The loss of the ships can be borne. But so many precious young lives! How could the base have been caught so much off guard at this juncture? And things will be harder still. I don't imagine that the Far Eastern and Pacific theaters of war will provide much cause for rejoicing for months and perhaps for years. For this very reason I was happy that the President promptly put the Japanese war within the universal frame and left no doubt that the chief enemy and archfoe is in Berlin. That is what must be defeated; everything else will follow in due course. And to this end a good beginning has been made in Russia. The whole German front pushed back, from Petersburg to the Black Sea! It seems incredible. It's more than the Marne. I wonder whether the Germans can be made to start a new advance in the spring?

Something disturbs me—not knowing whether the manuscript has reached you safely from New York. I made a mistake when I asked you to pass it on to Mrs. Lowe after you had read it. Please send it back to me instead—no hurry. I forgot that part of it is not yet revised. I must take care of that and transfer the corrections to the copies before these parts go off to be translated.

Yours,
T. M.

TO AGNES E. MEYER

Dear friend:

I am greatly reassured by your reasonable attitude toward that nasty prank on the part of the *New Yorker* woman. In fact it amuses me that you actually feel yourself shielded and protected by your two fellow sufferers. Naturally there is something in us which winces painfully at such wrongheaded exposure; but we would be foolish to take it seriously, not realizing how little others take it that way and how quickly they pass over it after having enjoyed a moment of malice. I have not yet seen the second installment of the drivel, but trust that my friends will no longer figure in it, so that I can do my wincing alone. Probably the political indiscretions will be served up now—I hear she quotes from my essay on Frederick the Great dating back to 1914. Won't *that* be a gracious taunt! Priceless, priceless.

But I must come to the defense of America when you say this country is more malicious and dangerous to helpless me than Europe ever was. You have no idea with what spite and nasty glee a reputation could be smeared in Germany. I find people here good-natured to the point of generosity in comparison with Europeans, and feel pleasantly sheltered in their midst. This irritating episode cannot change that feeling.

No, it does not look very Christmasy in the world; the star toward which, when all is said and done, humanity still goes on pilgrimage, is shrouded in a mist of blood. It is kind that you think of bringing pleasure to people in this clouded and profoundly troubled festival. I give you my warmest thanks for whatever may come.

America still has to learn the nature of this war. The disaster of Pearl Harbor shows how little notion she has of its evil radicalism, its total ruthlessness. It seems that for the present we shall be relatively impotent in the face of whatever the Japs undertake. I imagine still more grief is to come from that quarter. In compensation we can derive amusement from Adolf with his inner voices and his *"raison d'être."* (As conqueror of Gaul he is beginning to toss French phrases around, not always correctly.) His order of the day when he dismissed the generals and took command on his own was priceless. Nothing quite so romantic has been seen since the Maid of Orleans. Ah, that vicious toad—when will somebody trample on its head?

We were talking about God and religion today, and I said that with the best will in the world I can't tell whether or not I believe. Nevertheless, I sometimes suspect myself of believing; for without a faith I don't suppose one could hate *"l'infâme"* as much as I do.

I'm afraid that my questions may have prompted you to a second comment on the dialogue about God. Of course what you said encouraged me, but I remain somewhat disappointed by the chapter. It should have been the best in the volume, yet now I must be glad if something else turns out better. I am now working on the Tamar episode, a short novel in itself, and a curious subject.

And now to the main purpose of this letter: all good wishes and season's greetings to you and Eugene. He has suddenly taken it into his head to send me a box of cigars, whose looks proclaim their choiceness. I mean to thank him in English, but today there is no longer time.

> Yours,
> T. M.

TO ERICH VON KAHLER

Pacific Palisades
December 31, 1941

Dear friend Kahler:

For the New Year I want to wish you and Fine and your dear mother good fortune and health; not to do so would be a cold, unpleasant thing, and I am sure you too are wishing us the best tonight, even if you don't manage to set it down on paper. We are both *desperately busy* and therefore bad correspondents. For Christmas we made it a bit easier for ourselves by sending greetings by telegram. We told you, most sincerely, that we missed you, and have heard much the same from you. Where did you spend Christmas Eve—in New York or Princeton? It is truly a constant source of surprise, the places where we spend our days. On the 24th I went walking without an overcoat on my favorite promenade above the ocean, sat a long while on a bench in the sun—it is bearable at this season—and looked dreamily out at the blue theater of war.

I have been presented with an electric clock which I admire every morning, wondering how it contrives overnight to straighten out its calendar. How does the beast know that from the 29th to the 30th it has to change both figures, but from the 30th to the 31st only the second, whereas from the 31st to the 1st the first has to vanish? It comprehends what is necessary, and I can't understand how. But at the end of February we will certainly have to come to its aid.

Let me not forget your cake, which I think is the richest I have ever encountered in this category. It can scarcely still be called a cake, and confirms the saying that everything supreme of its kind goes beyond its kind.

Nothing came of our hopes to spend Christmas in Seven Palms House. But it's almost done; we shall be able to move in by the second half of January, and I shall, Heil Hitler, have the finest study I have ever worked in. Everything, in fact merely the floor coverings, runs into unnerving sums of money, and if I had not recently become Consultant in Germanic Literature[1] to the Library of Congress, with a small annual salary, I wouldn't know how we were going to manage. Had you heard about that yet? But I have the appointment and will occasionally have to deliver a lecture there.

We must only hope that this strip of coast will not be evacuated some day, with Seven Palms House becoming the quarters of some American colonel or perhaps later the Mikado! Americans are having bitter experiences. [. . .] But there is almost nothing that in the proper circumstances cannot be set right. For the coming year we can rationally only wish and hope that things won't go so badly that they can't sometime go better and finally go well again.

Have you read former Ambassador Davies's[2] *Mission to Moscow*? An excellent book, essentially composed only of his reports to Washington and extracts from a diary. But what clarity and foresight! No other diplomat has sent such reports home about Russia. America, it seems, has long been the only country the Russians trusted. Incidentally, in 1939 Roosevelt sent word to Stalin that if he really concluded a pact with Hitler, as certainly as day follows night H. would attack Russia after crushing France.

Over the holidays our little house was stuffed full. In addition to

---

[1] The appointment came on December 1, 1941. In his letter to Mann, Archibald MacLeish, the Librarian of Congress, wrote: "Certain friends of the Library of Congress have . . . made it possible for me to realize a hope which I have long entertained. That is, that the Library might count you among the scholars whom it numbers on its consultative staff. I am therefore now enabled to ask you whether you will do the Library the honor of becoming its Consultant in German Literature. Your duties in this office would not be arduous, but might be most rewarding, both to yourself, to the Library of Congress, to Germanic studies in the United States, and—who knows?—in its effects upon a future Germany, a future German literature, and German-American relations the future of which none of us can now foresee." From 1941 to 1944 Mann received $4,800 annually. He then waived the honorarium, but continued to hold the post until his death.

[2] Joseph E. Davies (1876–1958), diplomat. American ambassador to Moscow 1936–8. His book *Mission to Moscow* (1941) lent significant impetus to the American-Russian alliance during the war. In 1943 Davies served as President Roosevelt's special envoy, and in 1945 as envoy for the Potsdam Conference.

Golo, Erika was here, animating as ever, and my brother-in-law from Berkeley.[3] Then our little grandson, whom we took along with us from San Francisco for a few weeks to relieve his mother—a charming child, highly nervous, so it seems to me, but as such things go, on this very account particularly witty and winning.

Yesterday I made my German phonograph record[4] again, and was particularly insulting to Schicklgruber.[5] It does the heart good.

I am making steady progress on Joseph. [. . .] I have come to the story of Tamar, a big insert, practically a novella in itself. Do you recall? A remarkable female who shrank from nothing that would enable her to thrust her way into the sacred story. I cannot read enough of *Faust* and everything else that has been done along those lines, for after all I have a kind of universal poem under my hands, although only a humorous and bizarre one. I have never thought myself great, but I love to play with greatness and to live on a certain footing of familiarity with it.

Yours,
T. M.

[3] Peter Pringsheim, the physicist.
[4] These were recordings of radio addresses to Germany, subsequently published as *Listen, Germany!* (New York: Alfred A. Knopf; 1943).
[5] Adolf Hitler.

1942

———————— • ————————

TO CAROLINE NEWTON

Pacific Palisades
January 10, 1942

Dear Miss Caroline:

Many thanks for your friendly lines. Here on the coast, after a few brief days of panic and confusion, life has resumed its almost normal course. I needn't tell you that events constantly preoccupy and depress me—certainly they are not exactly cheerful.

I have had a rather strange experience with the *New Yorker* gossip. At first it vexed me very much, and I was indignant at the woman's treachery; but then I kept hearing from more and more Americans that they thought the article amusing and excellent, and that it really amounted to nothing but a tribute, by its very size alone. I find this point of view hard to understand, but apparently the thing looks entirely different to American eyes, and so I have calmed down about it. But still it pleased me that one of the victims, Mr. Angell of Pomona College, wrote a stern letter to the editors and sent a copy to Flanner herself.

Auden was here for lunch with us, while Erika was home. He was boyish and nice as always, and to my mind it is to his credit that he could play with the baby so well.

Thanks for the kind inquiry about Joseph. It's making good progress, although there are constant interruptions. Thus in the next few days I have to go to San Francisco for a Town Hall lecture, which also requires preparation. I suppose, poor *enemy alien* that I am, I shall have to obtain a permit to travel. I have written a letter to Francis Biddle,[1] since the role of *enemy alien* strikes me as particularly ludicrous, asking whether he

---

[1] Francis Biddle (b. 1886), American lawyer and writer; Attorney General of the United States from 1941 to 1945. Author, *Llanfear Pattern* (1927), *Mr. Justice Holmes* (1942), *Democratic Thinking and the War* (1944).

cannot make out some kind of safe-conduct for me. But no answer has been forthcoming from the honorable gentleman.

With good wishes for complete restoration of your health and capacity to work,

TO AGNES E. MEYER

Pacific Palisades
January 22, 1942

Dear Mrs. Agnes:

This time I am behindhand—you know that I was away for four days for a lecture with all the trimmings in San Francisco, and the pace was such that it was impossible even to think of writing. These Americans certainly know how to bleed you dry, not to say grind you down; they themselves have no nerves at all, and it never occurs to them that someone else might tire. One party lasted literally from six to one o'clock: dinner, followed by a mass reception, showing of a movie (very interesting—Singapore, Bali, Malaya—but I was already half dead). The lecture itself was a matinee in the theater, more than sold out, the entire platform occupied, so that I couldn't be present during the introduction; there was simply no room for me. It was a Town Hall affair; as usual I had to talk for eighty minutes, which is no trifle, and afterwards there were *questions*, which I consider a real vice of your great nation. A lunch in the hotel followed, and over the coffee the questions gaily continued. I always extricate myself in the most amusing way by not answering the question at all, but arbitrarily talking around it and saying whatever I *can* say. But the people are heartily content with that, at least they seem so, which again is extremely good-natured and *generous, God bless them.* That wish comes from my heart.

My neighbor at table was the President of Mills College, a splendid lady with a large, humorous face plus pince-nez, who most serenely kept her counsel about Golo. "*We enjoyed his visit very, very much, and so did he, we hope.*" That was all. It would have been utterly tactless to insist. The poor boy's prospects have probably shrunk to nothing since the war. No wonder; the colleges are under attack because of the foreigners they already have; how could they take on new ones?

While there we handed our infant grandson over to his parents— whom at first he didn't even recognize. We miss him intensely. There never was a more charming baby. He is my last love. May he become a good-natured, generous, humorous, and indefatigable citizen of this country.

It was very kind of you to have talked with Biddle once more. This way I at least have an indirect message from him. I understand, and have long been annoyed with myself for having even brought up my individual case. The small restrictions I am subjected to are not worth discussing right now. By nature I find firearms and explosives distasteful; our short-wave radio doesn't work anyhow; and for my *lectures*, which to be sure are distinctly *defense work*, I don't mind requesting travel permission from case to case. The question is only whether that will be the sum total of it. Already 400 California *publishers* have come forth with the lovely proposal that all *enemy aliens* be evacuated from the coastal states and banished to the interior of the country. Any small act of sabotage may suffice to bring about that sort of measure, and I wonder whether no exceptions will be permitted then and whether we will have to leave our new house and live in a hotel in Kansas City. After all, we do sometimes remember that we have been at war with Hitler longer than America. . . .

The house is rapidly being finished; in ten days or so we shall be able to move in, and we hope the crates from Princeton arrive in time. But even without them we can manage for the present. In any case, we have to arm ourselves with patience until everything is settled, and I can go on with Joseph even at my temporary desk with the bookshelves still empty. The Tamar story, I think, has turned out very well. It is a good portrait. Now the lean years are beginning in Canaan and Egypt simultaneously. But there is corn in Egypt.

Warmly,

Yours,
T. M.

TO MOLLY SHENSTONE

[*Original in English*]

Pacific Palisades
January 29, 1942

Dear Mrs. Molly:

You kindly dispensed me with answering your charming letter of January 21 and with thanking you for the beautiful gift which accompanied it. But I cannot make use of this permission and must tell you how happy I was to hear directly and personally from you and to receive that excellent and most vivid picture of our common hero.[1]

How well I remember the hours, after the French catastrophe, when we were sitting together in our Princeton home behind a helpful little drink and tried to give some confidence to each other! I am afraid we shall have more than one reason and opportunity to do so during the coming months and years. But each time, I am sure, we shall be *right*. [. . .]

Our moving into the new house is postponed from week to week and from day to day, but we are patient people. It is a rather paradoxical phenomenon that age gives patience—when time already becomes short, while youth with endless time before itself is always impatient.

Our warmest greetings to Allen!

Your friend,

TO ALBERT EINSTEIN

1550 San Remo Drive
Pacific Palisades, California
February 9, 1942

Dear Professor Einstein:

With the feeling that something must be done about the "enemy alien" matter, not for our sake but for the country's and its better impulses, some friends here and I have today drafted the enclosed telegram to the President, and would be much obliged if you would sign it together with Borgese, Bruno Frank, Count Sforza, Toscanini, Bruno Walter, and myself. Please cable me.

TO FRANKLIN D. ROOSEVELT

[Telegram in English]

Mr. President:

We beg to draw your attention to a large group of natives of Germany and Italy who by present regulations are, erroneously, characterized and treated as "Aliens of Enemy Nationality."

We are referring to such persons who have fled their country and sought refuge in the United States because of totalitarian persecution, and who, for that very reason, have been deprived of their former citizenship.

Their situation is such as has never existed under any previous

---

[1] Winston Churchill. Mrs. Shenstone had sent the famous photograph by Karsh.

circumstances, and it cannot be deemed just to comprise them under the discrediting denomination of "Aliens of Enemy Nationality."

Many of those people, politicians, scientists, artists, writers, have been among the earliest and most farsighted adversaries of the governments against whom the United States are now at war. Many of them have sacrificed their situation and their properties and have risked their lives by fighting and warning against those forces of evil which at that time were minimized and compromised with by most of the governments of the world.

It is true that the "Application for a Certificate of Identification" provides such persons with an opportunity to make additional statements as for their political status. But as, so far, no official announcement to the contrary has been made, these victims of Nazi and Fascist oppression, these staunch and consistent defenders of democracy, would be subject to all the present and future restrictions meant for and directed against possible Fifth Columnists.

We, therefore, respectfully apply to you, Mr. President, who for all of us represent the spirit of all that is loyal, honest, and decent in a world of falsehood and chaos, to utter or to sanction a word of authoritative discrimination, to the effect that a clear and practical line should be drawn between the potential enemies of American democracy on the one hand, and the victims and sworn foes of totalitarian evil on the other.

TO AGNES E. MEYER

Pacific Palisades
[postmarked February 18, 1942]

Dear Mrs. Agnes:

I am hastily writing to you again, this time from my own study, because of your letter concerning the problem of visiting.

It does seem to me, dear friend, that you do an injustice to your first visit on this coast, and it saddens me that you have so inadequate a memory of it—I mean, remember it as having been so inadequate. We devoted two whole mornings to one another, were undisturbed and alone for hours both days, talked, had a reading and a walk on the beach, and then I believe you once gave us the pleasure of coming to lunch with me *en famille*, in the sphere in which my life is lived. But the idea that you saw me only *en famille* is an illusion of memory, as is the breathless haste. I must say I remember all that more pleasantly than you do and think of it as being much more satisfying, and since nothing in this world is perfect, I would be delighted simply if it could be repeated just as it was. I grant, though, that it is quite a responsibility to ask you to come, fearing as I would that you would again go away with the sense that it was a waste of time. I don't want that and don't really know what I should do to keep it from happening. It's also a heavy responsibility to persuade you because I do not overestimate the charm and importance of my company, or even the comfortableness of it, and would understand only too well if you should not wish to see our good relationship *par distance* disturbed by my unpredictability as a human being. I am often tired and know that I can be deadly boring. But on the other hand, I also know—at least you have told me—that you have gathered strength and stimulation for your work from our personal exchange. And you know me well enough to realize that I am childishly eager to show you the new house, my new study—the final one I am destined for.

In short, I can only say I would be very glad—for one thing, because this meeting would be proof to me that we don't see each other less often than we used to because of my westward move. But if you have so little time that Florence must go to San Francisco to meet you, then how can I presume to ask you to come all the way here on my account alone? Such a meeting would in all likelihood turn out to be really breathless, and it would be, I repeat, too much responsibility for me to take. Why don't you let Florence stay here and come to visit her for a few days? That's how I would really like to have it. Seeing you again is a certain pleasure, seeing me again an uncertain one. Therefore I'd like you to come, of course, but not solely for my sake.

Happily, we still have time before March 25th to consider the question calmly. It would really be somewhat unnatural for you to be on this coast without seeing us. On the other hand, the distance from San Francisco to Pacific Palisades is not such a stone's throw as to justify coming for one hasty day. I must recognize that. For this very reason I rather wish that after settling your affairs you would let Eugene return alone and take a few days for a visit with Florence. Perhaps you can decide only at the last minute whether that is possible.

I must write a fifteen-minute broadcast for the Coordinator of Information.[1] Urgent *defense work.* . . .

The essay on the *Ring* is considerably older than the remarks in *Common Sense*.[2] It is a lecture delivered at the University of Zurich in

[1] Robert Sherwood.
[2] "In Defense of Wagner. A Letter on the German Culture that Produced Both Wagner and Hitler," *Common Sense*, Vol. 9 (January 1940).

1937. You see, my way of talking about Wagner has nothing to do with chronology and development. It is and remains "ambivalent," and I am capable of writing about him one way today, another tomorrow.

The lecture in *Mass und Wert* appeared in German, but I'm afraid I no longer have the issue. Perhaps Lowe-Porter has it; she is lagging quite far behind on the translation of the essay volume because she is simultaneously working on Joseph IV[3]—insofar as she is capable of work, for her health is bad and I am afraid I shall not have her much longer. Could it be that the issue is in your possession?

Lessing and Dürer will certainly go into the volume.[4] Then Goethe, Schopenhauer, Tolstoy, Platen, Storm, Freud—in short, everything that still seems to me presentable, including a good many political things such as the Bonn Letter, the *Atlantic Monthly* essay,[5] "Europe, Beware," and others—for example, the Berlin "Appeal to Reason"[6] of 1930. "Europe, Beware" emerged from a message to the *Comité permanent des lettres et des arts* of the League of Nations, in connection with a discussion on *"La formation de l'homme moderne."* The poor Frenchmen said at the time: *"Mais, cher ami, c'est très exagéré!"* Now an American journal of education, marveling at my prescience, has translated the message from French to English.

Yesterday I received a small book about Joyce (by Harry Levin;[7] New Directions books) in which there is a good deal about me by way of comparison. You might find it stimulating.

It was brave and patriotic of the *Post* to print a serious criticism of the conduct of the war. I hope the President had more to say in reply to it than that the capital is a "vicious rumor factory." But I incline to believe him when he says that something like a Cliveden set[8] exists and is malevolently active. There are secret victory celebrations over our defeats.

Cordially yours,

T. M.

---

[3] *Joseph the Provider*, the fourth volume of *Joseph and His Brothers*.

[4] As it turned out, this essay volume was not published in the planned form. Instead, a collection of political essays, *Order of the Day*, was brought out in 1942. The literary essays were published by Knopf in 1947 in *Essays of Three Decades*.

[5] "How to Win the Peace," *Atlantic Monthly* (February 1942).

[6] "Appell an die Vernunft," an address delivered in Berlin after the electoral victory of the Nazis.

[7] Harry Levin (b. 1912), professor of literature at Harvard. The book in question was *James Joyce*. Among his other works: *Toward Stendhal* (1945), *Toward Balzac* (1947), *Symbolism and Fiction* (1956), *The Question of Hamlet* (1959).

[8] Cliveden, the country home of the Astors, was considered the headquarters of a loosely associated group of persons influential in English life who were purported to be sympathetic to Hitlerism, or at any rate ready to appease Hitler.

P.S. Archie[9] has sent a check for two months, as I must mention with appreciation. Since he hit on the brilliant idea of my appointment, "economic problems" no longer exist for me. We can talk of something else, without prejudice to the grateful thoughts I privately devote to the matter.

TO LUDWIG MARCUSE[1]

Pacific Palisades
March 27, 1942

My dear Herr Marcuse:

A letter such as yours should have been answered at once—forgive me. Several times the hour I had set aside for it was snatched away.

How well I understand your agitation and your bitterness.[2] It is pure chance that I am so far not personally affected by the same decree. But since fervent protests by those of us who are unaffected have been useless, do you think it would make any impression if I were to join you? You are not familiar with the way Americans, or rather their authorities, think. If I came out and said: I cannot endure it, I want to be an *enemy alien* also, they would not burst into tears at all, but would take it casually as a resolve to lead the way by good example, and would cite it as removing all grounds for protest. The famous Muck[3] was interned throughout the last war, and Toscanini today, even when he is conducting for some "defense" cause, must obtain a travel permit the week before. That is democracy, or so it is called. Even the evacuated Japanese are told: If you are as loyal as you say, then don't complain and petition, but bow to the military necessities and willingly accept the sacrifice this country demands of you in a supreme *emergency. This is war.* You know the line of argument. Try to make these people understand that it is senseless and totally illogical cruelty (but often there is good sense and all too much logic behind it) to treat the German and Italian refugees, the expelled Jews, as hostile foreigners. To the Tolan Committee I said: "I am not thinking only of the refugees; I am thinking of the fighting spirit of this country. The terrible example of France looms before me. A nation which

---

[9] Archibald MacLeish.

[1] Ludwig Marcuse (b. 1894), writer, theater critic, professor of philosophy and German literature. Emigrated to France in 1933, to the United States in 1939.

[2] Marcuse, though expatriated, was considered officially an enemy alien, unlike Mann, who had Czech citizenship even though Czechoslovakia had by now ceased to exist.

[3] Carl Muck (1859–1940), conductor. Noted for his cool, almost pedantic interpretations and strict adherence to scores.

takes pleasure in victories over the closest enemies of its enemies does not seem to be in the best psychological state to defeat these enemies.'' I do not know whether I was understood, but I went so far as to say it. In general I went pretty far, and the only thing I deplore in your letter and in other less important ones I receive is that you turn to a person who is in any case doing his best. If I did nothing, no one would write me such letters. But since I do try to do something, I am called upon to do much more and to do it much better. I suppose that is only human.

I promise you that I shall continue to admonish and to warn to the very limits of immodesty and tactless interference in the affairs of my host country, which after all is engaged in a life-and-death struggle. The worst thing is that it seems too late to take affairs out of the hands of the military men. We urged that they should be allowed full powers to place what restrictions they wished on *enemy aliens*, but that the civil authorities should be the ones to define who is an *enemy alien*. However, in wartime the civil authorities are extremely submissive to the military, and the President, who knows very well what is going on, has the politician's instinct for the priority of questions.

I should like to believe, however, that the bark will prove to be worse than the bite. We have remonstrated most strongly against sweeping measures, pointing out that they can do a great deal of harm that could not afterwards be made good. Nevertheless, it appears that the sweeping measures will come first, and I don't know how far they will go. But relaxations, liberalizations, revisions will surely come also, if not collectively then at least individually, and if I should ever be able to be of use to you personally, it would truly give me pleasure.

TO ———

Pacific Palisades
May 4, 1942

Dear Herr ———:

I certainly should not like to interfere with the campaign, especially since the authorities in Washington seem to approve of it. But Americans do not look upon such matters the way we must. I have never thought the idea a good one, and have let it be known that to my mind an appeal to reason is a more dignified and perhaps more effective way to improve the status of the *enemy aliens* than through their making gifts. And what a gift! If it were only a matter of buying $10,000 worth of *war bonds* or contributing $10,000 to the American Red Cross. But a bomber! That is the crudest symbol anyone could find. If we consider what is going to come, what is justly and inescapably awaiting the German cities, we must certainly shrink a little from the prospect of our obituaries' reading that we ostentatiously contributed to it. Lübeck and Rostock were only samples, you know. Ghastly things will be happening—rightly so, I repeat. There will be whimpering beneath ruins, as in [Schiller's] *The Bell*. Cultural monuments may be reduced to rubble. Let the hands of a suffering and outraged world, which no longer sees any other way, do that; but not my hands. I can revile Hitler to my heart's content, and every month beg the Germans to send that "feebleminded tyrant" (which is what I called him last time) to hell along with his gang of robbers. Saying such things will not be to my detriment later on. But I simply would not like people in Germany after my death to be reading my books—or else not reading them—with the thought that I served as symbolic *chairman* for the symbolic financing of the not at all symbolic destruction "in those days." [. . .]

Perhaps my view of the whole thing is wrong, but I must act according to the way I see it.

With friendly regards,

TO AGNES E. MEYER

Pacific Palisades
May 12, 1942

Yes, my dear friend, what does "objective" mean—and what is the opposite of it? "Personal"? "Abstract"? "Passionate"? Or "chatty"? This last reminds me of old Fontane, whom I am now reading again evenings, or rather, nights before going to sleep, with indescribable pleasure, in spite of old-fashioned touches in his narrative manner. He has a virtuosity which forever enraptures me, especially his dialogue, which is mostly pure chattiness, but has incredible charm and truly supreme grace in its suppleness and stylization. Oddly enough, he did not develop this until his old age; he became more and more subtle, more and more a practitioner of the magic of intonation and of unobjectivity, or rather super-objectivity. In the end he met, in the humblest and most engaging fashion, Schiller's requirement that art "consume" the content by the form. Do you know him well? Given your North German traditions, you ought to find him to your taste. I recommend his masterpiece, *Effi Briest*, which I am now rereading. It is always a pleasure when our last reading of a favorite writer lies far enough back so that we can start reading him afresh.

Now, should what you wrote about Goethe in your last letter, which crossed mine, be placed in the category of objectivity or not? Perhaps not, because it was tied up with the personal, i.e., with me and the self-corrections of my life. In any case it was excellent, extraordinarily true and intelligent in its criticism, and I agree wholeheartedly. I have read it several times and, let me confess, also read it aloud in the family circle—for my brother particularly, who stayed with us for two weeks to recover from his wife (so we see it), and who was extremely interested by this American insight into the failings of our greatest man. He was actually a little envious that I had so clever a friend as you. Incidentally, in later years that monumental ego renounced individualistic imperialism to a large extent, at least didactically, and professed a kind of democratic communitarianism. I say "didactically" and secretly strike my own chest; for my conscience often asks me whether I too do not merely teach it, without having really laid aside the "inward," "German" concept of culture. But can I do more than profess my views, even against my own nature?

Your criticism of Goethe was not new to me, I assure you. Not to mention Börne and the "monstrously hindering effect" he ascribed to Goethe, there is also an essay on *Faust* by Turgenev which contains much of what you say. And as for me, all the unholy, disturbing, oppressive elements I assigned to Goethe in *The Beloved Returns* are connected with that. Do you remember that when He quotes the Chinese proverb, "The great man is a public misfortune," and the others laugh immoderately, Lotte secretly fears that someone may turn the tables by crying out: "The Chinese are right!"?

Ah yes, great men—at least those in the German style. And ah, the Germans altogether! I have lately been reading a good deal in Verdi's letters—artists' letters always attract me, and these particularly. In political matters also they are extraordinarily moving. His grief at the crushing of France in 1871 is prophetic. "The European war is unavoidable, and if France were saved we should be safe too."[1] He fears the worst from the Germans. "They are monstrously proud, hard, intolerant, rapacious beyond measure and scornful of everything that is not German. A people of intellect without heart—a strong people but they have no grace. . . . What now? I should have preferred to have our government follow a more generous policy and pay a debt of gratitude. A hundred

[1] Verdi's letter quoted in English.

thousand of our men might have saved France. Anyhow, I would rather have signed a peace after being defeated along with France, than to have been a passive spectator. That we are doing this will expose us to contempt some day. *We shall not escape the European war and it will engulf us. . . .*"[2]

How rightly he saw it—a simple composer of opera, but a man with the intuition of the cultured European. It was a failure of intuition that civilization did not take a common stand against that brilliant cannibal, Bismarck. And what progress we have made since then in the failure of intuition! Sometimes it is difficult to see why the civilized world should not go on being hoodwinked and overwhelmed forever.

But then again, something comes along like Churchill's most recent speech—splendid, *really heartening*. And what language, what biting humor, what a gay resplendence of the Word. Too bad that the Germans cannot compare that sort of thing with the ordure they are being offered. Nietzsche once said, in opposition to Darwin and the survival of the fittest: "The weak have more spirit." But the spirit of weakness has always made me rather uneasy, and I do not believe that it is any great help toward "survival." On the other hand, strength imbued with spirit— that is truth, that is a festival; and in fact, I don't imagine that there is any true strength without spirit.

Erika will be coming to visit you soon. She would like to arrange some South American propaganda business with the young Rockefeller,[3] and I hope she succeeds, for otherwise she will set off for England again. Even the flight to Washington makes me nervous. So many untoward things happen nowadays. But she is to bring you personal greetings, which are so much better than the written ones, however heartfelt.

Yours,
T. M.

TO AGNES E. MEYER

Pacific Palisades
July 25, 1942

Dear friend:

I can't tell you how much your letter has moved me, and how profoundly I sympathize with the dilemma from which you are suffering—or have suffered, for the end of the letter, after your confession, already implies

[2] Verdi's letter quoted in English.
[3] Nelson A. Rockefeller (b. 1908). The present governor of New York was at that time active in inter-American affairs.

enlightenment and shows that you are confident you can master your situation. If my advice can make things easier for you, I give it gladly and frankly. Let me begin by saying that the scene with your children thoroughly delighted me. What splendid young people! Can we wish the youth of America a better spirit, one with more promise for victory? It is a joy. YOUR CHILDREN ARE RIGHT. You wouldn't be their mother if you did not admit they are right, and I would have to be ashamed to the bottom of my soul before a young man like your son if I did not entirely share his opinion, fully accept his arguments. I already feel ashamed that I let him anticipate me in expressing that opinion, and if I were now to cry: "But my book! But the work in my honor, my biography, the God-seekers—after all, that is the main thing!"—it would be the height of ridiculous egotism.

Certainly the issue is not myself but you and your divided mind. I know what this book means to you, how attached you are to it, how you have grown in the writing of it. Because I do know, I have always suppressed the anxieties that I felt for your sake in connection with it. Haven't you noticed how I tried to make it easier for you, tried to persuade you not to take it too seriously? Do you remember the time you asked me whether you would do better to regard it as a majestic intellectual project or a practical, limited effort to make my work more accessible to the American public? Remember how decisively I urged the second course and assured you that you were particularly suited for it because of your dual cultural heritage? My thought at the time was to limit the work, to make it easier for you. You seemed to accept the advice; but not for long. The demands of the book grew and grew under your hand, more and more pertinent ideas poured in, its circles widened constantly, and at last you decided to do the "Tolstoy" section separately, solely in order to catch sight of land again.

Once again it worried me, and when you sent me that newspaper clipping which stated that you had withdrawn from certain social activities in order to find time for "other" tasks, I didn't feel at all happy about it, for I had to ask myself: "Can you take the responsibility for that?"

At the same time, I was innocent. But I would be making myself guilty, ridiculously guilty, if I did not unconditionally agree with your good children's remonstrances. I have never doubted that you will ultimately complete the great critical work you have undertaken. Since the task came your way, you will be able to go all the way with it. But there's no hurry. If my own work has time—I mean, lasting quality—

you can unconcernedly take time for yours. It would be no misfortune—on the contrary, it would actually be much more suitable—if the book were published only after my death; for I very much fear that you will be saying the kind of grand things about me that are better said posthumously than about a living person. In any case, militant devotion to this task is not compatible with the duties which these times, this war, impose upon you as a woman of national reputation. It must be put aside—*"for the duration."* We hear the phrase so often nowadays; in this case it is certainly appropriate. Your ideas, your strength, your energies now belong to your country, for whose sake the burden of that troublesome and damnably exacting book must be resolutely taken from you. I won't complain, I shall breathe a sigh of relief for you and for me when this decision is made. Nor does this mean that my work will have to do without your intellectual support and intercession. Why shouldn't you write a review of the small volume of political essays? Why not even publish an article about the last Joseph novel and take this occasion to speak of the work as a whole? I wouldn't even be surprised if, thanks to your fund of vitality, you managed the offshoot of the big book, the Tolstoy essay, and thus astonished your admirers by accomplishing "that too." But whatever you now do in a literary way will have to be a "that too," and the book in which you wanted to say everything cannot be fitted in. It will have to wait—which will certainly do it no harm.

What else could I rightfully reply to your moving letter? Probably I should have said it earlier.

In faithful affection,

Yours gratefully,
T. M.

TO GIUSEPPE ANTONIO BORGESE

Pacific Palisades
August 17, 1942

Dear Antonio:

May I give you a suggestion? You have no doubt read or heard of the letter of Mrs. Margaret McLean in the *New York Times* which bore the heading *Aliens held ungrateful* and the subheading *Lot here contrasted with what ours would be in enemy lands.* It was an unjust, narrow-minded, and foolish statement, which of course can only once again harm the so-called *enemy aliens.* Yesterday Bruno Frank brought me the text of his reply to the letter. It is only a few very cautious lines, which scarcely contradict her charges, but merely point out that here on the West Coast things are crucially different from New York.

My suggestion does not really involve all this, but rather the essay that Attorney General Biddle published in one of the recent issues of *Free World*.[1] This article has the tone we are familiar with from Biddle's previous official and unofficial statements. It is humane, wise, and just in a somewhat general and theoretical manner, but at the same time it is slightly veiled and commits him to little specific action.

I wonder whether you, in your threefold capacity as Axis refugee, American citizen, and member of the Board of Directors of *Free World*, ought not to take up your famous and formidable pen to answer Mr. Biddle politely and with grave emotion. The occasion seems to me favorable because here you would not be dealing with the member of the Cabinet but with Mr. Biddle simply as a writer and magazine contributor, with whom you can debate on the same plane.

Don't you think it's a good idea? I believe you could do a great deal of good by making such a statement, and *Free World* would be the richer by a brilliant contribution.

Greetings to all three of you!

TO AGNES E. MEYER

Pacific Palisades
August 20, 1942

My dear friend:

What—have my European pangs once more found their way into one of my letters? I can scarcely believe it. Shall I never learn prudence? "Culpable confidence and blind provocation"—not for nothing was I able to ascribe these fatal faults to young Joseph so credibly. They are the honorable author's own faults. Forgive me! I hate bad manners, and to judge my remarks by their reflection in your counterremarks, I simply behaved badly. But if you could hear the way I speak to the Germans, or at any rate to the Swiss and Swedes, every month on the British radio about our country here and its impending victory, you would not so readily misunderstand me and would not hold up Claudel's love and faith as an example to shame me. For I may say: In that, I am not inferior to

---

[1] An anti-Fascist monthly (1941–6) published in New York, edited by Louis Doliver. Thomas Mann was an honorary member of the editorial board. After 1945 *Free World* was published with a subtitle, "A Monthly Magazine for the United Nations." It later merged with *Asia* and *Inter-American* to become *United Nations World*.

him. His situation is harder than mine, you think. In many respects, certainly; I am aware that I am one of those who are still far too well off, considering the nature of the times. But he has the enormous advantage of being able to live in his own country, and of being not only read but even performed in his own language, whereas my work leads a translated shadow existence and not a line of it is accessible to my countrymen. Since the Nazis permit Claudel's plays to be given in Paris, he *cannot* have behaved so imprudently toward them as, say, I would have done. I think, therefore, that I can reassure you about him. I don't think that he is objectively putting himself into serious danger, and subjectively—well now, for the sake of his works a writer would venture even into the lion's den.

As though I meant to talk about Claudel! No, what I have on my mind is to ask you, please, not to believe that I harbor any improper feelings toward a country to which I owe nothing but good, and which the world will one day have to thank for tremendous things. When I consider merely that after the war America will certainly be the granary of the world and literally the "provider" of all nations!

> To all the people he giveth their meat
> To carry them over their hunger and need

is said of Joseph. That will be America's role. But as for the tragic sacrifices she is preparing to make, I have only one burning wish—that she may go on being spared them and that the war may come to an end before she has to make them in full measure. As a German I feel the most profound horror of having the death of America's best young men on my conscience, as it were. But on the other hand, if I had not done my best to prevent all this, I would be in Berlin today supervising the printing of the fourth volume of *Joseph*.

And now one more thing, dear friend. It is not good, not fair and reasonable, for you to imply that what you call my "impatience" takes on a wry, sardonic character from the fact that my sons are not yet soldiers. They can't help it. "*To join the army*" is not so easy a matter for them. Klaus has been trying for months to get in and has not yet succeeded, perhaps because he has not yet succeeded even in immigrating. Golo is in the same situation. He did *not* have the choice between teaching in the college and serving in the army, but between teaching and remaining inactive—which he could no longer endure. That was not dishonorable. When the war broke out, he immediately went from Switzerland to France in order to fight. He was thanked for that by being clapped into a concentration camp for three months. Here he simply has to wait until he is drafted—and until then he will fill to the best of his ability the modest, but difficult and demanding, teaching post he has obtained by his own competence. Any wish that the youth of America should die "so that" he can sit in safety is infinitely far from him. That is a nasty "so that" and I have never heard of any such *war aim*.

For all that, you are a wonderful woman, and your plan to fly to England to study social institutions there is splendid and exemplary. Exemplary because, you know, in America (may I say this?) there is on the whole little inclination to learn anything from the cousins across the water. The example of a personality like yours can be of the greatest benefit, quite aside from the direct results of your trip.

Poor Philip![1] It seems to be a case of a sorry squandering of fine potentialities. As for Bill,[2] I can only remind you of what I said above about my burning wish. When I say that, I am thinking above all of him, and of you.

I have plunged into the Library lecture and am writing away at it every day. It must convey my great gratitude, and I want it to be something fine and dignified. Altogether unthinkable that you may not be able to be present. Go to England in good time and come back—without an Oxford accent!—in good time.

Ever yours,
T. M.

TO KLAUS MANN

Pacific Palisades
September 2, 1942

Dear Eissi:

Let nothing break the good old custom that I write you a letter when something new of yours has been published.[1] My thanks for good, gay, and moving hours of reading come later than I had wished because our parental copy went from hand to hand and Mielein, who rightly sees it as a monument to herself (to use Medi's phrase), took over the book when I was in the middle of it, and has only recently given it back. Incidentally, I had only a short way to go.

---

[1] Philip Graham, Mrs. Meyer's son-in-law, who committed suicide in August 1963.
[2] The Meyers' only son, who was at this time completing his military training.
[1] *The Turning Point* (New York: L. B. Fischer; 1942), an autobiography written in English.

My opinion is of course biased, and emerges with a certain constraint since I am so paternally close to it all and think (feeling bitter in anticipation) that insensitive malice may make fun of the familial intimacy of these *confessions*. Probably, the world being what it is, that will crop up. There is an element of "Papa was so sick, you know,"[2] in the book, and at times I also had to think of Joseph's "culpable confidence and blind provocation." But what autobiography worth reading could do without this naïveté? When it is combined with cleverness and grace it is precisely what makes a good, an attractive autobiography, and I am certain that although we must expect some mockery, the preponderance of opinion will match my own: That it is an unusually charming, kind, sensitive, clever, and honestly personal book—personal and direct even in the adopted language which, it seems to me, is handled with surprising ease, authority, and naturalness. Involuntarily one looks for the name of the translator and can scarcely believe that it is a firsthand linguistic product.

Was it, as autobiography, a slightly premature undertaking? Some may say so, but if you had waited until you were fifty the early memories, which are always the best in confessions, might not show the freshness and bounce they have here. We parents certainly can be content with the figures we cut. The description of our "method" of education might be dangerous if it were to find imitators under unsuitable conditions. But the fine passage on motherliness, mother love, and filial gratitude will reconcile even the ill-willed, and the Papa who was so sick, you know, also turns out quite engaging, though somewhat mysterious with his *absentmindedness* and his melancholy humor. What can he have possibly said for "wretched and forlorn"?[3] I cannot remember the scene at all.

It is a tremendously European book, and perhaps will discourage the American reader because of its somewhat bizarre picture of pre-Hitler Europe, especially of the many bizarre chums it was your fate to encounter. But then when I read the chapter "Olympus"—which is of course the *pièce de résistance* of the book as a critical performance, and a fine, serious testimony to your capacity for devotion and admiration—I again have the impression that you present no superiority without *infirmité*, even though you warn against mistaking the *infirmité* for the superiority. It's a truly illustrious company you have assembled, but

[2] This phrase of Hofmannsthal's was a favorite expression in the Mann household. Hofmannsthal used to assume in a rather pampered, precious manner that everyone was always fully informed about himself and his circle.

[3] In *The Turning Point* Klaus Mann recalls one of his many departures from home. As he rode away, he writes, his father stood at the window and called out to him, "Come home when you are wretched and forlorn."

every one of them has his foibles. One is tempted to suspect that you willfully selected only those gods who have quirks. But if one tries to name some who haven't, one discovers that there are none who fill the bill.

At this very moment I am reading a letter from Eri, from whom I happily gather that friendly critics are lurking in the wings. Wonderful! Glorious if you were both at once, with the *United children*[4] and *The Turning Point*, to stand in the Bengal lights—pink and purple—of success. Although unfortunately, the T. P. probably is not for filming.

Keep well! I still can do no more than repeat what I said at the window.

We don't hear a word from Golo. Bibi and Gret are here with Anthony,[5] who is very tanned, with dark blue eyes and a worried expression. I daresay he looks like his father and me. After they have left with Frido, we shall be going to the movies often, until Erika comes.

My Washington lecture is being translated. Before she left, Erika cut it from 32 to 19 pages, and it will probably remain in this form, for once a passage has been deleted, it repels me.

TO HARRY SLOCHOWER

Pacific Palisades
September 8, 1942

Dear Dr. Slochower:

Many thanks for your kindness in sending me your essay on Goethe and Rilke in *Accent*.[1] It is a splendid contribution, and its first half especially, the study on *Faust*, fascinated me. I was particularly glad to see that you characterize the function of Mephistopheles ("Goethe's criticism of the Faustian upsurge") in much the same way that I do in my Princeton *Faust* lecture, incidentally a very inadequate and provisional piece which probably has never come your way.

The comparison of Goethe with Rilke—the confrontation of supreme competence and mastery of life's tasks with a cult of weakness enamored of nothingness—is, of course, scarcely flattering to modernity. A grandson of Goethe, Walter, used to say: "What do you expect—my grandfather was cock of the walk and I am a cockerel." Rilke might have

---

[4] Erika Mann's children's book, *A Gang of Ten*, written in English (New York: L. B. Fischer; 1942).
[5] Toni Mann, younger son of Michael Mann, born July 20, 1942.
[1] Summer 1942.

spoken in the same vein. But it cannot be denied that the cockerel has laid a few golden eggs.

TO FRIEDERIKE ZWEIG[1]

Pacific Palisades
September 15, 1942

My dear Madam:

My daughter has told me about the letter you sent her a few days ago. It pains me very much to learn of your feeling that I had not shown an attitude toward Stefan Zweig's death in keeping with the severe loss that the world of culture has suffered by the passing of this remarkable man. I understand that what offended you was my terseness, the fact that I limited public expression of my shock to a brief contribution to the memorial issue of *Aufbau*. Insofar as that was not simply a sign of my own tired and overworked state, it can be explained by the discouraging effect the great writer's tragic decision inescapably had, and which at least in my case was not conducive to literary activity in his honor. To write about a life work such as Stefan Zweig's is no small matter; it is a task to which one would have to give one's best. I was not in a psychological condition to do so.

He was a man of radical, unconditional pacifist disposition and convictions. In this war—a war whose coming one had to pray for and which could only be postponed by such a disgrace as Munich, a war which is being waged against the most infernal and unpacific powers that have ever attempted to shape human life in their own image—in this war he never saw anything but just another war, a bloodstained misfortune and a negation of his whole nature. He praised France for not wanting to fight and thus "saving Paris." He did not want to live in any of the belligerent countries; he left England, although he was a citizen, and went to the United States; later he went from here to Brazil, where he was received with the highest honor. And when it developed that this country too would be drawn into the war, he took leave of life.

There is a consistency about that which is above criticism. One can do no more to confirm one's character and convictions than by setting the seal of death upon them. Death is an argument that rebukes all rebuttal; the only appropriate response to it is to be mute. I say: to be mute. I was not and still am not inclined to seek a host of words.

---

[1] Friederike Zweig (b. 1882), writer, translator; first wife of Stefan Zweig.

You report (and I did not know it) that his wife was suffering from an incurable illness, and that this greatly contributed to the decision for a common death. Why did he not say so, instead of indicating that the motive of his act was despair over the times and the future? Was he conscious of no obligation toward the hundreds of thousands for whom his name was great and upon whom his abdication was bound to have a profoundly depressing effect? Toward the many fellow refugees throughout the world for whom the bread of exile is incomparably harder than it was for him, celebrated as he was and without material anxieties? Did he regard his life as a purely private affair and simply say: "I am suffering too much. Look you, I am leaving"? Could he concede the archenemy such a triumph—that once more one of us had furled his sails in the face of that enemy's "mighty, universal renewal," that one more of us had acknowledged bankruptcy and killed himself? That was the predictable interpretation of this act, and its value to the enemy. He was individualist enough not to care about that.

Please understand why I have remained silent, or almost silent! Herr Wittkowski[2] asked me for a contribution to his anthology. I did not regard him as a proper administrator of Stefan Zweig's literary legacy, but as the officious literary busybody I have to my discomfort found him for years. It seemed to me that he was merely seizing the opportunity of a famous man's passing to gather around himself the important names in world literature.

Believe me, dear madam, I mourn the extraordinary man whose name you bear as sincerely as do those who had the good fortune to be able to express their grief and their admiration in writing. All these eulogies are truly gratifying, and in the midst of sorrow I rejoiced in the impressive public honors given to Stefan Zweig by the country of his last refuge. May he rest in peace, while his name and work live among us.[3]

---

[2] Victor Wittkowski (1909–c. 1960), writer. Emigrated to Switzerland and Italy, then Brazil, where he associated with Stefan Zweig. Author of two slender volumes of verse and a book of stories, *Tibiae Tiberinae* (1940).

[3] On the tenth anniversary of Zweig's death, Thomas Mann wrote: "There were times when his radical, unconditional pacifism tormented me. He seemed ready to permit the domination of evil if that would prevent war, which he hated above all else. The problem is insoluble. But since we have seen that a good war, too, produces nothing but evil, I think differently about the attitude he then held—or at least, I try to think differently."

1942

TO AGNES E. MEYER

Pacific Palisades
October 15, 1942

Dear Agnes:

So you are safely back! It was a great event, a relief and joy when your letter arrived today, and my eyes flew eagerly over its lines. You have certainly been through grave, hard, moving experiences. Your picture of England is even darker and more painful than the one I had formed. But *"besiegt"*? Surely you mean the English word besieged. *Besiegt* as you know means "defeated," and certainly England isn't that yet, at least doesn't admit to being, any more than Russia does. My Führer's fury at the stupidity of his enemies who won't admit they are beaten is truly grotesque. They won't admit it, contrary to all the rules of war, which leads to their really not being, which in the end is going to cheat him out of his victories. All due to the "military idiocy" of his enemies. He's the only one who knows anything about war, as he proved before Moscow and Stalingrad.

I am hardly entitled to linger over the errors others make in mixing the two languages. Recently I actually said, *"Es ist wärmer bekommen"* (instead of *"geworden"*). A real German-American. All that remains is for me to start writing that way!

But what I wanted to say is that it's so good you're back. And how well it works out that we will soon be with you and can listen to your adventures! The Library lecture is set for November 17. The lecture was finished long ago and is being translated. [. . .] I think I have come out of the affair tolerably well, and *Joseph* was held up only a few weeks by the interpolation. I am presently working on the last chapters, and if it were up to me, the volume could be published in the spring. But Mrs. Lowe is still far behind, and I don't want to drive the dear old lady into hasty carelessness. Rather than that, let it be autumn of '43 before the book appears. It no longer really matters. Incidentally, she has sent me the translation of "Tamar," and aside from a few small errors it is excellent. *After all* I do suppose she is the best interpreter Knopf could have found for me.

Your articles on England—send them at once! I am more than eager. Copies of *Order of the Day* have come, and yours is going out to you at the same time as this letter. The book is very handsomely and carefully *manufactured*. What is inside it is not exactly overwhelming in itself. It is more of a *record* which shows that I said the things early.

We are very much alone now. Our entrancing grandson and the children all are going except Moni, who boards with us in silence. Erika is embarking on a *lecture tour* of fifty cities (God help her!). Golo has taken his teaching position in Olivet, Michigan, and is so busy that he gets up at three in the morning to prepare. Klaus, back in New York, has had —at least from the press—a warm, almost enthusiastic reception for his *Turning Point*, which does not surprise me, for it is a charming book and provides, in a personal, intimate fashion, a good picture not just of this *amazing family*[1] but also of the age against whose backdrop his life has been played.

That the English no longer have servants doesn't impress me at all, for the same will very soon be true in this country, at least out here in the West. Innumerable houses here are servantless, and since yesterday so are we, once again. Our Negro couple has returned to Texas; the husband is being called up. For us too there is no prospect whatever of finding new help, and my wife must do everything herself just like the British *ladies*. On top of that there is the difficulty with *oil* and *tires* which, given the distances out here, is a real calamity. But we shall have to prepare ourselves for far worse, and all this is not worth mentioning at all compared with the one thing that really matters.

We shall leave early, on November 8, and spend a few days in Chicago before we go on to Washington. From there we intend to visit New York, perhaps only for a few days, perhaps somewhat longer. My craving for an honest, not just fleeting, change of climate has become quite intense, and after all, I can do some work in the hotel. I've also written a foreword to *Listen, Germany!*—the twenty-five radio broadcasts to Germany. One always has one's hands full, which is good.

Once more, welcome back. It's good to know that you are in the country again.

Yours,
T. M.

---

[1] A phrase used by Harold Nicolson in his review of Erika Mann's *School for Barbarians*.

TO AGNES E. MEYER

Pacific Palisades
December 15, 1942

Dear friend:

It was thoughtful of you to let us know the hour of your broadcast. Yesterday we listened with much enjoyment, not letting a word escape us, moved by the warmth of your voice and by the feeling that your reports and exhortations will fall on fruitful soil in this country of good will. Thank you for this pleasure. How the voice brings the whole personality with it! If only the ether would soon transmit nothing but such voices of tried and true kindness and useful advice around the globe!

We came back on Sunday morning and have had hot, sunny days, which cool off with dangerous suddenness when the sun goes down. The trip with its many shifting scenes lies behind us like a dream—its high point came at the beginning with the evening in the Library, which I owe to you. It left me with a very good feeling. I am best if I can give and perform; on such occasions I stand up surprisingly well, although betweenwhiles I'm not much to boast of.

We are quite anxious about Bibi,[1] who was sick during our visit and is now lying in the hospital with an intestinal obstruction—a serious matter which, so it seems, will require an operation. Since he has just started his new job, this episode is at the least very troublesome. Nausea and pain had already seriously affected his performance. We must trust in the high level of American surgery. At bottom an acute organic illness, if it is not too bad, is easier to deal with than some intangible nervous ailment.

Klaus reports that he is at last going to be *inducted* on the 28th—which is a satisfaction to me also.

Economically—at least temporarily—there have been many unpleasant changes during our absence. Things look bad in the food markets: no butter, scarcely any eggs, scarcely any meat, even no vegetables. What nonsense—in this country! I regard it as a not very good joke, and indeed hear that the famine is to be switched off again on January 1.

Mountains of books and letters were waiting for me here—and at the same time the secretary cannot drive out daily because of the gasoline. I am hoping for what is called a B card for him as well as for us. Everybody here has one already; it is only we who missed the bus.

The gloriously heavy ashtray had also already arrived. Magnificent!

[1] Michael Mann.

Thank you—thank you very much. But guests who might admire it have become rarer.

This morning I resumed the *Joseph*, still somewhat hesitantly, with a feeling of strangeness. It must be finished by New Year's Day so that I shall have January free for the $1,000 story.[2]

I trust mother and child are well?

Yours,

T. M.

[2] The Moses story, *The Tables of the Law* (New York: Alfred A. Knopf; 1945) for which Mann had been offered this amount.

1943

———————•———————

TO AGNES E. MEYER

Pacific Palisades
January 5, 1943

Dear friend:

I didn't want to write you until I could make this announcement, which I herewith do, with some emotion: The *Joseph* is finished. Yesterday noon I wrote the last lines: They are friendly, understanding words addressed by the hero to his brothers, who with their father dead fear that he may after all decide to take revenge on them. So I have also included this biblical motif in the story. It allowed me to let the book fade out with the sound of Joseph's serene voice—to let him speak once more. And so it is done and may well stand as a monument of persistence and endurance, for I am more inclined to see it as that than as, say, a monument of art and intellect. I suggested as long ago as the *Betrach-tungen* that art is only an ethical way to give substance to my life, and today I still regard my work preeminently from this point of view. It is a life's occupation. That it may, beyond this, be worth something object-ively is a hope on my part, but not an assertion.

Since I wrote the above your two letters of December 28th and 29th have arrived, and I thank you with all my heart. [. . .] The holidays this year have a special meaning for us, both because of the conclusion of a work that has filled so many years and because of the impending tenth anni-versary of our departure from Munich (February 11th). And during these holidays you have shown us so much kindness, delicacy, *thoughtful-ness* that we think of you, dear friend, with emotion and veneration. Joseph bears the fine oriental title "Shade-giver of the King." You too are a shade-giver in many respects.

"Britain's Home Front"[1] has arrived safely—everything arrives very slowly, if it finds its way at all. These essays brimming with experience must surely be counted among the most instructive and engaging things available on the new England that has been shaped by the hard hand of war. I can understand the sensation they are making—more power to them. It is only too true that "what happens on our social front during the war will determine the nature of the peace." In this country there is probably far too much longing and false hope for a return to *"normalcy"* after the war. And nothing good is meant by *normalcy*. The military victory may be slow in coming, but it will come; our main anxiety already is the peace. Churchill, the old war-horse, does not understand these questions at all, nor does he want to; and it seems to me that F. D. R. has a strong inclination to make peace with the aid of the Church and South European Fascism—which would probably make World War III a certainty. This is my sole objection. For I am absolutely convinced that anything whatsoever is better than Hitler, and I feel personally capable of getting along with Communism as well as with a tolerably civilized clerico-Fascism.

Thank you for your information about the stones.[2] It is certainly fascinating, and young Tonio can well be pleased. His father is still peaky and worn, but on the road to recovery. In retrospect I regard the whole illness, serious as it looked, as a kind of nervous *fit* of a spastic sort.

With best wishes,

Yours,
T. M.

TO KURT WOLFF[1]

Pacific Palisades
January 20, 1943

Dear Kurt Wolff:

The George book[2] is in my hands—a precious gift. Thank you for making me one of the first recipients of this noble first fruit of your new publish-

---

[1] Agnes Meyer's report on her visit in England.

[2] A pair of precious jade cufflinks that Agnes Meyer had presented to Mann, with the request that he was to bequeath them to his grandson Tonio.

[1] Kurt Wolff (1887–1963), publisher, noted for the distinctive quality of his books in both Germany and the United States. His Kurt Wolff Verlag published many important German writers of the twentieth century, especially the Expressionists. In the United States he founded Pantheon Books and, subsequently, Helen and Kurt Wolff Books within Harcourt, Brace & World. His career as a publisher spanned fifty years, from Kafka to Günter Grass.

[2] *Poems* by Stefan George. A bilingual edition, translated by Carol North Valhope and Ernst Morwitz.

ing house. I have read a great deal in the book, with odd feelings. It is a curious experience, consistent with our whole destiny, to reread this movingly austere bequest in the language which we are now accustoming our ears and lips to. Without our transplantation, such a work could scarcely have come into being so soon: a work of devotion and craftsmanship, a lovely gift of the emigré German mind to a world which has so far known little about this noble representative of the German spirit. It has surprised me, for instance, that the name of Stefan George does not occur in the index of an American book of cultural criticism which otherwise has a remarkable range—*Art and Freedom* by H. M. Kallen.[3]

The choice in itself is excellent: adroit, intelligent, accessible—I am almost tempted to say popular. All the most attractive qualities in this proud and priestly temperament have been brought out—the heartfelt sweetness and naturalness, the Walter von der Vogelweide tone—without obscuring the autocratic, the austere, the harsh aspects. In saying this I am also speaking of the translation, which reflects the original as far as is humanly possible, thanks—as I know—to long, devoted work. Naturally there was a risk in presenting the German text as well—an open challenge to criticism. And criticism does take exception here and there, ungenerous though that is. For the side-by-side presentation says candidly enough: "See how we have had to grasp at straws, have had to fall back on weakening qualifications and rough equivalents." But the confrontation also expresses a justified pride: the knowledge that these translations can "stand alongside" the original and represent a real incorporation of rare emotional and linguistic material into the culture of our host country. The rhythmical suppleness is especially admirable. The Germans have always known how to appropriate foreign things. In the Diaspora they are beginning to transfer what is German to the foreign scene, and that too they do well. We must praise them where they deserve praise.

TO AGNES E. MEYER

Pacific Palisades
January 28, 1943

Dear friend:

I want at least to say good-bye before you set out on your new patriotic pilgrimage,[1] during which you will probably be somewhat inaccessible.

---

[3] Horace M. Kallen (b. 1882), professor of philosophy, New School for Social Research; author of *A Free Society* (1934), *Art and Freedom* (2 vols., 1942), *Patterns of Progress* (1950), *Cultural Pluralism and the American Idea* (1956), among others.

[1] Mrs. Meyer was setting out on a lecture tour.

But in compensation you will suddenly be with us in person and will have more to tell than I, sitting still as I do, have to write about. I shall do my part to have the *Moses* ready by then, but hardly imagine that you will have the time to listen to it. In any case it would have to be an extract, for in this *long short story* the *emphasis* is turning out to be on the "*long.*"

I have just returned from Hollywood, where in a small theater on the fifth floor of a department store, with some 350 ladies and 5 gentlemen, I had to listen to a *lecture* delivered by a practiced but simpleminded *stage* jackal on *Order of the Day* and *Listen, Germany!* Then I myself had to step forward and greet the audience; but I cut off all expectation of any performance on my part by saying: "*Everything I should add to this splendid analysis of my work could only be an anticlimax.*" That is how we must lie when we go out into the world. Nothing could have been an *anticlimax*. Even at that, I still had to sit there for another three quarters of an hour and sign books. What-all one doesn't do for popularity. Even Jefferson was, as I have just read in a book about him, "*thirsty for public praise*"—and that was "*the apostle of Americanism.*"

His successor in office has once more pulled a sensational prank with his flight to the African White House.[2] It was an exciting piece of news, although what can be released of the results of the meeting is naturally disproportionate to the importance ascribed to it by the high contracting parties. One must hope that the actual results will be more proportionate. *In any case, it will be a very long way to Tipperary*, in spite of Stalingrad and Rostov, which the Germans seem to be on the point of giving up. The nature of their reporting on the Russian defeat is once again grotesque. Suddenly the long-since-defeated Bolshevistic submen are far superior in numbers and equipment, and the poor, frail invader is waging a bitter defense of civilization against the craftily armed barbarian. It can be called a form of completely corrupted thinking, thinking that functions only as lie and crazy reversal of the truth. I wonder how much the people themselves are victims of this corruption.

Isn't it after all rather a pity that neither a Russian nor a Chinese emissary was present at Casablanca? Geography would have been no obstacle. A story is going the rounds that the crown prince of Italy and Señor Franco were present, which is ridiculous of course—and yet then again, not so stupid. I fancy (without becoming too disturbed about it,

---

[2] The reference is to the Casablanca conference between Roosevelt and Churchill and their general staffs, January 14–26, 1943.

since it is not my view that world history exists for our pleasure) that nothing much will come of "democratic peace." It will be a Catholic-Fascistic peace. Perhaps Europe no longer deserves anything better. But the Anglo-Saxon armies of occupation will probably serve to check the overdue revolutions in Germany, France, Italy, and Spain.

You always slap me down whenever I meddle in political matters, but I am convinced you will remember my predictions one of these days. In a pinch the Russians might upset all calculations, but we already often hear it said that after the defeat of Germany we shall have to confront the Russians. Will you come along to Moscow?

The Library pamphlet with the Joseph lecture has arrived, very handsomely printed. A copy must surely have reached you long ago. I only regret that the prefatory speeches by MacLeish and Wallace were not included. Then it would have been a complete memorial document for the participants.

We are having the rainy season now. Dripping days alternate with spells of hot, dry wind and blazing sunshine. The Borgeses are very happy with us and would love to stay here forever. He is working on a witty and spirited topical book, *The Cup for All*. They were in San Francisco for a few days, where they met Sforza again. He had already visited us here—an elegant, entertaining but, I think, somewhat windy man. Bibi is in good health, has seven pupils, and is very busy with rehearsals and performances. The children were enchanted by your modernistic hobbyhorse, which made a sensation here too.

And now, have a good trip, dear friend, and don't overstrain yourself. Sometimes I find myself already considering the topic of my talk next fall in Washington.

As always,

Yours,
T. M.

TO KLAUS MANN

Pacific Palisades
March 9, 1943

Dear Son:

There is a small Italian gathering in the living room, people whom Borgy has invited to a farewell party of tea and cocktails, but I have stolen away to write a letter to you for once. First because I know how important mail is for all of you, and secondly because I still haven't thanked you for the Gide book.[1] As I read, I kept thinking with pleasure that it was largely and perhaps wholly written here in our midst. It fascinated, entertained, and also instructed me; for your understanding of the man's soul and his art is precise and intimate because it is loving. I myself have some notion, and a deeply respectful one, of Gide's work, but I am not familiar with it line for line as you are. I don't think he could have wished for a better-versed portraitist and interpreter, and certainly no American could have been found to plead his cause as effectively as you. For that, a European was needed—and in general we shall be needed for quite a few things, even if after this war, as seems probable, we shall only be the Graeculi of the world. You have succeeded in making Greek highly accessible to the good-natured barbarians, in the most natural English, with serene, uneffusive enthusiasm, with anecdotes and all. I was startled by a good many features in the portrait—as, for example, that passage on the cigarette, the way he suddenly raises the silly things into the realm of high morality and vice, confesses that he cannot resist them, and maliciously speaks in the words of that unsympathetic character of his. An uncanny fellow—intricate, though by no means tricky. "Impious" in Hoffmann's sense probably fits better, and would no doubt appeal to him also. The most curious mixture of seducer and educator since—since Socrates, one is inclined to say.

I have been wanting for the longest time to write to you for both the reasons I mentioned above, but also because after all you are now defending us with arms and leading a difficult, new, strange, although all too ordinary life. But I have had too much to do. Besides my own work there are so many demands from outside: broadcasts to Germany, to Europe altogether, in English; to Australia, in English; articles for the Office of War Information on Germany's future, and so on—stupid stuff, but I can't always refuse, at least not when I don't buy many War Bonds (we *have* bought some). Chiefly during these past weeks, I have been busy with the Moses novella, which was commissioned as an introduction to a volume of stories on the Ten Commandments—I don't know whether anything will come of the plan at all. In any case, the realistic-grotesque story, whose subject, of course, is nothing less than the formation of civilized morality (the Golden Calf is a tragicomic relapse), greatly amuses me, and I have knocked off a hundred pages so rapidly that I felt I no longer have to be envious of your speed. After parting with some-

[1] Klaus Mann's *André Gide and the Crisis of Modern Thought* (New York: Creative Age Press; 1943).

thing big, I always allow myself to do something of this sort which I can handle effortlessly.

Unfortunate that old Lowe is still lagging so far behind on the translation of the *Joseph*. I could not write it in English myself—even you couldn't. But now it is questionable whether the autumn deadline can be kept. It would be a hard blow, because of the worsening paper situation and because after all, I cannot go on forever drawing royalty advances without the book's coming out.

The worst will soon be behind you. I was glad to hear of the major who is thinking of shunting you into the intelligence service. Saroyan seems to have landed there right off, you know, and is leading his author's life in uniform, as well as privately in between. That he has called his novelette *of the month* "The Human Comedy" is a pinnacle of rustic naïveté.

Good luck and honor!

Warmly,
Z.

P.S. I have written Coudenhove a letter calling it quits. It is much too ambiguous a salon.

TO BRUNO WALTER

Pacific Palisades
May 6, 1943

Dear Bruno Walter:

Your good letter of April 24th was a disproportionate reward for the small gift of the German broadcasts. Any word of thanks would have been too much for the Washington speech, which I sent only because it was meant for you, after all. But it is true that there has been too long a silence between New York and Pacific Palisades. Often, as I live busily along, I have felt it to be wrong and saddening, and I am glad we have broken the ice once more. Of course, the loss of contact was partly due to our having counted on seeing each other sooner: you were supposed to come last winter and didn't. That was a disappointment. But in any case, in your truest self you are always with us. The Walter *department* of our record library is quite large, you know. And recently, on that great afternoon[1] (it was a forenoon for us) there was a truly remarkable aboli-

[1] An uncut performance of the *St. Matthew Passion* in New York, with Bruno Walter conducting.

tion of distance: our excellent radio brought everything into the living room, even to the sound of the chorus standing up and sitting down again. For fifty-five minutes—the connection lasted that long—we were as good as there; everything audible was ours; and since (as is well known) you conduct exactly as I would conduct if I were a conductor, it was easy for me to imagine the by no means incidental visual concomitants. The choruses came over with a delicacy and purity that moved one to tears.

We live our by now deeply habituated waiting-room days among our palms and *lemon trees*, in sociable concourse with the Franks, Werfels, Dieterles, Neumanns—always the same faces, and if occasionally an American countenance appears, it is as a rule so strangely blank and amiably stereotyped that one has had enough for quite some time to come. But for the past few weeks, since our Swiss daughter-in-law has taken a *defense job* (she is a *tank cleaner*), we have had the two boys from San Francisco with us—hard on my wife, especially since the Negro maid works only very sporadically, but they bring gaiety and animation into the house. Tonio, the younger child, is still without much personality, but charming Frido has grown even prettier than last time, and is my daily delight. With clumsy tongue he is learning to talk now, and says, pointing to eye, nose, mouth, and chin: "*Augi, Nasi, Muhnd, Chien.*" When he has had enough of anything, or wants to console himself because there is no more of it, he says: " *'habt*" ["had"]. I find that perfect. When I am dying, I too shall say " 'habt." His farewell in all circumstances is "*Nacht.*" He has a specially intense response to music. He calls it "Itsch," and when the radio plays he is completely absorbed, simply sits and listens. Afterwards he comes and reports, with shining eyes: "*Itsch habt.*" I definitely must write about him, perhaps will include him in my next novel; for I have made up my mind to give the war time for one more novel, so that when it's over Bermann can march in through the Brandenburg Gate with four unknown books of mine. The completion of the Joseph is already well in the past; it was finished in January. Afterwards I wrote a longish Moses novella, a Sinai fantasy, for an interesting anthology to which Sigrid Undset, Werfel, Rebecca West, and others are contributing; each of the stories deals with one of the Ten Commandments and its violation by Hitler. The book has aroused great interest in advance and will be published in English (New York and London), German and Swedish (in Stockholm), French (in Canada) and Spanish (in South America). My Moses story forms the introduction. Werfel called it prettily: "Prelude for the Organ."

Now I have something very different in mind, something rather uncanny, tending in the theological and demonological direction. [. . .] the novel of a pathological, unlawful inspiration. The hero, incidentally, will be a *musician* (a composer). I intend to risk it—but can already foresee that I shall occasionally have to turn to you for advice and factual information, e.g., I am already wondering about the professional training of a creative musician. I suppose it takes many forms and does not necessarily include study at a conservatory? Hugo Wolf never seems to have studied at one. Nor Stravinsky either; he reports that the theory of harmony thoroughly bored him while on the other hand counterpoint was very attractive to him. He passed through his productive early development under the supervision of Rimsky-Korsakov. —Do you think I ought to read a treatise on composition? Do you have one? Incidentally, I also intend to ask Schoenberg[2] for advice.

You know that Erika is on her way to Europe, England, Sweden, possibly Russia. [. . .] A second vulnerable point is *Sergeant* Klaus, who wrote weeks ago that he would probably soon be setting out on "a long journey" (Africa, of course). We have heard nothing from him; he must be already on the way. Golo, still in his college, will be coming here in June to undergo a minor hernia operation. He says he is bursting with envy of his brother, and has only one thought: *to join the army*.

Keep well! A thousand gallantries to your ladies!

TO AGNES E. MEYER

Pacific Palisades
May 8, 1943

Dear friend:

You oughtn't to send on to me documents of such depressing stupidity and malice as the letter of Anne B. G.; rather you ought to agree with me that it's no reading matter for me. I cannot see how Klaus is to blame because the absurd female in her blind drive to vent her venom draws me, MacLeish, and by indirection, you too, into the controversy. What

---

[2] Arnold Schoenberg (1874–1951), Austrian composer and theoretician of music. Emigrated to the United States in 1933. A prolific composer and writer on musical subjects, Schoenberg is renowned for his creation of the twelve-tone technique. He and Thomas Mann became close friends in California; subsequently, Schoenberg became indignant over the inclusion of the twelve-tone technique in *Doctor Faustus* and accused Mann of appropriating his intellectual property. After a period of some acrimony on the composer's part, Schoenberg was mollified.

my antipolitical cultural credo of 1916[1] and my $90,000 sinecure[2] have
to do with Klaus's analysis of the relationship between Gide and Claudel
—a subject that surely has its place in a biography of Gide—is a question
the silly goose would undoubtedly not be able to answer. If you had had
the book at hand—an honor of which it is completely worthy—you would
know as well as I that Klaus's comments on Claudel are based on complete respect and irreproachable reverence for the man's genius. How
could it be otherwise? The author knows not only of your affinity for the
great poet, but also of my own long-standing admiration of his poetry—
something I expressed as far back as the *Betrachtungen* with a tribute to
L'annonce faite à Marie. For the rest, Klaus is absolutely correct in his
definition of Claudel's intellectual character as another form of the
French spirit contrasting with the attitude of Gide. If I were to write
about him, I could express myself no differently. Claudel's sincere hatred
of everything German and his contempt for Protestant culture one day
led him to call Goethe an ass. I think it permissible, when dealing with a
critic of such amusing candor, to be as truthful about him in turn: to say
that his political tendencies lie in the direction of a Catholic Fascism—in
other words, coincide with those trends which will probably exert the
strongest influence upon the shaping of the peace.

Of course a Catholic need not necessarily be a Fascist. There are
differences—demonstrated by the fact that Bernanos and Maritain have
left France, while Claudel's plays are, as I hear from you, being performed in German Paris, and he himself appears at the theater. I
believe you are needlessly worried about his personal safety. The news
that my son has "attacked" him could only improve his position.

It is curious. The bitterness could not be greater if Klaus had cast
aspersions on an American national saint, let us say Lincoln or Jefferson;
in fact it would have been more moderate. But Claudel has said: "To each
his own; justice consists in that"—a fine, conservative dictum, but what
has that to do with the boundless contempt of the Smith College girl for
"a conception of life in which economic equality is supposed to be the
highest attainable goal"?[3] There we have the political cloven hoof, the
venom and gall which pretend to be idealism. Ugh!

I am also depressed by your admission that your tour brought you
many a bitter and mortifying disappointment. I suffer with you, for I am

---

[1] *Betrachtungen eines Unpolitischen,* much of which was written in 1916.
[2] Thomas Mann's actual salary as consultant to the Library of Congress was $400
monthly. The writer of the letter had simply imagined the sum of $90,000.
[3] Quoted in English, presumably from the letter of Anne B. G.

grieved by everything that might shake the faith in this country which all of us entered with *such* enthusiastic faith. Of course, granted, everything is not as it should be. But isn't the nation great and good, and must we not admire the way this rich, pampered country is learning how to do without and wage war? Bizerta and Tunis have fallen a month sooner than anyone dared hope. Great things may be expected of the next few months, and even a setback, in fact especially a setback, would reinforce my gratitude for the sacrifices America is making to a cause which is so very much mine also. The real worry is whether the coalition can hold together, not just until the end of the war (Hitler's sole hope is that it will fall apart before then), but afterwards. For that will determine whether a durable peace can be created—durable because it courageously takes account of the new conditions. I have recently written to Alexei Tolstoy;[4] the letter has been sent to Russia. It will also be published here, perhaps along with his answer.

But incidentally: May the Allies win, win very soon, so that the unbearable misery in Europe will come to an end. What the victors then do with their victory does not bother me so much. Everything changes, and history will correct whatever they do wrong. Let us first have the victory! To be sure, it would be a shameful spectacle if the Allies were to start to scrap with one another.

We have our grandchildren from San Francisco with us. [. . .] Tonio is developing vigorously and is a sweet-tempered child, still unsuspecting that he is the proud possessor of extraordinary cufflinks. But Frido, who is beginning to talk—only German for the present, but that will soon change—is the most charming three-year-old I have ever seen. My heart swells when I as much as look at him. And we are very good friends.

I have not yet begun writing again, but am dreaming, taking notes, collecting, and preparing. Last night I was seduced into sketching the plan of the novel to a good friend, the writer Alfred Neumann. He was extremely excited—overwhelmed.

A long letter must come to an end. My very best wishes.

Yours,

T.M.

---

[4] Alexei Tolstoy (1883–1945), Russian writer, distantly related to Leo Tolstoy and, through his mother, to Turgenev. Joined the White Army in 1917; remained in exile in Paris and Berlin until 1923, then returned to Russia. Mann's letter to Tolstoy of April 28, 1943, was published in English in *The New Republic*, Vol. 108 (1943).

TO AGNES E. MEYER

Pacific Palisades
May 26, 1943

My dear friend:

I have been unwell for several days and could not write, not even letters.

In response to yours, may I reply as follows: We do not choose the hour in which a letter reaches the addressee and cannot estimate the psychological and physical state he will be in at the time of receiving it. Following your example, I might say you had "chosen" the moment when I was in the midst of conceiving a new book, and therefore in a state of great, easily shattered nervous tension, to send me the insignificant blather of the lady from Smith College—not in order for me to see how malignant and hate-filled the writer is, but so that I could see what a good-for-nothing my son Klaus is.

I have suffered bitterly and long from your having nothing but feelings of scorn and rejection for my children, for after all I love these children, by the same right that you love your children. I assure you, I can scarcely imagine a more horrible blow—to me personally—than that something should happen to your wonderful Bill in the course of the war. My thoughts must necessarily turn in many directions every day, yet running through them all is this anxiety, which also takes in the well-being of your daughters who are approaching their difficult hour. I have sometimes remarked to my family that I would not know how to go on if suffering should be inflicted on you through one of your children. But these feelings were certainly one-sided. Erika's lecture work, which is successful because of her great charm of personality and deep, passionate feeling for the moral and political questions of these times; her stay in England at the time of the worst blitz—to you all that was nothing but mischief making. And the Russians, you wrote, "have no time for tourists." For tourists! If only you knew how long I sat there, the letter in my hand, shaking my head.

You were right in your opinion that at least one of my sons should be in the army. Klaus literally fought to be taken in. Once a soldier, Klaus, although he was thirty-six years old and a totally untrained intellectual, went through the harsh *basic training* with the willpower of enthusiasm, and rose with surprising swiftness to the rank of staff sergeant. With humorously paternal pride I reported this to you. You sent not a word of appreciation or congratulation.

Now I have defended a talented, hardworking, and courageous son against what I consider the unjust charge that he made unseemly statements about a great poet who, moreover, is your friend. To my immense horror and astonishment, it develops that in so doing I myself have insulted and *"condemned"* Claudel—I who would never have breathed the faintest word against the cast of this man's mind, which is remote from my own, but which I hold in the highest respect.

It is Klaus who has written a book on André Gide, in which he necessarily referred to Claudel several times. He has done so in three or four passages—three times in a manner to which no one could possibly object. The fourth time he seems to have been guilty of an inaccurate description, based on false or outmoded information, of Claudel's attitude after the occupation of France. Who is called to account for that? I am. Klaus is young, and although not lightminded, lighthearted. He scarcely reads the attacks he has provoked by stirring up the Catholic wasp's nest; moreover, he knows nothing about our exchange of letters on this subject and has nothing on his mind but his soldier's life and the adventures before him. I, who am agitated by everything, who need peace and quiet as I do my daily bread, who can neither accomplish anything nor even merely live in the midst of bickering and quarrels, but instantly go to pieces—I must suffer for it, and on account of something I have had nothing to do with. I must see the shattering of a friendship which was dear to me.

It was dear to me. I understood how much I, the foreigner, possessed in having it, and I served it faithfully and with care. Serving is the very word. For years I have devoted to it more thought, nervous energy, work at the desk, than to any other relationship in the world. I have let you participate as well as I know how in my inner and outer life. On your visits I have read aloud to you for hours from new work no one else has seen. I have shown the most sincere admiration for your patriotic and social activities. But nothing was right, nothing enough. In my letters there was "no trace"—I no longer know of what, probably of humanity. You always wanted me different from the way I am. You did not have the humor, or the respect, or the discretion, to take me as I am. You wanted to educate, dominate, improve, redeem me. In vain I warned you, with all kindness and delicacy, that this sort of thing was an attempt on an unsuitable object, that at the age of nearly seventy my life was too thoroughly formed and fixed. I cannot but feel that your outbreak of wrath over such a letter as my next to last is merely the eruption of a profounder disappointment and embitterment taking an almost insignificant pretext to express itself.

I had wished so much—I cannot say how strongly—to give this relationship of ours a quality of balance and serenity, of calm, invulnerable cordiality. But now it has reached the crisis which probably threatened it from the first moment. Let us grant it and ourselves the tranquillity which alone can restore our psychological equilibrium. I, at any rate, need calm in order to find my way out of this torment back to myself and my tasks—it doesn't seem as if that were going to be easy. We can hardly forget what we owe to one another. I say to one another, for I was able to accept without loss of dignity and kindness and support, the easing of life that you offered, since you led me to believe that they were not unreciprocated benefits.

Our arrangement with the Library of Congress does, to be sure, seem to me to be so compromised and tainted by the denunciation of that fervent Claudel admirer that I had better suggest to Mr. MacLeish that I end my association with his institution, and announce this publicly. Otherwise I fear that he will feel personally implicated in the charges of corruption, favoritism, and waste of money which the lady has directed against him.

Full of good wishes for you and yours, I bid you a heartfelt farewell.

TO AGNES E. MEYER

Pacific Palisades
June 2, 1943

My dear friend:

Most certainly all bickering and quarreling must end; I am determined to end it, for it is destroying both of us. Much of it, in the past and now again, is probably due simply to my way of writing letters, to which I bring a certain linguistic passion. Then again, they may often sound involuted, although my aim was only to express myself with some precision. Misunderstandings are all the more likely since you—very naturally—do not read German quite as you do the language of this country and do not grasp some things properly, or else distort them in your memory. Twice in your letter of Friday you used the word "ridiculous" between quotation marks, as though I had used it. But I did not use it at all, and really don't know how I could ever bring myself to apply it to you or to our relationship. And I shudder at the imputation that I ever called you a simple, primitive soul. Furthermore, you read me as saying that you yourself had tainted our arrangement with the Library,

I wrote: "The publication[1] of *that fervent Claudel admirer* seems to me to have so compromised and tainted our arrangement with the Library of Congress that I had better, etc." I have meanwhile done what seemed right to me, and am awaiting the reply which will show whether, as I feared, MacLeish feels implicated by the charges which are tacitly brought against him. If those remarks were in the least representative, and if they express disapproval by even a part of public opinion, my association with the Library must be terminated. I do have some feeling for honor and dignity.

I wanted to correct the above mistakes; but with that, let us put the matter to rest. I would *not* wish, dear friend, that, as the phrase is, everything be as it was before. For it was not good and not right. It was too full of friction, too tense, too painfully emotional and charged with electricity. I want this crisis, which has caused the two of us so much grief and upset, to clear the atmosphere of such elements once and for all. It is a misery and a terrible burden on my conscience for me to imagine you as you describe yourself in your letter of Saturday. Never, never again! That must end—and it would have been very, very hard for me too, if that had necessarily meant the end of our friendship. But no one writes such letters as we have just been writing for the fun of it. They signify a termination, if not of a friendship, then at any rate of an era within a friendship. Once again, I wish and for my part will do my best to see that this painful crisis proves to have been epoch-making in our friendship, in a good, salutary, strengthening sense.

Thank you very much for *The British Home Front Compared with Ours*. That is indeed a *"Vital Speech of the Day"* and will remain a document of fine American self-criticism long after these days are past. You have never before spoken, I think, so clearly and convincingly, with such courageous incisiveness, in expressing your love and concern. I cannot imagine that such words will go unheard or fail to provoke thought. People like myself do not have your experience, but purely intuitively they share your concern, and at times anxiety rises that the war might last too long—for Hitler's sole but, alas, not entirely foolish hope is that the American *home front* will not endure a long war. I heard the remark from one of your *boys* that he could not finish his furlough fast enough and go back to where things are serious; that at home it is unbearable: dancing, lovemaking, indifference, complete ignorance of what is going on. Perhaps this referred only to California. Perhaps, too, the life of those

[1] Mann actually wrote "denunciation"; the change of this word and of the word order indicates that he was quoting from memory, not from a carbon copy.

at home always has something irritating about it for anyone coming from the front. But still, one wishes that the people at home recognized the gravity of the situation a little better—I do not think that is asking too much. What an encouragement to the enemy these strikes are! Do the workers ever consider what will become of them if Hitler wins? Of course they are entitled to more meat. But it is not my impression that this man Lewis[2] is concerned about the muscular strength of the *miners*. What is involved is a crass struggle for power, and one cannot help wishing that it will end in favor of the government and of the war.

I am writing again—on the novel for which the war in Europe, alas, will probably give me time. The thing is difficult, weird, uncanny, sad as life—in fact even more so, since idea and art always exceed and exaggerate life. To be palatable the story needs a leavening of cheerfulness, and for that a spirit of serene good cheer is needed. But until now I have never lacked this, even in worse times.

TO LUDWIG ALTMAN[1]

Pacific Palisades
June 20, 1943

Dear Herr Altman:

Thank you once again for the essay,[2] which I have read with great interest. Its central idea is certainly a truism. I was especially struck by the story about Tschaikovsky and the rich Russian noblewoman,[3] his friend on whom he never set eyes. I did not know the story and find it most remarkable.[4]

The decline of Schumann's genius was probably not so much the result of his marital felicity as of progressive paralysis—of which, to be sure, you could not very well speak.

It was good that I had the chance to chat with you. I hope we will see each other again sometime.

---

[2] John L. Lewis (1880–1969), the powerful president of the United Mine Workers.
[1] Ludwig Altman (b. 1910), organist and writer on musical subjects.
[2] "Our Great Symphonies Written by Lonely Men." *Opera and Concert*, November 1941.
[3] Nadezhda von Meck (1831–94), the widow of a Russian railroad magnate, who maintained a lively correspondence with Tschaikovsky and was of enormous help to him.
[4] Mann made use of this story in *Doctor Faustus*.

1943

TO KONRAD KELLEN[1]

Pacific Palisades
August 19, 1943

Dear Konni:

I hear that you are now at your preliminary destination, i.e., the site of your "basic training," have a fixed address, so to speak, unnatural though that may sound. This means that I can send you a few sympathetic lines on the very stationery you found for us, so that you won't think: "Out of sight, out of mind" and "He doesn't have to do KP and doesn't give a hang what others have to do!" For I do give a hang, but I can only let the things of this world take their course and try to alleviate matters by providing you with the familiar scrawl for reading matter. For once you don't have to copy or to translate it.

Yes, I have asked after you often in these weeks, and hesitate to offer prematurely, merely for my own reassurance, the hope that the worst may already be over for you—I mean, the worst in unusualness, if not in discomfort. In your case I imagine that it cannot be more than a case of getting used to not getting used to it all (Hans Castorp). Forgive the quotation from myself. What man shows perfect self-control in the presence of his secretary?

But that, too, is a kind of adjustment, and once the hard weeks of the "*basic*" are over (the time will surely pass quickly, given the never-changing tempo of the army), that adjustment will be at full strength. Then too, you will probably sail into the harbor of a somewhat less martial occupation. And my chief hope always rests on the fact that there is something about you which involuntarily keeps people, who on the average are not bad-hearted, from treating you too brutally.

Things go tolerably well with your successor. He comes only twice a week and types out his drafts, maintaining that he types faster than he writes. Dictating into the rattle of the typewriter is not pleasant, but I have grown adjusted to that too. Incidentally, I am cutting my correspondence to the bone, because I must produce the lecture—actually a lecture and a half, with interchangeable passages. For the past few days I made notes which I am now dictating to my wife. Quite often I say

---

[1] Konrad Kellen (formerly Katzenellenbogen) (b. 1913), friend of Erika and Klaus Mann. Emigrated to Paris in 1933, to the United States in 1936. Worked in a bank in New York for some time; became Thomas Mann's secretary, 1941–3. Served in the American army; subsequently became an officer and employee of the American military government. Worked in Radio Free Europe for eleven years, then as analyst at the Hudson Institute. Author of *Khrushchev—A Political Portrait* (1961).

alarmingly "leftish" things, but hope to cover these over and prevent a scandalous effect by strewing on top a good bit of conservative and traditionalist confectioner's sugar.

A lucky thing that Dr. Joseph[2] can read my handwriting. He is now beginning to copy the novel.

Do you know that Erika is in Cairo as a U.S. war correspondent? In uniform, with an officer's rank! Sergeant Klaus's reaction was very amusing; he is a soldier through and through and refused to take her rank seriously: "Why, she isn't on the payroll so she doesn't really belong to the Army."[3]

Well, *you* belong.

Lowe-Porter has asked her last questions and will now deliver. But the date of publication cannot be foreseen, *for manufacturing is becoming extremely difficult and correspondingly slow*, says Knopf.

I really must stop. What do you think—with all there is to do!

The war is going almost too well at the moment. We will no longer need you and Golo, who is also entering the lists against Hitler, or perhaps only against Hirohito, the Victor Emmanuel of the Rising Sun.

Wishing you the best imaginable,

Your old *boss*,

TO AGNES E. MEYER

Hotel Bedford
118 East 40th Street
New York, New York
October 27, 1943

Dear friend:

We returned from Montreal two hours ago, and once more I must thank you for your effective intervention in the passport affair, which was more, apparently, than Colston Leigh's[1] staff could cope with. But for you, the *re-entry permit* we applied for many weeks ago would probably not have come in time. The impression grows *that you are running the country*.

---

[2] Albrecht Joseph, Mann's secretary; also Franz Werfel's for a while.

[3] All correspondents officially accredited to the American forces were given the "assimilated rank" of captains; thus they were entitled to officers' mess and transportation privileges, but above all to treatment as officers under the Geneva Convention if they should happen to be captured. They were, of course, paid not by the army but by the periodicals for which they worked.

[1] Thomas Mann's lecture agent.

My experiences on this tour are moving and abashing. The general excitement, the overcrowded halls, the silent attentiveness, the gratitude —there is something confusing and incomprehensible about it all. In Montreal the police had to be called out when the overflow crowd refused to move and was threatening to crush in the doors. In Boston something like 1,000 persons had to be turned away. I ask myself every time: What do these people expect? After all, I'm not Caruso. Won't they be completely disappointed? But they aren't. They declare that it was the greatest thing they have ever heard. And they say to Katia: "You are a lucky woman." So I suppose it must be so.

Masses of letters and affairs have heaped up here. I don't yet see how I am going to handle them all. There is a lecture in Chicago on November 7th. On the 16th I speak at Columbia University. I hope others won't be inserted into the schedule. I would so like to get a little work done while we are here.

MacLeish needs the manuscript of the Library *lecture*[2] for printing. I can't send him the copy I am using. But didn't Miss O'Hara[3] make one or two carbons of her copy? I would be most grateful if she would send them to me, for I also need a copy for Fish Armstrong[4] or *The Atlantic. The Protestant* is also asking for it and is a possibility. But I must revise the manuscript for print.

I hope that you are altogether well again. At times I feel exhausted, but I am healthy and so far have not even caught a cold.

TO BERTOLT BRECHT

Pacific Palisades, California
December 10, 1943

My dear Herr Brecht:

I have read your letter with close attention. May I reply to it as follows.

In the middle of November I delivered a political lecture[1] at Columbia University in New York. A thousand people came to hear me, but—this is truly strange and, I suppose, truly German—among them was not a single one of the gentlemen with whom I was to hold tentative

[2] "The War and the Future," translated into English by Agnes E. Meyer.

[3] Mrs. Meyer's secretary of many years standing.

[4] Hamilton Fish Armstrong (b. 1893), American diplomat, author, editor. Editor of *Foreign Affairs* since 1928. Author of *Hitler's Reich—The First Phase* (1933); *Can We Be Neutral?* (1936) with A. W. Dulles; *When There Is No Peace* (1939); *The Calculated Risk* (1947); *Those Days* (1963), among others.

[1] "The New Humanism" (November 16, 1943).

consultations concerning a union of the anti-Hitler German exiles. One might have imagined that at least one or two of them would have been interested in the political statements of a man whom they regard as called, even uniquely called, to bring about that union. But not one had sufficient curiosity. If anybody had been present, doubts about where I stand, such as you express in your letter, could not have arisen.

In my lecture I did say that a certain general responsibility for what has happened, and for what may still happen, cannot be denied. For in some sense, all the individuals of a nation are responsible for what they are and do. However, I went on to cite the very arguments you use in your letter against equating what is German with what is Nazi. I also made the point that in our policy toward the defeated enemy, we must take into account the democracies' grave complicity in the rise of Fascist dictatorship, in the growth of its power, and in all the disasters which have come down upon Europe and the world. I spoke of this complicity of the capitalistic democracies in phrases which I thought would scarcely be accepted, let alone greeted with loud applause, as was actually the case. I have even poked a little fun at the bourgeois world's idiotic panic over Communism—have done so not only in New York but also in Washington, on the premises of the Library of Congress. I have said that it is not proper for us German refugees to give advice to tomorrow's victors on how to treat Germany, but I appealed to America's liberals and expressed the hope that our joint future will not be too heavily burdened by the measures taken by the victorious powers. It was not Germany or the German people who must be destroyed and sterilized, I said, but the guilt-laden power combination of Junkers, army officers, and industrialists, which has been responsible for two world wars. That is what should be destroyed. All hope, I said, rests upon a genuine and purifying German revolution, which the victors should not try to prevent but should instead favor and promote.

Such was the message of that lecture, and I hope you and your friends gather from these words that I am certainly not using the influence I possess in America to increase doubts of the "existence of strong democratic forces in Germany." But all this has nothing to do with the question which has seriously occupied me for weeks: whether or not the moment has come to set up a *Free Germany Committee* in America. I have become convinced that the formation of such a body would be premature. I have come to this conclusion not only because members of the State Department think it premature and do not want it now, but also out of my own reflections and experiences. The fact is—and if I remember rightly, it was discussed at our last meeting—that as soon as the public hears rumors of such a German group, uneasiness and mistrust arise among the representatives of the different European nations, and immediately the word goes out that any such German ring must be quashed. It is not only possible but probable that our union would be viewed as nothing but a patriotic effort to shield Germany from the consequences of her crimes. If we come forward now to excuse and defend Germany and call for a "strong German democracy," we would seem to be affronting the feelings of the nations which are groaning and almost crushed under the Nazi yoke. It is too soon to pose German demands and to appeal to the world's emotions in favor of a country which still has Europe in her power and whose capability for crime has by no means been shattered. Horrors can and probably will still take place, and they in turn will arouse the world's horror of this nation. Where will we be, if we have prematurely vouched for the victory of the better and higher impulses within Germany? Let her military defeat take place, let the hour ripen when the Germans themselves settle accounts with the villains with a thoroughness, a ruthlessness such as the world scarcely dares to hope for from our unrevolutionary people. That will be the moment for us on the outside to testify that Germany is free, that Germany has truly cleansed herself, that Germany must live.

1944

———————————————— • ————————————————

TO AGNES E. MEYER

Pacific Palisades
January 7, 1944

Dearest friend:

I am rather worried at not having heard from you for so long, not knowing where you are and how you feel. The aftereffects of the grippe can be so bad; a nervous depression is almost unavoidable. Have you overcome it? Has my post-Christmas letter reached you in Washington or at some Southern resort, or perhaps not at all?

What I wanted to tell you is that day before yesterday we took our citizenship examination and shall soon be, like our sons and grandsons, *cives romani*, for the final swearing-in still to come is only a formality. As a matter of fact, so was the recent procedure, though it was a very long one. We were at the bureau for almost four hours, although much of that time was devoted to waiting and to the hearing of witnesses. But our examination also was no joke, especially mine, since unlike Katia I had not studied for it. I was fairly knowledgeable about the form of government, the Constitution, and the administrative spheres, but when the lady conducting the examination began to talk about the administration and legislation of the states and cities, I proved to be utterly ignorant and could only display great astonishment at the autonomous powers of these communes—since I had to display something: "What, are you bold enough to make your own laws? I hope very much that they are in full harmony with the Federal laws and the Constitution."[1] She repressed a smile at this solicitude *faute de mieux*. I made my greatest hit with her in answering the question of why we had two Houses and not just a House of Representatives. That was primarily a matter of justice, I said, so that the smaller states, which send only a few congressmen, would not

[1] In English.

be at a disadvantage vis-à-vis the large states, since each is represented by two senators. *"That is a very persuasive answer,"* she said, astounded at the mixture of cleverness and ignorance I represented; and when we stood before the judge it turned out that she had slipped him a copy of *Buddenbrooks* so that I could write something in it for her. The judge thought what I wrote in it so touching that he was gripped by jealousy and insisted on having a dedication of his own, if only on a piece of paper, for which purpose he led me into his private office.

That's how it went. Afterwards we and our witnesses, Professor Horkheimer[2] and his wife, had a vigorous American meal in a restaurant, *pancakes with maple syrup, and coffee.* He told me that when they asked him on his honor and conscience whether I would be a desirable citizen he had answered: *"You bet."*

I have had an official letter from friend Archie in which he conveys to me the glad news that thanks to the generosity of certain patrons of the Library, he is in a position to extend my relationship with that institution for another year. Was I inclined to consent to the extension? I wrote back that he might believe it or not, but I didn't even have to think over the question and joined with him in feelings of gratitude toward those patrons. Wasn't that a lovely ceremony? [. . .]

I have at last received the proofs of *Joseph the Provider* from New York and am sending them to you. May you read them in the best of health and with forbearance for the boring parts of the book. Such an epical cake simply cannot consist of nothing but raisins. For me it all lies far in the past and scarcely interests me any longer. My concern now is with Adrian Leverkühn and the problem of how to make the musical technicalities that come thrusting forward *readable.* What is involved are such matters as polyphony in modern, essentially homophonic, harmonic instrumental music—for example, in Brahms and already in Bach. It is not genuine polyphony, inasmuch as it does not have real independence of the voices, as in the old vocal music. All that occurs is a transference of the polyphonic style to the thorough-bass technique, in which the middle voices function only as chord material. Adrian is already wrestling with such problems in his last year at secondary school.

---

[2] Max Horkheimer (b. 1895), philosopher and sociologist. Emigrated to France in 1933, to the United States in 1939. Taught at the New School for Social Research. Returned to Germany in 1949 to become *Rektor* of Frankfurt University and subsequently professor of sociology there. Author of *Studien über Autorität und Familie* (Paris, 1936), *Eclipse of Reason* (New York; 1947), *Studies in Prejudice* (New York; 1949), and others. Editor of *Zeitschrift für Sozialforschung* (1934–9) and *Studies in Philosophy and Social Science* (New York; 1940–2).

A cable has just come from Klaus; he has reached his overseas destination safely.

What will we witness in the months to come? The assault upon Europe is the most stupendous military undertaking in all history, and it is the peace-loving nations who have to undertake it. If it succeeds, we will have proof that it is not necessary to affirm war ideologically in order to accomplish tremendous things in it.

Warmly,

TO ROBERT SHERWOOD[1]

[Original in English]

Pacific Palisades
January 27, 1944

My dear Robert Sherwood:

I still owe you my thanks for the kind letter with which you answered my request concerning my son Klaus. It is probably due to your influence that his wish was fulfilled shortly afterwards. Since the first days of January he is overseas. We have already heard from him after his arrival in North Africa, where he stopped on his way to his destination. I just wanted to let you know about this, as you have shown such kind interest in the fate of the young man.

Gratefully yours,

TO AGNES E. MEYER

Pacific Palisades
February 16, 1944

My good friend:

I should like to know when you last heard from your son, and whether you have some idea where he is. I confess that not a day passes without my worrying about him, for your sake and his, and wondering how he is—I think of your feelings as a mother and tremble, as I do for my own wife. As far as I know, Bill is part of the Fifth Army, which seems to be in constant action in exposed positions. I was also tormented and worried by the news that American field hospitals had been bombarded. He could so easily be working in one of them. What a life for us all, with tragedy

---

[1] Robert Sherwood (1896–1955), the playwright, at this time held the office of Coordinator of Information.

so close every moment. The report that a son of Harry Hopkins[1] has been killed also gave me a stab of fright. I know that you have had direct news from Bill, and heard more about how he distinguished himself during the landing in Sicily, from a friend of his on leave. But that is some time ago. Have you received any letters since that friend's visit? I ask also because we would like to know at what intervals approximately you and Eugene hear from your soldier. You see, our eldest, who must also be engaged somewhere in that vicinity,[2] has been completely silent since the cable about his arrival.

I have not yet written to Knopf about the translation and probably no longer need to, since he says he will be visiting here in the near future. We can then discuss pending questions, and in any case, I shall ask him not to make any premature arrangements with someone else in regard to the translation. I shall tell him, as I do you, that the novel is an uncertain, far-reaching matter, and that we shall have plenty of time to make decisions about it. I am writing away at it slowly, without knowing whether or not certain passages will stand. The young adept has broken with music for the present and is studying theology in Halle—a broad field and a strange one. I keep being interrupted by outside demands which I find hard to refuse: I have just finished an article on Bruno Walter's fiftieth anniversary as a conductor, for the *New York Times Magazine*.[3]

Your comments on Joseph IV gave me a great lift. It is astonishing enough that under the present circumstances you managed to *read* the book. But you must never feel obligated to *write* about it—only if the desire to do so *est plus forte que vous*. Of course I am delighted that you have hopes of the book's being a publishing success. It is certainly an encouraging sign that the judges of the book club had confidence in it. To be sure, people greatly overestimate the wealth such a choice brings to me. For the present (since Knopf receives half of everything) it is merely $12,000—a useful sum, of course. It *may* double, even triple. But that depends on whether the judges have correctly divined the taste of the public. [. . .]

Golo gives a fabulous account of his army experience. He spent several weeks under the most primitive conditions in woods and fields

---

[1] Harry Hopkins (1890–1946), Secretary of Commerce, 1938–40; head of the War Production Board during the Second World War; Roosevelt's close associate and adviser.

[2] Unknown to his parents, Klaus Mann, with the Fifth Army in Italy, had been the only one in his training camp to volunteer for a number of hazardous missions.

[3] "Mission of Music. Tribute to Bruno Walter," *New York Times Magazine* (March 19, 1944).

somewhere. Suddenly he is ordered to report to Washington, i.e., to stand on a certain street corner and when a car stops to ask: "Is this the car of Mrs. Smith?" He is then taken into the car and whisked to a wonderful Mount Kisco-like country house, a palace with a large library, where he is set to studying along with a number of other bespectacled men, in order to become an instructor. Fantastic!

More American than anything you can possibly tell me about the light and dark sides of American civilization is the following item from the *front page* of the *Los Angeles Times*:

Bird to Sing at Funeral

Tacoma (Wash.) Feb. 14. Dickie, his pet canary, will sing, accompanied by a harpist, at funeral services to-morrow for John D. Dilderoy, 73.

I laughed till the tears came when I read that at breakfast, and went to my desk with my eyes still wet.

Cordially,

Yours,
T. M.

TO HARRY SLOCHOWER

Pacific Palisades
February 18, 1944

Dear Mr. Slochower:

Many thanks for sending me your essay.[1] It has helped bring me closer to Dewey's philosophy, something I badly needed.

I was extraordinarily struck by the quotation *"that ideas have been in fact only reflections of practical measures—so that what passes as psychology was a brand of political doctrine."*

What realism! Or, I suppose, what it really comes down to is a distrust of ideology. A strain of which we all have. It is easy to say: There will be no more wars when the capitalist economic system has collapsed. But after all we have experienced, can we doubt that come what may, human beings will find pretexts for slaughtering one another? Which is no reason not to speak in favor of socialism. But socialism too will probably not bring peace; that is more likely to be accomplished by

[1] "John Dewey, Philosopher of the Possible," *Sewanee Review* (Winter 1944).

physics through the unleashing of the uranium atom, for then the game will really be in deadly earnest.

I still regret we could not fit in a visit to Brooklyn during that trip. Nowadays there is no longer time enough for many things—let's hope there will be enough for that damnably difficult novel—one more novel! —which I have foolishly let myself in for.

All the best,

TO LION FEUCHTWANGER

Pacific Palisades
April 1944

Dear Lion Feuchtwanger:

It strikes me as quite amusing that I should be speaking to you via New York on this fine handmade paper,[1] and should be offering you my congratulations on your sixtieth birthday in this fashion, when we are after all neighbors on this faintly unreal coast and I have the pleasure of seeing you fairly often. Nor is anything going to stop me from personally calling at your palace by the sea on July 7 to give an encouraging handshake to my young colleague—my Lord, I was already sixty when Hitler was in the Maytime of his sins. That will be better than writing to you. But I would not want to be absent when the literary world gathers to pay collective homage between handsome covers, to you and your richly blessed life, although on holidays one would prefer not to be what one is on all other days: to wit, a writer formulating thoughts, weighing words.

Let me make it short and sweet! Let it be more a handshake than a congratulatory essay. It will scarcely have escaped your keen observation that I like you and by preference seek your conversation when we are in company together. That's easily explained. You are a dear, communicative person, a—forgive the word—simple-hearted soul whose good Munich speech produces a sense of well-being. You are in addition a knowledgeable, experienced person from whom one can learn things. And you have produced a varied, vigorous body of work, historically sound and clear and keen in its criticism of our own era—a blessed body of work which from the very start has won the widest sympathetic interest, first in Germany, then throughout the East and West, in Russia as well as in the Anglo-Saxon countries. In England, when people wish to give high praise to a book, I myself have heard them say: "It's nearly as good as Feuchtwanger."

---

[1] *Aufbau*, the New York newspaper, had sent out sheets of fine paper to friends of Feuchtwanger for their handwritten contributions, which were to be presented to the writer in an album.

Your life has always moved me to admiration and affection. You were born to fortune and success; the pair will never desert you. You are an encouraging example of the way in which the brightness of an individual's destiny wins out against the gloom of circumstances. The age has affected you, as it has all of us. You have suffered losses and calumny, have been torn from your roots, have gone through personal dangers—but I have never heard you speak of these things other than with laughter, and everything has turned out well for you. I think you were the first who contrived to establish in exile a more than worthy, a brilliant home. That was in Sanary-sur-mer, where together we spent the first months after our discharge as German writers. I would have liked to lead Goebbels through your rooms while I pointed out the view, so that he would eat his heart out. Now, untiringly active, an honored guest of this wide, already homelike country, you wait for the end of the idiotic episode which calls itself National Socialism—whose coming, you can well say, you did your best to avert. Since you are only sixty, young man, you will, unlike the undersigned, go on quite a way into what comes after. Whether I shall be very much the loser is a question we had both better leave aside. Unless all appearances are deceptive, we shall both witness the downfall of that disgraceful, murderous nonsense that expelled us from Germany. We shall celebrate its passing together and, each in his own hour, depart from life with the reassuring knowledge that, though all kinds of dubious literary phenomena are possible on the planet whose passing acquaintance we made, the utter limit of stupidity and baseness could not, after all, maintain itself more than a bare dozen years.

TO ERNST REUTER [1]

Pacific Palisades
April 29, 1944

My dear Herr Doktor Reuter:

Let me inform you, with gratitude, that your moving letter reached my hands safely, and that the copy, along with the pamphlet containing your memorable speech on Hauptmann, followed it soon after.

I am pressed by work and affairs, as well as somewhat weakened by a bronchial catarrh I brought back with me from Chicago—climatically a terrible place. But let me reply as follows:

[1] Ernst Reuter (1889–1953), Social Democrat politician. Mayor of Magdeburg in 1931. Emigrated to Turkey in 1933; 1939–45 professor of community science in Ankara. In 1947 Reuter became Mayor of Berlin, in 1951 Mayor of West Berlin.

For reasons of conscience and tact, I am repelled by a certain German refugee patriotism which has developed in the midst of the war. At a time when the enemy is still dangerously strong, when the gravest sacrifices must still be made if he is to be defeated, there are exiles who stand, as it were, with arms outspread in front of Germany, proclaiming that nothing unpleasant must be done to this country, since after all Germany has made the most remarkable contributions to Europe. At this moment, when we have so dim a picture of present-day Germany and of the forces within it which are still vitally concerned with the cause of freedom, I consider it premature—and as a German I regard it as unseemly—to give advice and prescribe courses of action to the men who, after the still-distant victory, will have to take those measures they judge necessary for securing the peace. The attitude of certain politically active refugees suggests not the slightest awareness of what Germany has inflicted, and continues to inflict, upon other nations. These refugees seem to feel not the slightest concern that they may be offending the all too justified feelings of those countries. Such people are warning against imposing an unwise and unjust peace upon Germany. My opinion is, on the contrary, that while a certain kind of peace imposed upon Germany might be unwise (and we must hope that the victors will show moderation and foresight), there simply cannot be such a thing as an unjust peace for Germany, after all that has happened.

This is my conviction, and I must act on it even though I incur only enmity by so doing. Or rather, I must avoid actions which are contradictory to it. But although I am on the point of becoming an American citizen and am surrounded by English-speaking children and grandchildren, I am and remain a German—for all the dubious honor and sublime misfortune this may signify. I am determined never to be unfaithful to the German language, to continue my life work to the end in it; and I long for nothing more than the moment when Europe will once again be open to my work and when I can once again enter into communication with those of my countrymen who still know and want to know something of me. You may be sure that whatever moral and spiritual weight I have, as you say, to throw into the scales will be at the disposal of the country in whose culture I am rooted, if there emerges from this war a matured, purged, penitent Germany that has forsworn the sinful and antihuman delusion of superiority which drove her into this catastrophe.

With my best wishes and regards,

1944

TO JOHN EASTMAN, JR. [1]

[*Original in English*]

Pacific Palisades
May 11, 1944

Dear Mr. Eastman:

Many thanks for your kind and detailed letter. I remember our meeting with such pleasure that I was very happy to hear from you again.

Your wish is very touching. But the way you suggest it, we cannot possibly do things. The gift of money which you received would hardly suffice to pay for one of my big manuscripts, some of which are already in the possession of American university libraries. Anyhow, money transactions between the two of us are not quite in place. Therefore, I am sending you, as a token of friendship, a few pages which I wrote a short time ago for an American periodical. The article is called "Vom Buch der Bücher und von Joseph" ("About the Book of Books and about Joseph"), and deals with my relation to the Bible and with the conception of the extensive work whose final volume will be published by Knopf next month. Of course, you cannot read my handwriting—but that would not be possible for you with one of my big manuscripts, either, and this way you have at least something authentic by me in your hands. It is a pleasant thought for me that you are the possessor of a small manuscript of mine.

Our stay in Chicago was marred a little by bad weather, but being together with our family there was a great joy. Elisabeth, the former "Kindchen," has very easily and happily become a mother for the second time, and during our visit was already well on the way to recovery.

Klaus is in Italy and writes that he has interesting and satisfying work. I am giving you his address below. Of course, he will be very happy to hear from you. Erika was scheduled to be in London by now, but her departure from New York suffered a delay, and she still seems to be staying there. Our second son, Gottfried, who is an American soldier in London, is expecting her longingly.

Please accept my best wishes for your well-being, and convey my kindest regards also to your mother.

---

[1] John Eastman, Jr., as a young man read Klaus Mann's *The Turning Point* and poured out his heart to the author in a sixteen-page letter. He subsequently met Klaus, and later the elder Manns. An ardent collector of Manniana, he donated his collection to the Colby Library in 1966.

1944

TO F. W. BRADLEY[1]

[Original in English]

Pacific Palisades
May 20, 1944

Dear Dean Bradley:

You have really given me a great pleasure with your interesting letter which bespeaks such wide knowledge of the German people and so much good will to understand it. Neither for me, the German, nor for you, the American, is it easy today to cling to this good will and to the hope that a Germany will emerge from this war that has become wiser and more mature through her dreadful experience.

What you write about German fidelity contains much psychological truth, although the word fidelity can, under certain circumstances, lose its dignity and beauty, namely if applied to the hopeless submissiveness to a regime of the boundless vulgarity of the National Socialist. The senseless lion's courage with which the German people's army continues to fight for the victory and perpetuation of this regime is a constant mystery and sorrow to me. I think you feel the same way. It is rather mortifying that not even today, when it is already rather late, are there men in Germany who have the strength and determination to lead the German people out of this horrible dead-end street. I am fearing more and more that a German revolution, if it comes, will come too late to possess any morally rehabilitating value, but will be a mere sign of utter collapse. Today, it is hard for a German who is rooted in the German culture and who intends to remain faithful to the German tongue, to look into the future of his country. However, the possibilities of change and regeneration of a whole people are great and unforeseeable, and therefore we shouldn't lose heart.

With repeated thanks and kind regards,

TO CAROLINE NEWTON

Pacific Palisades
June 9, 1944

Dear Miss Caroline:

You have showered me, or rather us, with precious gifts! Katia promptly pronounced her famous, "Tommy, you must," and so I am writing, and

---

[1] F. W. Bradley (b. 1884) was at this time dean of the University of South Carolina. He is noted for his studies of South Carolina place names and dialect.

would have done so without that. But my warm thanks must be expressed briefly, for people gave me a great deal to do on the 6th. The higher one's age rises, the more one is admired for, so it would seem, having stuck it out so long upon this planet. It does testify to a remarkably thick skin.

The day was certainly given a most dramatic accent by the apparently successful start of what we scarcely dared to believe in and what nevertheless had to come. Certainly the beginning was not the easiest part of the whole, and it means a good deal that it has succeeded. But for all that, it is only a beginning, and a gigantic piece of work still faces the stormers of Europe—who, to be sure, are giants themselves.

Let us hope. I have always wished so passionately that there would be peace on my seventieth birthday. I realize now that the wish can come true, at least as far as Europe is concerned.

We had no children and grandchildren with us on the day, and asked only a few good friends over for dinner. Erika is in England. If she was not in one of the first invasion bombers, that can only be because ladies were not admitted.

All the best to you, and our thanks once again.

TO KLAUS MANN

Pacific Palisades
June 25, 1944

Dear soldier—son:

This is to thank you for your interesting parcel of the end of April, especially for the letter, which I straightway took for a birthday letter and would have liked to thank you for promptly, at least after the highly dramatic accent June 6th was given. I must apologize to you, as to so many others, on the grounds of the illness that attacked me soon after the day, certain *intestinal troubles*, a kind of stomach and intestinal *flu* which is going the rounds here. Mielein, too, had a nasty touch of it for several days. It makes one very weak and depressed.

I had already seen the *Lettres* at some time or other, but there certainly is something special about it with the fragrance of Casablanca between the pages. I have shown your description of the ghostly round-dance to many people. It strikes me as more pitiable than horrible. They are carrying on German cultural life and do not realize what a quandary they are in. That Pree,[1] enormously intelligent as he is, should pick this of all times to go to Hungary and dither there about the "subtleties" of

[1] Emil Preetorius.

Far Eastern art is evidence of the torpor of their minds. And Godfather Drosselmeyer[2] with the Rhineland Poetry Prize! It's all too dreary.

You've heard all about us, of course, from Mielein. Day before yesterday we became American citizens. The newspapers published pictures and *stories*; it was also reported on the radio; and I hear that today, Sunday, there is to be an *editorial* on it in the *Washington Post*, at the same time as Ag's review of the *Provider*. My conscience twinged slightly on account of the dear Czechs, and I probably ought to write a letter to Beneš. But as everything stands, this step was right and necessary, not only to meet my obligations and the general expectations, but also because my Germanism is best sheltered in this great cosmopolitan community. Besides, I imagine that we shall be staying here. Of course I promise myself that many interesting things will come out of Europe, with France playing a major role in the life of the mind. But not many more of these developments will fall within my lifetime, and before they do come, something tells me, we still have some ordeals before us. The Nazis are determined to bring down with them everything in Europe they can lay hold of, and if we let them go ahead out of our tenderness toward Germany, they will wreak the maximum of destruction—and we will be partly to blame. How long will the war go on, and what will be left of the cities and countryside, if they defend every place all the way to Berlin as they are now defending Cherbourg? Is it conceivable that the German soldier will quit once Paris has fallen? Yes, you don't know the answers any more than I do.

Old Hesse (who, incidentally, is a few years younger than I) has completed his *The Bead Game*, and the two volumes have reached me. Passing strange. Takes place in a future after an era of wars and revolutions, in an artistic and scholarly utopia. The aged hero finally dies while swimming after a boy in too cold water. Just as I expected. At the same time there is no lack of almost alarming kinships with Adrian, and curiously enough a certain Master Thomas von der Trave,[3] who goes at things even more elegantly and ironically than "Joseph Knecht," plays a part in the book. Very mystifying.

Whether I shall finish with my own is something that, aptly enough, the devil alone knows. This biography of mine will be somewhat brasher and have more of the immediacy of life, I think, than Knecht's; but

---

[2] This was an occasional nickname in the Mann household for Ernst Bertram, who was in fact Elisabeth Mann's godfather. The name was taken from a story by E. T. A. Hoffmann.

[3] Lübeck, Thomas Mann's birthplace, is situated on the Trave River.

never has there been anything so easy to bungle, and the difficulties are mounting. Did I really have to load something of this sort on myself? But then again, how is one to pass the time otherwise? I already have more than 250 pages, of uneven value.

May you keep *well*! I would be happy to see you a lieutenant, for you deserve it.

Yours,

Z.

TO AGNES E. MEYER

Pacific Palisades
July 17, 1944

Dear friend:

I am much moved by your account of your reading of the *Betrachtungen*. Yes, I suffered quite a bit at the time, and for that reason the book has always remained secretly dear to me. In part, too, it is surprisingly witty out of sheer agony. American intellectuals might by now be "ripe" for it, for they are thoroughly tired of what they call my democratic Sunday sermons, and I would make more of a literary splash with the *Betrachtungen*. I realized once again how tired they are from the review of the *Provider* in the latest issue of *The Nation*;[1] it was apparent from the very first lines. The article, incidentally, is an honest piece of work. If only I knew how it comes about that I give the impression of Olympian arrogance. Basically all I want is to make people laugh, and for the rest I am the soul of laborious modesty.

I am sending you my reply to the letter in *The Atlantic*[2] in German. It naturally has a drier effect in the translation prepared here by Professor Arlt,[3] although Edward Weeks[4] of *The Atlantic* thought it "admirable." After all is done, it seems to me that I might rather have passed over the thing in silence. But perhaps it is just as well that I've said this once and for all, so that when such idiocies crop up again I can confront them with this reply.

[1] "The One and the Many: *Joseph the Provider*" by William Phillips (July 1944).

[2] Thomas Mann had published an article, "What Is German?" in *The Atlantic* (May 1944). This was attacked by Henri Peyre, professor of French at Yale, in the July issue. Mann's reply, "In My Defense," appeared in the October issue and was in turn answered by Peyre in the December issue.

[3] Gustave Arlt (b. 1895), then professor of German at the University of California, Los Angeles. Translator of Franz Werfel's play, *Jakobowski and the Colonel* (1944) and Werfel's novel, *Star of the Unborn*, among others.

[4] Edward A. Weeks (b. 1898), writer, editor, critic. Editor-in-chief of *The Atlantic*.

The chapter I told you about[5] is very decent and only a little eerie. I have no qualms about giving it to you to read. You will receive it as soon as it has been copied, along with the preceding chapters which belong with it.

A lady professor at Hunter College, Miss Anna Jacobson, is spending a semester's vacation here—she has taken this time off to write a book about "me." Why shouldn't she? It is an occupation *comme une autre*. Incidentally, it is not a biography. I see her sometimes to answer her questions, but cannot take any responsibility for the work in progress.

I am proud of your great success in Pittsburgh! But I don't like the picture. It is always an indiscretion to photograph a speaker, let alone a woman speaker, in the midst of the performance, with open mouth and heated eyes. I should have made some objections to that in the *Betrachtungen*. But one can't think of everything.

The Germans are pitiable. Golo and Klaus, who have to read their newspapers, sometimes send us gleanings. The populace is hoping for a miracle. A scientist is said to be working on a method for reducing New York to ashes within five minutes. "Only power," the newspapers say, "creates popularity. Since we have been sending the robot bombs across the Channel, we are loved again. The German people accompanies each of the hell-hounds with its heartfelt blessings." Unfortunate beings! But I am convinced that they will defend "Germany" to the last, and at the very end will wreak horrible havoc. There also exists an NN Plan. NN means *nach der Niederlage* [after the defeat]. Let us steel ourselves for what is to come!

Yours,
T. M.

---

[5] Thomas Mann had written in a letter to Agnes Meyer of July 6: "I actually wrote something good during my illness: Adrian's relationship to the prostitute from whom, although she has warned him, he contracts the disease, whereupon two doctors to whom he turns are eliminated by the devil. It is very gripping and mysterious. Bruno Frank thought it magnificent. The initial motif of the tropical butterflies ('Hetaera Esmeralda') recurs in it."

TO CLARA ZEMPLÉNYI NEUMANN[1]

Pacific Palisades
July 20, 1944

My dear Frau Neumann:

I have received your letter, and it has moved me deeply. I wholeheartedly share your feelings concerning what is happening to the Jews of Europe. Your horror, your shudders, your hatred—all that has been only too familiar to me for a long time. I have let no opportunity pass to say publicly how I feel and to try to arouse the conscience of the world. Only recently I wrote a contribution for a book dedicated to the Jewish leader Chaim Weizmann[2] which expressed my reverence for Judaism and my detestation of the crimes being committed against the Jewish people.

Now you call upon me to demand reprisals or the threat of reprisals in order to save the unfortunate Hungarian Jews. But you must consider that such measures represent a very grave moral problem. It is a big question whether the Allied nations, as fighters for freedom and humanitarianism, can allow themselves to descend to the level of an enemy so morally depraved as the Nazis, and to follow that enemy on the path of inhumanity. They have already been obliged to follow him a good part of the way, and have given him the diabolic satisfaction of seeing them involved in his blood-guilt. The Nazis, driven into a corner as they are, behave like desperados who have become utterly ruthless. They would answer measures such as you propose with similar measures, and perhaps quench their thirst for blood on American and English prisoners of war. Thus it might go on, one crime always evoking the next. Already it is difficult to see how, after everything that has happened, the nations will be able to live together after this war. The whole world bears the tremendous guilt of having, out of weakness, apathy, and even a certain sympathy, permitted Fascism and National Socialism to grow. Now it is engaged in a life-and-death struggle with them, and the annihilation of the enemy is the only way to put an end to the crimes. In response to your demand I can only reply that I would assent, though in silence and with shudders of horror, if measures such as you propose were undertaken in order to protect the 800,000 Jews. But as an individual and as a writer with a sense of responsibility, I do not feel able to call for such measures.

[1] Clara Zemplényi Neumann (1893–1960), Hungarian writer, at this time living in exile in Argentina.
[2] Chaim Weizmann (1874–1952), Jewish scholar and Zionist leader, first president of the new State of Israel (1948–1952).

1944

TO EDUARD BENEŠ

Pacific Palisades
July 29, 1944

My dear Mr. President:

It is a long time since I have had the honor and pleasure of meeting you, but often, during the cataclysms of recent years, my thoughts have been with you, and more than once I wanted to write to assure you of my lasting attachment, gratitude, and respect, and to tell you that my satisfaction at the turn of events has always been very largely determined by the thought of you and your country. But I knew that you were occupied with affairs of state, with travels—and what travels, with such importance for the future!—and I did not want to burden you. Now a change that could not have been foreseen in earlier times has taken place in my personal life and provides me with an opportunity to assure you of my unchanging and unchangeable loyalty and devotion.

My news is that my wife and I, after living in this country more than six years, have acquired American citizenship.

This is the outcome of a natural and unforced process of taking root in this soil, in a country which granted me honorable and generous hospitality after Europe became uninhabitable for people of my sort. Today I have two sons in the army, who by that fact are American citizens. One daughter is American by marriage, and I have American-born, English-speaking grandchildren growing up who, like their parents, will probably belong to this country forever. I myself am linked to quite a number of American universities by honorary degrees, and as consultant in Germanic literature I am attached to the staff of the Library of Congress, so that I am an American civil servant, as it were. I earn my living here as a writer and *lecturer*, but chiefly from my books which, painfully enough, have existed only in English translations for all these years. The expectation that I should not permanently enjoy the advantages of American life merely as a guest, but should take my stand as a citizen, was unmistakable, unanswerable, and psychologically justifiable. For as things stand today, is not my kind of Germanism best sheltered in the cosmopolitan universe which is called America? The idea of returning to Germany has long been very remote from me. The country, as an empirical reality (although not, of course, as a concept), repels me; I feel estranged from it and will be satisfied if my life work is once again accessible to those of my former countrymen who still can respond to it— I fear there will not be many left. In this respect I am counting more on

France, the land of the Czechs, Switzerland—in short, on *Europe*—which I am convinced will still remain the beacon of the world. I look to Germany only insofar as she may be capable of spiritually joining the new Europe.

Naturally I long to walk on European soil again, to breathe European air. But as far as I can foresee my future, I shall do so only as a visitor. I do not think that in the long run I shall turn my back upon this country, whose libertarian traditions and humanly beneficent atmosphere I sincerely appreciate. And I do not think I shall give up the home I have built here by the Pacific, the home which I have come to love and which is so favorable for my work.

But I must tell you, my dear Mr. President, that I have not taken this step without sorrow in my heart and faltering in my conscience. My life has made the step logical, but it could easily appear as ingratitude toward you and your lovable country, which made so handsome a gesture in granting me citizenship when my German citizenship was taken from me. The decree that I was no longer a German was too nonsensical to hurt me; but leaving the Czech community does hurt me, and what I should like to ask you is that you regard it, as I do, rather as a development than as an action.

When I think of the possibility of visiting Europe again, I look forward to paying my respects to you, Mr. President, at the Hradschin in Prague, as I have done several times previously. I shall not do so as a Czech citizen, to be sure, but as the citizen of a country that has contributed decisively to the liberation of your people, who have passed through such terrible suffering.

In sincere devotion,

TO BRUNO WALTER

Pacific Palisades
August 16, 1944

Dear Bruno Walter:

I am dictating these lines to Katia, so that we can jointly thank our dear old (and great) friend for his good letter of last month. Our thanks have been postponed all too long, chiefly because of a busy round of family visits, which have made heavy demands on Katia in particular. Not only was Michael's little family from San Francisco here (it's already a quartet), but Katia's brother Peter joined the party. He is on the point of exchanging his university post in Chicago for a scientific and industrial job in Pasadena.

Now all the birds have flown, which is both a relief and a loss. That is especially true of the grandchildren, who once again delighted our hearts—I need scarcely add that this time, too, it was charming and whimsical little Frido who occupied, amused, and moved us. I had to do a great deal of drawing for him, busses, palm trees, and railroads, and tell him stories—that is to say, one and the same story over and over: about the colored cook Myrtle and how she is so tired after washing dishes that she puts on her pink bathrobe, lies down on the bed, and snores. This snoring must be acted out in a special way, and must never vary. I was beginning to think I was thoroughly sick of it, but now I miss it.

Michael brought a great deal of music into the house, which suited me personally very well indeed. We had many string quartets, with extra guests and buffet dinners that Katia produced virtually by magic. The players were excellent. I need only mention Temianka[1] and van den Burg,[2] and Bibi also handled the viola very well. We heard wonderful things; a Mozart quartet particularly has remained with me, one of the six dedicated to Haydn—he seems to have taken special pains with those, and so of course they turned into something major. I had the chance to hear Beethoven's *Opus* 132 a second and third time—a tremendous work, tremendous especially in the lyrical movement and the indescribable last movement.

As for the other children, we hear frequently from Klaus as well as Golo. The latter is still doing intelligence work in London, but his last letter said that he hoped soon to be sent to France, where my former secretary, Katzenellenbogen, has been active since the beginning of the invasion. Klaus always sounds in good spirits and full of confidence, although at times the heat and the plague of flies in Italy must have been bad. The food and the supply of cigarettes seem also to have been rather unsatisfactory. What chiefly saddens him, he wrote, is the sight of the many beautiful old towns that have been badly shot up, and the misery of the populace, which apparently cannot yet be adequately relieved. You have probably had direct news about Erika through Lotte.[3] She does not write us often, but we know she is rushing back and forth between

---

[1] Henri Temianka, internationally known American violinist; conductor of the Temianka Little Symphony Orchestra, 1956–60.

[2] Willem van den Burg, Dutch cellist and conductor. For a long time first cellist of the Philadelphia orchestra under Stokowski; later active in San Francisco as a conductor and in Hollywood in movie work.

[3] Bruno Walter's daughter.

London and Normandy, and we read a small article of hers about her meeting and talks with the wounded. Whether this whole undertaking is worth the danger involved is something we parents, with our tendency to restrain, cannot judge. Her urge to be in the thick of things was overwhelming, and her impressions will certainly be useful for her lecturing once she is back safe and sound—which God grant. This prayer applies more than ever to our dutiful sons; indeed, what grief one feels for every life that must still be sacrificed. [. . .]

We are very eager, dear friend, to see the fruits of your year of rest—which in an intellectual sense has scarcely been that. There is hardly a book to which we have looked forward with such interest as your memoirs,[4] and I am only sorry that I cannot help out by finding the splendid congratulations you sent me that time. Those papers are resting quietly, well preserved in a box, somewhere in Oprecht's warehouse in Zurich. But you can surely take steps: you need only ask my New York literary agent, Dr. Franz Horch, 141 West 73rd Street, whom you probably know—I'm sure Lotte does. Recently he performed the amazing feat of finding in the *Public Library* an old essay of mine in the *Vossische Zeitung*, although I did not know even the approximate year of publication. It will be a simple matter for him to dig up your article from the *Neue Freie Presse*, since you can tell him the exact date it appeared.

We hope the holidays in Maine have done you good and will continue doing so. We have had an unusually cold and foggy summer—in fact, have so far been cheated out of summer. But in the last few days a spell of radiantly beautiful, yet not too hot weather has begun, and once again we are very glad to have settled down here.

I'm sure you understood why I did not send you the English edition of the fourth *Joseph* volume. Bermann's edition has now been published, insofar as one can speak of publication in the circumstances, and I am only waiting for additional copies to arrive to send you yours. I imagine I can mail it to the address on your letter.

Best wishes from house to house for a happy reunion under triumphal circumstances! We have had to wait a long time for what is now impending. But it will be good to depart this world one of these days with the knowledge that on this planet whose passing acquaintance we have made, all sorts of morally objectionable things are possible, but the maximum of stupidity and vileness still was not able to last more than eleven years and was swept away by the united forces of humanity.

[4] Bruno Walter: *Theme and Variations: An Autobiography* (New York: Alfred A. Knopf; 1946).

1944

TO *THE PRESBYTERIAN OUTLOOK*

[*Original in English*]

Pacific Palisades
August 26, 1944

Dear Sir:

When asked on my lecture tours by the gentleman who introduces me
how I like my name to be pronounced, the German or the English way,
I always declare that it should be pronounced the English way, that is:
my first name with a short o, and my last name like "man." Since having
become an American citizen I find this even more correct, and have
always thought it an advantage that my two names, the first as well as
the last one, lend themselves so easily to the English pronunciation. There
are more difficult cases: A former secretary of mine was called Katzenellenbogen. One day when driving his car he was to get a ticket, but
the officer despaired of ascertaining his name and finally let him go.

TO CORPORAL H. G. BIEHL

[*Original in English*]

Pacific Palisades
September 5, 1944

Dear Mr. Biehl:

Thank you so much for your kind letter. I fully understand that you are
disquieted and worried by the experiences you made among your comrades. I still hope that these experiences are not absolutely typical. On the
whole, one cannot say that the cultural life in America has been influenced by a bellicose hatred of everything German. Some books by German
emigrants have been greatly successful, and German music is being
cultivated without any scruples or fault-finding. And how could one do
without it if at all wishing to keep up a musical life?

On the other hand, it is of course not easy for simple people to wage
war and to risk their own lives fighting against a political power that had
become the greatest physical and moral menace, without the belief that
this power in its entirety and all its aspects is hateful and ought to be
destroyed. I must say frankly that I prefer the young American soldiers
who include the anti-fascist Germans in their antipathy to those who are
fascists themselves, which may also happen.

I have taken many an occasion to work on behalf of justice for the

German people, but this is not easy because the whole German people has become implicated in the monstrosities which the present German regime has inflicted on the world. I wish you would read an article I published in the May issue of the *Atlantic Monthly*, and which the editor has given the title "What Is German?" This, for instance, is a work by me in which I try to explain to the democratic world the simultaneous presence of great as well as ruinous features in the German national character. As was to be expected, the article has brought me a number of attacks, because it was interpreted as a recommendation of a soft peace.

That the hate of everything German should increase toward the now foreseeable end of the war is only too understandable in the face of the atrocities committed by the Nazis, and especially in England the conciliatory elements are being silenced by the horror of the robot plague. But we know that after the cessation of hostilities there shall be a cooling-off period before decisions are to be made on the peace to come. And on this period, whose name expresses the intention not to act on violent impulses, we must set our hopes.

TO ALFRED NEUMANN

Pacific Palisades
October 1, 1944

Dear Alfred Neumann:

It was very kind of you to send me Dr. Albersheim's[1] lecture. At bottom we are really interested only in what is "pertinent" at the moment; but our interest in that is feverish. Many thanks! And my thanks also to the author, if the piece was sent with his knowledge. I can well understand that the lecture should have created a stir. It provides much to think about. A *way out* must be found; many among the moderns feel that themselves—for instance, Toch.[2] Granted, the way will scarcely lead back beyond what was preparing in *Tristan* and *Parsifal* and then took its course. As for the *common man*, that's a dubious business: to consciously accommodate music to his desires—which as you know are not

---

[1] Gerhard Albersheim (b. 1902), musicologist. Emigrated from Vienna in 1939 to Scotland; has lived in Los Angeles since 1940, teaching at the Conservatory and at UCLA. Professor of music at Los Angeles State College since 1956. Occasional accompanist for Lotte Lehmann, Ezio Pinza, and Dietrich Fischer-Dieskau, among others. Author of *The Sense of Space in Tonal and Atonal Music* (1960).

[2] Ernst Toch (1887–1964), Austrian composer. Combined traditional, romantic elements with elements of the New Music. Emigrated to the United States in 1935; author of four symphonies, several operas, chamber and choral music.

only reactionary but also beneath the level of the good old things—is something I would think twice about.

Frau Katharina's[3] letter mentioned Camels—let's have them! That is, shouldn't we share them? And if that glorious woman could again dig up a few Pattys, I should be abjectly grateful.

TO MARIANNE LIDDELL[1]

Pacific Palisades
October 8, 1944

My dear Miss Liddell:

Your letter has given me great pleasure. I am always glad to hear from readers of the German edition, although this emergency edition, manufactured in Stockholm without my supervision and photographed in New York, swarms with errors, omissions, etc. Still and all, it is the German rhythm, my own sentences. How I envy music for needing no translation! One must imagine a music that was dependent on something like translation to understand the sadness of my state, and why the 1,800 German copies in America give me more pleasure than the 200,000 in English.

I wonder how the saga will seem as a whole, presented, say, in two volumes, as Knopf intends, and as Bermann will probably also do before long—unless it develops that the Germans' supposed craving to catch up on their reading was a completely mistaken notion. The book always was conceived as a whole, you know, and the division into volumes is more or less a matter of chance. I wonder whether posterity will see it only as a monstrous curiosity, or whether it will be regarded after all rather as a humorous song of humanity, sung in darkest days. Who can know! It's enough that a number of our better contemporaries take pleasure in it.

---

[3] Katharina (Kitty) Neumann, Alfred Neumann's wife. Toward the end of the war cigarettes (Camels) and cigars (Pattys) were in short supply, along with many other articles. Mrs. Neumann had developed such a faculty for obtaining scarce items that Thomas Mann sometimes jestingly called her the "Wonder Hen" because she laid miraculous eggs.
[1] Marianne Liddell (b. 1913), violinist, member of the Adolf Busch chamber orchestra.

TO AGNES E. MEYER

Pacific Palisades
October 11, 1944

Dear friend:

Little or nothing can be said against your criticism of Huxley, sharp though it is, and I am glad that I have decidedly kept my distance from the spirit, the ideology of the book[1] and of the man in general. This spirit is extremely Western European, overripe—decadent, as you cogently say. In Russia he would rapidly be brought to see reason, and we can only assent to America's rejecting him. It would not do for this mystical defeatism to win a following here. I, who have a certain weakness for decadence and feel quite at home in morbidity, taking a kind of pride in an insider's knowledge, was vexed by the total insensitivity of the reviews to the charms of the book *as a novel*—charms which you also must grant. The telephone scene with the former mistress at one end of the line, reading aloud to him from old letters, and the present mistress in the room; the uncle's death; the whole intrigue with the longed-for dress suit and the moral tangle from which the young man can no longer find a way out—all that and other things are new, *daring*, interesting, full of malicious liveliness. One must be a very firmly entrenched moralist simply to reject it out of hand. Yet I don't deny that at every step I was morally offended. Even the fact that the author uses his aversion to all carnality to trick out the story with descriptions of carnal pleasures is disquieting. But his icy coldness about everything that sears us, everything we hate and love, is truly outrageous. An Italian professor who leaves his country and goes into exile because of the dictatorship does not necessarily have to be portrayed as a fool; there must be something to such a man. And the way in which the author draws the exhaustion and disillusionment of a social reformer hardly indicates bitter pessimism or any indictment of this world which is so hard to improve, but is rather a brash, cynical mockery of the idiot who would have done better to think of the salvation of his soul.

It is not at all the book of an Englishman of today. Rather, it seems to have been written ten years ago, when the world did not understand and did not want to understand what events in Italy and Germany meant.

---

[1] Aldous Huxley's *Time Must Have a Stop*. In *The Story of a Novel* (New York: Alfred A. Knopf; 1961), p. 96, Thomas Mann comments that this book "gave me extraordinary pleasure—it is without doubt an audacious, top-ranking performance in the contemporary novel."

The first premise of the book is, after all, that a wealthy British family in Mussolini's Italy can lead its aesthetically decorative parasitic existence in complete indifference to everything happening there. The exiled anti-Fascist must live in England, and the Englishman in turn must live in beautiful Italy. One looks in vain for any awareness of the moral lethargy inherent in this situation, and no loftily ascetic superiority to the world can make amends for it.

But I am using up paper and time to tell you things you already know and have felt along with me. The book is exciting because it is a work of talent, and in literary terms an engagingly avant-garde performance. Yet it is reprehensible—you're right about that. But my own conscience is not so clear when the question of morbidity and decadence is raised. In that regard I have a long and rather sinister record—actually since *Buddenbrooks*. *Death in Venice*, too, isn't so unobjectionable, and right now in *Doctor Faustus* the atmosphere again is not exactly of the healthiest. In connection with all this, I imagine one must think of the novelist in that old sketch of mine, "At the Prophet's," of whom it is said: "He was on good terms with life."

At the moment the *Faustus* has entered a society-novel phase. Its scene is Munich, and I am digging in my memories of social life in the Munich of 1910. Adrian, of course, is poorly suited to the atmosphere of this simple-hearted Capua which was to become the "Cradle of the Movement."[2] I always had a premonition that this would be stupidity's fate.

My God, Aachen! So we have had to reduce it to ashes. Even though the inhabitants hung out white flags. *Poor people!* The Nazis want maximum destruction and chaos. Their ideas about this war, which they do not regard as a war like others, are totally sinister. Klaus and Golo should not be sent to Germany. They would be murdered in my place.

I don't want to end on this gloomy note, but rather with the wish that you are wholly at your best again psychically and physically and are looking forward to the future with confidence. Then I can too.

Yours,
T. M.

[2] i.e., of the Nazi Party.

TO ARCHIBALD MACLEISH

[*Original in English*]

Pacific Palisades
October 26, 1944

Dear Mr. MacLeish:

The schedule of my lecture tour next year is now almost completed, and I can give you my suggestions. On January 10, 1945, I shall speak in Tucson, Arizona, and hope to be in Washington on the 13th or 14th. For the speech in the Library I can offer you the days between January 15th and 18th. I personally would prefer the 16th or 17th. But I insist by no means on these two days.

I take the opportunity to ask you whether I may present to the Library the original handwriting of my Moses story which I wrote for the anthology *The Ten Commandments*. My special reason for this offer is the fact that the whole story is written on the particularly pleasant stationery of the Library—a misuse for which I can best atone by this dedication. Of course, I do not know whether the Library is at all interested in such treasures.

I am looking forward with pleasure to your kind news, and remain, with my best regards,

Faithfully yours,

TO AGNES E. MEYER

Pacific Palisades
November 17, 1944

My dear friend:

I hasten to write to you because I am afraid that Friend MacLeish may have alarmed you about the telegram I sent him (as well as the agent C. Leigh) last night. I have had to cancel the January journey to the East, for the following reasons. The indisposition which I have boringly kept referring to in my recent letters (rheumatic torments, chiefly) was only the harbinger of an acute illness which took the form of *intestinal flu* with high fever and kept me in bed for a week or so. I have been on my feet again for several days, but a troublesome affection of the nervous system, depression, lack of energy, such as usually results from the grippe, have lingered on. I might hope that by January all this would improve. But if the translation were to be ready in time, I would have to set to work at once and quickly write the lecture, a delicate task for which, I fear, I am not in the right spirits. All the same, I could manage to force it. But in addition, recovery from the acute illness has not freed me from the neuralgic facial pains which preceded it. Instead they have shifted to the teeth and caused a crisis which I had hoped to be able to postpone until after the trip. But now it must be faced, and that is a protracted process which will not be over by the time I'would have to leave. So I have had to adjust to the idea of giving up the visit to the East for this year.

This has not been easy for me, for I find it hard to forgive myself for abandoning such tasks. Besides, I am losing a great deal—the change of air, the recreation, the contact with the public, the stimulation and sociability of New York, and especially the chance to see you again, which I had been looking forward to with heartfelt pleasure and which now, because of this misfortune, has to be postponed indefinitely. It is very, very hard to bear. But the decision was altogether unavoidable and I must try to make the best of it.

At least I hope that this indefinable climate will find its way back to sunniness and thus give me some help. The damp, eternally foggy and cold summer we had is to blame for everything.

You keep well, and have patience with

Your afflicted but not despairing
T. M.

TO CHESTER M. DEUEL, JR.[1]

Pacific Palisades
November 28, 1944

Dear Mr. Deuel:

I would have thanked you sooner for your kind letter and manuscript if I hadn't taken to bed with a rather unpleasant case of the flu from whose aftereffects I am still suffering.

In the meantime I have read your manuscript and thank you for your confidence. It seems to me that this little work is not yet quite suitable for publication; forgive me for telling you this so openly. For one thing, in its purely formal aspects the little work does not seem quite balanced to me; I found quite a few abrupt changes from poetical expressions to everyday slang which did not quite please me; besides, the idea that the German soldier undergoes such a complete transformation

---

[1] Mr. Deuel was at this time a master sergeant in the United States Army.

simply by dying and becoming a spirit does not seem quite plausible to me. His American fellow soldier, it seems, also learns something through dying, but just what it is he learns does not become entirely clear to the reader. I do believe that the author feels and knows it, but there is here a lack of power to convey.

I was very much in agreement with the thought that this war must in any case be fought to the finish (no matter how one may theoretically think about war) to save the world from the evil which the victory of brute force and injustice would bring on all of us.

I hope that you do not hold my frank utterances against me, and thank you again for your confidence.

TO AGNES E. MEYER

Pacific Palisades
December 12, 1944

Dear friend:

I should say Dear Christmas Angel, for yesterday your dazzlingly beautiful gifts arrived. Our curiosity was too much for us and we opened the packages then and there, which no doubt is a violation of the spirit of Christmas. But how can you engender a Christmasy mood and show respect for Christmas packages in the kind of summer heat we've been having here for weeks? Weather conditions in these parts are ridiculous. All summer we froze in fogs, and at Christmas we have dog days.

Katia was fascinated by her pocketbook, which is truly an exceptionally tasteful and fine one. After she had looked at it for a while, I hid it from her again, so that she won't see it until it appears on the gift table. I was instantly delighted with the superlative cloth of the jacket. But to tell the truth, it has turned out to be somewhat too short and too close-fitting for me. I have tried it on again and again, but it does not appear as if it and I shall ever fit one another. This is all the more regrettable because in principle you have hit on the very thing: I so much wanted a silk lounging jacket, and it would have been difficult to find one out here. What can be done? Am I to hang the beautiful thing in the closet only to feast my eyes and hand on it now and then? Is an exchange still possible? I suppose I should send it back to the store immediately and start the process without waiting for your reply. But *if* it is to be exchanged, something might be done about choosing another fashion, *more informal*. This is a low-cut dinner jacket, not a work jacket. To fulfill its purpose perfectly it ought to be somewhat looser, as well as buttoned up rather higher.

All this sounds extremely ungrateful and carping. Those are traits alien to me, and yet I must exhibit them. Sad, sad! I would understand only too well if you, best of friends, were to have neither time nor desire to bother about the matter any more. If so, I shall bequeath the wonderfully beautiful thing to little Tonio, together with the jade cufflinks.

Such problems! I have put them first because the packages were yesterday's event. Today your letter arrived with the moving *letter to the editor*—and again I have to thank you for your noble, earnest, handsome, and energetic defense. The attacks must really have been nasty since MacLeish too was so furious over them. I am grateful that my own blood is not poisoned with the stuff. I promise myself from your antidote, a balm from Brangaene's coffer, the most purgative effect—even upon the letter writers and even if they understand nothing. The nobility and superiority of your words will somehow impress them and make them conscious of their own stupidity.

I suffer with you from the alarms, mistakes, and confusions of world events. I am even more an admirer of England than you. But what England is doing in Greece,[1] and apparently with the consent of the Labor Party, is gruesome; and in other events as well there is much reason for depression. [. . .] If we prove unable to cope with our task, the fault will not lie in the military realm, but in the intellectual and political realms. We have grown no wiser, or at any rate not significantly wiser, since the time of Spain and of Munich. We still fear socialism far more than fascism. But since these are the only alternatives, at least for Europe, we don't know what we want, and because of that everything can still go to pieces.

I had not realized that Archie's call to the State Department[2] would mean his leaving the Library, and I am sad about that. Let us hope he will be present this spring at the celebration, which we want to schedule as close to my birthday as possible, and to which I am looking forward with deep pleasure.

Ever yours,
T. M.

---

[1] After the withdrawal of the Germans, the British landed in Greece in October 1944 to prevent the National Liberation Army (EAM) resistance group from taking over the government. Under British pressure a coalition of the EAM with the royalist National Front (EDES) was formed. On December 1, 1944, the coalition ended, civil war broke out, and British troops came to the aid of the weak EDES. In bloody battles the British defeated their recent ally, the Liberation Army, which they considered to be thoroughly infiltrated by Communists.

[2] Archibald MacLeish had been appointed director of the Office of Facts and Figures in the State Department.

TO IDA HERZ

Pacific Palisades
December 26, 1944

Dear Fräulein Herz:

The lexicon[1] is original, interesting, and useful. Many thanks for the good choice and the kind thought.

We have had a typical children's Christmas, for the Swiss joined the Italian grandchildren and so there were four pairs of eyes dazzled by the glow of lights and gifts. The *living room* has turned into a wasteland of toys—we shall have to do a thorough housecleaning.

I hope you spent Christmas Eve cheerfully with good friends, in spite of the anxiety and disappointment we are once more suffering under. It is a frightful mess[2] and could have been avoided with a little more care and comprehension of the enemy's ruthlessness (but we have virtually no comprehension of that). Imagine the Germans reaching Paris again! I suppose we needed a lesson, but this one is a bit too much.

I was very relieved by a surprise telephone call from Erika from New York. She is back there, after a safe crossing on a troopship. I was secretly worried about her, since there was no knowing where she might be wandering around, perhaps in the vicinity of the German offensive. At the end of the month she is coming out here for a few days and will have much to tell us.

In this strangest of moments the B.B.C. has again commissioned me to make fortnightly broadcasts to Germany, especially to the occupied areas, small as they still are. But I spoke to them in the darkest days, and it is right for me to do so again. [. . .]

Have you received the *Joseph?* It was solicitously started on its journey.

All the best for the new year.

---

[1] Brewer's *Dictionary of Phrase and Fable*, which Ida Herz had sent as a Christmas present.
[2] The German offensive of Christmas 1944.

TO EARL J. MAYER

[*Original in English*]

Pacific Palisades
December 26, 1944

Dear Mr. Mayer:

I received your letter of November 6th and thank you very much for your confidence. Of course, it is quite impossible for me to tell whether or not you are called to be a writer. It sometimes takes very little, and sometimes immeasurably much to be a writer, depending on how one regards this profession and what one understands by it. To show you the way to becoming an author I am incapable of doing. This way everybody must find for himself, and he will find it if he is called.

At the present time, I believe you should not burden yourself with such plans and efforts at all. I think that you should first of all await your recovery and dismissal from the hospital and then, above all, tackle the not quite easy task of again taking root in civilian life. This seems to me of the greatest importance, and if later on you should like to approach me again for literary advice, I shall be happy to give it to you according to the best of my knowledge and ability.

With my best wishes,

1945

———————•———————

Pacific Palisades
January 5, 1945

Dear Alfred:

Today I write to you simply for reasons of curiosity because I want to know whether you have got in touch with Simon and Schuster in the matter of the English edition of *Das Gesetz*, and whether you have encountered any difficulties there. If this was the case, I will have to take Mr. Robinson to task, whom I suspect of sabotage in this matter.

I hope that you and Blanche have spent the holidays pleasantly. Of course, one is depressed now because of the military disappointments, and can hardly comprehend how so much carelessness and neglect was possible. The Germans seem to have imitated the Russians, who also knew how to feign impotence. It is reassuring to know that, after all, the Germans are not the Russians and we are not the Germans of those times.

We had quite a children's Christmas, just as it should be, with the two families from Chicago and San Francisco. For many weeks now we have had beautiful sunny summer weather and are being fully recompensed for a cloudy and cool summer.

With my kindest regards,

As ever with love,

1945

TO A. SULKA & CO.

[*Original in English*]

Pacific Palisades
January 12, 1945

Gentlemen:

As the smoking jacket you sent me did not fit—it was too small for me—
Miss Meyer instructed me to send it to her. However, when I received
Miss Meyer's lines, I had already dispatched the jacket to you. Therefore,
it will be best if you send the jacket to the address of Miss Meyer, 1624
Crescent Place, Washington, D.C.

TO FREDRIC WARBURG[1]

[*Original in English*]

Pacific Palisades
February 22, 1945

Dear Mr. Warburg:

Your kind letter of January 12th reached me safely. Unfortunately, a few
lines were cut out by the censor, presumably a sentence or two on the
back of the page. It is too bad that through this operation other things
were also eliminated on the other side. However, I suppose that it was
nothing of supreme importance.

I am deeply grateful to you for your report on my books. I am
particularly pleased that you were granted enough paper for the final
Joseph volume to print seven thousand copies. After all, I could not have
hoped for more.

After the conclusion of the *Joseph* series I have, as you may know,
written a story of smaller dimensions, a long short story, dealing with the
life of Moses, which was included as preface in the anthology *The Ten
Commandments*, published by Simon and Schuster. The separate German
edition of this story, entitled *Das Gesetz*, is uncommonly successful in
Switzerland, and therefore I am glad that now also Alfred Knopf is about
to publish a separate English edition of it. I shall advise him to send you
the galleys and would be very happy if this story, which has a strong
moral and timely touch and culminates in a curse of Hitler, would also
see the light of day in London. It will not require much paper or represent
a big investment.

[1] Fredric Warburg (b. 1898), Mann's English publisher.

I thank you very much for your kind inquiries as to the progress of my new novel. I have furthered it quite a bit in the meantime and believe that two thirds have been born. However, the subject matter is so difficult that I cannot rush it, but must rather proceed even more carefully than usual. So you don't have to worry about paper for this book yet. The translation has not yet begun, as I do not consider everything I have written as final. I believe I have already mentioned to you what the book is about: It is the fictitious biography of a modern musician, a composer, written by a surviving friend. The artist shares the fate of, let us say, Nietzsche and Hugo Wolf which, however, in my representation becomes less a clinical than a moral and theological affair. It is characteristic of the book that it contains a long conversation of the infected artist with the devil. Also, this work is by no means free from more or less secret relations to the events of the present and particularly to the fate of Germany.

That this fate is now on the verge of being fulfilled, and in the most gruesome manner, nobody can doubt. Oh, that everything were already over! Never before did a people have more cruel masters, masters who relentlessly insist that it perish with them.

Please accept my best wishes for your personal well-being and the course of your business.

TO BRUNO WALTER

Pacific Palisades
March 1, 1945

Dear Bruno Walter:

Erika writes me that you have read—Hofmannsthal would say indiscreetly—the fragment from the beginning of the novel in *Aufbau* and have had several technical criticisms to make of it, points which in your opinion are musically untenable. Naturally I am alarmed—although I cannot imagine what could possibly be wrong or disputable in these elementary matters. Does it have to do with the oft-asserted and oft-controverted coloristic character of the different keys? Or with the "discovery" of the compass of tonalities itself? Or with the fact that the young apprentice hits on enharmonic change as a means of modulation? Because that's all, you know. Nothing else happens in the section. And what I can't for the life of me understand is how anything of that sort could cause people to think that my model was Schoenberg.

Please enlighten me! If I have managed to slip some stupidities into these elementary mentions of music, and even some that the professional finds laughable, I shall rush to eradicate them all according to your instructions. Werfel, who does know quite a bit about music, said nothing to me when he heard me read the chapter. *Die Mahlerin*[1] was there, too. But what does *she* care whether I make a fool of myself? It's very good of you to keep a sharp eye out.

I no longer have the copy of *Aufbau*. That insignificant publication gave me no pleasure. I am therefore sending you a carbon copy of the typescript of the chapter, so that you can refresh your memory and let me know.

I have just had *a hell of a time* with my teeth. Impressions. Extractions, *toute la lyre*. Thanks to this, I of course have not regained the weight I lost because of the *flu* and am a nervous old man. Oh well, what can one expect? Perhaps I ought to interpolate a year of rest. But you could write on your year off, whereas I cannot very well conduct for relaxation. That is absolutely out of the question, say what you will. [. . .]

My lecture in Washington ("Germany and the Germans"—glare-ice!) is set for May 29th. Then we shall go on to New York for a few weeks. You will be there, won't you? I shall then tell you some more about the novel and what I mean to do with this intellectual musician who is my hero. The "new," the "radical" music, even the Schoenberg system, plays its part in the book, my dear friend. For there's no question about it: Music as well as all the other arts—and not only the arts—is in a crisis which sometimes seems to threaten its very life. In literature that crisis is sometimes concealed by an ironic traditionalism. But Joyce, for example, to whom I am closer in some ways than might appear, is quite as outrageous to the mind trained in the classical romantic, realistic traditions as Shoenberg and his followers. Incidentally, I can't read Joyce either, if only because one has to be born into English culture to do so. And as far as the corresponding music is concerned, you need fear nothing for me personally: at bottom I am committed to romantic kitsch from head to toe; to this day my eyes always overflow at a lovely diminished-seventh chord.

What the novel treats of is paralysis stemming from cleverness, from intellectual experience of the crisis—there is also a pact with the devil springing from the craving for an inspired breakthrough. A deep and many-faceted affair. Basically, music as such plays only a symbolic part—

---

[1] Alma Mahler Werfel (1879–1964), wife successively of Walter Gropius, Gustav Mahler, and Franz Werfel. Author of *Gustav Mahler* (1939), *And the Bridge is Love* (1958).

which, of course, does not obviate the necessity for having the details absolutely right.

P.S. I have just been considering whether it will be better to send you the whole beginning of the novel along with the chapter in question. Seen alone and entirely without atmosphere, the fragment is really too paltry.

TO GIUSEPPE ANTONIO BORGESE

Pacific Palisades
March 21, 1945

Dear Antonio:

It was very kind of you to send us your magnificent article[1] which, I note with satisfaction, meets with nothing but agreement and admiration among Americans of the higher type—and after all, it was addressed to the American conscience. We saw this only yesterday at a party which included the writer Nathan[2] and Maxwell Anderson.[3] There was only one opinion: that this was a most necessary and worthwhile admonition to American idealism, phrased with great dignity. I agree, and take pleasure in the way it exemplified the Platonic double sense of the word "good": how morality and aesthetics unite in it, and how beauty is the natural and appropriate dress of intellectual honorableness. Though "dress" is a somewhat misleading word. "Nature has neither core nor husk."

For the rest, I am almost sorry that out of discretion you substituted the case of Poland for the case of Italy—which is what you really meant, and from which clearer lessons could have been drawn. Isn't it a little facile and almost insidious to illustrate the defeat of idealism by reference to Russia and the Poles, who owe their liberation entirely to her, and to call upon the rest of us to at least acknowledge this fact? Are we supposed to say: "Russia has put this over on us; alas, all we can do is bow to the detestable facts"? That would be a poor way to prove to the Nazis the unity of the Allies which makes their cause hopeless. Roosevelt went to Yalta with many apprehensions and returned relieved because, by one

[1] "Europe Wants Freedom from Shame. A Realistic Warning: America Is Forsaking Its Idealism," *Life* (March 12, 1945).
[2] Robert Nathan.
[3] Maxwell Anderson (1888–1959), American dramatist. Among his plays: *What Price Glory?* (1924), *Winterset* (1935), *Both Your Houses* (1933), *Journey to Jerusalem* (1940).

means or another, the alliance had been preserved. "Politics is the art of the possible," Bismarck said. It is easy for pure intellect to mock or rage at the concessions which politics has to make, inasmuch as politics is a mediating and reality-shaping principle. Intellect is not obliged to shape reality. But what has to be shaped here is, to my mind, and *borné* though you may find this viewpoint, first and foremost the annihilation of the Nazi beast—which is making diplomatic offers to lay down arms in the West if only it is given leave to go on fighting against Russia alone. What a temptation to a world that once upon a time supplied a Munich! I shall never stop trembling for fear of a super-Munich; Yalta, bad as it may have been, has at any rate somewhat quieted this fear.

There are first-rate rapier thrusts in that masterly article. Why, then, such tilting with windmills as the remark that since America for all its size and population does not arouse anxiety in its sphere of influence, Europe need have no fear of Germany? Come now!

Here you have a bit of criticism of criticism. It cannot even scratch the skin of your essay as a work and an act.

Fatherly and grandfatherly greetings.

T. M.

TO UPTON SINCLAIR [1]

[Original in English]

Pacific Palisades
March 30, 1945

Dear Mr. Sinclair:

It is a shame that I haven't yet thanked you for the strange and beautiful book; but you know for yourself the many intrusions from outside against which we have to defend ourselves, and the innumerable small chores that have to be attended to every day.

I read *Mental Radio* with interest but without surprise. My skepticism is not of the kind which doubts everything, but on the contrary believes everything to be possible. I was very pleased that you insisted on your experiences and published this book, despite the protests from timid and doubtful souls. The remarks of these two types of people which you quote in the book belong to the most amusing passages it contains.

I think I already told you that I myself am apparently completely

---

[1] Upton Sinclair (1878–1968), American novelist, reformer, politician.

lacking in any occult gift. During the experiments of Dr. Schrenck-Notzing in Munich I always had the impression that my influence was rather impeding than furthering the accomplishment of phenomena. With regard to the transmission of thoughts I only know the familiar phenomenon occurring among old married couples: that one of them occasionally voices exactly the same thing the other has been thinking. But I suppose that cannot be called transmission; it is rather caused by many years of living together during which a parallel course of thinking has developed. On the other hand, my brother Heinrich has repeatedly assured me that in the hour in which our sister died, he heard her voice calling him by his name. She passed away in Bavaria, and he was at the time in the Austrian Alps.

With repeated and sincere thanks and my best wishes for your work and your personal well-being, I am

Yours cordially,

TO KOPPEL S. PINSON[1]

[*Original in English*]

Pacific Palisades
March 30, 1945

Dear Professor Pinson:

Thank you so much for sending me your piece "On the Future of Germany." I read it with great enjoyment and almost constant approval. I am sure it belongs among the most intelligent, impartial and fair-minded articles that have been written on the subject.

You can hardly imagine the fury a German has to face if he makes the least concession to the truth that National Socialism was not imposed on the German people from outside but has century-old roots in German life itself. The statement of this fact provokes the greatest indignation of the emigrated German intelligentsia, particularly of certain social-democrats who can hardly await the day when Germany will again rise as a strong, centralized democratic power—only to put Europe into her pocket again after a few years. Among these people a sentimental patriotism has broken out which seems fantastic to me.

I was all the more pleased with your open-minded utterances which are based on close familiarity with the German psyche. Particularly valuable to me are your remarks on pages 142–3 about the relative in-

---

[1] Koppel S. Pinson (1904–1961), professor of history at Queens College, New York.

effectiveness of the conception of the natural law and the Roman-Christian stoicism in German life which together form that religion of mankind which is so characteristic of the political and moral life of Western Europe. The German theologian Ernst Troeltsch has written an excellent book on the subject in which he emphasized his conviction that there are many elements to be found in the German tradition which, in the long run, do not at all exclude the reconciliation of the German mind with Western European culture.

With repeated thanks and kindest regards,

TO HERMANN HESSE

Pacific Palisades
April 8, 1945

Dear Herr Hesse:

It's a long time since you heard anything from your brother in spirit—or cousin at any rate—whom the winds have wafted to the Wild West. And yet you might well have expected to hear something from him, after that remarkable gift you have given the world of culture, and him too, me too, with your deliciously ripe and rich monumental novel, *The Bead Game*. But as you know, communication with Switzerland was cut off for months—at least to the extent that no mail was accepted on this side—and on top of that, while the bars were down I passed through a period of illness. [. . .] To be brief about it, whatever the form it took, it was a manifestation of old age, of which there's no more to be said. As a result, until I drop off, my trousers will be sitting too loosely about my waist. And yet I look fifty-five, especially when freshly shaved; and my doctor, who is completely sold on the modern idea that one's biological age is quite another thing from one's chronological age, advises me after every visit not to give way to any imaginary weaknesses. Well, one must merely look on with faint curiosity to see what lies in store. *The readiness is all.*

Grand and wonderful things have lain in store for you. At a time when others grow weary (and even the second part of *Wilhelm Meister*, which leaps to mind as a comparison, is after all a most weary, dignifiedly sclerotic omnium-gatherum), you have overtopped and crowned your life work with this treasure of purest thought—rich in romantic intricacies and imaginative, to be sure, but still perfectly controlled, coherent, a beautifully rounded masterpiece in which you yourself added up the very substantial "sum of your life, your existence."

The book was a surprise. I had not expected to have it so soon after its publication. How curious I was! I gave myself to it in different ways, sometimes reading rapidly, sometimes slowly. I love its combination of gravity and sportiveness—a tone familiar to me, more or less my own. Unquestionably the book itself has much the quality of a Bead Game, one of the supremely good ones. It is one of those organ fantasies upon all the materials and values of our culture, and exemplifies that stage in the evolution of the Game when the capacity for universality, for a position transcending the various disciplines, has been reached. Such a transcending is of course equivalent to the irony which ultimately transforms the whole thing, product though it is of deepest thought, into a roguish artistic jest. The root of its humor is that it parodies biography and strikes the pompous pose of the researcher. Yet people will not dare to laugh, and in secret you will be quite annoyed at their deadly sober reverence. I know how that is.

Among the feelings with which I read the book was also *dismay*—at a closeness and kinship which has struck me before, but this time is present in a particularly sharp and objective fashion. Isn't it strange that for some time now, ever since the completion of my "Orientalist" period, I have been working on a novel, quite a *"libellus,"* that both has the form of a biography and is concerned with music? The title is:

Doctor Faustus

The Life of the German Composer

Adrian Leverkühn

As Told by a Friend

It is the tale of a man's selling his soul to the devil. The "hero" shares the fate of Nietzsche and Hugo Wolf, and his life story, told to us by a pure, good-hearted, humanistic soul, has strong antihumanistic elements: intoxication and paralysis. *Sapienti sat.* Nothing more unlike your book can be imagined, and yet the similarity is striking—as happens now and then among brothers.

In closing: It is no wonder that such a "transcending" work as yours comes out against the "politicalization of Mind." [. . .] Very well, but we must first agree on what is meant. [. . .] If "Mind" is the principle, the power, which desires the good; if it is a sensitive alertness toward the changing aspects of truth, in a word, a "divine solicitude" which seeks to approach what is right and requisite at a given time, then it is political, whether or not this epithet sounds pretty. It seems to me that nowadays nothing alive escapes politics. Refusal is politics, too; it is a political act on the side of the evil cause. [. . .]

All the very best to you, dear Herr Hesse. Keep well, as I shall try to do, so that we may see each other again.

Yours,
Thomas von der Trave[1]

TO F. W. BRADLEY

[*Original in English*]

Pacific Palisades
April 11, 1945

Dear Mr. Bradley:

Thank you very much for your kind and interesting letter of March 30th. Your approval of my article in *Free World* was highly valuable to me. One should have thought that my painful concern with the fate of the German people and a feeling of solidarity almost bordering on the hypochondriac could be discerned in my statements. But in spite of that, the article has brought me attacks from a certain sphere of the German emigration, namely the social-democratic patriots who insist upon the clear distinction between the German people and the Nazis, who deny that National Socialism is deeply rooted in the German character and in German history, and who demand that full confidence be shown immediately to the defeated Germany and that she be given the possibility to become again a strong, centralized, democratic state—only to pursue her old power politics all over again. These are tendencies which I by no means dare support, and this attitude is being severely criticized.

But I cannot feel hurt by this accusation of unpatriotic disinterestedness toward my native country. During these last years I have done everything in my power to convince my former compatriots that for twelve years they have gone a path leading to disaster, and I have tried to approach them in exactly the way you suggest in your letter. In regular broadcasts, formerly once a month, now twice a month, I have appealed to the young people of Germany and to the whole German nation to get rid of their nefarious regime which has brought such great misfortune upon their country, and I have tried to reawaken those of their tendencies and traditions which in former times have earned the

---

[1] The name of the Magister Ludi in Hesse's *The Bead Game*. Mann recognized a portrait of himself in this character.

1945

German people the sympathy and love of the whole world. I have no idea whether these broadcasts have had any effect and whether, under the reigning terror, they could have had any effect at all, and in general it is very difficult for me to get a clear picture of the state of the country from which I have been separated for twelve years. What we learn about the behavior of the population since the partial occupation of Germany is not exactly encouraging, and neither are the remarks made by the Archbishop of Münster, Count Galen,[1] to an American newspaperman. These remarks seem to be characteristic of the state of mind of the Germans. I am afraid that the army of occupation will have to fight against many riotous outbursts of this people whose national pride is hurt by the defeat, and that a true reconciliation of Germany with the rest of the world is still quite far off. But it must and will be effected one day, and we can only put our hopes in the humanitarian and democratic traditions which are by no means lacking in Germany and which have only sunk into such fatal oblivion during the most recent part of her history.

With warmest regards,

TO ERICH VON KAHLER

Pacific Palisades
May 1, 1945

Dear, good friend:

What a pleasure your letter was! And we certainly shouldn't be casting stones about silence. We are in our own glass house as far as that goes, and can also only cite by way of apology the well-known botherations, the affairs and trifles, the cares, the routine, the demands of the times. What you write about present developments—all long anticipated, coming too late, and yet staggering as reality—we have read with unanimous applause, individually and all together. You are so right when you say that the German share should not be set apart from the general culpability of stupidity—which goes on proving itself invincible. But I must again insist that the Germans have played a special, terribly authentic role in the drama. Someone with so profound a knowledge of the German character in history would be the last to deny that.[1] [. . .]

[1] Count Clemens August Galen (1878–1946), Bishop of Münster; became a cardinal in 1946. He had taken a courageous stand against the bloodiest crimes of the Hitler regime, especially the euthanasia program for mental patients, yet subsequently opposed the occupation powers, for which reason Thomas Mann called him "unteachable."

[1] An allusion to Kahler's book, *Der deutsche Charakter in der Geschichte Europas* (1937).

You are right; what is the point of a long letter when we shall be seeing each other soon. Erika is with us, and on the 24th we shall be going by way of Chicago to Washington, where I am to speak in the Library on the 29th. On June 3rd or 4th we will in all likelihood turn up in the Bedford [Hotel] in New York, and on the 8th I repeat the lecture at Hunter College. But on June 6th we shall be at Bruno Walter's in the evening—he and Bronislav Hubermann[2] are going to play for us. You must come to that!

Whatever possesses you, reading the manuscript? I must say I was truly alarmed to hear it. The book is a secret, you know, and for the present a completely private experiment—as yet I can't imagine publishing it. I don't regard Lowe-Porter as a reader; she is a mute instrument, never lets out a peep. And here you are, simply going ahead and reading it. Please don't pass it on to anyone!

Roosevelt—let me not speak of it. This is no longer the country to which we came. One feels orphaned and abandoned. But I suppose it was just as well this way for him.

What a *porcheria* again, this ringing speech of Dönitz[3] to nation and army on the Führer's heroic death. *P.M.*[4] queried me by telegram today: *"Do you believe that Hitler is dead?"* I replied: *"Who cares?"*

Give my regards to Broch and all the heroes. See you soon.

TO HEINRICH MANN

The St. Regis
New York
June 9, 1945

Dear Heinrich:

I could not restrain my tears as I read your letter and also your magnificent essay[1] in the *Rundschau.* Let me thank you as well as I can, amid the unsought but still not exactly avoided brouhaha[2] of these days, for all your love and loyalty, which would not move me so deeply if I did not have the same strong feelings toward you.

For the rest, it is not so easy, what with all the accolades from kind people, to assume the right bearing, both outward and inward. There is

[2] Bronislav Hubermann (1882–1947), the celebrated violinist.
[3] Karl Dönitz (b. 1891), Hitler's Grand Admiral, who formed a new government after Hitler's death.
[4] New York afternoon newspaper, now defunct.
[1] "Mein Bruder" (June, 1945).
[2] The tributes and ceremonies celebrating Thomas Mann's seventieth birthday.

something comic about having a lump in one's throat. I have had to look at it all as a kind of test of the nerves, and play the part in spite of thorough skepticism, in fact melancholic knowledge, that it isn't really justified. [. . .]

Your contribution is of course the greatest piece in Bermann's issue. It is charming on the personal matters, especially moving in its memories of Papa (whom I too have thought of so often in the course of this life), and a wonderful document where it describes our fraternally dissimilar relationship to Germanism. The prose is unique. I have the feeling, not for the first time, that this condensed and intellectually pliant plainness is the language of the future, the idiom of the new world.

I'm looking forward to seeing you as soon as we are back.

T.

TO ALFRED NEUMANN

The St. Regis
New York
[*postmarked June 11, 1945*]

Dear friends:

God have mercy on me, what a brouhaha it is, but this is the way I wanted it after all. (*Did* I want it? Sometimes I tell myself I didn't. It just turned out that way.) And then again it's pure escape and restfulness, this living outwardly, doing nothing, and facing the world with a smile day after day. Only I simply can no longer bear to hear and read my name, and I feel glad that now in all likelihood the world will have done with me until I shuffle off. On which occasion it will make some fuss again, but then I won't have to play my part but will be performing my public duties merely as a bust.

In addition to his charming contribution[1] to the *Rundschau*, Alfred added so dear a birthday letter that I have wanted to thank him for days, but couldn't get to it. After my old brother, you, dear Neumann, are the first person I am writing to. It will take me months to catch up, but I wanted to slip in some expression, hasty though it must be, of my appreciation for those handsome signs of your friendship and faithfulness.

The *Rundschau* issue is really lavish, and some of the contributions are magnificent. A heap of telegrams from Europe (Sweden, Switzerland)

[1] "Thomas Mann liest vor" by Alfred Neumann (June, 1945).

gave me particular pleasure—our thoughtful tenants sent them on. We were relieved that Therese[2] sent one, along with the Oprechts.

It is humid and very hot here—not the most pleasant weather. Day after tomorrow we shall be going to the country for a few days, to Lake Mohank, I think. It is a Quaker hotel, so that we shall have to equip ourselves with a bottle of sherry. Then comes the *Nation* dinner,[3] then Chicago. And then we shall speed back to cool summer and to Niko.

To Kitty, the Wonder Hen, and to her fortunate spouse, all the best from both of us.

TO VICTOR REISSNER[1]

Pacific Palisades
July 12, 1945

My dear Herr Reissner:

I received your friendly lines while traveling. Of course one must not go too far in passing judgment on the statements of Bishop Galen and branding him as a follower of Hitler. That he has never been. But I too found his statements repugnant and depressing. Unfortunately they are all the more credible because many such patriotic follies are now coming out of that unhappy country. Certainly no one is more strongly affected by the prevailing misery there than I, and I understand very well the bitter feelings of many sincere opponents of Nazism who now have to suffer along with the guilty. But it seems to me that there are few if any signs of a proper understanding of what Germany as a nation has inflicted on the world, even from people who might be expected to understand. That understanding has not developed, or at any rate, not yet. In my radio address to the Germans I urged them not to imitate Galen's example; I said they ought to consider themselves not primarily as Germans, but as human beings who could not achieve liberation by themselves and who had to be led back to humanity by powers outside themselves.

---

[2] Therese Giehse, actress; close friend of the Mann household. Participated in Erika Mann's cabaret, *The Peppermill*. At the Zurich Schauspielhaus between 1938 and 1945. Now famous in all German-speaking regions, particularly for her roles in Brecht's plays.

[3] A testimonial dinner in honor of Mann's birthday, held on July 25, 1945. The money contributed by the participants was for the benefit of *The Nation*.

[1] Unidentifiable.

1945

TO HELEN LOWE-PORTER

Pacific Palisades
July 19, 1945

Dear Mrs. Lowe:

It is a relief to hear that you have not even read that *interview* and therefore could not have been indignant. Evidently only your good husband was. Our friend Kahler told me, looking very anxious, that your husband saw a grave insult to you in my general remark about the difficulty of translation, so much so that he was going to make you return my manuscript and refuse to translate it. Something had to be done, of course, and I hastily wrote that clarifying letter in Chicago.

But although it may have been unnecessary, it can do no harm, after all. For really I can never publicly praise all that you have done for my work often enough. Knopf, too, was delighted with my letter and told me so. He is very much attached to you and will always remain faithful, even if the New York press cuts up.

Recuperate well on your island. We are glad to be back in our summer coolness after the damp heat of the East. I am almost finished with my introduction to an edition of Dostoevsky's smaller novels, which Dial Press in New York is bringing out.[1] It was an interesting task for me. But within a few days I shall be able to return to the novel.

With warm regards, from my wife also, to you and your husband.

TO AGNES E. MEYER

Pacific Palisades
August 25, 1945

Dear friend:

I owe you thanks for several remarkable pieces of reading matter: First for Gide's obituary of Valéry, which is simple and warm and makes one envious of the unity of French literature, the higher solidarity among its representatives, however far apart they seem to be. And then for the expurgated chapter from *The Possessed*, which is not in my German edition of Dostoevsky, so that I knew of it only from Mereshkovsky. It is really a wild and gripping piece of writing, although its boldness goes beyond Dostoevsky's usual manner only in subject. I find it very coura-

---

[1] "Dostoevsky—in Moderation," Introduction to *The Short Novels of Dostoevsky* (New York: Dial Press; 1945).

geous and liberal of the Modern Library to have included it. Of course I should have read it, and it will sound rather ridiculous that I speak so mysteriously and out of personal ignorance of something that has been public knowledge for so long. Well, it does not matter. The gentlemen at Dial Press have not noticed that small point in my essay, and the critics of their edition will have an opportunity to show off their learning.

Are you at home? Or are you again (or still) engaged in serious, duty-bound adventures? You mean so well, work so hard, study, want so much to advise and help. I admire you and feel it almost rude to voice doubts as to whether you will be able to do anything to avert the impending nemesis. But the world scene looks threatening indeed. The peace has a gloomy character; no one can really believe in it, or wants to, and a cloud of anxiety of a totally new sort hangs over mankind. At the same time it would be sheer arrogance to say how things could have been done better, or should still be done. [. . .] We have reached the point at which the earth can be thrown out of its orbit by the reaction from explosions, so that it no longer circles around the sun. Of course, one might say simply: "So what?" But still, what a terrible shame that life might have to seek another refuge in the cosmos because it took so wrong a course on earth! Or shall we say that there is no right course for life, simply because it is life? One begins to doubt the wisdom of Creation. "It would be better if nothing were created," says Mephistopheles. "For my part I'd prefer the eternal void."

On the other hand, though, this war may have been the last; it's conceivable that humanity will muster up its instinct for self-preservation, and that with the peaceful utilization of the innermost natural forces the working day will be reduced to an hour. Then entertainment will have to be provided. Not everybody has a novel to write.

We have been having an admirable summer, almost always fair, with refreshing sea breezes combating the heat; and my health is good. I am working steadily on the German biography, but I have no idea what to think of it. Either it is something very novel and original, almost a work of genius, or it is trash. This dual possibility arouses my curiosity and keeps me at it.

As my friend you will be glad to hear that my birthday was cele-brated amiably and honorably almost everywhere in the world, even as far as South Africa. Articles and meetings all over, and congratulations coming from all quarters. A good man in Queenstown-Georgetown, British Guiana, asks my consent for the founding of a *T. M. society whose*

object would be to encourage the deeper study and discussion of my works.
What should I answer? *"In my opinion there is nothing more urgent than
that"*?

The children from San Francisco are here now, and when they go
they will leave the two grandsons with us for a few weeks. Frido is no
longer so ideal; he is rather more boyish, but very amusing, and speaks
English with a terrible Swiss accent.

The German press has come out with another article maintaining
that it is my duty to return and serve as psychiatrist to the nation. The
author is a certain Walter von Molo[1] who sturdily participated all along
and belonged to the Nazi Writers' Academy. The grotesque part of it is
that they are absolutely convinced over there of my tremendous influence
upon the decisions of the Allies, or at least the Americans, in German
affairs. If things go badly for the Germans—and how can they possibly
go any other way—I shall bear the blame because I did not intervene
enough. *Sancta simplicitas!*

Your *obedient servant,*
T. M.

TO WALTER VON MOLO

Pacific Palisades
September 7, 1945

Dear Herr von Molo:

I owe you thanks for a very friendly birthday greeting, as well as for the
open letter to me which you gave to the German press and which has
also been published in extracts in American newspapers. In it you
express even more vehemently than in your private letter the request, in
fact the demand, that I return to Germany and live there again, helping
"by word and deed." You are not the only one to direct this summons to
me; the Russian-controlled Berlin Radio and the organ of the united
democratic parties of Germany have also issued it, so I am told, with the
high-sounding argument that I have "a historic task to perform in Germany."

I cannot help rejoicing that Germany wants to have me back again—

---

[1] Walter von Molo (1880–1958), novelist. President of the Prussian Writers'
Academy 1928–30. His nationalistic emotionalism found favor with the Nazi regime.
For a time he was a champion of Hitlerism, but then retired to his estate. However, he
remained a member of the Academy and continued writing unmolested. Among his
works: A novel on Schiller in four parts, 1912–16; *Ein Volk wacht auf* (trilogy, 1918–22);
Geschichte einer Seele (1938; on Heinrich von Kleist); *Lebenserinnerungen* (1957).

not only my books, but myself as a person. Yet these appeals also have a somewhat disturbing and depressing effect upon me, and I hear something illogical, even unjust and ill-considered in them. You know only too well, my dear Herr von Molo, how difficult it is to help "by word and deed" in Germany today, given the almost hopeless situation which our unfortunate nation has got itself into. And it seems to me highly dubious whether an already old man whose heart muscle has felt the strains of these grim times can directly, personally, in the flesh, make much of a contribution toward raising up out of their deep abasement the people whom you so movingly describe. This is only by the way. It also seems to me that the Germans making these requests have given little thought to the technical, civil, and psychological difficulties standing in the way of my "reimmigration."

Are these twelve years and their results simply to be wiped from the slate, and is it possible to act as if they had never been? In 1933 the shock of losing the wonted basis of my life, of parting with house and land, books, mementos and all my property, as well as the shock of the deplorable attacks in Germany, the expulsions and repudiations—all that was hard enough, suffocating enough. I shall never forget how Munich's radio and newspapers launched an illiterate and murderous campaign against my Wagner essay, for this was the point at which I fully realized that return was cut off for me. I shall never forget the groping for words, the efforts to write, to reply, to explain myself—those "letters into the night," as René Schickele, one of the many departed friends, called these smothered monologues. What followed was hard enough too: the itinerant life from country to country, the passport anxieties, the hotel existence, while our ears rang with the shameful stories that made their way out of the lost country that was running amok, going from bad to worse, growing more and more alien. All of you who swore loyalty to the "charismatic Leader" (horrible, horrible, besotted education!) and carried on with culture under Goebbels did not go through any of that. I do not forget that later you went through much worse, which I was spared; but you never knew the angina of exile, the uprooting, the nervous shock of homelessness.

At times I was furious at your equanimity. I saw it as a breach of solidarity. If at that time the German intelligentsia, everyone who had a name and meant something in the world—doctors, musicians, teachers, writers, artists—had risen as one man against the disgrace, had declared a general strike, many things might have turned out differently. Instead, the individual, if he happened not to be a Jew, always found himself faced with the question: "Why should I? The others are going along. It can't really be so bad."

I say that at times I felt some fury. But I have never envied you who were sitting there inside, not even in your greatest days. For I knew only too well that those days were nothing but bloody foam which would soon dissipate. I envied Hermann Hesse, in whose companionship I found comfort and strength during the first weeks and months, because he had long been free, had broken away early, with the all too accurate explanation: "A great, important people, the Germans—who can deny it? The salt of the earth, perhaps. But as a political nation, impossible! As such, I want to have nothing to do with them." And he lived in beautiful security in his house in Montagnola, in whose garden he played *boccia* with his troubled, distracted guest.

Slowly, slowly, things subsided and arranged themselves. Some sort of domestic life was resumed, first in France, then in Switzerland; a relative calm, a settling down and sense of belonging emerged from forlornness; I picked up the work that had fallen from my hands, that had begun to seem irremediably shattered. Switzerland, hospitable by tradition but under the pressure of menacing, powerful neighbors and committed to neutrality as a moral principle, naturally showed a mild embarrassment at the presence of a guest without papers who was on such bad terms with his government, and called for "tact." Then came the invitation to the American university; and suddenly in this vast free country there was no longer any talk of "tact"; there was nothing but open, uncowed, outspoken friendliness, joyous, without reservations, in fact with the constant refrain: "*Thank you, Mr. Hitler.*" I have some reason, my dear Herr von Molo, to be grateful to this country, and reason to show my gratitude.

Today I am an American citizen, and long before Germany's frightful defeat I publicly and privately declared that I had no intention of ever again turning my back on America. My children, two of whom are still serving in the American army, are rooted in this country; English-speaking grandchildren are growing up around me. I myself am anchored to this country in many ways, here and there bound by ties of honor (in Washington and at the major universities which have conferred their *honorary degrees* upon me) and have built my house on this glorious, future-oriented coast. In its shelter I should like to pursue my life's work to its end—participating in an atmosphere of power, rationality, abundance, and peace. To put it bluntly, I do not see why I should not enjoy the advantages of my strange lot, after having tasted its disadvantages to the dregs. I especially do not see it because I cannot understand what service I can render the German people—which I could not also render from the State of California.

That everything has turned out as it has is not of my arranging. By no means! It is an outcome of the character and fate of the German people—a people tragically interesting and remarkable enough so that one is willing to put up with a good deal from them. But then one should also abide by the results, without trying to make the whole thing end in a banal: "Come home, all is forgiven."

I do not want to be self-righteous. For us on the outside it was easy to be virtuous and tell Hitler what we thought of him. I am not throwing stones, not at anyone. I am only alienated and "bashful," as we say of little children. In the course of all these years Germany has truly become alien to me. You must grant that it is a frightening country. I admit that I fear the sight of German ruins—both stone and human. And I fear that communication between one who watched the witches' sabbath from outside and you who joined in the dance and paid your respects to Old Nick would be difficult in any case. How can I be unresponsive to the effusive letters full of long-repressed loyalty now coming to me from Germany? They are truly emotional events for me—deeply touching. But my pleasure in them is somewhat checked not only by the thought that none of them would ever have been written if Hitler had won, but also by a certain ingenuousness and lack of sensitivity in them, by their naïve assumption that ties can be resumed as if these twelve years had never been. Books, too, have been coming. Shall I confess that I did not welcome them and soon put them away? It may be superstition, but in my eyes any books that could be printed in Germany from 1933 to 1945 are worse than worthless, and I am reluctant to touch them. A stench of blood and disgrace clings to them; they all ought to be pulped.

It was not right, it was impossible, to go on producing *Kultur* in Germany while all the things we know of were taking place. To do so meant palliating depravity, extenuating crime. Among the torments we suffered was the sight of German literature and art constantly serving as window dressing for absolute monstrousness. Strangely, no one seems to have felt that there were more honorable occupations than designing Wagner sets for Hitler's Bayreuth. To travel, with Goebbels's permission, to Hungary or some other Germanized European country and deliver clever lectures there as a form of cultural propaganda for the Third Reich —I do not say that was disgraceful; I merely say that I don't understand it and therefore shrink from reunion with a good many persons.

A conductor sent out by Hitler to perform Beethoven in Zurich, Paris, or Budapest incurred the guilt of an obscene lie—the pretense that he was a musician and making music, and no more. But above all, the music back home was already a lie. How could it be that Beethoven's *Fidelio*, preordained to be the festival opera for the day of German self-liberation, was *not* banned in the Germany of those twelve years? It was a scandal that it wasn't, that instead there were choice performances of it, that singers were found to sing it, musicians to play it, an audience to listen to it. What amount of apathy was needed for people to listen to *Fidelio* in Himmler's Germany without covering their faces and rushing out of the hall?

Ah yes, a good many letters are now coming from that alien, eerie homeland, transmitted by American sergeants and lieutenants. They come not only from important men, but from young people and ordinary citizens. And curiously enough, none of the latter advises me to hurry back to Germany. "Stay where you are," they say simply. "Spend your declining years in your happier new homeland. It is too sad here. . . ." Sad? If it were only that—and not also, inevitably, persistently malignant and hostile. Some Americans recently sent to me, as a kind of trophy, an old issue of a German periodical: *Volk im Werden*, March 1937 (Hanseatische Verlagsanstalt, Hamburg), edited by a highly placed Nazi professor, with an honorary doctorate. His name was not quite *Krieg* [War], but Krieck with a ck. It was grim reading. And I said to myself: Where people have been fed these drugs for twelve long years, I can't very well live. No doubt, I said to myself, you would have many good and loyal friends, old and young, there; but also many enemies lurking in ambush—defeated enemies, to be sure, but those are the worst and most venomous.

And yet, Herr von Molo, all this is only one side of the matter. The other side also demands a hearing. The profound curiosity and agitation with which I receive every piece of news from Germany, direct or indirect; the fact that I decidedly prefer such items to all news from the greater world as it is now reshaping itself, with such indifference to Germany's incidental fate—these reactions make me aware every day of the indissoluble bonds which after all still link me to the country that "expatriated" me. An American citizen of the world—very well. But how shall I deny that my roots are in Germany, that for all that I admire and feel enriched by foreign things, I live and have my being in the German tradition, even though the age has not permitted my work to be anything but a morbid and semiparodistic echo of the greatness of *Deutschtum*.

I shall always feel that I am a German writer. During these years in which my books have been kept alive only in English, I have remained faithful to the German language—not only because I was too old to change languages, but also because I am aware that my work has its modest place in the history of the German language. The Goethe novel, written in Germany's darkest days, smuggled in to you copy by copy, is not exactly a document of forgetfulness and infidelity. Nor do I have to say: "I feel shame for my peaceful hours; to suffer with you was a gain."[1] Germany has never left me in peace. I have suffered with you, and it was no exaggeration when I spoke in the letter to Bonn of my concern and distress: "My creative work emerged from daily wrestling with a mental and spiritual distress that has been with me every hour of my life for four years." I put that work of mine aside often enough. The half a hundred (or were there more?) radio messages to Germany which are now being printed in Sweden—those recurrent and repetitious pleas may testify that often enough other things seemed more urgent to me than "art."

A few weeks ago I delivered a lecture at the Library of Congress in Washington on the subject "Germany and the Germans." I wrote it in German, and it is to be published in the next issue of the *Neue Rundschau*, which was resurrected in June 1945. It was an attempt to explain on a psychological basis to a cultivated American audience how things could possibly have turned out as they did in Germany. And I had to admire the equanimity with which this audience, so shortly after the end of a ghastly war, received my explanations. Naturally it was not easy for me to follow a middle course between offering undue excuses and leveling charges which would also have been inappropriate for me to make. But it came off, more or less. I spoke of the beneficent fact that good often comes out of evil on this earth—and of the diabolic fact that evil often comes out of the good. I gave a brief account of the development of German *Innerlichkeit*. I rejected the theory of the two Germanys, one good and one evil. The evil Germany, I said, is the good Germany gone wrong—the good one caught up in misfortune, guilt, and doom. I was not standing there, I said, to follow the bad habit of recommending myself to the world as the good, the noble, the just Germany in a white dress. Nothing of what I had been trying to tell my listeners about Germany had come from cool, detached, outside knowledge, I said; rather I had it all inside me; I had experienced it all in my own person.

[1] From Goethe's *Des Epimenides Erwachen* (Act II, Scene 9).

That was, I think, what is called a declaration of solidarity, at the most critical moment. Not exactly solidarity with National Socialism—no, not that. But with Germany—which after all succumbed to it and made a pact with the devil. The pact with the devil is a profound thing, a venerable German tradition, and a German novel inspired by the sufferings of recent years, by suffering for Germany and because of Germany, would, I suppose, have to have this sinister agreement for its subject. But in our great national poem, the Evil One is in the end even cheated out of Faust's single soul. Let us not in any way suggest that the devil has now collected the soul of Germany. Grace is stronger than any pact signed in blood. I believe in grace, and I believe in Germany's future, however desperate her present may look, however hopeless the destruction seems to be. It's time to stop talking about the end of German history! Germany is not identical with the brief horror-laden historical episode which bears Hitler's name. Nor is it identical with the brief Bismarckian era of the Prusso-German Reich. It is not even identical with the mere two centuries which can be dubbed the era of Frederick the Great. It is on the point of assuming a new form, which perhaps, after the first pangs of change and transition, may yield more happiness and true dignity, may be more favorable to the genuine inclinations and needs of the nation, than the old condition.

Does Germany's defeat mean that world history is over? History is actually moving along at a most lively pace, and Germany's history is included within it. To be sure, there is always power politics to warn us against having any immoderate expectations. But doesn't the hope remain that inevitably the first tentative steps will be taken toward a world in which the national individualism of the nineteenth century will ultimately pass away? A global economy, the fading of political frontiers, a kind of depoliticalization of international relations in general, humanity's awakening to a consciousness of its practical unity, a first facing up to the world state—what the great struggle really is about is a social humanism going far beyond bourgeois democracy. And how could such humanism be alien and antipathetic to the German character? In the German's timidity in the face of the world there has always been such longing for the world; underlying the solitariness that turned the German character toward evil, no one can fail to recognize the wish to love, the wish to be loved. Let Germany expel arrogance and hatred from her bloodstream, let her discover love again, and she will be loved. In spite of everything, she remains a country of tremendous ethical potentiality, a country that can count on the competence of her people as well as on the help of the world. Once the worst is over, she can look forward to a new life rich in accomplishment and prestige.

In replying to you, my dear Herr von Molo, I have let myself range far afield. I beg your pardon. All sorts of things had to be tucked into a letter to Germany. Just this one more item: In spite of the great holding power which America has, the dream of feeling the soil of the old Continent under my feet once more is with me all my days and nights. If the hour comes—if I live, and if transportation conditions and the honorable authorities permit—I intend to make the crossing. And once I am there, something tells me that bashfulness and alienation, these products of only twelve years, will not prevail against an attraction that has longer memories, a thousand years of them, on its side. Until we meet again, then, God willing.

TO RUDOLF W. BLUNCK[1]

Pacific Palisades
November 19, 1945

My dear Herr Blunck:

I have received your friendly letter of November 6 and wish to express my sympathy for the discomforts that your brother, Dr. Friedrich Blunck, has to endure at the present time. But even if I could claim more influence with the British military government than I believe I have, I would be in no position to do anything about this matter. Your brother's attitude during the Nazi years offers me no opening, and people would be justifiably surprised if I were to intervene on his behalf.

Certainly no one is going to regard your brother as a *"war criminal"* in any narrow sense of the word. But you must consider that throughout the whole twelve years as president of the Nazi *Reichsschrifttumskammer* he held a prominent official position within Nazi culture, that he enjoyed all the advantages which accrued to him from this position, and so he can hardly wonder if, after the collapse of the regime under which he zealously worked, he suffers certain personal setbacks.

Ernst Wiechert,[2] a profoundly German writer who opposed the Nazi

---

[1] See letter of July 22, 1946, p. 505.

[2] Ernst Wiechert (1887–1950), writer. Sentenced to several months in a concentration camp in 1938 for his circular letters and speeches opposing the Nazis. Forbidden to publish during the war. Emigrated to Switzerland in 1948 and died there. Among his rather melancholy works, dedicated to "the simple life," are *Wälder und Menschen* (1936), *Das einfache Leben* (1939), *Rede an die deutsche Jugend* (1945). His collected works were published in ten volumes in 1956.

regime with great courage from the start and suffered severely as a result, quotes from a letter which your brother addressed to him while in office. At that time your brother wrote: "The new State for the first time in centuries, in fact perhaps since the times of Walther von der Vogel-weide, has restored the dignity of German art." That is quite a bit more than being "merely a German," as you characterize your brother.

We must comfort ourselves with the thought that the English camps are somewhat different from the Nazi concentration camps, in which a man like Ernst Wiechert languished while not the slightest protest was heard from his colleagues in Germany. It is likely that the imprisonment will not last very long, and we may hope that your brother will soon be able to put his considerable talent to work for the rebuilding of Germany and of his own life.

TO ALBERT EINSTEIN

Pacific Palisades
November 27, 1945

Dear Professor Einstein:

Forgive my troubling you, but I should like to ask your opinion and learn your position on two matters. I am enclosing a letter from a Mr. Alexander Stern in Nairobi, who reports that he is also turning to you with his proposal for a universal exiles' organization. I would very much like to hear your opinion of this project, which at first sight does not look un-reasonable, but which nevertheless strikes me as going much too far in its politically ambitious aims. If you simply refuse, I shall do likewise. If you set up conditions and limitations, I would be very grateful if you would let me know what these are.

Secondly, a musician named Franz Waxmann[1] came to see me today with the proposal that the international immigrants as a body show their gratitude to the country by presenting a gift. It seems that the famous portrait of President Washington by Gilbert Stuart is to be up for sale, and the idea is to collect $75,000 to buy it and give it to the White House. I have strong objections to this plan, which seems to me ill-advised in the present moral state of the country—the growing xenophobia, the growing anti-Semitism, etc. Moreover, it might well be said that such a collection ought to be organized for the starving children of Europe, rather than for

---

[1] Franz Waxmann, composer, chiefly of music for the movies, also for piano and string orchestra; conductor. Emigrated to the United States in 1934 and has since lived in Los Angeles.

a gift which has somewhat the air of toadying and of the desire to ingratiate ourselves. In this matter, too, I would be most grateful if you would inform me of your position.

TO FRITZ STRICH

Pacific Palisades
November 27, 1945

Dear Professor Strich:

That was a rewarding and important package: the Academy addresses,[1] among whom Burckhardt, Müller,[2] and Wölfflin[3] shine out; the fine essay on Stifter, which showed me more clearly than anything I have read how his pure, seemingly so unclouded work was carried out in spite of the distracting controversies of the day. Finally—though, good Lord, of course I read it first—the generous birthday essay in the Bund,[4] which I had not yet seen. Even if I discount some of those kind remarks as arising out of the festive occasion, evidently a few comforting things can be said about my journey upon this earth by people of good will. Many thanks for that, and for the whole generous *Xmas* present.

It so happened that at the time your package arrived I was rereading Stifter every night before going to sleep. I am among those who have read even *Witiko* conscientiously through to the end, and ever since I have regarded the work of that remarkable inspector of schools[5] as one of the greatest and most encouraging vindications of tedium in literature. His tedium is after all something different from the well-known *noble ennui*: it is a tranquil, pale, pedantic magic that takes a firmer hold than most "interesting" work, and is living proof of what degree of tediousness can be made possible in some circumstances. For the storyteller this is an important, and in fact truly exciting discovery. But aside from that and in spite of that, what an extraordinary storyteller the man is, every so often plunging ahead into extremes, even into pathological byways. As I reread (or, in the case of some stories, read for the first time) the *Studien*

---

[1] *Schweizerische Akademiereden* (Bern; 1945), edited by Fritz Strich.

[2] Johannes von Müller (1752–1809), historian and statesman; author of *Geschichte der schweizerischen Eidgenossenschaft* (5 vols., 1786–1808).

[3] Heinrich Wölfflin (1864–1945), Swiss art historian; successor to his teacher Jacob Burckhardt in Basel. Among his works: *Renaissance und Barock* (1888), *Kunstgeschichtliche Grundbegriffe* (1915), *Italien und das deutsche Formgefühl* (1931).

[4] "Thomas Mann zu seinem 70. Geburtstag am 6. Juni 1945" (*Der kleine Bund*, Bern, June 3, 1945).

[5] Stifter spent the latter part of his life as *Schulrat* for the public schools of Upper Austria.

and the *Bunte Steine,* and such feuilletonistic abnormalities as the description of the snowfall in the Bavarian forest and the frightening visit to the catacombs, I have become aware of his narrative genius with astonishment, with admiration that grows nightly. I keep talking about it to everyone. What a terrific thing *Abdias* is! And the children in the ice! and *Katzensilber,* in which such exquisite descriptions as those of the hailstorm and the fire are heaped one upon the other. And the absolutely unique milieu of *The Recluse.* There is something a little uncanny about the pedantic uncle with his "At breakfast." Moreover, the sensations that emerge from tedium are uncanny in the finest sense. —But I wish you had said much more about these narrative miracles and curiosities, which only a handful of lovers of Stifter are aware of, and which even they don't properly understand, and less about the philosophical, political, and moral matters—which these times do bring up, do demand, I know! And yet, even in regard to criticism of my own work—can you forgive me?— I have wished something similar. We are women, or half women, my dear friend. We always prefer to have our charm remarked on, rather than our virtue.

I know you are glad to be firmly rooted in Switzerland and attached to so estimable an institution. Would you respond to an invitation to teach in Germany, if it came? Well, you don't have to answer. Give my regards to our old friend Singer.[6] I have ordered his learned book;[7] it won't hurt me to have a few old German proverbs on hand as a counterpoise to my many stories of Jews—for which the Hebrew Union College in Cincinnati has recently made me a Doctor of Hebrew Letters. I forgot to mention this point in my letter of apology to Molo.

I often think how nice it would be to return to our evening skittles in Tegernsee at Bruno Frank's. He is dead now, and Werfel is dead; their widows have gone East; Leonhard Frank, an interesting man, has also gone there, and it is growing lonely. There is sociability enough, but scarcely anyone with whom one can have a real talk, at least in German. Day before yesterday we spent an evening at the home of Eisler,[8] the composer, with Charlie Chaplin. For three hours I laughed till the tears came at his imitations, scenes, and clowning, and was still rubbing my

---

[6] Samuel Singer (1860–1948), Austrian-born professor of German literature at the University of Bern. Among his principal works: *Deutsches Mittelalter und Renaissance* (1910), *Literaturgeschichte der deutschen Schweiz im Mittelalter* (1916), *Die religiöse Lyrik des Mittelalters* (1933).

[7] *Sprichwörter des Mittelalters* (3 vols., 1944–7).

[8] Hanns Eisler (b. 1898), composer, disciple of Arnold Schoenberg. Emigrated in 1933 by way of Russia to Hollywood, where he wrote a great deal of movie music. In East Germany since 1949.

eyes as we were getting into our car. Nobody so enlivens society as the gifted actor. They always want to perform, and so one is safe.

TO KARL KERÉNYI

Pacific Palisades
December 3, 1945

Dear Professor Kerényi:

A magnificent packet![1] And an inspiring testimony to your energy, humor, and creativity. My warmest thanks for all the stimulus and intellectual zest these essays provide. I have the impression that you are already playing a completely native and widely respected part in Swiss cultural life. Are you thinking at all of returning to your country? Certainly you have analyzed its problems with great shrewdness (and not without a note of emotional participation) in the *Neue Schweizer Rundschau.* You will soon be in a position to explain their own problems to the Swiss—for where are there no problems? In this colossally victorious and "powerful" country, the last refuge of bourgeois *complacency,* the atmosphere is gradually becoming so thick with them that one wonders how long things can go on without violent discharges. —Of course your scientific, anthropological contributions can just as well, or possibly better, go out into the world from Switzerland and in the German language. Only on this point, in regard to the language which after all is not your mother tongue (though you easily make me forget that), I should like to caution you to eternal watchfulness and discipline of the poetic conscience, whatever freedom it must have for the treatment of subjects like yours—the noblest there can be. "*Wie nahe eine solche Frage in der Zeit der 'Pariser Rechenschaft' lag, ebenso unmöglich erscheint sie . . .*" This is not a logical order in German. The simple "*So nahe—so unmöglich*" would be correct. Or else it could be put: "*Wie nahe auch eine solche Frage etc. —sie erscheint unmöglich, sobald etc.*" Such slips, naturally enough, are not *altogether* isolated. Hairsplitting? Pedantry? I can only once more plead the immense dignity of your subjects.

You see, in spite of the fascinating clan with the golden glint in their eyes (a wonderful idea!) and in spite of the tantalizing divine personality of the son of Maia,[2] forever luring one to further investigations, I fell

---

[1] It contained a number of essays by Kerényi: *Die ungarische Wendung, Bachofen und die Zukunft des Humanismus mit einem Intermezzo über Neitzsche und Ariadne, Die Töchter der Sonne. Betrachtungen über griechische Gottheiten, Hermes der Seelenführer.*

[2] Hermes.

most eagerly upon the Bachofen[3]-Nietzsche essay, which at this moment belongs in my circle (my magic or incantatory circle). For after all is said and done, to use a rather old-fashioned phrase, the perhaps impossible novel that I have been rolling uphill like a stone since May 1943 is basically a Nietzsche novel. Thus again it has a somewhat mythic atmosphere, although it takes place not three thousand years ago but in our own time, and really deals with the character and fate of Germany. Merely as a work of old age it has a certain kinship, though a remote one, with [Hesse's] *The Bead Game*. Nietzsche can be felt in it more strongly than Bachofen, who is no longer so vivid a factor in my work as he was when I was writing the *Joseph*. You understand perfectly to what extent my somewhat unsound remarks about him in the twenties were actuated by political alarm and by the tendentious distortions of his work. For in spite of all his feeling for the "pit" (without which there is no humaneness at all), he is anything but an obscurantist; rather, his system of thought ends in an affirmation of the religion of Zeus. The manner and the time of presentation seemed to me poor pedagogy, but I personally have never shied away from Bachofen; in fact, I have studied him almost as I did Schopenhauer. Just now, reading in your essay once again about his poetic concept of swampy substance and water plants and the symbolism of swamp fauna, I recalled with some amusement Potiphar's "holy parents" in *Joseph in Egypt*, the brother-sister couple who keep giving each other pet names such as "dear field-vole," "my swampbeaver," "buttercup" and "spoonbill" as well as "old mole" and "sparrow owl." They cannot do enough to demonstrate their archaic fealty to a prematriarchic "eon" and to parody Bachofen.

The best of everything to you. My European trip, insofar as I thought of it for next spring, is becoming more and more doubtful. In the first place, *Doctor Faustus* will probably not be done by then, and in the second place, people keep warning me about the disorganized conditions in Europe. To be sure, one can get there, but traveling on the Continent is evidently an adventurous improvisation which my nerves and innards would certainly not be up to. About this sort of thing I feel, sincerely against my own wishes, closer to Erasmus than to Goethe.

In spite of this, let us cling to the hope of seeing each other again.

---

[3] Johann Jakob Bachofen (1815–1887), philosopher and jurist, historian of ancient law, religion, and culture. He is considered the discoverer of matriarchy (*Das Mutterrecht*, 1861).

1945

TO CHARLES DUFFY[1]

[Original in English]

Pacific Palisades
December 14, 1945

Dear Mr. Duffy:

Many thanks for your kind lines of November 30th. You have by far overestimated my erudition. The thought of the medieval monk was far from my mind when writing about my Cipolla, and in case later philologists should find such an allusion in my story, I herewith want to state for all eternity that I did not have the slightest symbolical intention when naming the magician Cipolla.

Also, the pistol of our Mario is by no means a product of metaphysical speculation. The explanation of the fact that he carries a pistol lies rather in the circumstance that he is in love, and obviously unhappily in love, as it is quite clear from the story that his sweetheart prefers a more robust and handsome rival to him. The shot, or shots, which he fires at the mental tyrant Cipolla, who for a moment has conjured up love's happiness before his eyes, were originally intended for somebody else— not with full consciousness—but anyhow the pistol was in readiness.

Thank you very much indeed for your interest.

TO VIKTOR MANN

Pacific Palisades
December 15, 1945

Dear Brother Viko:

Yesterday, through the kindness of Herr Salm, your most recent letter arrived, with some more touching old photographs. [. . .]

I still owe you thanks for two other ample and detailed letters. In the second one of November 12th, to whom were you talking when you spoke of the outside world's complicity in the German disaster and in German sins? We who are outside have always been fully aware of that complicity; it is only that you don't know how steadily and how bitterly I pointed out the guilt of the democracies, especially in an essay called *This Peace*. I wrote the little book, which was published in English in

---

[1] Charles Duffy (b. 1903), professor of English at the University of Akron. This letter, along with some interesting speculations on *Mario and the Magician*, was published in *Monatshefte* (May 1959).

New York and in German in Stockholm, immediately after our arrival in Princeton, after the shock of the democracies' capitulation to fascism in Munich. In it I drew up the whole catalog of sins of the countries which had soon to atone for their false and immoral peaceableness by fighting the war. The whole thing could be foreseen so clearly that the present outcome seems outmoded and boring. Besides which, it is largely unsatisfactory, as you also quite rightly suggest in your letter. From this vantage point too, we see precisely the mistakes that are being made in the Allied treatment of Germany. The wrong people are shown preference, and harshness is applied where leniency is called for. On the other hand, it must be granted that it would be difficult to find any line that would please the Germans. [. . .]

Naturally we have been very interested in your activities in regard to the house in Herzogpark.[1] My conscience would not be entirely clear if it were to be restored at government expense on the assumption that we would soon be moving in. But the idea that a real house in Munich was waiting for us would have something heartwarming about it. One way or the other, we do hope to pay a visit there within a reasonable time.

A second package, whose most important contents are some woolen underclothing of mine (since under present conditions this sort of thing can't be bought even here), and which also has pictures of us and something in the way of nourishment, was started on its way to you about two weeks ago. I am concerned about its safe arrival. An alarming number of things go astray, and we don't know whether even the first package reached you. Theft is rampant everywhere—and no wonder, since people everywhere are impoverished and in need.

Alas, the manuscripts which Heins[2] had in safekeeping are probably gone forever. What he told Justizrat Veit,[3] incidentally, is untrue. We never asked to have the manuscripts taken across the frontier by a Czech courier. Rather, they were to be shipped directly to the United States along with the legally released personal property of a reliable acquaintance who held full written authorization from us.[4] This could have been done without any risk, and it remains unforgivable that Heins, to whom as our lawyer I had entrusted those things, refused to hand them over. If he

---

[1] The home that Thomas Mann and his family had abandoned in Munich.

[2] Valentin Heins, the lawyer who was supposed to look after Thomas Mann's interests within Germany during the early years of the Nazi regime.

[3] Adolf Veit (1873–1947), a member of the presiding board of the Bavarian Bar Association.

[4] This acquaintance had a diplomatic passport.

thought it his duty to turn the things over to the government, he should have done so the moment it was announced that my property was being expropriated; but in no case did he have the right to retain them against my express wish. The intention behind it can only have been to hold on to something of mine worth money—an intention that failed and that has inflicted considerable damage upon me.

Although this letter can no longer reach you for Christmas, let's hope it comes before the end of the year. Both of us wish you and Nelly[5] (whom we thank for her note) a very good, hopefully launched New Year —at least a better one, let us trust, than the year just behind you.

Warmly,

Yours,

T.

TO THEODOR W. ADORNO[1]

Pacific Palisades
December 30, 1945

Dear Dr. Adorno:

I have the impulse to write you about the manuscript I recently left with you; perhaps you are on the point of reading it. In writing to you I don't feel as if I were interrupting my work.

It excites me to know that this strange, perhaps impossible novel (what there is of it) is in your hands, for in the states of weariness which come to me more and more often, I ask myself whether I would not do better to drop it. So whether I stick at it depends somewhat on your response.

The point on which I feel I owe you an explanation concerns the principle of *montage*, which peculiarly and perhaps outrageously runs through this entire book without any attempt at concealment. I was struck by it again in a recent passage where it occurs in half amusing, half uncanny fashion; I was describing the hero's critical illness, and I included Nietzsche's symptoms word for word as they are set forth in his letters, along with the prescribed menus, etc. I pasted them in, so to

[5] Nelly Kilian Mann, Viktor Mann's wife.
[1] Theodor W. Adorno (1903–1969), philosopher, sociologist, and composer. Instructor in Frankfurt am Main, 1931–3. Emigrated to England in 1934, later to the United States. Professor in Frankfurt since 1950. Among his works: *Kierkegaard* (1933), *Dialektik der Aufklärung* (with Max Horkheimer), (1947), *Philosophie der neuen Musik* (1949), *minima moralia* (1951), *Drei Studien zu Hegel* (1963). See Mann's tribute to him in *The Story of a Novel*, pp. 42–8.

speak, for anyone to recognize. Another element of montage is the motif of the invisible feminine admirer and lover who is never met, avoided in the flesh: Tschaikovsky's Madame Meck. Well-known historical fact though it is, I am pasting it in and blurring the edges; I drop it into the story as if it were a mythic theme there for the taking, in the public domain. (For Leverkühn the relationship is a means of circumventing the devil's proscription of love, commandment of coldness.)

A further example: Toward the end of the book I obviously, using actual quotations, introduce the theme of the Shakespeare sonnets, the triangle in which the friend sends his friend to the sweetheart to do some wooing for him—and he "woos for himself." Of course I transform that: Adrian *kills*[2] the friend whom he loves, because in involving his friend with the lady painter he exposes him to murderous jealousy (Inez Rodde). But be that as it may, the borrowing still seems to me to have something bold and thievish about it.

To plead Molière's "*Je prends mon bien où je le trouve*" strikes me as an insufficient excuse for this conduct. It might be said that I have developed an inclination in old age to regard life as a cultural product, hence a set of mythic clichés which I prefer, in my calcified dignity, to "independent" invention. But I know only too well that quite early in life I went in for a kind of higher copying: i.e., in describing Hanno *Buddenbrook's* typhoid fever, the details of which I unabashedly lifted from an encyclopedia article and then "versified," as it were. The chapter has become famous. But its merit consists only in a certain poeticization of mechanically appropriated material (and in the trick of indirectly communicating Hanno's death).

The case is more difficult—not to say more scandalous—when it is a matter of appropriating materials which are themselves already poetic—that is, when a real literary borrowing is involved, performed with an air that what has been filched is just good enough to serve one's own pattern of ideas. You rightly presume that when I say this, I have in mind the brazen—and I hope not altogether doltish—snatches at certain parts of your essays on the philosophy of music. These borrowings cry out all the more for apology since for the time being the reader cannot be made aware of them; there is no way to call his attention to them without breaking the illusion. (Perhaps a footnote: "This comes from Adorno-Wiesengrund"? It won't do!)

It is curious: my relationship to music is fairly accepted; I have

---

[2] The italics throughout this letter are Mann's and do not indicate words in English in the original.

always been adept at literary music-making, have felt myself to be half-and-half a musician, and have translated the technique of musical inter-weaving to the novel. Only recently, for instance, Ernst Toch in a con-gratulatory note certified me outright as "musically initiated." But in order to write a musician-novel which occasionally even seems to aspire to become, along with other things, a novel of music, more is needed than mere "initiation." Scholarship is wanted, and that I simply lack. Which is one reason I was determined from the start, since the book in any case is based on the principle of montage, to shrink from no borrowing, no appropriation of other men's property. I trust that the borrowings will serve as an independent function within the pattern of the whole, will acquire a symbolic life of their own—while at the same time continuing to exist *intact in their original places* in works of criticism.

My hope is that you will share this view. The fact is that my own musical education has scarcely gone beyond the late romantics, and you have given me the ideas about contemporary music that I needed for a book which, among other things, deals with the *situation of art*. Just as in the case of little Hanno's typhoid fever, my "initiated" ignorance needed precise details to enhance the illusion and serve the purposes of the pattern, and I would be deeply obliged to you if you would intervene and correct them wherever these details (which I have not borrowed ex-clusively from you) are awry, misleading, or expressed in a way which experts might find ludicrous. *One* passage has been subjected to expert examination. I read the part about Opus 111 to Bruno Walter. He was *enthusiastic*. "Why, that's magnificent. Nothing better has ever been said about Beethoven. I had no idea you had penetrated so deeply into him." And yet I do not even wish to set up the expert as the absolute judge. The musical expert in particular, always so very proud of his arcane know-ledge, is for my purposes all too ready to come forth with his superior smile. It could be said, cautiously and *cum grano salis*, that something may give the impression of being right, may sound right, without being altogether so. —But I am not trying to ingratiate myself with you.

I have pushed the novel along to the point where Leverkühn, at the age of thirty-five, in a first wave of euphoric inspiration and in an incredibly short time, composes his principal work, or first principal work, the *Apocalipsis cum figuris*, after the fifteen Dürer prints or also directly after the text of the Revelation. Here the problem is to imagine and characterize convincingly a work which I think of as a very *German* product, an oratorio with orchestra, choruses, solos, a narrator. I am really writing this letter to keep my mind on the matter, which as yet I don't dare attack. What I need are a few significant, suggestive *specific* details (I can manage with only a few) which will give the reader a plausible, even a convincing picture. Would you think about the problem, along with me: how the work—I mean Leverkühn's work—can more or less be described; what sort of music you would write if you were in league with the devil; could you suggest one or two musical characteristics to further the illusion? I have a notion of something satanically religious, demonically devout, at once stringently disciplined and criminally loose, often mocking art, also something reaching back to the primitive and elemental (Kretzschmar-Beissl reminiscence), abandoning bar divisions, even the order of tonalities (trumpet glissandi); furthermore, something scarcely performable: ancient church modes, *a capella* choruses which must be sung in untempered tuning, so that scarcely a tone or interval on the piano occurs, etc. But it's easy to say "etc."

I have just learned that I shall be seeing you sooner than I thought, since arrangements have been made for a conference on Wednesday afternoon. Well, I could have said all this to you face to face. But then again, there is a propriety and reassurance for me in your having it in your hands in black and white. Let it be the groundwork for our conversation, as well as a record for posterity, if there should be a posterity.

1946

———————•———————

Pacific Palisades
[postmarked January 28, 1946]

My dear Professor:

It was a great pleasure to receive your letter, and along with it the amusing drawing provoked by a phrase in my battle cries. My thanks and congratulations to the artist. The fifty-five radio addresses have now been published as a collection, and to my own surprise they do not seem monotonous, although they persistently say the same thing. [. . .]

I would not place the end of the bourgeois cultural era in 1933, but back in 1914. The shock we experienced then was, of course, based on the feeling that the outbreak of the war marked the end of a world and the beginning of something utterly new. Since then everything has been in movement, tossing and churning, and will go on that way for a long time. How can you ask me to define in a word or two the new things that will develop out of the struggles and convulsions we have been passing through in this mutational crisis? I am hardly the person to do so, for I am a child of bourgeois individualism and by nature (if I am not careful to correct myself) very much inclined to equate bourgeois culture with culture per se and to regard what is coming after it as barbarism. But my sympathy with mutating life teaches me that the opposite of "culture" as we knew it is not barbarism, but *community*.[2] I am thinking primarily of art. One typical aspect of the postbourgeois world will be that it will liberate art from the solemn isolation which came about after *the emancipation of culture from cultus*,[2] when art was elevated to the role of a substitute for religion. Art will be freed from its lonely dependence on an educated

———

[1] Pierre-Paul Sagave (b. 1913), professor of German literature, Aix-en-Provence. Among his books: *Réalité sociale et idéologie religieuse dans les romans de Thomas Mann* (1954).
[2] Mann's italics.

elite called "the public," which already no longer exists, so that art will soon be entirely alone and well on the way to extinction unless it can find the way to the "people"—that is, to express it prosaically, to the masses. I believe that art's whole attitude toward life will change; its mood will be serene and *more modest*.[3] It will shed a good deal of its gloomy ambition, and will show a new innocence, indeed innocuousness. The world of the future will regard it—and art will again regard itself—as the handmaiden of a community which will embrace far more than "education" and will perhaps not *have*[3] culture but *be*[3] something like it.

Well, I have indulged in prophecy. But your question tempted me to it, and I fear I have returned too little by returning too much. Make the best of it.

TO BRUNO WALTER

Pacific Palisades
February 25, 1946

Dear friend:

Have no fear, your warning was scarcely necessary. Similar advice has been coming from everyone, as well as from Germany itself; so I now say like Gerhart Hauptmann when people wanted him to run for president: "After mature consideration I would not dream of it."

Even without a visit to the Fatherland the trip to Europe would have buffeted my after all somewhat precarious health. I shall surely do better first to finish my novel, which makes enough demands on my strength.

Incidentally, our late friend Werfel used his last eighteen months very well. *Star of the Unborn* is a terrific thing, excellent, arresting— mystical, of course, but with humor. Granted, as prose the book has no quality, which puts it in a different category from Dante. But as an achievement of the imagination it is most impressive. You'll see.

Warmly,

Yours,
T. M.

[3] Mann's italics.

1946

TO JONAS LESSER[1]

Pacific Palisades
March 21, 1946

Dear Herr Doktor Lesser:

Your manuscript came several days ago, and for once I had all the leisure I needed to read it promptly from beginning to end, since for more than a week a really nasty grippe has kept me in bed—really the best place for reading. I am still extremely tired from the whole bout, and can only thank you for your work and congratulate you on it.

What shall I say, since I can say only a little? I was moved by the incredible exactitude with which you study my work as literature, and at the same time somewhat alarmed by this movingly affectionate exactitude. Will the public stand for it and not find it exaggerated and improper for modern work whose author is still living? I don't know. We must hope that there are at least a handful of people whose sympathy with the work will make them follow all these precise references, interpretations, and combinations with interest. At one point it seems to me (though should I say this, in view of the chief concern I have just mentioned?) that the intensity of your observation curiously falls off. I refer to the little chapter on the dwarfs. It is indeed apt to describe the dignified Dudu simply as a Nazi, but to do so is to overlook the sexual satire which is the main thing in the characterization of the two little people. All Dudu's dignity, solidity, and "pomposity" is founded, of course, on his capacity for begetting, on his quality as a substantial married man; and Beauty's whole distaste for him is founded on his own dwarfish purity, his nonparticipation in sex. I don't want to expatiate on it except to say that at this point your critique has omitted a few things. It also surprised me that for all your loving analysis of the language and, if I may put it that way, the lexical fullness of the book, you omitted the bickering scene between the two dwarfs, although that would have been so much to your purpose. Moreover, this scene belongs in the context of your comparison of the *Joseph* with the *Ring of the Nibelungen*, for it is definitely reminiscent of the quarrelsome meeting of Mime and Alberich.

Just two more minor comments. The word "parody" seems to me to be used too often, and occasionally in a fashion that might confuse the

---

[1] Jonas Lesser (b. 1896), author and critic. Editor in Paul Zsolnay Verlag, Vienna, until the Anschluss. Emigrated to London, where he now lives. Author of many essays on Thomas Mann and reviews of his books. His chief work is *Thomas Mann in der Epoche seiner Vollendung* (1952), to which this letter refers.

reader. Furthermore, I should like to warn you against such stylistic turns as "You remember," etc. They seem to me somehow out of place in a book of criticism, and I would stick to the more conventional "We will recall."

I trust that these few dry remarks make it clear that your magnificent, affectionate commentary has given me much pleasure. I am grateful to you, and wish you the gratitude of the public. The manuscript is going back to you well packed.

TO AGNES E. MEYER

Pacific Palisades
April 3, 1946

Dear Princess:

Please forgive me for dictating this, but I would not want you to go without any news from me, and writing is too strenuous for me at the moment.

What I have to tell you is that my trip East is now definitely postponed. Along with this grippe, which I can't seem to throw off, a minor lung condition has come to light. It has certainly been there for a long time and explains some of the fatigue I have suffered in recent months, in fact for a good deal longer. This means that recuperation will be a lengthier business than after a simple virus infection; afternoons my temperature is rather high and I must spend a large part of the day in bed. What I miss most are my walks, which the doctors (our family doctor and a specialist who has been consulted) absolutely forbid for the present. The doctors promise that I'll be well in about three months, but that is certainly tribulation enough.

Please inform Luther Evans[1] of the state of affairs. If we are determined to find a silver lining, we may say that autumn in Washington is certainly a better season than late May.

Warm greetings from

Your faithful

---

[1] Luther Evans (b. 1902), Librarian of Congress 1945–53; Secretary General of UNESCO 1953–8. Author of *The Virgin Islands, from Naval Base to New Deal* (1945), among others.

1946

TO FREDERICK ROSENTHAL[1]

Billings Memorial Hospital
Chicago
May 14, 1946

Dear Dr. Rosenthal:

From my sickbed, which for the most part is no longer a bed but an armchair, I want to write you the first note I have been capable of. By your preliminary treatment you had a large share in the remarkably smooth and fortunate course of this surgical affair; for the penicillin therapy you put me on at home kept me free of fever on the journey and during the entire week preceding the operation here, and that surely helped matters.

I was in the best of hands here too, to be sure, and the whole thing was carried out with such solicitude and gentleness that there was never any question of real suffering. Moreover, my good-natured and patient constitution helped the helpers.

Today the weather was sunny and I was allowed outside for the first time, still using the wheelchair; but between whiles I am walking with little difficulty and only have to be careful not to move too rapidly and get out of breath.

We plan to set out on the 24th and be back home on Sunday the 26th. Seeing you soon and telling you about the operation in greater detail, as well as showing you my enormous scar, is among the things I am looking forward to.

Please give my brother my greetings.

TO ERICH VON KAHLER

Billings Memorial Hospital
Chicago
May 15, 1946

Dear friend Kahler:

Many thanks for your delightful, entertaining visit by letter. I am in no condition to return so much goodness with anything good, for my life at present is as impoverished in thoughts as in deeds; it's really a case of rather too little of anything. And yet I may say that I went through this

---

[1] Frederick Rosenthal (b. 1902), specialist in internal medicine in Berlin, 1932; practiced there until 1936, then emigrated to the United States. In Beverly Hills, California, since 1938. Dr. Rosenthal was the first to diagnose Mann's lung illness.

whole unexpected adventure with serious attentiveness, although without any thoughts worth communicating, and can be content with myself insofar as the thing may be thought of as an opportunity to show fortitude. I can even pride myself on having accomplished a few "deeds" in the active sense of the word, for in this situation I displayed an almost uncanny psychological preference for passive accomplishments. I went in for being a model patient, a role which after all has its dubious aspects. [. . .] At the same time the business was no joke, as the tremendous scar running from my chest to my back distinctly shows. Without codeine I still would not be able to take the pain of the healing process. But I am walking effortlessly, was outside in the wheelchair yesterday, and must only avoid moving too rapidly, since I still tend to be short of breath, and probably will for months to come.

I cannot praise the hospital enough; Adams[1] proved to be first-class, and the preliminary and postoperational treatment was perfect; every factor was taken into consideration. I have gone through the whole gamut: bronchoscopy, blood transfusions, pneumothorax, etc.; but everything was done in the most considerate, most progressive manner.

We mean to set out on the 24th and hope to drive into our flower-filled garden on Sunday the 26th, with Erika. My mind must be devoted entirely to finishing the novel. It deserves that on the whole, although some things may have gone wrong in the details. Toward the end I was writing it against the counterpressure of the illness. But in a work that deserves the name, not everything has to be successful. I am reading— for the first time as a whole, I think—[Gottfried Keller's] *Green Henry*. It has its weaknesses, prolixities, vexations, but is truly a *work* after my own heart.

Isn't the last issue of the *Rundschau* excellent? Not least because of your splendid essay. A quotation from Nietzsche, incidentally: "I am speaking about democracy as of something *to come*."

Thanks once more for your visit. I hope we shall see one another soon. Give Broch my best regards and remember me to your dear mother.

Yours,

T. M.

---

[1] William E. Adams (b. 1902), specialist in lung surgery at Billings Memorial Hospital in Chicago. Dr. Adams saved Mann's life.

1946

TO ANNA JACOBSON

Pacific Palisades
June 9, 1946

Dear Miss Jacobson:

My warmest thanks for your good and faithful birthday letter. I am doing tolerably well. Not that I can set all sails as yet; but in the mornings I tinker with the manuscript a little, stroll around the garden, which is in magnificent flower, and can even indulge myself with half a cigar after dinner.

On the whole, I don't mind that my constitution was given this testing. The doctors declare that a man of thirty could not have come through the operation any better. I suppose I am the type who can say of himself, like Nietzsche: "But aside from my being a *décadent*, I am also its opposite." I imagine he should have put it: "the opposite of one."

I assume that you did not read the Kästner[1] article[2] in context, but only those two misleading sentences. It is about the most outrageous thing the Germans have yet attempted against me, and a classical example of Saxon *Heemdicke*.[3] "To G. I shall never return," dear Annette Kolb wrote me in 1933. It has become a household phrase with us.

TO GOLO MANN

Pacific Palisades
June 16, 1946

Dear Golo:

How pleased I was at the long review of your book[1] in the *New York Times*: we promptly clipped it for you while we were in Chicago, staying at the good old Windermere. Gentz occupied and entertained me for an entire week, which otherwise was given over to the preliminaries for my operation. I must say, even in translation, which does somewhat smooth

[1] Erich Kästner (b. 1899), novelist, journalist, poet; author of many juveniles, including *Emil and the Detectives*. He was forbidden to publish in Hitler's Germany; his nonpolitical work of that period appeared chiefly in Switzerland. After the war Kästner became feature editor of the Munich *Neue Zeitung*.

[2] "Betrachtungen eines Unpolitischen," *Neue Zeitung* (January 19, 1946).

[3] Thomas Mann is imitating the Saxon pronunciation of the word *Heimtücke*, meaning "treacherous spite." In spite of his vexation, Mann was ready to vouch for Erich Kästner's integrity a year later at the meeting of the International PEN Club held in Zurich in June 1947.

[1] *Secretary of Europe, The Life of Friedrich Gentz* (New Haven: Yale University Press; 1946).

503

it down and make it similar to a certain type of American book, it is a distinguished, delightfully intelligent, original, fascinating book that does honor to its author and will certainly bring him practical honors and promotion. I can't go into it any further, but did want to congratulate you on this fine and felicitous publication.

Now I have received, through the mediation of the politically Germanophile German-Amercian journalist Lochner[2] (hm!) the enclosed letter from Berlin, which is causing me a good deal of perplexity—in fact real embarrassment. Ought I to accept the chairmanship or honorary chairmanship of this German League for Freedom, which clearly lacks any broad base, and in so doing perhaps identify myself with all sorts of patriotic sentiments these people will probably be forced to attach to their desire for peace and reconciliation? The word "reconciliation" is used in a very strange sense in Germany, you know, the implication being that it is imperative to reconcile Germany—and how, indeed, is any German peace organization going to keep this conception out of its demonstrations, proclamations, lectures, and so on?

On the other hand, I don't like to be always withdrawing, saying no, separating myself from Germany. Mielein, too, doesn't want me to do that, and is rather inclined toward acceptance. I wanted to ask your advice, to lean on your knowledge of the conditions. Can this group be taken seriously? Are they fit to associate with? After all, I shall have to count on something of a *stir* in the world press if a German peace league boasts of having me as president. It is a great responsibility. And why just this particular chance list? Why aren't some of the Heidelberg people on it—Vossler, etc., in short, the people of good will in Germany who can think beyond the limits of the Reich? Please look into the matter and decide.

Enough of that. At the moment I feel like Uncle Viko's nursemaid Hanne who would blow on a yarn reel for him, and when he wanted more would say: "No, my angel, I can't do more."

Warmly,

Z.

---

[2] Louis P. Lochner (b. 1887), journalist, radio commentator; Berlin chief of the Associated Press 1919–46. Author of *Herbert Hoover and Germany* (1960), among others.

1946

TO ERICH VON KAHLER

Pacific Palisades
June 20, 1946

Dear Erich:

Is it possible, Prince? Can an omission like this trouble your conscience? A perfectly ordinary seventy-first birthday! It's kind enough that you thought of it afterward.

I am tolerably well, and if I were more obedient and did not keep on the go so much mentally and physically, I would probably be further along by now. Still, I have gained five pounds since we have been back— *quite satisfactory*.

Having Erika here is very dear and delightful—she is writing a book about Europe. We laugh a great deal about the United States chaos— *the biggest chaos the world ever saw*.

Cordially,

Yours,
T. M.

TO HANS FRIEDRICH BLUNCK

Pacific Palisades
July 22, 1946

My dear Herr Blunck:

"Consternation" is the only word I can use to describe the feeling with which I read your letter and memorandum. They are not the only ones of their kind; why am I the recipient of these reports, declarations, justifications from Germany? I do not have the power to bind and loose, you know. And if I am taken as representative of the "world," why, this world is currently behaving so inadequately that one hardly needs to make apologies to it. Everyone must try to settle with his own conscience.

My comment on you was quite by the way, not voluntary, but elicited by your brother's letter. I *could*[1] only reply that it would look strange for me, who so ostentatiously turned my back on the Third Reich, if I were not to allow my name to be used to influence the Occupation authorities in favor of a literary spokesman and dignitary of that Reich.

You maintain that you were nothing of the kind, and I do not want to class this argument with the general phenomenon that nowadays

[1] All italics in this letter are Mann's.

everybody insists he "wasn't." But when I read such sentences in your statement as: "When Hitler in 1933 was called to the chancellorship by President von Hindenburg and *took the oath of loyalty to the Weimar Constitution,* I trusted the solemn declarations that all citizens would have the same rights. I assumed that a brief period of transition to a *new constitution* was involved. . . . After the death of Rudolf Binding I was invited to take a seat in the German Academy in Munich. My activity was limited to . . . offering advice and proposals for *instruction in the German language abroad*—" when I read such things I can only lift my eyes to heaven and say: "Almighty God!" Is so much blindness possible? Can any intellectual have so completely lacked insight and feeling for the horror that was going on? Did Hitler's magic consist in his ability to make people believe he would be the protector of the Weimar Constitution? Before he issued a new constitution? And the "instruction in the German language abroad"! Every child in the whole wide world knew what was meant by this euphemism, namely the undermining of the democratic forces of resistance everywhere, their demoralization by Nazi propaganda. Only the German writer did not know. He had no problem; he could be a purehearted simpleton and cultivate a placid temper, without moral indignation, without any capacity for detestation, for anger, for horror at the altogether infamous *Teufelsdreck* which National Socialism was to every decent soul from the first day on.

And you were invited to be a member of the Nazi Academy in Munich. Now just imagine: to my way of thinking, no colleague should ever have been willing to take the seat from which I was expelled in the most offensive manner immediately after Hitler took his "oath to the Weimar Constitution." Does that strike you as very conceited? But I do not stand alone in holding this view. It is shared by the entire intelligentsia. Only in Germany do people lack any feeling for such solidarity, any sense of pride, any courage to protest and take a stand. There they are only too ready to take the side of arrant evil—as long as it looks as if "history" were going to prove the evil right. But a man of letters, a creative writer, ought to know that although life allows all sorts of things, it stops short at absolute immorality.

This letter is degenerating into a philippic, which was the last thing I had in mind. I am scarcely qualified to be a rigid judge of ethics; I am the last to cast a stone and do not in the least regard myself as an authority before whom motions for acquittal should be brought. But nothing can ever dispel my grief and shame at the horrible heartless and brainless failure of the German intelligentsia to meet the test with which it was confronted in 1933. It will have to achieve many glories before that can be forgotten. May God grant it the strength and inner freedom to do so. This is both my general hope and at the same time a very personal wish for your work and future happiness.

TO AGNES E. MEYER

Dear friend:

Your latest letter has brought good—best—perfect news.

Florence came to lunch with us yesterday; she is looking well, laughs readily, and is obviously in good spirits. At our request she had brought her camera, and she took a lot of pictures in the garden. She told us the glad news about your visit, though she surmised, with a pretense of woe, that you were probably coming more for my sake than for hers— which, of course, I could only answer with sardonic laughter.

Many letters come from Germany, written very small to save space, with long explications, excuses, and declarations of love.

People have urged me to translate Hersey's reportage on Hiroshima into German. But I am not the least interested in having the Germans read it. As a piece of American *self-criticism* it is excellent, but the Germans have material enough for gloating as it is.

See you soon.

Yours,
T. M.

TO VIKTOR MANN

Dear Vikko:

Your good letter of August 7 arrived several days ago and gave us a great deal of pleasure. It is only common sense that you should stipulate your needs and wishes in regard to extra food. Katia will do her best to follow your suggestions. We can only hope that everything she so faithfully packs reaches you safely. "Many things are lost in the night," as it goes in the Eichendorff poem and Schumann song.

Whenever anyone wants to reprint something from *The Beloved Returns* he invariably hits on the passage you are worried about—a sign that people are amused by the impudent anachronism I allowed myself there. Of course the allusion to the late unlamented Adolf can't be called anything else. Today I might not even include it, but at the time he was not yet "the late." I'm not overly repentant about it. Fundamentally I don't think it so foolish and impossible that Goethe's thoughts, since they were already dwelling on the Germans, should have sailed off into still unverifiable anticipations. There are curious examples of that. Look into Keller's works sometime at the poem, *Die öffentlichen Verleumder*.[1] It is quite incredible. The pretext for the frenetic description of this plague was quite trivial—some petty yellow journalist in Zurich, I am told. Yet how the imagination, stirred by a morsel of reality, drifted off into prophetic visions of horror! It is in fact a divination of National Socialism, down to the final phrase that someday it will be talked about "as the Black Death." That sort of prophecy can come true.

But I have caused a good deal of comic confusion. Perhaps you heard the story that the British prosecutor[2] in Nuremberg quoted Goethe on the Germans, thinking that the quotation was authentic, when it was really from *The Beloved Returns*. The wide-awake British press loudly proclaimed that it wasn't from Goethe at all but from my novel, and the embassy in Washington asked me, quite abashed, what the truth of the matter was. I replied that I would guarantee that everything Goethe thinks and says in my novel might very well have been thought and said by him, so that in the higher sense the prosecutor had quoted correctly after all. I don't quite know whether that consoled Lord Inverchapel[3] and the Foreign Secretary[4] at whose request he wrote. It remains an awkward incident.

At present Bibi and Gret are visiting us with their sweet boys. Eri is still here too, but she has given the first of her *lectures* with great success and soon she will be taking off again. In compensation a visit from Golo is in prospect. [. . .] Furthermore we are expecting Katia's twin, old Klaus, and his son[5] all the way from Japan. I am leaving room for greetings from Erika.

Warmly,

T.

P.S. I go ahead and smoke. My lung is really perfectly all right.

[1] The Public Slanderers.
[2] Lord Hartley W. Shawcross (b. 1902).
[3] British ambassador in Washington, 1946–8.
[4] Ernest Bevin (1881–1951).
[5] Klaus Hubert Pringsheim (b. 1923), associate professor of political science at McMaster College, Hamilton, Ontario, since February 1966.

1946

TO DAVID GUY POWERS[1]

[Original in English]

Pacific Palisades,
October 24, 1946

Dear Dr. Powers:

I received your kind and interesting letter of October 15th, and thank you for the honor you do me with your inquiry. However, I am afraid that my reply will be very unsatisfactory, for the simple reason that you are wrong to presume I owed my successes—if I may talk of successes— to my skill in getting along with people. That is not at all possible in the case of a writer who exerts his influence through the written and molded word—an influence, deeply personal though it may be, is nevertheless indirect. I have always lived a very secluded life, and it was certainly not my way of handling people which has won me friends for my person and my work. I can hardly call myself a judge of human nature in the practical sense of the word, and I believe that this is true of many portrayers of humanity whose work shows much psychological insight. In my opinion, these insights spring from self-observation and self-criticism rather than from particular attention to others.

I may be justified in adding that I have indeed written the story of a personal success due to the art of treating people. It is the four volumes of my Joseph novel. Through an artistically executed religious and mythical fraud, this charming young man knows how to give people the impression that the lives of Adonis and Osiris are re-embodied in his own life, and to amaze and captivate everybody around him. And in spite of dangerous traits in his character he is able to achieve the highest honors in a foreign country.

The fact that I could tell this story may prove that I, as a poet, know something of the art of handling people, but it is probable that I could not have written this success story if I myself were a Joseph.

---

[1] David Guy Powers (1911–67), professor of speech at Queens College, New York.

1946

TO ERIKA MANN

Dear Erikind:

Unfortunate Inez has just shot poor Rudi dead in the streetcar, with which the next to last part of our slenderized little book[1] is concluded. For a few days now I shall do nothing but write letters, which should be a blessing for you, my faithful child, in your hectic solitude. Know that we miss you very much! There is a good, enlivening spirit in the house, more *vigor*, when you are here. But as the time flies (every evening I'm worn out, but it flies) you will "soon" be here again—although I cannot really believe it will be by Christmas. Enough that you are coming in the spring, when I shall be finished with Adri and doing the Nietzsche lecture. With that, we will travel East in May, perhaps even to the Far East.[2] It is only in your company that I would dare undertake it, even though Hohenberg[3] writes again that life there is completely normal and comfortable.

Yesterday we said good-bye to the San Francisco family. The parents have been in Mexico almost all this time, and they left the boys with us. The children bothered me so often with clock, globe, elephant's tooth, and *music box* when I wanted to sit quietly; but now that they are gone I sadly miss them and took leave of them with kisses of blessing.

The enclosures are not particularly important. That people today when quoting Goethe quote only from *The Beloved Returns* is not a healthy state of affairs. I have called the attention of *The German American*[4] to its mistake, as the phrase goes in the story of the gentleman with the lobster mayonnaise.[5] And I wonder what rubble-strewn alley in Dresden it is that has been named after me. It certainly won't be very grand.

At the moment Alfred Knopf and Henry Wallace are here from the East. We have already had dinner at Eddie's[6] with the former; he talked

---

[1] Erika Mann had made a number of proposals for cutting *Doctor Faustus*, which the author accepted.

[2] I.e., Europe.

[3] Arthur Hohenberg, lecture agent in Brussels.

[4] A New York monthly founded in 1942.

[5] A favorite anecdote in the Mann household: Lobster mayonnaise is offered to a diner at a banquet. "With both hands he reached into the bowl and smeared his beard and face. When the waiter called attention to his mistake, he said: 'Excuse me, I thought it was spinach.' "

[6] Edwin Knopf (b. 1899) Alfred Knopf's brother.

a good deal about the *pocket money* he has given Lowe-Porter, $2,400, to be exact. *"Since she took the money, Tommy, I am sure she will do her best."* Henry drew a *colossal* crowd here. Hulle[7] and Herzog wanted to attend the *mass meeting*, but it was quite hopeless: 11,000 inside and 5,000 outside. We wanted to greet him at least at the "private" *cocktail party* which was held at Ciro's, Sunset Boulevard, but gave up, since we would never have got to him and even less got away. Objectively speaking, of course, this is very gratifying. In the end things are not so bad with the *Democrats*.

Fare you well, dear child, and do honor to the *amazing family* everywhere. You ought to give at least one lecture in Washington.

[End of letter missing]

TO FREDERICK ROSENTHAL

Pacific Palisades
October 28, 1946

Dear Dr. Rosenthal:

May I turn to you for medical information which I hope will not put you to too much trouble? What I need are a few characteristic details about the (lethal) course of meningitis (cerebrospinal meningitis would probably be best) in a three- or six-year-old child. What would be the initial symptoms and the later ones? What is the treatment? What is the antitoxin? If the child were living in the country, could the requisite cranial puncture be undertaken at home? The child had better not be moved to the city and a hospital (even for the purpose of isolation) because of the swift course of the disease. What is the usual duration of meningitis? Would the child have to suffer greatly? Does unconsciousness come soon? The conditions are such that the treatment, at least in the beginning, is in the hands of an ordinary country doctor.

I would be extremely grateful to you for some data.

---

[7] Paul Hulschinsky, interior decorator and film designer; an old friend of the Mann family who was in charge of the furnishings for the Pacific Palisades house.

1946

TO FREDERICK ROSENTHAL

Pacific Palisades
November 5, 1946

Dear Dr. Rosenthal:

Many thanks. You have given me everything I need—even more. But one can never know too much, even if a good deal only remains "a ghostly presence behind the scenes," as Fontane says. I am deeply touched by the trouble you have gone to.

I am quite well. I suffered absurd torments from my skin ailment, but finally landed with a Russian-Jewish woman doctor named Segetz—it was really a landing after the storm. The wise woman cured me completely in the course of five visits, after S. with his X-rays had done nothing but harm and a man named P. also completely failed. I assume that you would have recommended Dr. Segetz to me. In any case Willy Speyer, who was also saved by her, told me that he met her through you. In this special and very delicate case she is actually the only one *who knows what should be done.*

I had the same thing, only far less seriously, after being bedridden for some time with erysipelas. This time it was obviously a complication following the long business. Even in the throes of the most severe sciatica I have not had such nights, and now the pain is gone as if by magic. Send every such patient to Segetz!

All the best, and once again my thanks.

TO AGNES E. MEYER

Pacific Palisades
December 1, 1946

My dear friend:

How glad I was to see that you had cleared out for at least a few days and were resting where it is good and peaceful. I fear that you have been taking on too much lately, and are on the point of doing so again—but can one scold you for your self-sacrificing disposition? Which of us can settle down snugly nowadays? One way or another we are all consuming ourselves and painfully taking part, whether we want to or not, in the birth of a new world. If my disposition were not a curious mixture of excitability and phlegm, where would I be? I've gone through quite an assortment of experiences, you know, have hated and despaired and fought, and along with everything else have still sung my songs. You are not wrong to consider me fairly hardboiled. I've learned not to be afraid of "demons." They are unhappy, unfortunate beings who soon come to a bad end. What does this man Lewis have in that thick skull of his? Does he want to bring things to a *showdown* that will make him dictator? He will be crushed. But what you say about this buffalo's imperviousness to hatred impresses me. When I think how I shudder at every show of hatred that I arouse (unintentionally, by my sheer existence), I am struck by something like admiration for the man. He must have nerves like telephone wires.

America as a whole is not in the happiest state—morally damaged by a war which was a necessity, but simply as a war was after all evil and harmful. Those are the antinomies of this vale of tears. Now we are experiencing a great lowering of morale, raw avarice, political reaction, race hatred, and all the signs of spiritual depression—although in seeing this we must not forget the abundance of good will and sound sense this country still enjoys. As a German I am naturally inclined toward pessimism, and occasionally I fear having to go through the whole disaster, somewhat modified, once again. And then there would be no further exile—for where would I go? But the historical, intellectual, and material conditions really are quite different and far more favorable here. America will make it all right. But if fascism comes, I can point out that I was once Senator Taft's[1] dinner guest. That perhaps may save me from the concentration camp.

We have the house full of family. Katia's twin brother is here from Tokyo with his young son, and Golo and Moni arrived this morning. Our civilian lieutenant colonel is good and tired of his bogus lord's existence in Germany, he says it is a corrupting and intellectually debasing existence, and he will not return there. He wavers between a professorship (for which he is born, I think) and a financially more advantageous *educational job* offered him by the State Department. For a few weeks, at any rate, we shall have him with us, which makes me happy. He is very sorry to have missed you and most warmly returns your greetings.

The house guests, who in their turn attract guests, are somewhat distracting, but I am bending every effort to finish the novel and think I am going to have it done by February. Mrs. Lowe has already received 720 manuscript pages and is at work on them. The printing of the German edition is also under way—in Switzerland this time—and I am

---

[1] Robert A. Taft (1889–1953), U.S. Senator, 1939–53, and a leading Republican.

expecting the first proofs. This is the first time in a long while that I myself can supervise the printing of a book. My hope is that the *Faustus* will be published in Germany too, once my books can come out there. But that is taking longer than one would have thought.

Had I written you that I was reading Conrad? If not, it's a curious coincidence that you too happen to be reading him. I have found him extraordinarily fascinating, especially *Victory, the Nigger of the Narcissus,* and above all *Nostromo,* in which South American corruption is so magnificently portrayed. As a storyteller he has absorbed too much of the outward manifestations of life to be very "inward." But he is a man and very often a true poet.

And what a poet Blake is! Your quotation—a famous one, incidentally—is proof of that. I have paid tribute to him by having Adrian Leverkühn compose several odd pieces to texts of Blake, for example, "Silent, Silent Night." —An American friend, Dr. Angell of Pomona College, has just lent me *The Portable Blake,* a good selection edited by Alfred Kazin.[2]

Well, this has become a long Sunday letter. Greetings—and *more power to you.* I often think that if the world were ruled by a few sensible women, it would be better off.

Yours,

T. M.

TO ELISABETH MANN BORGESE

Pacific Palisades
December 14, 1946

Good Medikind:

The most modest item on your want-list, a Christmas note from Signor-papale, is being promptly and gladly furnished. Though what shall I tell —since you know all about what goes on here, the jolly company in the house, and so on. But I want to send you, our grand Antonio, and the dear fascinating child all my good wishes for a gay Christmas Eve and a good New Year, which I am afraid is going to be quite well along before we see each other again. I was much impressed by your account of the Geneva meeting.[1] for which Antonio of course would be the only possible delegate. Here, too, it looks more and more as if we shall cross the ocean.

---

[2] Alfred Kazin (b. 1915), American critic and editor. Among his works: *On Native Grounds* (1942), *A Walker in the City* (1951), *Starting Out in the Thirties* (1965).

[1] The first international meeting of various organizations advocating world government eventually took place in Montreux (August 17–24, 1947). Borgese was not present.

1946

The problem would still be Germany. Although it is now the vogue there, apparently, to speak decently of me, I shudder at the prospect, and think that we shall ask Uncle Vikkoff[2] to come to Zurich instead.

Actually I am not thinking beyond completion of the novel, but that really can't drag on much more—I am counting on February or thereabouts. I don't dare let the thing become much longer, for I have already numbered the 809th manuscript page; and in any case virtually everybody appears in it, some of them even under their own names—like the Reiffs[3] in Zurich. Simple as that. Reisi[4] has been informed that he has been tucked into the book. Bermann thinks he can only be delighted, but that "only" is perhaps a word too much. Nevertheless he is urgently needed to introduce a note of cheer, for the work as a whole is distinctly sad and turns sadder and sadder toward the end—how could it be otherwise? Last night I read two chapters to Mielein, brother-in-law, his son, and Golo—the section where charming Nepomuk Schneide-wein, a kind of Ariel, comes to Pfeiffering and dies of meningitis, because after all Adrian is not permitted any softer emotions. The child, an elfin, idealized Frido, is certainly the loveliest thing in the whole book; and then the devil takes him. All of us were close to tears.

I was also close to tears today when your dear, thoughtful present arrived—the Schumann album. And imagine, every single record is broken. What a misery! I have put off thanking you for the lovely present all through this letter because I have to add such depressing news. The album was packed without excelsior, just between cardboard, but it must in addition have been brutally knocked about. The question is: Was the store responsible for the packing? It was certainly inadequate, for in the past records have always come in excelsior, and it seems to me that the firm ought to replace the album. But we are not quite certain, for it looks like your handwriting on the carton. Did you have a part in sending it? As I say, I have the impression that the parcel was treated with particular roughness just because it was marked fragile. People are so spiteful nowadays.

[2] Viktor Mann.

[3] Hermann Reiff (1856–1938), silk manufacturer, married (second marriage, 1914) to Lilly Sertorius (1866–1958). The Reiffs, art-loving, hospitable, tactful patrons of the arts, played a unique part in Zurich society. Swiss and foreign musicians, actors, writers, painters, etc., would mingle at the Reiff home with diplomats, gentleman farmers, manufacturers, and princes. The Reiffs paid little attention to the matter of compatibility among their guests. Rival and hostile conductors might find themselves sharing a bathroom, but no one was offended. In his simpleheartedness and lack of bias, the host succeeded in establishing harmony, at least for the time being.

[4] Hans Reisiger.

Three persons have become too fat here: Niko, Golo, and myself. Niko from gluttony, Golo probably from the substantial army rations, and I from the operation. A gain of twenty pounds since you saw me! And all my trousers too tight. But I am told I'll lose again later on.

I actually offered the article for the students of.F.W.G.[5] to Henry Wallace for his *New Republic*, but then withdrew it because I quickly found I no longer liked it. It says too little on the one hand, and on the other hand too much. At best it may have been the right sort of occasional piece for that particular moment.

Once again, a lovely Christmas!

H.P.[6]

TO HANS POLLAK[1]

Pacific Palisades
December 29, 1946

My dear Dr. Pollak:

You were very kind to send me the school edition of my sketch, "Das Wunderkind,"[2] and the issue of *The Australian Quarterly* with your essay, "How Shall the Teacher of German Present Germany?" My warm thanks for this interesting material. I was particularly struck by the way your article discusses, with suitable circumspection, the responsibility of German intellectual life for the tragic course of events in Germany. I fully understand that you as a teacher draw a sharp dividing line between the high level of German thought and the reality which today has plunged the world into such profound doubt of the soundness and validity of German thought in general. As a teacher, I say, you are right to declare that "certainly no writer of the past bears the responsibility for the fact that the Junkers and industrialists put Hitler into power" and that neither Hegel nor Nietzsche can be held accountable for modern demagogy.

Nevertheless, I have scribbled a dubious *hmm* in the margin. Does it not disparage and diminish the realm of the intellect to acquit it of all responsibility for its consequences, its real manifestations? That Hegel, Schopenhauer, and Nietzsche contributed to shaping the German mind

---

[5] Federal World Government.

[6] Herrpapale, a variant of the jocular Signorpapale.

[1] Hans Pollak, at this time a member of the German department of the University of Western Australia.

[2] "The Infant Prodigy." In *Stories of Three Decades*.

and its relationship toward life and the world is as undeniable as the fact that Martin Luther had something to do with the Thirty Years' War, whose horrors he explicitly took "upon his neck" in advance. To deny the guilt of intellectual leaders seems to be belittling them, and we Germans today have every reason to be concerned with the ambiguous role of German thought and the German great man, and to ponder it.

But once more I say, why should you as a teacher become involved in such futile speculations? You are right to put them aside, at least as long as you are teaching, and to point out to your students the greatness and goodness to be found in this sphere, whatever disasters may also flow from it.

Once again my thanks, and my best wishes.

TO EMIL PREETORIUS

Pacific Palisades
December 30, 1946

Dear Pree:

I do not want the year to come completely to an end without once more writing you a word of friendly remembrance, although it will not reach you until long after the beginning of A.D. 1947. Don't take my long silence amiss; my recovery after that operation did not go so very fast after all. A good deal of fatigue lingered and has almost become chronic as a result of low blood pressure, which is further aggravated by the climate here. Often after I have done my morning stint I can no longer bring myself to face any personal correspondence—I've "had enough for the day." I am staking everything, you know, on finishing the monster of a novel that has already occupied me for two and a half years, this *Doctor Faustus*, which has assumed such dimensions because too much of the times and art and the pain of the times and the predicament of art has tried to enter it. But that won't happen to me again. No more novels, I vow. In the years that still remain to me I definitely intend to do only short things that can be tossed off rapidly: essays, reminiscences, a *short story* now and then. I conceive it as very pleasant and unburdened; I am no longer fit for Atlaslike tasks. *Buddenbrooks*, *The Magic Mountain*, the *Joseph* story with the Goethe book tucked in, and now this—those are enough skyscrapers for one life, and for mine surprisingly many. I have had patience—which Schopenhauer called heroism. Good fellow, he thought his one-and-all, clung to through thick and thin, heroic. Poor fellow, much good he did humanity with his particular song of life.

Whereupon things went up to the icy heights of Nietzsche, and then they went incredibly fast, incredibly deep down.

At the moment I am imagining and composing for my musician the Symphonic Cantata, with which he bids farewell to the life of the mind— *The Lamentation of Doctor Faustus* (after the chapbook), an ode to sorrow, since Adrian's destiny obviously does not include the Ninth Symphony's "Joy," whose heralding must therefore be canceled. It is a most expressive work, for man's first and truest expression is lament, and as soon as music freed itself for expression, at the beginning of its modern history, it became *lamento* and "*Lasciatemi morir*." Well now, lamentation is certainly a most contemporary theme, and even *your* "civilization and its discontents" probably refers to more than the material inadequacies and privations which, I at least try to pretend to myself, cannot be so acute in your rural Bavarian setting as elsewhere in German lands—frightful, frightful! I become sick at heart listening to the tales brought back by travelers to Europe—Dieterle, for example. How could anything come out of such a life but despair at life itself?

How odd; I had come to just this point when your letter of last month reached me. What shall I say to it? That you Germans should be writing in a hearty and confident spirit? It would be asking rather too much. What you heard about me was nothing new, nothing recent. They had read it in the letter to Molo, in a much-criticized passage where I spoke of the troubled emotions with which I receive products of the Third Reich. Both we outside and you inside have a rather morbid sensitivity concerning this Third Reich. Enough. I only want to make the point that I began spontaneously writing this New Year's greeting yesterday, and today your letter arrived.

1947

———————————•———————————

TO AGNES E. MEYER

Pacific Palisades
January 28, 1947

Dear friend:

If my *news* was good, your reply is even better. Welcome in advance to this coast. So at last, on April 1, I shall hear one of your famous lectures.

Expect us, then, on the 29th—or else on the day before. I have chosen the last Tuesday of the month so that we can also gain some time for the Chicago family. We will certainly stay only two days at Crescent Place. Nowadays that is enough of an imposition.

A few days ago Bonn sent me (after a tactful previous inquiry) a new copy of my honorary doctor's diploma, with solemn letters from the *Rektor*, the dean of the philosophical faculty, and, no less, the American *officer* for university affairs. So here I am once again a German "Herr Doktor"—who would have thought it!

If I live until tomorrow noon, which in view of my weight gain of twenty pounds can scarcely be doubted, the last line of *Doctor Faustus* will have been written.

As ever and for ever

Yours,
T. M.

TO THE DEAN OF THE PHILOSOPHICAL FACULTY OF THE UNIVERSITY OF BONN

Pacific Palisades
January 28, 1947

My dear Dean:

I owe you my cordial and solemn thanks for the restoration of my honorary doctorate, and for the eloquent and significant letters with which you and the *Herr Rektor* accompanied the document. I have reread with some emotion the dignified Latin text of the lost diploma, which so kindly sets forth the reasons for my work's being honored, and I need not assure you, my dear Professor, that it warms my heart to know that I am once again linked to a German university as a member of its philosophical faculty.

If anything can diminish my gladness and gratification, it is the thought of the dreadful price that had to be paid before your celebrated academy found itself in a position to revoke the step forced upon it in the past. Poor Germany! The frantic fluctuations in her history have probably been visited on no other country and people.

Personally, I have been led by strange ways indeed, and in my youth could never have dreamed that I would spend my latter days as an American citizen on this palm-grown coast. But at bottom destiny has always been well disposed toward me, and I cannot but marvel at the way the individual always triumphs over the general, wins through against circumstances. I live here and do my work as I used to in Munich's Herzogpark, and my "de-Germanization," to use Nietzsche's word, has not progressed very far after all. On the contrary, I find that in these happier foreign parts I have become all the more conscious of my Germanism. Especially during the past two and a half years I have been occupied with a novel—or whatever the thing should be called—which I hope to complete within a few days and which is something so utterly German that I have the gravest fears concerning its translatability—or rather, I am already resigned on that matter.

May I ask you, my dear Dean, to give my best regards to *Herr Rektor* Konen. With cordial good wishes for your personal well-being, for the University of Bonn, and for the old homeland,

TO ERIKA MANN

[*Telegram in English*]

Pacific Palisades
January 29, 1947

keen glorious child[1] must know that Adrian's sad story was definitely brought to a happy end today

[unsigned]

---

[1] In Wagner's *Die Walküre* Wotan calls Brünnhilde "*Du kühnes, herrliches Kind.*" Thomas Mann often jokingly applied the phrase to Erika Mann. "*Kühn*" actually means "bold," but Thomas Mann preferred the cognate "keen" for the sake of sound.

1947

TO FRITZ GRÜNBAUM[1]

Pacific Palisades
February 29, 1947

Dear Dr. Grünbaum:

The question has frequently been thrown at me, and I have always tried to explain plausibly that I am not the right person to answer it. I myself left everything obscure, you see, in the uncertain semidarkness of the carriage lanterns, and so it hardly does for me to decide afterwards between reality and unreality.

Every time I am called upon for a decision, my impulse is to declare both sides right. But when all is taken into account, I must admit that the balance inclines slightly more toward the side of unreality. There is much in the text that decidedly suggests, insofar as there is anything decisive about the whole thing, that it is a reverie, something that "one does not start at" because it is emanating from oneself. In reality Goethe would scarcely allude to the nodding of Lotte's head—that comes from her. He would also not speak so much in iambics—that comes from Lotte's having just been to the theater. For she too speaks in verse: "Ah, it is wonderful to make a sacrifice, etc." He would also scarcely conclude his speech with the final words of *The Elective Affinities*, and if he were there, Mager would probably see him when he helped the lady out of the carriage. Once he is called "the Mantle Wearer"—that is a mythological name, you know; I think Wotan was called that. And the way his voice at the end "died away" and her "Peace to your old age"—that, too, is slightly ghostly.

I suspect that she has so deep a longing for a concluding dialogue which will bring matters to some resolution that she simply produces the scene for herself. But even so, it is still not possible to speak of pure unreality. What we have here may be a phantom dialogue, which comes about because the woman's longing meets that of her old friend, a dialogue of phantoms in which Goethe speaks his thoughts, although he is not sitting physically beside her, and which therefore has a higher reality.

You see how muddled we storytellers are in our thinking. Don't take it amiss. In any case, the meeting in the carriage is not historic, as the dinner is. Goethe did not fetch Lotte from the theater.

In connection with this letter, I have been dipping into the book again. When all is said and done it is close, very close to my heart, and those were good days when I was writing it.

---

[1] Unidentified. The letter was addressed to Herzlia, near Tel Aviv, Palestine.

1947

TO MANFRED GEORGE

Pacific Palisades
March 11, 1947

Dear Manfred George:

I am herewith returning Furtwängler's[1] defense to you by registered airmail. I have read the memorandum and can imagine what an excellent critical piece *Aufbau* will publish on it. For there is no question that it offers many points for attack, for all its skillfulness and all the impressive facts it advances. As far as I am concerned, after some consideration and some moments of temptation, I have finally decided to take no position on it. After all, it was I who publicly censured Furtwängler's position, and if he now defends himself it is not up to me to defend myself in turn against his defense. The way I am, the reply would inevitably lead me far afield, and I would be ashamed of this long-windedness. So many more important and more urgent things must be said right now that it would seem to me sterile and obstinate, especially after such a long silence, to engage in a polemic against an already four-month-old memorandum of self-defense by a conductor who is suing for the right to practice his art in Germany again. For a periodical that continuously discusses events in Germany, it is quite a different matter.

From Furtwängler's memorandum, as from so many other documents, I see once again what an abysmal gulf lies between our experience and that of the people who remained behind in Germany. Communication across this gulf is completely impossible, and although at first I refused to believe it, I have more and more been forced to realize that even my statements during the war and afterwards were felt inside Germany to be only ignorant babble which in no way approached the experience of the Germans; my "political" writings were felt as comforting and strengthening only outside Germany. Thus I have it from a reliable source that my letter to Bonn, which after all did go round the world and, I can venture to say, was everywhere regarded as in a way saving the honor of German intellectuals, "hurt" the philosopher Karl Jaspers when he read it—the same Jaspers who has delivered such an excellent address on German guilt. This strictly in confidence. I am telling it to you only so you will understand my decision no longer to "hurt" the

---

[1] Wilhelm Furtwängler (1886–1954), conductor and composer. In charge of the Berlin Philharmonic, 1922–45 (reappointed in 1950), at times also conductor of the Leipzig Gewandhaus Orchestra and the Vienna Philharmonic. Composer of symphonies, a piano concerto, and two violin sonatas; author of *Gespräche über Musik*.

Germans and to leave them their Furtwängler if they want him. Enough of this. [. . .]

In any case, thank you for your consideration. With my best regards,

TO VIKTOR MANN

Pacific Palisades
March 27, 1947

Dear Vikko:

Your good letter of February 10 has arrived safely, and the preceding one too. I don't think there have been any gaps in the correspondence. It is a pleasure to me to know that my English letter[1] gave you all a certain sense of security. And a joy to hear of the impression that *The Beloved Returns* made upon you.

I'm not pleased that of all things, the *Saturday Evening Post* issue is going the rounds among you. The picture was quite good, I grant. But the interview with the agent Colston Leigh was much distorted. This is evident if only from the fact that Erika, who at the moment is probably the best lecturer in his stable, is not even mentioned. He never said the things the article quotes him as saying about me. I *"lecture"* little, but when I give a lecture, as I shall shortly be doing in Washington and New York, people certainly do not come merely *to look at me*. This was hardly their impulse even at the start, when my English was much worse but I toured the whole continent with *The Coming Victory of Democracy*.

Ro-Ro-Rowohlt[2] has indeed written me a good long letter. [. . .] I have passed it on to Bermann, who says that newspaper-type printing of books is nothing new, that things of that sort were done in the past, and that he himself is planning a similar venture in cooperation with Suhrkamp. He means to write to Rowohlt himself. There is surely no doubt that this cheap mass printing of books is an excellent way to familiarize broad strata in Germany with authors whose image has grown quite dim to them—and I am one of those authors.

Our visit to Munich, Vikko, is a very serious problem that we are thinking about and discussing a great deal. If I could come and go quietly as a private individual, the matter would be very simple. But I would be

---

[1] Thomas Mann had written a letter in English expressing the hope that the American occupation authorities would permit Viktor Mann and his wife to retain possession of their home.

[2] An allusion to the series of paperback books called *rororo* inaugurated by the Rowohlt publishing house after the war.

coming officially, you know, and inevitably with a good deal of stir; I should have to present myself to the public—and to be frank, with each passing day the idea looks more and more ticklish. Considering the way things are developing in Germany, the kind of atmosphere once again forming there (and once again, the other countries share in the blame, but that is another matter), it does not surprise me that everyone begs me not to go. [. . .] Wiechert, now in Switzerland because he could no longer endure it, declared to the Stockholm *Tidningen* that if Hitler came back tomorrow, sixty to eighty per cent of the people would receive him with hurrahs. I won't quote the other things Wiechert has to say about the country's degradation and ugly hopelessness. But because he once very mildly and pallidly whispered something about "guilt," he has been branded as a "traitor," stones have been thrown through his windows, and he was constantly threatened, until he had to ask for American protection and a guard was posted in his house. That's Wiechert for you, a conservative, nationalistic man. And now what about me, whom the champions and avengers of German honor classify as so much worse, so much Redder? Do you think that my stay would come off without "disturbances"? Everyone here predicts them. Not that I would be afraid for my life. But imagine the awkwardness and shamefulness of the situation! The military government would feel obliged to protect me, although by law a naturalized American has no claim to protection in his country of origin. No matter; if they grant me the visa they will have to watch over me and prevent unpleasant incidents. Am I to go around Munich with an *M.P. bodyguard*? Inevitably I would be speaking publicly; let's say I should have to deliver a lecture at the university. Very well then: police cordon, checkup of members of the audience, tension, fear of riot. And what should I, what can I say to the Germans, sensitive plants that they are today, sore, thin-skinned, overwrought? They obviously don't see that Germany is in precisely the straits her leaders wanted her to be in if they were going to lose the war. But saying anything against these leaders without criticizing the Occupation (which I can do here, but not there) would be in itself unpatriotic. At bottom the Germans don't want any slurs cast at their Third Reich. So we must speak only of the future! But that lies completely in darkness, and we have no idea what we ought to wish, hope for, recommend. [. . .] Saying anything would be empty posturing, evasion, lying, comforting wishy-washiness—and even at that, it would be impossible to avoid giving offense.

I shall say nothing about the effect on my nerves of the lamentations, the petitions for help, the agonizing belief in my "influence" which would overwhelm me (I am already saying "would" although these are only speculations). I suppose you have also privately pictured all this for yourself and asked yourself, as I ask myself, what purpose would be served by a visit which I would end as soon as possible with feelings of profound relief. The Americans, too, would probably breathe easier once I was gone. My impression is that they would not gladly grant me an entry permit—it would probably be granted, but not gladly—because they would rightly fear "*trouble*," which they don't like. We shall have to look into it more closely in Washington. It is possible that from that quarter the answer will be a simple No.

Painful is certainly a mild word for the disappointment we would all feel if our plans for the reunion, cherished so eagerly on both sides, were to be blasted by the harsh requirements of reason. But there is no real necessity for that to happen, even if things turn out as I expect. I think my Americans in Munich are ready to grant me one wish, and Erika (who is with us at the moment) has offered to help get permission for you to come to us when we are in Zurich, where I am to read a piece on Nietzsche on June 3, at the International PEN Club Congress. It would be nifty if you came—a bit of a change for you and for us a harmless compensation for renouncing a not so harmless undertaking.

Warmly,

T.

TO HEINRICH MANN

Savoy Hotel
London
May 22, 1947

Dear Heinrich:

A greeting from this venerable capital before we leave it again—as a sign of remembrance in the turmoil of the world. God knows why one plunges into it instead of sensibly staying "at home." It was probably the feeling that at last I had to exert myself in some other way, after the long exertion at the desk. Certainly plenty is happening. The ten days in New York alone were grotesquely lively after the customary uniformity. The crossing on the giant ship[1] was somewhat marred by a continuous rolling because the ship is so tall—not restful at all. The arrival in Southampton with two thousand people and their masses of

[1] The *Queen Mary*.

baggage was confused to the point of being catastrophic. The first days here I had to fight a gastric and intestinal affliction, in spite of which I went through everything: *interviews, press conferences, receptions, broadcasts,* and, to a great throng, the *lecture* in London University. The Nietzsche lecture, simplistic as it is, went over well here, as it did in Washington and New York. [. . .]

We are flying to Zurich on Saturday morning. I hope a warmer spring awaits us there. Here it has been dark and cold the whole while. London seems quite downcast, and in spite of diligent repairs, traces of the ordeal the city has been through are visible everywhere. The nervous strain caused by the bombs and V-missiles must at times have been scarcely endurable, and one wonders whether any other nation would have endured it without screaming for peace at any price. Everybody believes in the necessity of preserving the Labour government except for fascistic soapbox orators, one of whom I listened to. I saw only indifferent or disgusted faces in the audience. Even conservatives like Harold Nicolson are joining the party.

I hope you are faring well. Warm greetings from Katia and Erika.

T.

TO THE EDITORS
OF THE *NEUE ZEITUNG*[1]

Flims
Graubünden
June 25, 1947

Dear Sirs:

The writer Manfred Hausmann[2] is spreading a story, through German newspapers,[3] that in 1933 I wrote to Minister of the Interior Frick begging for permission to return to National Socialist Germany, pledging that—very much in contrast to my previous conduct—I would hold my tongue and no longer interfere in political affairs, that I was dead set against going into exile. Such was the tenor of my letter, according to Hausmann, who maintains that it was never answered. His point is that

---

[1] An American newspaper for German civilians founded in October 1945. It ceased publication in 1955.

[2] Manfred Hausmann (b. 1898). Among his works: *Kleine Liebe zu Amerika* (1931), *Abel mit der Mundharmonika* (1932), *Alte Musik* (1941). After the Second World War he turned to a kind of Christian existentialism and wrote *Das Worpsweder Hirtenspiel* (1946), *Liebende leben von der Vergebung* (1953), among others.

[3] Hausmann's essay, *Thomas Mann sollte schweigen* ("Thomas Mann Ought to Keep Quiet") was first published in the *Weser-Kurier*, May 28, 1947.

I would gladly have returned to the Third Reich at the time, but had to stay outside because I did not receive permission to go back.

The absurdity of this allegation is obvious. In 1933 I needed no "permission" to return to Germany. That return was precisely what was wanted: by the Munich Gestapo, so that it could take revenge for my struggle against the rising evil; by Goebbels's Propaganda Ministry for reasons of international prestige and so that the Academy of Literature would be able to use my name. More than one very broad hint (by the *Frankfurter Zeitung*, for instance) gave me to understand that the past would be forgotten if I returned. Bermann-Fischer, who then hoped to be able to maintain his publishing house in Berlin, promised to meet me in his car at the border and take me to Berlin. He sent the editor of the *Neue Rundschau*, S. Sänger,[4] to Sanary-sur-mer to persuade me to return home. I refused. Recently published diary passages from the years 1933–1934[5] reflect the deep horror I then felt of Germany and which, I fear, I shall never again be able to shake off entirely. They also express the unshakable conviction that nothing but misery, nothing but bloody ruin for Germany and the world, could come out of that regime—and with it my pity for the German people even then, that they should have invested such intensity of belief, enthusiasm, proud hope in something so patently macabre and depraved. By my public statements in Switzerland, my declaration of belonging to the refugee movement, I forced the Nazis to the expatriation which was the last thing Goebbels wanted. "As long as I have anything to say, that won't be done." And now the story is spread that I was pleading for permission to take the oath of loyalty to the Führer and enter the *Kulturkammer*. Hausmann vouches for it.

Why he attacks me from the rear with this senseless slander, what I have done to him to deserve this I do not know. Is he enraged because today I "will not" do what I then supposedly "could not" do? Not two years have passed since he wrote to America to our mutual publisher that he was in deep despair in Germany, a stranger in his own country. The German people are hopeless, he wrote, corrupt down to the roots, and he longed for nothing better than to shake the dust of Germany from his feet and be able to go abroad. Today he speaks of an "admittedly impoverished and unfortunate but still relatively democratic Germany" which I, out of some nastiness, refuse to return to. Certainly there is

[4] Samuel Sänger (1864–1944), writer, publicist; for many years editor of the *Neue Rundschau*. Emigrated to France in 1939, to the United States in 1941; died in Los Angeles. Author of biographies of John Ruskin and John Stuart Mill.

[5] In *Twice a Year*, XIV–XV, Fall–Winter, 1946–7.

something terribly weird about the German sense of balance—and who would wonder at that?

In my agony at that time I wrote a good many "letters into the night" (such was René Schickele's phrase for them). If among those appeals addressed to a Germany being rapidly swept away toward its destruction there should also be a letter to Frick, and if Manfred Hausmann has contrived to obtain possession of this letter, he ought to publish it in its entirety instead of peddling an obviously falsified summary of its contents. I am certain that any such document[6] from the year 1933 would not be to my dishonor, but to the shame of the man, since gone to his judgment,[7] who as Hausmann observes with a kind of satisfaction, "did not respond to it."

TO KITTY AND ALFRED NEUMANN

Flims
Graubünden
July 14, 1947

Dear Alfred Neumann and Madame Wonder Hen:

It is not in the least nice that you should not have had a word from me during this entire trip, but you know and can imagine how we have been living since Washington and New York (how long ago that is!). It has been a breathless round of demands, festivities, performances; likewise tensions, agitations, and the fending off of importunities, which come, of course, from Germany. There have been official and unofficial invitations; messengers have appeared and insisted. But I have been unable to bring myself to go [. . .] and am doing my best to lessen the rancor; have written to German newspapers, done a reading in St. Gall for the benefit of the Munich orphanage, etc.

The Nietzsche lectures turned out well in English (especially in London) and even better in German in the Swiss cities. But the best thing was after all the reading from *Faustus* in the Zurich Schauspielhaus; the situation tied in perfectly with the farewell celebration of 1938, when I read from *Lotte*—so perfectly that the whole nine intervening years of life seemed to have vanished. I did the Fitelberg chapter (the temptation by the "world"), and there was great amusement and re-

---

[6] The letter was ultimately found in German archives, dated the spring of 1934; it was published, with Mann's consent, in the *Neue Zeitung* of August 8, 1947, and proved the absurdity of Hausmann's charges.

[7] Wilhelm Frick was sentenced to death at Nuremberg and executed.

sponsiveness. Opus 111 came at the end. When Zurichers really like
something, they combine their applause with a trampling which produces a kind of thunder. Erika was ecstatic. Since then she insists that I
must write a comedy with parts for the two of us to act. Well, I suppose
I'm not quite young enough for that.

Here it is very lovely and healthful after all the flurry: glorious,
still fir forests with picturesque cliffs and gorges out of Doré, and the
sight of the ledges, pinnacles, and high meadows of the surrounding
mountains is also a change from the eternal Pacific. There was (and is) a
suitcase full of neglected correspondence to work through, an Augean
stable, and in addition I have read the proofs of the novel here—with
mixed feelings. It is a strange work, perhaps too much so, and along with
some really remarkable things it has plenty of prolixities, weaknesses,
flaws. Bermann claims that the copyright matter with America has now
been settled and that the German edition can be published this autumn.
I have not yet seen him. He also telegraphed that cheap editions of my
books and those of others (editions of 150,000) are now coming on the
market in Germany.

You've been having vexations, my friend? I'm sure they came from
the source of all vexation, Germany. I would guess it was some nastiness
in connection with your Munich novel.[1] But you'll tell us about it.

Wasn't the business with Niko exciting? After Gottlieb's[2] letter we
could no nothing but mourn for the dear creature. And then he simply
came trotting home. When all is said and done, he's the smartest of us all.

On the 20th we are returning to Zurich. From there we shall have
all sorts of expeditions, including one to Italy to Mondadori and to
Lucerne for a meeting with Hesse. Then come a few weeks in Holland,
and on August 29th we board the little *Westerdam* in Rotterdam. We
could even have had the *America*, but shrank from the trip to Cherbourg,
which is said to be involved and bothersome.

We met my Munich brother at the border and even took him to
Zurich with us. The cooperation of a French border officer made it
possible. [. . .]

To a good reunion!

---

[1] Alfred Neumann's *Es waren ihrer sechs*, a novel about a resistance group at
Munich University.

[2] Ernst Gottlieb (1903–1961), writer, photographer, musicologist. Emigrated to
the United States in 1939. Cofounder, with Felix Guggenheim, of the Pacific Press,
which produced de luxe editions of German books for bibliophiles. From 1946 to 1961 publisher of facsimile editions of rare books on music. Among his works: *Walter Rathenau*
(1929).

1947

TO HERMANN HESSE

Baur au Lac
Zurich
August 10, 1947

Dear Hermann Hesse:

At the last moment (we are flying today), thank you for your kind note. The "Nationals"[1] in Lucerne kept their word, insofar as we definitely did not have to pay for the royal suite which they had gotten ready for us and which we had not asked for.

It was a good reunion, which we shall think back on all through the year. But I can't say how tired I am of all the bustle, and it is highly unpleasant that in Holland it will in a minor way start all over again from the beginning. I will be glad when we are on board ship, and I have secret doubts whether I shall let myself in for the dance again next May (which would be only eight months). I do leave Switzerland reluctantly, though. No getting around it, it's a charming country, and the crossing of the Alps recently, when we went to Stresa by car, made a deep impression on me. (How did they ever manage it with the elephants that time?) Besides, if one comes from far away and not too often, one picks up many Fränkli.[2]

I have heard vexing news from Washington about the copyright matter, and it once again becomes probable that the German edition of the book will have to be postponed another eight or nine months—which would be painful for me, but for Bermann, I think, a severe financial blow. From Dr. Benedikt[3] (formerly of Vienna), who has read the proofs in Sweden, I received a gratifyingly enthusiastic letter.

May you and Frau Ninon fare very well; we both send our greetings to you.

---

[1] The Hotel National in Lucerne.

[2] A jocular Swiss diminutive of franc; Mann was very fond of the word.

[3] Ernst Benedikt (b. 1882), Austrian writer, journalist, painter. Editor-in-chief of the Vienna *Neue Freie Presse*. Arrested by the Gestapo in 1938. Emigrated to Sweden in 1939, where he remained. Among his books: *Die Quellen künstlerischen Schaffens* (1913), *Kaiser Josef II* (1937), a volume of poems, *Von Neuem blüht . . .* (1962).

TO KLAUS MANN

Dear Eissi:

I have somewhat expanded the Goethe *outline*,[1] added a few poems such as "Sah ein Knab' ein Röslein Stehn," and set up an extra category for epigrams in verse and prose (from the *Divan*, the *Epigrams in Rhyme*, and the *Maxims*) because I especially like his aphorisms and coined proverbs. In my opinion neither the *Trilogie der Leidenschaft* nor a certain dialogue between Hatem and Suleika in the *Divan* should be omitted. "Du beschämst wie Morgenröte dieser Gipfel ernste Wand"[2] is indispensable, and likewise her "Magst du meine Jugend zieren mit gewalt'ger Leidenschaft." I must admit that the division into *Love and Youth* and *Wisdom* rather confuses things, for the *Trilogie* is not *Youth* and the love songs of old age not *Wisdom*. Something to joke about in the preface.

I have sent Dial Press a complete list of the contents as I would like to have them, together with a long letter in which I display all our scholarship in regard to existing translations. My letter confesses that I can no longer foresee how many pages the book will have, but asks them to consider whether it would be a misfortune if the project turned into a two-volume edition (boxed). In addition I have asked to what extent they can and are willing to participate in locating and choosing the existing translations. To my mind this participation cannot go very far. Above all, it is important to determine which of the prospective poems and epigrams are untranslated or have to be newly translated, so that I can turn to Auden, Spender, or Prokosch, or two of them, or all three, concerning specific assignments. Quite apart from my contract with the publishers, I think it would be sensible for you to enlist Bubi K.[3] right away, so that he can provide the clarifications which I need for my correspondence with the poets.

Kahn[4] is copying out the epigrams and aphorisms for me. I don't

---

[1] Mann was editing *The Permanent Goethe* for Dial Press, and consulted his son Klaus frequently on details.

[2] See Mann's comment on this poem in *Last Essays*, p. 98.

[3] Oskar Seidlin (b. 1911), writer and German professor. A boyhood friend of Klaus Mann, Seidlin (formerly Koplowitz) emigrated to Switzerland in 1933, to the United States in 1938. Professor of German literature at Ohio State University from 1946 on. Among his works: *Essays in German and Comparative Literature* (1961) and *Von Goethe zu Thomas Mann* (1963).

[4] Hilde Kahn, at this time Thomas Mann's secretary.

know whether I shall receive the little volume of letters from Insel. You had best send me yours. I'll have the copying done here.

The whole business is certainly going to cost a great deal of trouble and racking of brains—more than $2,000 pays for. But if I collaborated at all, I had to do the whole thing.

Tonight Erika arrived. A very good thing that she can recuperate here from the traveling and the kidney attack before she goes on tour again. —Your comparison of present-day Paris with the Vienna of 1918 strongly appeals to me. Sad, sad. A democratic senator recently took off his jacket and declared, in shirtsleeves, that we no longer have a single friend in the world.

You have some, and deserve them. Keep in good spirits! What Mielein meant was "tired from living," not "tired of living."

Warmly,
Z.

TO HOWARD L. NELSON[1]

[Original in English]

Pacific Palisades
October 3, 1947

Dear Mr. Nelson:

I want to thank you for your kind letter of July 27th, and also for the enclosures, these two photographs which give me such a stirring picture of the remaining, ghostlike outlines of my grandparents' house. The Buddenbrook bookstore, which was established in the ground floor of the building, was, of course, not permitted to retain its name until the war, but only until the Nazis seized power. Then the house was renamed Wullenwewer-Haus by the ignorant Nazi rabble, although this Lübeck senator did not live in the eighteenth but in the sixteenth century.

I am not surprised about the melancholy impressions you are gaining in Germany. On my trip to Europe, from which I just returned, I have avoided my native country, which has taken on such a deeply sinister character during the past one and a half decades. I am in correspondence with several good friends over there, partly young people whom I do not know personally, and I am convinced that, as before, there are decent, intelligent, and well-meaning men in Germany. But I am afraid

---

[1] Howard L. Nelson, at this time American vice-consul in Bremen, had written to Mann about the Buddenbrook House in Lübeck.

that the people as a whole never found any other fault with the monster Hitler than that he lost the war, and I am also afraid that this people as a whole are even today hoping to regain their military power as soon as possible—and thanks to the unfortunate world political constellation, their chances of doing so are not too bad.

But no more gloomy political remarks! I just wanted to thank you for the intelligent interest in my life's work which is expressed in your letter.

With kindest wishes and regards,

TO AGNES E. MEYER

Pacific Palisades
October 10, 1947

Dear friend:

[. . .] I frequently wonder whether and to what extent you still feel at all concerned about me, and of course that makes me vaguely timid about writing. Nevertheless, the inveterate need to tell you about myself continues. Tolerate it as well as you can!

Among my children you think well of Golo—very rightly and to my delight, for he is a splendid fellow and I am happy to have him in the vicinity once more: as professor of history at Pomona College, whence he drives over to us on weekends in his little Ford. Erika, who came home from Europe by herself (from Switzerland she went to Prague to visit our friend Beneš and then to Poland), is keeping us company while awaiting the beginning of her *lecture* season. It may well be the last, for given her principles (which are by no means Communistic) and the paths we are now taking in these United States, opportunities for expressing her opinions will probably dry up more and more. She is clever and lively enough to manage in some other way. I myself am no longer signing any of the multitudinous appeals with which the desperate Left is making a nuisance of itself, for I have little desire to play the martyr once again. I still would rather think that what is taking place is a certain moral relaxation of the country after the strains of the Rooseveltian period of genius. For the rest, I console myself with a neat phrase that I heard from Harold Nicolson in London: "In America," he said, "one must distinguish between weather and climate. The weather is bad there right now, but the climate is good." The climate is good! And an obscurely uneasy sense of America's growing unpopularity in the rest of the world is also present.

For personal reasons the case of Hanns Eisler touches me closely. I know the man very well; he is highly cultivated, brilliant, very amusing in conversation, and I have often had splendid talks with him, particularly about Wagner. As a musician he is, in the opinion of all his colleagues, first class. Since the Inquisition has turned him over to the "secular arm" for deportation, there is the danger that he will land in a German camp. I hear that Stravinsky (a White Russian!) means to start a demonstration in his favor. But I have wife and children and am not inquiring further into the matter.

Since I am, after all, a novelist, I have followed the trial against that young couple for murdering their parents, and its outcome, with a certain excitement. The acquittal is a phenomenon that I cannot yet get out of my head. One could, by paying sufficiently, obtain a look at the correspondence of the two young people during their time in prison awaiting trial. Ernst Lubitsch,[1] for example, has read these letters and reports that they can scarcely be surpassed for obscenity; but on the other hand there is not the faintest suggestion in them of any thought about their own case, the mystery of how their parents died. During the trial the two exchanged infatuated looks, obviously on instructions from the defense lawyer; for after the acquittal the girl up and declared she did not intend to marry her friend *"and she would leave it to us to figure out why she doesn't care."* What can the *cheering crowd* in the courtroom have had to say about that? Do you at all understand why the people were rejoicing, what about? To judge by the pictures, the couple themselves had no special charm. Does the public rejoice at the fact that people can commit a crass crime *and may get away with it?* That would not be a very healthy kind of rejoicing. It seems to me the very height of cynicism that the defense attorney means to sue for the insurance—thus making a mockery of the theory that the deaths were suicides. I think that the housewife who held out all alone to the last, and finally agreed to the "not guilty" verdict against her will, is going to be proved right in her feeling that somehow punishment will catch up with the culprits.

Now, though this comes ridiculously late, I must give you a friendly reproof—which is really a plea that you explain and set me right. In your unforgettable speech here to the teachers' organization, in which you so bravely criticized Hollywood, you went strangely astray, unless I am entirely mistaken, in your choice of the specific object. I refer to your denouncing Sherwood's *The Best Years of Our Lives* as a *disgrace* to

---

[1] Ernst Lubitsch (1892–1947), motion picture director. Of German birth, he came to Hollywood in 1923. Among his successful films: *The Student Prince* (1927), *Trouble in Paradise* (1932), *The Merry Widow* (1934), *Heaven Can Wait* (1943).

American movie production and to the country itself. My dear friend, how many corrupt and corrupting pieces of hackwork there were to pillory instead of this film! At the time I had missed it, but yesterday I saw it by chance, and I must say it belongs among the finest things of its kind to have come my way—unsurpassed in its naturalness, profoundly decent in its opinions, brilliantly acted, and full of genuinely American life. Tell me, for heaven's sake: Where in this film do you see any hate-mongering, debasement, appeal to evil instincts, or anything that is a disgrace to the country? The difficulties of readjustment to civilian life by the returning soldiers are portrayed with discretion, humor, and kindness; the women are touching except for the one vulgar creature who belongs in the general scheme; the men as individuals, with their class-shaped destinies, are completely true to life—as the world to which they return is true to life. Wasn't it permissible to sound the note of tragedy, that every time the *boys* come back, the ideals for which the war was fought have been betrayed and sold out? Do you object to the fact that the man who has the crudity and political baseness to say to the returned cripple, "We fought the wrong people," is knocked down? If not, what is it you object to? I must acknowledge a priori the superiority of judgment of an American woman such as yourself. Since I would like to be an American, I cannot help wishing to see and think as you do. I earnestly beg you: Would you explain for my instruction, if you can find the time, your reasons for condemning the film?

When I am feeling livelier I consider all sorts of writing projects: a medieval legend novella which, with *The Transposed Heads* and the Moses story, could form the third piece in my "Trois Contes"; working up the Felix Krull fragment into a modern picaresque novel set in the hansom-cab era. Comedy, laughter, humor seem to me more and more the soul's salvation; I long for them after the minimal portion of these in *Faustus,* and promise to find a plethora of gaiety despite the gloomiest of world situations. One who wrote the *Joseph* at the time of Hitler's victories will not let whatever is coming get him down, insofar as he lives to experience it. Your experience, dear friend, will extend farther than mine, and perhaps you will occasionally think of me as you go through it.

1947

TO MR. GRAY[1]
[Draft]

Pacific Palisades
October 12, 1947

Dear Mr. Gray:

The two remarks in Bob Nathan's *living room* probably were not spoken quite as Mr. Lyons[2] reproduces them. Feuchtwanger could not possibly have said: "I'm going home to Germany," for he has no more intention of doing so than I have. Moreover, he would not praise Germany as a country "where real culture can be found" in contrast with America any more than I would—and in an American writer's house to boot! As I know our friend Lion, he advocates a linguistic patriotism; he sees the life of German literature as attached to the life of Germany. He probably argued that a language cannot exist in the air, that without the backing of a nation and state it is a dead and toneless language, and that therefore we German writers have an interest in the political existence of Germany. There is a great deal of truth in this argument.

As far as I am concerned, I have occasionally read comments on myself to the effect that I must always be a patriot because I am one by nature, and that since I have abandoned my German patriotism I have become an American patriot. The remark Mr. Lyons ascribes to me seems to confirm this, and truly I may well have said something of the sort. At one time my faith in America's humanitarian mission was very strong. In the last few years it has been exposed to slight strains. Instead of leading the world, America appears to have resolved to buy it—which is also a very grandiose thing after its fashion, but does inspire less enthusiasm, you know. But even under these circumstances I still remain an American patriot, a fact which is confirmed to me by the grief I feel as I observe the growing unpopularity of America in the rest of the world. The American people are not responsible for this development and do not comprehend it. Those who try to explain the reasons for it are more and more reduced to silence. We can already see the first signs of terrorism, talebearing, political inquisition, and suspension of law, all of which are excused by an alleged state of *emergency*. As a German I can only say: That is the way it began among us, too. But I express this warning only in a low voice, as incidentally and unpretentiousiy as I am doing it here, and would not express it at all if I did not believe in my heart that this great country deserves our love, our concern, and our confidence.

[Unsigned]

[1] Unidentified.
[2] Perhaps Leonard Lyons, the columnist.

1947

TO ALBERT EINSTEIN

Pacific Palisades
October 14, 1947

Dear Professor Einstein:

I am writing to you about a matter which touches me closely, on personal grounds as well as on grounds of principle. You are familiar, at any rate in general outline, with the story of the composer Hanns Eisler, whom I know well and whom all his colleagues consider an excellent musician and a brilliant, highly cultivated person. Since the Inquisition has turned him over to the secular arm for deportation, he is in danger of landing in a German camp, and his friends here would like to try to help him avoid this fate. He hopes, upon what grounds I do not know, that he will not be deported if he states that he is willing to leave the country voluntarily. To that end he needs entry papers to another country, and he is thinking of Czechoslovakia, where as an artist he has friends and followers. A telegram has been drafted, the text of which I enclose, which is to be sent as a diplomatic message to President Beneš through the Czech consulate general in San Francisco. It could, of course, tremendously further the matter if you would add your name. The other signers are only my brother Heinrich and myself and, I hope, also the American writer William L. Shirer,[1] whose cooperation I am requesting by this same mail. Since the matter is urgent, would you please let me know by telegram.

TO OTTO BASLER

[*Telegram in English*]

Santa Monica
October 20, 1947

Kindly airmail important Swiss reviews Faustus.

---

[1] William L. Shirer (b. 1904), American journalist. War correspondent, political commentator for the Columbia Broadcasting System. Author of *Berlin Diary* (1941), *The Challenge of Scandinavia* (1955), *The Rise and Fall of the Third Reich* (1960), among others.

1947

TO CHARLES BURKHART[1]

[Original in English]

Pacific Palisades
October 18, 1947

Dear Mr. Burkhart:

Your letter has safely reached me via Bern. I have been back from my trip to Europe for a few weeks.

Above all, I am naturally pleased with the interest you are taking in my *Stories of Three Decades*. The sympathy of musicians has always been particularly valuable to me, because I owe a great deal to music, have learned much from it and, already at an early stage, have instinctively practiced the art of translating the technique of musical composition into the literary, the narrative field. That you have noticed this shows fine observation, and you will find it confirmed upon further reading of my works—which must be desirable to me for other reasons, too.

I am not surprised to hear that orthodox Christian education has been repugnant to you, and I am just as little surprised by the fact that you have returned, of your own free will, to Christianity as a religious moral law. You and I are, of course, not talking about dogmas and Christian mythology when we confess to this *religio*. Christianity was an enormous revolution, or rather: a real mutation of the human conscience and of human world-consciousness, a spiritual event which can never be effaced, unless it be through a complete relapse into a criminal, atavistic state, such as was represented by German National Socialism, for instance. Christianity and the conception of civilization have become one, and we are all living and breathing in it.

With regard to the relation between Christianity and art, it must be said that only in its radically puritan and picture-hating forms has Christianity taken an opposing stand toward art (with the exception of music). The Catholic Church, especially, has cultivated the fine arts and blended them into her ceremonies—apparently because, due to its sublimated sensuality, the Church recognized in art a helper, a middle-man between the divine and the earthy sphere. That it is indeed: a messenger between above and below, between mind and life, and its roots in the senses have seldom burdened its conscience. The great painters of madonnas cared little whether, perhaps, sensuous-erotic

---

[1] Charles Burkhart (b. 1928), pianist and teacher of music at Queens College, New York.

538

motives entered into their devout doings. Only a puritan fanatic like Savonarola would point this out to them—much to their contrition. But fanatical puritanism is a wrong against humanity, whose charm, difficulty, and dignity lies in the very fact that it belongs simultaneously to a corporeal and a spiritual world, and whose perfect representative is art. Art may well feel guilty before the pure mind, but it atones for its sensuous-erotic roots through sublimation in its creations and through purifying form.

The problem which occupies you has often been touched in my writings, the meditative as well as the narrative ones. There exists a critical counterpart to the *Stories of Three Decades*, entitled *Essays of Three Decades* (Knopf, 1947), which contains studies on Schopenhauer, Goethe, and Tolstoy, which, quite verbally, are "essays" on this theme. Also my novel *The Magic Mountain* may offer you some inspiration. Of course, I do not presume that you will find enlightenment especially in my books and could not be much better instructed by greater and wiser authors. But since, anyhow, the topic cannot be exhausted within the frame of a letter, your question after further works by me that might "help to clear the muddy waters" must be welcome to me.

TO RICHARD BRAUNGART[1]

Pacific Palisades
November 7, 1947

My dear Herr Braungart:

I now have your friendly letter of September 25 as well, and only want to say a reassuring word to you about the apparition scene in *The Magic Mountain* which has so perplexed you. This ghost scene is led up to, as you know, by the already occult events concerning the little Swedish girl. That our good fellow Hans Castorp sees his deceased cousin in the as yet unknown uniform of the impending world war is a piece of poetic license which derives its realistic empirical background from experiments in Dr. Schrenck-Notzing's[2] laboratory. I had sat in on several such experiments. Perhaps you are familiar with the essay *Occult Experiences* which I published while I was writing *The Magic Mountain*. It sets forth my ambiguous relationship to this whole realm, a relationship not

---

[1] Richard Braungart (b. 1872), essayist and biographer.
[2] Albert von Schrenck-Notzing (1862–1929), parapsychologist. Among his controversial books: *Materialisationsphänomene* (1914), *Physikalische Phänomene des Mediumismus* (1920).

of complete incredulity, but of disdain. *The Magic Mountain* by its whole nature offered the opportunity to make fictional use of this material. But the end of the chapter, Hans Castorp's departure from the séance room, makes it plain that he feels what he has seen is unworthy, sinful, and repulsive.

TO HERMANN HESSE

Pacific Palisades
November 25, 1947

Dear Herr Hesse:

I am in possession (it is something to possess) of your good letter of October, with the charming postscript from Frau Ninon and that fine correspondence about *The Bead Game*. From which one can plainly see how pure, lofty, and penetrating the effect of this "incommensurable" work is. Once again I perceive how nothing is really interesting except the incommensurable. I think the word was first applied to Goethe's *Faust*, by himself, and *Faust* remains the paragon to which one's thoughts turn when any example of that extraordinary genre appears again. I have just been looking into *Faust II* once more, in connection with putting together a Goethe anthology. Can you understand how it is that people so frequently take it as boring allegorical mystification? I was once more completely *transporté* and heartened by it—much though there is to say against the exotic growth that it is, with its dubious hero, its Catholic-opera conclusion and its mixture of revue and universal poem. But how superb it is after all in every passage, how witty and humorous in the treatment of myth, on the Pharsalian Fields and the Peneius, and of the mystery of Helen. How right, everywhere, because of jesting, wise, lyrical language. Moreover it is so completely comprehensible, and one might easily be tempted some time to write a totally fresh, intimate commentary on *Faust* which would relieve people of their all too pious timidity in the face of this sublime, serene, by no means inaccessible work, exceptional as it is, bold and humanly fallible as it is.

The Bead Game in a sense belongs to the family, differentiated by its prose dress—such things are done in prose nowadays. E. R. Curtius has written an excellent piece on it in the German magazine *Merkur*—you will have seen the essay, of course; I complimented the author on it very highly in Zurich, but otherwise he was not very agreeable, politically beyond the pale—I noticed in him a kind of intellectual atrophy and even debasement to be found in almost all those who spent the whole time stuck inside Germany—a quality that at once repels and saddens.

Europe already lies far behind, like a dream to which my thoughts often return with pleasure, especially the resumption of ties with Switzerland, and seeing you again. Everything was "again"; at the end, to top it all off, there was the once-again visit to a favorite place, the Huis ter Duin in Noordwijk "aan Zee." Nowadays, eight years afterwards, the hotel is as bad as it is expensive, but the grand terrace, the beach, the sea, are glorious, and I did my writing again in the sandy hut. As the ship sailed into the Hudson here, the passport official said: "*Are you THE Thomas Mann? Welcome home!*" Ah well—*home*. I suppose so. I have long since ceased to know what *home* really is; at bottom I never have known. On that matter see *Voyage with Don Quixote*,[1] a part of which I read you once upon a time in Montagnola, when it was freshly written.

To think that you would like to hear the old essays again! There are better ones in the volume *Adel des Geistes*; the shorter ones especially, I think, are worth reading—the one on Storm and the one on Platen,[1] which, to my pride, won applause from Croce. After all, he is a scholarly critic, which I am certainly not. I prefer merely to offer intimate homages, and at the same time to tell a few tales out of school.

At the moment I am doing nothing definite, am inwardly trying out this and that (what would you say if I developed the Felix Krull fragment into a regular picaresque novel, for entertainment in my old age?) and keeping an eye on *Doctor Faustus*, which has now entered the European world. [. . .] My first act, when the mail comes, is to rummage through it to see whether there are any comments from Sweden or Switzerland about the book. There have been a good number which reverberate somewhat with the excitement which is peculiar to the book in spite of and because of its tediousness. Do you have it, by the way? Distrusting the publisher, I ought to have sent it to you myself, but so far only a few copies that I urgently needed here have reached me. As soon as more arrive, one will go out to you—unless I hear beforehand that you already have it.

Cordial greetings from house to house, from couple to couple.

[1] Included in the volume *Essays of Three Decades.*

TO FREDRIC WARBURG

[*Original in English*]

Pacific Palisades
December 13, 1947

Dear Mr. Warburg:

Thank you for your kind letter of November 27th. The few cuts and corrections, the list of which I have sent to Mrs. Lowe-Porter, will hardly cause a delay in the delivery of the manuscript. These small changes can be effected in Mrs. Lowe's manuscript with a few strokes of the pen. The reason why I decided upon them—most of the cuts refer to musical theory—is simply my desire to make things a little easier for my translators.

Mrs. Lowe writes me that, principally, her task is done. She adds, however, that she is not completely satisfied with the solution of the extremely difficult problem. Given a few more months, she believes to be able to turn out a really perfect translation. I wonder whether it is not advisable to grant her the extension of time, and am about to put the same question to Alfred Knopf. I think it possible that he will agree to it in the interest of the book, and because he recently told me that the present dark situation of the book market would make a delay in the publication of this book more desirable than lamentable. The right moment for this year's Christmas business has anyhow been missed, and you have probably been considering next spring for the publication. If you and Knopf should be willing to grant Mrs. Lowe some more time, the book will probably not be ready before the fall of 1948. But don't you think the result would be well worth waiting for? To make a really adequate translation of this book particularly is a task requiring the utmost in talent and linguistic artistry. Mrs. Lowe certainly possesses these qualities, and is a systematic and scrupulous worker who strives for perfection. I would be very happy to grant her the time she thinks is necessary to do her best.

I was greatly interested to learn of your acquisition of the 2,000 copies of *Essays of Three Decades*. I had already learned of the book's publication in England through a very favorable review by Peacock. What you tell me about the prospective reprints also "sits smiling to my heart," to quote *Hamlet*.

With the kindest season's greetings, I am

1948

TO WALTER KOLB[1]

Pacific Palisades
January 4, 1948

My dear Herr Oberbürgermeister:

I have your letter of November 27—incidentally, it reached me only yesterday—and sincerely thank you for inviting me to come to Frankfurt for the centennial of the assembly in the Paulskirche,[2] and to speak at the reception in the Palmengarten.[3] I deeply appreciate the honor you show me, and do not find it easy to decline. Nevertheless I must, and it is better that I do so at once rather than after long hesitation.

I am already an old man, somewhat wearied by a life work at which I have labored hard, and by the shocks that the times have inflicted upon all of us. My health has also become delicate, and I must try to budget my strength—not out of miserliness, but to keep myself for my family a while longer, and if possible to accomplish a bit more. To cross first this continent and then the ocean is no longer a trifle for me; my present working schedule also leaves no room for it, and so I had renounced such a strenuous project for this year and probably also for next. Your letter did make me waver somewhat in this decision, but only temporarily. I must leave it at that.

The German edition of a novel that I wrote during the war is on the presses at this very time. It represents a return, after many intellectual wanderings, to the German urban world of my first book, *Buddenbrooks*,

[1] Walter Kolb (1902–56), member of the Social Democratic Party of Germany from 1920 on. In public service 1924–33, then disqualified for political reasons. Repeatedly arrested and imprisoned by the Gestapo. Mayor of Frankfurt am Main from August 1, 1946, until his death.

[2] The National Assembly that met in the Church of St. Paul, Frankfurt, on May 18, 1848, marked the beginning of constitutional government in Germany.

[3] The famous greenhouses in Frankfurt, often used for public receptions.

and has had quite a response in Switzerland. I think the novel may possibly dissipate or at any rate temper a good many misunderstandings that have formed in Germany regarding my relationship to the old homeland. This book will make many people realize more strongly, I think, than any speech I might make at the commemoration of the Paulskirche assembly that I am not exactly a deserter from Germany's destiny.

Permit me to set down here my deeply felt wishes for the welfare of the German people, for their spiritual salvation, their psychic and physical recovery—although I suppose the physical ought to be put first. All this, to be sure, is indissolubly connected with the weal and woe of the rest of the world, and with the question of whether the world can overcome—without some new, shattering catastrophe—its difficult crisis of transition and the antagonisms stemming from that crisis. But a son of Germany may be permitted to focus his wishes upon the land of his traditions. By no means last of all, those good wishes include the beautiful, shattered city whose head you are, and whose name brings so many cherished memories to me. May I hope, for dear Frankfurt, the renewal of her ancient glory.

With my respect and regards, my dear Mayor Kolb, I am

Sincerely yours,

TO HEINZ-WINFRIED SABAIS[1]

Pacific Palisades
February 9, 1948

Dear Herr Sabais:

I am most grateful for your letter and your essay,[2] which Professor Jockers[3] sent to me. Together they constitute the best thing that has come to me from Germany since I don't know when. I very much approve of your good, keen, and pure-intentioned intellectual work, and although you and those who think as you do may rightly call themselves a "forlorn handful," a voice such as yours cannot help but give people courage and

---

[1] Heinz-Winfried Sabais (b. 1922), writer. Editor of the *Neue Literarische Welt*, 1951–3. Author of *Mein Acker ist die Zeit* (poems, 1948), *Deutsches Bekenntnis zu Goethe* (1949), *Deutsche Lyrik der Gegenwart* (1959), *Götter, Kaiser, Diktatoren* (1965).

[2] "Vom klassischen zum modernen Humanismus," published in two monthly issues of the magazine *Aufbau* (1947).

[3] Ernst Jockers (b. 1887), professor of German literature at the University of Pennsylvania; emeritus, 1957.

actually inspire the faith you demand: that German intellectuals will take an active part in building the world we are hoping for.

In your arguments I find a great kinship with my own thoughts and feelings, especially all you say against the vanity and bigotry of those who imagine themselves sole possessors of the truth. I am also in sympathy with your call for "safeguarding the springs of progress," or as it might also be put, for a kind of religious spirit which consists in obedience to and constant regard for the changing aspect of truth. In the still largely misunderstood Joseph novels, I used the term *Gottesklugheit*—meaning man's prudence in uniting his will with that of God and not insisting on remaining in states "which He wishes us to go beyond." I call such obstinacy *Gottesdummheit*, stupidity before God, a state which necessarily leads to catastrophes, and in which ultimately there is a longing for catastrophe as a way out. What we like to call the "Western world" has long been living is such a state, although some sense of what the world spirit demands is gradually finding its way into the West—as far as the Atlantic. Democracy refuses to recognize that it has ceased to have any moral existence except in the form of socialism. Rather than admit that, it throws itself into the arms of Fascism—which is real dereliction, besotted breach of duty—and sets the world on fire. It is very polite of you to regard "the century of the common man" slogan, which only a "forlorn handful" believes in, as the Western world's credo. The other slogan of the "American century," which contains a great deal of ungodly stupidity, is incomparably more popular; and if "we" do not succeed in buying the world away from socialism, there remains the A-bomb. How much more is needed before the climate here approximates that of Germany around 1930?

On the other hand, I share all your concern for "keeping individuality from being overpowered by the apparatus of social organization" and approve every one of your warnings against the total politicalization of man and the Machiavellism which results from that. Realism and awareness of the ever-changing aspects of life in the "dialectic of events" are good things, but they also harbor the germ of cynicism and a comically jesuitical adroitness in manipulating ideology, tactics, rhetoric. The human conscience should not be delegated to the Politburo, do you think?

There is nothing more touching and more engaging than your call for the union of politics and morality in humanism. I also gladly accept the definition of optimism you give, although I am no great admirer of the Creation; I regard the exploding universe more as a devil's joke than as a reason for crying hosannah, and must plead guilty to some of the mystic's partiality for nothingness and dissolution. But I live, and am fundamentally pervaded by the identity of life, optimism, and ethics. Let us substitute a warmer, more comprehensive word for it: *Sympathie*. From that springs all I do, in the way of entertaining and advising.

I know why I cannot feel any real rapport with the justly celebrated Albert Schweitzer: he is too theoretical for me; he speaks of optimism and ethics instead of sympathy. He is said to play the organ very well, and yet I can never see him as an artist. Goethe strikes me as preferable. He had the sympathy which comes directly out of life, without concern for optimism or pessimism—and at the same time there is certainly more poetry in his Mephisto's nihilism than the philistine imagines. *Wilhelm Meister* contains a magnificent sentence which covers our whole situation of the today: "The human pack fears nothing more than reason; if it understood what is fearsome, it would fear stupidity; but the former is uncomfortable, so that people must push it aside; the latter is merely ruinous, so that they can wait for it to work." Brilliant! Conclusive! Goethe's alleged "last word," calling for more light or something of the sort, was certainly not spoken; there has been a good deal of fraud about that story. But what he really said at the end, and meant, is clear: "There is really only one thing to do—go forward." Let us abide by that, and if Germany also abides by it, she will live.

TO ARNOLD SCHOENBERG

Pacific Palisades
February 17, 1948

Dear Herr Schoenberg:

That certainly is a curious document.[1] It touched me, showing as it does the zeal with which your disciples stand guard over your glory and honor. But so much strained malice, which at the same time so completely misses the mark, also has its comic aspect.

---

[1] A "Hugo Triebsamen" had purportedly sent Schoenberg an extract from an imaginary *Encyclopedia Americana* of 1988, and Schoenberg forwarded it to Mann with a bitter comment. The extract stated that Thomas Mann, originally a musician, was the real inventor of the twelve-tone system, but that after he became a writer he silently tolerated its appropriation by a thievish composer named Schoenberg. With the publication of *Doctor Faustus*, Mann had claimed the musical system as his own intellectual property.

In a cordial letter of reconciliation dated November 25, 1948, Schoenberg admitted that he had invented Triebsamen and his letter: "My synthetic Hugo Triebsamen, whom I manufactured out of Hugo Riemann and Dr. Rubsamen. . . ." His purpose had been to make Mann realize how seriously his character, Adrian Leverkühn, had endangered Schoenberg's posthumous fame.

I imagine every Hottentot nowadays knows who is the creator of the so-called twelve-tone system. Anyone who as much as picks up a book like *Doctor Faustus* certainly knows. Why then does this Triebsamen pretend that I was passing myself off as the inventor of the system? In a novel that attempts to give a picture of an epoch as a whole, I have taken an enormously characteristic cultural phenomenon of the epoch and transferred it from its real author to a fictional artist, a representative and martyr of the age. Surely every review of the book, in whatever language, which in any way discusses its presentation of music, will hardly fail to mention your name. There are naturally other grounds for doing so besides the references to the row technique. Why doesn't Triebsamen also make a fuss about the idea of transforming the horizontal into the vertical—a ramification of an idea clearly taken from your *Theory of Harmony*? Didn't he notice that the whole musical theory of the book is saturated in your ideas, in fact that by "music" what is really implied all along is Schoenbergian music?

The novel of the epoch identifies "music" with Schoenbergian music. That's not doing any damage to your historical stature.

But surely all sins are punished on this earth! Utilizing large portions of reality in my montage, I concocted a fiction composed of all sorts of elements ("Much do the poets lie," says Homer), and now your loyal Triebsamen in his turn spins a wild farago about my ambition to be a composer, my early acquaintance with you, my later differences with you, etc. No one is going to understand such jumbled nonsense, especially since the book hasn't even appeared in English yet. What is this piece of writing supposed to be, anyhow? A letter? An article? As I have already said, as a testimony of embattled devotion there is something touching about it. And yet as I read it I cannot help recalling that old groan: "God save us from our friends."

I am sorry, my dear Herr Schoenberg, that your attention has been riveted upon this aspect of the book. The whole thing would have interested you. Now, alas, I suppose you are lost to it as a reader. And yet it was a well-intentioned gift we tossed over the wall to you!

Let us hope that you are all past the *flu* and that everyone is in good health.

1948

TO FREDRIC WARBURG

[Original in English]

Pacific Palisades
March 4, 1948

Dear Mr. Warburg:

You have given me a very touching surprise with your kind letter of February 19th. I did not expect that you would read my novel before the printing of the galleys, and much as your impatience pleases me, I must almost regret the fact that you made the acquaintance of the book through the unfavorable medium of a faint carbon copy. Considering the volume of the book, yours is, indeed, an impressive reading feat, and I can only be proud of the impulsiveness with which you familiarized yourself with the work.

Your reticence in the judgment of this strange work is only too justified. I myself share this reserve completely and don't let my head be turned by the enthusiastic hymns of praise which are reaching me from Europe, and now also from Germany. It is a work whose rank and value will remain undetermined for some time. Only posterity will be able to decide these questions. But already today the reading public recognizes that I have written this work in particular with my innermost feelings, I can almost say with my heart's blood, and I am glad to note that you too seem to understand this. Of course, much of the book's natural music is being lost in the translation, but I am convinced that even a poor translation (and I know Mrs. Lowe-Porter's rendition will be anything but poor!) cannot destroy the substance of a work.

The short review from the *London Times Literary Supplement* is the first English-language echo to reach me. It sounds a bit thin, and we must hope that warmer and deeper-probing utterances will follow. I was especially surprised that at the end the author speaks of a "loosely woven net of ironically glittering prose." I should say that I was never less ironical than in this very serious, confession-like tome, and as concerns the "loosely woven net," this is in truth an extremely tight-knit composition in which, musically speaking, "no note is free," and in which all elements are interrelated.

Please accept my best thanks, dear Mr. Warburg, for your personal interest in this work whose English publisher you are. May it bring honor to your firm.

1948

TO ERICH VON KAHLER

Pacific Palisades
March 6, 1948

Dear, good friend:

I can't tell you, or can tell you only with awkward brevity, how your essay has moved and pleased me. A few days ago I broke my shoulder bone in a clumsy fall at someone's house, and I am still all bandaged. For the first few days I was pretty miserable, but now it's not so bad.

Your essay is the first discussion of the book that goes far beyond the ordinary reviews, a study written from a high vantage point of philosophical criticism that takes in my whole life and life work, with remarkable perception of its unity. Honoring the work, it also honors the life, not only on a moral basis, as effort, but as an existence guided and shaped by an inner "daimon." So naturally I find your essay deeply gratifying and feel thankful for so much intelligent friendship and insight.

After having read the essay twice in this form, I look forward with pleasure to seeing it again in print. What stirred me most, perhaps, were the things you said about the almost savage directness of the book. That directness kept exciting me all along, and even now makes me feel as if the novel were still my own secret. It startles me that you use the word "montage," for in my own mind I have used it frequently, and the idea of montage is in fact one of the premises of the book.

One might almost think that the final paragraph directed against certain simpleminded notions regarding my comfort and safety strikes a banal note compared with all that comes before. But in the final analysis, it is by no means a bad idea to set that matter straight, both for the Germans and for people like Döblin.

TO HEIDI HEIMANN[1]

Pacific Palisades
March 10, 1948

Dear Miss Heimann:

[. . .] The Britten records arrived in excellent condition a few days after your friendly letter, and I want to thank you for your sympathy with my musician and music novel, as well as for the thoughtful and valuable gift. We played the records at once and listened to the songs with your text

[1] Heidi Heimann, journalist and art historian; in London since 1936. Wrote "Thomas Mann's 'Hermesnatur' " (1957) for the English Goethe Society.

in hand. It is sensitive, clever, original music, and surprisingly moderate in harmony; I had imagined the man rather "wilder." At any rate, Adrian Leverkühn might well be very happy to have done some of these things, such as the nocturne with the "dying, dying, dying," and the sick rose.[2]

It was time I learned something about this interesting composer. At present he is much talked about in this country, and his *Peter Grimes* is supposed to be coming to Los Angeles. Some years ago my second son lived for a considerable time in the same house with Britten, in Brooklyn. It was a kind of bohemian colony, to which Wystan Auden also belonged. Back then, the young musician seemed not to have given the impression of genius. I suppose it was the story of the ugly duckling.

With my thanks once again, and the friendliest greetings for Ida Herz also,

TO BLANCHE KNOPF

[Original in English]

Pacific Palisades
March 10, 1948

Dear Blanche:

Above all I want to thank you very much for your and Alfred's sympathetic lines. My shoulder bone is improving satisfactorily under expert care, and I can already slip my arm into my coat sleeve again and only have to wear it in a sling. In a few weeks the whole stupid incident will be forgotten. I sincerely hope that Alfred's leg is making similarly good progress. That was indeed a more serious matter!

From Mrs. Lowe, who is about to return to the United States, I received yesterday the enclosed Translator's Note to *Doctor Faustus*. It is an intelligent utterance, and I can well understand that Mrs. Lowe feels the need to point out the enormous difficulties of her task. I am only afraid that her characterization of the book might have too discouraging an effect and might give the impression that this book is terribly highbrow and accessible only to the highest developed intellect. I think that in paragraph 4 the sentence "addressed to no other audience than an intellectual, even a cosmopolitan one," should be shortened in such a

---

[2] Benjamin Britten's *Serenade*, opus 31 (1943), containing musical settings of the poems "Nocturne" by Tennyson (with the refrain, "Dying, dying, dying"), "The Sick Rose," by Blake, and "Ode to Sleep," by Keats. Miss Heimann wrote that she was giving Mann the record because she was "thunderstruck at Leverkühn's choice of texts."

manner that it simply reads: "addressed to no other audience than a cosmopolitan one." That would modify the matter somewhat.

The book is, in fact, no insurmountably difficult treatise but, at least in part, an entertaining, even exciting novel. It would certainly not be desirable to make the public scared of it.

I myself also include today a note which I promised to add to the English as well as all other foreign- and subsequent German-language editions of the novel. You can imagine that it was Maestro Schoenberg who, worried about his posthumous fame, asked me to do so, and I could not refuse his wish. The note should be placed at the end of the book, *not* on the last page of the text, of course, but at some distance from it, so that its disenchanting effect is kept at a minimum.

With many regards from Katia and myself to you and Alfred,

TO BRUNO WALTER

Pacific Palisades
March 26, 1948

Dear friend:

Many thanks for your sympathy. There is something quite embarrassing about receiving flowers, wine, and nice letters as the reward for such clumsiness. The step at Horkheimers is universally hated, and no doubt a good many others have stumbled over it, but still not quite in that way. I must have been exceedingly eager to be off.

Incidentally, it is odd what a shock such a bone fracture is to the whole organism. I knew at once that something dreadful had happened, and I am told that I was deathly pale as I stood up. Most people faint, the doctor said. Fever followed, too. But it was only the first week that was really unpleasant. The break is healing very rapidly for an (to put it mildly) adult, and at times I can already leave the sling off. But one's whole being is involved in the organic process, and such healing certainly costs energy. The incident has left me fatigued; also intellectually sluggish and disinclined to work—although I can scarcely call that an exceptional state.

As her father I must thank you for your hospitality to Erika. She has been back with us since day before yesterday, to my delight. She is an intrepid, splendid, amusing child, you know. *Da brach sich sein Blick, er gedachte, Brünnhilde, dein.* Wonderful passage! But now we are looking forward to many a wonderful passage in the *Missa.* Do well on the 18th, with the aid of that noble talent of yours, to which I shall never fail to pay tribute.

The best of good wishes from the three of us to you and Lotte.

Schoenberg insists on my having a postscript stating that the twelve-tone technique is *his* and not the devil's invention. Pfitzner's telegram[1] to Frank is not bad either. You musicians are a fine lot!

TO ELLIOTT E. COHEN [1]

[*Original in English*]

Pacific Palisades
March 26, 1948

Dear Mr. Cohen:

Privately and quite belatedly I want to express to you my regret about the fact that you were obliged to publish the unpleasant and strongly hostile letter of Mr. Flint. It was really humiliating for me: all other letters received by you were demonstrations of grateful appreciation for some offering by *Commentary*, and only my contribution had to provoke this utterance of disgruntled superiority.

One is quite pretentious in Cambridge, Massachusetts, and I had been forced to use great simplicity in my description of Nietzsche's spiritual development. As you know, the article in question was the text of a lecture I first held at the Library of Congress (abbreviated to about half of its length), and later in New York, London, Zurich, and Amsterdam, always under the lively interest of large audiences, among which there may have been many people to whom up to now Nietzsche's name had been familiar only in the stupid connection Nietzsche-Treitschke-Bernhardi, and who received, for the first time, a more intimate insight into this mind. It may have been a mistake to publish this popular lecture as an essay.

There is nothing left for you to do but to ask Mr. Flint to continue with the reevaluation of Nietzsche which I began so clumsily on his own and far superior level, and to show you the true and real Nietzsche who

[1] In a later letter to Hermann Hesse, Mann writes: "Hans Pfitzner . . . has been cleared of the charge of Nazism. Yet he was a member of the 'cultural senate' and all. Before Reich Minister Frank was hanged, Pfitzner sent this telegram to him in his last hour: 'Dear friend, all my thoughts are with you.' I must say, that is so *au delà*, goes so far in folly and quixoticism, that it reconciles me to the acquittal."
[1] Editor of *Commentary*.

is needed today. Or should he be one of those who don't accomplish anything themselves, but only sit back and wait for others to do something in order that they may write supercilious letters?

TO ROGER SENHOUSE[1]

[*Original in English*]

Pacific Palisades
April 18, 1948

Dear Mr. Senhouse:

Thank you so much for your expression of sympathy on the occasion of my accident. Its consequences are almost overcome now, and if I wanted to, I could again give the Hitler salute with the broken arm. The fracture has healed just as fast as the chest operation of some time ago. It seems I am a tough thistle.

Thank you for the new British translation of the Nietzsche lecture. I am curious to hear what Mrs. Lowe-Porter, who also received a copy, has to say about it. It may be more British than the one I have used so far, but, frankly speaking, I do not think it is better. The reason may be that, quite generally, I do not like the translations of my writings, but this much is objectively true:

There are some awkward passages and misunderstandings in it, as in other translations. For instance: "The highest praise that can be paid to Wilde" is not the same as the German: "Wenn man Wilde sehr loben wollte, so vergliche man . . ." And on page 23, the phrase: "This estimate of him is merely childish" is more crude and inept than "This distinction is naïve" from the American text. Nor do I like the passage on page 25: "How out of date, how academic even." I think "timebound and theoretical" is much better.

These are only a few examples. I shall now wait for Mrs. Lowe-Porter's judgment, but in any case I am sending you the revised American translation of the article as it was published in the January and February issues of the New York periodical *Commentary*. Please be kind enough to check this text, which Erika and I have edited together very carefully. I am almost certain that you, too, will prefer it in the end. And why shouldn't the article of a naturalized American like me have an American touch? I don't think the English readers will mind this. Do you intend to publish the lecture as a pamphlet?

[1] Roger Senhouse (b. 1899), editor at Martin Secker & Warburg Ltd., Mann's English publisher.

1948

I have no idea what I wrote to Preetorius at the time. The American sponsored *Neue Zeitung* in Munich asked me by wire for the permission to print this letter, and as I was convinced I had not written anything bad, I gave the permission. The Zurich paper *Die Tat* seems to have reproduced the letter later. I haven't seen it yet.

I am very happy that you did not read the *Faustus* in the only half-legible typewritten copy, but are waiting for the proofs. Dear Mr. Warburg was too curious and has atoned for it.

Erika is staying with us and sends you her best regards. She spent a few days at the hospital because of a harmless little operation. As soon as she is well again, I shall ask her about the copy of her interview with Beneš. Letters reach her under my address.

This year we intend to stay quietly at home and not to travel. But the year 1949 will probably find us in Europe—and England—again. I had a very friendly invitation from Oxford to speak there in German about Goethe. It is the so-called Taylor lecture, and at the same time I was invited to become the honorary president of the Undergraduate German Literary Society. This post was held during the last twenty years by Gerhart Hauptmann.

Again many thanks and best wishes for your well-being.

TO VIKTOR MANN

Pacific Palisades
May 11, 1948

Dear Viko:

Just a few lines to show you how far the news of your "Thoughts and Memories" has already traveled. I found the enclosed story today in the New York *Aufbau*, a German-Jewish weekly which reaches readers not only in the United States but also in Canada, New Zealand, Australia, etc. The account does sound rather strange, and I am sending you the clipping chiefly on account of the alleged title[1] of your book, which certainly must be a misunderstanding. I cannot deny the allegation outright, since I don't have the facts. Yet I am certain that you would never have thought of anything so tasteless (as well as tactless toward Heinrich). Have you any idea how this title got into the newspapers, and can you do anything about it? If you will send me a brief correction, I'll pass it on to *Aufbau*.

---

[1] The incorrect title given by the article was "Thomas and His Brothers." The book in question, later published posthumously, was Viktor Mann's memoirs, *Wir waren Fünf, Bildnis der Familie Mann.*

554

I hope your spring is as lovely as ours here. Everything glows with color; quite as in the poem,[2] a gentle wind blows from the blue sky, and not only are the lemon trees blooming, but they are heavily hung with fruit.

Erika had to undergo an operation at the Santa Monica Hospital—a female matter. She is with us now, recuperating well and writing letters for me under the secretarial name of Homer Smith. Frequently callers on the telephone ask for this *gentleman.* At which times he just happens to be on vacation.

Many greetings to you and Nelly!

T.

TO VIKTOR MANN

Pacific Palisades
July 3, 1948

Dear Viko:

Here is a clipping from *Aufbau* to reassure you. I suppose the item was prompted by your publisher. I myself would probably have done nothing, with the feeling that such things are after all hardly read, quickly forgotten, and ultimately corrected by reality. In fact, I was sorry to have bothered you about it when I saw that these idiocies have almost spoiled your pleasure in writing the book. God forbid! It is only that you had not so far experienced what we all know: as soon as one steps into the public realm there are vexations to be put up with, whether they spring from malice or silliness. Usually it's both.

Then again, I suppose it is just as well that I did call your attention to these possibilities. We too have been conferring about the right title. We rather liked "I Remember: From the Life of a Family." But your "Portrait of a Family" is just as good—perhaps with the subtitle "Reminiscences." "We Were Five," nice in itself, really sounds too much like Neumann.[1]

We have already given Frido the portrait of the Swiss ancestors. And what you have in mind for him later on is truly touching.[2] No, we didn't laugh; rather, we were as moved as we were surprised. He wants

[2] Mignon's song, *Kennst du das Land . . .*, from Goethe's *Wilhelm Meister.*
[1] Alfred Neumann's book was entitled *Es waren ihrer sechs* ("There Were Six of Them").
[2] Viktor Mann planned to bequeath all the family heirlooms in his possession to his great-nephew, Frido. This plan came to nothing because of Viktor's unexpected death the following year.

to become an *in*gineer in Brussels (where an uncle on his mother's side has a factory), and so there he will be, when all of us are no longer around to see it, sitting among the old things. Strange, strange.

The Lübeckers have received my monster parcel of books, translations, newspapers, etc., and act as if they were in seventh heaven. They want to found a T. M. Society for all Germany, rebuild the house on Meng Strasse exactly as it used to be, etc. Sheer farce. The new director of the city library also wrote me, but poor Wendt added a few penciled lines. In fourth form he was my favorite classmate—imaginative, nice, and silly, although head boy. All through Gymnasium he remained a model pupil. But much later, when I once asked him why I had never heard anything of him since, he wrote: "I suppose that is only because you do not move in academic circles." In Elbing, where he was on the school board, I found him so fat and stupid that it was a pity—he also seemed to be rather generally held in contempt. Now he seems to be dying mentally and physically. It is very melancholy. A human life off to a good start and breaking down early. Incidentally, they tell me he was much impressed by the samples from my parcel, which were brought to his bed. "I am proud to be your friend," he wrote. Poveretto.

Enough now. I hope you are both in good health and managing well with food. Are you pleased with the new currency? Has the mark "inner" value? Do the people believe in it? Will it supersede the black market and the cigarette currency? I suppose its introduction puts the final stamp on the division of Germany. And yet that division surely cannot last long.

TO THEODOR W. ADORNO

Pacific Palisades
July 12, 1948

Dear Dr. Adorno:

Heartfelt thanks for your sympathy.[1] Klaus, physically restored, is for the present staying at Bruno Walter's along with Erika, who is giving him spiritual care. I am somewhat angry with him for having tried to do that to his mother. She is understanding about everything—and so am I. That has spoiled him.

The situation remains dangerous. My two sisters committed suicide,[2] and Klaus has much of the elder sister in him. The impulse is present in

---

[1] Klaus Mann had made a suicide attempt.
[2] Carla Mann in 1910; Julia Löhr-Mann in 1927.

him and is favored by all the surrounding circumstances—except that he has a parental home he can always rely on, although naturally he does not want to be dependent on it.

It is a good sign that he curses the *publicity* that followed the incident on the grounds that "this makes it so hard to start over again."

Your article on Egk[2] is shot through with the most serious kind of wit. It amused me tremendously. I gave it to my brother-in-law to read, so that he could see how strict and traditionalistic things are in the realm that he, like our dear, good Bruno Walter, despises as antimusical.

See you soon.

TO WERNER SCHMITZ[1]

Pacific Palisades
July 30, 1948

My dear Herr Schmitz:

Thank you for your letter. Ever since Europe was thrown open again, I have made inquiries about Ernst Bertram, but have been able to obtain only vague, half-reassuring information. I am glad, therefore, that one of his students sends me news. I would have been even happier if he had written to me himself sometime during these years. But I suppose he is too proud for that, and also bears me too great a grudge because I had to oppose what he believed in.

If you ask me my opinion of his case, of the "classification" he has been assigned, it is this: Ernst Bertram is a good, fine and pure person, of extraordinary intelligence, and for many years he was my and my family's best friend. What alienated us more and more, to my sorrow, was the increasingly political virulence of his professional interest in German culture, his romanticizing of things Teutonic, his surrender to a myth of blondness and idealized nationalism—in other words, his enthusiastic faith in the rising "Third Reich," a faith which could not be shaken despite all my warnings, all my expostulations on the ominous aspects of this mass movement. How many conversations I remember! He saw roses and marble where I saw nothing but diabolic filth, a poisonous intoxicant for the populace, innate murderousness, and certain ruin for Germany and Europe. Communication between us ceased to be

---

[2] Werner Egk (b. 1901), composer and conductor; director of the Hochschule für Musik in Berlin, 1950–3.

[1] Werner Schmitz (b. 1919), librarian, writer; author of numerous magazine articles on literary, oriental, social, and cultural subjects.

possible. He perceived the crudeness well enough; but his own tender nature hailed the barbarian invasion from within, since there was no longer any to come from outside. He looked to it for the renewal of the culture, purification, exaltation, glorification of the Fatherland. And he remained true to this faith, *unselfishly and personally untainted*,[2] not only at the time of Hitler's sham victories, at the time of the ravishing and plundering of Europe, but on down to the death throes of the National Socialist state, down to the days of the militia and the were-wolves.

In that context, what does it signify that he was not a Party member? He was too aristocratic to be a card-carrying member of anything. But the assertion that he was "never a National Socialist" is untenable. Of course he was not one like the man in the street, but he was one as a student of myth, as an idealist and visionary. You even say that he did not belong to the *Reichsschrifttumskammer*. Is that possible? As far as I know, no one could write and publish in Germany without having entered that association and taking the oath of loyalty to the Führer. But Bertram did write and publish: a book on freedom of expression (at least he was free to express himself), articles, proclamations, and speeches, which we outside shuddered at. He was a champion and spokesman for National Socialist *Kultur*, and given the inseparability of realms, he naturally did not restrict himself to cultural matters alone. He was political. He called upon Austria to beg to be annexed to Hitler's Germany. His mutiny against Rust[3] in the name of "academic freedom" resembles the parochial politics of certain Lutheran clergymen who accepted all the atrocities of the "national state" until the moment that it infringed upon the interests of their church—and who then, I grant, in several cases took upon themselves the martyrdom which, thank God, was not granted to our staunch defender of academic freedom.

And now? Ernst Bertram has been removed from his teaching post. This is senseless in view of the reinstatement of many incomparably more dangerous, politically cruder types in public service. Such people are again being trusted with office and power. But is it senseless for Bertram himself? After the disastrous shipwreck of all his racist ideals, can he desire to teach young people once again? Can he want to do so in a Fatherland occupied by what he called "termite peoples"? In short, I ask myself whether you are really speaking and acting for him, as he would wish it, when you canvass for supporters to favor his reappointment.

[2] Mann's emphasis.
[3] Bernhard Rust (1883–1945), Hitler's minister of science and education.

Yes, as you say, those are threadbare reasons which, according to your letter, have been officially given for his exclusion. Bertram never really belonged to the George circle, although he was quite close to it. His Protestantism and Germanism rebelled against the imperial-Roman and Jesuitical tendencies of that sacred clique. Also, there were probably too many Jews in it for his taste. (He would never have stood for Gundolf's[4] becoming a full professor, he said.) —The idea of an "elite" which he advocated is by no means alien to democracy. —And to call Nietzsche, the European, the condemner of Bismarck and Wagner, a "forerunner of the Third Reich," is a crude simplification. No doubt about that—just as there is no doubt that Bertram's early work on him is the essence of beauty, musicality, and innocence. That book will be republished frequently, and will always be admired. It can stand the light of any day— whereas we can conclude without malice that Bertram's writings of the Nazi period cannot stand the light of the present day and had better not be reissued. That matter can, I think, easily be left to his own desires and discretion.

The same principle applies to his future production. I would regard it as wrong and undignified to impose a ban on his writing and publishing. Here is someone who ought to be master of his own silence and speaking out; and as things are, we may expect silence rather than speech from a man of his pride. But if some day he presents the major book on Stifter he was once planning (I do not know what became of that project), I see no reason why German culture should deprive itself of such a contribution by any foolish interdict.

Finally, the denial of his pension. I confess that sobering recollections mingle with my feelings of protest: recollections of Jewish scholars who in 1933 were thrust from their professorial chairs and their laboratories. Their colleagues of German blood made few inquiries about how they were faring. I have a brother-in-law, a highly respected theoretical physicist, who also would once have been entitled to a pension in Germany and today does not know how he is to support his declining years. But be that as it may, I will not condone it if the same hardship is to be inflicted on the great mythographer of Nietzsche, who has taught so many young men whose intellectual services Germany is now dependent on. It ill becomes the generous country that pensioned off its princes to send a noble-spirited, misguided professor into the economic desert.

To sum up: I am against Bertram's being recalled to an academic

---

[4] Friedrich Gundolf (1880–1931), leading German literary critic and prominent member of the Stefan George circle.

teaching position. He probably does not wish it himself. Moreover, he must be close to the age limit. But I am decidedly for his being granted a decent retirement salary and the right to determine his own rules for his creative work.

TO AGNES E. MEYER

Pacific Palisades
September 7, 1948

Dear Agnes:

Naturally our letters crossed. That's the way it always is, and each time we should have been patient for one day more. But which day is it? That is what we would have to know.

Your opinion of the manuscript is certainly absolutely correct. Just send it back to me—I have the rest of it. But if you have already sent it to the author, that's all right too. He always writes me in English and behaves like an American. I am inclined to think he is one, for he sometimes writes about America in a way that he would scarcely permit himself as a German. But Americans sometimes do write that way. During the war I once received a letter from a G.I. in the Philippines who said: "*I envy you your swift, sure maturity, your heritage of culture, your relentless self-discipline. Such things are hard-won in European civilization. Here in America they are almost nonexistent.*" Well, if he says so himself . . .

Curious. The concern you express about Fitelberg is a matter that our Klaus raised when I first read the chapter to the family. He commented that the portrait could seem anti-Semitic. Others, including Jews, insisted that was not so, and really Saul is a charming, clever fellow who has a good many astute things to say about the parallels in the fate of Germans and Jews. Granted, he is only one Jewish type; God knows there are others more serious and dignified. The unfortunate thing is that Jewry also comes off so badly in its other representative, the Fascist Breisacher. But it is too late to change any of that. The book wanted it so. And after all, what sort of picture do the other people in the novel present? It is an aquarium of many fantastically shaped fish, and the only truly agreeable characters are Frau Schweigestill and Serenus Zeitblom.

What does it matter if you are not ready with your article on *Faustus* when the book comes out in October? Let the run-of-the-mill reviewers have their say first. Then you can rectify some of their idiocies. Above all, I am looking forward to your militant article in *The Atlantic Monthly*. You really are a kind of feminine Winkelried.[1] I admit, however, that heroism of this sort sometimes strikes me as futile. The wave of reaction will be rising a good deal higher; we can do nothing about it. The Roosevelt era is going to have to be demolished even more thoroughly, for it was after all just one great *un-American activity*. Dear friend, let me confess to you that I already hate the Thomas-Rankin Committee and its wretched activities almost as much as I once hated Hitler. I subscribe to that with my full name.

Yours,
Thomas Mann

TO WILLY BAUER[1]

Pacific Palisades
September 14, 1948

My Dear Herr Amtgerichtsrat:

I am much obliged to you for your friendly and confidential letter of August 5, and wish first of all to express how moved I was by everything you tell about yourself, your career, your courageous life and suffering. Your whole human and political bearing, your path from son of a Berlin workman and part-time student to Socialist Party official, member of the Reichsbanner, and brave defender of the Republic, has made a deep impression on me. I am truly happy to be in touch with someone so representative of human decency.

About the affidavit you have asked me for in behalf of that unfortunate man Blunck—may I in turn ask you to excuse me. I cannot testify for Blunck, not in any respect; and to testify against a colleague, and cause him to be given an unfavorable classification, as it is called in Germany nowadays, is also repugnant to me. All these years I have lived far from Germany, but I knew of Blunck's presidency of the *Reichsschrifttumskammer*, knew he was considered an exponent of Nazi culture and was enjoying the concomitant advantages. I therefore saw in him one of those sinister figures, alien and incomprehensible to me, into which a good many familiar persons were transformed in those days.

---

[1] Arnold Winkelried, a Swiss hero (possibly legendary) who at the battle of Sempach in 1386 threw open his arms and embraced so many of the enemy spears as he fell that he cleared a path for his comrades to attack.

[1] Willy Bauer (b. 1907), retired district magistrate, at this time serving as prosecutor of a denazification tribunal.

After the collapse of Nazi rule, Blunck wrote to me in the warmest and most respectful terms, and like so many others, represented matters as if the whole thing had been a misunderstanding. I did not quite believe that, but I replied in a decent and friendly way, not censoriously. Quite recently, before your letter came, he again wrote to me, without mentioning the forthcoming denazification trial. Of course I have never promised to come to his defense, and if he cites me among those who are prepared to bear witness to his democratic or even socialistic principles, that is a false citation. I would prefer to remain entirely outside the whole affair, and I herewith request you to allow me to.

With many thanks and my highest respects and regards, I am, my dear Herr Bauer,

TO HELEN LOWE-PORTER

Pacific Palisades
October 3, 1948

Dear friend:

Two days ago copies of the English *Doctor Faustus* reached me. I promptly sent my compliments to Alfred Knopf on the handsome format (the Dürer symbolism on the *jacket* is really very fine), and now I want once more, and this time from direct acquaintance with the work, to give you my earnest and heartfelt thanks for your tremendous and faithful feat of interpretation. I regard as unjustified the doubts expressed in your witty little preface as to whether your translation may be conceded beauty as well as fidelity. As you know, my relationship to the English language is not intimate enough for me to be really qualified to give praise. But I have read a great deal here and there in the volume, and I find that the translation reads like an original, like a work of English prose, which does mean that you have contrived to find equivalents for the frequently strange devices employed in the German, and have skillfully adjusted the differences between the languages. In doing that, it seems to me, you have also found the equilibrium between exactness and beauty.

You have done quite right in simply letting German words stand occasionally. It is curious, however, that in one case you did not do so where it would have been particularly appropriate. I am referring to the Fitelberg chapter, where the visitor speaks of Anatole France and makes the joke that a German writer cannot call himself "Deutschland," he must be content with "Deutsch"—and then he would be giving himself a Jewish name. Here "Deutschland" and "Deutsch" should unquestionably have remained in the original, for "Deutsch" is a well-known Jewish surname, whereas "German" is no name at all. A German warship, moreover, is of course not called "Germany" but "Deutschland." This point should be changed at the first opportunity.

Forgive this minute stricture—upon a performance that is on the whole so extremely admirable. Now let us see what American criticism and the American public will make of the novel. If they don't like the book, it will not be your fault.

What have you decided about your *Faustus* essay? It interests me very much. Will it appear first in a magazine?

Greetings from my wife and Erika.

I came out for Wallace very strongly. The man is too touching to leave him in the lurch. Dewey will be elected anyway and an impressive demonstration for Wallace seems highly desirable to me.[1]

TO ERIKA MANN

Pacific Palisades
November 6, 1948

Dear Erikind:

Heartiest good wishes for your forty-third, spoken straightforwardly and without euphemisms. Good lord, that's no age at all, you know. How silly and unfinished I was at that time of life! [. . .] I enclose the finest birthday present I could think up.

The Munich affair[1] is certainly disgusting, and I suppose not without its dangers. We shall have to wait and see whether the yellow sheet itself publishes Eissi's reply. If not, and if the *Neue Zeitung* prints it, there is little point in my protesting also. Especially since Klaus means to go on with the libel suit. I doubt that it will be successful. When these people speak of "agents" they add "in effect," and thus are probably covered legally. All the same, you yourself could make a German newspaper admit that it had distorted your remarks on Poland. What I might do, perhaps, is express my astonishment in the *Neue Zeitung* that German newspapers are allowed to publish denunciations of British and American citizens. I could call that an impudent abuse of their licenses.

For a few days I was thoroughly depressed by the dreariness of the

---

[1] These sentences in English.

[1] A Munich weekly, *Echo der Woche*, had editorially called Erika and Klaus Mann "leading agents of Stalin in the U.S.A."

American *Faustus* reviews. The nadir was reached by Hamilton Basso[2] in *The New Yorker*. But the New York *Herald Tribune* was very decent; the *Atlantic* is now out, and at the same time there is a full-scale treatment in the *Saturday Review of Literature*. So it doesn't look so bad after all. Only they all place such dreadful stress on the G-e-r-m-a-n allegory. My own fault. I know it.

If I live and keep my strength I'll throw them *Felix Krull*, which consists of nothing but pranks, so that at last they'll stop regarding me as a *ponderous philosopher*.

I hope all hearts go out to you on your *campaign*. To a certain extent the outcome of the election has cleared the air.

I'd really like to hear nothing more about the *Confessions*,[3] and let them lie for an indefinite time. But I suppose it won't be feasible and would also be unjust, since I have given Schoenberg so much credit in the postscript. But then I have made too much of my indebtedness to Adorno. These matters can be abridged, eliminated, and generalized, I should think.

Why shouldn't I know that Frido has written to Till? That surely does not harm the story.[4]

The very best of everything for the new year and forever.

Z.

TO KLAUS MANN

Pacific Palisades
November 12, 1948

Dear Son:

Yesterday a young lady from Western Union phoned us and said that last year on November 11 we had telegraphed a birthday greeting to Professor Borgese in Chicago; she only wanted to remind us that the time had come round again. Business must be very bad there. Or was it *pure kindness*? She did not remind us of your forty-second, probably assuming correctly that it would not be necessary. We think without reminders of how the girls stood around you at that time and exclaimed, *"Der schöne Bub!"*

---

[2] Hamilton Basso (b. 1904), novelist and journalist. Associate editor, *New Republic* 1935–7. Among his books: *Courthouse Square* (1936), *Festival* (1940).
[3] *The Story of a Novel.*
[4] "Till" was an imaginary character invented by Erika for her nephew Frido. Till supposedly lived in the deep woods near Columbus, Ohio, and wrote letters to Frido. Although Erika was nowhere near there, she contrived to have all Till's letters bear the Columbus postmark.

and how at nine you were almost taken from us, and again recently, and are thankful from the bottom of our hearts that we are spending your birthday together with you, though far apart, that you have stayed on for us and the many who love you, and will stay on in your gifted and intelligent and yet, of course, sad-hearted lovableness, your brave willingness to do your part, and your unflagging hard work.

So you are planning a new novel.[1] That's fine, and I am so curious that I would almost wish nothing else would come your way to tempt you and keep you from it. The starry-eyed one[2] seems to have failed— anyone who counts on the movies is throwing himself on Satan's mercies.[3] But it is a pity, because the project would have brought you here. On the other hand, Brother Korda[4] telephoned to say he was off for London and that he definitely hopes to have you follow soon. So be it. I hope it comes about, both for you and for myself. Since his last visit, when he gave me an intelligent and fascinating sketch of some of his own ideas about the film, I believe that you would get along well with him and that with your combined forces something really delightful would emerge. But we must probably assume that this too will fade away, for as I said, this whole realm is untrustworthy, insubstantial as the wind; and I have much more confidence in your novel.

I have good cause to be bitter about the largely miserable press *Faustus* has been having here (*New Yorker*! The ultimate!), but I am too cheerful to feel that way, first of all because I am back at work on the little legend novel[5] and then because of the highly amusing outcome of the elections. As you know I was for a Wallace manifesto, and pitched in to help because like everyone else I was convinced that it would be Dewey. This surprise delights me. For years the real mood of the people has been systematically veiled and distorted; the country was supposed to be *definitely* Republican and the era of Roosevelt finally buried. All the reactionaries felt themselves borne along on the *wave of the future* and imagined they could commit any sort of impudence. Suddenly the whole sham has fallen apart. It is a clear victory for F.D.R. and a clear expression of the people's desire to continue to be governed in his spirit. In domestic matters first of all, of course; but it's bound to affect foreign

---

[1] Klaus was planning a novel about a suicide—to purge his own longing for death.

[2] Christopher Isherwood.

[3] Paraphrase of a line from Wagner's *The Flying Dutchman*, Act I.

[4] Zoltan Korda (1895–1961), brother of the producer Sir Alexander Korda, was to be director of a *Magic Mountain* movie; Klaus was to collaborate on the scenario. The plan came to nothing.

[5] *The Holy Sinner* (New York: Alfred A. Knopf; 1951).

policy too. Even the harrying of Communists may let up (especially since Parnell Thomas is going to the jug for corruption), so that Schulze-Wilde's[6] juvenile delinquencies will probably cease to be of interest to you.

Sister is returning tomorrow. I've missed her greatly.

Fondly,

Z.

TO ALFRED A. KNOPF

[Original in English]

Pacific Palisades
December 4, 1948

Dear Alfred:

Miss Lamar sent me the copy of your letter to Mr. Sulzberger, and I want to tell you how deeply your words have moved me. Katia and I discussed at length how wonderfully humane it was of you to react this way and to give the powerful newspaperman a piece of your mind. Certainly your words will not fail to make an impression on him and on whomever may read them. Because everybody must feel that this is not a publisher writing who is annoyed because he sees his business endangered, but a man who feels that an injustice has been done at an important place and who protests against it.

I believe it was Lichtenberg who said: "If a book and a head collide and it sounds hollow, it is not necessarily the book that is at fault." That must serve to comfort me, and also there were several intelligent voices which compensated me for the rudeness of the *Times*. After all, you have a few very presentable utterances for your advertising, as for instance the write-up in the *Saturday Review of Literature*, which surely is just as important as the *Times*. In the papers on our West coast too, which, however, do not carry so much weight, there were friendly and respectful comments, and my fellow countryman Lion Feuchtwanger wrote a review for the Los Angeles *Daily News* which he concluded with the words: "Most readers will agree that *Doctor Faustus* is a great book with grave things to say. It conveys insights and sensations such as can be found in no other book of the past decade."

It is remarkable how differently this work is being reflected in people's minds. I can only hope that the confidence you placed in the value and the future of *Doctor Faustus*, and for which I am deeply

[6] Harry Schulze-Wilde, editor of the Munich newspaper *Echo der Woche*. See note 1 in the preceding letter.

grateful to you, will be confirmed. The book has come from my heart, it cost me much anguish, and contains many things from my life. After its publication in Europe it displayed a power of reverberation as none of my previous books. I am inclined to believe that in the end also American critics will come to the conclusion that this work is not quite such an everyday occurrence.

I wish Mr. Hellman had known of your so very characteristic letter to Sulzberger when he drew your profile for the *New Yorker*. It would have made a good point in his article. I must say that I have read his piece, as far as it has been published, with almost undimmed pleasure, —no matter how you yourself may think about it. Of course, it contains the usual *New Yorker*-style caricaturing and sarcasms, but on the whole Hellman could not help but draw the portrait of an unusually *pittoresque* personality of great attractiveness who far surpasses the average publisher's type. Naturally there must always be some material for laughs in these portraits, but I think this is the best of its kind that has come to my attention. And I also believe that despite its various errors it will mean enormous publicity for you and your house. Let me know sometime whether you hold very contrary views on the subject.

Coming back to the part of your letter concerning our friend Helen Lowe-Porter, I want to say that I did not read Professor Levin's review, but the derogatory treatment of her achievement as a translator hurts me very much. It is my impression and the impression of better judges than myself that Miss Lowe did what was humanly possible, and I would be very sorry if she should take the disparaging remarks of the *Times* to heart. Also in this respect, I trust, time will turn out to be a better judge than *Times*.

As ever and more than ever,

Cordially yours,
T. M.

TO *THE SATURDAY REVIEW*
OF LITERATURE

[Original in English]

Pacific Palisades
December 10, 1948

Sir:

Arnold Schoenberg's letter both astonished and grieved me. Our personal correspondence on this matter had been of a thoroughly friendly character in all its phases. Not so long ago, when I sent him the English edition of *Doctor Faustus* with my appended statement, the maestro thanked me cordially with an air of complete satisfaction, so that I was led to believe that the "Leverkühn Case" was settled and disposed of. Now I regret to learn that it not only continues to annoy him but actually irritates him increasingly, although he still has not read the book.

If his acquaintance with the book were not based exclusively on the gossip of meddling scandalmongers, he would know that my efforts to give the central figure of the novel "qualities a hero needs to arouse people's interest" were neither limited to the transfer of Schoenberg's "method of composing with twelve tones," nor was this characteristic the most important one. Quaintly enough, he calls this technique his "literary property," though actually it should be called a musical system that has long since become a part of our cultural pattern, used by countless composers throughout the world, all of whom have tacitly purloined it from its originator. The universal dissemination and the wide employment of this technique are the very factors underlying the basic error of which I accuse myself. I sincerely believed that every child in our cultural area must at one time or another have heard about the twelve-tone system and its initiator, and that no one on earth, having read my novel, could possibly imagine that I was its inventor or was trying to pose as such. This opinion of mine, I must say, was confirmed by many Swiss, German, Swedish, and, more recently, French reviews of the book, in which Schoenberg's name was quite casually mentioned. It was he himself who enlightened me with respect to my error. Serious misunderstandings, he informed me, would result from my book, unless I did something about it. Everybody except him, he said, kept receiving credit for his creation, and, if he knew anything about the breed of musicologists, they would attribute his theory to me a hundred years from now because I had developed it in my novel. His contemporaries, he added, were withholding so much from him that he had, at least, to guard his name and fame for posterity.

His concluding word moved me, no matter how absurd his apprehension seemed. It is quite untrue that it required "much pressure" to induce me to give him due credit. As soon as I understood his concern I gave instructions to include in all translations, as well as in the German original, the appended statement which now appears in the English edition of *Doctor Faustus*. It was intended as a bit of instruction to the uninformed, and I worded it as objectively as possible. "Take note," it says in effect, "there is a composer and music philosopher living among us, whose name is Arnold Schoenberg; he, and not the hero of my novel, is the one who, in reality, thought out the twelve-tone composition method." The statement does not raise the question who is whose contemporary. If Schoenberg wishes, we shall, all of us, consider it our greatest and proudest claim to be his contemporaries.

As soon as I had received the first copies of the German edition I sent him one with the inscription: "Dem Eigentlichen" ["To the real one"]. It meant: "Not Leverkühn is the hero of this musical era; you are its hero." It was a bow, a compliment. I have always addressed Arnold Schoenberg, the uncompromising and bold artist, with the utmost respect, in personal contact as well as in my letters, and I shall continue to do so.

The idea that Adrian Leverkühn is Schoenberg, that the figure is a portrait of him, is so utterly absurd that I scarcely know what to say about it. There is no point of contact, not a shade of similarity, between the origin, the traditions, the character, and the fate of my musician, on the one hand, and the existence of Schoenberg, on the other. *Doctor Faustus* has been called a Nietzsche-novel and, indeed, the book, which for good reasons avoids mention of Nietzsche's name, contains many references to his intellectual tragedy, even direct quotations from the history of his illness. It has also been said that I had bisected myself in the novel, and that the narrator and the hero each embraced a part of me. That, also, contains an element of truth—although I, too, do not suffer from syphilitic paralysis. But it has not occurred to anyone to speak of a Schoenberg-novel.

Instead of accepting my book with a satisfied smile as a piece of contemporary literature that testifies to his tremendous influence upon the musical culture of the era, Schoenberg regards it as an act of theft and insult. It is a sad spectacle to see a man of great worth, whose all-too-understandable hypersensitivity grows out of a life suspended between glorification and neglect, almost willfully yield to delusions of persecution and of being robbed, and involve himself in rancorous bickering. It is my sincere hope and wish that he may rise above bitterness and suspicion and that he may find peace in the assurance of his greatness and glory.[1]

---

[1] Although a German draft of this letter exists, it is here printed as it was originally published in *The Saturday Review of Literature*, January 1, 1949, except for two minor corrections.

1949

———————•———————

TO ELLIE BOMMERSTEIN[1]

Pacific Palisades
February 19, 1949

My dear Fräulein Bommerstein:

I am sincerely grateful to you for your kind explanation. I was aware of Hauer[2] and his original authorship of the twelve-tone system at the time I wrote my reply to Schoenberg. But I deliberately repressed the name, rather than provoke the unhappy man even more. Your data, however, significantly extend my knowledge of the matter, and your letter will be valuable to me if I should once again have to defend myself seriously against Schoenberg's complaints.

TO ARCHIBALD MACLEISH[1]

[Original in English]

Pacific Palisades
February 27, 1949

Dear Archie:

Your letter, beautiful like a poem and as heartening as the word of a friend, has been in my hands since yesterday. With how much joy have I read it, and yet with how much regret. Why? Because I shall be far away from New York on May 27th. This, of course, is the Goethe year,

---

[1] Not identifiable.

[2] Joseph Matthias Hauer (1883–1959), Austrian schoolmaster, composer, and music theorist who developed a twelve-tone system of his own before Schoenberg. He called the elements of his system "tropes" and elaborated his ideas in several books: *Vom Wesen des Musikalischen* (1920), *Deutung des Melos* (1923), *Zwölftontechnik, die Lehre von den Tropen* (1926).

[1] MacLeish was then secretary of the American Academy of Arts and Letters, New York.

and I could hardly have hoped to dodge its obligations. A fairly long program of duties has been composed: at the end of April we are to leave for Chicago where the dance begins; subsequently, I shall speak in Washington on "Goethe and Democracy"; there follows New York; then England; then Sweden; finally Switzerland, and, perhaps, Austria; in short, the summer will have all but ended by the time we return to California. On the day of the Annual Ceremonial of our Academy, alas, I shall have to speak at the University of Lund, Sweden—an engagement to which, between you and me, an honorary degree-giving is to lend additional weight.

It may be quite useless for me actually to pose the question which I keep asking myself. Prior to my flight to Europe, I am scheduled to stay in New York from May 3rd until and including the 10th. But only May 6th and the evening of the 7th are as yet occupied. And I wonder whether it would be even remotely possible to advance the date of the Ceremonial to either the 4th or the 5th, or the forenoon of the 7th, or else to the 8th, 9th, or 10th of May? I do not, to be sure, really believe in this possibility but merely ask in order to show you how sorry I am at the thought of being prevented from personally accepting the honor that is to be bestowed upon me, and from conveying my thanks in person.

I herewith accept that honor—it sounds strange indeed, when ever since yesterday I have been feeling like a child on Christmas! —Believe me, I am keenly appreciative of your institute's generous gesture, the value and significance of which I fully recognize. It has been said, mockingly, that I, more than any other writer, consider myself worthy of any distinction received from the contemporary world. Just how I managed to cause this misunderstanding, this utter miscomprehension of my basic mood and disposition, I should well like to know. In looking back I tell myself: you just muddled through. For I am too deeply aware of the precarious nature of my personal relationship with art to ever part with a finished work—any work—with the faintest hope for worldly success. Whenever success did come, I was amazed, amused and touched; also, I was disquieted and objectively concerned with the question of what had brought it; I went through all sorts of emotions; but not once have I felt self-satisfied and "worthy." Praise has yet to shake my skepticism. Often there was too much acclaim, fit—as I told myself in advance—to provoke certain critics to judge my efforts with ill-tempered and exaggerated severity.

Time will set it all right. I am full of joy and gratitude because my American colleagues of the Academy have decided to bestow upon me so rare a distinction. What pleases me peculiarly is the fact that I should thus be honored soon after the publication of a work of my old age which, though I deem it curious rather than exemplary, stems from the very depths of my being. Goethe has said it beautifully: "Rarely do we satisfy ourselves; all the more comforting is it to have satisfied others."

TO LAVINIA MAZZUCCHETTI

Pacific Palisades
March 14, 1949

Dear friend:

I must quickly dictate; otherwise I shall never finish. How charming of you to have once again found the time and the mood to chat with me or for me so copiously. Your letter is interesting from the first to the last word, and I am especially grateful to you for the Italian enclosure. It seems to me that Dallapiccola[1] is absolutely right. The less this mortifying affair is exploited in public debates and shouted from the rooftops, the better. In my reply to Schoenberg I was more concerned with sparing him and his painful sensitivity than with defending myself. For the rest, I have paid due acknowledgement in my notes on *Faustus*, and as far as I am concerned the case is settled, except for the lingering regret that Schoenberg has taken the matter so wrongly and foolishly. I do not feel any irritation with him and have no interest in others' launching polemics against him. Which does not mean that I am not delighted with Dallapiccola's personal viewpoint, as I was also grateful for the long article that Dr. Schuh[2] devoted to the case in the *Neue Zürcher Zeitung*. There is a real friend, who always comes to one's aid at bad moments. I shall never forget his support in 1933 when the Munich lynching parties were up in arms against my Wagner essay. This time too he has found the right words, and his article is a comprehensive appreciation of the book as well.

Your Italian lecture evening must have been enchanting. The interest it aroused is plainly evident from the two notices. You could certainly draw on abundance, for the number of interesting contemporaries you have met from childhood on must be extraordinarily large. I am deeply touched that you found room to include me, and in so kind a light, at the end of your recollections. These things are comforting

---

[1] Luigi Dallapiccola (b. 1904), leading Italian composer; "dodecaphonist."
[2] Willi Schuh (b. 1900), musicologist; music editor of the *Neue Zürcher Zeitung*; prolific writer on musical subjects.

counterpoises to other slightly disturbing incidents, such as the strange pro and contra meeting in Zurich, which I have heard of for the first time through you. What strange people! And what can possibly be the source of the hatred I inspire in a good many of my fellows? Probably it is simply that every—how shall I put it?—intenser life arouses enmity; and ultimately one has to console oneself rather arrogantly with Goethe's quatrain:

> Es will der Spitz aus unserm Stall
> Uns überall begleiten
> Doch seines Bellens lauter Schall
> Beweist nur, dass wir reiten.[3]

[. . .] How odd that you will be sixty years old this summer. But for a long time doctors and physiologists have agreed that age is something entirely relative and personal, quite apart from the number of years, and that people of fifty, sixty, and seventy can be of entirely different ages. That is the case with you. You have more vitality than many a young thing, and I trust I shall find you once again in that refreshing, cheering, and entertaining state of vivacity at the beginning of June in Zurich.

Bondy's[4] "Weimar in Hollywood" escaped my notice, like so much else. Was it a case of the dog again? The last piece I read about myself by him, in the *Weltwoche*, was rather interesting, though self-aggrandizing. Most cordial greetings, and once again thank you for your copious parcel.

TO HANS REISIGER

Pacific Palisades
March 19, 1949

Dear Reisi, I must thank you for a charming letter, passed on to the whole family, and altogether for the finest kind of reading matter: the chapter from your *Salamis*,[1] earnest, on the highest level, intelligent, humanly warm and poetic; then the *Herder*,[2] which arrived only day before yesterday and in which I have already read a good deal. I am only sorry that you have not provided the collection—which truly reveals Herder's whole

---

[3] The dog that guards our stable tries
To keep forever at our side
His barking and his yapping cries
Prove only it is we who ride.

[4] François Bondy (b. 1915), distinguished French man of letters, editor of *Preuves*, frequent contributor to *Encounter, Hudson Review*.

[1] *Aeschylos bei Salamis* (1952).

[2] *Johann Gottfried Herder—Sein Leben in Selbstzeugnissen, Briefen und Berichten* (1942).

personality and his time—with an introduction of your own in the manner of your unforgettable Whitman essay.[3] Weren't you sufficiently in sympathy with Herder to write one? I would understand that. For all his high-mindedness, he had a good many low-spirited, unfortunate, tactless traits in his character. That this visibly degenerated in his old age speaks badly for his basic disposition. I am delighted to see that research work has once again made you creative and inspired the idea of the Bückeburg novella,[4] which you speak of with such precision and vividness that it sounds already finished in your head. This means that the physical ailments, which you sometimes reported to us in so patient a tone, have not been able to affect the freshness, curiosity, and enterprise of your spirit. [. . .] I too want to be more humorous again, after the gloom of *Faustus*, which, however, was also not exactly of a feeble kind, I think.

I myself haven't been spared some of the aforesaid ailments. An eye infection, which was causing constant obscuring conjunctivitis, would not go away and was beginning to make reading and writing impossible for me. A pleasantly apathetic doctor who did nothing caused the thing to drag on. Only recently, on my wife's and Erika's insistence, have I had a bacteriological check and suitable treatment, which is beginning to take effect.

The real interruption to my work has not come from that, but from your vicinity. I had prepared for my spring trip to England, Sweden, and Switzerland by knocking together a Goethe lecture, after which I returned to my legend novel. Then came a correspondence with Munich officialdom, the upshot being that I was made honorary chairman of the literary section of the new Academy of Fine Arts. And when I had accepted that (after quickly righting the balance by accepting the Weimar Goethe Prize), Preetorius wrote to say that now I must come to Munich in June for the Goethe ceremonies and speak at a solemn public occasion. I had been half and half hoping all along that this cup of seeing Munich again would pass me by, although I realized that in the long run it would not be possible. I had declined friendly invitations from Frankfurt (where I recommended Unruh instead of myself), and likewise from Leipzig and Weimar (+++ Zone). So then, was it to be Munich alone? It is true that I would not be up to a tour of the country as far as Lübeck, etc., and the point could easily be made that the visit to the city in which I spent forty years of my life must stand symbolically for all Germany. But my

---

[3] The introduction to Reisiger's translation of Whitman, *Walt Whitmans Werk* (1922).
[4] *Herder in Bückeburg* remained unwritten.

confusion is vast since this prospect has opened up. I have not yet consented, but I shall probably have to, and my peace is gone.[5] I suppose I should not take it all so hard, but I cannot help feeling that this return after sixteen years of alienation is a ghostly adventure and a veritable trial. For so very long, "being taken to Germany," "falling into the hands of the Germans," was a nightmare. And what am I to say? It is all terribly complicated. So I must put everything aside and embark on inward efforts to put together a speech—and then again I cannot do it, for there is a block. The awareness of how much we and they have drifted apart in all these years prevents me from finding the right tone. A bad situation—although I suppose in some auspicious hour the right thing will come to me. But I fear that the degree of reconciliation which the "German" aura of *Faustus* may have brought about will be undone again by the memoirs now being published which deal with the years during which it was written. The perspective, the nature of experience, was so different. My birthday rejoicing at the Allied landing in France, for example, and how fervently I wished for the downfall of that spawn of hell—altogether, my hatred, which was the only really deadly hatred I have known in my lifetime and which people in Germany did not feel, for otherwise the evil could not have lasted. Given all that, communication is difficult. Of course it isn't absolutely necessary to talk about those matters; I might simply restrict myself to the (very doubtful) future and to *old Goethe*.

Would you come to Munich if I did decide to go? If we stay in Switzerland, we certainly hope to be able to attract you there.

All the best for your health, your work, and our reunion, one way or the other.

TO FELIX BRAUN[1]

Pacific Palisades
March 29, 1949

Dear Herr Felix Braun:

"Flirting" is certainly an *understatement*, but just as certainly it is not meant in any derogatory sense, since everything I say about Werfel in those recollections[2] is colored with the warmest affection. He was a dear,

---

[5] *Meine Ruh' ist hin*: from Gretchen's song in Goethe's *Faust*.
[1] Felix Braun (b. 1885), Austrian poet, novelist, playwright. Friend of Hofmannsthal and his circle. Emigrated to London in 1938, returned to Vienna in 1951.
[2] Prepublication in the Vienna *Die Presse* of a chapter from the forthcoming *Story of a Novel*, describing a sickbed visit to Franz Werfel. See *The Story of a Novel*, pp. 68–70.

enthusiastic, richly talented man and artist, and I miss him greatly. The word "flirting" alludes partly to the childlike element which was part of his nature, and which also underlay his hunger for intuition and image, for a symbolic body for the spirit. The Church offered him that. He never saw in it more than a symbolically theatrical, even operatic (he loved opera) representation of spirituality on earth, and he did not identify with it any more than that.

The "temptation to become a convert" did come to him. He rejected it in humble language, addressing the Archbishop of New Orleans with the utmost sincerity. I have seen the letter. His arguments are good; and only one of them is always cited, which I too cite.[3] The man of God has not "*released*" the others, and besides, they would have led me too far afield.

Rest assured that I call no one a liar or poseur who is seeking peace of soul—wherever he finds it. Another archbishop has recently declared that there are only three kinds of people: *Communists, convinced Christians, and amiable nonentities*. I count myself among the last.

TO FRANCIS BIDDLE

[*Original in English*]

Pacific Palisades
April 14, 1949

Dear Mr. Biddle:

As brief as your question[1] must be my reply, for I am in the middle of the preparations for a lecture trip to the East and to Europe on which we will depart in a few days.

One could not deduce from the inclusion of my portrait in the strange rogue's gallery of *Life* magazine that I participated personally in the World Peace dinner at the Waldorf Astoria. Actually I just sent a sympathetic telegram to Professor Shapley, whom I estimate very highly as a genuine American patriot and peace lover. It was this sentiment

[3] "He had steadfastly rejected the temptation to become a convert on the grounds that it would not do for him to deny his Judaism at a time of Jewish martyrdom." *The Story of a Novel*, p. 70.
[1] Francis Biddle had written to Thomas Mann: "I saw in the April 4 number of *Life* that you were at the Cultural and Scientific Conference for the World Peace dinner at the Waldorf Astoria.

"I am genuinely interested in knowing the reasons that impelled you to go, and thus to lend the authority of your presence at a meeting which apparently was largely dominated by Communists, and used chiefly as a sounding board for Communist propaganda. . . .''

which I expressed to him. Furthermore, I wired to Secretary Acheson, asking the Department of State for an explanation of the mystifying fact that, although the delegates of the eastern countries were given their visas, the invited guests from western Europe and South America were kept away with the exception of a single Englishman, due to the Department's refusal to issue them the necessary visas. My inquiry received a polite but completely insincere reply, containing only formal arguments. The truth is, of course, that the State Department wished to brand Shapley's peace conference as purely Communistic while at the same time they wished to prevent the invited Europeans from expressing certain feelings existing over there towards America and her foreign policy. It is, after all, not difficult to understand that Europe does not like the prospect of becoming the victim of the Russian-American conflict and would prefer to have the two giants settle their rivalry on the North Pole instead.

If I were alone with my doubts regarding the wisdom of our foreign policy I would, of course, tell myself that I have been in this country for only ten years, have been a citizen for only five years, and that the native-born Americans must know better—and I would keep my mouth shut. But since I find that a great number of mentally high-ranking and distinguished Americans are sharing my doubts, I should consider it cowardly if—for fear of losing my popularity—I were to refuse them my name and my support.

I am neither a dupe nor a fellow-traveler and by no means an admirer of the quite malicious present phase of the Russian revolution. But I consider a war between the United States and Soviet Russia a horrible catastrophe with immeasurable consequences for the entire civilization; it would certainly forever destroy the very things America pretends to be fighting for. Yet, the danger that this unspeakable misfortune might come to pass is growing so menacing that I can well understand the grievous fears of people like Professor Harlow Shapley. No economist will be able to tell you how we can ever withdraw from the cold war without an economic crisis, and the solution to the latter, of course, would be nothing but actual warfare. If well-meaning Americans make the attempt to call together the outstanding intellectual leaders from east and west in order to have them debate—on a purely cultural and spiritual basis—the dangers of our present political situation and its possible peaceful settlement, I cannot regard such an undertaking as subversive or criminal; on the contrary it seems highly welcome to me.

The course of the meeting has, naturally, been grossly misrepresented by the politically coordinated press. I am informed to the effect that the overwhelming majority of the speakers divided the blame for the present impasse evenly between east and west. The Russian delegation was repeatedly applauded, but one should not find that objectionable. What is wrong with treating the guests from that great, uncanny country with friendliness and encouragement in an effort to show them that in America today there are still a great number of people of good will?

Only so much, dear Mr. Biddle. Perhaps I will have an opportunity to talk the matter over with you personally.

TO NELLY MANN

Hotel St. Regis
Fifth Avenue and Fifty-fifth Street
New York
May 10, 1949

Dear Nelly:

It pains me that the turmoil of departure and the hectic days in Chicago, Washington, and here have kept me from telling you how much I sympathize with your grief, not to speak of my own sense of loss. I know how stunned, how incapable of taking it in, you must have felt at first. The two of you have belonged together so long, and this sudden, terribly premature parting is so cruel. How grievous, too, that our Viko had to go when his hopes were high, when his life was taking a new turn. And he the youngest of us brothers—what an unforeseeable decree of fate, how hard to accept!

Ever since our reunion we had felt anxious about him, I admit. As early as the first war his heart must have suffered damage from the rheumatic fever he had then, and two years ago in Switzerland he showed signs of strain through all his gaiety and liveliness. Still, who would have thought it! Heinrich himself, distinctly feeble, was also overwhelmed by the news.

Who knows whether it was not a premonition of his approaching end that led Viko to write the book of memoirs? In it the charm of his personality is preserved, and in it he will live on.

Let us cling together in love and memory of him, in loyalty to what he was. The publisher in Konstanz has sent me the funeral address, which was very fine and truthful.

Your feeling of loneliness, dear Nelly, must be deep and bitter.

But you are not alone in your sorrow for your husband, that most lovable of men.

Our plane is leaving for England in a few hours. We hope to see you in Switzerland.

Your brother-in-law,

TO ALFRED KNOPF

[*Original in English*]

Hotel Baur au Lac
Zurich
June 20, 1949

Dear Alfred:

Many thanks for your kind letter of June 3rd. It was thoughtless indeed that we did not leave you our different European addresses which we knew in advance. Now, of course, we received your letter with some delay, and I hasten to thank you for your good wishes to my birthday. Katia too was touched by your thoughtfulness.

Many adventures lay behind us, and some more are ahead. The stay in England was very pleasant, and particularly the ceremony of giving the degree, in the beautiful old hall of the fourteenth century, in its stiff dignity was amusing and moving in the same time. In Sweden the tragic news[1] reached us, and our first idea was to give up the whole trip. But eventually I decided to fulfill my lecturing obligations, and I believe this was the right thing to do. Of course everything is now saddened and darkened, but Switzerland is as attractive for us as ever. In a few days I shall be through with my lectures, and then we shall have some rest in the mountains, in Hotel Schweizerhof-Vulpera, Schuls-Tarasp, Unterengadin. But the most difficult part of the trip is still ahead, the visit in Frankfurt, where I am to receive the Goethe-Preis. About August 1st we hope to start for home, perhaps by boat this time, and we shall inform you when we are due in New York. I wished we were there already!

With love from both of us to you and Blanche affectionately as ever,

Yours,
Tommy

---

[1] Klaus Mann had committed suicide in Cannes on May 21, 1949.

TO HERMANN HESSE

Vulpera
July 6, 1949

Dear Hermann Hesse:

My last letter had scarcely been sent when, much delayed, your and your wife's kind words about the death of our Klaus arrived. I thank you warmly for them, in the name of our whole family.

My thoughts dwell sorrowfully on his abbreviated life. My relationship to him was difficult, and not without feelings of guilt, for my very existence cast a shadow on him from the start. Yet as a young man in Munich he was a high-spirited prince who did a great many provocative things. Later, in exile, he became far more serious and moral, and truly industrious as well; but he worked with such facility and speed that there is a scattering of flaws and oversights in his books. Who can say when he began to develop the death impulse which was so mysteriously at variance with his surface sunniness, geniality, facility, and cosmopolitanism? Inexorably, in spite of all our support and love, he destroyed himself, for at the end he no longer reacted to thoughts of loyalty, gratitude, consideration for others.

Nevertheless, he had a splendid talent. Both his *Gide* and his *Tschaikowsky* are very good books, and his *Vulkan,* aside from the parts he could have done better, is perhaps the best of the refugee novels. If some day we collect his most successful things, it will be seen that his going is a great pity. Much injustice has been done to him, and much is still being done now he is dead. I think I can say for myself that I always praised and encouraged him.

I have had ridiculous trouble and agony preparing a lecture for Germany. On top of that, there are irritations and regrets on both sides over travel dates that cannot be coordinated. It would have been so good if we could have met in Sils or somewhere around here. Well then, until next year!

1949

TO LUDWIG KUNZ [1]

Amsterdam
August 5, 1949

My dear Herr Kunz:

Thank you for your letter and the lovely flowers.

It is certainly reasonable to speak of a cultural crisis and time of change, with all the difficulties and painful adjustments accompanying such periods. All of us feel the crisis in our bones, of course, and all of us have difficulty maintaining a tolerably sensible, just, and decent attitude. But it is *not* correct to say that the all-embracing crisis has had a "leveling" effect upon literature. Literature is too variegated and differentiated, according to the personalities of the writers. Moreover, there are a number of first-class works whose "importance" derives precisely from their bearing the traces of the crisis and more or less directly confronting it. These works appear to have come predominantly from elderly writers, probably because their horizons are wider, their culture and experience richer, than those of the young who have been born in the midst of dissolution. For my part I regard it as an advantage to have known the last quarter of the nineteenth—the bourgeois—century.

Broch's *Virgil*, my brother's latest novel *Der Atem*, Hesse's *The Bead Game*, a good many things by Aldous Huxley, even my own *Faustus* are greater and, as documents of the age, more illuminating than anything produced so far by the young. Let us hope that they grow in strength and continue the evolution of our inheritance. Western culture has had to withstand a great deal, and will not go into a decline this time, either.

I must leave for the ship bound to America. High time.

TO PAUL OLBERG [1]

Pacific Palisades
August 27, 1949

My dear Herr Olberg:

I gladly answer your Open Letter because it is yours, and hope that in doing so I am not falling into the error you wrongly take me to task for: that of making needless and unbecoming apologies.

[1] Ludwig Kunz (b. 1900), editor, critic, and translator; has lived in Amsterdam since 1938.

[1] Paul Olberg (1878–1960), journalist, writer, active Social Democrat. Born in what was then the Russian Baltic area, he served terms in Tsarist prisons before he was out of the Gymnasium. Ultimately fled to Berlin from the Soviet Union, and in 1933 from Berlin to Sweden. Author of *Brief Aus Sowjetrussland* (1919), *Rysslands Nya Imperialism* (1940), *Polens Öde* (1944), *Antisemitismen in Sovjets* (1953).

Your letter is well-meaning but excessively anxious. I do not at all feel that by delivering my "Address for the Goethe Year" in Frankfurt and Weimar I surrendered anything, repudiated my exile or my attitude during the war. Concerning the "National Revolution" of 1933 I said: "Germany seemed to me poisoned, not exalted. Distorted and alienated, it no longer offered me air to breathe. . . . There was no returning. . . . If my searing hatred of the corrupters of the country had been resolutely shared by the German middle class, by the German people—Germany need not have come to this present pass." Here I was interrupted by applause. Do you call that an apology?

Nowhere and never have I said that the Nazi horrors must be forgotten. (I have repeatedly said the very opposite.) And never have I held that the present state of mind of the German masses is particularly gratifying and a source of hope. This is not so, for reasons due partly to the German people themselves, partly to an unfortunate world situation which favors the bad elements in Germany and represses the good ones.

I went back to our old homeland because it seemed to me impossible, on the occasion of Goethe's two-hundredth birthday, to speak on Goethe in Sweden, Denmark, and Switzerland, but not in Germany. I went also with the faint hope that my visit might possibly lend some support to those disadvantaged better elements in Germany, even though that support could only be spiritual and moral. It almost seemed for a while as if this had been the case.

I went to Weimar because I am grieved by the "deep gulf," as you put it, which runs across Germany, and because I think it should not be deepened but if possible bridged, even if only momentarily and symbolically. The people there were grateful to me for not forgetting them, for not treating them like Germany's prodigal children who must be shunned like plague victims, but for coming to them also and addressing them as if they too were still Germans.

Perhaps you do not know that the political regime in Thuringia is not a pure one-party system. There are non-Communists in the government, and this is even truer of the Weimar town council. Thus Mayor Buchterkirchen of Weimar, from whom my invitation came, is a Christian Democrat. The opening speech at the ceremony in the admirably rebuilt National Theater was delivered by Churchwarden Hermann, chairman of the Town Council—a clergyman, that is. You would have been astonished at things he was permitted to say, and the Protestant liberties he took. In Eisenach the formal reception for me was attended by the bishop of the diocese. There he was, with his golden cross on his chest, to thank me for having contributed the 20,000 Ostmarks of the Goethe Prize for the rebuilding of Weimar's Herder Church—a use perhaps not quite to the taste of Communists.

They turned our ride through Thuringia into a popular festival such as writers rarely if ever have been given, with flags, flowers, garlands, banners, toasts, singing children, and town bands. I owe all this to an affection I have never purchased by any avowals of loyalty to communism. Thinking aloud in public, I said that in the vast land of Russia, autocracy and revolution for many decades waged a cruel struggle one against the other, but they joined hands in the end, so that we now have an autocratic revolution which uses the same sinister methods as the Tsar's police state, although for quite different purposes. This observation was taken very ill by the Russian press. Nevertheless, I reserve the right to make a distinction between Communism's relationship to the idea of humanity and the absolute vileness of Fascism. I refuse to participate in the hysterical persecution of Communists and the incitement to war. I speak in favor of peace in a world whose future for many years now has been inconceivable without communistic features. And all this obviously earns for me, within the territory of that social religion, a certain trust which I have not sought, but which I cannot bring myself to regard as a sign of my moral and intellectual illness.

You talk a good deal about political liberties and the rights of citizens—and seem to forget what you said previously about the use to which these benefits are usually put. It is an outrageous use. The authoritarian people's state has its cruel aspects. Yet it brings with it the blessing that, inside it, stupidity and brazenness, at long last, must hold their tongue.

In the East Zone I have not seen any filthy, libelous letters and idiotic, abusive articles such as occur in the West—and not only just "occur." Do I owe this courtesy merely to the threat of Buchenwald—or to a kind of popular education which, more thoroughly than in the West, instills respect for a stand such as I have taken?

The East puts out stamps with a portrait of Gerhart Hauptmann—far be it from the West to make such gestures. It is easy to say: "They only want to use culture as a front, exploit it, trick themselves out with it." There is more to it than that.

The men in charge, so I heard and read, are extremely eager to make my life work accessible to the people and especially to the youth, to expose them as much as possible to its "critical realism" and its "humanism." That is true. Quite early, in fact in 1945, there were lectures in

Weimar on my books, especially on the Goethe novel, and eminent Communist historians and literary critics devoted major essays to my work. —I am no "fellow traveler." But it appears that I can count some clever Communists among my fellow travelers.

For all its sincerity, my dear Herr Olberg, your letter has a note of repetitious cliché, of mechanical parroting and deadness, and I can only wonder that you thought you were saying something new. Violence is of course an evil thing, and concentration camps a terrible educational method. But attempts to bring about socialism without violence, such as Beneš made, have also failed; and the English experiment in socialism is running into every kind of opposition. For the rest, a few profoundly ironic scenes concerning the destiny of ideas on earth, the inevitable guilt that they incur, and the devil's hand in the game, may be found in the Second Part of *Faust* (Act V).

Among the Communist functionaries of the German East Zone there are of course some lickspittle, self-serving and power-hungry despots. But I have looked into other faces and seen resolute good will and pure idealism—the faces of people who work eighteen hours a day and sacrifice themselves to make a reality of what they believe to be truth, and to create those social conditions inside their country which, as they say, will prevent a relapse into war and barbarism. Seldom or never did I see these faces smile. They have an ascetic seriousness—austere calm, determination, and a religious concern with the improvement of earthly things. Humanly, this spirit is hard to resist. Only by avoiding contact with it can we properly hate it and go on happily playing ideals off against it which often have become mere cant concealing self-interest.

TO EMIL PREETORIUS

Pacific Palisades
October 20, 1949

Dear Pree:

Many thanks for your letter, whose warmth is some compensation for the thwarting of our star-crossed reunion. It is good to know that there are a considerable number of people in the land of G. who do not altogether say No and Ugh to the mere fact of my existence. They do not determine the general physiognomy of Germany, and their sort never has determined Germany's character and fate. But I comfort myself that in the higher sense they are the ones who count, and all the shouting and spewing of the stupid majority fundamentally mean nothing—not in the long run, and scarcely even for the moment. I have never overestimated myself, but I know what I know, and all sensible people know it too.

It was really my fault that our meeting could not take place. You had made your arrangements for August 28 and I insisted on an earlier date, out of impatience to be on my way home. So I should not have been surprised that you were engaged on that day. As your friend I am certainly delighted to learn what engaged you, especially since it opens the possibility that we may meet here rather than there. As for Germany, though I don't want to commit myself for good and all, I almost think that I went there at the last moment that was possible for me, and that there will not be another visit. I shall never be able to keep myself from saying bluntly how things stand there, and that increases the hatred and would, shamefully, necessitate an ever larger police guard.

Certainly "Munich" came off quite pleasantly and without sour notes. The big press conference; the Academy's reception in the Prinz Karl Palais, at which Penzoldt[1] spoke very nicely; the Goethe lecture; the banquet in the evening at the Rathaus—it all went along nicely and amicably and innocuously, really just as if nothing had happened, whereas the sight of the city was an emphatic reminder of what had happened. To see this whole portion of an outlived past reappearing in a tattered and battered state, with the faces of people so much aged, had something ghostly about it, and I did a great deal of looking the other way. I also chose not to visit our house in Herzogpark. I'm so unfeeling as to have little emotion about the past, and find Jean Paul dreadfully sentimental when he says: "Memory is a paradise from which we cannot be expelled." Why paradise? I must always live freshly in new things.

Incidentally, I have written a short account of my German travels for the New York *Times*. It is being syndicated in Europe by the New York Press Corporation, so perhaps you will be able to read it somewhere, in some language or other. I put special emphasis on my experiences in the East Zone, that is to say, in Weimar. What a fuss because I went there! And yet the city of Frankfurt itself sent a delegation to the Weimar Goethe ceremonies. I was given a most cheerful and positive report of them by the highly intelligent town councillor Reinert,[2] with whom we became good friends in Frankfurt.

Yours with all good wishes,

---

[1] Ernst Penzoldt (1892–1955), writer and sculptor. Mann had a very high opinion of Penzoldt as man and artist.

[2] Hellmut Reinert (1891–1962), assistant to the Mayor of Frankfurt am Main from 1921 on; town councillor after 1945.

1949

TO WILLY STERNFELD

Pacific Palisades
November 3, 1949

Dear Herr Sternfeld:

I want to return Pechel's[1] letter to you and thank you for telling me of your correspondence with him. He is a decent person and should be intelligent enough to realize how that phrase I wrote in 1945 about the uncanniness of German books was intended and felt. Among my friends in Germany who are capable of some empathy with the experiences of those outside, none has blamed me for it, and none has insisted that I solemnly recant. Really, it's all old hat. Since then I have provided the dear Germans, to their delight, with totally different reasons for indignation—for example, with that letter to the Swedish journalist,[2] which I truly need not have written. It was pure cockiness. I said that in view of the behavior of the West German press, one might give thanks that in an authoritarian democracy impudence and stupidity at last had to keep their mouths shut. That, too, was the product of a mood—not really tenable, of course. For as you know, I am not in favor of violence and police-state methods. But wasn't it a nasty piece of foolishness to do away with licensing for the German press? If it was not something far worse than foolishness. General Clay[3] has just spoken quite candidly in Washington (so I am told by the Indian ambassadress) about the way things are going in Germany. No one applauded him, for the city is swarming with sinister Germanophiles. But he did speak the truth, and I speak it also if I need to, and did so years ago when I alluded to the profound regret Americans were feeling that instead of beating Russia with Germany, they were beating Germany with Russia. This regret still gnaws at our American hearts, and we'll never forgive Roosevelt for it.

---

[1] Rudolf Pechel (1882–1961), writer; honorary president of the German Academy for Language and Literature. Editor and publisher of the *Deutsche Rundschau* from 1919 on; the magazine was banned in 1942, and Pechel was sentenced to a concentration camp. He was released at the end of the war. Author of *Deutscher Widerstand* (1947), *Deutsche Gegenwart* (1952), among others.

[2] Paul Olberg. See page 581.

[3] Lucius D. Clay (b. 1897), military governor of the American Zone in Germany, 1947–9.

1949

TO WALTER KOLB

Pacific Palisades
December 2, 1949

My dear Mr. Mayor:

Thank you ever so much for sending me the text of the speeches delivered at the anniversary celebration in St. Paul's.

I have read Grimm's[1] address with sincere admiration, and your own speech with the somewhat embarrassed emotion which such eulogies inspire in a modest person. Quite aside from its subject, incidentally, I find the speech as such excellent. One of the less amiable letters I received from Germany suggested that I probably wrote it myself. People overestimate me.

TO ARNOLD SCHOENBERG

Pacific Palisades
December 19, 1949

My dear Herr Schoenberg:

Your *character document* in the magazine *Music Survey*,[1] which the editors have been considerate enough to send to me (other things of this nature have been withheld from me), made me aware to my great dismay that at the time, I don't know how many years ago, you were only lending, not giving, me your *Harmonielehre*. In truth this undeniable fact had entirely slipped my mind; imperceptibly I had come around to conceiving of the loan as a possession—perhaps because in a higher sense it had really become a possession to me. This is an attempt at a psychological explanation which does not condone the act. Rather, I must sincerely beg your pardon. At the time you explicitly mentioned how rare the copy was, so that it is even less forgivable that I made you wait so long before returning this valuable book. Indeed, why didn't you ever remind me?

I am now hastening, after so shamefully long a time, to return your property to you by mail. I studied the book very thoroughly, and I can only hope that this did not leave obvious traces.

P.S. Let me take this opportunity to ask a question. Since I am now faring

---

[1] Adolf Grimm (1889–1963), educator and politician. Member of the German resistance. Jailed 1942–5.
[1] "Further to the Schoenberg-Mann Controversy," by Arnold Schoenberg, published in the Fall 1949 issue of *Music Survey*, a quarterly that appeared from 1948 to 1952.

587

worse and worse under the hail of your attacks, may I, in extremity of need, publish your letter of October 15, 1948, written upon receiving the English edition of *Doctor Faustus* with the note at the end, in which you thanked me for complying with your request, declaring yourself fully satisfied, and added: "I was firmly convinced that I could expect nothing else from you, as I would not have from myself, and I am very glad that my confidence has been rewarded in this manner"—?

At that time you did not take the explanatory note as an "act of revenge." How it has since become one in your eyes, I do not know. But I ask myself in vain how the impulse to "revenge" myself upon you is supposed to have come over me. Even that insignificant diary remark[2] about your *Jacob's Ladder* was set down at the time *Faustus* was being written, and so on purely chronological grounds revenge could not have been in question.

You are thrashing away at a scarecrow of your imagination—not at me. That kind of thing does not generate any desire for vengeance. However you insist on being my enemy, you will not manage to make me yours.

T. M.

TO IDA HERZ

Pacific Palisades
December 25, 1949

Dear Fräulein Herz:

Many thanks for the handsome, practical, and ingenious object. I am very fond of such things. But it is not right that with my interdict against any more books because they are crowding us out, you should be put to possibly greater expense!

I hope a pleasant Christmas Eve awaited you. Ours was passed— with the Borgeses, Walters, Klaus Pringsheim and son, and Golo and a young American friend—amid a German-English confusion of tongues, the music of new records, and the frolic of children; somewhat fatiguing, but enjoyable. The American student, who had never before participated in anything so Continental, was intoxicated. "*Gee, Golo,*" he said.

---

[2] "At this time Schoenberg sent me his book on harmony, the *Harmonielehre*, and the libretto of his oratorio, *Jacob's Ladder*, whose religious poetry I found impure. On the other hand, I was all the more impressed by his extraordinary textbook, hose pedagogic attitude is one of sham conservatism, the strangest mingling of piety toward tradition and revolution." *The Story of a Novel*, page 52.

"That was quite an evening! The champagne, the conversation—it was out of this world."

Our phonograph has been miraculously renovated and is now adapted to the new records which run up to half an hour and allow an entire symphony to be heard without interruption. Wonders of the modern age! "But are we happier because of them?" the philosopher asks.

A good New Year!

Yours,

T. M.

TO MARTIN G. SCHMIDT[1]

Pacific Palisades
December 31, 1949

Dear Herr Schmidt:

Thank you for your letter. Nothing moves me more than the kind of decency that emanates from it. I cannot possibly go into all it deals with and all the questions it asks. Just this much: My attitude is in large part explained simply by my geographical position. We derive our moral feelings from the life around us, and the faults and sins of the "West," along with its hypocrisy, are all too frequently thrust at me. I can only ask you not to be misled by the nasty gossip of the newspapers about me, and to believe that I mean well and seek truth—all the while making mistakes like any other mortal—and shall, God willing, pass with fair honors the scrutiny of a posterity that will have journeyed far beyond our furious conflicts.

With cordial good wishes for the New Year,

---

[1] Now known as Martin Gregor-Dellin (b. 1926), writer, editor, organizer of the Thomas Mann Exhibit of the German Federal Republic. Author of *Jakob Haferglanz* (1956 and 1963), *Richard Wagner im Spiegel von Thomas Manns Prosawerk* (1958), *The Lamp Post* (New York: Alfred A. Knopf; 1964), *Möglichkeiten einer Fahrt* (1964), *Einer* (1965).

1950

---•---

TO THEODOR W. ADORNO

Pacific Palisades
January 9, 1950

Dear Dr. Adorno:

Many thanks for your ample, interesting letter. It has been read repeatedly and read aloud, and yesterday I told your good wife all about it
when she had lunch with us. At last, I might say. For the longest time we
could not manage to see each other because I was often ill and hardly fit
for society: an infectious inflammation and swelling of the ear passages
at times reduced me to virtual deafness, a most depressing state, with my
nights disturbed by a tormenting itch. A time-consuming treatment
brought improvement, but then a violent sore throat developed, which I
still have—probably the same infection that has fled elsewhere as a
result of the exorcisms. I don't know, but the air here seems to be full of
such phantoms all the time, and I find it significant that you are feeling
so energetic back there in our alien homeland. Basically we in this foreign
land that has become so homelike are living in the wrong place, which
confers a certain air of immorality upon our existence. On the other
hand, I rather enjoy it. Besides, I am very much attached to our house,
which is so completely right for me, and I also love the country and the
people, who have certainly remained good-natured and friendly, although
the political atmosphere is becoming *more and more unbreathable.*
Recently the Beverly Wilshire Hotel refused its hall for a *dinner* of the
Arts, Sciences and Professions Council because a *communist like Doctor
Mann* was to speak at it. To be sure, this produced such an uproar in the
community, and such a hail of telegrams descending on the hotel, that it
capitulated and let us have the hall. When my throat is better, I intend to
go there and deliver a speech, a limpid one as befits my years. Yet I
should think I have a full citizen's right to protest, for this year I have had

to toss $16,000 in taxes into the maw of the Cold War. Is that what I wrote *Faustus* for? Absolutely not!

Would you believe that Schoenberg has fired still another broadside at the book and at you and me? This one was in the London magazine *Musical Survey*, but the article was so silly that the editor apologetically called it a *character document*. Among other things Schoenberg declares that bad luck dogs anyone who has sinned against him; of two ladies who did so, he says, one broke her leg and the other suffered some similar misfortune. It is truly beyond belief. But I have written him again to say that although he may insist on running around as my enemy, he will not manage to make me his.

For a while I am continuing to smile at the Confidence Man from a distance, for *The Holy Sinner* is not yet finished, although far advanced. Actually, nothing whatsoever stops me from working in the mornings.

The penitent is now on his savage stone, and in order to rationalize his nourishment I am borrowing (or the monk is) the idea from Epicurus (and Lucretius) of the earth's *uberi* and the "milk" they yielded for the nourishment of the first men. Such a tube which reaches down into the earth has remained for Gregorius. One has to find such shifts. Incidentally, it seems to me that Hartmann[1] hints at something similar.

We all send our best regards and hope you will go on enjoying your philosophizing with the children.

TO ALFRED A. KNOPF

[*Original in English*]

Pacific Palisades
January 21, 1950

Dear Alfred:

I had a very gratifying letter from Helen Lowe in which she informs me that she has read the manuscript of my legendary novel (as much of it as I had sent her), that she likes the story, and that she has already started on the translation. How quickly her work will proceed, she is, of course, unable to say, but she assures me that she will do her best. At present she has no library at her disposal, but she hopes to get established where there is a moderately good one for the type of literature she needs for her stylistic inspiration.

---

[1] Hartmann von Aue (b. c. 1165), the medieval poet on whose *Gregorius* Mann based *The Holy Sinner*.

Her main concern seems to be whether she has enough strength to work without a secretary and typist the first time. She adds: "You and Alfred must think about this and let me know." It seems we really have to make a decision in this matter. I know that you have previously facilitated our friend's work in England by contributing toward the salary of a secretary. Since it is very important to me that the translation progresses swiftly so that it can be published approximately at the same time as the German edition, I am prepared to share the cost of hiring a secretary with you.

I received your charmingly bound speech on the beginnings of your publishing career, and thank you very much for the pleasure I derived from reading it.

I take this opportunity to enclose for your German lector a letter I received from a German writer-acquaintance of mine by the name of Alfred Gold. Mr. Gold has written his memoirs, and the table of contents he attaches reads very attractively. I would be grateful if the matter could be handled at your office and Mr. Gold be informed directly of the result.

As ever with love,
Yours,
Tommy

TO MAXIMILIAN BRANTL

Pacific Palisades
March 19, 1950

Dear Dr. Brantl:

My warm thanks for your telegram and your kind letter. You were a loyal friend to Heinrich;[1] for friendship and loyalty do not mean agreeing with everything a man's mind leads him to, but believing in his sincerity and not abandoning him even in error, or in what might look like error.

A great writer deeply rooted in the European and especially the Latin tradition and, as certain books of his show, gifted with a truly prophetic political instinct of a kind very rare in Germany, he commanded the language of the future—even more so as he grew older—and consequently was properly understood by very few during his lifetime. But it was so moving to see in his fiction and essays how a highly cultivated, austere, and brilliant mind sought plainness, strove to reach

---

[1] Heinrich Mann, who died on March 12, 1950, in Santa Monica.

social community and the common people, without in the slightest surrendering his aristocratic quality. Especially in his book of memoirs, *Ein Zeitalter wird besichtigt*, this mixture of limber intellectuality and plainness, is everywhere new, remarkable, and future-oriented.

He was ill a great deal of late, and also much aged in appearance, but he planned to leave in about six weeks for East Berlin, where wealth and the highest honors were awaiting him. He wanted to and did not want to; the adventure loomed before him and all of us as something frightening, and it actually remained not quite believable. On his last night he stayed up unusually late and listened to music with pleasure for a long time, and it was hard to persuade him to go to bed. Then, in his sleep, came the cerebral hemorrhage, without a sound or a movement. In the morning he simply could no longer be awakened. His heart went on functioning until about noon, but he never regained consciousness. Let us not be ungrateful. It was at bottom the most merciful solution.

The funeral was dignified. A minister of the Unitarian Church and Lion Feuchtwanger spoke, and a quartet played a beautiful slow movement of Debussy. Then I followed the coffin across the warm greensward of the cemetery of Santa Monica. R.I.P. The way things are going aboveground, we need not so especially mourn his passing. [. . .]

TO SHINJIRO KIRISHIKI[1]

[Original in English]

Pacific Palisades
March 21, 1950

Dear Mr. Kirishiki:

With many thanks I acknowledge the receipt of your touching letter of February 6th which I read attentively, and not myself alone, but also my wife and daughter participated in your confessions and discussions.

You must forgive me if I cannot go into your arguments as thoroughly as they deserve. I am about to leave on a lecture tour for which I have to make my literary preparations, and am sorely pressed for time. But I do want to tell you that I have full understanding for the particular difficulties of Japanese intellectual life in its precarious position with occidental civilization on the one hand and genuine Japanese conventions on the other. It is certainly not easy for a spiritually striving young

---

[1] Shinjiro Kirishiki (b. 1927), a Japanese student who wrote Mann a seven-page letter in which he poured out his heart about the predicament of postwar Japan.

Japanese to find the right road between romantic veneration of the old traditions and increasing Western modernity. But life has become difficult for all of us today, and for everyone it is an extremely subtle task to reach the right viewpoint with regard to the old customs and a radically changing world. One must have faith in oneself and make it a matter of personal sympathy and integrity to decide and to do what is right.

You say that I am expected in Japan and would be warmly received. I have been told so before and am deeply moved by this friendliness. For a long time now it has been my desire to see your beautiful and strange country. But my life is far advanced, and if I travel at all, it is understandably the old places of Europe to which I owe my education that attract me. Sometimes I am doubtful, especially in moments of fatigue, whether at my age I will still be able to visit Japan. But I cling to this dream and am glad and grateful in the knowledge that I have friends there who would welcome my coming.

With repeated thanks for the confidence expressed in your letter, I am, dear Mr. Kirishiki,

TO JULIUS BAB

Pacific Palisades
March 24, 1950

Dear Herr Bab:

Thank you for your kind letter and for the excellent article on Viktor's book. We were all extremely surprised by his writing it. It is truly engaging—warmhearted and deft—and a great success in Germany, not only for the now departed author but more or less for the whole house. [. . .]

Of course one does have to wink somewhat, or else say straight out, as the phrase in the well-known story goes: "*You must not believe everything the horse says.*" Old Heinrich, to whose family sense the book strongly appealed, showed some surprise when he read about his going to his little brother for advice on his novels. He remarked gently: "Curious, I can't remember that at all. I suppose it was one of his notions." I feel rather the same way in regard to Permaneder's outburst. He had quite a few "notions," you see, which do very well for his charming book, but which literary history should not absolutely rely on.

This between ourselves.

I am thoroughly shaken and exhausted by all these partings. A son and two brothers—the youngest and the eldest—all in one year. Left behind and alone, one must try to keep going for a while longer, until permission comes, as people say here, *"to join the majority."*

TO WALTER H. PERL

Pacific Palisades
March 25, 1950

Dear Dr. Perl:

[. . .] I am sure your review of *The Story of a Novel* will be fine. People here do not care at all for unqualified eulogies. Criticism is supposed to criticize, and nothing is to be praised to the skies—to that extent democracy still prevails in this country. However, you as a professor of German may well be overestimating my unpopularity for having strayed into the "politics of the day" (as you call the crisis in culture and humanity through which the world is passing, and from which I cannot very well escape into the "nonpolitical"). In spite of everything, there are hordes of people in this country who are still friendly toward me. Besides, I have not strayed any more into the day's politics than I did in 1933. I did not, of course, initiate the protest against the arrest of the lawyers defending the Communist Party leaders, but I signed it because word for word, and in very good words, it spoke the truth. It was directed against a crude breach of justice; the people were illegally charged because their activities were not illegal, and their lawyers were certainly entitled to immunity. These lawyers, be it noted, were released again under the pressure of a still tolerably healthy public opinion. Only German professors and Fascists can be annoyed at that.

Please understand that I am not on the point of becoming a martyr for a cause which is not mine; I can never endorse the totalitarian state. But a good many people here are on their way to becoming martyrs— namely, all those who oppose the destruction of democracy, a process which is in full swing under the guise of protecting that democracy. Doesn't it all strike you as dreadfully familiar, dreadfully like Germany? "Something very wrong must have happened . . ."[1] —oh yes, things are happening and things are building up which were previously inconceivable in a country before the coming of Fascism. The "cold war" is bringing physical and moral ruin upon America; that is why I am against

---

[1] A quotation from *An Exchange of Letters.*

it—and not "against America." If the Mundt[2]-Nixon[3] bill[4] should be passed, I shall take precipitate flight, along with my seven honorary doctorates.

If, as you say, you want to remain connected with my work, I think you can do so without undue scruples, even as a member of the Congregational Church. There are American Christians, like the Rev. Stephen Fritchman[5] of the First Unitarian Church of Los Angeles, who have strayed into the politics of the day even farther than I have.

TO AGNES E. MEYER

Pacific Palisades
March 27, 1950

Dear good friend:

Many thanks for your faithful letter, and rest assured that I perfectly understand and altogether approve of Dr. Evans's decision. Please tell him that, and thank him, too. As things now stand, there is nothing more reasonable than to silently drop the idea of the *lecture* before protests start coming in. To be sure, at the close of my address I do provide a strong and reasoned repudiation of communism in addition to a word for peace, but I realize that I have forfeited my chance to make this declaration in the Library. Perhaps everything would still be all right if I had not written that letter to the Swedish journalist, which was truly a foolish prank—completely unnecessary. Nothing compelled me to write him, and the letter contains sentences which were far too much the expression of a momentary mood and provoked by passing irritability. As I wrote them I had no idea that they would be broadcast and that they would eventually reach this country. But on the other hand, Mauriac[1] is quite right in what he says about the *parole écrite* and the culpability of *irréflexion*—more right, at any rate, than in his judgment on America, which again is far too much the expression of a mood, namely the proud

---

[2] Karl E. Mundt (b. 1900), Republican Congressman and subsequently senator from South Dakota. At this time a member of the House Un-American Activities Committee.

[3] Richard M. Nixon (b 1913), then also a member of the House Un-American Activities Committee.

[4] The bill, a manifestation of the antiliberal tendencies of the McCarthy era, passed the House but did not come to a vote in the Senate. Its principal provisions were subsequently incorporated into the Internal Security Act of 1950.

[5] Stephen H. Fritchman (b. 1902), Unitarian clergyman; since 1948 minister of the First Unitarian Church of Los Angeles.

[1] François Mauriac (b. 1885), French writer. Nobel Prize, 1952.

European's touchy attitude concerning the Marshallization and coloniza-
tion of Europe, although Europe has herself to blame for her misery. But
such voices of protest are being heard from England too.

Let me hope, at any rate, that I shall be able to deliver the lecture
in Chicago and New York; for I would be reluctant to admit in Europe
that I am no longer allowed to speak in America. That would be shaming.
For me, I mean, of course.

Take no oaths, dear friend, that America and Russia will never come
to a real war. Nobody knows where the *cold war* may lead. In any case it
will not lead to anything good. It is only making Russia more angry, if
that is possible; but here it is destroying democracy and leading to
general madness. My depression, intensified by all the final partings in a
single year—first our son, then my youngest brother in Germany, now
the eldest—is beyond describing.

Please go on believing that I mean well in spite of all the blunders
the confusion of the times causes me to commit, blunders from which
perhaps we are saved only if we concentrate solely on our own welfare.

TO AGNES E. MEYER

Hotel Baur au Lac
Zurich
May 21, 1950

Dear Princess:

It is high time that you had some greeting and a very hearty one, from
our travels—again and again I meant to write but could not in the rush
of moving about and meeting all the demands on me. The interval since
we saw you and Eugene at the Hotel Carlyle—a mere three weeks and a
bit—feels much longer that that because it has been so busy. Our flight
to Stockholm went smoothly and pleasantly, and we had a fine time in the
city. The lecture there was organized by the Swedish PEN Club, whose
president, Prince William of Sweden,[1] introduced me with a particularly
fine speech in German to an audience that was movingly receptive.
Living quietly as I do, I never realize how many affectionate friends I do
have in the world, and the manifestations of that friendship on such
occasions bewilder me even more than they gladden me. It was even
wilder in Paris. The reception at the Ritz, organized by the publisher of
Docteur Faustus, was a tumult; for three hours I had to sign books in a

---

[1] Prince William (1884–1965), second son of King Gustav V, president of the
Swedish PEN Club, author of travel books, essays, poetry, fiction and dramatic works.

librairie while people stood *in line* on the street under police supervision; and the lecture in the Sorbonne had to be transferred to the large *amphithéâtre*. Two thousand people came—it is a long time since anything like that has occurred, I was told—and the conduct of this crowd too was extraordinary. I find it foolish, for fame is founded on foolish and confused reasons; but I report it because it may amuse you.

What it leaves me with is fatigue and a sense of *humbug*, but at the same time a quiet feeling of joy that in some way I can be something to people. Incidentally, it had literally slipped my mind how beautiful Paris is. A glorious city! It happened to be the day of the Maid, with a grand parade in front of her monument outside our hotel, and at night the architectural complex from Notre Dame to Sacré Coeur was enchantingly illuminated with spotlights. Magnificent.

Then we drove here by way of Chaumont and Belfort in our little English car, enjoying the most agreeable weather, and entered Switzerland with feelings of homecoming. Tomorrow we are driving to the Ticino for a week—to Lugano to visit Hermann Hesse, an old friend, in Montagnola—but then we shall spend the greater part of June here. My lecture in the Schauspielhaus is on the 5th, and I follow it up a few days later with a reading from the Gregorius. We still do not know where we are going in July, but by the beginning of August we shall certainly set out for home by way of London.

I am enclosing a few newspaper items, one French and one German, from Heidelberg. The latter especially is a fine sample of how my ideas and hopes are being received in Europe. May America, great and good and only badly overwrought, not misunderstand me! I am attached to her and truly mean very well by her. I tell nobody that I was not allowed to speak in Washington, and only stress that I lectured in Chicago and New York. The South German Radio has had me make a tape recording of the lecture "The Years of my Life"; it will be broadcast in Germany on my birthday. It closes with the following words:

"One who has lived for seventy-five years knows something of the mercifulness of time and its patient fulfillment. He has also built up a certain affection for this green earth, and when—how soon!—he sinks into her arms, he wishes for the generations of men who move about aboveground in the light that their fate may not be misery and the shame of brutalization, but peace and gladness."

Faithfully yours,

TO ALBERTO MONDADORI[1]

Hotel Baur au Lac
Zurich
June 19, 1950

Dear Alberto Mondadori:

Many thanks for your letters. My wife will be undergoing an operation tomorrow at the Hirslanden Clinic, and we are very preoccupied.

Let me answer your questions as follows:

In *The Magic Mountain*, disease is not represented as a state of grace, but almost as a vice. In *Faustus* it is a means provided by the devil to induce creativity in an artist inhibited by knowledge.

Twelve-tone music is a brilliant attempt to reimpose order and lawfulness on music, which was falling into subjectivity and arbitrariness. It aims at objectivity, strict composition.

The figure of Adrian Leverkühn has nothing whatsoever to do with Arnold Shoenberg in character, fate, circumstances.

The question of the situation in Germany would lead me too far afield. I would not want to supply the enemies I have there with material for fresh bickering and abuse. Besides, I have many good and loyal friends there.

If I signed the Stockholm Motion against the Atom Bomb,[2] I did so because it was represented to me not as a Communistic action, but as a purely humanitarian one. Many non-Communists who are convinced of the necessity of preserving peace have signed it. It is abominable that the word "peace" should be brought down to the level of a Communist Party slogan.

TO LION FEUCHTWANGER

Dolder Grand Hotel
Zurich
June 25, 1950

Dear Lion Feuchtwanger:

I think you have received a preliminary card of acknowledgement,[1] but God knows you have certainly deserved my direct and personal thanks,

---

[1] Alberto Mondadori (b. 1914), son of Arnold Mondadori, founder and head of the Italian publishing house; poet, film director, founder and editor of several periodicals. Now vice-president of Mondadori Publishers.

[2] This was a lapse of memory; in fact Thomas Mann refused to sign the motion. See also letter of April 3, 1951, p. 611.

[1] For birthday greetings.

which would have gone off to you sooner had I not been living for weeks in the midst of various excitements—all very gay at first and then very grave and depressing. For my family waited until the festivities were over before telling me that my wife would have to undergo an immediate operation. Not to have it would involve even more dangers than are in any case connected with surgery at her age and with an illness gallantly ignored for a long time. The operation was successful, and after days of danger (problems with the circulatory system, bladder, intestines) we seem to be over the hill. Convalescence is a matter of two or three weeks. I have of course been at the Hirslanden Clinic a good deal, which takes time and means that I had to neglect other obligations. In spite of all the encouraging signs and the confidence of the doctors, I still feel anxious. It was hard to see so brave a soul, who has never had the slightest tendency to self-pity, suffering so cruelly for days on end. The really effective pain-killers had to be used sparingly. Well, as I say, it is going better now. [. . .]

Our return home will be delayed somewhat. We plan to spend a few weeks in the middle of July in the mountain air of Sils Maria, and it will probably be the middle of August before we set out for home, by way of London, at a forced-march pace.

Good luck and blessings for your splendid work.[2] Greetings to Marta.[3]

TO IDA HERZ

Dolder Grand Hotel
Zurich
July 4, 1950

Dear Fräulein Herz:

In haste; my wife is visibly much better; the healing process is going along most satisfactorily, and in about a week we shall be able to have her convalescing at the hotel. After another four or five days we all shall go up to Sils Maria; I am counting on the air there to restore her strength completely.

I very much wonder whether I ought to advise you to leave London where you live in honor and have work which is to your liking, for America, whose present atmosphere is anything but alluring. And would

---

[2] Feuchtwanger's novel about Goya, *This is the Hour.*
[3] Marta Feuchtwanger, who gave her husband's magnificent library of 30,000 volumes to the University of Southern California.

the position of custodian of the T.M.C.[1] constitute work commensurate with your energies? For they will be unable to use you academically, you know, and even for posts as archivists they probably want people with *degrees*. Your comment on the Morea affair is so truly English in spirit (and so very much after my own heart) that you would feel extremely alienated over there. We must discuss all this face to face.

I am delighted that they are so appreciative of your doubtless major contribution to the exhibit.[2] If you are ready to part with it for good, you ought to set a price that corresponds to the sacrifice you are making. The distinction Angell makes between *"the least you feel you could afford to sell it for"* and *"its intrinsic worth to you"* strikes me as meaningless.

I repeat, it's heavy weather in America now; I am afraid you would inevitably feel homesick for a less malignant atmosphere.

The chances are that I myself will be going to Yale at the end of August, and will spy out the terrain.

Your sympathetic telephone call touched us all very much. My wife and Erika send their regards.

TO AGNES E. MEYER

Pacific Palisades
August 30, 1950

Dear Agnes:

I am truly grateful to you for your long, well-meaning letter. It was waiting for me yesterday on my return to *privacy*, a *privacy* which in the future I shall manage to guard strictly. The lecture grieved you, but not to have sent it to you would have been unfriendly and shown lack of trust. Anyhow, it will probably be my last, and if you read its final sentences over once more you will see that they are a rather fitting farewell from an old man who has been well-intentioned toward humanity and therefore toward this country as well. Someone I met in Switzerland, who had heard "The Days of My Years" in German in New York, told me that at the final words his eyes had filled with tears. From this I would gather that after all there must be something comforting and helpful in it for a great many people, in the midst of the present hubbub of ideological hatred and fury. In Stockholm, where I spoke under the auspices

[1] The Thomas Mann Collection at Yale University.

[2] The Yale Library organized an extensive exhibit of manuscripts, notes, letters, diaries, source books, editions, and translations in connection with Mann's seventy-fifth birthday.

of the PEN Club, with Prince William of Sweden presiding, a professor of physics came up to me afterwards and said that if I only knew what despairing letters he was receiving from American colleagues about the state of their country I would understand why my lecture had made him happy.

People are wrong to spread tales abroad about America. I would never do that and in Europe have always emphasized my attachment to this country. In the lecture, too, I speak with some self-mockery as an American patriot, precisely where I call upon America to use her power and wealth for the building of world peace. What I say about the "financing of peace" is not at all original and not even un-American, for Senator McMahon[1] has already made such proposals.

I do not want to "abandon America to socialism" (which may be an inevitable necessity for Europe) any more than you do; but it grieves me that this land of pioneers and liberty is at present supporting the old, worn-out, rotten and corrupt forces throughout the world, and that America in a time of inexorable change plays the *policeman* of the status quo. I do not stand alone in this grief. Read a book like *Philosophy of Peace* by John Somerville.[2] Here is one man who tells the truth—and not out of malice and disloyalty.

If it comes to the large-scale war which General MacArthur is trying to ignite in Asia, all of us who have terrible doubts about American foreign policy would probably fare badly. Concentration camps and military tribunals would soon be set up. But the war probably will not come. Europe does not want it, and Acheson and Truman have rejected with alarm the wild pronouncements of MacArthur and the Secretary of the Navy. Though under heavy pressure from domestic politics and the criminal McCarthy campaign, they do not want total insanity and global catastrophe. And so I will probably be allowed to stay here in the house that is dear to me, on the patch of American soil that is my own, to stay and continue my life and my work a while longer—with the comforting awareness that I shall not lack sympathy and respect here any more than in Europe. I have just come from New Haven, where I saw the astonishing birthday exhibition which the Yale Library has put together from the documents of my life and work. [. . .] I am well aware that such honors

[1] Brien McMahon (1903–1952), Senator from Connecticut from 1944 to his death. Author of the McMahon Act for Control of Atomic Energy. A proponent of the international control of atomic weapons.

[2] John Somerville (b. 1905), professor of philosophy. Testified in three trials of alleged Communists as a non-Communist expert for the defense. Author also of *Soviet Philosophy* (1946), *The Communist Trials and the American Tradition* (1956).

are accorded me not because of my political statements but in spite of them. Yet I still have a few things to "contribute," and where something like this *exhibition* is possible; I myself am also possible, I think, for a while longer.

We have been in St. Moritz, where Katia recuperated very well from her operation. The Upper Engadine remains for me the most beautiful, most inspiring landscape in the world. During this whole trip I have done no work, except for a short piece on "Michelangelo's Eroticism" in connection with an Italian-German edition of his poems, whose force has deeply moved me. Once again, how inseparable greatness and suffering prove to be. The piece will be published only in German, in a Zurich art magazine. I would really be glad to have *The Holy Sinner* appear only in German, for I am already shuddering at the stupidities of the critics who will be going by the English version. The Germans are a thoroughly unbearable people, but I am after all a German writer through and through and a devotee of the German language, and I do frequently dream of ending my life in a German-language area, in Switzerland.

Incidentally, *Harper's Magazine* intends to publish "The Years of my Life" in the October issue, in the abbreviated spoken version. What daredevils! Won't such publication be an *un-American activity*?

Keep well, and do believe that I sincerely appreciate the trouble you have gone to in your letter, out of friendly concern.

TO KLAUS W. JONAS[1]

Pacific Palisades
October 8, 1950

My dear Herr Jonas:

Many thanks for your good letter and the warmhearted report[2] on the truly astonishing exhibit at Yale. Thornton Wilder said that to his knowledge no living author has ever been honored by such an exhibition here. But this is just what is producing a certain irritation in a good many people. The *New Yorker*, for example, commented on Dr. Angell's *T. M. Reader* that anyone looking at the book would never believe I was still alive and contentedly dwelling in my California house. I might be a

[1] Klaus W. Jonas (b. 1920), professor of German literature at the University of Pittsburgh. Author of *The Maugham Enigma* (1954), *Carl Van Vechten* (1955), *Fifty Years of Thomas Mann Studies, A Bibliography of Criticism* (2 vols., 1955, 1966), and others.

[2] An article on Yale's Mann exhibition, published in the New York *Staatszeitung und Herold* (June 24, 1950).

major author, all right, *"but not that major."* This is not the only reaction of that sort to the fuss being made over me. Naturally I can't help being pleased that what I am has also succeeded in winning zealous, affectionate friends. Indeed, I feel this to be a reassurance and protection against many hostile attacks, especially of a political nature. But still, the honors these friends arrange make me fear the envy of the gods, and the envy of men even more. I ask myself, therefore, whether a plan[3] such as yours should not be postponed until my passing—unless it turns out that there was nothing to me after all.

I cannot, therefore, "hail" your project in the sense of saying: "Excellent. That will fill an intolerable gap. The public and scholars will rejoice, and I certainly deserved it long ago." I must be able to say that I just barely countenanced it, for I do not want to be guilty of it. Anything of that sort must be done behind my back.

Please do not take this as a spurning of faith and love. These I always think fine, even when they are directed toward myself.

TO HENRY HATFIELD[1]

[Original in English]

Pacific Palisades
December 27, 1950

Dear Mr. Hatfield:

Many thanks for your letter of December 19th with the pleasant enclosures. A few days ago, also the Thomas Mann issue of the *Germanic Review* arrived, and I need not tell you that its display of intelligent critical interest in my life's work has given me great pleasure. I am very grateful to its editors—particularly, of course, to you personally—for the preparation of this number.

I never actually saw the study by Holthusen[2] which is also mentioned in this issue, but have again and indirectly learned more about it. It is indeed quite something that in the end he calls me the last great depicter

---

[3] The plan for Jonas's *Bibliography of Criticism.*

[1] Henry C. Hatfield (b. 1912), professor of German literature at Harvard University. Editor of the *Germanic Review*, 1947–53. Author of *Winckelmann and his German Critics* (1945), *Thomas Mann* (1951; 1962), *Schnitzler, Kafka, Mann* (with J. M. Stein; 1953), *Aesthetic Paganism in German Literature. From Winckelmann to the Death of Goethe*, and other books, as well as many articles, essays, and reviews in the field of German literature. Editor of *Thomas Mann: A Collection of Critical Essays* (1964).

[2] Hans Egon Holthusen (b. 1913), writer, specialist on Rilke. His "The World Without Transcendence," a violent attack on Thomas Mann, has been translated by Henry Hatfield and published in *Thomas Mann: A Collection of Critical Essays.*

of European decadence. I am curious to know when the very last one will appear. For if Mr. Holthusen himself does not personify European rebirth, I don't know just where it is to be found.

The concluding paragraphs of your book give promise of much that is kind and heartwarming about the whole. I must admit, however, that my interest in writings about myself has greatly decreased with the years, and I cannot promise to read your work from the first to the last word. But I will no doubt read in it and acquaint myself with its chief intentions, and shall gladly inform you of my impressions.

With my warmest wishes for the New Year, I remain, dear Mr. Hatfield,

1951

———————•———————

TO ROBERT J. HAVIGHURST[1]

[Original in English]

Pacific Palisades
January 11, 1951

Dear Mr. Havighurst:

Your telegram arrived yesterday. A few days ago, I co-signed a letter from the Committee for Peaceful Alternatives to the President of the United States, —a strong and very well put warning against German rearmament, a document which, I presume, will also be released to the press. I thus took a stand on the issue at stake, and can only repeat that I share the grave apprehension with which you view the proposed re-militarization of a country that—according to solemn decisions but five years of age—was to remain demilitarized forever. Your appeal, more-over, rightly stressed the fact that it is precisely the best elements within Germany itself who vigorously oppose remilitarization.

The demonstration you plan to stage against a project so dangerous in every respect has my full approval.

Even so, and much to my sincere regret, I cannot come to Chicago in the foreseeable future. You mention some "schedule" of mine into which this trip might be fitted. Well, there is no such thing. I am a writer, chained, as it were, to his desk; and I am also an old man who could not, during the winter, leave California for the East without impairing his health. Besides—*and more important*: if this country is to be told, resoundingly and in public, that she has taken a wrong and pernicious road, then, to my mind, it should be a clear-sighted native, a one-hundred-percent American who should do the telling, rather than

---

[1] Robert J. Havighurst (b. 1900), chairman of the Committee for Peaceful Alternatives. Author of many works on education and society; professor of education at the University of Chicago since 1941.

an immigrant with a European accent and a novelist to boot, to whose political credit precious little is being placed.

With every good wish,

TO ERICH VON KAHLER

Pacific Palisades
February 1, 1951

Dear Erich:

You cannot imagine how it troubles me that I haven't yet thanked you for your friendly *Season's Greetings*, or even for your splendid essay in the magazine of the *Atomic Scientists*.[1] The essay truly strikes me as written from the depths of my own heart. And really, agonized as we all are by so much falsehood, the ring of truth almost brings tears to the eyes. If only I did not have the feeling that it is all in vain. The good books, the commentators who, rarely enough, still risk a word of warning over the radio—none of that has the slightest influence. Obstinately and inexorably nemesis takes its course, following the vilest laws, and sometimes I catch myself thinking: just as well; let it come the way they insist on having it. Human wickedness deserves a visitation such as the earth has not yet seen—and this civilization of grabbers, fools, and gangsters deserves to perish.

How hardworking you are! Right after the political essay comes this one on aesthetics in the *Rundschau*.[2] It is very rich and fine criticism. And yet I know you must simply have stolen the time to produce these good things.

With my energies plainly dwindling and a sense of depression growing, I have managed to put together nothing but trifles since the summer. [. . .] But since *The Holy Sinner* is out of the way and in print, I have taken up the ancient *Felix Krull* once again and am continuing it, letting him saunter on into the unknown without any real faith that I shall ever finish it. I suspended work on it in 1911 to write *Death in Venice*, and it is truly curious to take up the old fragment again after four decades and all I have done in between. I have actually resumed on the selfsame page of Munich manuscript paper (from Prantl on Odeonsplatz) where I stopped at that time, unable to go on.

God knows whether we shall be coming East in the spring. I no

---

[1] "Foreign Policy Today," *Bulletin of the Atomic Scientists*, Vol. VI, No. 12 (December 1950).
[2] "Was ist ein Gedicht," *Neue Rundschau*, Jahrgang 61, Heft IV (1950).

longer have lectures, at any rate, and it would only be a stopover on the way to Switzerland, which as things stand has by degrees and rather without any special grounds become my favorite country, and where I should gladly spend the last brief years of my life. We must see.

Cordially,
T. M.

TO OTTO BASLER

Pacific Palisades
February 4, 1951

Dear Herr Basler:

Thank you for your letter and the "documents."[1] They are very fine ones, and our dear, great Hermann Hesse is a curious person. He always represents himself as ancient and worn-out and tired of the world and opinions (as he has just done again in the postlude to the *Badegast*, which I have read with much pleasure), and then suddenly, out of healthy annoyance, he hits out like a young champion, so that the sparks fly. It does the heart good.

You cannot imagine how shaken I was by the news of the dreadful Swiss avalanches. What a disaster! The whole world should be drawn together in sympathy for the suffering of that good country. But it was a day's sensation, a *headline*, no more. You say, at least it comes from the Creator's hand. Are you so sure? Related events here and striking abnormalities of the climate indicate that it may not be altogether absurd to connect these things with the infamous nuclear explosive tests being held in the deserts of this country. Uncanny light effects at tremendous distances, and slight earthquakes, accompany them. I would not be in the

---

[1] Hesse had sent the following sharp reply to a letter from a reader in Germany: "Dear Sir, I have received your letter and would have been delighted with it if it had not contained that tract on my dear colleague and friend Thomas Mann.

"You Germans expatriated this man, stole his property, threatened his life, and in every way persecuted and reviled him—and now you stand there and judiciously consider whether you ought to forgive him such-and-such a step or permit such-and-such words of his to pass. We wretched foreigners watch this spectacle and it makes our hair stand on end. Instead of your criticisms and your insults, you ought to ask his forgiveness on your knees. But then it is well known that not a soul in Germany shares in the guilt for what you have brought down upon the world and yourselves since 1933.

"Since you refuse to, I feel shame in your stead for these unforgivable acts. With greetings, yours, H. Hesse."

Hesse sent several copies of this letter to other correspondents, and received a touching reply from a young poet in Hamburg.

least surprised if nature, abused by human hubris, were not to avenge herself in all kinds of unforeseen ways.

Cordially,

T. M.

TO PROFESSOR PHILIP MORRISON[1]

[*Original in English*]

Pacific Palisades
February 18, 1951

Dear Professor Morrison:

Your letter has touched me deeply, and I sincerely thank you for it. It is the most likable communication I received in this unfortunate matter.

I fully understand your viewpoint, and I sympathize with it, without, however, being able to share it. Unlike a pure work of art which must be created exactly to the artist's innermost design and not with a view to the greatest popular success imaginable, a political action, if it is to make sense, must primarily strive to be successful. No American peace movement generally believed to be Communist-inspired or controlled could at the present possibly succeed. The Communists, to my mind, should be the first to realize this. They should not only not insist on prominently figuring on each and every list naming America's fighters for peace, but should also formally decline any invitation to initiate, sponsor or co-sponsor any peace crusade or the like in this country. Rightly or wrongly, their manifold activities in the asserted service of peace have not for years past been accepted as so many expressions of either their love of humanity or their spontaneous, sincere, and unalterable hatred of war; instead they keep being discounted and attacked as the "comrades'" faithful execution of certain plans by the Politburo.

I know well that the *Times* has, indirectly, lied and falsified as only a newspaper can. But the trouble is that they were given the chance to do so, and you cannot imagine how many friends and acquaintances sent me the *Times* story with its sensational headline, accompanied by exclamations of horror and fear lest I might possibly be deprived of my passport or even my young citizenship. My decision, however, to keep away from any and all collective actions from now on, and to say what I

---

[1] Philip Morrison (b. 1916), professor of physics, Cornell University; took part in the development of the atom bomb at Los Alamos. He had invited Mann to join the American Peace Crusade.

have to say absolutely on my own, —this decision is not based so much on fear and the desire for security, although, of course, I would not like to experience again what I went through in 1933 and in my old age find myself without a place to hang my hat, —this decision, as stated in a short notice to the United Press, is based rather on the fact that of late it has become increasingly difficult, if not impossible, promptly to discern the true character of any group one is asked to join. Furthermore, as I must admit to you in confidence, it is due to a true inner withdrawal of my interest from the destinies of this country which, in my opinion, has embarked on a wrong and ruinous course. If it refuses to hear this, I don't want to impose.

Of course, I have no objection to your having shown your kind letter to me among your friends.

With the expression of my sincere esteem, I remain, dear Professor Morrison,

TO ALFRED A. KNOPF

[*Original in English*]

Pacific Palisades
March 28, 1951

Dear Alfred:

Your letter made me very happy indeed.[1] That's what I call a susceptible publisher! May the American public react the same way, that's all we can hope for. As a matter of fact, I myself couldn't help finding the book quite nice when I read the German proofs. It is light, it is serene, it has a certain aloofness without being cold, and I think it *is* something that I could do it right after *Doctor Faustus*. So you see how self-complacent I am.

The translation I didn't see yet. It must have been quite a tour de force, because the book is full of linguistic tricks and jokes of all kind. But if you are satisfied, there will be no reason for me to be exacting.

Very soon I shall dictate to my secretary some notes about the origin and the historical background of the story. *The Holy Sinner* seems to be the final title of the English version. Not bad.

Yours as ever,
T. M.

---

[1] Knopf had written: "I found the book utterly entrancing. As sheer narrative, it seems to me to be perhaps your best work."

1951

TO THE EDITORS OF *AUFBAU*

Pacific Palisades
April 3, 1951

Dear Sirs:

During the past week the most mistaken charges have been repeatedly leveled against me in public. The campaign began on March 26 with an article by Eugene Tillinger[1] in a magazine called *The Freeman*, which indeed makes very free with its slanders. Regrettably, on March 29 the United Press took up Mr. Tillinger's "revelations," thus assuring them the kind of wide distribution that *The Freeman* neither deserves nor enjoys. On March 20 the U.P. sent an abbreviated version of my rebuttal over its wires. But in the first place, it is common knowledge that denials are printed by only about 10 percent of the publications which first carried the matter to be denied; in the second place, the U.P. version of my reply seems to me altogether inadequate. I therefore wish to explain briefly the true facts of the matter for the readers of *Aufbau*.

Mr. Lyle C. Wilson, Chief of the U.P. Bureau in Washington, comments on March 29 on the *communist-front activities* of which I have been guilty—according to *The Freeman*—and from which I have not desisted, even though in certain specific cases I have untruthfully denied such "activities." "*Without making use of the ugly word itself,*" Mr. Wilson writes, "*the magazine states Mann lied on at least two occasions in denying specific communist activity.*"

I have had to reach the age of seventy-five and to live in a foreign country which has become home to me, to be publicly accused of lying by witch-hunters who—and this is what is so confounding—give no credence nor even pay attention to any one but their "witches."

Mr. Tillinger, to offer an example, is still unaware on March 26 that on February 12 and with full publicity (via U.P.) I announced my withdrawal from an organization—the American Peace Crusade—to which I had belonged for a few days. And thus as far as he is concerned, one of my principal "*front activities*" consists in my remaining a member of a group which incidentally includes a large number of good liberal Americans along with several sponsors who have been denounced as Communistic. *The Freeman* does not listen. Fascinated to the point of

---

[1] Eugene Tillinger (d. 1967), free-lance journalist; secretary of the short-lived anti-German organization founded by Rex Stout, the Committee to Prevent World War Three. Wrote for extreme rightist publications such as *Plain Talk*, which later merged with *The Freeman* when this magazine was founded.

611

stupefaction by the propaganda speeches of its "witches," it produces two "proofs" that I twice told falsehoods.

First, there is a photostatic reproduction of the so-called Stockholm Peace Declaration in its French version, bearing my signature. This "document" was not new to me. Months after its publication and weeks after my return from Europe, it was shown to me as part of a *photomontage* which allegedly pictures me signing the Stockholm Declaration in Paris in the spring of 1950. For the occasion I am wearing a suit which I took with me to Europe in the summer of 1949, but not in 1950. Likewise visible in the picture is the black mourning tie which I had tragic reason to wear in May 1949. I have been unable to learn, and do not care, how this picture was manufactured. But what I know, and what I have truthfully stated, is that I did *not* sign my name to the Stockholm declaration.

For his second item "documenting" my lying, Mr. Tillinger offers a clipping from *L'Humanité* (the newspaper of the Communist Party of France) which reproduces a few sentences that I addressed to M. Joliot-Curie in the late fall of 1950. These sentences, taken from a personal letter to the great French scholar, were an attempt to tone down the sharpness, which I found humanly repugnant, of the *refusal* that I felt obliged to send to M. Joliot Curie. I wrote him that I could not participate in any way in the Second Congress for World Peace which he was convoking. My personal efforts in behalf of peace, which I too regard as humanity's most urgent task, would not have the slightest practical significance if they should become entangled with *"propaganda displeasing to this country."*

M. Joliot-Curie was not authorized to release the whole letter, let alone misleading parts of it. That he nevertheless did so was not good.

But in any case: *In no way and in no sense did I participate in that congress.*[2] I publicly (via the Associated Press this time) denied reports to the contrary, and I am decried as a liar because Mr. Tillinger believes only his "witches."

I have replied to him and *The Freeman* and suppose I may count on my answer's being printed in that organ. But this whole thing remains a symptomatic disgrace as well as a sinister absurdity. Ex-Communist renegades and former Soviet spies—trained traitors each and all—put themselves forward and are accepted as principal defenders of democracy. People who cannot distinguish black from white and—so they allege, at least—consider the most primitive tricks of Communist propaganda as

[2] Mann's emphasis.

better coin than the word of a man of hitherto unquestioned integrity, set themselves up as defenders of decency and freedom.

I am not a Communist and never have been one. Neither am I a "fellow traveler," nor could I ever be one where the destination was totalitarianism. I felt it an honor and a joy to become a citizen of this country. But hysterical, irrational, and blind hatred of communism represents a danger to America far more terrible than native communism. Indeed, the persecution mania and the mania to persecute that we have succumbed to and that we seem on the point of surrendering ourselves to, body and soul—these cannot lead to anything good. Unless we change our course immediately they will surely lead from bad to worse. That is something which on this occasion has to be said.

TO ALVIN JOHNSON[1]

[Original in English]

Pacific Palisades
April 18, 1951

Dear Dr. Johnson:

I have read your letter[2] over and over again. Here is my reply:

I do not like too much open-handedness in the use of the word "genius," particularly in reference to myself. It is almost with impatience that I reject such appellation. As an artist, I was not without courage, but in my deepest heart I have always been a modest person whose best and most fruitful gift was the power of admiration which made it possible for me to learn. Now as in my youth, I am looking up to the truly great creations of the past which I see high above my own, and which alone deserve the name of "genius." Even the remotest connection with these stars is meritorious. It creates a certain intimacy with greatness, such as I

---

[1] Alvin Johnson (b. 1873?), teacher and writer. Taught political economy and political science at Columbia, Chicago, Cornell, and Stanford Universities. Editor of *The New Republic*, 1917–23. Director of The New School for Social Research in New York, which he transformed, during the Nazi years, into a virtual haven for refugees. Among his works: *Introduction to Economics* (1909), *The Professor and the Petticoat* (1914), *Deliver Us from Dogma* (1934), *The Public Library; A People's University* (1938).

[2] Johnson had written to Mann on April 6 pointing out that Hermann Broch was in the hospital with "coronary complications" and rather reproachfully urging Mann to recommend Broch for the Nobel Prize. "You wrote appreciatively of Hermann Broch, but you had committed yourself to someone else for the next Nobel Prize. But you are not committed for the following year, are you? And your nomination is equivalent to election. May I beg a few words, not committing yourself, to be sure, for your position is too responsible for commitments, but expressing an opinion that the prize for the later year could hardly do better than Broch. . . ."

have expressed in my Goethe novel. But my self-esteem had enough sense never to go beyond the "Anch'io sono pittore."

It is doubtful to me whether greatness and genius exist at all at the present time. Even in our most fortunate moments, we all have but a trace of it. And here, perhaps above all others, I think of our friend Hermann Broch. From my previous letter you know the high esteem in which I hold him. He is a noble and prolific thinker and a frequently auspicious poet. His *Sleepwalkers* is an admirable work, and I consider his *Virgil* one of the most extraordinary and profound experiments ever to have been undertaken with the flexible medium of the novel. When occasionally expressing this opinion publicly, I encountered much frowning opposition, even from people who should have had more understanding. How, they asked, could I praise his books? Abstruse and sophistical, they called them, almost impossible to read. I remained firm in my conviction, and shall always come out for this conviction and for our important contemporary, —of that both you and Broch may be assured.

I am deeply grieved to learn that Broch is ill and discouraged by his illness. I also regret that his condition leads him to believe "I never will consider him worth my backing." What hypochondria! Good heavens, I am sure I need his "backing" more than he does mine. He belongs with those minds upon whose good opinion we base our belief in ourselves and in the benign judgment of posterity. But now we are concerned with the backing of his candidacy for next year's Nobel Prize. How could I refuse it? You are exaggerating, indeed, when you say that "my nomination is equivalent to election." My influence is by no means strong enough to persuade the committee in Stockholm to give the prize to an intellectual figure that is probably quite foreign to them and which it may not consider to be sufficiently world-renowned and acknowledged as to be suitable for the honor. This board never had the ambition to *establish* a world reputation; its task, rather, seemed the confirmation and crowning of an already existing one. Too narrow a goal, maybe. But then the board never set out to surprise the world nor did it ever consider it the purpose of the prize to assist needy writers financially.

In certain scholarly American circles, Broch enjoys great respect. He was awarded several fellowships, as well as the title of Poet Resident of Yale, and as he could not live on that, he was also given a lectorship. To the broader public, his name has an esoteric quality that inspires reserve and, I am afraid, is not encouraging to the Stockholm committee. Bearing in mind that Joyce and Kafka passed away without receiving the prize, one dares hardly hope for it in Broch's case. Altogether the "pride" of us

Nobel Prize winners is greatly dampened by the thought of who did *not* get it. Certainly the by-passing of Broch (or at least a delay in his choice) would be more excusable than is the omission of Ibsen, Strindberg, and Tolstoy. In the opinion of the Swedish trustees, the outline of Broch's stature may not yet be sharp and distinct enough to assure them of world-wide approval in case of his selection. Much of what he has to say to mankind is still buried within himself, it has not yet completely ripened, not yet become fully audible and penetrated the consciousness of the world. His readers and admirers form an elite—and the judges in Stockholm are not used to basing their decisions on the opinion of an elite.

Despite all this, I think it possible that the energetic intervention by an American group of prominent scholars might make an impression on the Stockholm board. As for myself, I am so thoroughly convinced of the important place his two chief works, and particularly his *Virgil,* are occupying in the history of literature of whose development they are representative, that I would not exclude myself from such an action because of any faint-heartedness. My name, dear Dr. Johnson, is at your disposal when you and the other American friends of Hermann Broch will appeal to the Stockholm Prize Committee for next year's Nobel Prize.

TO ERICH VON KAHLER

Pacific Palisades
April 23, 1951

Dear friend:

Thank you for your good, kind letter. And above all, our sympathy for your grief over your mother. "You know, 'tis common . . ." And you were expecting the inevitable. Nevertheless, it is a totally unique shock and wrench, as I very well remember from my own experience. Good that you are so busy and hopeful in so many directions, even though all this furthering, arranging, and building is done under the pressure that weighs so heavily on us all. I know exactly what you mean by "acute depression." I myself am nothing but a bundle of nerves, trembling at every thought and word. Only yesterday I let myself break down and weep listening to the *Lohengrin* prelude—simply in reaction to all the baseness. Have people ever had to inhale so poisoned an atmosphere, one so utterly saturated with idiotic baseness? We live in a world of doom from which there is no longer any escaping. Your "Are you crazy?"

anecdote[1] is striking enough, except that in my opinion the man sailing westward is just a trace crazier, for despite the fact that dear Switzerland may be even more pro-American than some Americans, it seems to me that in general the European mentality does not come up to the barbarous infantilism we have here, especially not since the notable turn toward pacifism the Roman Church has taken. It knows why.

For the rest, we are a long way from forming any definite plans. Erika, who is ordinarily the element of practical energy in the house, is much too sick to take any such thing in hand. She had to have a very serious operation, from which she is only slowly recovering. First of all, then, we must wait until she is well. But in other respects too there are so many affairs in suspension: the sale of the property, the purchase by Yale Library of my entire "posthumous papers," including diaries I have kept since 1933, for which some uncowed philanthropist must come forward—and other things. The farthest we will go—and Katia prefers this idea—is that we shall rent the house, if possible, for a year and spend that time in Europe, first of all in Gastein; the baths attract me because of arthritic-rheumatic difficulties with my hip and arm. But even this temporary step is quite uncertain. It is also a question of money. We know nothing at all. [. . .]

TO WILLIAM HART[1]

[*Original in English*]

Pacific Palisades
May 1, 1951

Dear Mr. Hart:

Your kind lines have touched me very much. It was a real pleasure for me to hear of your warm interest in my life's work, and it is almost surprising for me that among my books you prefer *The Beloved Returns*, a book for which I myself have retained a certain loyalty and affection. Surprising is your sympathy for this work only because it was the most difficult one to translate, and its transference into English was a veritable tour de force for Mrs. Lowe-Porter which could succeed only partially. The English title alone, *The Beloved Returns*, means a certain stylistic depreci-

---

[1] One friend is sailing from New York to Europe and another in the opposite direction. As their ships pass on the high seas they recognize one another and both cry out in horror simultaneously: "Have you gone crazy?"
[1] Unidentifiable.

ation of the whole. In German the book is simply called "Lotte in Weimar," and the English title has something very foreign to me.

It was a good time when I wrote this book. I began it in Switzerland and finished it in Princeton, where we lived for two years before settling down in California. For a long time, even while writing *Death in Venice*, I had wished to make Goethe's person and life the topic of a story. But I always lacked the courage until a light and humorous approach offered itself with the anecdote about the visit of the aged Charlotte Buff in Weimar. The novel was a long interpolation in the Joseph novels, for I wrote it after the completion of *Joseph in Egypt* and before starting *Joseph the Provider*. Thus the different pieces of a life's work are connected like links of a chain.

With repeated thanks for your kind interest,

TO KENNETH OLIVER[1]

[Original in English]

Pacific Palisades
May 4, 1951

Dear Dr. Oliver:

It is difficult to find words to describe the pleasure your kind letter gave me. To learn that, under the guidance of a distinguished teacher, young American students of literature are occupying themselves so thoroughly with my life's work could only give me great joy and satisfaction. I congratulate myself, and I also congratulate your pupils—namely on their receptiveness and their enthusiasm—quite apart from its incidental object. Admiration, quite generally, is our greatest asset, a wonderful gift, the prerequisite of all our growth and development. Where would I be today if it hadn't been for my ability to admire, to look up to that which is high above me, and to view the good, the great, and the masterly with amazement and discernment? We only learn through admiration.

I am moved to hear that this group of young people desires a personal contact with me and expects possible furtherance of their studies and insights through a conversation with me. Believe me, I deeply regret having to disappoint you in this respect. But I am an old man whose health is no longer very steady, and who is profoundly disturbed by the

---

[1] Kenneth Oliver (b. 1912), author of *Our Living Language* (rev. ed. 1964) among other works; chairman of the division of humanities and fine arts at Occidental College 1961–7, professor of English and comparative literature since 1948.

perniciously tense and disaster-laden atmosphere in which we are breathing today. Nervous and tired, I live very secluded, occupied only with my work and shy with regard to "social" obligations and discussion, especially as I do not muster the English language sufficiently for me to be able to express myself freely and adequately on complicated subjects—and that is what we are concerned with. My pleasure at such a get-together would be mixed with too much effort and shortcoming, and for you and your group it would be a disappointment. It is better, therefore, to give up this idea.

If during the planned studies of my writings some questions should arise which you should like to have answered by the author himself, I will be very glad to do so to the best of my ability by letter.

I have no very clear picture of how my books present themselves in the English translation in which your pupils have to read them by necessity. Doubtless, Mrs. Lowe-Porter has accomplished all that is humanly possible, but she herself is most fully aware of the existing difficulties which my German style puts in the way of a translation into another language, and while working on her English version of *Lotte in Weimar* (*The Beloved Returns*—a title entirely unnatural to me!) she once said to me, almost with contrition: "I am committing a murder!" She was certainly too harsh with herself, and I am reporting her utterance only because it is important to me that you and the young friends of my work realize that you are dealing with a shadow, a reflection, not really with the object itself. The translation communicates my ideas, more or less, but what is an idea deprived of its native form? In art, content and form are too much one and the same to permit the content to remain entirely unchanged when lifted from its primary form and poured into another.

A translation, though in itself a great achievement, may arouse quite erroneous impressions about the spirit of the original. For instance, I have occasionally heard the American critics call my style "Olympian," "pompous," and "ponderous"—and at first would not trust my ears at these characterizations. None of these attributes are in the least pertinent, believe me! Complete lucidity, musicality, and a serenity which lightens what might be heavy—this is what my prose has always tried to achieve. In addition to that, I admit, there is a playful tendency towards irony and subtle parody upon tradition. It is especially these elements which are jeopardized by the translation and may cause my English style to appear stilted.

Please excuse these remarks which I hope do not seem pretentious.

They are only meant to show you how eager I am for your students to regard my novels in the proper light and perhaps to offer a kind of compensation for the personal interview.

With my best wishes for your seminar, I remain, dear Dr. Oliver,

TO JULIUS BAB

Pacific Palisades
May 30, 1951

Dear Herr Bab:

My warmest thanks for your intelligent, calm study of *The Holy Sinner*. Anything is possible when the New York newspaper for political and scholarly affairs[1] publishes no less than two articles at once on the book.

Of course a writer can be permitted to do that sort of thing only once. It cannot be repeated. But I have done all my things only once, and there is no reason to leap to the conclusion that every experiment is a "blind alley" in which the author will now be stuck for all eternity. Basically every one of my books has been a blind alley, from which it was impossible to go any further in that particular direction, yet each time I emerged to go on to new things.

The linguistic jokes are perhaps carried a little too far, and in Germany there has been considerable talk about my corrupting the language. They're fine ones to talk! A German living abroad, Joachim Maass,[2] could write me: "But my deepest and heartiest pleasure in this book is the language. . . . When I consider what we younger writers, and especially the German generations after us, have or should have to learn from that. . . . The way the language plays with its awareness of its origins, with the game quite often becoming serious—that is, producing an unsuspected enrichment by its gay excursions into dialect and polyglotism. . . ." He really must feel that way; what point would there be in flattering me? From Hesse, Reisiger, and others I could quote similar remarks. It is after all a supranational medieval world of my own whimsical invention, and I simply could not conceive it except as linguistically piebald. It's curious, isn't it, how naturally the Low German of the fishermen on the half-English Channel Island merges with the English, as for example in *"Dat's nu'n little bit tou vul verlangt!"* *"Dat's"* is already the English "That's," and the following " 'n little bit" fits in

---

[1] A pun in German on the name of the New York German newspaper *Staatszeitung*.
[2] Joachim Maass (b. 1901), writer. Emigrated to the United States in 1939. Taught German literature at Mount Holyoke College.

smoothly, although it is no longer Low German, but pure English, so that the reader hardly notices the mixture. Actually I arrived at the Middle High German through Nepomuk Schneidewein in *Faustus*—he deepens the linguistic perspective of the book with his Swiss German, which establishes the link from the baroque German of Luther back to the medieval German. That was the starting point, if you would like to know. *"Waetlich"* (fine, stately) you would have found in a Middle High German lexicon. I assume it is connected with the more modern *weidlich*. I hardly think that these old words offer a serious obstacle to the reader. Their meaning is always clear from the context—even in the case of the fragments of Old French—which, incidentally, in a certain case are "not even meant to be understood." They are borrowed from an Old French dialogue between Adam and Eve about the apple (as the scholars would surely be discovering soon) and the *"Fais le! Monique, ne sez que est! Es il tant bon? Tu le saveras!"* is comprehensible enough, I should think.

Sibylla's prayer to the Virgin is a borrowing (a rather free one, so that I may say the best verses are mine) from the Vorau Lament for Sins of the middle of the twelfth century. You mention the overly Goethean verses that Grigorss (not Grigorsch!) once murmurs under his breath. But aren't these really much prettier:

> *Stella maris bist du genannt*
> *nach dem Stern, der an das Land*
> *das müde Schiff geleitet.*
> *So hast du auch bereitet*
> *Ankunft dahier,*
> *Ankunft bei mir*
> *dem so genehmen Knaben,*
> *dem muss ich Gedenken tragen,*
> *beides, bei Tag und Nacht. . . .*
> *Gern, Fraue, das ist wahr,*
> *Küsst' ich ihn auf das Haar*
> *Und, gäb' er Freude kund,*
> *dann auf den Mund!*[3]

It is hidden by being set as prose, as are also the parodied *Nibelungenlied* verses Maître Poitevin falls into when he tells about Grigorss' "diversion" on the drawbridge. That one hero cuts another through

---

[3] "Stella maris art thou called from the star that guides from far the weary bark to land, thus likewise hadst thou planned the way to me of the so lovely boy in whom I have such joy by day and night. . . . Gladly, Lady, that is sooth, would I kiss him on the brow, and if he joy did show, then on the mouth." (*The Holy Sinner*, p. 200 f.)

slantwise with a single stroke so that the victim never notices until he tries to stoop and falls apart—there is actually a passage to this effect in the *Nibelungenlied*. The Maire is decent enough to say: "That I made up in song, it really did not happen." You make a keen and profound observation when you say that underneath all the jokes I am very serious about the religious core of the legend, the idea of sin and grace. My life and thinking has, for a long time now, been dominated by this idea; and really, is it not pure grace that it should be granted me, after the exhausting work on *Faustus*, to bring off this religiously merry little book?

TO GORDON T. WICK [1]

[Original in English]

Pacific Palisades
June 4, 1951

Dear Mr. Wick:

I received your kind letter of May 17th and hope you will find it forgivable that I cannot do very much with it and do not quite understand what kind of an answer or advice you expect from me. It seems you have read none of my books but only heard a few things about me, for instance about the "breadth of my knowledge" and the "diabolical perversion of my soul." I must confess that I do not quite recognize myself in this characterization. But what has chiefly astonished and depressed me in your letter was the remark that you are incapable of admiration, except in the case of physical beauty. Now, while physical beauty certainly is something very enjoyable, its contemplation does not lead anywhere. An artist, I should think, ought to be capable of admiration for great works of art and great masters. The faculty to admire and to look up appears to me as a prerequisite of any kind of learning and spiritual growth. It is by no means necessary that you read my books. But you should study the great works of world literature, and study them with intense admiration in order to become able to create something yourself that need not be equal to them, but that will yet be related to them due to the fact that it went through their school.

---

[1] An American sailor.

TO ALFRED A. KNOPF

[*Original in English*]

Pacific Palisades
June 8, 1951

Dear Alfred:

Yesterday I wrote you in order to express my pleasure about our success with the Book-of-the-Month Club. It is with some reluctance that I am approaching you already again, for I hate to bother you, and yet I would like to expose some doubts regarding our financial arrangements. You know how much I appreciate your thoughtfulness in this matter, and it is, of course, a great advantage for me, to receive the income from the new book in installments. However, now *The Holy Sinner* has become a Book-of-the-Month selection I wonder whether the annual payments we have decided upon are not too low. In normal times it would doubtless be an excellent thing for me to avoid high taxes and to have an income of $10,000 assured for as many years as possible, maybe for the rest of my life. But unfortunately we do not live in normal times, and nobody can overlook the existing danger of inflation. Under these circumstances it might not be wise to extend such installments over too long a stretch of time, I do not think longer than three years.

I perfectly realize that the Club is not what it used to be. For *Doctor Faustus* they paid me about $25,000, but in this case I had to share the royalties with Somerset Maugham, and so it might not be exaggerated to expect about the same amount this time, plus the proceeds from the regular edition. You are, of course, much more able than myself to estimate the total income. I feel it would be reasonable to set one third of it as annual payment, starting this year, since it is quite possible that we publish another book of mine in three years.

Now we have already signed a contract which gave you and your lawyer quite some trouble. As long as this is still a private arrangement between ourselves it probably might be subjected to amendments in view of a changed situation. If it has already been presented to the income tax authorities this letter is perhaps completely futile, and anyway I repeat my excuses for my scrupulousness.

Cordially as ever yours,

1951

TO ALFRED A. KNOPF

[Original in English]

Pacific Palisades
June 17, 1951

Dear Alfred:

Thank you so much for your fine birthday gift. I am greatly enjoying the excellent cigars.

Perhaps you read that I managed to stir up a new scandal? J. R. Becher is a German poet of no little importance who was very nice and hospitable to me when I visited Weimar, and delivered an enthusiastic speech in my honor. Why shouldn't I congratulate him to his 60th birthday in spite of the fact that he is a Communist? So did many non- and anti-Communist German writers, including Döblin and even Hermann Hesse. Feuchtwanger too contributed to the little book of honors. Why do people scold only me? I must always be the victim. —But this too will be forgotten soon.

We are planning to go to Europe for some months in July. We shall leave the 4th and expect to be, after a stay in Chicago, in New York the 9th of July only (St. Regis). Will you be there at that time?

As ever yours,
T. M.

TO CHARLOTTE KESTNER[1]

Pacific Palisades
June 18, 1951

My dear Fräulein Kestner:

My thanks for your charming letter of May 25. It was a most touching and curious experience for me to hear from a direct descendant of the heroine of my Goethe novel, moreover, one who even bears her name, and I take pleasure in answering, although with the utmost simplicity, the questions you have asked.

Above all, you can be certain that the anecdote elaborated in my novel, the visit of Hofrätin Kestner in Weimar in 1816, is absolutely historical. Goethe mentions very briefly and dryly in his diary for

---

[1] Charlotte Kestner (b. 1895), the great-great-granddaughter of Charlotte Buff, the heroine of Goethe's *Werther* and Mann's *The Beloved Returns*. A former nurse, she lives in France.

September 25th of that year: "Dining with Ridel and Madame Kestner from Hanover." In actuality the only persons invited to the lunch were Charlotte's relatives, at whose home she arrived on September 22. She stayed with them and not, as I represent it, at the inn Zum Elefanten. Moreover, only this small group was present at the lunch; it was not a dinner for sixteen persons as I have described it. Charlotte Kestner was accompanied not by her elder daughter Charlotte, but by one of the younger ones named Clara. There is a letter from Clara to her brother, who if I am not mistaken was named Georg, describing the stay in Weimar and the visit with Goethe. Apparently this daughter had somewhat the same sobering impression of the great man as her mother. The note that Charlotte addressed to Goethe from the Elephant after her arrival is my own invention; on the other hand, the passage from the letter on page 437[2] is historical; it is taken from a letter to her son, Legation Councillor Kestner.

Many of the details of the novel are drawn from contemporary documents. Thus Frau von Schiller, Friedrich Schiller's widow, mentions in a letter the nodding of the old lady's head. I make use of that psychologically and as a leitmotif. As for the story of the white dress and the bows, of which one is missing, it has only a very slight historical foundation. Frau von Schiller in that same letter dwells on the fact that Lotte had dressed in white like a young woman, but she does not mention the bows; forgivably or unforgivably, I added them.

I must ask you to be content with these sidelights. I have written to you in German because I trust that Lotte Buff's granddaughter will not have forgotten the language.

TO GEORG VOLLMER[1]

Pacific Palisades
June 25, 1951

My dear Herr Vollmer:

My best thanks for your friendly letter of May 26. The curious Symbolum Veritatis[2] accompanying it would surely have been something for Adrian Leverkühn, the hero of my *Faustus* novel.

[2] Of the first English edition (New York: Alfred A. Knopf; 1940); page 391 of the Stockholm *Gesamtausgabe*.
[1] Georg Vollmer (b. 1892?), civil servant. Since 1946 head of the German headquarters of the Rosicrucian Society in Darmstadt.
[2] A chart showing the astrological relationships of Jacob's blessing.

In regard to your inquiry about the meaning of the prelude to *Joseph and His Brothers*, I can say only that this essayistic fantasy is meant to be a sort of overture to the novel, a way of preparing the reader for the journey into the well of the past. Of course, all sorts of motifs from mystical systems of thought (things I picked up here and there) play a part, but the prelude itself does not, as you assume, form part of a larger whole. Nor does it express a definite philosophy except for one passage on page 53,[3] where something is said about the soul involved with nature and the spirit detached from the world, the principle of the past and the principle of the future. It states that each of the two principles purports to be the "water of life," that each accuses the other of dealings with death, and that in this neither is quite wrong, since nature without spirit or spirit without nature cannot truly be called life. The great hope lies in their union—that is, in the genuine penetration of the spirit into the world of the soul and in a hallowing of the one through the other which should bring about a humanity blessed "with blessings from heaven above, blessings of the deep that lieth under."

That is the humanism—call it a philosophy, if you will—which permeates the entire book and, like a principal motif in an opera, is sounded for the first time in the prelude.

TO LION FEUCHTWANGER

Strobl am Wolfgangsee
August 6, 1951

Dear Lion Feuchtwanger:

We both finished your great novel[1] on shipboard—where, incidentally, a number of the passengers were reading it. We could devote ourselves to it entirely, for we have never had so gentle a crossing. The ocean was peaceful as a river throughout the eight days, and although halfway across we picked up an *emergency* appendicitis case from a small American warship for operation (in response to a radio call; a Dutch ship was also there at once; you can't get a doctor that quickly in Los Angeles), we nevertheless arrived in Le Havre early.

Both of us were brimming over from our reading and talked a great deal about it; we also described the book to Erika, who has now taken it over. Goya's *Caprichos*, as you present them, seem to me the best parable

---

[3] Page 48 of the first American edition (New York: Alfred A. Knopf; 1934).
[1] *This is the Hour.*

for the book itself: "all Spain" is in it, the Spain I once quickly and super-
ficially surveyed on a tour—seen here with vastly greater exactitude, of
course, and with all the historical background, studied thoroughly: a
somberly brilliant giant painting. It gives the strongest sense of the
immutable character of the country, its special, half non-European
nature, which comes out, say, in the sinister role still played there by the
Inquisition even in the age of Voltaire—a harrowing and fascinating
chapter. The number of vividly alive personalities against a background
painted at once minutely and in broad strokes (among them so ludi-
crously believable a character, so original in its alloy, as that of Prime
Minister Don Manuel); the life of the great painter himself with its
anxieties and honors; the host of references to the present which you
impress on the reader without the slightest insistence—it is all so excellent, gripping, instructive, rich, and strong—I can only congratulate
you on a work whose success with readers there and here, *hic et ubique*,
seems to me guaranteed.

The trochees that conclude the chapters, frequently rather odd to
look at, strike a note of caricature that suggest Spanish models with which
I am unfamiliar. They are a caprice which I understand very well indeed
—perhaps in contrast to a good many other readers. People—especially the
Germans—think that prose is something beneath verse; but it can also be
something above it, can include verse and playfully produce it out of its
own body. That sort of thing may give the impression of juggling and
overexuberance, but it really springs from a sovereignty that can afford
all kinds of whims. At its height, the novel can do anything.

From here we are going to Salzburg for a few days, then to Gastein—
Haus Gerke. That will be on the 15th. Three weeks later we will be
back in Zurich, where we have taken quarters in the Waldhaus Dolder.

All the best to both of you; we'll be seeing you at the beginning of
October.

TO IRITA VAN DOREN[1]

Bad Gastein
Austria
August 28, 1951

Dear Mrs. Van Doren:

You will testify that you have had to write me twice before I agreed to

[1] Irita Van Doren (b. 1891), literary editor of the *New York Herald Tribune*,
1926–63.

contribute to your Author's Number.[2] There is much too much talk about me, and I am reluctant on my own part to add to it. On the other hand, it is true that many errors about me as a writer and a man circulate in both Europe and America, some of them undeservedly creditable, others undeservedly painful to me. Perhaps, then, I should not lose the opportunity to take up a few of these and in all sincerity set matters right.

For example, I sometimes notice with embarrassment, that on the basis of my books people regard me as a virtually universal mind—a man of encyclopedic knowledge. What an illusion! In reality I am, for a (forgive the phrase) world-famous writer, almost inconceivably ill-educated. In school I learned nothing but reading and writing, the multiplication table, and a little Latin. I resisted everything else with dull obstinacy and was considered a hopeless lazybones. This was premature, for later on I did develop into a hard worker when it became necessary to supply the scholarly foundation for a work of fiction, that is, to collect information in order to play literary games with it—or strictly speaking, to scandalously misuse it. Thus I became in turn an expert in medicine and biology, a firm Orientalist, Egyptologist, mythologist and historian of religions, a specialist in medieval culture and poetry, and so on. But the worst of it is that as soon as I finish the book for whose sake I run up such expenditures of scholarship, I forget with incredible speed everything I have learned and go about with an empty head, in wretched awareness of my total ignorance. It is therefore easy to imagine the bitter laughter with which my conscience responds to the eulogies on my learning.

On the other hand, I do not think I deserve certain opprobrious and vexing characterizations frequently applied to my manner of writing and my whole way of thinking, especially in my new—or no longer so new—homeland, America. I have seen epithets like "Olympian," "pompous," "ponderous," and things of that sort used to describe my writing, and I could not believe my eyes—especially when it was suggested in addition that I am a conceited man who majestically takes the praise and honors of the world as his due, and even makes a point of going out after such honors.

How false all that is! Just as false as the notion of my vast learning. My friends know that I have not a trace of Olympian airs, that all

---

[2] This letter was published, with some omissions and in a different translation, in the *New York Herald Tribune Book Review* for October 7, 1951, along with statements by other writers, under the general heading: "Some of the Authors of 1951, Speaking for Themselves."

solemnity, affectation, exaltation, all prophetic and arrogant pretensions are wholly alien to my nature and my taste—and that "ponderous" is an adjective which, if it were apt, would signify the failure of all my efforts. My ambition is to make the difficult easy; my ideal is clarity. And if I write long sentences, which the German language in any case inclines to, I make a point of trying (and successfully, I think) to preserve complete lucidity and fluency. Once, at the beginning of the Joseph stories, I wrote purely for fun a sentence that goes on for one and a half printed pages. The translators, of course, broke it up into many short sentences. But let anyone who knows German read that sentence aloud and see whether he loses the thread even once. It is neither *pompous* nor *ponderous*; it is funny, and serves as an example of a self-mockery which is not altogether foreign to my writings—and is probably the reason I am so often misread.

This mockery is closely related to a parody, not cynical but affectionate, of tradition. Such may well be the attitude of a writer who in an age of endings and transitions finds himself at once playing the part of a straggler, consummating and completing the past, and the part of an innovator undermining and dissolving it. It is the role and situation of the ironic conservative. I have ascribed an entire novel, *Doctor Faustus*, to the pen of a pious humanist and upright Gymnasium teacher, and a Swiss critic[3] could say of this book: "Contact with so much as a single page of this work estranges us from all the traditions of the German novel. . . ." There follow some exaggerations about the means by which that is done; my only objection, aside from the exaggeration, would be that the gloom of the book hindered the critic from mentioning as one of those means, and the principal one, its humor.

The fact is that I consider myself primarily a humorist—and this kind of self-image is incompatible with Olympianism or pompousness. Humor, I am inclined to think, is an expression of amiability and comradeship toward those with whom we share this planet—in short, of fellow feeling, of an intention to do good to men, to teach them an appreciation of charm and to spread liberating merriment among them. Incidentally, it is more closely akin to modesty than to arrogance and conceit, and if modesty in praising itself did not cease to be modesty, I would call myself a modest person. I regard my life work as the result of an extremely personal and very precarious coming to terms with art. It is far from exemplary, and when I hear myself being called the "fore-

[3] Eduard Korrodi: "Thomas Manns 'Doktor Faustus'," *Neue Zürcher Zeitung* (October 22, 1947).

most novelist of the age" I want to hide my head. Nonsense! I am no such thing; Joseph Conrad was, as people ought to know. I could never have written *Nostromo*, nor the magnificent *Lord Jim*; and if he in turn could not have written *The Magic Mountain* or *Doctor Faustus*, the account balances out very much in his favor. I have often been stupidly vilified, but far more often immoderately acclaimed; and please believe that I have never encouraged such homage. Never in my life have I lifted a finger to "advance my cause," to invite honors, or to promote the publication of books concerning me.

I live a rather withdrawn life, see few people except when I am traveling, and concern myself with nothing but my tasks as they come along, each growing out of the last. While I am working I do not think of the public and of success, and if success comes it is a fortuitous event that falls upon me out of the clouds. Or rather, I myself fall out of the clouds and down to earth with a thud, for I have never yet finished a book without being convinced of its unreadability. Individually, in fact, they often are unreadable, and it is not this or that book which has produced the success, but the whole. A long life filled with work has gradually made a certain impression.

But I have never been conscious of my "position" in the world. My imagination fails me at this point, and I go on as if no one were concerned about me, although I ought to know that here and there people are lying in wait for me to expose my faults so that they can raise a hue and cry about them. I lack any feeling for personal politics—a deficiency which I have scant hope of mending at this late date.

There, set down in haste, you have my confession. I am afraid it violates your space requirements, and with the ocean to cross, will probably arrive too late for your Author's Number anyhow. I do not know whether I would say "Too bad," about that, or "Just as well" and "So much the better."

TO KENNETH OLIVER

[*Original in English*]

Pacific Palisades
October 12, 1951

Dear Professor Oliver:

I am ashamed for thanking you only today for your letter of July 12th. It reached me in Europe, from where I have just returned, but at the time I was unable to answer it due to frequent changes of residence and a mineral-water cure which I took at Bad Gastein, Austria.

Now that I am back, the waters of my European and American correspondence reach up to my chin, and to reply to each individual letter properly is almost impossible. Let me say only this:

You will find scattered references to what I have called the new, or third, humanism in my essays. What I had in mind was a new approach, born of suffering, to the idea of man, to the mystery of this species, at home in two worlds, the spiritual and the natural, for whom, because of this, life is much more difficult than for any other creature. It is the actual experience of this mysterious difficulty which might lead to a new feeling of sympathy with and awe of human existence, a sympathy which might bridge the seemingly unbridgeable gulf of contrast and hostility mentioned in your letter. I cannot and will not venture into the political realm now. But I am convinced that peace is the great commandment of the world hour, and that another war would destroy all hopes one might have for humanity for an incalculable period of time. If I have occasionally participated in the so-called peace propaganda, I did so not out of fondness for Russian totalitarianism from which I have recently explicitly distanced myself in a lecture entitled "The Days of My Life." That I could have been accused of communistic leanings can only be explained by the understandable nervousness prevalent in this country today, which is largely the product of a propaganda that is not always carried out with a sufficient sense of responsibility. When I speak for peace, I do not speak for Russia and Stalinism but for humanity, whose destiny has remained close to my heart up to the late years of my life.

Please be content with these few and insufficient words, and let me thank you most warmly for attaching importance to my thoughts and my endeavors.

TO HERMANN HESSE

Pacific Palisades
October 14, 1951

Dear Herr Hesse:

What splendid, truly engaging reading your *Letters* are! As soon as we were back I picked the book out from the fifty others that have accumulated here, and in the past several days have spent my reading hours, after dinner and evenings, almost exclusively with it. It is remarkable how the book holds me. I say to myself: "Now hurry up and skip a few. Here are all these other books that you're at least mildly curious about." But nonetheless I go on reading, letter after letter, until the last. It is all so agreeable—that touching mixture of reserve and warm responsiveness, as pure in language as in thought (but I suppose they are the same), full of a gentle and yet virile, consistent wisdom which is belief within unbelief, trust within skeptical despair. At bottom the whole of the human situation is in this book, as a historical and intellectual phenomenon. Certainly it is there in the very wise comments to Fiedler about the Church and the august intellectual rank, but historical sterility, of pure religiousness. And it is particularly refreshing when every so often your patience snaps and you speak plainly—about political matters, in which (to my reassurance and reinforcement) we entirely agree, or, say, when you refuse, so stoutly and so merrily, to let yourself be played off against me. Do believe, if the reverse should ever happen (but I don't suppose there is much danger), I would also give the donkeys a piece of my mind. I am quite proud that a goodly number of these charming documents of a personality are addressed to me—more than I imagined. I have also reread in this context your handsome congratulations for my 75th birthday, and can only return your hope and wish: Stay among us for a long time to come, dear Hermann Hesse. To all higher spirits you are a support and a beacon, and for me our friendly solidarity is a constant comfort and encouragement.—

We had a pleasant, smooth flight with Swissair from Zurich-Kloten to New York. The plane lands only twice, in Ireland and in Newfoundland, and the eight night hours in between these two stops constitute the actual trip. We slept through it very well in our "excellent reclining seats." In Chicago (in damp heat; the Middle West is a climatic horror) we stayed for three days with Medi, whose adventurous spouse happened to be in Italy, before undertaking the 36-hour journey to our coast. Chicago has an excellent museum of natural history which we visited not just once, but at my insistence a second time. It displays most vividly the beginnings of organic life—in the sea, when the earth was still waste and void—the entire animal kingdom, and the appearance and life of early man (reconstructed in sculptures based on skeletal finds). The group of Neanderthal men (the terminus of one line of evolution) in their cave is something I shall never forget, as well as the earliest artists, who are shown devotedly crouching down to paint pictures of animals on the cave walls, probably for magical purposes. I was utterly fascinated.

One feels a curious stab of warmth and sympathy at the sight of those faces.

Last night Erika also came back, via Canada. That is good.

With cordial good wishes to you and Ninon,

TO JENÖ TAMÁS GÖMÖRI

Pacific Palisades
November 15, 1951

Dear Herr Gömöri:

Many thanks for your letter. I was delighted to hear from you again, and of course the enclosed poem[1] was especially interesting to me. How eloquently it expresses the impossibility of translating any literary creation from the language in which it is begotten, out of which it is born, into another language! It is rather widely acknowledged that poetry cannot really be translated. But few know that the same holds true for all superior prose, that it is denatured, its rhythm is shattered, all its finer nuances fall by the wayside. Often, in fact, its innermost intentions, its spiritual posture and intellectual aims, are distorted beyond recognition, to the point of total misunderstanding, no matter how hard the translator tries for faithful reproduction. Few, I say, know this—the more sensitive translators are themselves most likely to be aware of it. A good many of them have told me their woes. I remember very well, for example, that my American translator and friend, Helen Lowe-Porter, during her work on the English version of *Lotte in Weimar* said to me with a sigh: "*I am committing a murder.*"

Oddly enough, badly written books are best suited for translation and quite often gain considerably by it. On the other hand, among the best there are a few extraordinarily lucky strokes, such as the German Shakespeare translation and Tieck's German version of *Don Quixote*— amazing instances of great works of literature being really incorporated into the cultural stock of another nation. And if I may descend to my own case once again, every Frenchman tells me that the late Maurice Betz's transmutation of *Zauberberg* into *Montagne magique* is another such lucky stroke. That is my feeling too when I leaf through the translation. It is a real re-creation of my novel in different linguistic material; it has become a French book—and alas, what a German book it still is!

[1] A German translation of a Hungarian poem commenting on the impossibility of translating even the opening line of Mann's short story, "Little Herr Friedemann."

Yet who would wish to discourage the peoples of the world from translating, merely because it is *fundamentally* impossible? The penchant of the Germans for things foreign, and their craving to acquaint themselves with foreign literature insofar as they are able, is not their worst trait. They have always been the most zealous of translators, and there were periods in which they significantly raised the level of their own culture by translation. The German poets of the Middle Ages—Wolfram, Gottfried, Hartmann—actually did little more than translate from the French. And let us not forget that important modern writers of other countries—Ibsen, Strindberg, Hamsun, even G. B. Shaw—attained world fame via Germany, as a consequence of the German ardor for translation.

I do not know a word of Russian, and the German translations in which as a young man I read the great Russian writers of the nineteenth century were very feeble. Nevertheless, I consider this reading among my greatest cultural experiences. If a book has substance, I do assure you, even in a bad translation a good deal remains. And very few people are so familiar with a foreign language that they can grasp every nuance of the original the way the native-born do. All in all, I am inclined to think that you lose less by reading a work in the original than by reading it in your own language, but not *much* less, if the translation is decent.

There now, I have after all written a kind of defense for translation. But do not take it to mean that I am not completely in agreement with the laments and the standards expressed in your poem.

TO HENRY HATFIELD

Pacific Palisades
November 19, 1951

Dear Dr. Hatfield:

Your "realistic" essay[1] is first-rate. I read it as soon as it came and thoroughly enjoyed it. Your discussions of *Simplicissimus* and the picaresque novel particularly fascinated me—for personal reasons, since picaresque jests happen to be occupying me once again.

In the neo-Russian of Marxist criticism, "realistic" means, of course, only that which is "pertinent to society." But on those terms what good art wouldn't be realistic? In the final analysis accuracy, "authenticity," the striking resemblance to real life, is what always gives us pleasure in

---

[1] "Realism in the German Novel," *Comparative Literature*, Vol. III (1951).

art, in the rendering of psychological as well as objective states. As a young man in Munich I frequently used to see a great comedian of the old type, of the so-called "ideal school": Ernst *von* Possart. But what humor he would wring from extremely elocutionary diction, especially in tragedy, when he would say, for example: "Such wise children seldom live long."[2] Or: "So wicked a man cannot be; it is impossible."[3] —We may stylize and symbolize as much as we like—without realism it doesn't do. Realism is the backbone; it gives a work the ring of truth. What else have I done in *Joseph* and *The Holy Sinner* if not real-ize? The "earth milk" on the barren stone is only an old mythologem dating back to Epicurus and still earlier. But in the story it plays a realizing, realistic part.

Thanks and regards.

TO PAUL AMANN

Pacific Palisades
December 23, 1951

Dear Dr. Amann:

A thousand thanks for your richly chatty letter and for the Riemer study. I have not the slightest objection to make against anything in it, nor to the quotations from the letter, although about all that emerges from them is that I did not really know the answer myself. The essay is decidedly interesting, and if *Modern Language* had not published several things on me quite recently, I would have no doubt of its being accepted there. In any case it is a handsome comparison of history and poesy (tolerant toward the latter), and ought to appear in print.

I have written all sorts of additions to the Krull memoirs, but I am always in peril of falling into a "Faustian" sprawl and losing control of the form. Thus I bring the hero, who is an amorist, into contact with the idea of Being itself, which perhaps is only an episode between Nothingness and Nothingness—as life on earth is only an incident with beginning and end, since the inhabitability of a planet is limited. At the same time all things pass imperceptibly into one another: Man into the animal realm, the latter into the vegetable realm, organic into inorganic being, the material into the immaterial, into scarcely-yet-being and into non-

[2] From Shakespeare's *Richard III*, Act III, Scene 2, as Possart spoke the words. Actual wording: "So wise so young, they say, do ne'er live long."
[3] From Shakespeare's *Othello* in Possart's version. Actual wording: "Fie, there is no such man; it is impossible."

being, without space and time. Primal creation: How and when did the first vibration of being (electromagnetic or whatever) appear in the void? This is the true primal creation, the first newness. The second is that addition to the inorganic which we call life—something added without any addition of matter. A third addition in the realm of the organic and animal is the human element. Transition is conserved, something indefinable comes in, as when the turning point to "life" was reached. Love, understood as a sensual stirring in the face of the transitory quality of Being—not only of life, not only of man. And Being itself, then, perhaps an evocation by love out of the void? —But all this must strike you as incomprehensible gibberish. A small grandson of mine said as he came out of church: "When you start to think about God, you get combustion of the brain." A new phrase, and not a bad one.

I beg your pardon and wish you very happy holidays.[1]

[1] Translation (by Richard and Clara Winston) copyright 1960 by Wesleyan University Press. Reprinted by permission.

1952

━━━━━━━━ • ━━━━━━━━

TO ERNST BERTRAM

Pacific Palisades
January 16, 1952

Dear Ernst Bertram:

Thank you for the fine gift of your book.[1] I can well understand that you do not wish to send these scenes, epigrams, and songs, irradiated as they are with all that is highest and noblest, out into a world which truly is becoming more and more a great wasteland. It is fitting that instead you entrust them in a private printing to a few whom you believe will know how to receive them. I am happy that you count me among those few.

Your work has many overtones of farewell—as indeed, much of contemporary writing, the best and finest of it, often seems to me like a hasty recollection, a summoning up and recapitulating of the Occidental mythos once more—before the night falls, a long night, perhaps, and a deep oblivion.

Well, it is said: *"Ein ewig Auferstehn sei ihm die Menschenbrust."*[2]

TO A. M. FREY

Pacific Palisades
January 19, 1952

Dear Herr Frey:

Thank you for your two letters. It moves me that *The Story of a Novel* has been so much on your mind. Originally I felt impelled to write it only by the moral obligation to give Dr. Adorno *credit*, to use the Ameri-

---

[1] *Die Fenster von Chartres* (privately printed; 1951). The dedication was: "With thoughts of Thomas Mann. Ernst Bertram 1951."
[2] "May he be ever resurrected in the hearts of men."

can phrase, for what I brazenly took from him and what he gave me in collaborating on the musical aspects of *Faustus*. An act of loyalty. But then, of course, the thing became a sample of what an autobiography built around each book of mine might be. I tried something similar with the *Joseph* opus, although hardly going into such detail about the surrounding outward circumstances. It would probably be difficult to reconstruct my whole life around the works, though this is the pattern of *The Story of a Novel*. But the book may well stand as *pars pro toto*, for in essentials and *mutatis mutandis*, each of the others developed pretty much along the lines described here.

On the whole I feel great timidity about directly autobiographical writing, which seems to me the most difficult kind of all, an almost impossible task from the point of view of literary tact. I am by no means sure that I have not offended against that tact more than once in *The Story of a Novel*. I have not had the little book translated into English[1] in part because of its only too correct predictions about the evolution of post-Rooseveltian America, but in part simply from the feeling that confidences are unbecoming to the lonely. We poor Germans! We are fundamentally lonely, even when we are "famous." No one really likes us, and except for a few specialists in German literature no one in other cultures feels like bothering about us. [. . .] Of course it is only natural that those who are native to the Anglo-Saxon culture and language should be concerned with their own realm and with one another, and should be irritated at also being expected to pay attention to someone who has suddenly descended from nowhere with his seemingly demanding, although in reality very timid, *Germanic approach*. Young Toynbee,[2] a son of the philosopher of history, recently wrote a clever little article about me somewhere: "The Lonely World Citizen,"[3] in which he derived my isolation directly from my Germanism. He said very amusingly that if an English critic were asked to name the ten most prominent figures in contemporary literature, he would suggest four Englishmen, three Americans, and three Frenchmen. If he were then reminded of me, he would snap his fingers and exclaim: "Oh yes, a place has to be found for him too." Toynbee also said very neatly that my novels are very

---

[1] The English translation was published posthumously (New York: Alfred A. Knopf; 1961).

[2] Philip Toynbee (b. 1916), writer, son of the historian Arnold J. Toynbee (b. 1889). Critic and editor on *The Observer*. Author of *The Savage Days* (1937), *The Barricades* (1943), *The Garden in the Sun* (1953), *The Fearful Choice* (1958), among others.

[3] "Thomas Mann: The Isolated World Citizen," *The Observer*, London, Observer Foreign News Service, No. 5589 (1951).

different from one another, but that taken all together they bear no similarity to any other novels being written today.

A German—a world citizen—then again, as a world citizen extremely German—and as a German again peculiar—there one stands, read in denaturing translations which obliterate whatever charm the original has—a great, unloved name. I don't know whether I may add "unloved because unknown." Everything German is unspeakably unpopular, that is clear, and it is a great *malheur* to be a German writer, an insuperable handicap. What a privilege to be born into English or French culture. How much easier a life! To be German makes for timorousness. It does not encourage one to attempt autobiographical confidences.

You too—if you wrote in English or French, how much better off you would be. Your stories would not turn sour on you, and something like the *Verteufeltes Theater*[4] would not make the rounds of the publishers for years had your name been Fry instead of Frey. Even Goethe says: "A German writer—a German martyr"—even he.

It would certainly make an intriguing study to interpret "the birth of Venus" in cosmological rather than mythological terms. I am very fond of such reading. Jeans[5] at one time fascinated me. Recently a few highly interesting books of this kind have been published here: *The Universe and Dr. Einstein* by Lincoln Barnett,[6] and *Is Another World Watching?* by Gerald Heard.[7] The former is strictly scientific, the second a piece of scientific humbug, but very entertaining. It takes up the riddle of the *"flying saucers"* and pretends to explain it along strictly scientific lines: The idea is that our irresponsible fumbling with atomic forces has aroused concern among the inhabitants of Mars (insectlike in structure and very advanced), so that they wish to observe us from those vehicles that have been so frequently sighted and see how close we are to unleashing cosmic disaster.

Enough for today.

·   ·   ·

[4] A novel by Frey, published at last in 1957.
[5] Sir James Hopwood Jeans (1877–1946), English physicist, astronomer, and writer. From 1912–46 professor of astronomy at the Royal Institution. Among his books: *The Universe around Us* (1929), *The Mysterious Universe* (1930), *Through Space and Time* (1934), *Physics and Philosophy* (1942), *The Growth of Physical Science* (1947).
[6] Lincoln Barnett (b. 1909), writer. Among his books: *The World We Live in* (1955) and *The Treasure of Our Tongue* (1964). *The Universe and Dr. Einstein* was published with a foreword by Albert Einstein in 1948.
[7] Gerald Heard (b. 1889), English writer. His mystic philosophy strongly influenced Aldous Huxley and others. Among his books: *The Ascent of Humanity* (1929), *The Human Venture* (1955), *The Five Ages of Man* (1963). Likewise the author of many detective stories, such as *A Taste for Honey* (1941).

P.S. One of these days when we are in Zurich I must read you an assortment of oddities from *Krull*.

TO CAROLINE NEWTON

Pacific Palisades
April 15, 1952

Dear Caroline:

How your essay delighted me! My warm thanks. It is unpretentious and full of real sympathy, such as the professional critics, of course, cannot call up. For the rest, you are right: "A hundred years will tell the tale." I shall lay my head to rest without having any notion of what I have been worth—and shall be worth. Perhaps I have received too many honors in my lifetime and have already squandered my reward. But then too, there has also been plenty of spiteful disparagement, which may mollify Fate. If I have aimed at making people laugh (as I also do in *The Holy Sinner*), that may likewise be connected with the need to placate. My "humor" is really skepticism toward myself. "Thou comest in such a questionable shape . . ."

I did not choose the picture I am sending you because I think it a particularly good one, but because our late Niko, your gift, figures in it. We shall never see his like again.

The changes in our personal life that the newspapers have prematurely reported are still a while away. The likelihood is that this year, just as in the past few years, we shall go to Gastein and Switzerland and be back in the autumn.

All good wishes for your health.

TO HERMANN WEIGAND

Pacific Palisades
April 29, 1952

My dear Professor Weigand:

I most certainly have read your "essay"—and a very successful essay it is. You rightly assume that I was curious about it, and I am especially grateful to you for not having made me wait for the offprints. That island, *The Holy Sinner*, already lies far back along the stream, but it was indeed a most entertaining and unusual sojourn I had there, and to hear a person like you discuss it so completely and painstakingly has been very exciting. Really, you have done great honor to this somewhat over-exuberant experiment of my old age, even by the length of your study—so much honor that I am in danger of not taking your warnings and misgivings to heart. This danger, I must admit, is increased by a certain frivolous confidence I have in my "feeling for language," which I do not really think is *slipping*, and by the thought that the linguistic escapades of *The Holy Sinner* constitute something quite unique and unrepeatable, a stylistic amusement more or less justified by the fluidity of language at the time in which the novel is cast. It is taking too pessimistic a view to assume that I am on the downhill path, that the manner of the writing is unfortunately the outcome of exile. Never again will I *bosten* and *swaggern*,[1] you can be sure of that, and I am not hopelessly attached to the coinage *ausfigurieren* [to figure out]. Several times, incidentally, you see symptoms of depravity where there are none. *Jemandem die kalte Schulter zeigen* [to show somebody the cold shoulder] is excellent German, and Goethe always or almost always uses *überall* [everywhere] in the sense of *überhaupt* [on the whole, altogether]. It is not English, only rather old-fashioned German; and *aufbringen* [to bring up] a child has a somewhat similar overtone. It seems to me that Goethe could have used it in all innocence for *aufziehen* or *auferziehen* [rear, raise]—if he did not actually do so.

I also want to say this: I had not the slightest notion that *The Holy Sinner* might represent the fulfillment of Adrian Leverkühn's dreams of an art of the future liberated from isolation. I am all too aware that I am not the man for such fulfillments. This late form of a legend is "late" in every sense, as late as I am myself. That is no compelling argument against it—and me. "And yet how much the one word twilight says," Hofmannsthal tells us. Still, it is significant that the little book cannot be published in the "East"—in the Russian Zone of Germany, in Czechoslovakia, Hungary—because it is "alien to the people."

I used the passage from the letter of Bishop Paulinus about ancient St. Peter's because I was delighted with its magnificent Latin sentence structure, which seemed to me well suited to the occasion. My Roman gentlemen also Latinize occasionally in their speech.

But the idea that the highly intellectual Faltonia (my adjective *starkgeistig* is formed on *esprit fort*: how un-German!) bears any resemblance to "Mrs. Mann," and that the tone between her and Probus has the slightest similarity to that between us, is a complete misunderstanding. My good wife, although acute and quick-witted, is anything but a

---

[1] Anglo-German verbs constructed from *boast* and *swagger*.

bluestocking. She is a housewife through and through, and her literary activity is limited to writing letters to children and grandchildren.

Do you really think that Hartmann treated the sinful love scene between the children so much more discreetly than I? He is fairly explicit about the "wrestling," you know, and there are other places where I had considerably more filling-in to do than here. I added the killing of the fine dog partly to give the scene a bloody and frightening quality, and partly so that the narrator could comment that this act was worse than all the rest. Although he despises Nature because she allows such physical goings-on, he does not exaggerate the importance of sex. Perhaps he has a dim notion that incest is really a taboo arising out of privilege. It was permitted to gods and kings and forbidden only to the common folk. Isis and Osiris were sister and brother, and people tend to forget that Hera and Zeus were also. All of mythology teems with marital unions of brothers and sisters, sons and mothers. And such minglings extend from the Near East down to the Christian mystery of the Mother of God. Not for nothing does Sibylla pray: "Thou of the Highest child, mother and bride."—

Are doctors disqualified as readers of *The Magic Mountain*, and Egyptologists as readers of *Joseph*? Why should they be? I have always had some of my best readers among medical men—*The Magic Mountain* actually influenced lung therapy—and musicians. Moreover, I know more than one Orientalist who was delighted with the *Joseph* on altogether professional grounds. For *The Holy Sinner* I delved in a good many dictionaries, for my own entertainment traced every word I wrote back to its roots, and in so doing had in mind that I was extending a friendly invitation to fun-loving philologists—you yourself very much included. And with what enthusiasm you have accepted this invitation and handed it on with your recommendation to the younger generation!

Let me say a word here about my reputation of being a *"second Leonardo"* and my dazzling pseudo universality, which in reality is everywhere only *skin-deep*. Of course you are right. Nowadays real universality is not possible, of course, and in my case what actually exists is a kind of brilliant ignorance. Perhaps I am too good at display, the "show window," at the *manipulation of esoteric material.* Perhaps I have always acquired knowledge solely for a purpose, for the moment, and in order to play with it. And yet I should not like to see the—*sit venia verbo*— Faustian expansiveness, which distinguishes my books from other contemporary works, represented entirely as mere swindle. At least I try to give it authenticity, and my "dabbling" with various branches of knowledge has always had a peculiar intensity of empathy which has allowed me to achieve a creative familiarity with new fields that astonished the specialists. In the course of a long life I have truly dwelt under many roofs, have learned a good deal, parasitized a good deal, and am fairly justified in saying that nothing human is alien to me. Even in these times it is possible for a man to construct out of his life and work a culture, a small cosmos, in which everything is interrelated, which despite all diversity forms a complete personal whole, and which stands more or less on an equal footing with the great life-syntheses of earlier ages. I think that this "gift of unusual concentration,"[2] this intense organization of my life, has made more impression upon people than the display of encyclopedic knowledge.

But enough! The charm of your criticism lies precisely in your ability to arouse interest by unmasking. It is a kind of enlightenment that does not disillusion. And after all, keeping a close check on art and the work of an artist can only strike me as a congenial and familiar approach. Nietzsche once called the artist an intolerably sensual and vain monkey. *Right he is.*

You couldn't possibly discover all the sources from which I "dug up" material. Aside from Gregorovius, there was also the book by a Catholic writer from Munich named Joseph Bernhard, *Der Vatikan*, from which came several specimens of sagacious papal decisions (of Leo I, I think) that I transferred to my Gregorius. Old English names are taken from an illustrated work in many volumes, the *Handbuch der Kunstwissenschaft*, a project initiated by the late Professor Fritz Burger, edited by Dr. A. E. Brinckmann, Potsdam, Akademische Verlagsanstalt. That is, I used the volume on early English and Irish art. Other important books were *Kleinere deutsche Gedichte des XI. und XII. Jahrhunderts*, edited by Albert Waag, Halle an der Saale, Verlag Max Niemeyer, 1916, in which the *Vorauer Sündenklage* and the *Arnsteiner Marienlied* may be found. These, along with Hartmann, were my principal Middle High German reading and sources for words. The *ubele wuoftal* and the *wurmgarten*, for example, come from there. I took over the following almost literally:

> *Ein teil dû mirs sculdig bist*
> *daz dû mir helvest umbe got:*
> *wande dû den êwigen lop*
> *durch die sundaere imphienge*
> *unde ne wêre nie niemen*

[2] A leitmotif in *The Holy Sinner*; H. T. Lowe-Porter translates the phrase "gift of pulling himself together."

mit sunden bevangen,
sôwaeriz unergangen
daz got mit dir getân hat[3]

In the original, the prayer is being offered by a man, so I rewrote it as follows:

Ein Teil du mir's schuldig bist
Sag ich mit Frauenlist, etc.[4]

[. . .] You see, I am already making it easier for the young philologist you encouraged to attack these problems.

I should also mention a rather trivial little book, bought secondhand: *Deutsches Leben im 12. und 13. Jahrhundert. Realkommentar zu den Volks- und Kunstepen und zum Minnesang,* by J. Dieffenbacher (Leipzig: Göschen'sche; 1907). It supplied all sorts of material on hunting, falconry, riding, tournaments, marriage, and so on. Among my notes there is a whole list of old German names for dogs, from which I picked *Hanegiff.* I no longer remember where I got the names. In short, there was throughout a curious melange of frivolity (mixing up different centuries) and pedantic care. I suppose that was part of the underlying idea of this singular opusculum.—

One word more about *Der Grüne Heinrich*[5] as a gap in my education. I was not really unfamiliar with the book when I read it in the hospital "for the first time." I meant, for the first time with awareness, pleasure, and the admiration which in my youth I had for Tolstoy, Turgenev, Thackeray, Flaubert, the Goncourts, and Keller's own stories, such as *Die Leute von Seldwyla.* The place of *Der Grüne Heinrich* was more or less occupied by *Wilhelm Meister,* in somewhat the way as the place of Stefan George was occupied by Platen. I didn't need it, or at any rate thought I didn't, and was surprised by the pleasure that my belated close reading gave me from the first word to the last. I read the second version edited in 1926, from the posthumous manuscripts by Jonas Fränkel and

---

[3] One thing you owe to me,
That you help me with God.
Since you have received eternal praise
Because of sinners
And if no one had ever
Been enmeshed in sins,
Then never would have happened
What God has done with you.
(Compare *The Holy Sinner,* page 201.)

[4] One thing you owe to me
I say with woman's guile.

[5] See *The Story of a Novel,* p. 183 f.

published by Eugen Rentsch in Zurich, but was not under the illusion that the novel had first appeared in this form in 1926. The first version (Brunswick, 1854) has been included in this same collection of Keller's works, and stands in my library right beside the volume containing the final version. Oddly enough, the later parts of the story are no longer told in the first person, but in the third. A curious case.

With sincere gratitude,

P.S. In my letter to Dr. Auerbach[6] the phrase should read: *"die Ernährung des Büssers"* rather than *"die Erwöhnung des Büssens."*

In your text, where you quote the verse about the prince *nommé* Grimald, the exclamatory *"Ahí*, war das *ein Sündenpaar!"* (instead of *"das war"*) would be more correct.

TO FREDERICK ROSENTHAL

Pacific Palisades
May 5, 1952

Dear Doctor:

I must appeal to you once more for medical information, as I did when I was working on *Faustus.*

The question is one of cancer of the uterus. A woman, a society lady, about fifty years old, with whom it has already "ceased to be after the manner of women," falls passionately in love with her son's young tutor. In this psychic state, which contraverts her physiological state, there occurs a bleeding months after the onset of menopause (there might also be several at the usual intervals). The fact delights her inordinately. It also makes her behavior toward the young man much bolder, since she takes the matter as a kind of miracle of love, a reanimation of her physical femininity as a consequence of psychic forces, of emotion. Instead it turns out that the bleeding derives from an advanced cancer of the uterus and that the supposed new springtime is a cruel deception of nature, namely death.

The story really happened. Whether an operation was attempted or whether it was too late for one, I don't know. In any case, the woman died. —At what stage of the development of cancer (which as is well

---

[6] Erich Auerbach (1892–1957), professor of Romance languages in Marburg, 1929–35. Taught at the University of Istanbul, 1936–47; then at Yale University from 1950 until his death. Author of *Mimesis* (1946) and many other books.

known takes place imperceptibly in the uterus, without pain signals) is it likely that such a bleeding would occur which could be mistaken for renewed menstruation? Probably in an extremely advanced stage, wouldn't it be? What does the operation involve, if one is undertaken? Removal of the entire uterus? And if the affected organ is removed, wouldn't the patient live? By what signs does the physician recognize— often too late—the presence of cancer of the uterus? Is the bleeding after cessation of the sexual functions an unmistakable sign of cancer—and at the same time of the hopelessly advanced stage of the disease? How long does it take for a carcinoma to develop from the initial stages to the point where it is no longer operable? The uterus itself is insensitive; but wouldn't the presence of cancer manifest itself, or at least arouse suspicion, by a change in general health or physical decline? Why is it so often recognized too late?

Some purely physiological questions: What happens to menstruation during the climacteric up to the final termination of fertility? Does it become gradually irregular in amount until it ceases entirely?

I do hope that answering this barrage of questions will not give you too much trouble. Choose a time for it that is good for nothing else![1]

TO ERICH VON KAHLER

Pacific Palisades
June 5, 1952

Dear, good friend Erich:

Your book[1] has given me such pleasure, I have read so deeply in it, and now I can thank you for it only with impoverished, tired words. For some time I haven't been feeling very well (without, incidentally, having any specific reason), and at the same time I am always, as Luther so expressively puts it in a letter (I like to quote the phrase, which certainly applies to you toc) "overladen, overcrowded, overwhelmed by affairs." I am longing for Gastein, and our departure, first for Switzerland, is really near. We are flying to Chicago on the 24th. There we shall stay for a few days, and from the afternoon of the 26th to the 29th, when we fly on to Europe, we shall be in New York, Hotel St. Regis. There we do hope to see you this time, so that I can clasp your hand for the gift of your book—unless you yourself precede us to Europe. I have the impression

[1] Dr. Rosenthal supplied the requested information, which was eventually incorporated into Mann's short novel, *The Black Swan.*
[1] *Die Verantwortung des Geistes.* Collected essays (1952).

that you had this in mind. Just as well; then we shall meet somewhere over there.

Your book—I simply love its voice, that anguished vibrato which testifies to the distress of heart and mind out of which it was all written, the distress we all share. It testifies also to the compassionate concern of a man whose wisdom might easily have made him scornful and cold, but who continues to concern himself with the fate of poor, poor, stupid, stupid humanity. I was again deeply moved by the magnificent *Faustus* study,[2] profoundly stirred by the birthday article on the "Responsibility of the Intellectuals." But everything else is on the same high level, every stirring and, one would imagine, irresistible plea to take thought. Let him listen who has ears to hear! In any case I feel that the existence of such books—the fact that at least they are written—somewhat saves the honor of humanity, if "man" as an experiment should prove to be a mistake refuting the whole of Creation.

See you soon!

TO AGNES E. MEYER

Pacific Palisades
June 20, 1952

Dear Agnes:

What is involved is the centuries-old Accademia dei Lincei in Rome. Thanks to a generous patron, it has established international prizes for art and literature, which are being given out this year, and I am the first recipient of the major International Literature Prize (the money value is five million lire—about $8,000).

Two members of the Academy who are especially well disposed toward my work—Professors Bianchi Bandinelli[1] (Siena) and Luigi Russo[2] (Pisa)—nominated me for the prize, and their proposal was unanimously adopted at the session of June 7 held in Rome. The official citation, written by Professor Francesco Flora[3] (Milan), states that the

---

[2] "The Secularization of The Devil."

[1] Ranuccio Bianchi Bandinelli (b. 1900), professor of archaeology. Direttore Generale delle *Antichità e belle Arti*. Prolific writer on Etruscan, Roman, and Greek art.

[2] Luigi Russo (1889–1961), historian of literature; professor of Italian literature in Florence, rector of Pisa University, director of the famous Scuola normale superiore of Pisa.

[3] Francesco Flora (1892–1961), professor of Italian literature at the University of Bologna. Prolific writer on literary history, noted for his articles on various trends in contemporary literature such as Futurism, Hermeticism, etc. Author, among other books, of *Storia della letteratura italiana* (1940–2; 1947), *Scrittori italiani contemporanei* (1952).

prize is intended to honor not only my "mighty" literary work, but especially "the real example of a living humanism which transcends the divisions of our times and thus provides guidance to all creative spirits."

This judgment is truly moving, given the character and work of the Academy, for its humanistic interests are largely philological, historical, and archaeological.

Yours ever,

TO HANS REISIGER

Zurich
November 1, 1952

Splendid Reisi:

I am already finished with your fine, noble-spirited book,[1] of which you gave me far too modest an impression when you described it to me, almost contemptuously, at Gastein. Even calling it a "story" is too modest, though correct to the extent that it is not a novel and also not a history, but a poem, a song, an elevated, enchanting, colorful song sparkling with judicious, sound *aperçus* on the human condition. Anyone with a trace of youthfulness in his heart must call it simply glorious. How boldly, accurately, distinctly it is all seen and how magnificently stated— a flower of conscientious study which intuition, fresh imagination, fine principle, and staggering linguistic artistry have raised to the heights of poetry. I shall never forget the picture of that fatal battle, and cannot admire enough the vividness of the characters, especially of Xerxes in all his greatness, abandoned by the gods and tragically deceived. There even totalitarian despotism is given its aesthetic due—as altogether the magnanimous, forgiving, and nevertheless extremely firm view from above down upon the human scene—in other words, justice—constitutes the purifying, stainless morality of the book.

I have been trying to say quickly and all at once what moved me during the reading, and lingers as happy emotion. I cannot do more. I am bedeviled by all sorts of obligations, as well as by the impending reorganization of our life, which is already in progress. [. . .] The next step is Frankfurt; then, only too quickly, within this very month, a whole week in Vienna, which promises to be gay. The shocks of so many deaths, Neumann, Oprecht, then Hans Feist,[2] obituaries to write or to speak, have

---

[1] *Aeschylos bei Salamis* (1952).
[2] Hans Feist (1887–1952), doctor, later translator of Croce, Pirandello, Giraudoux, Cocteau, Jules Romaing, and Christopher Fry, among others.

come in between. I am not working and have the somewhat abnormal feeling of consuming myself in mere outward affairs. Well, things will settle down eventually. Imagine, we have rented two stories of a house on the heights of Erlenbach, right beyond Küsnacht. It has a magnificent view over the whole Lake of Zurich. The year's rent comes to approximately the wages of our Negro woman *help* in California. On December 15, two weeks after the return from Vienna, we mean to move in. Until the furniture arrives from Pacific Palisades, we are being provided with everything we need as a loan from the furniture house of Pfister, entirely free of charge, even the cost of delivery. Altogether, people are charming to us here; even in government bureaus there is always the refrain: "It is an honor to us." To be welcome does make one feel good after all. The purpose of our stay is set down in the residence permit as: "Passing of the evening of life and literary activity." That is very pretty, you know. Let us hope that it will be a passing *with* such activity. And let us hope also that this move makes for no bad blood in America. In certain quarters there has already been nastiness enough. [. . .]

Read Adorno's *Versuch über Wagner* (Suhrkamp). It is in a way a challenging but extremely intelligent book, which I found profoundly interesting. *Salamis* and this work of criticism—there could not be any sharper contrast in reading matter. Both types attract me. But I think there is more benediction on yours!

Keep your heart open for me.

TO TOR BONNIER [1]

Waldhaus Dolder
Zurich
November 17, 1952

Dear Herr Bonnier:

I am turning to you about a matter close to my heart and which, I suspect, will seem important to you also.

It concerns Strindberg's daughter, Kerstin.[2] As you know, she spent some time in a Stockholm psychiatric clinic because of grave psychic disturbances. She was discharged, apparently cured or distinctly im-

[1] Tor Bonnier (b. 1883), head of the Albert Bonnier publishing house 1938–42, and still on the board of directors. Bonnier promptly and generously acted on Mann's request in this letter.
[2] Kerstin Strindberg (1894–1956), August Strindberg's highly gifted but mentally unstable daughter; she wrote, drew, and painted, but never published or exhibited anything.

proved, and is now in Switzerland. I have known Kerstin for a long time, and she was always a good friend of my children also. Yesterday I spent several hours with her, and my impression was that while she absolutely cannot be called mentally ill, she is physically and psychically in a bad state and urgently needs looking after and psychiatric treatment. After all, staying in the general ward of an insane asylum, even though her condition may have made it necessary, is probably a severe shock under any circumstances, and given her unstable temperament, a certain amount of disturbance afterwards is only too natural.

It seems to me that Kerstin could not find better facilities for the care she needs than right here in Switzerland, where the doctors are especially skilled at treating such conditions, and I already have in mind a small private sanatorium run by a physician who to my personal knowledge is very trustworthy. For a month's stay the sum of 1,000 francs would be ample, and this could be of decisive importance for Kerstin's life.

My feeling is that the daughter of the greatest Swedish writer of our time has the right to count on help in so critical a moment, and you will understand that my first thought was to turn to Strindberg's publisher.

I did, however, gather from something Kerstin said that she herself possesses some modest savings which she is keeping for times of utmost need and would not like to touch under any circumstances. It would not be easy to prevail on her to finance the stay at the sanatorium from this source, and the anxiety attendant on any such decision would undo the possible benefits of treatment.

May I, since I am already appealing to you on Kerstin's account, go a step further and suggest that her pension might be increased somewhat to keep pace with rising prices? To be free from pressing financial anxieties would undoubtedly be of major psychic importance to her at this moment.

Please, dear Herr Bonnier, do not take offense at these suggestions, which spring from concern for Strindberg's daughter.

With many regards to you and your wife from both of us,

1953

---•---

TO IDA HERZ

Erlenbach-Zurich
January 16, 1953

Dear Fräulein Herz:

You received my small New Year's gift gratefully, and it's not right that we haven't yet thanked you for your pretty Christmas gifts. I must make up for it. The extremely practical *lighter* is, to be sure, not suitable for the car, at least not for the Fiat we have now (with a little Swiss flag fluttering on it). But it will certainly do me good service on the desk— better than the American benzine lighter I have at present, which is called "Senator." True to its name, it fails all the time.

Our California things—furniture, books, pictures—have just arrived, and we are living in chaos. I confess that I am writing you from the Hotel Waldhaus Dolder, to which I have escaped from the turmoil. But it will be an odd experience indeed to live here among all these things.

I go about with the rosette of an *officer* of the Legion of Honor in my buttonhole. I am excessively vain about it, just like a Frenchy.

TO AGNES E. MEYER

Erlenbach-Zurich
February 8, 1953

Dear friend:

Certainly I received your letter in which you so reassuringly approved my staying in Switzerland. But unfortunately it seems that my letter didn't reach you—the one in which I thanked you and also spoke about the "interviews on America," which you rightly warned me against. I have given no such interviews, but in Vienna, which I had not visited for fifteen years, I was forced to hold a press conference at which, among other things, I was asked (probably by someone on the "left") what I thought about the restrictions on freedom in America. I replied that American democracy felt threatened and, in the struggle for freedom, considered that there had to be a certain limitation on freedom, a certain disciplining of individual thought, a certain conformism. This was understandable, I said, and on the other hand it did honor to the country that much opposition was stirring, especially in intellectual circles, against this wartime regimentation. The matter could not have been put more discreetly, more sparingly. But the craving for *headlines* naturally distorted my words, so that it might appear as if I as an American citizen had had the gall to say something deprecating or even critical of America while abroad. I do not have the gall, you can be sure of that.

I was recently offered the opportunity to publish in America my views on conditions there. Through its Geneva correspondent, the *New York Times* asked me to express my opinions in an interview or article "on the realities and dangers in the current trend of American policy toward restriction of entry and investigation (and castigation) of nonconformist opinion in all walks of life—everything, in short, that will be suggested to you by the names McCarthy and McCarran."[1] A remarkable invitation. But I asked myself: "Would Agnes M. advise me to do it or not to do it?" "She would advise me against it," I answered myself, and so I said: "*No, thank you.*"

In that same earlier letter I also told you that shortly before Christmas the French government awarded me the Officer's Cross of the Legion of Honor, the official reason being: "*Cette distinction est un hommage rendu par la France à l'exceptionelle valeur et à la signification mondiale de votre œuvre littéraire ainsi qu'à la lutte que vous n'avez cessé de mener dans l'intérêt de la liberté et de la dignité humaine.*" That is a fine attestation, and the finest words of welcome Europe could offer me on my return.

I was alarmed to hear that you and Eugene were seriously ill during the holiday season. *Virus pneumonia* is no joke; there is something most uncanny about it. Now it is over, thank God, and the big inauguration party at your home, after your rest in the South, must have been a major event! [. . .]

---

[1] Patrick A. McCarran (1876–1954), chairman of the Senate Internal Security Subcommittee and author of the McCarran Act, which provided for registration of all aliens in the United States and stiffened the rules for granting immigration or visitor's visas to political suspects.

You seem not to have liked my little study in praise of transitoriness.[2] It was not aimed at human hubris and complacency in general, however. I merely meant that it would be good if out of all our sufferings a new feeling of solidarity for mankind would emerge, a unifying sympathy for man's precarious position in the universe, between nature and spirit; in short, that a new humanistic ethical system might form and enter into the general consciousness and subconsciousness. It might have a salutary influence upon the spiritual climate here on earth—for the climate is unbearable everywhere right now. But those are pious wishes. Even Christian wishes, if you will. To me "Christian," in spite of Nietzsche, still is not a term of abuse.

Cordially,
T. M.

TO MAX RYCHNER [1]

Erlenbach-Zurich
April 11, 1953

Dear Dr. Rychner:

You have written most magnificently about the chatty book.[2] My best thanks.

I was amused by your slipping in the word "philosopher," because it reminded me of my former homeland across the sea. In America I was often called a philosopher, and each time I couldn't help laughing, for the term is used far more naïvely than in your review. Over there every patently sensible idea elicits the remark: "*That's good philosophy*."

Good Lord, when I read something like the latest issue of the *Neue Rundschau* with its contributions by Kahler, Adorno, Karl Löwith,[3] etc., I feel completely swamped by intellectuality and tell myself that I must never again attempt to write criticism. I feel more at home with the "spirit of narration" and am glad to be telling stories again. My story about the woman[4] is finished, and now I am actually mulling over the

---

[2] "Lob der Vergänglichkeit" (1952). Included in *Altes und Neues* (1953).

[1] Max Rychner (1897–1965), Swiss literary critic, essayist, poet, journalist. President of the Thomas Mann Society of Zurich.

[2] *Altes und Neues. Kleine Prosa aus fünf Jahrzehnten.* A collection of Mann's shorter pieces.

[3] Karl Löwith (b. 1897), professor of philosophy in Marburg, Sendai (Japan), Hartford, Conn., New School for Social Research, New York; at Heidelberg since 1952. Among his works: *Kierkegaard und Nietzsche* (1933), *Jacob Burckhardt* (1936), *Von Hegel zu Nietzsche* (1958), *Heidegger, Denker in dürftiger Zeit* (1960).

[4] *The Black Swan* (New York: Alfred A. Knopf; 1954).

old material for the *Krull,* rereading the pages and trying to recover its specific musical "tone."

TO LAVINIA MAZZUCCHETTI

Erlenbach-Zurich
April 19, 1953

Dear Lavinia:

We think of you a great deal, wonder how you are, and talk about the inconsolably heavy blow[1] that has struck you so suddenly, evidently out of a blue sky. We wanted to visit you, but couldn't manage it with all the things that always have to be taken care of before a journey. Tomorrow, then, we are flying. I am rather looking forward to seeing Rome again, but as usual feel reluctant to travel. We want to be back by the end of the month. Bandinelli has tried to lure us to Siena, but we prefer to fly back directly. After all, I shall have to leave again in the second half of May for England (Cambridge[2]) and then for Hamburg.

How sad that you cannot be with us in Rome. As soon as we are back we hope to see you and clasp your hand. We are so deeply sorry about your loss. But we trust in your courage. In any case, the term of life is running out for us all. Katia will be seventy in July, and I am close to seventy-eight, feel my strength slowly ebbing away, and think about death a great deal. Though it has always been on my mind.

Until we see you again, dear friend.

TO FRIDO AND TONI MANN

[*Picture postcard*]

Rome
April 30, 1953

Dear Frido and dear Toni:

Greetings from Rome at the moment of our departure. This card shows you St. Peter's Cathedral. Yesterday I visited the Pope, His Holiness Pius XII.[1] He was very amiable. Soon we'll be seeing each other again, dear boys. I am looking forward to that.

Your Grandpa

[1] Lavinia Mazzucchetti had lost her husband, the Swiss writer Waldemar Jollos.
[2] At Cambridge Mann was awarded an honorary doctorate on June 4, 1953.
[1] Pius XII (1876–1958), Apostolic nuncio to Bavaria 1917–20; nuncio to Germany 1920–29; elected Pope in 1939.

1953

TO GOTTFRIED BERMANN FISCHER

Erlenbach-Zurich
May 27, 1953

Dear Dr. Bermann:

Many thanks for your letter. How glad I am to hear that our new volume has given you pleasure. It really wasn't a bad idea. I too have seen that the collection is winning many friends.

Your Mexico trip was obviously a good idea also. For me our Rome journey was a similar, but then again quite different, experience. Tired and weak though I often feel, I take joy in the youthful receptivity I can still muster for such an occasion. I was stirred by the perspective of millennia that opens out there, and strengthened in my European pride. You know, this continent ought to reaffirm itself in a sense of its ancient dignity and historical tempering, and carry its head higher instead of abasing itself before money and stupid power.

I had decided from the first that if I were going to be in Rome I would visit the Pope, and although there was hardly time for obtaining an audience, it was, remarkably enough, arranged within a few days with the aid of the Academy and of a gentleman from the *Osservatore Romano* (!). After a slow journey through the anterooms, it proved to be a tête-à-tête of about a quarter hour, yet it was for me a remarkable and stirring moment in my life to stand before this white figure who represents so much. He was most cordial, but looked distinctly tired from the virus infection that he had passed through at approximately the same time I did. "The sickness," he said, "all very well. But the cure. That is what lingers." He speaks excellent German, and I had the impression that he recalls with the greatest pleasure the time he was nuncio in Germany, which was evidently the best period of his life. In 1949 in front of the Wartburg[1] the Mayor of Eisenach told me that he had stood on the same spot with Cardinal Pacelli, who had looked up at the walls and said: "That is a blessed castle." Which is certainly an extraordinary pronouncement for a Catholic prince of the Church. I reminded him of it, and said that the words had made such an impression upon me because they showed that the *homines religiosi* are fundamentally of one mind and that denomination is after all not of such great importance. He expressed lively agreement, and the "unity of the religious world" actually formed the core of the conversation. As a sign that it must end

---

[1] The castle associated with Martin Luther.

(for so many are always waiting), he gives one a small silver medallion with his portrait as a memento, and one genuflects once again, which I found very easy and natural to do. I think back on the episode with a certain tenderness.

We will be setting out again very soon—to Cambridge, England, where they again want to place a doctoral hat upon my unlearned head, and from London (Hotel Savoy) to Hamburg for two readings at the Goethe Society and the University. We intend to be back before the middle of June, unless the weather should be good enough for us to go to the North Sea for a few weeks. But it will probably be too cold.

I hope, then, that we shall be seeing one another during the summer, which we probably shall simply spend here upon our airy height. An invitation has come from America, a joint one from three large Quaker colleges, to lecture to them in the autumn. Good people! But in the words of Thoma's[2] rapscallion: "I'm not that dumb."

I am much reassured to hear that the mimeographing for copyright purposes has been started.

Katia and Erika send their best regards.

TO KUNO FIEDLER[1]

Erlenbach-Zurich
July 19, 1953

Dear Reverend:

Thank you again for your very good letter and the picture. The *Corriere* would like contributions from me, but I have nothing to offer.

Here a family festival is impending: my wife's seventieth birthday. Children and grandchildren are gathering; every bedroom is occupied, the table is long, and I am distracted. I also cannot help thinking a great deal about all the living together and bearing everything together for forty-eight years. Death will part our hands, and each goes into the loneliness of his nonbeing. How strange it all is.

---

[2] Ludwig Thoma (1867–1921), writer. His *Lausbubengeschichten* and *Filserbriefe* were very popular. Mann knew him from the time they had worked together on the magazine *Simplicissimus*.

[1] Kuno Fiedler (b. 1895), pastor, writer on theological subjects. Began to correspond with Mann in 1915; officiated at the baptism of Mann's youngest daughter Elisabeth. Made himself so unpopular under the Hitler regime that he was given an indefinite prison term. He escaped from the prison, reached Switzerland, and served as pastor in the Engadine.

In September we intend to spend a few weeks in the Ticino. We hope to see you there. Have already reserved rooms in the Villa Castagnola.

Yours,
T. M.

TO ERNST ALFRED PHILIPPSON[1]

Erlenbach-Zurich
July 22, 1953

My dear Professor:

I am afraid I have not yet thanked you for the handsome gift of your essay on the genealogy of the Germanic gods,[2] although I have written to others (Karl Kerényi) about it. It is an excellent book, most scholarly and always fascinating—at least to me, whose affinity for the sphere of myth you so kindly confirm in your dedication. Much in the book was entirely new to me—for example, Wodan-Odin's original link with the realm of the dead, like Osiris. And I was impressed again and again by your conception of the sequence from primitive religious numinosity to playful mythmaking and systematic theology. Forgivably, it is the second of the three that the novelist rejoices in.

Your suggestion that "even the Christians could not dispense with the symbolic genealogy of their myth, where the relationship of God the Father to the Son had to be cast into a humanly familiar formula" is most striking. But then to add the Holy Spirit to that! At which point the happy tenor of mythic genealogy comes to a halt. The Trinity, the One equal to Three and Three equal to One, is probably the strangest formula dogma has ever imposed on faith.

Many thanks for all the instruction and stimulation.

TO OTTO BASLER

Erlenbach-Zurich
August 2, 1953

Dear Herr Basler:

Your kind message on my wife's birthday has given both her and me deep pleasure. She sends her warm thanks, and only wonders about the

---

[1] Ernst Alfred Philippson (b. 1900), professor in the department of Germanic languages and literature at the University of Illinois since 1947. Coeditor of the *Journal of English and Germanic Philology* and of *Texte des späten Mittelalters und der frühen Neuzeit.*

[2] *Die Genealögie der Götter in germanischer Religion, Mythologie und Theologie* (Illinois Studies in Language and Literature, XXXVII, 3, 1953).

"plums and spinach." Good heavens, of course they may occur side by side, but could scarcely go as a mixed dish. Not that we know of. —Somebody who once saw me crumbling graham bread into honey at breakfast asked: "I suppose that is a North German dish?" Ever since, we have always called it "My North German dish."

Yes, the old Privy Councillor's wife[1] was an imposing personality, a legend to her children and children's children. How in the world could you have caused her to think that dreadful thing[2] of you? But I'm sure she was only playacting—which she did professionally in her youth, you know.

And now you are off to Germany? What takes you there? Lectures? Or mere curiosity about that forever uncanny place? I hope for a report.

The Black Swan is coming out in September. I shall be glad when the story is presented all at once, as a whole. The Germans have read it only in monthly installments, for which this particular story is most ill-suited.

I am alternately reading Dostoevsky and Balzac. What wild greatness! One bows one's head—before the Karamazov's and before *Splendeurs et Misères des Courtisanes*. Different as they are, these two monstrously great ones have something in common that separates them from all the rest.

TO HANS REISIGER

Erlenbach-Zurich
September 8, 1953

Dear, good Reisi:

Many thanks for your dear and good letter of August 28. I would have answered more promptly if so much were not always going on here, and if in particular my afternoon correspondence hours were not so often stolen from me by teatime visits. Everybody passes through Zurich, and everybody wants to call. Sometimes it is very nice, but more often it's a mere waste of time, and I fend off as many as possible.

I enjoyed Eberle's[1] essays on the familiar places. He is a good travel writer with a fresh eye and a happy gift for communicating. Do give him my regards and thanks. I was taken back to the time of my own inspec-

---

[1] Frau Geheimrat Pringsheim, Katia Mann's mother.
[2] Undoubtedly "playacting," Frau Pringsheim had addressed Otto Basler, a Swiss to the core, as a "Hitler spy" on the occasion of his first visit in Küsnacht.
[1] Josef Eberle (b. 1901), publisher, writer; author of numerous travel books and four volumes of poetry in Latin (1954–61).

tion trips and even back into the novel[2] itself, to which Eberle alludes at one point. Your fondness for it always does my heart good. The opus is little known, too expensive and too time-consuming a project for people in search of reading matter nowadays. Nevertheless, I think you are right in your estimate. That was one of life's pinnacles—which at seventy, in deepest agitation, was once again continued or even surpassed in *Faustus*. The things that have come since are postludes—let's not quibble about it. They are as good as ordinary things can be, as is the case with *The Black Swan*, which I do not esteem very highly, rather disgruntled and spoiled by earlier work as I am—or with the *Krull*, which moves along only at a wearisome pace, interrupted by a hundred disturbances and spells of fatigue, basically by my no longer being in the mood to go on. Nevertheless, now and again I do manage to strike off some amusing things.

You also have, I see with sympathy, your trials and troubles, such as the years bring with them. My doctor here, Dr. Mäder on Bahnhofstrasse, always says: "The decades—you must consider that." Of course I consider that, and actually my feeling is that at seventy-nine one should let doctors alone. Life has not been child's play for you or for me either, or if it has, it's been thoroughly strenuous play. God be praised that the clouding of the vitreous humor was nothing serious—at any rate there was no detachment of the retina, concerning which I have always heard nothing but bad. Dr. Gscheidel vividly reminded me of the dentist Gosch in Munich, who in treating a root used to say every other minute: "Oh dear, this won't work!" Most encouraging.

A thousand copies of *Salamis*—why, that isn't bad at all, my friend. And it certainly was a critical success. On top of that, Athens![3] I am impressed. I do hope it works out. It would be very fine and solemn.

In July we had a turbulent time because of my wife's seventieth birthday, which was celebrated on the scale that she deserves, though she didn't want it. Children and grandchildren gathered, every room of this little house was full, and Swiss friends gave a party at the Eden au Lac, with many fine speeches. They'd also arranged a serenade of chamber music under our windows on the birthday morning. The Swiss press participated kindly, and the Frankfurt *Neue Zeitung* had a handsome, cordial article written in real friendship by Bruno Walter, who incidentally is here right now.

•

[2] *Joseph and His Brothers.*
[3] A Greek translation of Reisiger's *Aeschylos bei Salamis* was planned, but the project fell through.

Erika is in Göttingen, trying to save what can be saved in a *Royal Highness* film. [. . .] But at the end of the week she will drive us to Lake Geneva, where rumor has it there are reasonably priced and at the same time stately houses for sale between Vevey and Lausanne. I have an unconquerable distaste for *mesquinerie*, and this place, though most beautifully located, is a little *mesquine* in comparison with our house on San Remo Drive, which has now been sold, although below its value. My study doesn't even have room for a sofa, although I need one for work, since sitting stooped for hours at the desk is not good for me. —All in all, one ought to have more money, don't you think?

From Geneva we intend to go to Lugano (Hotel Villa Castagnola) for two weeks, one major reason being to greet the Hesses again, whom we have not seen since our return to Switzerland. We will be back at the beginning of October. May we invite you to be our guest then, as in the days at Küsnacht? You could work as you pleased, and the whole vicinity here, on and above the lake, is so charming. We would take drives, go to the theater and the opera, listen to our good record player, read things to one another, etc., as in the old days. As Medi used to say: "With Herr Reisiger, Herrpapale is always so cheerful."

P.S. I suppose it will strike you as incongruous that I invite you to a house which I myself have called a little *mesquine*. Really, conditions here are rather cramped, and your quarters would not be appropriate to your station. My wife says she would put you up in the Sonne in Küsnacht, a very prettily situated and well-run hotel. In Gastein, after all, we also lived apart.

TO CLAIRE GOLL[1]

Erlenbach-Zurich
December 12, 1953

Dear Madame:

Many thanks for your kind letter. It is remarkable that you should happen to write me about *Royal Highness* just now. The book has always been a Cinderella among my works, but now it is having a kind of popular resurrection because it is one in Fischer's series of low-priced

---

[1] Claire Goll (b. 1901), writer, wife of the writer Ivan Goll (1891–1950). Among her works: *Le tombeau des amants inconnus* (1944), *Education barbare* (1944), *Arsénic* (1945), *Journal d'un cheval* (1953), *Le ciel volé* (1958).

books, because of a pompous German color film which is shortly to be "premiered," because of various radio versions being made from the film, and so on. *Habent sua fata libelli.*

I am glad to hear that you had a good time in California. It is hardly likely that I shall see that artificial paradise again, even if I should sometime revisit New York. Our house is now sold, and we are on the point of buying another here. At present we are only renting, and I am an inveterate homeowner.

Michael seems to be having pleasant successes in Japan. We are beginning to suspect that he will stay there. And why not?

You women can be amazing. Also living in New York, but writing in French, there is a certain Marguérite Yourcenar[2] who has composed the memoirs of Emperor Hadrian with an almost maddening fictional authenticity that is based, by the by, on tremendously solid scholarship. Do you know the book? It is the finest that has come my way in a long time.

TO AGNES E. MEYER

Erlenbach-Zurich
December 20, 1953

Warmest congratulations, dear friend, on the brilliant success of your book,[1] and everything good for the New Year for yourself and your whole household. Has Claudel told you about our meeting in Zurich? He was very charming to the *protestant maudit*. The first word he spoke was your name.

Yours,
T. M.

[2] Marguérite Yourcenar (b. 1903), French writer. Professor of French literature at Sarah Lawrence College. Of her ten books, *Coup de Grâce* and *Hadrian's Memoirs* have been published in English.

[1] *Out of These Roots. The Autobiography of an American Woman* (1953). Mrs. Meyer's flyleaf dedication read: "For Thomas Mann with gratitude for the innumerable hours of enchantment which his works have given me."

1954

———————————•———————————

TO FRIDO MANN

Erlenbach-Zurich
January 18, 1954

Dear Fridobutz:[1]

It was very sweet of you to have written us so soon. We are glad to hear that you both have adjusted to the place again easily and happily. It must be very jolly and pleasant being five to the room, and the dire consequences of skiing in slush—namely broken tip, headache, splattered windbreaker, and all that—must be long over and forgotten by now. Of course I imagine the broken ski tip is the worst of it, but still it's better than a broken ankle.

Here too all the snow disappeared in a single wild stormy night of föhn. That is a real relief for drives into town.

Aunt Eri was here for twenty-four hours and today, with skies clearer than we have seen them in a long time, has left for Arosa. She told us all about her trip. The Russians in East Berlin heartily invited her to Moscow, and said that if I came too, my, what vodka and caviar there would be! But I'm not allowed to go wherever I want to; people like me have to have themselves examined by their best doctors all the time, and then I would have to go to just the place they thought most healthful for me. But I think I won't go at all; the idea makes me rather uneasy. They said to Eri in a very threatening tone that she had better see I stayed in good health. As though they could sentence her to forced labor if I caught a cold. We laughed so much over that.

Adieu, my good boy; you stay in good health too. When we have the house in Kilchberg and you go to school in Zurich, say, you'll be able to live with us all the time. That would be nifty.

[1] *Butz* = bogey.

The best of greetings from Mielein and me to both of you. Give our regards to Maria[2] and Boris[3] too.

Your loving Grampa

But you mustn't say anything about East Berlin and the Russians, not in school and not to Mamms and Papps or to Piffi and Pfiffi.[1]

TO FRIDO AND TONI MANN

[*Picture postcard*]

Taormina
February 14, 1954

This little donkey pulls the brightly painted cart laden with all sorts of small goods through the village and is not afraid of Mount Etna in the background, which sometimes spews fire.

The best of greetings to you both from your far-traveled

Kilchberg grandparents

TO ERIKA MANN

Taormina
February 15, 1954

Dearest Eri:

Everything has just arrived, three letters and three packages. I am touched by the faithful giant's labors you have performed,[1] also confused, because weak in head and legs. I have only glanced through everything and will work over it later. I have never felt quite right about 20mans[2]

[2] Maria: housekeeper of many years, first for Michael, later for the Thomas Mann family.

[3] German police dog, taken over by Michael; his full name was Boris Godunov.

[1] Mamms and Papps: Herr and Frau Fritz Moser, Frido's Swiss grandparents. Piffi and Pfiffi: cousins in the Moser family.

[1] Erika Mann had gone through the entire manuscript of *Felix Krull*, searching for possible small discrepancies between the early fragment and the body of the 'Memoirs' written forty years later. She had proposed a fuller treatment of 'Lord Kilmarnock' and revisions in the section devoted to the Twentyman family, suggestions which Thomas Mann later followed. The dedication in Erika Mann's copy of *Felix Krull* reads: "To Eri, to whose keenness I owe many things in this book, above all 'the Lord,' in love and gratitude. Z. Kilchberg, October 3, 1954."

[2] Originally there had been a whole chapter in *Felix Krull* devoted to the Twentyman family. It was cut from the book, but later published separately in the *Neue Rundschau* ("Ein nachgelassenes Kapitel aus 'Felix Krull,' " Jg. 68, Heft 2, 1957).

and was loath to sacrifice them to the Scottish laird. He may be in Erlenbach, but there is the unhappy possibility that I destroyed him,[3] and then I have no idea what to do. I won't be able to deal with this major change until we are back, in any case, and perhaps for the time being, shall send the publisher only the early pages, so that they can start setting.

Whatever comes of it, I am warmly grateful for your conscientious labors.

We have spent a week here, filled largely with sickness, and with the sun seldom appearing. We shall have to spend another week rather shakily, perhaps slowly becoming less shaky. Then I should like to go to Rome, and to Florence for a little. At the moment I am only impatient and anxious to be back in Erlenbach to look around for the Scotsman. I do hope that I kept those pages.

We are more than glad you are feeling better. We'll see you again at the beginning of March.

Feuchtwanger writes that Dieterle has gone to great lengths to persuade Columbia to base the film on the novel, but in vain. But that would not even have been necessary; their merely using a few motifs and characters (Mai-Sachme, Montkaw, Pharaoh Amenophis IV) would have sufficed to connect the film with the book, without a full sale, and at the meager cost to them of twenty or thirty thousand dollars. I keep wondering whether that proposal could not still be made at this late date.[4]

I wrote a lengthy letter about *sex* some weeks ago to your cellar doctor[5] in Berlin, but have received no answer.

Have magnificently congratulated Marcuse[6] in *Aufbau*. I manage to do everything.

Z.

---

[3] Mann had in fact destroyed the few pages dealing with the Scottish aristocrat. The new chapter (Book Three, Chapter 2) was written as soon as Mann returned to Erlenbach and includes Felix's experiences with Miss Eleanor Twentyman as well as with Lord Kilmarnock.

[4] Nothing came of the film Dieterle was planning, based on the biblical Joseph.

[5] Dr. Paul Orlowski, whose office had been smashed by bombs, set up his consulting room in the cellar of his home in Berlin.

[6] An article congratulating Ludwig Marcuse on his sixtieth birthday (*Aufbau*, November 5, 1954).

1954

Erlenbach-Zurich
March 21, 1954

Dear Ida:

Many thanks for *The Doors of Perception,* but I cannot really share your enthusiasm for the book. It represents the last and, I am tempted to say, the rashest development of Huxley's *escapism,* which I never liked in him. Mysticism as a means to that end was still reasonably honorable. But it strikes me as scandalous that he has now arrived at drugs. I have a guilty conscience nowadays because I take a little seconal or phanodorm at night in order to sleep better. But to cast myself by day into a state in which everything human is indifferent to me and to succumb to wicked aesthetic egotistic pleasure would be repugnant to me. Yet this is what he recommends to everybody, because otherwise man's lot is at best idiocy, and at worst suffering. What a use of "best" and "worst"! His mystics should have taught him that "suffering is the swiftest beast that bears us to perfection," which can't be said of *doping.* And being rapt over the miracle of a chair and absorbed in all sorts of color illusions has more to do with idiocy than he thinks.

The Hamburg physician Frederking[1] warns that only a person extremely experienced in psychotherapy can cope with the states of excitement produced by mescaline intoxication. (And Huxley is not experienced; he is a dilettante.) Indications for the use of mescaline are strictly limited, the doctor goes on to say, and it is impossible to predict whether the results of a mescaline experiment will be in any way rewarding. Now, given the eloquent endorsement of this famous writer, many young Englishmen and especially Americans will try the experiment. For the book is selling like mad. But it is an altogether—I do not want to say immoral, but must say, irresponsible book, which can only contribute to the befuddlement of the world and to its incapacity to meet the deadly serious problems of the times with intelligence.

We are about to move into our own home: in Kilchberg on Lake Zurich, Alte Landstrasse 39. The packers appear on the 25th, and now I shall have to charge myself with *escapism,* for I cannot endure the turmoil and am moving into the Hotel Waldhaus Dolder for two weeks.

---

[1] Walter Frederking (1891–1964), neurologist and psychotherapist. Introduced the ergot derivative LSD XXV into psychotherapy in the fifties, after having previously experimented with mescaline.

1954

TO SIEGFRIED MARCK [1]

Alte Landstrasse 39
Kilchberg am Zürichsee
May 23, 1954

Dear Professor Marck:

My cordial thanks for your fine, far-ranging, rich book, *Grosse Menschen in unserer Zeit*. It fascinated and moved me—that too; for how could I fail to be moved by what you have to say in it about "me," about Joseph especially, and the ultimate melancholy that surrounds his charming personality. I suppose that after all he is my favorite son, in spite of Adrian and Grigorss—though it is the latter who speaks the words which you would rightly like to set as a motto over everything I have done: "I thought to offer God an entertainment." To entertain has always been my desire and aim, but would anyone take such great trouble about it if men alone were the object? Art, they say, strives toward perfection. But after all, that is not an entirely earthly striving. —Incidentally, in the Krull memoirs, as I realize while reading proofs of the First Part, I have been guilty of such unseemly things that observations like this are hardly in order.

Your book is excellent, whether it deals with Dewey or Roosevelt (especially with him) or the various Frenchmen. But it teems with truly frightful typographical errors, the kind that actually obscure the meaning. The errata list only a few of them. For whole sections it is like reading uncorrected proofs. You should have gone to the expense of airmail so that you could take care of the corrections yourself. There is no depending on publishers' proofreaders.

We now have a house of our own again, much more spacious and attractive, and also more convenient for getting to the city, than the place we rented in Erlenbach. The view out over the lake, alive with sailboats and regatta vessels, and the built-up hilly shore opposite us, is charming. Recently we gave a *housewarming party* (called *Huusröiki* here) for thirty-six persons, headed by the municipal president. You too must visit us sometime!

[1] Siegfried Marck (1889–1957), philosopher, historian, and sociologist. Professor of philosophy in Breslau (1924). Emigrated to France in 1933, to the United States in 1939. From 1941 on taught at Roosevelt College, Chicago. Among his works: *Germany: To Be or Not to Be?* (with Gerhart Seger, 1943). *Grosse Menschen in unserer Zeit* (1954) contains an essay on Thomas Mann.

TO GEORGES MOTSCHAN [1]

Kilchberg am Zürichsee
May 26, 1954

Dear Georges:

It seems to me that I have not yet sufficiently thanked you and your dear wife for the "bread and salt" which you recently brought us in so transfigured a form to our new and final Swiss home. That must be put right—and I must add that it was a joy to us to see you two among the good friends who celebrated our housewarming with us. Of course! If anyone could not be spared, it was our faithful gentleman chauffeur through Red Germany. May he come to see us often with his lovelier half. I very much regret that I didn't give her a kiss at the moment of welcoming you. Afterwards there was no opportunity.

TO ERIKA MANN

Kilchberg am Zürichsee
June 7, Whitsunday, 1954

Poor dear Erikind:

Thanks—a thousand thanks. Your terribly, piercingly touching letter was delivered yesterday in time, together with a late batch of a dozen telegrams, and I wept a little over it, in the midst of laughter. Along with the apprehension, the doubts, the melancholy that hang over my later years I have grieved, as I told you, over what you have had to undergo there, the ordeal of the stomach test, the gruesome experience of that "healing sleep," and all that. I was also furious at the doctor who sent for you just when he was leaving, but of course I did not have quite the right view of the situation. In any case I am calmer now and more confident about you, for although at the moment you are leading a thoroughly wretched existence, I see to my comfort your patient, courageous good will and take heart, trusting in your future once the crudest immediate aspects of the treatment are successfully past and your fundamentally sound constitution can once more take over, somewhere in the mountain air. Something certainly had to be done—we all felt that it couldn't go on the way it has been doing, and should also have realized that the resetting would not be a simple thing. It is certainly astonishing and a very hopeful

---

[1] Georges Motschan (b. 1920), born in Russia, the son of Swiss parents. In 1949 he drove Mann to Frankfurt, Munich, and Weimar during Mann's first postwar visit to Germany.

sign that even in the last days before your deciding on radical treatment you were able to produce such lovely, graceful, engaging things as your children's stories. The capacity to give pleasure, even in the midst of misery, is surely a guarantee that you have the *resources* in yourself to find your way back to joy.

In that I see a certain father-daughter resemblance between us, for only recently I too was able to add a few amusing sidelights to the *Krull*, things that look as if they sprang from good humor, which was not the case—or at any rate, the good humor was extracted from ill humor. It is only too plain to me, I must admit, that after the "original" speech about love, nothing of any moment follows, and the end of the volume is rather slack and offhanded. My view of the whole is distinctly disgruntled, and I am steeling myself for its publication with some embarrassment. Certainly it's not a very dignified production. Is it right for a man to celebrate his eightieth birthday with such compromising jokes? What's wanted less than weary wantonness?—to put it in proverbial terms. Often I can't help thinking that it would have been better if I had departed from this earth after the *Faustus*. That, after all, was a book of seriousness and a certain power, and would have been a neat finale to a life's labor, whereas now with *The Holy Sinner*, though I happen to love it, there begins an overhanging epilogue that probably would be better lacking. I have no impulse to go on spinning out the *Krull*, at least for the present, although it would be relatively easier than starting a new enterprise, as I am now trying to do. Actually I can only say that I am trying to try. I have vaguely in mind something like a little portrait gallery of the Reformation period, brief sketches of Luther, Hutten, Erasmus, Charles V, Leo X, Zwingli, Münzer, Tilman Riemenschneider, showing how within the framework of contemporaneity, their personal standpoints and viewpoints, and their individual destinies contrast in a well-nigh comical manner. But I don't really have any proper conception (as yet); I am studying a good many things, but know only vaguely what I want, and sometimes think I have completely forgotten how one goes about attacking and accomplishing a work. In other words, perhaps the talent, or the energy to work things out, has leaked away—a horrible feeling, for without work, that is, without active hope, I wouldn't know how to live. Every time I feel this way, all I can do is to remember that only recently I managed to turn out something quite talented and successful, and that distraction and fatigue, which are not necessarily permanent, are responsible for my present plight.

I should not bother and depress you with my moods; that is the last thing you need. Yesterday passed in the pleasantest way, amid flowers and a sweet shower of letters and telegrams—a faint foretaste, though, of the silly fuss that will be stirred up next year, to which I look forward with some misgivings. In the morning there was an emissary from Mondadori, Signor Federici[1] from Milan, who brought a precious piece of embroidery. In the afternoon Michael and Frido together performed very neatly and cleanly a quite difficult violin sonata of Mozart, and in the evening we had a small party with the von Salises,[2] Lotte Walter, Emmie,[3] Golo, Michael, and Gret. I presided between Frau von Salis, a nice, natural person, and Lotte. We can look forward to the Brahms Haydn Variations, which Kuzi has just conducted enchantingly in Florence. But I am looking forward even more to the *Natürliche Tochter*[4] in the Schauspielhaus on Friday, third performance. I know I shall listen fascinated to every word of this old chestnut.

Therese[5] recently invited us to dine with her in Zug, in a solid, respectable inn with attached butcher shop; we had good lake fish in herb sauce and cherry torte. Very good raspberry liqueur with the coffee, and Mielein promptly gave me a bottle of the same for my birthday, along with a beautiful, soft cashmere bathrobe and other nice things. Bermann presented a complete *Tristan* with Furtwängler conducting. Another glorious record is the Tschaikovsky violin concerto of Isaac Stern, performed with the lightest touch, absolutely masterful.

Now I stop. You can't write down everything, after all. The house is a daily pleasure; in the next few days we shall also be obtaining a fine, much bechromed Plymouth, and in short, I ought not be dejected. At the end of July or the beginning of August we shall be going to St. Moritz, Suvretta House, where you too can make your way and become even healthier than you already will be by then.

Lovingly,

Z.

---

[1] Federico Federici, at that time secretary at Mondadori Publishers.

[2] Jean Rudolf von Salis (b. 1901) and his wife Elisabeth von Salis. A historian and writer, he was a professor at the Swiss Institute of Technology in Zurich. Author of *Rilkes Schweizer Jahre* (1936), *Weltgeschichte der Neuesten Zeit* (1951–60), *Im Laufe der Jahre* (1962), among others.

[3] Emmie Oprecht.

[4] By Goethe.

[5] Therese Giehse.

1954

Kilchberg am Zürichsee
June 8, 1954

To my astonishment my seventy-ninth birthday has been remembered in
so many places all over the globe, in such a number of kind letters, that I
am incapable of expressing my appreciation other than in this summary
form. I ask each one of you to regard my thanks as entirely personal and
most cordially directed to himself alone.

TO ERICH VON KAHLER

Sils Maria, Engadine
Hotel Waldhaus
August 12, 1954

Dear friend Kahler:

It troubles me that I haven't written you for so long. You know how it is:
work, affairs, all sorts of minor illnesses, and added to that, the more and
more frequent weariness of my years. Oh well. Your letter of the middle
of June is here, with the account of your sickness, the operation, and what
it has cost you to recover. Although I went through a similar thing when
I too was seventy, these lung operations are, I think, the most pleasant
kind. Once the decision to operate was taken and carried out, I actually
did not experience the time in the hospital as a period of suffering, and
quickly and effortlessly cleared out. A kidney affair such as yours is
undoubtedly much nastier, and I have the impression that you were
unfortunately subjected to a grueling trial of patience. But it's a relief to
know that you are on the way to recovery, in fact by now must certainly
have your full strength back—and that despite your rashness in burden-
ing your convalescence with the McCarthy *hearings*! Yes, my friend,
what is there to say about them? I don't mean only that *performance*, but
the whole thing. One sits mute between the stools. Such is the situation of
every decent person today, and all the frothy nonsense one has to swallow
in silence is not exactly good for the kidneys. But we go on living out our
day, which after all is already reassuringly reddening in the west, and
wish the best for those who will have to keep on with it a while longer.

Since finishing the Krull memoirs—as far as they go for the time
being (440 pages)—I have done very little. The moving and setting up
house were partly to blame for this lack of production. [. . .]

Now I am already beginning to think, as far as the strenuous air up here permits, about the festival speech I am to deliver next May at the official Schiller celebration. I could not refuse that, impossible though the task really is. It has to be attacked naïvely and personally, and I must try to pour into it something of the glorious magnanimity and the enormous intelligence of the poet and his work. The combination of intellectual pride and the popular touch is almost unique.

I have just been reading a nineteenth-century thing on his burial and the fate of his bones—an utterly scandalous affair which Goethe allowed to take its course without lifting a finger. And even twenty years later when the skull, dug up with much toil out of the refuse (it remains doubtful whether it was the right one), was buried at the Grand Ducal Library in the base of Dannecker's bust of Schiller, Goethe was not present. He sent August.[1] He was always unwell whenever anything was happening that might stir him to too much emotion. I should not be reproached for having called attention, in *The Beloved Returns*, to the ludicrous element in his majesty. Not, incidentally, that Schiller was entirely unridiculous. But in a certain sense he was "greater," more largehearted than his friend, and Goethe knew it, too.

I was so happy to hear that you will be taking in dear old Helen Lowe! She is looking forward to the feeling of being sheltered in your house, and now after all wishes, almost longs, to translate the *Krull*. But I don't know whether Knopf can be persuaded. She is after all very, very feeble with age. On the other hand she is the only one who can translate certain passages of the book, verses, doggerel, and altogether strike the tone. I don't know what to advise. Possibly the assignment has already been made.[2]

Do you know a Prof. Erich Heller[3] of the University of Wales? He is supposed to write a book[4] for Secker & Warburg for my eightieth birthday, and has sent me an extraordinarily clever volume of essays, *Enterbter Geist*[5] (Suhrkamp), which together with essays on Goethe, Burckhardt, Nietzsche, Rilke, Kafka, and Kraus also contains a piece "From Hanno Buddenbrook to Adrian Leverkühn"—critically interesting, half flatteringly negative. I would be curious to hear your opinion of it.

My wife and Erika, who is with us, send warm regards.

[1] Goethe's son.
[2] *Felix Krull* was in fact translated by Denver Lindley.
[3] Erich Heller (b. 1911), professor of German literature at Northwestern University since 1960. Emigrated in 1939 from Prague to England, taught at Cambridge and Swansea. Guest professor at Hamburg, Harvard, Heidelberg, etc.
[4] *The Ironic German. A Study of Thomas Mann* (1958).
[5] *The Disinherited Mind* (1954).

TO AGNES E. MEYER

Kilchberg am Zürichsee
August 22, 1954

Dear Agnes:

Back from Sils Maria for a few days, we are leaving tomorrow for the Rhineland, where I have readings in Cologne and Düsseldorf. Before we go I want to write you about Faulkner's latest novel, that curious book you sent me because you wanted to hear my opinion. I don't know whether you are still interested after all this time, but I should like to tell you, although I do so with hesitation, for I read the book with vacillating feelings—as you probably did too; otherwise you would not have asked me. I don't like to judge and never condemn, for anyone sitting in a glass house had better not throw stones, and when I think how "ambivalently" the first volume of the Krull memoirs will be received this coming autumn, I think I would do better not to let out a critical peep.

This much can be said: For a foreigner the novel is distinctly hard to read, and I would be surprised if Americans and Englishmen didn't also find it rough going. I am taken to task for my long sentences, and my style is called *pompous* and *ponderous*. But good Lord, it is graceful toe-dancing compared with the overcrowded, overburdened, dragging, and thoroughly opaque periods that Faulkner for some reason thought appropriate for this book. He is reinforced in the high opinion he has of the novel—in part quite rightly!—by the fact that he worked for nine years on it. But that's just it: the reader feels the labor too much; the asthmatic manner makes it felt. He sweated over the book—certainly not in vain, but he did sweat, and that should never be noticeable, for art must make the difficult seem easy.

The book is entitled *A Fable*. It really ought to be called *A Parable*, and the parable is carried out importantly, portentously, rather pedantically. There is the Christ-sergeant with his twelve disciples, complete with a Peter and a Judas. He is correctly born in the stable of an inn, suffers sacrificial death between two thieves, and Mary, Martha, Mary Magdalen (from Marseilles)—they are all there. Did you perhaps find it a little cheap, to have this biblical text coming on in disguise solely in order to send pious shivers down the reader's back? I could scarcely disagree. Everything is arranged too systematically, too plainly; and there is no reminiscence here of Kafka with his religious dream-vagueness, comedy, unpredictability, and profundity.

At the same time the novel has great merits—I am sure you will agree. The author's knowledge of military matters is impressive, and the fantasy with which he deploys that knowledge is poetic. The way the opposing generals confer on the restoration of discipline so that the war can be continued may well be called satire in the grand manner, and there is grandeur in the dramatic dialogue between the sergeant who wants to die for the redemption of humanity and the commander with his tempter's offers. The finest thing in the book is the writer's love for man, his protest against militarism and war, his belief in the ultimate triumph of goodness. You were moved by that, I imagine. I was also, and if, as may be assumed, the book proves a tremendous success, I shall be very, very glad. [. . .]

All the best to you.

Yours,
T. M.

TO RICHARD BRAUNGART

Kilchberg am Zürichsee
September 29, 1954

Dear Herr Braungart:

Don't worry about that. I would of course never have permitted any changes or cuts, and no one over there[1] ever made any such suggestion to me. They have much too emphatic a respect for "culture" to do anything of the sort. The editions are therefore completely correct, and the demand is great. *Faustus* has just had a reprinting of 10,000 copies, and they would print more if they had more paper.

The only thing that might possibly conform with your fears is a certain stereotyped quality to the jacket copy, where they rather clumsily try to adhere to the "line." But the public and I can take that into the bargain. The main thing is that all my work is now available, unfalsified, in Germany No. 2. The craving for "free" literature over there is great. The classics, too, reverently untampered with, are being printed and sold in huge quantities.

---

[1] In East Germany.

1954

TO FRANZ THEODOR CSOKOR [1]

Kilchberg am Zürichsee
October 29, 1954

Dear Herr Csokor:

Many, many thanks for your remembrance, and especially for the magnificent gift of the trilogy,[2] to which I turn again and again with admiration, although my old head is preoccupied with difficult work. Ah yes, how fine to sit in the autumn sun if the world—and one's self—allows it. You are looking forward to your seventieth? Be prepared! I am ten years further along, and I confess to you, I am fearful. For with the decades things get noisier and more strenuous every time, and in my case they are complicated by the fact that "the whole" of Germany (you understand) thinks up "honors," which inevitably cause awkward situations. The complications will start with the Schiller celebration in May, for Weimar demands its share. Well, I hope to get through with a more or less whole skin this time, and I shall not reach ninety.

---

[1] Franz Theodor Csokor (1885–1969), Austrian expressionist playwright, novelist, poet, director. Joined the partisans in Yugoslavia during the war. President of Austrian PEN since 1947; has also served as president of International PEN.

[2] *Olymp und Golgatha. Trilogie einer Weltwende.* The three plays forming the trilogy are *Kalypso, Caesars Witwe, Pilatus.*

1955

————————•————————

Kilchberg am Zürichsee
January 8, 1955

Dear Lavinia:

No, we don't forget you, never, never. Only, as your intuition told you, "our Schiller" so thoroughly captured me that I had to neglect everything while working on it. It has turned out a sizable essay, around 100 pages, from which the speech will now have to be extracted. This is to be done in Arosa, where we are going shortly for a few weeks in hope of a little sun; here, the eternal blanket of mist is enough to drive one to melancholia—to which in any case I have a strong tendency. That is the reason for the Felix Krull jokes, which I never dreamed would be such a hit. This very month the third printing (up to sixty thousand) is to go out. It's plain that people are longing for the kind of entertainment which also occasionally gives them food for thought.

After once again going over Schiller's collected works, especially the *Wallenstein*, I wrote the essay with real love and admiration. Of course there are elements of touching absurdity in him. But woe to anyone who fails to recognize his specific greatness.

For Christmas we were lent the boys from Fiesole. Frido, now fourteen and a half, has shot up to a lanky handsome fellow with an appealing nature. He remains my favorite. We have virtually brought him up—I carried him in my arms, drove him around in the car. And then there remains the link with him because of the child Echo in *Faustus*. He feels that and responds to it; and the whole relationship is somehow virtually sacred for me.

Katia is active and keeping well—as I too am trying to do. Erika is working on films in Munich, but we shall meet in Arosa (Hotel Excelsior).

A thousand good wishes.

1955

TO AGNES E. MEYER

Kilchberg am Zürichsee
February 9, 1955

Dear Princess and friend:

You must have been surprised and even offended by the delay in my
thanks for your letter of December 27, which I read several times. The
reasons for my silence are these: An essay on Schiller, which I think I
have already mentioned, took such complete possession of my mind for
weeks and months that I was good for nothing else, so that I was forced
ruthlessly to neglect my correspondence—even the most important, even
the dearest. Unfinished letters piled up alarmingly on my desk. In the
middle of January, in a thoroughly exhausted state, I went up to Arosa
(1,800 meters) with Katia, hoping for sun and recuperation. I took the
whole heap with me, hoping to work through it up there, chiefly by
dictation; but above all I wanted to write to you. Things turned out very
differently. We had been there for only a few days when I was struck
down by a virus infection, with chills and high fever. At the start it was
extremely nasty. It was a complete collapse, with very low blood pressure
and great weakness. The doctor there suppressed the fever with penicillin and treated me as best he could. But after I had been on my back
for some weeks more, Katia and Erika insisted on a consultation with the
head physician at the Cantonal Hospital in Chur, who came up, examined
me, and recommended that I be taken to his hospital, because in my
reduced condition I could no longer cope with the mountain air. I was
then carried down in an ambulance and spent my "vacation" in the
hospital, weak and without appetite. In that state I had to submit to many
blood tests and X-rays, and also to a curious extraction under anesthesia
of marrow from the breastbone. Not much information came out of all
this, but the doctors were worried by a drastic lowering of blood pressure.
That can't be looked into again for another two weeks or so, and will
probably prove to be a mere concomitant of the infection, from which I
am slowly recovering.

Day before yesterday I was able to return to Zurich and our own
house, where my convalescence is being supported by vitamin injections
and heart-strengthening drugs. The comfort of the house and the home
food is doing me good. I can also be out of bed the larger part of the day,
which makes this letter to you possible, dear friend—though it is incidentally somewhat against orders, for actually I am still forbidden to do
any kind of work. But my need to write you is reinforced by what you

675

say about your giving away the cabin and once more coming across sections of your manuscript on the works of T. M. I'm sorry about the cabin. I have spent so many lovely hours at that wonderful place, and especially remember a breakfast at which Archibald MacLeish delivered himself of a moving speech in my honor. I was always proud of this man's warm feelings toward me; he seemed to me a representative of the best America. Seeing those old, closely written pages again must have been an odd experience for you, and the thought of it is touching to me. For in those days I was always moved to profound gratitude by your active, affectionate, and diligent concern with my artistic life, touched to the point of shame, and these feelings were always accompanied by a certain apprehension for your sake. I saw quite well that you were attempting too much, plumbing too deeply, stretching the framework too far, trying to include too much in your undertaking, to be able—given the multiplicity of your talents, occupations, and obligations—to persist in this complicated task, which after all was too confining a task for a person like yourself, whose nature is not merely literary. As it turned out, you were simply not permitted to continue, and you know how emphatically in agreement I was when you decided to put the work aside *for the time being* because your country demanded other and more urgent things of your energy. But what you did was certainly not done in vain, and I would readily believe that nothing better has been written anywhere about the problematical subject than the pages you have just been leafing through.

(February 10) I had to pause here yesterday to catch my breath. I wanted to say that the offer from the Library of Congress to take your private papers under its wing is honorable and sensible. I can think of no better place for the preservation of the fragments of your work on "me" than this one, and likewise for the letters which at that time you drafted in inspired German and—unfortunately—never sent. Many a dissertation by young literary scholars, from every imaginable point of view, will be written about my scribblings, and I completely agree with your idea that future students will derive profit from your notes, if they are publicly accessible. As for my own many letters to A. E. M., I think that they should not be rescued from oblivion unselectively. A limited number of them which can perhaps be conceded some substance might be given to the Library. The majority fulfilled their one-time purpose and may well vanish. [. . .]

Tomorrow, February 11, Katia and I are celebrating our golden wedding anniversary—very quietly. Erika, Golo, and Medi Borgese have come for it, but we are keeping to the family circle and making no fuss about the day, which incidentally is the very one on which we left Munich twenty-two years ago, never suspecting that we would not return. Ah yes, life was strange. I should not wish to use a more complimentary adjective, nor would I gladly go through it again. No doubt you feel differently. I daresay you would repeat the whole from the beginning with the greatest pleasure.

We are deliberately letting this anniversary pass quietly in view of the festivities coming up in May and June: I mean the Schiller celebration and my eightieth birthday. In my weakened condition I contemplate these exertions with some anxiety, for I always lack the imagination to think beyond the state in which I happen to be at the moment. In any case I have limited my activities in honor of the poet, whom I sincerely love, to the two principal places in his life: Stuttgart and Weimar. In Stuttgart President Heuss[1] will take part in the celebration and also deliver an address. I mean to endure with a military stoicism whatever it is that people intend to do with me for June 6. I have always liked Andersen's fairy tale of the Steadfast Tin Soldier. Fundamentally it is the symbol of my life. And the word "symbol" reminds me of an extremely vivid childlike wish-dream I recently had: I dreamed that for my birthday you gave me a ring with a beautiful gem—an emerald—and the ring was to be the symbol of a chain which extended from me here across the ocean to the city of Washington, D.C. There was the most amazing distinctness about the way I saw the ring with the green stone, this link in the chain, and I reveled in it like a child—like the child I am, to the extent that I top it off by confessing the dream to you. If you find it as childish as it probably is, don't waste a thought, let alone a word, on it.[2]

I have written a few rather good things about Schiller, especially about *Wallenstein*, the antipodal friendship with Goethe, and also about *Tell* and *Demetrius*. The essay will be published in various magazines and as a separate little book (*pamphlet*). I had already completed it when I came upon an additional letter of 1795 to Wilhelm von Humboldt which I found extraordinarily moving and which I must return to later on. Schiller speaks of an idea for an Olympic idyll about the marriage of

---

[1] Theodor Heuss (1884–1963), president of the German Federal Republic from 1949 to 1959.
[2] Mann's family gave him a ring with a green stone, a tourmaline, for his eightieth birthday.

Heracles and Hebe—"all mortality would be dissolved, everything would be pure light, pure freedom, pure potency; no shadows, no barriers, nothing of that sort would be visible." "I feel literally giddy," he says, "when I think of this task, when I conceive the possibility of accomplishing it. To present a scene in Olympus—that would be the summit of pleasure. I do not entirely despair of it, if only my mind could be perfectly free and washed entirely clean of all the refuse of reality; I would then once more summon up all my strength and spiritual resources, even though they were to be entirely consumed on this project." —Isn't that fearfully moving? The plan, at which he never made even a stab, is mentioned nowhere else in his notes, in none of his lists of titles and possible subjects. It has something transcendental about it, something going beyond life, no longer earthly and reserved for a spirit that has passed on, although his life was to continue for another ten years. Basically he yearned for transfiguration, shadowless, untrammeled, "pure light, pure freedom." Goethe in his old age, when his daughter-in-law had said something deprecating about Schiller, answered her: "You are all far too wretchedly earthbound for him."

I can do no better for a close to this letter. With a thousand good wishes, I am

> Your old protégé,
> Thomas Mann

TO GUIDO DEVESCOVI[1]

Kilchberg am Zürichsee
May 1, 1955

My dear Herr Devescovi:

I am much indebted to you for sending me your essay on *Doctor Faustus* and for the very kind dedication that accompanied it. To my shame I must confess that I read Italian poorly and was not always able to follow your train of thought precisely. But it is curious how much we do understand when we ourselves and our work are involved. Whenever something concerns this book, which has remained closer to my heart than all the others (probably because it was most costly to me), I suddenly fancy myself a proficient reader of languages even more foreign to me than Italian, which has been halfway familiar to me since my youth.

[1] Guido Devescovi (b. 1890), professor of German language and literature at the University of Trieste. Author of poems and critical essays on Goethe, Grillparzer, Musil, etc.

What emerged most clearly from your penetrating study is your enormous knowledge of German literature, which I in particular have every reason to admire. How much you have absorbed of German culture and thought, how much you have read—just the things by me and about me alone are staggering: fifteen pieces on *Faustus* that I myself have never even seen. —Fortunately, I suppose I must say, for there are evidently a good many hostile and negative statements in the lot, and it is astonishing that all the derogatory material you have had to digest was unable to smother your sympathy with the novel, your feeling for its curious and radical directness. For me the book still has some of the character of a Leyden jar which one cannot touch without receiving an electric shock. But I grant you, the stupid and the fundamentally antagonistic are immune.

I have never seen that pamphlet by Holthusen. It was not sent to me, and I did not ask for it. Subsequently he seems to have withdrawn some of his pulverizing criticism. When he was upbraided for it at the time, he is said to have answered: "Something had to be done. He was crushing us all, you know." Certainly that was not the intent of this book born of pain, which occupies a place outside of literature, so to speak.

Among the remoter things to which your knowledge of the literature —certainly extraordinary in a foreigner—extends is the essay by Rychner, "T. M. und die Politik." It was a clever piece, high in quality, but has since been surpassed by an essay of Alfred Andersch in the new magazine *Texte und Zeichen* (Vol. I). The essay is entitled "Mit den Augen des Westens, T. M. als Politiker," and contains the psychologically most accurate statement so far made, particularly about my relationship to the "East." Permit me the hint.

I was especially moved by your remark: "*La figura di Heinrich Mann, oscurata dalla grande ombra del fratello per tanto tempo, appare oggi sempre più nella sua giusta luce e grandezza.*"[2] May that be true! His status is officially very high in the Communist part of Germany; but with few exceptions, one of which you cite, the West is silent about him. Even his beloved Italy and his still more beloved France show little receptivity to his life work, entirely Latin in schooling and character though it was, for all the peaks of sheer genius in it, such as *Die kleine Stadt, Professor Unrat, Henri IV*, and the late masterpiece, *Ein Zeitalter wird besichtigt.* I can assure you that a chariness concerning the obscuring "grande ombra" has marked my whole life since *Buddenbrooks.* Granted,

[2] "The figure of Heinrich Mann, obscured by the great shadow of his brother for such a long time, is today appearing more and more in its true light and greatness."

I too have contributed to the Europeanization of the German novel, but my way of doing it was more traditionally German and closer to music, sounding a more ironic note than his—a dubious advantage, but a real one precisely in the eyes of the Germans and of Latin students of German literature. At the same time, my basic attitude toward him and his somewhat formidably intellectual work was always that of the little brother looking up at the elder. It is expressed autobiographically in *Royal Highness*, where Klaus Heinrich says to his brother, the Grand Duke: "I have always looked up to you because I always felt and knew that you were the more distinguished and superior of us two and I am only a plebeian compared with you. But if you deem me worthy of standing at your side and bearing your title, *and representing you to the people*, although I do not consider myself so very presentable and have this hindrance here with my left hand, which I must always hide—then I thank you and am yours to command."

I represented "Albrecht" to the people *per tanto tempo*, with all that feeling for family which both of us had. Harold Nicolson once wrote something about "that amazing family," and this gave me more pleasure than any praise of me alone. For the rest, I feel quite sure that posterity will establish justice insofar as the hierarchy in this *family* is concerned. But it was an indescribable shock to me, and seemed like a dream, when shortly before his death Heinrich dedicated one of his books to me with the words: "To my great brother,[3] who wrote *Doctor Faustus*." What? How? He had always been the great brother. And I puffed out my chest and thought of Goethe's remark about the Germans' silly bickering over which was greater, he or Schiller: "They ought to be glad that they have two such boys."

TO HERMANN HESSE

Kilchberg am Zürichsee
June 10, 1955

Dear Hermann Hesse:

You know from your own experience what I have been through and how things stand with me. I have composed a beautiful card and had it printed; it should be ready for sending today or tomorrow; but a card won't do for you. This letter cannot be adequate either, but at least my thanks must be written to you at once, my friend, for the kind words, so

[3] *Grosser Bruder* means both "big brother" and "great brother." Heinrich Mann was, of course, the "big" brother in the sense of being the elder.

unmistakably bearing the stamp of your mind, which you addressed to me in the *Neue Rundschau* and elsewhere, words expressing an attachment which I cherish as you do, and subtle mockery of the fools who do not understand it, are put out by it, and would like to destroy it.

Inwardly tired and skeptical, outwardly as disciplined and affable as possible, I have put a great deal behind me: first the Schiller journey and the visit of state in Lübeck, then the birthday tumult here, which lasted for four days and is only slowly subsiding. The dear world, with dear Switzerland in the van, has done everything in its power to turn my head, but I can still put up quite a healthy resistance. What amused me most was the degree of "Doctor of Natural Sciences" that E.T.H.[1] imaginatively conferred upon me. Now that is something new and original, for a change. Moreover, strictly between the two of us, I shall soon become a Swiss, via the township of Kilchberg. The Bundesrat seems willing for this to be carried out on an altogether exceptional basis, as we may construe from Petitpierre's[2] having appeared at the celebration in Conrad Ferdinand Meyer's house, where he delivered a speech in German with the most delightful French accent. Nor was this French accent missing from the rest of the festivities—to my great pleasure, I confess. A volume, *Hommage de la France à T. M.*, arrived with articles and congratulations from many French writers and statesmen. I find it all charming, although I haven't even thought of reading it yet.

But I did want to say that a temperate telegram came from the German Minister of the Interior, Schröder.[3] He must have wrung permission for that from Adenauer[4] in a difficult conversation.

Keep well, you and Ninon, whom we were somewhat cross with because the Etruscans so completely supplanted us with her.[5] Shame creeps over me when I reflect that you meanwhile have lived in soberly composed, sensible peace, whereas I have surrendered my life to a kind of festive dissolution. Your firmness in the face of such temptations is exemplary. But when does one seriously try to follow good examples?

---

[1] Eidgenössische Technische Hochschule, the [Swiss] Federal Institute of Technology.

[2] Max Petitpierre (b. 1899), Swiss politician; member of the Bundesrat (Federal parliament) 1944–61; president of the Confederation, 1950, 1955, and 1960.

[3] Gerhard Schröder (b. 1910), German politician; minister of the interior, 1953; foreign minister, 1961.

[4] Konrad Adenauer (1876–1967), chancellor of Germany, 1949–63.

[5] Ninon Hesse had come to Zurich to see the exhibition "Art and Life of the Etruscans."

1955

TO CAROLINE NEWTON

Kilchberg am Zürichsee
June 25, 1955

Dear friend Caroline:

You were so sweet to think of my eightieth birthday, and it was a great pity that your fine plan to be here then didn't work out. So, now that things have settled down a bit, I must send you my warm greetings. I also want to say how grateful I am for your telegram and the magnificent flowers.

Everything went very nicely; there was almost an overabundance of honors, and I must say that the present homeland of my choice, Switzerland, thoroughly overwhelmed me. But from every country in the world there came newspaper articles, special issues, thoughtful gifts, and a torrent of letters that to this day I have not yet been able to look through. I was touched that Alfred Knopf flew here from New York just for three days—what's more, in an overcrowded tourist plane—and spent three days with us in the friendliest and most unassuming way. We have never been closer.

The American press, too, paid a great deal of attention to the "event," especially considering that you people over there normally make much less fuss about birthdays than we do in Europe. Just today the mail brought a very friendly article from the *Nation*.

Naturally all the children and grandchildren were here, and we had a lovely intimate evening at the home of our friend Emmie Oprecht— but still and all, it's good to know that the celebrations are finally over. All the more so since I had just completed a most strenuous lecture tour through Germany, in connection with Schiller's 150th birthday. For that occasion I wrote a longish essay on him, which I mean to send you tomorrow.

Naturally I am delighted to hear that your translation of *Wilhelm Meister* is finished, or at any rate very close to being. Katia and I are looking forward to reading Goethe in English before too long. But above all, we hope that your health has improved again. By now you are probably in Vermont, where you always feel so well. Next week we will be going to the North Sea—to Noordwijk in Holland, Huis ter Duin, where we have stayed several times with great pleasure.

Keep well, dear friend Caroline. Both of us send you our warmest greetings.

1955

TO FRIDO MANN

[*Picture postcard*]

The Hague
July 4, 1955

Dear Frido:

Greetings from the Netherlands. It seems to me I have not properly told you that I—and incidentally all of us—very much liked the first movement of your sonata. Good luck with the continuation. And with the story also. In Amsterdam I received a splendid decoration to put round my neck, Commander Cross of Orange-Nassau, and am going to visit the Queen. Tomorrow we go to Noordwijk.

Your Grampa

TO KARL BACHLER[1]

Noordwijk am Zee
Holland
July 8, 1955

My dear Herr Doktor Bachler:

Thank you very much for your letter of the 2nd and for the interest which you and your newspaper have taken in the coming production of *Fiorenza*. I understand that Herr Lippert,[2] the new manager of the Bremen theater, intends to put it on early in September. I need not say that as the onetime author of this play or nonplay, thoroughly hybrid product that it is, I strongly share this interest, not to say this curiosity. I suppose it is always an experiment when *Fiorenza* is brought to the stage, but I am looking forward to it with special suspense and with a degree of confidence.

When an experienced practical man of the theater like Managing Director Lippert (though he is not a practical man in the ordinary sense, but a person of culture) decides with enthusiasm to throw his great name as a director into the scales for the sake of this product of my youth, it supports my own conviction that the work contains elements which are suitable for the theater—indeed, which cry out for it. I am thinking not so much of the several rewarding parts it offers to actors as of its dialectical tension, which is so closely akin to dramatic tension that it might almost

---

[1] Karl Bachler (b. 1905), editor-in-chief of the *Weser Kurier* in Bremen; student of literature, art history, and history. Among his books: *Der Pritschmeister Ferber* (1929), *August Strindberg* (1931), *Das englische Drama* (1947, 1948).
[2] Albert Lippert (b. 1901), theater manager and actor.

be considered one and the same. Whenever I try to recall what motivated me at the time, what I had in mind when I cast this work in scenic and dialogue form without seriously worrying about the theater and its requirements, even its time limitations, I realize that it was the dialectical, contentious and contradictory, profoundly discursive character of the material. I saw the aesthetic and the religious temperaments engaged in rivalry for the highest prize: dominion, power. This polarity of the concepts of everlasting festivity and of sanctifying spiritualization is embodied in Lorenzo and his humanistic retinue (that coterie of artists) on the one hand, and in Savonarola on the other. I did not conceive of Savonarola in terms of religious history, as a forerunner of the Reformation. Rather, I regarded him in purely symbolic terms as the great antagonist of beauty, the ascetically pessimistic critic of life. He is the somber, fascinating prophet of pure spirit—an artist too, but "simultaneously a saint" who "makes morality possible again" in an age and world of pampered esthetes who lend themselves to every new stimulus.

Dialectics and symbolism are a temptation for the theater, even when no consideration has been given to the needs of the stage. And in fact the stage has repeatedly taken up this "play"—despite the adaptation it requires. In earlier years I have seen it given in various cities: In Frankfurt, where Carl Heine[3] tried his hand at it, with boldness and some success; in Munich; with Reinhardt in Berlin; in Bochum (under Saladin Schmitt[4]); above all, shortly after the First World War, in Vienna, where a variety of circumstances joined to create a production which happily assuaged my theatrical guilty conscience, as other performances had not really done. The place was the Academy Theater, the sponsor a literary association which assembled a cast consisting of some of the best speakers among the members of the Burgtheater and the Volkstheater. That is important, because these scenes, so dependent on stylized language, must be spoken well. But what chiefly promoted the effect was something in the atmosphere of the times, the state of mind of a society that revolutionary events had plunged into dubieties, crises, and intellectual strains. It therefore reacted to the dubieties and strenuous intellectuality of these dialogues as to something familiar, "relevant" to the present, appropriate. For curiously enough, though written in a time of deepest peace—a decade before the catastrophe, when everything

---

[3] Carl Heine (1861–1927), director and theatrical critic in Hamburg and Frankfurt. He directed the premiere of *Fiorenza* on May 11, 1907. Author of several plays and monographs on the theater.

[4] Saladin Schmitt (1883–1951), managing director in Bochum from 1918–49. Part of the time he also acted as managing director of the Duisburg Opera (1921–35).

seemed stable—this quasi-drama had something anticipatory in it which made it closer to the spiritual situation of 1919 or 1920 than to that of 1904. This seems to occur often with works of the imagination.

I have been trying, not altogether in vain, I think, to follow the reasoning which may have prompted Bremen's new managing director to make another attempt with *Fiorenza* at the present time. He may seem foolhardy, but perhaps he is only clever enough not to be overly prudent. Do we not live in times of even greater stress than those days in Vienna when Ferdinand Onno[5] played the Prior of San Marco with unforgettable intensity? Is this not a time of crisis, of ideological struggles, a time in which the ascetic and dictatorial spirit of political Dominicans pits itself against "freedom," "beauty," refined aestheticism, and sensual pleasures? The dialogues on the day of Lorenzo the Magnificent's death can serve as parables and parallels for these times. And then there is the matter of the theater's evolution in the past generation. With the continual development of stage techniques, the theater has cut remarkably free from its old rules, and the audience, too, has a totally different conception of an evening's entertainment. It is an audience receptive to epic, intellectual, symbolic drama, to the dissolution of staid acts into a rush of fragmentary scenes passing rapidly across the stage.

Are these some of the considerations, my dear director, that have made you so sanguine about such a reckless undertaking? Am I to undermine your faith? Talk you out of it? I come very close to sharing it myself. Moreover, recklessness is the very essence of the theater. So I can only wish you good luck—you and your courageous artists.[6]

TO CARL JACOB BURCKHARDT[1]

Huis ter Duin
Noordwijk aan Zee
July 14, 1955

Dear Minister Burckhardt:

I was delighted by your friendly letter, and no less, or scarcely less, by your news of the shipment of wine (of your own raising?) that awaits us in Kilchberg. Cheers! And many thanks.

[5] Ferdinand Onno (b. 1879), actor.
[6] This letter was printed in the program notes for the Bremen performance of *Fiorenza*.
[1] Carl Jacob Burckhardt (b. 1891), Swiss diplomat and historian. Friend of Hofmannsthal. League of Nations Commissioner in Danzig 1937–9, then president of the International Red Cross. Swiss ambassador to France, 1945–50. Among his books: *Richelieu* (1935), *Erinnerungen an Hugo von Hofmannsthal* (1940), *Meine Danziger Mission 1937–9* (1960).

We have been here for ten days—just the two of us. Erika was with us in Amsterdam, but then flew to London on business and is now taking a cure in the mountains above Lucerne. We shall stay until about the end of the month. I have always been tremendously fond of the coast and like it even in the fog we have now. I am writing you in my beach hut, which faces the gently rolling ocean.

Day before yesterday we visited the Queen at her country seat, an hour from here by car, to thank her for the wonderfully beautiful decoration I received from her (or with her approval): a magnificent thing, Commander Cross of Orange-Nassau, the prettiest plaything for big children. Her Majesty regaled us with coffee (at 11 A.M.; the Dutch drink coffee at all times of the day) and was plain and dignified. She is distinctly anticeremonial, which has its dangers; for she simply gave no token when the audience was at an end, so that we stayed much too long, I think. Thank God, that was not mentioned in the newspaper. —Her eldest daughter is not a good student, and the Queen is anxious about her final examinations. We refrained from saying that we hardly thought there was any cause for worry. Moreover, this might really be the wrong attitude. The princesses' studies at school are treated with most democratic seriousness.

We are looking forward to seeing you again in Switzerland where, *after all*, it is best!

TO KONRAD KAHL[1]

*Cantonal Hospital
Zurich
July 30, 1955*

My dear neighbor:

Many thanks for your kind attention, the lovely flowers. The lilies are altogether charming, capricious in form, almost like orchids; they are keeping splendidly and give me pleasure every day.

Let us hope that neither you nor I will be condemned to a long enchantment on the mountain—not seven years, and not seven weeks either. My progress is said to be good, at least as far as the chief illness which has brought me here is concerned. But along with that always comes a variety of associated vexations and minor torments which thrust themselves unduly into the foreground.

---

[1] Konrad Kahl (b. 1914), interior decorator and businessman; essayist by avocation. Herr Kahl was in the hospital room next door to Mann, and sent him flowers.

1955

TO THEODOR W. ADORNO

Cantonal Hospital
Zurich
July 30, 1955

Dear Dr. Adorno:

Many, many thanks for your letter. Yes, I have been cheated out of a week of lovely weather in Noordwijk and shall now be losing I don't know how many weeks of normal and upright life because of this unexpected illness, one wholly alien to me, which at first I thought was rheumatism but which under medical examination has proved to be a quite severe circulatory disturbance, an inflammation in a vein of the left leg.[1] That sort of thing calls for great care, a long period of lying absolutely still (with all the peculiar concomitants, which I had never known before), and most precise treatment. I am certainly receiving that perfectly here, having been taken in charge by the well-known specialist in internal medicine, Professor Löffler.[2] I do not have any pain worth mentioning, although there are all the subsidiary annoyances which commonly go with a major illness. But every such thing is tedious; I shall scarcely get away in less than four weeks, of which only one has passed. *Pazienza!* What I have entered into is Magic Mountain time.

Something of the sort had to come. I was quite astounded when after my wild life of May and June the usual reaction of sickness postponed its arrival. Then, while I thought I was recuperating on the magnificent beach at Noordwijk, enjoying my role as Commander of Orange-Nassau (*"Je Maintiendrai!"*), nature had thought up something quite new and surprising for me—this. The witty, quietly inventive female!

You will find the Hesses in the Waldhaus, but not me. Even if I should be discharged from here while you are still staying up there, 1,800 meters would be beyond limits for me for the time being. I'll look forward to meeting you in Kilchberg, then, on your way back. You will enjoy seeing our house, which in its beautiful situation and unpretentious comfort makes the perfect last establishment.

---

[1] Mann was in fact suffering from a thrombosis. On the course of his illness, see Erika Mann: *The Last Year of Thomas Mann* (New York: Farrar, Straus & Cudahy; 1958).
[2] Wilhelm Löffler (b. 1887), director of the medical clinic of the Cantonal Hospital, Zurich, 1937–57.

1955

TO THE MICHAEL MANN FAMILY

Cantonal Hospital
Zurich
August 9, 1955

Dear people:

My warm thanks. It was so sweet of all of you to gather together for that family letter, which was a comfort and a joy to me. I need both, for it is a most wretched existence I am leading at present, and the end is not yet in sight. Lying in bed all the time, with a leg wrapped in alcohol or aluminum acetate. It doesn't hurt, but this immoblie mode of life has so many unpleasant complications, of which for decency's sake I mention only the various frantically itching eczemas which the eternal bedwarmth brings on, especially on the feet, which have to be painted constantly with a white menthol mixture that produces chills. In short, it is a nuisance, and I hardly feel like eating anything.

Every afternoon I can sit up in a chair for an hour, and then Mielein plays music for me on the phonograph lent by Motschan. But my nerves can't take much of it, and I do better to read Alfred Einstein's[1] book about Mozart—which is very good, isn't it, Bibi? I was particularly interested to learn that M. had no feeling at all for nature or architecture or any kind of visual effect, but always derived his stimuli solely from music itself. He made music out of music, as it were, a kind of artistic inbreeding and filtered production. Very odd. He was also an aristocrat and had, unlike Haydn, little fondness for the popular touch. In this he was like Goethe. His whole life long he suffered from his physical smallness and unprepossessing appearance. He really must have looked like nothing at all.

The boys have described your circumstances in Forio d'Ischia with great vividness, especially Frido, who has made remarkable progress in handwriting and expression. But Toni also writes very briskly and energetically. I think I too would enjoy your kind of life for a few weeks. When you have a clear sea for bathing, sun all day, and a kerosene lamp and candles at night, who needs electricity and running water? But then you will certainly feel that you are living in regal splendor when you stay with Medi.

---

[1] Alfred Einstein (1880–1952), musicologist and critic. Emigrated by way of Italy and England to the United States in 1933. Among his books: *Mozart* (1945), *Music in the Romantic Era* (1947), *The Italian Madrigal* (1949).

Good healing for Bibi's wrist, and love and all good things for each of you.

Your Z. and G.

TO LAVINIA MAZZUCCHETTI

Cantonal Hospital
Zurich
August 10, 1955

Dear friend:

My present misery was necessary to give me the chance for a closer examination of the *Ponte* issue, which brought your fine birthday essay.[1] I feel keenly how many thanks I still owe you for this warmhearted commentary on my personal life and our long years of friendly exchange. Alas, these thanks will not be set down in a form worthy of the kind of praise you lavish upon my letters in your article. My head is empty and my stomach heavy, as though I had eaten much too much, although I eat virtually nothing. But these weaknesses, as well as the itching eczema brought on by the eternal bed-warmth, are only side effects of the major trouble—the stoppage in the leg, which is undergoing steady improvement—so that hope of return to my normal existence is approaching closer. Afternoons I am already allowed to sit up in an armchair. They promise me that in a few days they will let me promenade a little in the corridor, and once I am permitted to go down to the garden I shall be as good as back home. Free movement in fresh air—we don't know what it means to us as long as we take it for granted. But if this dreary intermezzo should on the whole cost me only four or five weeks, thanks to the modern injections, I shall have got off very easily. It is actually part and parcel of such circulatory disturbances that they are tediously protracted, and in the past one could lie immobile for half a year with such an ailment.

You cannot imagine how sorry I was to depart prematurely from Noordwijk—or rather, to be departed per ambulance. It is such a lovely place, the most magnificent beach I know, and in my hut there, thanks to the stimulating air, I even wrote a few trifles, although a great deal of sand sifted onto the paper. I felt especially well, and there of all places this had to happen to me. But that's what comes of Schiller's celebrating the 150th anniversary of his death and I my eightieth birthday. I simply

---

[1] "L'uomo Thomas Mann" [*Il Ponte* (anno 11), a monthly review of politics and literature published at Florence.]

carried things too far—or let myself be pushed too far, and Rome, Paris, Oslo—for the present I must drop all such plans.

Keep well, and once again thanks for *Il Ponte*. Medi Borgese's piece[2] is also very touching and droll, and there were so many other good and friendly things in the issue. Please express my warmest gratitude to the editors.

This was Mann's last letter. His condition took a sudden turn for the worse, and he died two days later, on August 12, 1955.

[2] "Infanzia con mio padre" (translated from the English).

Italicized page numbers indicate letters to the person after whose name they appear. A boldface page number indicates a brief biographical note about the person after whose name it appears.

Index

Index

Index

Index

Index

Index

Index

Index

Index

Index

Index

Index

Index

Index

Index

Index

Index

Index

Index

Index

Index

Index

THE PRINCIPAL WORKS
OF THOMAS MANN

American Editions in Translation published by Alfred A. Knopf, New York

1916 ROYAL HIGHNESS
A Novel of German Court Life
Translated by A. Cecil Curtis

1924 BUDDENBROOKS
Translated by H. T. Lowe-Porter

1925 DEATH IN VENICE AND OTHER STORIES
Translated by Kenneth Burke
Contains DEATH IN VENICE, TRISTAN, *and* TONIO KRÖGER *(out of print)** †

1927 THE MAGIC MOUNTAIN
Translated by H. T. Lowe-Porter
Two volumes

1928 CHILDREN AND FOOLS
Translated by Herman George Scheffauer
Nine stories, including LITTLE HERR FRIEDEMANN *and* DISORDER AND
EARLY SORROW *(out of print)**

1929 THREE ESSAYS
Translated by H. T. Lowe-Porter
Contains FREDERICK THE GREAT AND THE GRAND COALITION *from* REDE
UND ANTWORT; GOETHE AND TOLSTOI; *and* AN EXPERIENCE IN THE OCCULT,
from BEMÜHUNGEN *(out of print)*

1930 EARLY SORROW
Translated by Herman George Scheffauer (out of print)*

* Included in *Stories of Three Decades*, translated by H. T. Lowe-Porter.
† *Death in Venice*, translated by Kenneth Burke, reissued as a separate volume, 1965.

1930   A MAN AND HIS DOG
       Translated by Herman George Scheffauer (out of print)*

1930   DEATH IN VENICE
       A new translation by H. T. Lowe-Porter
       With an Introduction by Ludwig Lewisohn (out of print)*

1931   MARIO AND THE MAGICIAN
       *Translated by H. T. Lowe-Porter (out of print)**

1933   PAST MASTERS AND OTHER PAPERS
       Translated by H. T. Lowe-Porter (out of print)

       JOSEPH AND HIS BROTHERS
1934   I JOSEPH AND HIS BROTHERS [The Tales of Jacob]
1935   II YOUNG JOSEPH
1938   III JOSEPH IN EGYPT
1944   IV JOSEPH THE PROVIDER
1948   *The complete work in one volume*
         Translated by H. T. Lowe-Porter

1936   STORIES OF THREE DECADES
       Translated by H. T. Lowe-Porter
       Contains all of Thomas Mann's fiction prior to 1940 except the long novels

1937   AN EXCHANGE OF LETTERS
       Translated by H. T. Lowe-Porter (out of print)

1937   FREUD, GOETHE, WAGNER
       Translated by H. T. Lowe-Porter and Rita Matthias-Reil
       Three essays (out of print)

1938   THE COMING VICTORY OF DEMOCRACY
       Translated by Agnes E. Meyer (out of print)

1938   THIS PEACE
       Translated by H. T. Lowe-Porter (out of print)

1940   THIS WAR
       Translated by Eric Sutton (out of print)

1940   THE BELOVED RETURNS
       [*Lotte in Weimar*]
       Translated by H. T. Lowe-Porter

       * Included in *Stories of Three Decades*, translated by H. T. Lowe-Porter.

A Note About the Editors

RICHARD WINSTON, *the author of* CHARLEMAGNE: FROM THE HAMMER TO THE CROSS (*1954*) *and* THOMAS BECKET (*1967*) *has, in the course of over thirty years, translated more than a hundred full-length books from five European languages, including the works of some of the foremost German writers. His wife and collaborator, novelist Clara Winston, is the author of* THE CLOSEST KIN THERE IS (*1952*), THE HOURS TOGETHER (*1962*), *and* PAINTING FOR THE SHOW (*1969*). *They have two daughters and live in Halifax, Vermont.*

A Note on the Type

This book was set on the Monotype in a type face called Walbaum. The original cutting of this face was made by Justus Erich Walbaum in Leipzig in the early 1800's; the modern, by the Monotype Corporation in the 1930's. Young Walbaum began his artistic career as an apprentice to a maker of cookie molds. How he managed to leave this field and become a successful punchcutter remains a mystery. The type face that bears his name may be classified as "Transitional." The slight human irregularities in its cut are a strong factor in its modern appeal.